International Corporate Reporting

Visit the *International Corporate Reporting, Fourth Edition*
Companion Website at **www.pearsoned.co.uk/roberts** to find
valuable **student** learning material including:

- Suggestions for revision work
- Guide to essay writing and assignments
- Making best use of the book's 'exhibits'

Fourth Edition

International Corporate Reporting
A Comparative Approach

CLARE ROBERTS

PAULINE WEETMAN

PAUL GORDON

FT Prentice Hall
FINANCIAL TIMES

An imprint of **Pearson Education**

Harlow, England • London • New York • Boston • San Francisco • Toronto • Sydney • Singapore • Hong Kong
Tokyo • Seoul • Taipei • New Delhi • Cape Town • Madrid • Mexico City • Amsterdam • Munich • Paris • Milan

Pearson Education Limited

Edinburgh Gate
Harlow
Essex CM20 2JE
England

and Associated Companies throughout the world

Visit us on the World Wide Web at:
www.pearsoned.co.uk

First published in Great Britain by Financial Times Professional Limited 1998
Second edition 2002
Third edition 2005
Fourth edition 2008

ISBN: 978-0-273-71473-6

British Library Cataloguing-in-Publication Data
A catalogue record for this book is available from the British Library.

Library of Congress Cataloging-in-Publication Data
Roberts, Clare B.
 International corporate reporting : a comparative approach / Clare Roberts,
Pauline Weetman, Paul Gordon.-- 4th ed.
     p. cm.
 Rev. ed. of: International financial reporting / Clare Roberts, Pauline Weetman,
Paul Gordon. 3rd ed. 2005.
 Includes bibliographical references and index.
 ISBN-13: 978-0-273-71473-6 (alk. paper) 1. International business
enterprises--Finance. 2. Accounting--Standards--International cooperation.
I. Weetman, Pauline. II. Gordon, Paul. III. Roberts, Clare B. International financial
reporting. IV. Title.

 HF5686.I56R634 2008
 657'.96--dc22   2008001028

10 9 8 7 6 5 4 3 2
11 10 09 08

Typeset by 73 in 9/12 Stone Serif.
Printed by Ashford Colour Press, Gosport

The publisher's policy is to use paper manufactured from sustainable forests.

Contents

v

Supporting resources

Visit **www.pearsoned.co.uk/roberts** to find valuable online resources

Companion Website for students
- Suggestions for revision work
- Guide to essay writing and assignments
- Making best use of the book's 'exhibits'

Extensive teaching materials for instructors
- Tutorial assignments for every chapter
- Additional exam questions and solutions to questions in the book
- Projects for extended study, including outlines, resources and solutions
- PowerPoint slides and more

For more information please contact your local Pearson Education sales representative or visit **www.pearsoned.co.uk/roberts**

Preface

Introduction

This fourth edition takes as its theme 'harmonization of measurement and disclosure in financial statements: diversity in reporting assurance, governance and the management perspective'. The title 'International Corporate Reporting' reflects the importance of the combined corporate report which balances financial statements, explanatory descriptions and an ever-widening range of disclosures to provide assurance on the quality and reliability of the financial statement.

January 2005 marked a significant stage in the move towards acceptance of international financial reporting standards (IFRS) as the basis for harmonizing financial statements. It was the date from which listed companies in member states of the European Union (EU) were required to apply IFRS in their consolidated financial statements, in place of the accounting standards of their home countries. Beyond Europe other countries have taken a range of attitudes. Some have adopted IFRS in full; some have revised their national standards to incorporate the main aspects of IFRS with some local variation; others are still considering their options.

The fourth edition of this book reflects the significant progress towards national acceptance of IFRS as a basis for global harmonization, on the one hand, and the desire to retain some element of national identity and control, on the other hand. The national identity remains most apparent in the regulation of assurance of the quality of financial statements and in the wider narrative reporting that accompanies the financial statements.

We are sometimes asked, 'Is there any need for a course in comparative corporate reporting now that IFRS are widely applied?' We answer that in an ideal world there would be no continuing scope for a comparative study of international financial reporting because harmonization would be complete. In reality, differences persist. Although the International Organization of Securities Commissions (IOSCO) endorsed IFRS in 2000, it left an option for individual securities commissions to scrutinize IFRS and add further conditions to them. The IASB has faced the challenge of establishing confidence in its independence as a standard setter, while having no direct powers of enforcement or scrutiny. In the period from 2000 to 2005 we observed the legislators of two major economic groupings (the EU and the USA) using the language of 'convergence' while preserving territorial positions. Since 2005 we have seen progress in discussions between the EU and the Securities and Exchange Commission of the United States to eliminate the need for European companies to reconcile IFRS-based financial statements to US GAAP in annual reports. The tensions in this discussion pulled from two directions: the European Commission retained its right of political control over the legal process across member states while the SEC awaited reassurance about mechanisms for enforcement of high-quality international accounting standards that would retain a level playing field for US companies.

Corporate failures of companies with a high profile have caused a major loss of confidence for investors in global markets. To restore confidence, the processes of corporate governance and assurance (including audit) have been revised significantly in many countries, although regulation remains primarily under national laws. We are now aware that the implementation of any system of financial reporting is critically dependent on the quality of the corporate governance and assurance mechanisms of the national regulator.

As a separate aspect of accountability for social and environmental matters, there has been increasing emphasis on corporate social reporting (CSR) to the point where high-quality CSR information is seen as essential by those evaluating investment possibilities. Information about responsibilities to employees, customers, communities and society in general is now a common feature of many annual reports. It is part of the wider focus on narrative reporting to explain the activities of the business.

In this fourth edition we aim to provide insight into the areas of comparability, and the persistence of diversity, in the corporate annual reports of listed companies across global markets. We also indicate how national diversity may continue to be significant for non-listed companies and for reporting in a national context. All the developments we have described in this introduction are fascinating to researchers and we have built into the text a wide range of examples of research studies in this area that will be of interest to students and may offer ideas for their own future research projects.

Aim of the book

This text aims to bring to undergraduate and postgraduate courses in accounting and finance an awareness of similarities and differences in accounting practices and an ability to analyze the causes and consequences of those similarities and differences. There is a strong emphasis placed on IASB standards as the focus of comparison.

The book aims also to familiarize students with the growing body of research into international accounting practices, giving detailed explanation of research methods that may encourage students to apply such techniques in project work.

Structure of the book

The book is divided into four modules (Parts 1 to 4) each of which deals with a separate aspect of international corporate reporting. The full text is suitable for a full 15-week semester but the modular structure allows lecturers to plan selectively for shorter courses.

The fourth edition starts in Part 1 with a general overview of issues relating to global accounting standards. It sets the scene for a deeper subsequent study of specific regulatory regimes. Chapter 1, new to this edition, explains the arguments for and against a move to global accounting standards and points to some of the continuing unresolved issues. Chapter 2 focuses on investors and companies to ask how reducing international diversity will affect a wide range of corporate decisions. Chapter 3 explores the complex framework of assurance mechanisms that have been established to give credibility to international and national reporting practices. It reflects the actions taken by a wide range of institutions, both statutory and voluntary, to enhance confidence in financial reporting. Chapter 4 reflects the importance of narrative reporting in achieving transparency in financial reporting through disclosure. Chapter 5 explains how harmonization through IFRS has been improved, and how convergence with US standards required continuing action, in three areas: business combinations; segmental reporting; and foreign currency translation.

Part 2 presents the well-regarded analytical focus of the book by setting the analytical framework for the study of accounting practice and explaining the methods used in various types of comparative reporting study. The institutional framework is described in Chapter 6, covering in general terms the influence of the political system, the economic system, the legal system, the tax system, the financing system and the accounting profession. Cultural influences on accounting rules and practice are critically evaluated in Chapter 7 using well-known academic sources. Classification of accounting systems, as presented in Chapter 8, provides a framework indicating international similarities and differences. Practical approaches to measuring international differences in accounting rules and practices are presented in Chapter 9, drawing on methods established in the research literature that are suitable for student project applications.

Part 3 describes the forces that are shaping the development of international standards. The development of the IASB as a standard-setting board with international recognition is explained in Chapter 10, with an explanation of the procedures used in setting international financial reporting standards. Chapter 11 explains the US background to the US GAAP which offer a rival to IFRS as a potential system of global accounting standards. Chapter 12 describes the accounting environment in the EU with 27 member states committed to the application of IFRS since 2005. Chapter 13 explains some of the circumstances in which accounting standard setting has become a political process that may override the logic and symmetry of a purely technical process.

Part 4 describes how a selection of countries have moved towards adoption of IFRS. We have included in our selection two countries with strongly established capital markets (the UK and Japan), three countries with established capital markets in Europe (France, Germany and The Netherlands) and two countries that are still at relatively early stages of development of capital markets (Poland and China). In these country chapters we relate accounting developments to the institutional environment within which accounting practice operates.

Particular features

We have retained from previous editions the features that students and lecturers have identified as particularly helpful:

- *there is a strong emphasis on IASB standards* as a basis for convergence of accounting measurement and disclosure, with explanation of how the work of the IASB is receiving careful and serious attention from standard-setting authorities in many countries;
- *experienced researchers* show how the methods used in research papers may be understood and applied in undergraduate honours and postgraduate courses;
- *a consistent framework for analysis* shows how students may seek to explain harmonized accounting and national reporting differences in the context of an institutional framework and a cultural perspective;
- *focus on accountability* in corporate reporting;
- *description of corporate governance and assurance initiatives* that have developed out of Enron and other major corporate failures;
- *transparency and disclosure through narrative information* in annual reports, explaining the legislation and guidance available and giving examples of the range of practices that have emerged;

- *the development of financial reporting practices across Europe* is integrated in one chapter with particular reference to Poland as the largest economy entering the EU in the 2004 enlargement.
- *examples of accounting practices* drawn from published accounts;
- *names of major companies* in each country are given as a guide to students intending to investigate further;
- *case studies* are drawn from practice and from research studies to illustrate the general points of principle contained in early chapters;
- *end-of-chapter questions* encourage students to analyze and compare the information within and between chapters;
- *an accompanying Lecturer's Guide* assists students and lecturers in the practical exploration of the wealth of material available for study of aspects of international accounting. This Guide is available free to lecturers adopting this text and can be accessed via a Supplement download site at **www.pearsoned.co.uk/roberts**.

New features of this edition are:

- An extended discussion of the arguments for and against development of global accounting standards (Chapter 1).
- A discussion of some of the political pressures faced by the IASB when a regulator, such as the European Commission, adopts IFRS and requires their use.
- Updating of source material to reflect the rapid rate of change in all aspects of corporate reporting.

Flexible course design

The material in this book is sufficient for a full semester's course of study, in the typical half-year semester lasting around 15 weeks. For shorter periods the modular structure allows selection of relevant material. For a course focusing on the broad issues of globalization in corporate reporting, Part 1 provides a self-contained programme of five chapters. For a study of research methods in comparative financial reporting, Part 2 gives a framework in theory and a description of comparative accounting research methods and their application. Part 3 provides a more specific course of four chapters linking the development of the IASB, the strength of the US accounting system and the power of the EU in supporting its choice of global accounting system. Part 4 provides more country-specific material. It would be possible, for example, to develop a short course on the development of accounting in China by linking Chapters 6, 7, 10 and 17. A framework for institutional and cultural analysis is provided in Chapters 6 and 7, the process of developing IASB standards is explained in Chapter 10 and the specific developments in China are contrasted in Chapter 17.

Target readership

This book is targeted at final-year undergraduate students on degree courses in accounting or business studies. It is also appropriate for use in a core module of a specialist postgraduate MSc taught course or an MBA. It has an international perspective, in its basis of IFRS, and so is not restricted to study within a particular country. It is also a useful basis for research students in planning research projects in comparative financial reporting.

The book should also be of interest to professional readers and general management because it focuses on analysis of financial statements rather than techniques of preparation of accounts.

Support material: project work and tutorial guidance

For students learning about comparative reporting practices, it is essential to have first-hand experience of that practice. This means students must handle, read, observe and think about accounting information as it appears in practice. It may be in printed annual reports; increasingly it is also available on company websites.

As a first step in familiarization we have included selected exhibits in the country chapters. In the student section of the Lecturer's Guide we suggest questions that will help students to think about the exhibits and may help the tutor in guiding discussion. We also suggest tutorial question sheets for every chapter.

The next step for students is to carry out project work with company material. In this way they discover the practical problems of reading and understanding annual reports that we have all experienced as researchers and that equity analysts experience in practice. To make efficient use of class time we have provided project material in the Lecturer's Guide available via the Supplement download site. We also give the project assignment sheets and instructions for students. The projects and relevant materials cover:

- relating perceptions of culture to accounting values;
- comparisons of accounting policies and harmonization measures;
- disclosure and measurement practices, with the comparability index;
- assessment of voluntary disclosure;
- reconciliation statements; and
- the use of web-based materials.

Companion Website

On the Companion Website, www.pearsoned.co.uk/roberts, lecturers will find project material that can be downloaded, as well as tutorial notes and guidance on end-of-chapter questions. Lecturers will find overheads for lectures and ideas on how to plan and assess teaching.

Acknowledgements

The authors have used much of the material of this text in their respective teaching assignments with final-year and postgraduate students and are appreciative of feedback from students in several universities.

They are grateful to the following reviewers of the international chapters for the first edition: Chris Kelly (**Australia**), Professor Zhengfei Lu (**China**), Professor Jean-Claude Scheid (**France**), Professor Dr Wolfgang Ballwieser (**Germany**), Professor Derek Bailey (**Hungary**), Professor Kazuo Hiramatsu (**Japan**), D. H. van Offeren (**The Netherlands**) and Professor James A. Schweikart (USA).

In respect of the third edition the authors are grateful for helpful observations from Professor Steve Zeff, Professor Simon Gao and Professor Jason Xiao, Dr Nazli Mohd Anum Ghazali and Dr Marek Schroeder.

This fourth edition has been helped by comments provided by anonymous reviewers, through the publisher.

Particular thanks for encouragement and support with previous editions must go to Richard Whitbread, Anna Herbert, Sadie McClelland, Paula Harris and Paul Mitchell at Pearson Education. For this edition we thank Tim Parker and Amanda McPartlin.

Publisher's acknowledgements

We are grateful to the following for permission to reproduce copyright material:

Exhibit 1.2 from Herman and Thomas (1995), Combination of tables from paper, *Accounting and Business Research* and Types of compliance with IASs. Wolters Kluwer. This material is copyright protected and is derived by kind permission of the copyright holder and publishers, CCH and Wolters Kluwer, from its periodical *Accounting and Business Research/Accountancy*; Exhibit 1.3, Mission statement of the Publish What You Pay coalition, Publishwhatyoupay; Exhibit 1.4 (Rahman, A., Perera, H. and Ganesh, S. (2002) 'Accounting practice harmony, accounting regulation and firm characteristics', *Abacus*, 38(1):46–77. Published by Blackwell Publishing Limited; Exhibit 2.1 (Fraser, P. and Oyefeso, O. (2005) 'US, UK and European stock market integration', *Journal of Business Finance and Accounting*. 32(1–2):161–181). Published by Blackwell Publishing Limited; Exhibits 2.3 and 2.4 from Lane, P.R. and Milesi-Ferretti, G.M. (2004) 'International investment patterns', IMF Working Paper, WP/04/134, July. International Monetary Fund; Exhibit 2.19 from *Accountancy* May 2001: pp. 98–99, Wolters Kluwer. This material is copyright protected and is derived by kind permission of the copyright holder and publishers, CCH and Wolters Kluwer, from its periodical *Accounting and Business Research/Accountancy*; Exhibits 3.3 and 4.4 reproduced by permission from US Securities and Exchange Commission; Exhibit 4.1 from Patel, S., Balic, A., Bwakira, L., Bradley, S. and Dallas, G., Transparency and Disclosure Study – Europe, (April 2003). Published by Standard & Poor's, a division of The McGraw-Hill Companies Inc.; Exhibit 4.2 from BT Annual Report and Form 20-F (2004), p. 154. © BT Plc; Exhibit 4.8 from Motorola Annual Report (2002) © Motorola Inc.; Exhibit 4.14 from *Michelin Annual Report* (2006), p. 156, www.michelin.com. Michelin; Exhibits 4.15, 4.16 and 15.9 from *GlaxoSmithKline Annual Report* (2006). GlaxoSmithKline plc; Exhibit 5.11 from *SAB Miller Annual Report 2004*. SABMiller plc; Exhibits 5.18 and 10.13 from *Roche Annual Report* (2006), F. Hoffmann-La Roche AG; Exhibit 7.1 (Gray, S.J. (1988) 'Towards a theory of cultural influence on the development of accounting systems internationally', *Abacus*, 24(1):1–15). Published by Blackwell Publishing Limited; Exhibit 7.11 from Radebaugh, L.H., Gray, S.J. and Black, E.L. (2006) *International accounting and multinational enterprises*, 6th edition, p. 50. Reprinted with permission of John Wiley & Sons Inc.; Exhibit 8.9 (Gray, S.J. (1988) 'Towards a theory of cultural influence on the development of accounting systems internationally', *Abacus*, 24(1):1–15). Published by Blackwell Publishing Limited; Exhibit 8.10 from Nobes, C.W. (1984) *International Classification of Financial Reporting*. London: Croom Helm. © Cengage Learning Services Ltd 1984; Exhibit 8.11 (Nobes, C.W. (1998) 'Towards a general model of the reasons for international differences in financial reporting', *Abacus*, September, 34(2):162–187). Published by Blackwell Publishing Limited; Exhibit 9.7 reprinted from The Conservatism Principle and the Asymmetric Timeliness of Earnings, in *Journal of Accounting and Economics,* Vol 24, pp. 3–37, with permission from Elsevier, (Basu, 1997); Exhibits 10.16 and 10.20 © Stora Enso; Exhibits 11.1, 14.1, 15.1, 16.2, 17.1 and 17.19 from *The Economist Pocket World in Figures*, 2008 Edition, Profile

Books Ltd; Exhibit 11.7 from *Southern Co. Annual Report* (2006), pp. 53 and 54, The Southern Co.; Exhibits 11.15 and 11.19 reproduced with permission from The Dow Chemical Company; Exhibit 11.21 from *General Motors Annual Report* (1996) pp. 59, 99, General Motors Corporation; Exhibit 14.10 from Hoogendoorn, M. (1996), 'Accounting and taxation in Europe – a comparative overview', *The European Accounting Review*, 5 (Supplement) pp. 783–794. © M.N. Hoogendoorn; Exhibit 14.14 from Total, Registration Document 2006, pp. 112, 168. © TOTAL S.A. April 2007; Exhibit 15.7 (True and Fair Override) from *Kingfisher Annual Report* (2004), p. 27, © Kingfisher plc; Exhibit 16.10 Reproduced with permission from 'History of Accounting and Auditing System in Japan' in English. Website of the Japanese Institute of Certified Public Accountants (JICPA) Copyright © 2008 by the JICPA. All rights reserved. Used with permission; Exhibits 16.11 (Organization of the Financial Accounting Standards Foundation, 2007) and 16.12 (Organization of the ASBJ [2007]). Financial Accounting Standards Foundation, Japan; Exhibit 16.14 from Consolidated Accounts in Journal of Accounting and Public Policy, McKinnon and Harrison, p. 209, (1985) with permission from Elsevier.

In some instances we have been unable to trace the owners of copyright material, and we would appreciate any information that would enable us to do so.

Plan of the book

Part 1 GLOBALIZATION – CONVERGENCE AND DIVERSITY		
Chapter 1 Global accounting: what and why?	**Chapter 2** Investors and listed companies	**Chapter 3** Confidence and assurance
Chapter 4 Transparency and disclosure		**Chapter 5** Choices in global accounting

Part 2 CONTRASTING HARMONIZATION AND DIVERSITY ACROSS CORPORATE REPORTING SYSTEMS			
Chapter 6 Institutional and external influences on accounting rules and practices	**Chapter 7** Cultural influences on accounting rules and practices	**Chapter 8** Classification of accounting systems	**Chapter 9** Measuring harmonization and diversity

Part 3 SIGNIFICANT INFLUENCES ON INTERNATIONAL ACCOUNTING PRACTICES	
Chapter 10 Developing the IASB's accounting standards	**Chapter 11** The United States of America
Chapter 12 Harmonization across the European Union	**Chapter 13** Some debates on global standard setting

Part 4 FROM NATIONAL TO INTERNATIONAL STANDARDS			
Chapter 14 EU member states	**Chapter 15** United Kingdom	**Chapter 16** Japan	**Chapter 17** China

PART 1

Globalization – convergence and diversity

Introduction to Part 1

In Chapter 1 we ask why there have been differences between accounting systems and whether now is the right time to move from national to global accounting systems. We also consider the contenders for the long-term role of global standard setter.

In Chapter 2 we focus on investors and companies to ask how reducing international diversity will affect a wide range of corporate decisions. We ask how investors cope with different forms of corporate reporting and how companies make efforts to communicate with an international readership.

Chapter 3 reflects the embedding of recent years' changes in corporate governance and assurance across many countries. There were events, particularly the Asian economic crisis of 1997 and the collapse of Enron in 2001, that severely shook confidence in accounting information. Restoring confidence and providing assurance in the integrity and reliability of financial reporting has created a new approach to regulation around the world. Chapter 3 leads with the Sarbanes–Oxley Act of 2002 in the USA, and then explains the procedures taken in a range of countries in recent years to establish or reinforce confidence in the financial reporting systems of companies.

Chapter 4 turns to transparency, which is a key theme of regulators seeking high-quality financial reporting. It discusses the meaning of transparency and gives examples of regulation and practice seeking to improve transparency in corporate reporting. It also indicates those aspects of corporate reporting where diversity in national practice will continue for some years to come.

Chapter 5 brings this part to a conclusion with a description of accounting practice in three areas where diversity under national regulation was considerable. It outlines the problems of a series of technical issues and contrasts the IASB and FASB positions on each. Some items are under attention in the short-term convergence project of the two bodies; others will remain different for longer; and some differences have disappeared under some controversy.

Purpose of Part 1

Part 1 forms a self-contained module that provides a general overview of issues relating to global accounting standards. It sets the scene for a deeper subsequent study of specific regulatory regimes in Part 3 and specific countries in Part 4. However, it could also be taken as a stand-alone short course to broaden the perspective of students in honours year or masters study after acquiring a national perspective in a traditional course on financial accounting.

Learning outcomes

Specific learning outcomes are set out at the start of each chapter, but overall, on completion of Part 1, the student should be able to:

- present arguments for and against the movement towards global accounting standards;
- explain why information is needed, and how it is supplied, to investors in global capital markets;
- explain and discuss the mechanisms for audit and assurance that have developed in recent years in response to crises of confidence caused by major financial collapses;
- explain and discuss the meaning of 'transparency' in corporate reporting and the developments aimed at improving transparency;
- explain and discuss accounting issues facing multinational companies in business combinations, segmental reporting and foreign currency translation.

1

Global accounting: what and why?

Learning outcomes

After reading this chapter you should be able to:

- Explain the types of differences that may exist between financial reports from different companies or countries.
- Discuss the arguments for and against global accounting standards.
- Explain why global standards may or may not be appropriate for developing countries or for small and medium-sized companies.
- Understand the arguments used in support of possible alternative global standard setters.

1.1 Sources of differences between accounting systems

Whenever the accounting rules permit more than one alternative treatment for the same event, or whenever an accounting rule requires the use of judgements, estimates or forecasts, different individuals and different companies are likely to produce different figures. Similarly, they may decide to disclose voluntarily different amounts or types of information. This means that, at least when talking about relatively large or complex organizations, no two accountants or two companies will report the same set of events in exactly the same way. While differences will exist inside a single country, you may expect two companies from different countries to show even greater differences.

The differences between two sets of accounts may be due to three factors:

- differences in the rules of different countries;
- differences in the ways in which the rules are interpreted or implemented;
- differences in preferred practices (including voluntary disclosure practices).

Each of these types of differences will be briefly explored below.

1.1.1 Differences in accounting rules

The most obvious reason why companies use different accounting methods or report different information is because the rules or regulations in each country are different. Differences can exist at all levels of the accounting system. For example, recognition rules may be based on different definitions of an asset (e.g. using either legal ownership or economic control-based definitions) or the relative importance accorded to various accounting principles may be different, in particular the matching or accruals principle and the prudence or conservatism principle. Countries can also adopt different valuation methods, ranging from strict historical cost to full current cost systems. Disclosure rules can also vary across countries. Differences in disclosure regulations include differences in the scope of the financial statements (whether only group or group plus individual company accounts), differences in the types of organizations regulated (whether all large organizations or all limited liability companies or only listed companies) and differences in the amount of information demanded.

At least until relatively recently, no two countries had identical accounting systems. In some cases – such as those of the UK and Ireland, or the USA and Canada – the differences were generally relatively few and relatively minor. In other instances, even of geographically proximate countries such as, for example, the UK and France, or the USA and Mexico, the differences have been much greater, including some quite fundamental differences. As described in Part 3, this is the main reason why the International Accounting Standards Board (IASB) has been so involved in setting accounting standards. Since it first started in 1973 the standards issued have over time covered more contentious areas of accounting and have gradually contained fewer options. As discussed in Chapter 10, the IASB has become more and more successful in reducing international diversity in accounting practices as more countries have begun to use international standards rather than purely domestic standards. Exhibit 1.1 provides some details of the current status of international standards worldwide.

If we look at the position prior to any really significant impact of IASB on practices, then we can see some major differences in accounting rules. For example, Nobes (1988)

Exhibit 1.1   Status of international accounting standards as applied to listed companies

Not permitted	Permitted	Required	To be introduced
Argentina	Bermuda	All of EU	Brazil 2010
Bangladesh	Bolivia	Australia	Chile 2009
Canada	Israel	Egypt	India 2011
Colombia	Mexico	Ghana	Japan 2011 for existing standards
Japan	Paraguay	Hong Kong	
Malaysia	Sri Lanka	Jordon	
Pakistan	Switzerland	Kenya	
South Africa	Zambia	New Zealand	
Thailand		Philippines	
Tunisia		Russia (piecemeal introduction from 2006)	
USA		Uruguay	
		Venezuela	

Source: www.iasplus.com/country/useias.htm (at August 2007).

describes 12 major differences that then existed between the rules in the USA and the UK:[1]

- Inventories: UK generally does not permit LIFO (Last In, First Out), while it is commonly used in USA.
- Deferred tax: USA provides for full deferred tax, UK only provides to the extent that liability is likely to arise in future.
- Foreign currency translation: UK permits use of average or closing rate for translation of income statement, USA only permits use of average rate.
- Fixed assets: USA does not permit upward revaluation.
- Goodwill: USA requires amortization, UK permits amortization or immediate write-off to reserves.
- Subsidiaries: only USA requires consolidation of all subsidiaries.
- Pooling: different definitions of when this method can be used.
- Dividends: USA does not provide for declared dividends.
- Extraordinary items: USA does not permit inclusion of gains or losses on disposal of businesses.
- Capitalization of interest: USA requires capitalization in certain situations, UK permits capitalization as one option.
- Oil and gas: different rules apply in certain situations.
- R&D: USA requires expenditure, UK allows capitalization in certain situations.

---

[1] As reported in Weetman and Gray (1991).

While this is a list of rules that differs in their application in the two countries, it may be instead that a particular rule only applies to one country. For example, as discussed in Chapter 5, group or consolidated accounts were not required in much of Europe until relatively recently. Other examples of areas that are regulated in some countries but not others include accounting for financial instruments or pension costs.

1.1.2 Differences in the interpretation of accounting rules

Even where the rules of two countries are identical, they may be interpreted or applied in consistently different ways by companies in different countries. Many areas of accounting entail the use of estimates, forecasts or judgements. For example, to calculate economic depreciation rates you must first decide on the most suitable allocation basis, the useful life of the asset and its residual value. All of these involve the use of estimates, forecasts and judgement. Similarly, non-current asset valuation depends upon expectations of whether the company is a going concern or not (IAS 10) while inventory valuation demands the prediction of 'estimated selling costs and estimated costs of completion and the estimated costs necessary to make the sale' (IAS 2).

Alternatively, different accountants may interpret rules in slightly different ways. For example, treatment of a lease may depend upon how they interpret 'major part of economic life' or 'substantially all of fair value' (IAS 17), while revenue recognition demands interpretation of 'significant risks and rewards of ownership' and 'continuing managerial involvement to the degree usually associated with ownership' (IAS 18). The treatment of contingent assets and liabilities (IAS 37) depends upon exactly what is meant by terms such as 'probable' (does this mean, for example, 95 per cent certain, or is an event with an 85 per cent chance of occurring still probable?) and 'remote' (is this an event with a 10 per cent chance, a 5 per cent chance or only a 2 per cent chance of occurring?).

The use of judgements, forecasts and estimates and the interpretation of ambiguous terminology mean that identical events may be measured and reported in different ways by different companies. Obviously, there may be differences inside a country, but the differences may often be much greater in an international setting. One reason for this is differences in the culture of countries, as discussed in Chapter 7, so that individuals tend to act in predictably different ways in the countries. For example, Davidson and Chrisman (1993) looked at the first 24 IAS published in both English and French in Canada. They found that the translations of ambiguous terms such as 'likely', 'normally', 'usually' or 'remote' were not always consistent and that, in almost half of the cases looked at, English- and French-speaking students interpreted the terms in significantly different ways. Similar differences also exist when applying local standards in different countries. Schultz and Lopez (2001) found evidence that auditors from France, Germany and the USA interpreted similar domestic rules in different ways. In this case, when asked to decide upon the amount to estimate for warranty costs, the French accountants were the most conservative in their estimates as well as the ones most affected by the way in which the actual question was framed, whether in optimistic or pessimistic terms (similar to the alternatives of describing a glass as being half full or half empty).

Doupnik and Richter (2003) looked both at translations, as Davidson and Chrisman did, and at untranslated rules, as did Schultz and Lopez, and supported both sets of conclusions. Using US and German auditors and IAS uncertainty expressions, they found that there was a translation effect in that Germans working in English tended to use less of the continuum of certainty/uncertainty (they were asked to put quantitative measures from 0 to 100 per cent against uncertainty terms) than did German speakers working in

German.[2] This was not simply a country effect, in that there were no differences between Swiss, Austrian and German auditors. There was also a culture effect in that native German-speaking accountants working in English and US accountants working in English often attributed significantly different point estimates to the same term. Doupnik and Riccio (2006) found that cultural differences could explain different interpretations of probability measures in Brazil (as a Latin American country) compared with Anglo-American interpretations.

These findings are probably to be expected. While accounting is often described as a science, implying extremely high levels of objectivity, we will see in Part 2 how accounting rules and practices are influenced by a wide variety of factors. For example, we will see how the link between taxation and financial reporting and the creditor versus shareholder orientation of the financial statements might affect attitudes towards income measurement. Similarly, it seems reasonable to argue that culture may affect how someone interprets particular rules. For example, a person coming from a society that is relatively unhappy with uncertainty may interpret 'probable' in a more restrictive way than will someone coming from a society that is more comfortable with uncertainty.

1.1.3 Differences in preferred accounting practices

A distinction must be made between accounting regulations, or *de jure* issues, and actual practices, or *de facto* issues. The political and economic systems of countries differ, as will be discussed in Chapter 6. This means that companies from different countries may want to report different pictures. For example, income smoothing may be more prevalent in some countries than in others, while companies in some countries may consistently choose to report more conservative figures than companies in other countries (see Chapter 9).

While the earliest international standards contained a large number of options, later standards have considerably reduced the amount of choice available, but choice has not been entirely eliminated. For example, companies may choose between historical costs or revalued historical costs for tangible non-current assets (IAS 16) and between recognizing all borrowing costs as an expense or capitalizing borrowing costs on acquisition, construction or production of a qualifying asset (IAS 23). Similarly, IAS 31 permits choice of method for consolidating joint ventures, while IAS 2 permits the use of FIFO (First In, First Out) and weighted average for inventory and IAS 7 permits the disclosure of direct or indirect cash flow statements.

While it is relatively straightforward (although not necessarily easy) to compare the accounting regulations of two countries, this may tell us relatively little about how similar the accounting practices of companies actually are in areas where discretion exists. *De facto* practices may differ considerably across countries, even if there are few *de jure* differences. Alternatively, if all companies, irrespective of country of domicile, choose wherever possible to use similar methods, *de facto* differences may be less than the *de jure* differences.

An idea of the prevalence of differences in actual practices can be seen in the work of Herrmann and Thomas (1995). They looked at the actual practices of large companies in a number of EU countries in 1991–92, again before the IASB had a significant effect on international harmonization. The EU encompasses a range of countries with very different

---

[2] For more on translation effects see, for example, Evans (2004).

Exhibit 1.2   Accounting differences and similarities in the EU, 1991–92

	Belgium	Denmark	France	Germany	Ireland	Netherlands	Portugal	UK
Fixed asset valuation:								
Historical cost	19	12	24	30	5	24	0	9
Modified historical	4	18	6	0	19	6	20	21
Depreciation:								
Straight-line	17	28	26	2	23	30	20	30
Straight-line and declining balance	6	2	4	28	1	0	0	0
Goodwill:								
Write-off	0	18	0	9	17	25	0	29
Capitalize	20	5	30	20	3	2	8	1
R&D:								
Expense	4	15	19	3	10	9	0	25
Capitalize	9	0	0	0	0	4	10	1
Inventory:								
Lower cost/market	22	26	29	30	24	17	7	30
Cost	1	4	1	0	0	8	13	0
Market	0	0	0	0	0	5	0	0
FIFO	2	9	5	0	8	9	2	7
LIFO	6	0	2	15	0	1	0	0
Average	8	2	11	3	0	0	9	2
Combination	3	1	6	1	0	1	8	3
Foreign currency balance sheet translation:								
Current	17	21	30	19	21	27	9	29
Temporal	3	0	0	11	0	1	0	1
Foreign currency income statement translation:								
Average/actual	20	4	29	24	13	18	6	26
Current	0	17	1	6	5	9	2	4
Total	23	30	30	30	24	30	20	30

legal and corporate financing systems. As discussed in Part 2, the literature suggests that these differences will lead to significant differences in accounting requirements and the attitudes of companies towards accounting measurement and disclosure. However, they are also countries that have all had to enforce EU accounting Directives which, while not designed to make accounting practices identical, were designed to introduce harmonious accounting practices and reduce the number and importance of differences. Exhibit 1.2 illustrates their findings that substantial differences existed in the actual practices used by these companies.

Jaafar and McLeay (2007), examining data from the 1990s, show that there was limited convergence in accounting practices for inventory costing, goodwill on consolidation and depreciation of fixed assets. They also question a measure of harmonization that focuses on convergence on one accounting practice only. They argue that comparability is achieved if firms use the method that is appropriate to the circumstances. We discuss the 'harmonization or standardization' debate in section 1.4.4.

1.2 Possible advantages of a single set of global accounting standards

It is generally agreed that both companies and users benefit from accounting regulations. Financial statement information is used in a wide variety of decision-making contexts and is used directly or indirectly in a range of different types of contracts. For example, shareholders need to know what profits have been earned by a company and without financial statement information they would be unlikely to invest in the stock market. Debt providers likewise need to know the financial status of the firm and many debt contracts are couched in accounting terms, with debt covenants designed to protect the interest of debt holders against the competing interest of management or shareholders. Management often receive performance-related bonuses while performance-related pay is not uncommon. It is also difficult to believe that suppliers would extend credit or customers enter into many types of long-term contracts without access to reliable accounting numbers.

Of course one possibility is for the firm and the shareholder, debt holder, employee, customer or supplier to negotiate at the start of each contract exactly what information is to be provided and what accounting rules are to be used. However, this would prove impossible in practice and firms would generally prefer to use one set, or at least a limited set, of rules for all contracts as this decreases their transaction costs. Similarly, the external parties who may be contracting with a number of individual firms would be faced with lower contracting costs if all firms used the same accounting rules.

This suggests that there will be many benefits to companies and users in having a single set of agreed accounting rules. However, as discussed in Part 2 of this book, this does not mean that all companies or all users would easily agree on what this set of rules should look like. This will be a problem inside any one country, but in an international setting this is likely to be even more of a problem. However, if we ignore for now the problems involved in deciding what this set of rules should look like, and if we assume that a set of acceptable rules can be found, then we can explore the potential advantages of a globally agreed set of accounting rules.

1.2.1 Companies as preparers and users of financial statements

Many companies are affected by international accounting differences. A company that engages in any form of international trade may have to use foreign financial statements or prepare financial statements using the rules of other countries. A company that exports or imports goods may want to assess the creditworthiness of its trading partners. A company that wants to borrow money from foreign bankers or other lenders may have to produce financial data using the rules that these potential lenders are familiar with. However, it is multinational companies that will be most affected by international accounting differences. Local accounting rules will have to be used in the financial statements of foreign subsidiaries if these are the statements required by local tax authorities, minority shareholders or debt providers. However, most countries require companies to produce group accounts using consistent accounting methods across all subsidiaries. This may mean that if rules differ across countries the company has to produce two sets of financial statements for some of its subsidiaries – one using local generally accepted accounting principles (GAAP) for local reporting purposes and one using parent company GAAP for consolidation.

If a company is listed on a foreign stock market it will have to meet the listing requirements there. At present stock exchange regulators, particularly the Securities and Exchange Commission (SEC) in the USA, may require a foreign registrant company to prepare financial statements using a set of accounting standards familiar to the stock exchange. Even if the company does not have to produce a full set of financial statements, it may have to produce a 'reconciliation' statement explaining the differences between reported profit and reported net assets under two different sets of accounting standards.

These multiple reporting requirements may involve substantial extra direct costs – there may be additional data collection, collation and auditing costs. There may also be extra indirect costs due to differences in reporting requirements. The existence of different accounting systems may result in the same event being reported in two, or more, very different ways. This may create confusion and dysfunctional behaviour inside the company. If there are two sets of figures each apparently measuring the same events, which is 'correct'? Which one should local management seek to maximize? What should they do if the two accounting systems conflict, so that actions that increase reported earnings under one system reduce earnings reported under the alternative set of rules?

The benefits to multinational companies of having one set of global accounting standards therefore may include:

- reduction in costs of production, collation, dissemination and auditing;
- reduction in the risk of uncertainty and misunderstanding by managers inside the company due to lack of comparability of the information produced within the group by the parent and subsidiaries in different countries;
- more effective communication with investors and other international users of the accounts;
- comparability with other companies in the industry, both nationally and internationally;
- comparability of contractual terms, such as lending contracts and management performance bonuses;
- reduction in excuses for non-disclosure based on national perceptions of secrecy; and
- sharing and extending best practice.

1.2.2 Investors

Portfolio theory tells us that shareholders should invest in a diversified portfolio. While the maximum benefits of diversification are achieved if an investor invests in a portfolio of shares representing a proportionate spread across the entire stock market, considerable benefits can be obtained if the investor buys considerably fewer companies than this provided these are carefully chosen. Just as in a domestic setting investors can reduce their risk by investing in a more diversified portfolio of companies, they can further reduce their risks by investing in companies from many different countries. With increasing ease of international investment, individual shareholders are increasingly investing in foreign shares either directly or indirectly via investment in internationally diversified investment funds (see Chapter 2 for more on this).

However, if companies from different countries produce figures using different methods or provide different information, then their statements will not be comparable with each other. Normally, not enough information is given to allow the user to convert the reported figures to those that would have been produced under a different set of accounting rules. The reader of foreign financial statements may thus have great difficulty in understanding what the figures mean.

For example, if a Japanese investor is interested in a UK company, she may compare its financial statements with a similar Japanese company and find that the UK company appears to be more profitable. This may be because the Japanese company really is less efficient than the UK one. Alternatively, it may be more efficient than the UK company, but it uses accounting methods that reduce its reported earnings in comparison to its UK competitor. If the Japanese investor knows that Japanese accounting rules are different, but she cannot measure the impact of these differences, she may decide not to invest in the UK at all or she may decide to invest in UK companies only if they appear to be very much more profitable than their Japanese alternatives. Whatever investment decision she finally makes, she will probably have made a different decision from that which she would have made had the Japanese and UK companies used the same accounting methods.

For *investors*, the benefits of global accounting standards therefore lie in having assurance about the comparability and the high standard of the accounting information provided. Global accounting standards should:

- reduce the cost of obtaining information by reducing the need to learn different accounting systems and eliminate the need to adjust the reported information to make it more comparable;
- reduce the likelihood of making poor decisions by reducing the risk of misunderstanding different accounting systems; and
- reduce the risk of missing investment opportunities through avoiding unfamiliar national accounting.[3]

While international standards should bring benefits to all investors, whether professional or amateur, they are likely to be of most benefit to individual investors who have less knowledge and experience of different accounting systems and less ability to deal with a great deal of complex accounting information and have less information processing power.[4] Such investors are also likely to be less able to obtain information from other sources and are therefore more dependent upon financial statements than are professionals. Improved disclosures should allow them to compete on more equal terms with professionals.

These direct advantages should lead to other more indirect advantages,[5] namely:

- reduce processing costs, which should increase the efficiency with which stock markets incorporate information in their prices;
- reduce barriers to cross-border acquisitions and divestments so increasing takeover premiums available to investors; and
- increase demand for share investment, which may decrease company's cost of capital.

---

[3] Miles and Nobes (1998).
[4] Hirshleifer and Teoh (2003).
[5] Ball (2006).

1.2.3 Other groups affected by international differences

If companies or shareholders make different decisions because of international differences in accounting, other groups will also be affected. If differences in disclosure rules affect a company's foreign location decision, then local communities, actual and potential employees and governments will all be affected. Similarly, stock market listing decisions affect the stock market(s) themselves, other stock market participants and the balance of payments of countries. Shareholders' investment decisions have secondary impacts or implications for other companies that are not invested in, and for the economy as a whole.

But it is not only companies and shareholders that use financial statements. Employees of foreign-owned subsidiaries and their trade union representatives may use financial statements in negotiations on pay or conditions. Host governments may use financial statements to help them in economic planning. Customers, suppliers and lenders may want to gauge the creditworthiness or future prospects of foreign-owned companies. They may not have the power to demand information produced under local rules and they will have to rely upon financial statements produced under unfamiliar foreign rules. This may mean that they have to spend extra resources in learning about the accounting differences and in calculating their impact on the reported figures. Alternatively, they may be unable or unwilling to do this. In this case they are likely to be misled by the financial statements and they may make wrong decisions because of this.

Finally, accountants have to audit the statements of multinational groups, including foreign subsidiaries. The problems and additional expenses involved in having to understand and audit figures produced under multiple accounting jurisdictions may be considerable.

For *national governments*, accounting information gives a basis for taxation and for ensuring that companies operating in their country show sufficient care for the resources used in the country.

Very often we see cases where the national accounting regulations of one country look much like those of another and it seems wasteful of time and effort to develop national rules that are almost identical to established rules that appear to work well elsewhere. So if the national government can accept a set of global standards there are benefits in:

- reducing the cost of setting and monitoring national accounting regulation;
- avoiding duplication of effort across national boundaries;
- encouraging international flows of capital across national borders;
- giving greater confidence to international investors and lenders.

While developed countries are likely to benefit from the reduced costs of standard setting, the benefits may be much greater for developing countries. Standard setting is expensive and these countries are less able to afford a high-quality standard-setting system.[6] They are also countries that tend to be the host rather than home to multinational companies. This raises particular concerns for domestic standard setters. The fear is that multinationals are mobile, they are able to move to other countries and they will do so if faced with particularly severe or unpopular regulations. This may mean that developing countries are unable or unwilling to produce standards that such companies

---

[6] Chamisa (2000).

do not support. For example, this argument is behind the Publish What You Pay (PWYP) campaign. This is an international campaign started in June 2002 by George Soros and a number of non-governmental organizations (NGOs) with the aim of helping citizens in resource-rich developing countries hold their governments accountable for the management of revenues from oil, gas and mining industries. It currently has over 300 NGOs worldwide as coalition members. It has called for the disclosure of payments made by the companies in those industries to governments on a country-by-country basis, as is illustrated by the PWYP mission statement extract reproduced in Exhibit 1.3. This campaign was started as no single developing country would have the power to introduce these measures, but if countries act together then multinational companies would have to comply as they could not simply move to an alternative resource-rich country. As discussed in Chapter 13, the PWYP campaign has been active in lobbying on the proposed new international segment standard.

These pressures leading towards the use of global accounting standards have been shown graphically by Rahman *et al.* (2002) in Exhibit 1.4.

1.3 Possible disadvantages of a single set of global accounting standards

While many writers wholeheartedly support the introduction of global standards, there are others who argue that the disadvantages outweigh the advantages either in all cases, or for at least some countries and some companies.

There are several reasons why sceptics are dubious about the advantages of global standards. If the standards are to be successful they must reduce diversity, so that some existing methods of accounting will no longer be permitted. Global standards can only be set if national governments and standard setters agree to them. This means that there must be a reasonable level of support for the proposed rules. Typically, exposure drafts are issued, comment letters and hearings take place and the final standard emerges with a relatively high level of international support. As discussed in Chapter 13, this is a political process and like any political process is dependent upon consensus and will probably be influenced by lobbying activities.[7] The likelihood of any particular method being acceptable is dependent not simply upon its theoretical acceptability or the extent to which it meets the conceptual framework, but also on its international acceptability to companies, governments, accountants and users. This is likely to result in a set of 'one size fits all' regulation with local differences or characteristics being ignored. A country or company with unique needs or characteristics may be forced to accept what is suitable for the majority and will no longer be able to adopt a different method of accounting more suited to its own circumstances. Thus, amongst those who ask more fundamental questions about convergence on one set of global standards, some ask 'what creates true harmony?' McLeay *et al.* (1999) argue that the level of harmony depends on adopting the same accounting method under the same circumstances (such as across the same industry), and different methods under different circumstances rather than forcing uniformity on all companies regardless of circumstances.

This discussion leads to the following possible disadvantages or limitations of global standards.

---

[7] Zeff (2002).

| Exhibit 1.3 | Mission statement of the Publish What You Pay coalition |

The Publish What You Pay coalition calls on:

- **Multi-national, private and state-owned extractive companies** to disclose a net figure for all types of payments (royalties, taxes, bonuses etc) made to governments for every country of operation in their annual financial accounts, and to disclose to which level of government payments are made;

- **Governments of resource-rich countries** to:
  - ○ Require disclosure of payments by all extractive companies operating in their territory on a company-by-company basis and by payment type;
  - ○ *Publish What You Earn*, i.e. disclose fully revenues from resource extraction;
  - ○ Independently audit and verify this information in line with best international practice. This can be achieved by way of full implementation of the Extractive Industries Transparency Initiative and compliance with international codes and standards on natural resource and fiscal transparency, such as the IMF *Guide on Resource Revenue Transparency*;
  - ○ Put in place mechanisms for sub-national reporting of payments and revenues;
  - ○ Establish open, participatory and transparent budget processes at national, regional and local levels in order to consult with civil society on the effective allocation and management of revenues from resource extraction and public finances in order to promote broad-based economic and social development;

- **Governments of OECD countries** to require country-by-country disclosure of payments of all extractive companies registered or listed on financial markets in their country;

- **Bilateral and multi-lateral financial institutions**, including the World Bank Group, IMF, regional development banks, export credit agencies and private sector banks, to require *extractive companies* to comply with the Publish What You Pay requirements on transparency of payments as a pre-condition of all project support, and *governments* to have in place a functioning system to account for and independently audit revenues from extractive industries in return for non-humanitarian/non-emergency development, technical and financial assistance;

- **Donor organisations to promote the empowerment and capacity building of civil society organisations** across resource-rich countries in order to allow citizens to hold their government accountable for the management and expenditure of revenues received from the extractive industries.

In addition to these measures:

- Extractive companies and local authorities should disclose information about **social investments** and **payments to local budgets** made by extractive companies. These payments and investments can be important factors of sustainable social and economic development and thus the public should be involved in the process of managing these revenues;

- To promote full accountability of companies and governments in the management of resource revenues we also call for the public disclosure of **extractive industry contracts** and for **licensing procedures** to be carried out transparently in line with best international practice. As contracts typically include schedules, formulas and other determinants of the government's potential revenue streams (such as revenue sharing arrangements, taxes, royalties, bonuses, social benefits, etc., and exemptions from any of these) fulfilling the public's right to access these contracts (with exemptions for provisions that are genuinely commercial confidential information) will help inform citizens about how much their government is supposed to receive from resource extraction, which can then be compared with how much the government actually receives. Contract transparency can thus help civil society understand whether governments have struck deals with extractive sector projects that are in the public interest, and then whether promised revenues actually materialise.

Source: www.publishwhatyoupay.org/engliah/pwyp_mission_statement.doc.

16

Exhibit 1.4 A model of the pressures towards increased harmonization

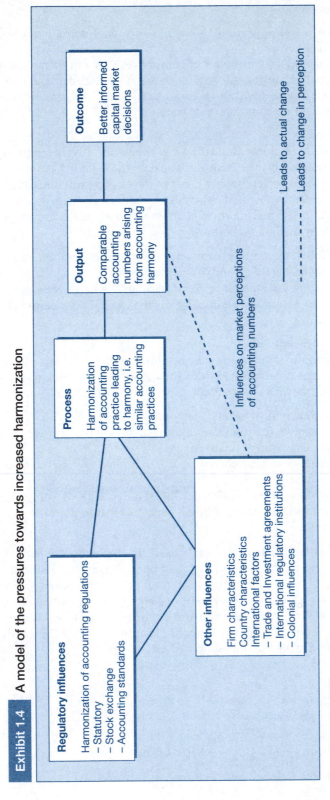

Source: Rahman et al. (2002).

For *national companies*:

- they have less opportunities to influence an international standard setter than a domestic one;
- their business and economic circumstances may not be faithfully represented by the prescribed accounting procedures of the global standard; and
- they may be faced with high costs of changing from one set of standards to another with little or no commensurate benefits.

For *investors*:

While the use of global standards may appear intuitively appealing for investors, they may not understand the basis on which the standards have been written, particularly the strong focus on serving the needs of developed capital markets. This is likely to be a particular problem for smaller investors who lack the expertise and skills of the professional investors so placing them at an even greater disadvantage. This means that disadvantages may include the following:

- using global standards gives an appearance of comparability but hides real differences in commercial activity; and
- the use of global standards, particularly in the early years of changeover, can cause confusion nationally, especially if the global standards are seen as reducing precision.[8]

For *national government*:

The attraction of saving costs may be outweighed by the loss of control over the nature and content of the accounting standards. Also the government still has the task of ensuring compliance with the standards. Limitations for national governments are:

- there is no reason to believe that 'one system fits all';
- harmonizing on full disclosure may be detrimental to developing countries by putting them at a competitive disadvantage;[9]
- developing countries may not be able to influence global standards as much as developed countries;[10] and
- comparability of financial reporting standards needs comparability of compliance and without this the potential benefits of international standards may not be realized.[11]

To a large extent the argument for or against a single set of global standards is actually an argument about globalization premised upon the assumption that the most important, if not the only important, users of accounting information are international capital market participants.[12] If purely national companies dominate an economy, if the economy has few international investors, or if the national accounting system is designed with a wide concept of accountability in mind to serve the needs of other local user groups, then many of the supposed advantages of global standards are unlikely to materialize.[13]

---

[8] Barth *et al.* (1999).
[9] Kirby (2001).
[10] Rahman (1998).
[11] Ball *et al.* (2003); Holthausen (2003); Chen *et al.* (2002).
[12] Hopwood (1994); Arnold and Sikka (2001).
[13] Lehman (2005).

Ball (2006) lists many features of the world as it affects accounting that look more local or country specific than global, namely:

- extent and nature of government involvement in the economy;
- politics of government involvement in financial reporting practice (e.g. political influence of managers, corporations, labour unions, banks);
- legal systems (e.g. common versus code law; shareholder litigation rules);
- securities regulation and regulatory bodies;
- depth of financial markets;
- financial market structure (e.g. closeness of relationship between banks and client companies);
- the role of the press, financial analysts and rating agencies;
- size of the corporate sector;
- structure of corporate governance (e.g. relative roles of labour, management and capital);
- extent of private versus public ownership of corporations;
- extent of family-controlled businesses;
- extent of corporate membership in related-company groups (e.g. Japanese *keiretsu* or Korean *chaebol*);
- extent of financial intermediation;
- the role of small shareholders versus institutions and corporate insiders;
- the use of financial statement information, including earnings, in management compensation; and
- the status, independence, timing and compensation of auditors.

This suggests that for many companies and users who are not involved in international transactions, there may be few, if any, benefits of global standards. However, the advantages or disadvantages of such standards cannot be considered in isolation of consideration of what the standards actually require. If a global standard setter manages to introduce a set of standards that meet the needs of the local economic–political environment, then that may bring benefits to all preparers and users even if they are not involved in any international activities. If instead it sets standards that are less appropriate or useful than the existing domestic standards, then that will bring few advantages even to companies or investors involved in international investment activities.

1.4 What should global standards look like?

1.4.1 FASB standards or IASB standards?

Two systems of accounting have been frequently advocated as the optimal set of international standards. Some believe that generally accepted accounting principles in the USA (US GAAP) are based on a high-quality set of standards written by the Financial Accounting Standards Board (FASB standards) that would be acceptable anywhere in the world. Others believe that a better approach is to draw on the international financial reporting standards (IFRS) of the IASB.[14] Some feel that IFRS are too closely influenced by the Anglo-American model and have a homogeneity that does not recognize national

---

[14] Leuz (2003).

diversity.[15] Mutual recognition of different approaches, with benchmarks to guide comparability, would be more respectful of different identities and is an alternative favoured by some.

The US regulators take the view that US standards are of a high quality and question anything that does not meet the detailed content of US GAAP. Other countries take the view that US rules are biased towards US needs and want to have a direct involvement in setting a truly international set of standards. This second view has been helped greatly by the European Commission recommending that, from 2005, all listed companies in EU member states should apply IFRS. This debate is not yet resolved and Part 3 of this book discusses this area in much more detail.

Some have argued that having a monopoly standard setter rather than competitive standards may lead to poorer standards.[16] Instead, they suggest that companies should be allowed to choose to use all the FASB standards or all the IASB standards. Investors will be more likely to invest in companies using high-quality standards that are attuned to their needs, so giving companies a financial incentive to use the 'better' set of standards. The market will decide which set of standards is more useful and the standard setters in turn will have an incentive to meet these demands as they wish their standard to be used.

This argument of course focuses entirely on stock market participants who have a direct relationship with the company and have the market power to purchase effectively the preferred set of standards. It ignores the need of other users such as governments, suppliers, customers, employees or the general public who may also have preferences, but lack the market power to influence corporate choice.

1.4.2 Global standards and developing countries

Others question the suitability of either US GAAP or IFRS. Both are written for companies in highly developed capital markets. They are then used as a basis for an accounting system in developing economies that have little or no capital market transactions, and may not be appropriate to such economies.[17] There have been stages in the development of the IASB, and its predecessor IASC, when projects were begun with the intention of focusing on developing economies, but relatively little has emerged.

While there has been much debate in the past on the usefulness to developing countries of either international accounting standards or developed countries' standards, there has in contrast been relatively little evidence provided whether in support of or against the use of such standards. This is inevitable as it is impossible to prove empirically which set of accounting standards is most appropriate – obviously you cannot run a scientific experiment with some countries having to use international standards and other countries being forced to use alternative standards.

Perera (1989) argues that Anglo-American or by extension international accounting standards are unlikely to be useful to developing countries as they tend to differ from developed countries in terms of the political–economic system, business ownership structures, users of accounting information and country-wide and corporate cultures. In particular, the capital market will generally be less important while the small-company

---

[15] Hoarau (1995).

[16] Sunder (2002); Dye and Sunder (2001).

[17] Larson and Kenny (1995).

and NGO sectors are relatively more important. The accounting profession is typically less strong and accounting technology is less available. The government is often more important and is more involved in managing the economy. Perera suggests that instead what is needed is a system where it is easier to prepare and use information and where there is better integration of financial accounting, management accounting and public sector and national income accounting. Such a system must recognize that generally the profession is not as strong as it is in countries such as the UK or USA with accountants and managers generally not being as well trained and that the government and the culture of the country both tend to favour a more uniform system of accounting. Hove (1986) instead is most concerned with the fact that developing countries tend to play host to multinational companies. Reflecting similar concerns to those of the PWYP Group, he argues that any system of accounting must concentrate less upon issues of measurement practices and must instead pay more attention to the needs of the country, in particular its development needs, and the need of the government for information. Particularly important are likely to be information on matters such as taxation, balance of payments, employment and environmental impacts. He also argues that the accounting education system of most developing countries is currently too similar to that of the western countries and that it overemphasizes technical competence and does not sufficiently train accountants to consider the impacts of what they are doing and whether or not alternatives exist that would be better for the country. Tyrrall *et al.* (2007) examine the case for implementing IFRS in Kazakhstan, using interview research to explore the problems faced in IFRS implementation. They question the presumption of IFRS relevance to the needs of developing countries but find acceptance that the country had no choice but to proceed with IFRS adoption.

Others, such as Chamisa (2000) in contrast, argue instead that western accounting as reflected in international standards is useful for developing countries in that many developing countries have stock markets and that they need to develop these further if they are to be successful.

Larson and Kenny (1996) argue that these different perspectives reflect different theories of economic development and different views on appropriate standard-setting strategies. Specifically, they identify three possible accounting setting strategies. Harmonization strategies are based upon the view that accounting is universal, similar transactions and events occur everywhere and the accounting system should likewise be similar everywhere. Exhibit 1.5 provides a simple summary of this type of argument.

The harmonization strategy is most appropriate if the strict form of modernization theory holds in practice. This says that economic development is a process with discrete development stages that all countries must pass through and today's developing countries can replicate the processes used in the past by other countries. So if accounting systems have been developed and found useful in the wealthiest countries of the west, they

---

Exhibit 1.5 An argument in favour of global accounting standards

> Accounting is essentially concerned with measurement, so it would be reasonable to expect that principles of measurement should be the same in any country. The language used to add words of explanation may differ but the reported values should not be affected by barriers of language. Companies operating and reporting in more than one country should not experience different measures of financial outcomes solely because of the accounting principles of the country in which the head office is located.

will also be useful for, and should be used by, developing countries which wish to emulate the economic success of these countries. However, it is unlikely that today's developing countries can simply follow the same development path that was earlier followed by the developed countries. When the developed countries industrialized, developed their stock markets, grew their multinational companies, established their accounting professions or started setting accounting rules they were the first countries to do so. Developing countries tend instead to play host to multinational companies and must compete in the international economy with very much richer and more powerful developed countries. What was useful or appropriate for developed countries and what helped them develop may not be appropriate in the very different world facing today's developing countries.

The second approach to standard setting is the naturalistic or situationist strategy. This implies that while many transactions are universal, there will also be some environment-based differences and the accounting system needs to be adapted to reflect these differences. This approach would be more appropriate if a more flexible form of modernization theory holds. The flexible modernization theory argues that while all development processes will show similarities and all countries will tend to go through a similar process, it will differ from country to country. Similarly, accounting should be similar, but it must adapt to unique circumstances in each country, a so-called contingency theory of accounting.[18]

The third standard-setting strategy is the particularism or evolutionary strategy which argues that environments are so different that accounting regulations and practices need to be developed by each country. This fits best with dependency theory and world system theory which argue that there is no universal process of development. Indeed they argue that the present structure of economic relationships is such that it prevents the poorest countries from achieving significant economic growth. This implies that the solutions to their economic problems may be very different from the processes that were adopted by the wealthier countries. Likewise, the accounting systems that are optimal for these countries may also be quite different.

Even if either the naturalistic or particularism view is accepted it does not necessarily mean that developing countries should not use international standards, although they will probably need to be supplemented by additional disclosure and perhaps also measurement requirements covering a variety of areas of particular relevance to developing countries such as social, environmental and international trade information. It may be that while international standards are far from perfect, they may be better than the alternatives available. Creating an accounting system is expensive and time consuming and requires a high level of technical ability across a relatively large group of individuals. Most developing countries have lacked the necessary resources for this. In practice therefore most have either willingly or unwillingly imported many or even all of the accounting practices and rules of a developed country, as discussed in Chapter 6. If this is the case and if a country is faced in practice with two alternatives, import for example US rules or import international rules, it may well prefer the international rules. This may be because importing rules from the USA or from a past colonial master such as the UK may be politically unpopular, or it may be because at least with international standards developing countries have some input into the standard-setting process, however small, whereas they have absolutely no voice in the standard setting of the USA or any other individual country.

---

[18] See, for example, Talaga and Ndubizu (1986); Wallace (1990).

A final possibility may be to develop regional standards used by a group of countries. While no two countries are identical and developing countries encompass a wide range of countries differing greatly in terms of wealth, development, types of natural resources and industries, and political, social and cultural factors, there are similarities between at least some of them. Therefore, it might be argued that rather than each country developing its own standards, an alternative is for groups of similar countries to develop their own accounting systems. For example, the OCAM plan is used in member states of the Customs and Economic Union of Central Africa (UDEAC) or the so-called Francophone African countries.[19] This is based upon the French Plan Comptable and it has some clear advantages in terms of simplicity and uniformity.[20] However, it has had no impact on accounting practices in any countries outside this relatively small group of countries and other regional groupings have generally been far from successful in developing regional accounting systems.

1.4.3 International standards and small and medium-sized enterprises

Just as there has been debate on whether or not a single set of global standards is appropriate for developing countries, there has also been a similar debate on whether a single set of standards is appropriative for companies of all sizes. As discussed in Part 3 of this book, the types of organizations that are covered by standards vary considerably around the world. At one extreme is the USA where only listed companies are required to produce statements using prescribed accounting standards. In the past the FASB and AICPA have both considered the appropriateness of introducing a second set of GAAP for smaller corporations[21] with the latest study occurring in 2004–05.[22] This wide-ranging survey of lenders, investors, owners, managers and accountants concluded that the existing so-called 'big-company GAAP' would be of some value to smaller companies, especially as they help to ensure greater consistency and comparability. However, there was also general agreement that big-company GAAP contained several rules that were not decision useful for smaller entities and that ideally small-company GAAP should be different. It was also felt that the benefits of developing a specific set of small-company GAAP would outweigh the costs and that the best way forward was to develop a new set of GAAP rather than start with existing GAAP and then introduce a series of exemptions. Some of the more important differences between small companies and large companies were felt to be:

- Capital succession considerations or planned transfer of ownership.
- Different capital structures including sole proprietorship and partnership.
- Income and estate tax planning considerations.
- Common use of loans backed by personal guarantees.
- Ownership typically more closely held and often involved in management of business.
- Stewardship needs are more important than valuation needs.

While this study is not without its critics,[23] many of the views espoused have also been seen in the international arena where similar debates have been taking place. While

---

[19] United Nations (1991).

[20] Elad (1995); Elad (1996).

[21] FASB (1981); AICPA (1976); AICPA (1981); AICPA (1995).

[22] AICPA (2005).

[23] AAA (2006).

some countries require all companies to use international standards, others require listed companies to follow international standards and unlisted companies instead to follow domestic rules, with some countries such as the UK having a simplified set of rules for its smallest companies.

In June 2004 the IASB issued a discussion paper followed in February 2007 by an exposure draft (ED) on an international standard for small and medium-sized enterprises (SMEs). While initially these were defined in terms of size criteria, this is now to be left to individual countries because what counts as small will vary across countries. However, the proposed standard is aimed at all companies that do not issue public debt or equity (except financial institutions) and that publish general purpose financial statements. The ED suggests that IFRS for SMEs are suitable for a typical SME with about 50 employees. In many countries that would be quite a large entity. It leads to the question of whether there needs to be further refinement of the accounting principles for very small enterprises (micro-entities). Aspects of this ED are contentious and are still being debated, especially questions such as:

- How is an SME defined?
- Should a 'top-down' approach be adopted with the standard being based on existing GAAP or should a new set of GAAP be introduced?
- Should only the disclosure rules differ from big-company GAAP or should at least some measurement and recognition rules also be different?
- Exactly which areas should be covered?[24]

The idea of such a standard has generally been favourably received with there being a relatively high level of agreement that international standards impose too high a cost on the smallest entities. For SMEs the costs of compliance seem to outweigh the benefits. However, there is more debate on whether small-company GAAP are really an appropriate issue for international standard setters or whether they are an issue best left to domestic standard setters.

As discussed above, most of the benefits of global standards accrue to stock market participants or to multinational companies. It is far less obvious that purely domestic companies would benefit from them. These are the companies that will be most likely affected by purely local environmental differences and so are the companies that would perhaps most benefit from domestic rules that can best reflect any unique environmental features. The debate on the appropriateness of global or international standards therefore depends upon whether or not there is currently a local alternative to international standards in existence. If there is not and SMEs have currently to follow international standards then a simplified and more appropriate set of international rules is probably a very good idea. However, if there is currently a domestic alternative then the case for an international standard depends upon the answer to two questions. Firstly, to what extent are SMEs really part of an international economy? It may well be that smaller countries will most benefit from international GAAP for SMEs as the smaller the country is then the more likely it is that its small companies will be involved in international trade and have to deal with customers or suppliers from other countries who are not familiar with domestic rules. Secondly, what are the specific circumstances of that country – how different are domestic small-company GAAP from international big-company GAAP and how difficult or expensive will it be for a company to move from

---

[24] See, for example, Sian and Roberts (2006); Sian and Roberts (2008); and the IASB website www.iasb.org.

domestic to international rules? And what exactly are the differences between domestic and international rules? Are the differences of particular importance and is the information produced when using domestic rules very much more useful or appropriate to the specific needs of local SMEs?

1.4.4 Harmonization or standardization?

Even when there is agreement that the benefits of global accounting standards outweigh the limitations, there is still a question of 'What kind of standards?' Do we want harmonization leading to harmony, or standardization leading to uniformity? **Harmonization** is a process by which accounting moves away from total diversity of practice. The end result is the state of **harmony** where all participants in the process cluster around one of the available methods of accounting, or around a limited number of very closely related methods. **Standardization** is a process by which all participants agree to follow the same or very similar accounting practices. Where this agreement is achieved, the end result is a state of **uniformity**.[25]

Those who support an aim of achieving harmony take a liberal view of what is meant by similarity of accounting method. It may be achieved as a result of natural forces such as changes in culture, growth of economic groupings, international trade, political dependency, or evolution of new securities markets. Such forces cause enterprises, accounting organizations or national regulators to learn from and imitate each other's practices. International organizations seeking to promote harmony are usually formed by groups of like-minded individuals or representatives of national organizations who try to use powers of persuasion and argument to promote harmonization.

Those who support an aim of achieving uniformity take a much stricter view of what is meant by the same or very similar accounting practices. Achievement of uniformity within a defined period of time requires the intervention of a regulator or facilitator. The regulator may try to use powers of persuasion and argument to establish a body of support but eventually the powers of enforcement are used to ensure full compliance, with penalties being applied for non-compliance.

Summary and conclusions

If each country is left completely free to set its own standards, the rules set are likely to be quite different in different countries. This will be the case in particular if the legal system, economic–political system or cultures of the countries are very different. If differences in the accounting rules reflect differences between countries, then they will probably be magnified by differences in the ways in which the rules are interpreted and in the free choices companies make in terms of which methods to use and what to disclose voluntarily.

While accounting might well develop in each country to meet the specific needs of that country, this may not necessarily be optimal for either the companies or the users of financial statements if a wider perspective is instead taken. Companies increasingly operate internationally, they either trade with foreign companies or have subsidiaries operating in a number of countries, and either list on foreign stock markets or have foreign

---

[25] Tay and Parker (1990).

investors investing in their shares in the domestic stock market. Similarly, investors may wish to invest in foreign companies while other users such as governments, employees, debt providers or suppliers may also be interested in the activities of companies from foreign countries. To the extent that producing or using financial statements produced using different rules imposes additional costs or adds to the difficulty or confusion of preparers or users, all will benefit if companies use only one set of rules wherever they operate. It may be therefore that each country will benefit from international cooperation and that the benefits of using one set of rules will outweigh any disadvantages of having a set of standards that are not optimal from when the particular unique, local, country-specific environment is considered.

Key points from the chapter:

- Differences between corporate reports of two companies from different countries may be due to differences in the rules of the two countries; differences in the ways in which the rules are interpreted or implemented; and differences in preferred practices (including voluntary disclosure practices).

- The arguments in favour of global accounting standards are expressed in terms of benefits for preparers, investors and regulators in terms of transparency, comparability, cost saving and understandability.

- The arguments against global accounting standards are that apparent comparability of rules may hide underlying real differences in the transactions and events that are reported; national control of standard setting is lost; the standards are being used in developing countries without regard for their specific needs; and giving monopoly position to one organization may reduce quality through lack of competition.

- Global standards could develop by different routes. At present the competing claims are from IFRS of the IASB and the US GAAP based on FASB standards in the USA.

- Initiatives on global accounting harmonization and standardization are focused on public listed companies; the needs of small and medium-sized enterprises that are not listed on a stock exchange present a separate challenge that remains under debate.

Questions

The following questions test your understanding of the material contained in the chapter and allow you to relate your understanding to the learning outcomes specified at the start of this chapter. The learning outcomes are repeated here. Each question is cross-referenced to the relevant section of the chapter.

Explain the types of differences that may exist between financial reports from different companies or countries

1 Why might different preparers interpret the same rules in different ways? (section 1.1.2)

2 Why might this be a particular problem in an international setting? (section 1.1.2)

3 Why might different companies prefer to adopt different accounting rules and techniques? (section 1.1.3)

4 Why might this be a particular problem in an international setting? (section 1.1.3)

Discuss the arguments for and against global accounting standards

5 Explain the arguments in support of and against the development of international accounting standards from the perspective of companies. (sections 1.2.1 and 1.3)

6 Explain the arguments in support of and against the development of international accounting standards from the perspective of investors. (sections 1.2.2 and 1.3)

7 Explain the arguments in support of and against the development of international accounting standards from the perspective of governments. (sections 1.2.3 and 1.3)

8 Discuss the relative merits of harmonization and standardization as ways of achieving global comparability in accounting rules and practices. (section 1.4.4)

Explain why global standards may or may not be appropriate for developing countries or for small and medium-sized companies

9 Explain why the Publish What You Pay campaign was started and what its objectives are. (section 1.2.3)

10 Assess the arguments for and against developing countries adopting international standards. (section 1.4.2)

11 Assess the argument for and against requiring SMEs to use international accounting standards. (section 1.4.3)

Understand the arguments used in support of possible alternative global standard setters

12 What are the advantages and disadvantages of adopting US standards as global accounting standards? (section 1.4.1)

13 What arguments may be used in support of and against allowing more than one set of standards to be used internationally? (section 1.4.1)

References and further reading

AAA Financial Accounting Standards Committee (2006) 'Financial accounting and reporting standards for private entities', *Accounting Horizons*, 22 June: 179–194.

AICPA (1976) *Report on the committee on generally accepted accounting principles to smaller and/or closely held businesses.* New York: American Institute of Certified Public Accountants (AICPA).

AICPA (1981) *Tentative conclusions and recommendations of the special committee on accounting standards overload.* New York: American Institute of Certified Public Accountants (AICPA).

AICPA (1995) *Standards overload: problems and solutions.* New York: American Institute of Certified Public Accountants (AICPA).

AICPA (2005) *Private company financial reporting task force report.* New York: American Institute of Certified Public Accountants (AICPA).

Arnold, P.J. and Sikka, P. (2001) 'Globalization and the state-profession relationship: the case of the Bank of Credit and Commerce International', *Accounting, Organizations and Society*, 26(6): 475–501.

Ball, R. (2006) 'International financial reporting standards (IFRS): pros and cons for investors', *Accounting and Business Research.* International accounting policy forum: 5–27.

Ball, R., Robin, A. and Wu, J.S. (2003) 'Incentives versus standards: properties of accounting income in four East Asian countries', *Journal of Accounting and Economics*, 36: 235–270.

Barth, M.E., Clinch, G. and Shibano, T. (1999) 'International accounting harmonization and global equity markets', *Journal of Accounting and Economics*, 26: 201–235.

Chamisa, E.E. (2000) 'The relevance and observance of the IASC standards in developing countries and the particular case of Zimbabwe', *International Journal of Accounting*, 35(2): 267–286.

Chen, S., Sun, Z. and Wang, Y. (2002) 'Evidence from China on whether harmonized accounting standards harmonize accounting practices', *Accounting Horizons*, 16(3), September: 183–198.

Davidson, R.A. and Chrisman, H.H. (1993) 'Interlinguistic comparison of international accounting standards: the case of uncertainty expressions', *International Journal of Accountancy*, 28(1): 1–16.

Doupnik, T.S. and Riccio, E.L. (2006) 'The influence of conservatism and secrecy on the interpretation of verbal probability expressions in the Anglo and Latin cultural areas', *International Journal of Accounting*, 41: 237–261.

Doupnik, T.S. and Richter, M. (2003) 'Interpretation of uncertainty expressions: a cross-national study', *Accounting, Organizations and Society*, 28: 15–35.

Dye, R.A and Sunder, S. (2001) 'Why not allow the FASB and IASB standards to compete in the US?', *Accounting Horizons*, 15: 257–271.

Elad, C.E. (1995) 'The value added accounting principles of the OCAM plan: a theoretical appraisal', *Research in Accounting in Emerging Economies*, 3: 53–82.

Elad, C.E. (1996) 'Implementing the OCAM plan: two contrasting case studies', *Advances in International Accounting*, 9: 47–72.

Evans, L. (2004) 'Language, translation and the problem of international accounting', *Accounting, Auditing and Accountability Journal*, 17(2): 210–248.

FASB (1981) *Financial reporting by private and small public companies*. Stamford, CT: Financial Accounting Standards Board (FASB).

Herrmann, D. and Thomas, W. (1995) 'Harmonisation of accounting measurement practices in the European community', *Accounting and Business Research*, 25(100): 253–265.

Hirshleifer, D. and Teoh, S.H. (2003) 'Limited attention, information disclosure, and financial reporting', *Journal of Accounting and Economics*, 36: 337–386.

Hoarau, C. (1995) 'International accounting harmonization: American hegemony or mutual recognition with benchmarks?', *European Accounting Review*, 4(2): 217–233.

Holthausen, R.W. (2003) 'Testing the relative power of accounting standards versus incentives and other institutional features to influence the outcome of financial reporting in an international setting', *Journal of Accounting and Economics*, 36: 271–283.

Hopwood, A.J. (1994) 'Some reflections on the harmonization of accounting within the EU', *European Accounting Review*, 3(2): 241–253.

Hove, M.R. (1986) 'Accounting practices in developing countries: colonialism's legacy of inappropriate technologies', *International Journal of Accounting*, 22: 81–100.

IASB (2004) *Discussion Paper, Preliminary views on accounting standards for small and medium enterprises*. London: International Accounting Standards Board (IASB), June.

IASB (2007) *Exposure draft: International financial reporting standards for SMEs*. London: International Accounting Standards Board (IASB), February.

Jaafar, A. and McLeay, S. (2007) 'Country effects and sector effects on the harmonization of accounting policy choice', *Abacus*, 43(2): 156–189.

Kirby, A.J. (2001) 'International competitive effects of harmonization', *International Journal of Accounting*, 36(1): 1–32.

Larson, R.K. and Kenny, S.Y. (1995) 'An empirical analysis of international accounting standards, equity markets, and economic growth in developing countries', *Journal of International Financial Management and Accounting*, 6(2): 130–158.

Larson, R.K. and Kenny, S.Y. (1996) 'Standard setting strategies and theories of economic development', *Advances in International Accounting*, 9: 1–20.

Lehman, G. (2005) 'A critical perspective on the harmonization of accounting in a globalizing world', *Critical Perspectives in Accounting*, 16: 975–992.

Leuz, C. (2003) 'IAS versus US GAAP: information asymmetry-based evidence from Germany's new market', *Journal of Accounting Research*, 41(3): 445–472.

McLeay, S., Neal, D. and Tollington, T. (1999) 'International standardisation and harmonisation: a new measurement technique', *Journal of International Financial Management and Accounting*, 10(1): 42–70.

Miles, S. and Nobes, C. (1998) 'The use of foreign accounting data in UK financial institutions', *Journal of Business Finance and Accounting*, 25(3) and (4): 309–328.

Nobes, C.W. (1988) *Interpreting US financial statements*. Guilford: Butterworths.

Perera, M.H.B. (1989) 'Accounting in developing countries: a case for localized uniformity', *British Accounting Review*, 2(1), June: 141–157.

Rahman, S.F. (1998) 'International accounting regulation by the United Nations: a power perspective', *Accounting, Auditing and Accountability Journal*, 11(5): 593–623.

Rahman, A., Perera, H. and Ganesh, S. (2002) 'Accounting practice harmony, accounting regulation and firm characteristics', *Abacus*, 38(1): 46–77.

Schultz, J. and Lopez, T.J. (2001) 'The impact of national influence on accounting estimates: implications for international accounting standard-setters', *International Journal of Accounting*, 36: 271–290.

Sian, S. and Roberts, C.B. (2006) *Micro-entity financial reporting; perspectives of preparers and users*. International Federation of Accountants, SMPC Information Paper, December. New York: International Federation of Accountants (IFAC).

Sian, S. and Roberts, C.B. (2008) *Micro-entity financial reporting; some empirical evidence of the perspectives of preparers and users*. International Federation of Accountants, SMPC Information Paper. New York: International Federation of Accountants (IFAC).

Sunder, S. (2002) 'Regulatory competition among accounting standards within and across international boundaries', *Journal of Accounting and Public Policy*, 21(3): 219–234.

Talaga, J.A. and Ndubizu, G. (1986) 'Accounting and economic development: relationships among the paradigms', *International Journal of Accounting*, 21, Spring: 55–68.

Tay, J.S.W. and Parker, R.H. (1990) 'Measuring harmonization and standardization', *Abacus*, March: 71–88.

Tyrrall, D., Woodward, D. and Rakhimbekova, A. (2007) 'The relevance of International Financial Reporting Standards to a developing country: evidence from Kazakhstan', *International Journal of Accounting*, 42: 82–110.

United Nations (1991) *Accountancy development in Africa: challenge of the 1990s*. New York: UN Centre of Transnational Corporations.

Wallace, R.S.O. (1990) 'Accounting in developing countries: a review of the literature', *Research in Third World Accounting*, 1: 3–54.

Weetman, P. and Gray, S.J. (1991) 'A comparative international analysis of the impact of accounting principles on profits: the USA versus the UK, Sweden and the Netherlands', *Accounting and Business Research*, 21(84): 363–379.

Zeff, S.A. (2002) '"Political" lobbying on proposed standards: a challenge to the IASB', *Accounting Horizons*, 16(1), March: 43–54.

2 Investors and listed companies

Learning outcomes

After reading this chapter you should be able to:

● Understand why investors might want to invest in foreign companies and the
approaches they may take.

- Understand the reasons why companies might list on foreign stock markets.
- Understand the additional costs of listing on foreign stock markets.
- Evaluate published research seeking to explain the foreign stock market listing choices of companies.
- Understand the different approaches that companies can take when reporting to foreign investors and the factors that affect this decision.

2.1 Introduction

As discussed in the previous chapter, the demand for global standards derives from a variety of different factors, but clearly one of the most important has been the continuing internationalization of business and the concomitant increase in the number of international investors. With the almost universal adoption of IFRS, many of the barriers or additional costs of international listing will rapidly fall while increased access to technology makes it easier for investors to access rapidly and cheaply relevant information and invest internationally.

However, the increasing use of IFRS does not mean that all companies will use identical measurement and reporting practices; investors will increasingly be interested in companies with unfamiliar domestic languages and currencies, different views on disclosure or differences in how apparently identical accounting rules are implemented.

The chapter begins by looking at investors and explores the reasons why they might want to invest in foreign companies and how they might use (or not use) financial statement information in their investment decision making. It then turns from demand to supply and the decisions of companies to make international listings. The possible reasons for companies to want a foreign listing are explored and some of the additional costs are described. The empirical research on choice of listing location is reviewed for evidence regarding the factors driving the choice of listing location. The chapter then examines the different approaches that a company can take to reporting to its foreign statement users, and it finally looks at some of the empirical studies that have examined stock market reactions to the disclosure of information using different GAAP.

2.2 Approaches to international equity investment

2.2.1 Why shareholders invest internationally

Reading through this book you may gain the impression that prior to the general acceptance of international standards the sensible investor should not have invested in foreign companies or foreign stock markets, while after their widespread acceptance investors can easily invest in companies from any country. Both of these conclusions would be somewhat simplistic. Even when each country used different accounting methods there were clear economic advantages in investing internationally, which investors understood despite the problems of non-comparable accounting practices. Even after the adoption of international standards in many countries, some substantive differences in disclosures will persist. In addition, different equity transaction methods, different currencies and different languages all make it more difficult and more expensive to invest in foreign markets.

There are clear benefits to investing in foreign companies and foreign markets. For example, if an investor had invested $1,000 in the US market in 1985 she would have an investment worth $3,818 ten years later. If the investment had been made in the Thai market instead it would have been worth $16,212, or $23,209 in Mexico, $48,023 in the Philippines or $64,707 in Chile.[1] However, this is past history. An investor deciding now to invest in Chile might instead find in ten years' time that this was the worst decision she could have taken. Which stock markets have been particularly good or bad investments in the past is not relevant today. All that is relevant is the fact that stock markets have not all moved together – in any one period, some stock markets will be doing well and others will not be doing so well.

A cautious investor in the domestic stock market would not invest in only one or two companies. No investor can consistently pick winners. To be successful in picking companies, investors must make better or more accurate predictions than do other investors. For example, if you think a company will grow and make lots of profits in the future and if other investors also think the same, they will also buy the shares and the share price will increase now, before these profits are made. If in future periods your prediction proves correct and the company is successful, the share price will not then increase as this is not new information, but simply something that everyone already expected. It has already been reflected in the share price due to increased demand in earlier periods. You will only benefit if you are better at predicting which companies will perform well in the future than are other investors; in other words, if you have special knowledge, insights or skills that others do not have. While you might choose well and make a lot of money, you might equally well choose badly and lose money instead. It is well established that, over time, all ordinary investors can hope is that they do as well on average as the market does. The semi-strong form of the efficient market hypothesis generally holds in active stock markets of developed countries. Share prices react quickly and correctly to all new information and no investor is able consistently to outguess the market. This means that investors should invest in a well-diversified portfolio of shares. This allows them to minimize their risk for any given level of return (or maximize their expected return for any given level of risk). At least in theory investors should diversify across all available shares and invest in the market portfolio. In practice, if they choose different types of companies, a well-diversified investment in approximately 40 stocks should be sufficient to gain most of the benefits available from diversification in any single market.

Diversification brings benefits because the returns made from different equities are less than perfectly correlated. While some companies might be doing particularly well with rising share prices, other companies will instead be performing less well. Similar considerations apply to international investing. There has been a great deal of interest in the literature in the question of the extent to which different stock markets are co-integrated or the returns from different stock markets are correlated to each other. Studies in the 1970s and 1980s tended to find relatively low levels of correlation. For example, one of the earliest studies of the benefits of international diversification[2] calculated that this lack of co-integration meant that a well-diversified international portfolio would be typically only half as risky as a similar-sized portfolio of US shares. However, more and more investors are accessing foreign markets, more companies have listed internationally since then and many economies are becoming more integrated

---

[1] Melton (1996), p. 28.
[2] Solnik (1974).

into the global economy so that the level of co-integration is rising and the benefits from international diversification are falling. For example, Taylor and Tonks (1989) looked at the UK, USA, Japan, The Netherlands and West Germany, from 1973 to 1986, and found that the UK market had become more integrated with the others following the abandonment of exchange controls in the UK in 1989. Similarly, Corhay *et al.* (1993) found that the stock markets of the UK, France, Germany, Italy and The Netherlands had become more integrated during the 1975–91 period, while Smith (1999), in a study of stock market correlations before and after the 1987 stock market crash, provides evidence that European stock markets became more highly correlated both with each other and with the USA after the 1987 crash.

Exhibit 2.1 reports the correlations between the monthly returns from eight European markets and the USA for the 27-year period, January 1974 to January 2001. This shows a picture of very high correlations across all these exchanges. Fraser and Oyefeso (2005) conclude that there is evidence of a common stochastic trend linking all the markets such that, if the period were sufficiently long, there would be perfect correlation across the markets. However, there are significant short-run deviations from this trend, especially with respect to the US and UK markets. This implies that investors can gain from short-term diversification across the markets.

There are a number of reasons why stock markets are not perfectly correlated in the short term. Different economic and political policies, different trade patterns, industrial structures, corporate policies and investor behaviour all mean that companies in different countries will tend, on average, to perform somewhat differently. In any one period companies from one country will tend to perform relatively well, but in other periods, companies from other countries will instead tend to perform better. However, the convergence of stock markets is likely to continue, due at least partially to the increasing use of IFRS which will help reduce market segmentation by reducing barriers to investment caused by different accounting requirements.

Obviously investors cannot invest in all companies in each market. Instead they will choose a smaller number of companies to invest in that approximately replicate international markets. One attraction of investing in a foreign stock market is that the investor can sometimes invest in different types of companies or different industries. For example, a UK investor wanting to invest in an electronics manufacturer could not invest in a UK manufacturer of any significant size but might instead decide to invest in a US or

Exhibit 2.1   Correlation matrix of real stock market returns, 1974–2001

	Belgium	Denmark	France	Germany	Italy	US	UK	Spain	Sweden
Belgium	1								
Denmark	0.982	1							
France	0.977	0.982	1						
Germany	0.983	0.989	0.983	1					
Italy	0.945	0.954	0.958	0.954	1				
US	0.877	0.884	0.887	0.881	0.887	1			
UK	0.905	0.917	0.917	0.915	0.918	0.877	1		
Spain	0.942	0.943	0.948	0.944	0.938	0.886	0.907	1	
Sweden	0.940	0.951	0.942	0.946	0.937	0.896	0.910	0.926	1

Source: Fraser and Oyefeso (2005).

| Exhibit 2.2 | Sectoral distribution of the 50 largest companies, selected countries, 2007 |

	UK	France	USA	Japan
Financial sector	11	8	12	8
Mining, oil & gas	7	1	3	1
Computers, IT & electronics	–	4	10	8
Telecommunications	2	1	2	4
Utilities	4	4	–	3
Chemicals & pharmaceuticals	2	3	7	4
Construction	–	6	–	2
Industrial	3	7	6	13
Media and Entertainment	5	5	4	2
Food, drink & tobacco	8	2	3	1
Retail	5	3	2	1
Other	3	6	1	3

Source: Derived from FT 500 (July 2007), http://news.ft.com/reports/ft500.

Japanese company. French or Japanese investors wanting to invest in a large drinks or food manufacturer would have more choice if they looked to the UK rather than their own countries. Exhibit 2.2 lists the industrial sectors of the 50 largest companies, by market capitalization, from the UK, France, the USA and Japan. This gives a good idea of differences in the industrial composition of the major companies in these countries.

All the evidence shows that individual investors are increasingly investing internationally. For example, Exhibit 2.3 shows the proportion of domestic shares owned by foreign investors in a number of countries as at the end of 2001, while Exhibit 2.4 shows the areas which attract foreign investors.

These exhibits show that the stock market is particularly important in the UK and the USA and is relatively less important in the Euro area and Japan. However, it is the UK and the Euro areas that are most dependent upon foreign investment, with over one-third of domestic shares being owned by foreign investors. This is in marked contrast to the USA, where domestic companies are primarily owned by Americans, with only 13 per cent of their shares being owned by non-Americans. This is despite the USA being the preferred location for foreign investment by investors from both the Euro area and

| Exhibit 2.3 | Importance of foreign investment in various stock markets |

	Domestic stock market capitalization as % of world	% domestic stocks owned by foreign investors	Domestic GDP as % of world GDP
Euro	15.9	36.5	19.6
Japan	9.3	16.7	13.4
UK	8.9	35.6	4.6
USA	48.9	12.9	32.3
Rest of world	17.0	N/A	30.1

Source: Lane and Milesi-Ferretti (2004).

Exhibit 2.4   Pattern of foreign investment in various stock markets

Host	Source			
	Euro area	Japan	UK	USA
Euro area	–	16.8	43.7	28.6
Japan	7.3	–	9.9	10.6
UK	22.2	13.0	–	21.7
USA	45.2	54.3	24.3	–
Rest of world	25.4	15.9	22.0	39.1
	100%	100%	100%	100%

Source: Lane and Milesi-Ferretti (2004).

Japan. Perhaps surprisingly, UK investors instead prefer to invest in the Euro zone, suggesting that differences in accounting practices might be a larger deterrent to foreign investment than are differences in language.

It might be expected that the importance of foreign investors will increase in all markets over the next few years. It is becoming increasingly low cost and a straightforward procedure for investors to invest in foreign stock markets. The simplest way for the ordinary investor to do this is through investing indirectly in foreign markets by buying unit trusts or other similar investments which themselves invest in foreign markets. Exhibit 2.5 lists just some of the types of funds that UK investors can buy, all of which in turn invest in foreign equities and all of which can be bought in pounds sterling. This means that individuals or private small investors need not invest directly in the shares of foreign firms. They do not therefore have to bother with the costs and inconvenience of dealing in different currencies or languages. Instead, all they need to do is decide which type of domestic fund they wish to invest in and then choose among the alternative funds. In these cases, the decision is not based upon an individual company's financial statement information but is based upon economic data and information about the performance and costs of the competing funds.

However, this does not mean that financial statement information is not used by stock market participants – the investment funds must decide upon suitable companies

Exhibit 2.5   Examples of UK funds investing in foreign equities in various countries and groups of countries

Regional funds	Global, Europe, North America, Asia Pacific, Latin American Emerging, Far East
Country funds	America, India, Switzerland, Korea, China, Japan, Russia
Growth funds	American, Asian, German, Japanese, European growth
Small company funds	American, European, Asian, Korean, Emerging markets
Tracker	American, Europe, Japan, Pacific
Other	Global ethical, Global technology, European ethical, Japan technology

Source: Based on list of funds, www.ft.com (August 2007).

to invest in. Professional fund managers and analysts will need to compare companies from different countries. The next section therefore looks at the alternative investment strategies that can be adopted by anyone, whether an individual investor or professional fund manager, wishing to invest directly in equities from different countries.

2.2.2 Passive investment strategies

Three different strategies have been identified which investors can use to cope with accounting diversity.[3] At one extreme, investors may decide not to rely upon company-specific information at all. Instead, they could adopt a passive or index-based strategy. In the international arena this would involve deciding how much to invest in particular countries on the basis of non-accounting factors. Factors considered might include relative GNP, past and forecast country growth rates and the size of the stock market. The investor would then choose a portfolio of shares from each country that mirrored or represented the country's total stock market. The objective is to match the returns of each stock market invested in, rather than to outperform it. Passive investment strategies are being used increasingly by US and UK institutional investors investing in their domestic stock markets. Such an approach was initially developed as a way of reducing transaction costs as it involves less share trading. Shares are only bought or sold when the portfolio no longer adequately mirrors the market due to changes in the market caused by such factors as new issues, mergers and takeovers. These types of portfolios are often called 'trackers' or 'tracker funds', because they are designed to mirror or track the market.

Because passive investment strategies reduce the need to analyze financial statements, they can also be a useful response to problems of lack of accounting information or lack of understanding of the accounting information provided. They may therefore be particularly useful for investors wishing to diversify into international markets. However, some financial statement information will still be needed when choosing an adequately diversified portfolio and to ensure that it remains well diversified.

2.2.3 Active investment strategies

The opposite approach is to adopt an active investment strategy based, at least partially, on accounting information. Here, investors try to assess whether or not a company will be a good investment. They will use accounting information as well as other information (economic information including forecasts, company information from newspaper reports and stockbroker reports and possibly company visits) to assess the strength and weaknesses of companies and their management and the companies' likely future prospects. Using all of this information they will buy or sell shares whenever they have new information or whenever market conditions change in an attempt to 'beat the market'.

While more and more companies and countries are using IFRS, not all companies are currently doing so. If the statements produced use unfamiliar GAAP and the company itself does not restate these into more familiar GAAP, then the investors can adopt one of two approaches. Firstly, they might restate the figures provided into a more familiar set of accounting principles. This would mean that the figures could then be more easily compared with the figures provided by companies from other countries. This approach

---

[3] Choi and Levich (1997).

is based upon the assumption that stock markets are reasonably well integrated. Companies from different countries can then be compared one with the other: 'Is the company a good investment compared with alternative investments from other countries?' The investors then choose the best companies to invest in irrespective of their home country.

The second approach is to become familiar with various foreign GAAP and then to use a local perspective when analyzing foreign financial statements. This approach is often called a 'multiple principles capability'; it is premised upon the opposite assumption, that markets are not integrated but are segmented. It assumes that companies can be usefully compared only with other companies from the same country and a company's performance should therefore be assessed only in the context of the local market: 'Is the company a good investment inside that market or not?'

2.2.4 Mixed investment strategies

An intermediate investment strategy is also possible which adopts aspects of both a passive and an active approach. This would involve adopting a passive strategy and using an index approach for all of those countries or industries where the investor has insufficient information or where the available information is based upon unfamiliar accounting rules. Where investors are familiar with the information provided and sufficient disclosures are made, they would instead adopt an active investment strategy.

2.2.5 Actual investment strategies

Relatively few studies have looked at how investors actually manage in a world of accounting diversity. Choi and Levich (1996) questioned 400 European institutional investors, 97 of whom replied. Two-thirds of these placed high reliance upon accounting information when selecting foreign equities and only four did not use accounting information at all. Eighty-five per cent of the respondents compared investments across countries rather than deciding upon the amount to invest in each country and then selecting from among potential investment targets inside it. When asked about accounting differences, only 23 per cent replied that differences in the quality of financial reporting limited their investments in Europe and 14 per cent cited accounting differences as a reason for limiting investments. (Liquidity, currency and market risks were all mentioned by at least 40 per cent of the sample.) Nearly half (42.3 per cent) of the respondents said that they might increase their investment in Europe if a common set of accounting and reporting concepts were introduced. These respondents were equally divided on whether they would prefer IAS or US GAAP disclosures.

The respondents were also asked about how they dealt with differences in accounting principles and disclosure practices. The findings are reproduced in Exhibit 2.6.

Two different approaches were taken when the accounting principles were different. Respondents either placed more emphasis upon other information, including the services of investment advisors, or attempted to restate the figures using more familiar GAAP. Again when the disclosure practices were different, two approaches were taken. Respondents either sought more information or changed their investment strategies to cope with the increase in uncertainty. Miles and Nobes (1998) found that fund managers and analysts working in UK financial institutions developed a range of approaches to foreign accounting data and did not all have accounting expertise but used other information to learn about company performance.

| Exhibit 2.6 | Dealing with differences in accounting principles and disclosure practices, 1996 |

	No. of Respondents	Percentage
Differences in accounting principles:		
Place higher weight on other information	64	66.0
Restate foreign accounts	49	50.5
Use information and analysis from investment advisory services	41	42.3
Attach a low weight to accounting information	10	10.3
Differences in disclosure practices:		
Visiting company to collect information	46	47.4
Assigning higher risk rating to company	44	45.4
Attending company road shows	42	43.3
Avoiding investment in companies with less disclosure	34	35.1
Requiring higher expected returns from companies with fewer disclosures	26	26.8
No answer	13	13.4

Source: Choi and Levich (1996), pp. 294–295.

2.3 Foreign stock market listing

2.3.1 Stock market segmentation

The extent to which stock markets are integrated with each other or are instead segmented is an important question, as this affects the ease to which investors can invest in foreign stock markets and companies can list in foreign markets.

At one extreme stock markets could be completely segmented. Here, foreign investors are unable to invest in the local market and/or foreign companies are unable to list in the local market. This is usually the result of government-imposed restrictions. The popularity of measures to restrict entry to domestic stock markets has decreased greatly in recent years and many barriers have been dismantled. However, some countries, especially developing ones, still have government-imposed restrictions. These can take various forms including foreign currency controls and even the blanket prohibition of foreign ownership of certain types of companies or limits to how much of a company can be owned by foreign investors.

At the other extreme, stock markets can be completely integrated. Investors from all countries will have equal access to all securities and foreign companies can list freely without incurring more transaction costs than do domestic companies. Foreign and local markets will therefore be equally accessible. If this were the case then rationale investors should hold a worldwide portfolio of stocks. There would also be no incentive for companies to list on foreign stock markets as investors could instead invest in these markets themselves at no additional costs.

Obviously, in practice most markets will be neither completely segmented nor completely integrated. However, stock exchanges are becoming more integrated. For example, the Paris, Amsterdam, Brussels and Portuguese Stock Exchanges have combined to form Euronext while in the first six months of 2007 the London Stock Exchange announced the rejection of a takeover bid by NASDAQ, the signing of a memorandum of understanding with Tel Aviv Stock Market to facilitate trading in dual-listed stocks, and an agreement with Tokyo Stock Market on access arrangements (all in February). In March, it announced the signing of an agreement with the Johannesburg Exchange for the provision of technology services and in June announced a cooperation agreement with the Bahrain Stock Exchange and the takeover of the Borsa Italiana.

Given that stock markets are in practice still partially segmented, foreign investors and/or companies can trade on foreign markets but they face additional transaction costs or restrictions that are not faced by domestic investors and/or companies. Companies may find it easier to issue their stock on foreign markets rather than relying on foreign investors buying their shares on its domestic exchange. If a company wants to attract substantial numbers of foreign investors it may have to go to them – the transaction costs faced by the company entering a foreign stock market will be less than the aggregate transaction costs incurred by large numbers of foreign investors all entering the domestic stock exchange.

2.3.2 Importance of cross-listing

The number of companies that were listed on foreign stock markets reached a high point in 1997 when 4,700 companies had a listing on a foreign stock market.[4] Since then there has been a remarkable decline in the number of such companies, so that by the end of 2002 the number had fallen to 2,335. Similarly, the median percentage of foreign to total listings has fallen from 14.6 per cent in 1995 to 9.6 per cent by 2004, with foreign listings accounting for 5.8 per cent of total trading in 2004.

Chapter 6 provides more details of the number of companies listed on the major exchanges, and if these figures are compared with similar data reported in earlier editions of this text we can see how the decline of cross-listing has affected particular exchanges, as shown in Exhibit 2.7, which provides figures for the main markets of each exchange. This shows how London has in particular been affected by these changes, with New York and NASDAQ being far less adversely affected.

There are a number of reasons for the increase in the number of companies delisting from foreign stock markets. However, before exploring the reasons for delisting the reasons for listing on a foreign exchange will be examined.

Exhibit 2.7	Number of foreign companies listed on major stock exchanges.		
	1996	2003	2006
NYSE	305	466	451
Tokyo	67	32	25
NASDAQ	416	343	321
London	533	381	343
Euronext	N/A	346	256
Hong Kong	22	10	8
TSX (Toronto)	58	38	52
Deutsche Borse	N/A	182	104
Swiss	233	130	92

---

[4] Karolyi (2006).

Some foreign listings are important in the sense that many shares are traded each year, while others are relatively unimportant, with very few shares being traded. Similarly, different companies seek foreign stock market listings for different reasons and companies may list in different countries for different reasons. A number of motives for foreign listing have been suggested.

2.3.3 Public share offering

Exhibit 2.8 provides some anecdotal evidence illustrating the importance of foreign stock markets as a source of finance. (Note that these companies were randomly chosen; they are not unique and many other companies could have been chosen as illustrations.) For example, only 9 per cent of Nokia's shares are owned by domestic investors while less than one-third of Nestlé's shares are owned by domestic shareholders and Norsk Hydro has more than twice as much of its stock owned by foreign investors as by Norwegian non-state investors.

Listing in a large foreign market to obtain funding is especially important for companies such as Nokia or Nestlé, which are large but come from relatively small countries. If they had to rely only on domestic investors they would be unlikely to be able to obtain

---

Exhibit 2.8 Selected European companies: listing and ownership patterns

Stock market	Year of entry	Ownership	%
Nokia Finland (December 2006)			
Helsinki	1915	USA	52
NYSE	1994	UK	11
Deutsche Borse	1968	Germany	9
Stockholm	Delisted 2007	Finland	9
		France	5
		Switzerland	3
		Others	11
Nestlé, Switzerland (December 2006)			
Swiss		Swiss	32.5
USA – ADR		US	34.5
Paris delisted		UK	8.1
Frankfurt delisted		France	3.6
UK delisted		Germany	5.4
		Other	15.9
Norsk Hydro, Norway (March 2007)			
Oslo		Norway state	43.8
London		Norway private	16.7
Euronext – Paris		Individuals living in:	
Germany		UK	13.8
NYSE		USA	13.8
(was listed in Stockholm, Switzerland and Amsterdam)		Others	11.9

Source: Extracted from annual reports: www.nokia.com, www.Nestle.com, www.hydro.com.

Exhibit 2.9 Foreign companies listing on the NYSE, January 2006 to June 2007

Country	Total number	IPO	Country	Total number	IPO
China and Hong Kong	11	9	Canada	11	1
Central and South America	5	4	EU	8	6
India	2	1	Japan	1	1
Bermuda and Barbados	5	4	Israel	1	1

Source: NYSE.com (September 2007).

sufficient funds at a reasonable price. In recent years, new listings that seek funds or IPOs (Initial Public Offerings) are particularly common from developing countries. For example, Exhibit 2.9 shows the new listings on the New York Stock Exchange by foreign companies in 2006 and the first six months of 2007. Of these 44 new listings, 27 were IPOs, with many coming from China and Central and South America.

2.3.4 Other types of share issues

As also seen in Exhibit 2.9, many companies sought a listing on the NYSE without making a new share issue. There are a number of other reasons why companies might want foreign listing(s). One of the most publicized foreign listings was Daimler-Benz's listing on the NYSE in 1993 – the first German company to list there. By the time of its merger with Chrysler in 1998 it had still not raised any new finance on the NYSE.

Increasingly, companies issue shares to their employees. Director share options and share-based employee pay schemes are now popular. They are seen as a way of ensuring the long-term loyalty and commitment of the workforce and they may also be tax efficient. While companies obviously hope that most employees will not sell their shares, they must be given the opportunity to do so. If a company wants to extend these schemes to cover foreign employees, it may have to list in the foreign country so that employees have a local market in which they can trade their shares. A company may also wish to issue shares, not for cash, but to finance or partially finance acquisitions. Again, if it wishes to offer shares for foreign takeovers, it may have to provide these potential shareholders with the opportunity to sell their shares in their local stock market(s).

Similarly, a large foreign ownership may help to protect the company from being taken over. Foreign ownership can make takeovers more difficult and more expensive to organize, while shareholders in countries such as Germany, with no history or culture of hostile takeovers, might be less willing to sell their shares to such bidding companies.

2.3.5 Share listing as a signalling device

There are several other potential benefits of a local listing.[5] It may provide the company with extra publicity, which in turn encourages brand recognition and customer loyalty. It may also signal to customers and potential customers the long-term commitment of the company to the country. Again, this may lead to increased sales. Foreign listings may

[5] Radebaugh et al. (1995).

also signal that the company is now a major international player and may therefore increase the company's prestige.

A local listing may also change the perceptions of other groups such as local communities, governments and local authorities and pressure groups. It might help to improve the operating climate facing the company. The political benefits of a local listing may be particularly great in countries that are economically or politically less stable. The company will also want to reduce its risk in these countries, and one way to do this is to ensure that local operations are financed locally. A local listing will mean that the local affiliates can be financed in a more balanced way by local equity as well as local debt. This can be important in reducing the exchange rate or currency risk faced by a company. If all shareholders are situated in the parent's country, the foreign subsidiary's earnings will have to be converted into the parent currency before dividends are paid. Having local shareholders avoids this need to convert currencies, as local earnings can be used to pay local currency dividends.

2.3.6 Additional costs of foreign listings

Selling shares in a foreign country can often be very expensive. There will always be extra direct costs – various registration and listing charges have to be paid and these can be substantial. However, these may be the least of the extra costs incurred. There will often be other costs caused by differences in the regulatory systems:[6]

- different underwriting practices
- different registration and regulatory requirements
- different initial and continuing disclosure requirements
- different control and oversight systems with respect to share dealing practices
- different clearance and settlement procedures.

This may mean that the company has to plan and organize share issues in different countries in quite distinct ways. Different accounting and reporting systems may also be necessary and extra auditing costs may be incurred.

Once a company has done all this and has managed to issue shares in more than one market, it will be faced with further additional costs if it wants to keep an active presence in the foreign market. If it fails to maintain investor interest, there may be substantial share flowback – the shares that were initially issued in the foreign market will be sold back to domestic shareholders. This happened, for example, with some of the UK privatization issues such as British Telecom, with many of the shares that were initially issued in the USA finding their way back to the UK fairly soon after issue.[7] To prevent this happening the company will have to maintain an active investor relations department in the foreign country. This department will be responsible for keeping the press, financial analysts and stockbrokers well informed about the company. Without this activity, there is unlikely to be much press or analyst interest and therefore less interest by ordinary shareholders. Similarly, the interest and loyalty of institutional investors may have to be managed actively. The company will need to organize systematically such measures as company briefings and meetings with financial analysts. This will obviously be far easier and more successful if there is a well-organized local investor relations department to manage the relationships.

---

[6] Hanks (1997).
[7] Tondkar *et al.* (1989).

Different listing and reporting requirements (not only GAAP but also non-financial disclosures and frequency of reporting rules) can result in substantial extra direct and indirect costs. Direct costs are fairly easy to quantify – any extra information, production, dissemination and auditing costs. In most cases these will be relatively small, but in those cases where the company's existing information systems have to be redesigned to pick up or process different information, there may be very substantial one-off setting up costs. Indirect costs are very much more difficult, if not sometimes impossible, to quantify, and they can be larger than the direct costs.

The provision of any extra information has the potential to induce extra political costs and competitive disadvantage costs. Political costs may arise when the new information causes the perceptions of employees, the general public, pressure groups or the government to change. For example, the company may report higher earnings under foreign GAAP, thus changing perceptions regarding the extent to which the company is exploiting its market position or its labour force. Such changing perceptions may mean that the company is faced with a more difficult operating climate – employees, customers, local communities and the government might become more suspicious and less cooperative. Competitive disadvantage costs arise when a company is made to disclose information that is of value to its competitors. This could happen when a company is forced by foreign reporting requirements to disclose information that is not disclosed by other domestic companies. Examples might include requirements to disclose detailed segment information, research and development and advertising expenditures, or information about environmental contingencies.

Political costs will generally be incurred only if foreign GAAP reporting results in larger earnings or the disclosure of particularly sensitive information. In contrast, investor resistance or reluctance to invest can occur whenever the two sets of figures are different. It does not matter if earnings are increased or decreased; all that matters is that they have changed.

2.4 Listing behaviour of companies

2.4.1 The London Stock Exchange (LSE)

2.4.1.1 LSE listing requirements

The listing requirements of the LSE are influenced by the EU. The EU has issued several Directives on listing which, like the accounting Directives discussed in Chapter 12, have had to be incorporated into the laws of all EU member states.

Several Directives are particularly relevant to the harmonization of stock exchanges in the EU.[8] Exhibit 2.10 shows the early effects of these Directives on the LSE.

The first of these Directives, in 1979, established minimum conditions for the admission of securities to a stock market listing. In the following year a second Directive coordinated the requirements for the publication of listing particulars. The third, in 1982, set disclosure requirements for interim statements of listed companies. These three Directives had relatively little impact on the London or Paris Stock Exchanges. However, they led to significant increases in the disclosure requirements of a number of exchanges including the Amsterdam and the German Stock Exchanges.[9] The 1987 Directive was

---

[8] Scott-Quinn (1994).
[9] Tondkar *et al.* (1989).

Exhibit 2.10	EU stock exchange Directives, 1979–90

1979 79/279/EEC	Co-ordinate conditions for admission of securities
1980 80/390/EEC	Co-ordinate information in prospectuses
1982 82/121/EEC	Publication of half-yearly reports
1987 87/345/EEC	Mutual recognition of listing prospectuses
1989 89/298/EEC	Prospectus used for simultaneous public offer all EU states
1990 90/211/EEC	Allow single document for listing and public offers

particularly important, as it was the first one to introduce the concept of mutual recognition. It ensured that member states recognized all prospectuses issued by companies listed on any EU member state's exchange as long as the prospectus was approved by the authorities in that country.

Full mutual recognition can be seen clearly in the listing requirements of the LSE. The LSE accepts all documents that have been approved by any competent authority in another EU member state if they are in English or if a certified translation is provided. In addition, its listing requirements are such that it accepts all accounts 'prepared and independently audited in accordance with standards appropriate for companies of international standing and repute'. This would automatically include accounts drawn up under US GAAP.

More recent Directives continue to have an impact on the harmonization of disclosure and on competition between stock exchanges through the EU's Financial Services Action Plan, designed to create a single European capital market. The Prospectus Directive 2003/71/EC, the Market Abuse Directive 2003/6/EC and the Transparency Directive 2004/109/EC (see also Chapter 12) are intended to create a level playing field across the EU. While these Directives largely reflect good practice already established in the LSE, they offer a challenge in potentially reducing the differential advantage of the LSE over other markets.

2.4.1.2 Listing of foreign companies on the LSE

The LSE had a position of international prominence by the beginning of the nineteenth century. It helped to finance business in much of the Commonwealth (particularly important was the financing of the South African mining industry) and other parts of the world. For example, up until the mid-1880s much of the US insurance industry, agriculture and railways were financed from London. The importance of the London market can be seen in the example of another US industry, brewing. By 1886, 15 American breweries were listed in London[10] (see Exhibit 2.11).

A study by Gray and Roberts (1997) looked at all foreign companies with full listings of equity shares (not debt) on the LSE at the end of 1994. They looked at when the companies were first listed, where they came from and what industries they operated in. The number of companies seeking a new listing increased each year, reaching a peak of new listings per annum in the mid-1980s and declining after that (with 63 of the sample companies having listed during the period 1980–84, 58 in 1985–89 and 34 in 1990–94). The 293 companies identified came from 26 countries. Over one-third (108) came from the USA and 63 came from South Africa, while Australia, Bermuda, Canada, Japan and

---

[10] Reckitt (1953).

Exhibit 2.11 American breweries registered on the LSE, 1896

Company	Date of registration
Bartholomay Brewing Co., Rochester NY	April 1889
St Louis Breweries	Dec. 1889
City of Chicago Brewing & Malting Co.	June 1890
San Francisco Breweries	Unknown
City of Baltimore United Breweries	Nov. 1889
Milwaukee & Chicago Breweries	Dec. 1890
United States Brewing Co.	May 1889
New York Breweries	Aug. 1889
New England Breweries	March 1890
Denver Breweries	June 1889
Cincinnati Breweries	Oct. 1889
Springfield Breweries	March 1890
Washington Breweries	April 1888
Indianapolis Breweries	Nov. 1889
Chicago Breweries	April 1888

Source: Reckitt, E. (1953), p. 31.

Sweden all had ten or more companies listed on the LSE. The South African companies had generally listed much earlier than had the companies from other countries. This reflects the historical links between the UK and South Africa and the importance of UK finance in the development of South African mining. In contrast, the majority of the US companies listed during the 1980s. This was partly due to the break-up of the large telecommunications companies and the creation of a number of smaller companies, known as 'Baby Bells', partly due to the international expansion of US business at this time and probably partly due also to fashion or 'follow-my-leader' behaviour by companies. European companies have a long history of listing in London – Royal Dutch Petroleum and Unilever (The Netherlands) both listed in the 1940s, SKF and Electrolux (Sweden) in the 1950s and Thyssen, Bayer and Hoechst (Germany) in the early 1960s.

The LSE produces a list of all listed overseas companies and from this it is possible to get an idea of what types of companies are currently listed. Derived from this list, Exhibit 2.12 lists all the countries with more than ten companies listed on either the

Exhibit 2.12 Number of non-UK corporate issuers on the LSE, July 2007

Country	No. of registrants	Country	No. of registrants
Australia	46	Bermuda	46
British Virgin Islands	24	Canada	54
Cayman Islands	37	Germany	10
India	27	Ireland	77
Israel	28	Japan	16
The Netherlands	23	Russia	21
South Africa	14	South Korea	13
Taiwan	10	US	82

Source: Derived from data at www.lse.com, September 2007.

| Exhibit 2.13 | Companies listing in London, January 2006 to July 2007 |

	Total number	AIM IPO	AIM other	Main market IPO	Main market other
Australia	21	9	11	0	1
Bermuda	16	6	5	1	4
British Virgin Islands	22	15	4	3	0
Canada	25	11	10	0	4
Cayman Islands	27	20	5	2	0
Netherlands	12	6	3	3	0
Ireland	20	11	6	3	0
Russia	14	0	0	13	1
USA	32	23	8	1	0

Source: www.londonstockexchange.com.

main market or the newer and smaller Alternative Investment Market (AIM) which was established in 1995 for small and high-growth companies.

AIM has been very successful in attracting foreign company listings. For example, 234 foreign companies were admitted to London in 2006 or the first seven months of 2007. Of these, 175 were listed on the AIM and 59 on the main market. Most listed via IPOs with 116 of the AIM market and 45 of the main markets listers issuing IPOs. Exhibit 2.13 lists all countries that were home to ten or more of these companies. From this it can be seen that many of the companies came from the developed countries (i.e. Europe, North America and Australia) or were from the offshore financial centres of Cayman Islands, British Virgin Islands or Bermuda, countries where companies locate due to either their tax rules or their disclosure rules. However, it is also particularly noticeable how popular London has become as a place to issue IPOs by relatively large Russian companies. In contrast, only two companies from India (one AIM and one main market) and two companies from Hong Kong (both AIM) listed, while no Chinese companies listed on either market.

2.4.2 The USA

2.4.2.1 American Depository Receipts (ADRs)

Most foreign (non-US) companies trade their shares in the US through American Depository Receipts (ADRs). Rather than offering shares denominated in their own currency they repackage their shares as ADRs. An ADR is a certificate that is evidence of ownership of shares in a company based outside the USA. Each certificate is backed by a stated number of shares. ADRs are popular with US investors because the procedures for sale and purchase are simplified and dividends are paid in US currency. There are various different types of ADRs (see Exhibit 2.14).

ADRs can be sponsored or unsponsored. Sponsored ADRs are administered by one bank only, which has been appointed by the issuer. In contrast, unsponsored ADRs allow more than one bank to carry out depository services. Such ADRs usually trade on the over-the-counter (OTC) market and cannot be traded on any stock market.

The easiest and cheapest of these various ADRs are Level One ADRs and Rule 144A offerings. Issuers of Level One ADRs need only file their home country reports with the Securities and Exchange Commission (SEC). However, these ADRs cannot be traded on any US stock market or NASDAQ. Trade can take place only on the electronic bulletin board or the

Exhibit 2.14   Types of ADR

Level One	Trade over-the-counter (OTC) Not seeking to raise capital, minimal SEC registration, sends SEC the public reporting documents required in its home country
Level Two	Traded on stock exchange or NASDAQ Not seeking to raise capital. Full SEC registration procedures. Reports to SEC on form 20-F
Level Three	Allows issuance of new shares; gives greater visibility in US market Full SEC registration and reporting requirements on form 20-F
Rule 144A	Placed and traded only among Qualified Institutional Buyers SEC registration not required
Global DR	DR structured as combination of Rule 144A private placing and public offering outside USA SEC registration not required

Source: Summarized from information on ADRs, JP Morgan, www.adr.com, September 2004.

so-called 'pink sheets'. This market tends to be characterized by its expense and trading margins are typically large. However, it is still an important market. Similarly, Rule 144A offerings cannot be traded on any stock market. Instead, the shares can be offered only as a private placing to a qualified institutional investor. The advantage to the issuing company is again that it avoids the disclosure rules involved in a stock market listing.

A non-US company can go further and issue Level Two or Level Three ADRs on any stock market or on NASDAQ. In these cases, the SEC is very much in favour of a 'level playing field' – in other words, US investors must not be less protected when investing in a foreign company than when investing in a domestic company and US companies must not be disadvantaged in comparison with foreign firms when seeking equity finance. This means that the same measurement and disclosure rules should apply to foreign and domestic companies. However, foreign companies that qualify as foreign issuers[11] (if a majority of shareholders, directors, assets or business is American, the company is treated as a domestic issuer) can opt for Level Two ADRs and take advantage of certain concessions with respect to the information required and the measurement rules used.

As at the start of September 2007, 1,827 individual companies had various types of ADRs. Exhibit 2.15 lists all countries that are home to more than 20 of these companies.

Exhibit 2.15   Countries with more than 20 companies with ADRs

Argentina	24	Italy	25	South Korea	41
Australia	144	Japan	155	Taiwan	64
Brazil	76	Mexico	47	Turkey	21
China	85	Netherlands	40	Ukraine	52
France	46	Poland	32	UK	140
Germany	43	Russia	87		
Hong Kong	114	South Africa	59		

Source: Summarized from ww.adr.com.

---

[11] Hertz *et al.* (1997).

This demonstrates the range of countries that have companies with ADRs. Particularly noticeable are the developed countries of Japan, Australia and the UK. Also well represented is South America, traditionally an area that has looked to the USA for capital, and several countries that are increasingly joining the western capitalist system, in particular Russia, Ukraine and China.

If a foreign company wishes to trade shares on NYSE, American Stock Exchange (ASE) or NASDAQ, it must also register with the SEC and file its annual report. Since May 2002 this has to be via an electronic submission on EDGAR (see section 11.4.2.3). The annual filing normally meets the requirements of Form 20-F which includes information about the business and financial information as well as other items of information, in particular details of the shares or securities registered (see Exhibit 2.16). This is the equivalent of the Form 10-K lodged by US companies.

Exhibit 2.16	Information to be included in Form 20-F

PART I

Item 1. Identity of Directors, Senior Management and Advisers

Items 2 & 3 [where 20-F is used for a new offer of shares]. Offer Statistics & Expected Timetable; Key Information

Item 4. Information on the Company
  A. *History and development of the company.*
  B. *Business overview.*
  C. *Organizational structure.*
  D. *Property, plant and equipment.*

Item 5. Operating and Financial Review and Prospects
  A. *Operating results.*
  B. *Liquidity and capital resources.*
  C. *Research and development, patents and licenses, etc.*
  D. *Trend information.*
  E. *Off-balance sheet arrangements.*
  F. *Tabular disclosure of contractual obligations.*
  G. *Safe harbor.*

Item 6. Directors, Senior Management and Employees
  A. *Directors and senior management.*
  B. *Compensation.*
  C. *Board practices.*
  D. *Employees.*
  E. *Share ownership.*

Item 7. Major Shareholders and Related Party Transactions
  A. *Major shareholders.*
  B. *Related party transactions.*
  C. *Interests of experts and counsel.*

Item 8. Financial Information
  A. *Consolidated Statements and Other Financial Information.*
  B. *Significant Changes.*

Item 9. The Offer and Listing.

Item 10. Additional Information.

Item 11. Quantitative and Qualitative Disclosures About Market Risk.

Item 12. Description of Securities Other than Equity Securities.

PART II

Item 13. Defaults, Dividend Arrearages and Delinquencies.

Item 14. Material Modifications to the Rights of Security Holders and Use of Proceeds.

Item 15. Controls and Procedures.

Item 16A. Audit committee financial expert.

Item 16B. Code of Ethics.

Item 16C. Principal Accountant Fees and Services.

Item 16D. Exemptions from the Listing Standards for Audit Committees.

Item 16E. Purchases of Equity Securities by the Issuer and Affiliated Purchasers.

PART III

Items 17, 18. Financial Statements.

Item 19. Exhibits. [These include the Certification by the officers of the company]

Source: www.sec.gov/about/forms/secforms.htm, Form 20-F.

The rules contain a number of accommodations to the practices of other jurisdictions including:

- interim reporting as per home requirements;
- acceptance of IAS 7 (cash flow accounting), FRS3 (Business combinations) and IAS 21 (hyperinflation); and
- acceptance of home country or IAS GAAP plus a reconciliation statement.

The reconciliation statement starts with domestic or IAS earnings and equity and lists all the significant differences between these and US GAAP. Each difference is quantified so that the total difference between the two sets of earnings and equity is explained. Exhibit 9.1 provides an example of the reconciliation statement of a UK company, British Telecom. The reconciliation statement must be included in the notes to the accounts, so it is considered by the auditors when they consider their opinion of the financial statements. This means they should declare an exception to the statements if the reconciliation statement does not include all material departures from US GAAP or if the quantification of the effects of the accounting differences are misstated.

A reconciliation statement coupled with a full set of home country GAAP statements may be used providing these are based on a 'comprehensive body of accounting principles'. While this is not defined, SEC staff have indicated that this is taken to include the principles followed in all OECD member countries.[12]

---

[12] Hertz *et al.* (1997).

2.4.2.2 Listing of foreign companies on the NYSE

While relatively few foreign companies have listed in London since 1990, the same cannot be said for New York. As shown earlier in Exhibit 2.7, the number of foreign companies listed on the main market in London fell by approximately 40 per cent from 1996 to 2006 (533 to 343 companies) while in contrast the numbers on the NYSE increased by approximately 50 per cent (from 305 to 451). At the beginning of September 2007, the NYSE had 428 foreign companies from 45 countries listing common shares. Exhibit 2.17 provides a list of all countries that are home to at least ten registrants.

It is interesting to see the differences between this list and the pattern of companies listed in London as shown in Exhibit 2.12. Only six countries appear on each list, namely Bermuda, Canada, Germany, India, Japan and The Netherlands. As might be expected, far more Canadian, Central and South American companies are listed on NYSE than on London, as are more companies from China. In contrast, the NYSE has fewer companies from British Commonwealth countries such as South Africa, Australia and India and also less from Israel, Russia and other East European countries.

One significant difference between the two markets lies in the timing of the listings. The NYSE has a few companies that have maintained listings from the 1950s or earlier, such as Alcan Aluminum and Canadian Pacific from Canada, KLM and Royal Dutch Petroleum from The Netherlands and Shell Transport & Trading from the UK. However, the majority of the listings have occurred since the mid-1980s, although very recent years have seen a fall in the number of foreign registrants. For example, there were 60 new listings of foreign registrants in 2000 followed by 51 in 2001, falling to 16 in 2003 and then increasing slightly to 29 in 2006 and 15 in the first six months of 2007. While most of the new listings in this period came from Europe and Canada, it is noteworthy that several more came from each of South Africa, Brazil, Korea, Taiwan and Puerto Rico, while the NYSE is increasingly popular with Chinese companies with four listing in 2006 and seven listing in the first six months of 2007.

Only a minority of the foreign companies listed have issued full public offerings on the NYSE. All but one of the Chinese (see Exhibit 2.18) and the majority of companies from South and Central America, India, Hong Kong and from various mainland European countries such as France, Italy and Spain have made public offerings, suggesting that the need for funds was the main reason for seeking a listing. In contrast, relatively few of the companies from Australia, Canada, Japan or the UK have made public

Exhibit 2.17	**Number of non-US corporate issuers on the NYSE**

Country	No. registrants	Country	No. registrants
Argentina	12	Germany	14
Bermuda	30	India	12
Brazil	31	Japan	19
Canada	80	Mexico	16
Chile	15	Switzerland	10
China	26	The Netherlands	15
France	14	UK	32

Source: www.nyse.com, September 2007.

| Exhibit 2.18 | An example of the information provided by the NYSE on its foreign registrants: China |

Company	Symbol	Industry	Share Listed	Type	IPO
CHINA (24 ADR & 2 non-ADR Issuers)					
Acorn International	ATV	Consumer Products marketing	5/3/07	A	IPO
Aluminum Corp of China Ltd (Chalco)	ACH	Aluminum Production	12/11/01	A	IPO
American Oriental Bioengineering	AOB	Pharmaceuticals	12/18/06	A	
China Eastern Airlines Corp Ltd.	CEA	Airlines Operation	2/4/97	A	IPO
China Life Insurance Co. (China Life)	LFC	Commercial Life Insurance	12/17/03	A	IPO
China Netcom Group Corp.	CN	Fixed line telecom.	11/16/01	A	IPO
China Petroleum & Chemical Co. (Sinopec)	SNP	Petroleum & Petrochemical	10/18/00	A	IPO
China Southern Airlines Co. Ltd.	ZNH	Commercial Airline Service	7/30/97	A	IPO
China Telecom Corporation Ltd.	CHA	Fixed-Line Telecoms	11/14/02	A	IPO
China Unicom	CHU	Telecommunications	6/21/00	A	IPO
CNOOC Limited	CEO	Crude Oil & Gas Expl.	2/27/01	A	IPO
Guangshen Railway Company Ltd.	GSH	Rail Transportation	5/13/96	A	IPO
Huaneng Power International, Inc.	HNP	Holding Co./Power Plants	10/6/94	A	IPO
LDK Solar Co.	LDK	Solar Wafer Manuf.	6/1/07	A	IPO
Mindray Medical Internat. Ltd.	MR	Medical Devices Manuf.	9/26/06	A	IPO
New Oriental Education & Technology Group Inc.	EDU	Private Educational Services	9/7/06	A	IPO
PetroChina Co. Ltd.	PTR	Oil and Gas Exploration	4/6/00	A	IPO
Qiao Xing Mobile Communication	QXM	Mobile Comm. Handsets	5/3/07	A	IPO
Semiconductor Manuf. Internat. Co.	SMI	Semiconductor Mfg.	3/17/04	A	IPO
Simcere Pharmaceutical Group	SCR	Pharmaceuticals	4/20/07	A	IPO
Sinopec Shanghai Petrochemical Co.	SHI	Petrochemicals Prod'n	7/26/93	A	IPO
Suntech Power Holdings Co. Ltd.	STP	Solar Cell Manufacture	12/14/05	A	IPO
Tongjitang Chinese Medicines Co.	TCM	Speciality Pharmaceuticals	3/16/07	A	IPO
Trina Solar Ltd.	TSL	Solar Power Products	12/19/06	A	IPO
Yanzhou Coal Mining Co. Ltd.	YZC	Coal Mining	3/31/98	A	IPO
Yingli Green Energy Holding Co. Ltd.	YGE	Solar Energy	6/8/07	A	IPO

Source: www.nyse.com. Data as at 7 August 2007.

offerings, suggesting that the decision to list may not have been driven by a need for new funding. As discussed above, these companies may have sought a listing for a number of other reasons.

2.4.2.3 NYSE Global Shares

The NYSE has developed Global Shares, which can be traded on either the NYSE or the home country market without converting the shares traded in one market for shares traded in another. Canadian companies have used this model to trade in the USA since 1883. The Global Share enables other non-US companies also to trade on the same terms as North American equities. They are intended to enable virtually seamless cross-border trading, allowing non-US companies to increase liquidity and pricing efficiency in the US market while permitting US investors access to the home market shares on the same terms as local investors.

An example of the use of Global Shares may be seen in DaimlerChrysler. The merger between Daimler-Benz AG and Chrysler Corporation in November 1998 marked the first time a company outside the USA or Canada directly listed the same common shares on both a US exchange and its home stock exchange. The principal features of the Daimler-Chrysler share are as follows:

- The DaimlerChrysler (NYSE: DCX) Global Shares trade on the NYSE, the Frankfurt Stock Exchange and multiple exchanges around the world.
- DaimlerChrysler shares are quoted in US dollars on the NYSE and local currencies on other markets.
- Dividends are payable in euros or US dollars. For US shareholders, a New York transfer agent handles the conversion and payment process.
- Separate transfer agents in the USA and Germany clear trades via a computer link between the New York custodian of shares (Depositary Trust Company – DTC) and the Frankfurt custodian (Deutsche Börse Clearing – DBC).

Global Shares provide an alternative to the ADR facility for non-US companies but have the advantage that buyers may make direct purchase of equity in a company, obtaining lower costs than through intermediaries. The shares function in the same way as those of US companies and allow US investors to trade a non-US security outside market hours and receive dividends at the same time as shareholders in the company's home country.

2.5 Empirical research into stock market listing choices

A number of studies have looked at the factors that help to explain listing choices or where and why companies list on foreign stock exchanges. One of the first of these was by Saudagaran (1988), who tested four hypotheses. These were that the likelihood that a company has a foreign listing is a function of:

- the relative size of the company in its domestic stock market (capitalization or market value of company's equity to total market capitalization);
- importance of foreign sales (foreign sales to total sales);
- importance of foreign investment (investment in foreign countries as a proportion of total investment);
- importance of foreign employees (employees in foreign countries as a proportion of total employees).

Looking at 223 companies with shares listed in at least one of eight foreign countries, the study found support for the importance of the company in its domestic local stock exchange and the importance of foreign sales. It failed to find any support for the other two hypotheses (foreign investment and foreign employees).

Later studies have looked instead at the importance of disclosure levels in different countries. Biddle and Saudagaran (1989), using a similar sample, found support for the hypothesis that companies tend to be indifferent across exchanges with levels of disclosure that are less than domestic disclosure levels. In contrast, they are progressively less likely to list on exchanges in countries with higher disclosure levels. Alternative explanations of listing behaviour were also considered – the importance of industry membership; geographic location (whether located in the same geographic area or not); importance of country of listing as an export market (industry exports to country as proportion of industry exports to all sample countries); and the relative importance of the company to its domestic stock market. Even when all of these alternative explanations were also taken into account, disclosure levels still helped to explain listing choice. These results were confirmed by a later study (Saudagaran and Biddle, 1995), which looked at the listing behaviour of 459 multinational companies from the same eight countries (Canada, France, Germany, Japan, The Netherlands, Switzerland, UK and USA) in 1992.

While these are interesting results, some care should be taken in interpreting them. It should not be assumed that the results will always hold across all countries and all time periods. This type of study suffers from two serious limitations. Firstly, it looks only at the position at one point of time. It tries to explain the decision to list – a decision that may have been taken many years earlier – by looking at contemporary economic, corporate and accounting factors. Secondly, these studies looked only at certain countries.

One other study (Gray and Roberts, 1997) suggests that the factors determining listing choices may differ across companies from different countries. Gray and Roberts instead tried to explain the number of registrants from each foreign country that were listed on the LSE in 1994. They ran a regression with the dependent variable being number of companies listed from country X and the independent variables being:

- disclosure level (more or less than UK);
- size of economy (GDP);
- economic development of country (per capita GDP);
- importance of national stock market (market capitalization to GDP);
- trade with the UK (exports and imports to UK as a proportion of all exports and imports of country);
- level of domestic investment (domestic investment to GDP);
- cultural affinity to the UK (English speaking, EU member or Commonwealth member).

While the model was relatively successful in explaining the number of foreign registrants (adjusted R^2 of 61 per cent), Gray and Roberts found no evidence to suggest that disclosure levels were significant. Instead, the only factors that helped to explain the number of companies listed were GDP, stock market capitalization and domestic investment rates. More companies were listed from countries that were large, had relatively important stock markets and high needs for capital as measured by domestic investment levels.

A single country study by Yamori and Baba (2001) on the opinions of Japanese managers in 1996 found that the managers believed strongly in the favourable effect of overseas listing in terms of increasing prestige and widening the shareholder base, but regarded disclosure and financial reporting requirements as the main obstacles to overseas listing. They pointed out that the subsequent moves in Japan to align more closely with IFRS, together with the economic impact of the recession that occurred after 1996, would require their conclusions to be tested against the change of circumstances.

Later studies have looked at a range of factors affecting listing choice including differences in disclosure levels as well as geographic proximity, cultural similarities and trade patterns. For example, Pagano *et al.* (2001) and Sarkissian and Schill (2005) found that cultural and geographic proximity were important explanations of listing choice. In a later study, Pagano *et al.* (2002) documented the differences between European companies listing in the USA (primarily large, recently privatized with expanding sales growth) and European firms listing on other European stock exchanges (not growing as fast and with significant increases in leverage). Henderson *et al.* (2006) extended this body of work by examining not only equity issues but also debt issues. In practice, corporate bonds are more likely to be issued internationally than is equity. They documented how during the period 1990 to 2001 approximately ten times as much debt as equity was issued outside the home country, representing 20 per cent of total corporate bond offerings in comparison with the 12 per cent of equity issued outside the home country. Again, they found regional patterns in listing preferences as well as decisions apparently being affected by the state of various markets. Listing of equities were more common when stock markets appear overvalued and bond issues tended to precede market interest rate rises. Ndubizu (2007) instead looked only at firms cross-listing in the USA for the period 1985 to 2003. He documented how firms appear to manage earnings prior to listing by changing the timing of discretionary accruals. However, he found little difference between firms raising capital or IPO firms and other firms. This suggests that it is not the desire to increase demand and so the price of the new share issue that influences earnings management behaviour. Instead, he suggested that this behaviour may be due to a desire to report good news and so increase investor recognition.

These studies suggest that listing choice is determined by the specific combination of firm-specific features and stock market features. For example, Chemmanur and Fulghieri (2006) show how companies can benefit from listing on exchanges with high disclosure requirements only if they can also produce high-quality information at a relatively low cost. Thus, they argue that in the long term, while the number of stock markets may continue to fall, there will still be a range of different markets with different disclosure requirements. However, if a company does list on a market with stricter disclosure requirements, the evidence suggests that it may reap several advantages. Looking at the impact of cross-listing in the USA, the evidence seems to suggest that this is a good thing for the company in that analysts' coverage increases, as does the accuracy of their forecasts, and that is associated with higher valuations.[13] One reason for this may be that such listings seem to encourage firms to adopt a disclosure package more in line with that typically found in the USA in that they are also associated with improved disclosures, less aggressive earnings management and the increased willingness to disclose bad as well as good news.[14] It also appears that the increase in investment by US shareholders following cross-listing is greatest for firms with weak accounting practices, firms that are most likely to improve their accounting practices after cross-listing. However, the attractiveness to investors also depends upon other factors: in particular, cross-listing does not increase the attractiveness of companies that are closely held or companies from countries with weak shareholder rights.[15] Finally, it appears that it is institutional investors in the USA that are particularly attracted to non-US listers that provide US GAAP-compliant information.[16] However, before we can gain a full understanding of the importance of disclosure requirements we really need to know more about the role played by financial intermediaries, both analysts and investment bankers, and how they react to disclosures and foreign listings under different circumstances.[17]

Rather than examining the relative importance or impact of accounting regulations, research in the finance literature instead initially tended to focus upon the impact of

---

[13] Lang *et al.* (2003a).

[14] Lang *et al.* (2003b); Khanna *et al.* (2004).

[15] Ammer *et al.* (2006).

[16] Bradshaw *et al.* (2004).

[17] Karolyi (2006).

cross-listings on share price behaviour. Theoretical research argued that firms could successfully circumvent restrictions or additional costs faced by international investors and that they would therefore reap the advantages of reducing segmentation and reduce their costs of capital.[18] Empirical research found that cross-listing has little impact on US firms[19] but that in contrast non-US firms listing in the USA appeared to reap significant benefits.[20] However, the market segmentation hypothesis has been criticized, especially by Stulz (1999), for a number of reasons. For example, if cross-listing reduces a firm's cost of capital, one would expect to see more cross-listed firms than there are. Many companies that cross-list come from countries that are relatively well integrated, for example Canadian companies in the USA, while listing patterns over time appear to bear little relationship to changes in market integration or segmentation.

Stulz suggested that in order to explain why some companies cross-list while others from the same country do not, the corporate governance characteristics of the individual firm must be looked at. Corporate governance rules have been tightened in most countries over the last couple of decades to limit the ability of management and controlling shareholders to reap benefits at the expense of outside or external shareholders. However, corporate governance regulations vary quite significantly across countries, while individual companies similarly have quite different corporate governance characteristics. If a company has weak corporate governance structures in place and has powerful controlling shareholders then it will be particularly expensive for it to list on a stock market with higher corporate governance regulations such as the USA. Companies in this position will only cross-list if they can reap specific benefits, such as raising extra funds for high–growth opportunities.[21] This helps explain why fewer firms are cross-listing. With the Sarbanes–Oxley Act in the USA increasing significantly the corporate governance regulations (see Chapter 11 for more on this), the costs of listing have increased, while the benefits are reducing as markets are becoming less segmented.[22] Sarbanes–Oxley also helps explain a number of delisting decisions. The Act imposed various compliance costs on all firms, but it also requires firms with weak corporate governance structures to change their practices. Thus, it is no surprise to find an increasing number of companies delisting that had significant insider controlling interests and weak corporate governance.[23]

2.6 Methods of reporting to foreign users

2.6.1 Foreign language statements

As we have seen, there are a significant number of firms that cross-list, often on a number of different exchanges, and many more issue debt internationally. However, even if a company does not issue debt or equity internationally, it may still have significant numbers of foreign investors. Companies could just ignore the fact that these foreign

---

[18] Alexander *et al.* (1988); Eun and Janakiramanan (1986); Errunza and Losq (1985).

[19] Howe and Madura (1990); Lau *et al.* (1994).

[20] Foerster and Karolyi (1999).

[21] Coffee (2002); Doidge *et al.* (2004).

[22] Bris *et al.* (2007).

[23] Leuz *et al.* (2006); Hostak *et al.* (2007).

investors exist and that they may be used to quite different types of narrative disclosures, different currencies or different languages. While this appears to be a costless alternative, there may be substantial indirect or hidden costs in doing this. If potential lenders cannot even understand the language in which the reports are written they are far less likely to buy the shares. Many companies therefore translate not only their annual reports and accounts but also their entire set of web pages, including the investor relations pages, into foreign language(s).

Foreign language annual reports may be just abridged reports (typically the financial statements, the accounting policies, the Chair's statement and a very brief overview of activities) or complete word-for-word translations of the entire annual accounts and report. Most large European companies produce complete English-language versions of their annual report including all the narrative disclosures. The only costs involved in doing this are the cost of translation and any additional printing costs, so it tends to be a fairly cheap alternative. It is therefore an acceptable method of reporting to foreign users if:

- the foreign users are relatively unimportant; or
- the accounting and reporting systems of the two countries are very similar to each other.

If there are relatively few foreign users or they are relatively unimportant, it will not be worth spending any more on any of the more expensive alternative ways of reporting to foreign users – the additional costs would outweigh the advantages. Alternatively, the foreign readers may be very knowledgeable about the differences in the accounting systems internationally. As we saw in section 2.2.3 above, some investors are able to adopt a multiple principle capability and are able to cope with differences in accounting methods. Here, there would be no advantages to the company in using other more sophisticated, but more expensive, reporting methods. Finally, there may be little point in doing more if there are few material differences between domestic and foreign GAAP statements. Even if the two countries both use IFRS, there may be differences in other aspects of the annual reporting package. For example, Leventis and Weetman (2004) found that listed companies in Greece reporting in Greek and English produce, on average, a larger amount of voluntary disclosure than those reporting only in Greek. This suggests that the target of producing the English-language report may drive the content of the Greek-language report.

2.6.2 Convenience translations

Even if shareholders are presented with a complete set of accounts in their own language, they may still be confused by the use of a different or unfamiliar currency. While this is obviously less likely to be a problem, the use of a different currency can make it more difficult to get an accurate impression of what is going on. Some companies therefore go one stage further and also translate the currency they report in – the 'convenience translation', so called because it is not a complete method of foreign currency translation, such as the closing rate or temporal method. Instead, all the figures, both the current year and past year(s), are translated at one exchange rate.

Convenience translations are relatively rarely found in European reports, but many large Japanese companies provide such statements. Exhibit 16.1 (Sumitomo Mitsui) illustrates the provision of a convenience translation for the latest year for the notes to the accounts. As is common with Japanese companies, this company actually goes slightly further and also reformatted its accounts to present them in a form more familiar to foreign (US) readers. In many cases this is not simply a case of presenting the same information in a slightly different form, but also involves the provision of additional information.

2.6.3 Reconciliation statements

One example of this is the reconciliation statement produced by many companies listed in the USA, as described above in section 2.4.2. The benefits of this type of reconciliation statement depend upon several factors. Some companies would argue that there are no benefits. Instead, they would argue that producing two sets of figures will increase uncertainty. However, if the users are relatively sophisticated they should be able to understand why two sets of GAAP may result in different earnings or equity figures and should not be deterred from dealing with the company. Indeed, some users are sufficiently powerful to demand that statements are drawn up in familiar GAAP. For example, banks when lending large sums of money will often be able to demand whatever information they require. Similar powers are held by governments and tax authorities.

It appears that the SEC insistence on the preparation of a reconciliation to US GAAP (except by Canadian companies) may partly reflect a concern for insufficiently conservative accounting practices, as well as a desire to see extensive disclosure. In its response to the SEC on the acceptability of IAS, FASB in June 2000 recommended that companies using IAS should provide reconciliations to US GAAP, although as discussed later in Chapter 10 the IASB and the SEC are working towards removing this requirement.

There has been a considerable amount of interest in the academic literature on the usefulness of reconciliation statements. There is a high level of agreement that when a company produces two sets of accounts, in particular US GAAP full sets of accounts as well as domestic GAAP accounts, then both sets of accounts contain useful information in the sense that the markets react to both sets of accounts. There is rather less agreement on the usefulness of US GAAP reconciliation statements with much of the evidence suggesting that such statements are not informationally useful.[24] However, others suggest that they are useful, but that the usefulness depends, as might be expected, at least partially upon the time period being considered and upon the country of the disclosing company and the specific items being considered.[25]

Street *et al.* (2000) used a comparability index (see Chapter 9) to examine the US GAAP reconciliations of 33 companies whose annual reports complied with international accounting standards in 1997. From the three years of data available in Form 20-F they found that the overall adjustments were significant only in 1996 with an adjustment of 20 per cent from IAS profit to US GAAP. They concluded that the gap between IAS and US GAAP was narrowing. They also found examples of non-compliance with IAS, some of which were material in relation to the reported earnings. They pointed out that if the SEC were to be persuaded to abandon the requirement for a reconciliation, there would need to be greater assurance from the preparers and auditors of accounts.

Studies of the impact of reconciliation statements have generally examined the impact of disclosures upon share returns, although one more recent study has instead explored the issue of the impact of disclosure upon analysts. In that study, Hora *et al.*

---

[24] See, for example, Rees and Elgers (1997); Chan and Seow (1996).
[25] See Fulkerson and Meek (1998); Rees (1995); Barth and Clinch (1996).

(2003) tested the effect of foreign GAAP earnings and Form 20-F reconciliations on the revision of analysts' forecasts. The data related to the years 1988 to 1995. They found abnormal revisions around the announcement date of earnings prepared under foreign GAAP and around the filing of Form 20-F. They concluded that the foreign earnings and the reconciliations convey information to the analysts. One problem with this research design is that Form 20-F contains a mass of information alongside the reconciliation statement, so the analysts may have been reacting to some other aspect of Form 20-F.

Other studies have instead examined the impact of information released in the UK by UK companies cross-listed in the USA. These studies generally support the conclusion that US investors react to UK earnings announcements and annual general meetings and that they are able to use UK GAAP reports to help them value the stocks in the US market.[26]

This body of work has generally been taken to mean that US GAAP information is of a better quality than are other GAAP. However, all that can really be concluded is that US GAAP statements and reconciliation statements provide different, new information from that provided in domestic GAAP statements. However, it appears that both domestic GAAP and US GAAP statements are, when provided, useful to investors.

2.6.4 Use of IFRS

The IASB used to list on its web pages all companies that voluntarily stated their compliance with international standards. This list was then used in a number of studies to examine the questions of how good the compliance was with international standards and who actually complied with the standards voluntarily. From this it is clear that, prior to IFRS 1, many companies claimed compliance when this was less than complete. For example, the 2000 survey of 1999 accounts identified 165 companies claiming compliance with international standards; however, only 102 of these were fully compliant with the rest adopting various levels of compliance of 'IAS lite' as shown in Exhibit 2.19.

An earlier survey of 1996 accounts was used to look in detail at 49 companies' accounts.[27] This identified the areas of non-compliance, with the areas of the highest non-compliance shown in Exhibit 2.20.

One obvious question is 'which companies did not voluntarily comply fully with international standards?' Street and Bryant (2000) suggest that the level of compliance is associated with a number of factors. In particular, compliance is higher on average among companies that are listed in the USA or that file in the USA than among companies that are not either listed or filed in the USA. Obviously, one reason for this may be the US listing per se, but it may be instead that US listing status is highly correlated with some other variable such as size or country of domicile, which is the real reason for the level of compliance. Further testing using multiple regression found that compliance was positively associated with listing status as well as with the type of audit report compliance statement and the use of international auditing standards. In other words, the main factors were the extent to which the company's auditors, and presumably therefore the company, are serious about the use of international standards. Surprisingly, they did not find that variables such as size, profitability or industry helped explain compliance.

A second important question that could be asked about the impact of international standards is 'which companies claim to follow international standards (even if this

---

[26] Olibe (2002); Olibe (2006); Frost and Pownall (1996).

[27] Street *et al.* (1999); see also Taylor and Jones (1999).

Exhibit 2.19	Types of compliance with IAS	

		Number of companies
1	Full IAS compliance	102
2	Full compliance with national standards that comply with IASs	4
3	Full compliance with exceptions specified in the accounting policies	10
4	Full compliance with exceptions specified in the notes, but outside the policies	3
5	Accounting policies comply with IASs or are based on IASs or the principles in IASs	4
6	As 5 but with specified exemptions from full compliance	4
7	IAS used only when there are no equivalent domestic standards	12
8	IAS used only for selected items or when permitted by domestic requirements	13
9	Reconciliations from domestic GAAP to IASs	6
10	Summary IAS financial statements	4
11	Unquantified description of differences from IAS treatments	5
Total		165

Source: *Accountancy*, May 2001, pp. 98–99.

compliance is less than complete)?' Again using the IASB list of companies following IAS in 1996, El-Gazzar *et al.* (1999) found that the most important variable appearing to explain whether or not a company complied voluntarily was internationality, as measured by the percentage of foreign sales. Also important were membership of the EU, size, profitability, debt ratio and the number of stock markets listed on. Different stock markets have different listing requirements. In most cases, companies can choose whether to follow local GAAP, international GAAP or some other internationally accepted GAAP such as US GAAP. Which of these three a company will choose depends upon the costs of compliance or non-compliance. Obviously, as a company increases the number of stock markets it lists on the costs of using local GAAP in each market will increase, so that it becomes more and more advantageous to use just one GAAP. However, this need not be IASB GAAP, but could be US GAAP. Ashbaugh (2001) provides evidence to suggest that the decision on whether to use IASB or US GAAP will depend upon the particular circumstances of the company. In most cases, it will prefer whichever of these two alternatives is the easiest or cheapest to do, namely the alternative that requires the least number of accounting changes from its domestic GAAP.

Probably the most important question is simply 'is IAS information useful to the market?' There is some limited evidence on this. Harris and Muller (1999) looked at the impact of 20-F reconciliation statements that recast information from IAS to US GAAP. They found that the impact on reported figures was generally smaller for their sample than was reported in studies of domestic GAAP to US GAAP reconciliations, implying that US GAAP were more similar to IAS GAAP than to GAAP in many other countries. The results on market impact were not unambiguous, differing somewhat

Exhibit 2.20 Level of non-compliance with international standards

Standard	Area	Number of companies
IAS 2 Inventories	Use of 'lower of cost and market' rather than 'lower of cost and net realizable value'	13 of 47
IAS 8 Net profit/loss	All items of income and expense included in net profit/loss	13 of 49
	Strict definition extraordinary items	10 of 10
IAS 9 R&D	Disclose accounting policy	10 of 43
	Disclose amount charged to expense of period	10 of 43
IAS 16 Property, plant & equipment	Reconcile carrying amount at beginning and end of each period	15 of 49
IAS 18 Revenue	Disclose accounting policy	27 of 49
IAS 19 Retirement plans	Disclose general description of plan	14 of 23
IAS 21 Foreign currency	Disclose amount of exchange difference included in net profit/loss	15 of 48
IAS 22 Business combinations	Disclose cost of acquisition	11 of 31
	If useful life of goodwill exceeds five years, justify period	14 of 38
	Reconcile beginning and end period goodwill	13 of 42
IAS 23 Borrowing costs	Disclose capitalization rate	14 of 14

Source: Derived from Street *et al.* (1999).

depending upon the models used to measure the impact. However, they concluded that there is some evidence that US GAAP reconciliations are useful even from IAS GAAP, in that they were value relevant when using models based upon returns rather than prices per shares. This does not of course necessarily imply that US GAAP are somehow 'better' than IAS GAAP, simply that they may provide different information.

One interesting study that throws further light on the question of whether US or IAS GAAP are more informationally efficient was carried out by Leuz (2003) who looked at companies on the German Neuer Markt (new market), a market for smaller high-growth companies. These companies were allowed to use either US or IAS GAAP. Neither of these was used for taxation purposes and the decision on which to use did not affect any other features of the regulatory environment they face. He found no evidence of any significant differences in information asymmetry; in other words, there were no significant differences between companies that used US or IAS GAAP in terms of bid-ask spreads, share turnover, analysts' forecast dispersion or initial public offering under pricing. Similarly, Daske (2006) found no evidence that listed German companies managed to reduce their equity cost of capital by voluntarily adopting IAS or US GAAP, suggesting that the change in accounting rules did not increase demand for their shares.

Ashbaugh and Pincus (2001) instead looked at the question of the impact of IAS adoption on analysts' forecasts. While this study used voluntary adoptees of IAS during the period 1990–93, a period when IAS offered significant choice, they did find that the voluntary adoption of IAS resulted in improved forecasts and that the improvement was greater for those companies with the greatest change in GAAP.

These findings support the conclusions drawn by Barth *et al.* (1999) in a study that uses mathematical proofs to show that international harmonization, of itself, is not necessarily a good thing. Rather it depends upon whether or not greater harmonization results in more or less precise GAAP and increasing or decreasing price informativeness of the resultant information. The empirical studies here show that moving from domestic to IAS GAAP is generally perceived by the market as being desirable. However, stock markets would probably have found the move from a position of international disharmony to the widespread adoption of US GAAP informationally useful as well. The question of whether or not US GAAP or IAS GAAP would have been found most useful in the context of stock market informativeness remains currently unresolved.

While share ownership is increasing in a large number of countries, accounting systems have developed in different ways under different environmental pressures. In particular, as discussed in Chapters 4 and 5, not all countries have developed their accounting systems in response to the needs of stock market participants. The possible effects of this on stock market participants have been explored by Ali and Hwang (2000). They explored the value relevance of financial accounting data across 16 countries (i.e. the extent to which accounting earnings and the book value of equity can be used to explain share returns). They found that the value relevance of accounting information is lower in countries with:

- bank-orientated financial systems (i.e. high debt–equity ratios);
- private sector bodies not involved in the standard-setting process;
- an accounting system belonging to the 'continental' cluster rather than the 'Anglo-American' cluster;
- tax rules that significantly influence financial accounting measurements;
- less spent on external accounting services.

Summary and conclusions

This chapter looked at the effects of international diversity in accounting practices. In particular, it sought to provide answers to the questions of how do investors cope with accounting diversity and how can companies adapt their listing behaviour and their disclosure policies to cope with accounting diversity?

Given the often very different figures that can be produced under different GAAP, it is not immediately obvious why investors would want to cope with the additional problems and uncertainty involved in investing in foreign companies. However, we saw that the benefits can be substantial and, at least for the individual or private investor, it is getting easier and easier to invest in foreign companies indirectly through the ever-increasing number of investment funds that exist. However, this does not remove the problem of how to cope with accounting diversity – the investment trusts still have to decide which companies they should invest in. The chapter therefore looked at the somewhat limited evidence there is regarding how investors cope with accounting diversity. This suggests that foreign investment might well increase as accounting diversity is reduced.

The chapter then moved on to look at the listing behaviour of companies. Taking as its starting point the evidence showing that many companies list on foreign exchange(s), the chapter looked at the reasons for this phenomenon. We also saw that one response to the increase in international investment by individual shareholders and the increasing co-integration of stock markets may be the continuing decrease in attractiveness of international cross-listing by companies.

Key points from the chapter:

- Companies may have to list on a larger exchange if they want to raise a large amount of equity capital. This is especially the case for companies from relatively small countries or countries with relatively inactive stock markets.

- Not all companies list to raise new funds and companies also list on foreign exchanges for a range of reasons including risk management, issuing shares to employees and for takeovers, and signalling to customers, the general public or governments.

- The USA demands the highest level of disclosure from foreign registrant companies – requiring, for example, a reconciliation statement explaining differences from US GAAP.

- The reconciliation affects direct and indirect costs. The ways in which the USA has reduced these costs by allowing a variety of different methods of selling of shares were also discussed.

- Studies on stock market listing behaviour provide clear evidence that differences in listing requirements have been important; however, this is not the only consideration and the extra disclosure costs do not appear to be an insurmountable barrier.

- While most companies may potentially benefit from the advantages of reducing segmentation, companies with poor corporate governance structures and with powerful inside shareholders will be faced with substantial extra agency costs if they have to follow the corporate governance rules of US stock markets.

- Increasingly more companies are likely to face the question of how best to report to foreign users. Existing practices range from translation into foreign languages, through translation of the currencies and account formats, to complete statements under foreign GAAP.

Questions

The following questions test your understanding of the material contained in the chapter and allow you to relate your understanding to the learning outcomes specified at the start of this chapter. The learning outcomes are repeated here. Each question is cross-referenced to the relevant section of the chapter.

Understand why investors might want to invest in foreign companies and the approaches they may take

1 Why might investors wish to invest in foreign companies? (section 2.2.1)

2 Describe the composition of the optimal portfolio that investors can invest in and describe how they might go about investing in a suitable portfolio. (section 2.2)

3 Identify and describe the alternative investment strategies an investor can adopt when deciding which shares to invest in and, in each case, describe the role and use of financial statement information. (section 2.2)

Understand the reasons why companies might list on foreign stock markets

4 Why do companies list on foreign stock markets? (section 2.3)

5 What actions might a company have to take to ensure that it maintains a large active shareholder base in a foreign country? (section 2.3)

6 Which types of companies are particularly likely to seek a listing on a foreign stock market? (section 2.3)

7 If a company wanted to trade its shares in the USA, what alternative methods are available to it? What would you advise it to do? (section 2.4.2)

Understand the additional costs of listing on foreign stock markets

8 What are likely to be the main additional direct costs incurred by a company seeking a listing on a foreign stock market? (section 2.3.6)

9 What are likely to be the main additional indirect costs incurred by a company seeking a listing on a foreign stock market? (section 2.3.6)

Evaluate published research seeking to explain the foreign stock market listing choices of companies

10 What is the empirical evidence of foreign listing behaviour on UK stock markets? (section 2.4.1)

11 What is the empirical evidence of foreign listing behaviour in the USA? (section 2.4.2)

12 What does empirical research tell you about the factors that affect a company's choice of where to list? (section 2.5)

13 If you wanted to test empirically for the factors that affect a company's choice of where to list, how would you go about getting the information you needed? What problems do you think you would encounter? (sections 2.4 and 2.5)

Understand the different approaches that companies can take when reporting to foreign investors and the factors that affect this decision

14 Describe each of the main methods that a company could adopt when reporting to its foreign users. (section 2.6)

15 Describe the relative advantages and disadvantages of each of the methods identified above. (section 2.6)

16 What does empirical research tell us about the usefulness of reconciliations statements and statements produced under alternative GAAP? (sections 2.6.3 and 2.6.4)

References and further reading

Alexander, G., Eun, C. and Janakiramanan, S. (1988) 'International listings and stock returns: some empirical evidence', *Journal of Financial and Quantitative Analysis*, 23: 135–151.

Ali, A. and Hwang, L.-S. (2000) 'Country-specific factors related to financial reporting and the value relevance of accounting data', *Journal of Accounting Research*, Spring: 1–21.

Ammer, J., Holland, S.B., Smith, D.C. and Warnock, F.E. (2006) *Look at me now: what attracts US shareholders*, National Bureau of Economic Research Working Paper, June.

Ashbaugh, H. (2001) 'Non-US firms' accounting standard choices', *Journal of Accounting and Public Policy*, 20: 129–153.

Ashbaugh, H. and Pincus, M. (2001) 'Domestic accounting standards, international accounting standards, and the predictability of earnings', *Journal of Accounting Research*, 39(3): 417–434.

Barth, M.E. and Clinch, G. (1996) 'International accounting differences and their relation to share prices: evidence from UK, Australian and Canadian firms', *Contemporary Accounting Research*, 13(1): Spring.

Barth, M.E., Clinch, G. and Shibano, T. (1999) 'International accounting harmonization and global equity markets', *Journal of Accounting and Economics*, 26: 201–235.

Biddle, G.C. and Saudagaran, S.M. (1989) 'The effect of financial disclosure levels on firms' choices among alternative foreign stock exchange listings', *Journal of International Financial Management and Accounting*, 1(1): 55–87.

Bradshaw, M., Bushee, B. and Miller, T. (2004) 'Accounting choice, home bias and US investment in non-US firms', *Journal of Accounting Research*, 42(5): 795–841.

Bris, A., Cantale, S. and Nishiotis, G.P. (2007) 'A breakdown of the valuation effects of international cross-listing', *European Financial Management*, 13(3), June: 498–530.

Chan, K.C. and Seow, G.S. (1996) 'The association between stock returns and foreign GAAP earnings versus earnings adjusted to US GAAP', *Journal of Accounting and Economics*, 21: 139–158.

Chemmanur, T.J. and Fulghieri, P. (2006) 'Competition and cooperation among exchanges: a theory of cross-listing and endogenous listing standards', *Journal of Financial Economics*, 82(2), November: 455–489.

Choi, F.D.S. and Levich, R.M. (1996) 'Accounting diversity', in Steil, B. (ed.) *The European Equity Markets*. London: Royal Institute of International Affairs.

Choi, F.D.S. and Levich, R.M. (1997) 'Accounting diversity and capital market decisions', in Choi, F.D.S. (ed.) *International Accounting and Finance Handbook*, 2nd edn. New York: John Wiley & Sons.

Coffee, J. (2002) 'Racing towards the top? The impact of cross-listings and stock market competition on international corporate governance', *Columbia Law Review*, 102: 1757–1831.

Corhay, A., Rad, A.T. and Urbain, J.P. (1993) 'Common stochastic trends in European stock markets', *Economics Letters*, 42: 385–390.

Daske, H. (2006) 'Economic benefits of adopting IFRS of US-GAAP: have the expected cost of equity capital really decreased?', *Journal of Business Finance and Accounting*, 33(3&4), April/May: 329–373.

Doidge, C., Karolyi, G.A. and Stulz, R.M. (2004) 'Why are firms listed in the US worth more?', *Journal of Financial Economics*, 71: 205–238.

El-Gazzar, S.M., Finn, P.M. and Jacob, R. (1999) 'An empirical investigation of multinational firms' compliance with international accounting standards', *International Journal of Accounting*, 34(2): 239–248.

Errunza, V. and Losq, E. (1985) 'International asset pricing under mild segmentation: theory and test', *Journal of Finance*, 40: 105–124.

Eun, C. and Janakiramanan, S. (1986) 'A model of international asset pricing with a constraint on the foreign equity ownership', *Journal of Finance*, 41: 1015–1124.

Foerster, S.R. and Karolyi, G.A. (1999) 'The effects of market segmentation and investor recognition on asset prices: evidence from foreign stock listing in the United States', *Journal of Finance*, 54: 981–1013.

Fraser, P. and Oyefeso, O. (2005) 'US, UK and European stock market integration', *Journal of Business Finance and Accounting*, 32(1–2): 161–181.

Frost, C. and Pownall, G. (1996) 'Interdependencies in the global markets for capital and information', *Accounting Horizons*, 10(1): 39–57.

Fulkerson, C.L. and Meek, G.K. (1998) 'Analysts' earnings forecasts and the value relevance of 20-F reconciliations from non-US to US GAAP', *Journal of International Financial Management and Accounting*, 9(1): 1–15.

Gray, S.J. and Roberts, C.B. (1997) 'Foreign company listings on the London Stock Exchange: listing patterns and influential factors', in Cooke, T.E. and Nobes, C.W. (eds) *The Development of Accounting in an International Context*. London: Routledge.

Hanks, S. (1997) 'Globalization of world financial markets: perspective of the US Securities and Exchange Commission', in Choi, F.D.S. (ed.) *International Accounting and Finance Handbook*, 2nd edn. New York: John Wiley & Sons.

Harris, M.S. and Muller, K.A. (1999) 'The market valuations of IAS versus US-GAAP accounting measures using Form 20-F reconciliations', *Journal of Accounting and Economics*, 26: 285–312.

Henderson, B.J., Jegadeesh, N. and Weisbach, M.S. (2006) 'World markets for raising new capital', *Journal of Financial Economics*, 82: 63–101.

Hertz, R.H., Dittmar, N.W., Lis, S.J., Decker, W.E. and Murray, R.J. (1997) *The Coopers and Lybrand SEC Manual*, 7th edn. New York: John Wiley & Sons.

Hora, J., Tondkar, R.H. and McEwen, R.A. (2003) 'Effect of foreign GAAP earnings and Form 20-F reconciliations on revisions of analysts' forecasts', *International Journal of Accounting*, 38: 71–93.

Hostak, P., Karaaoglu, E., Lys, T. and Yang, Y. (2007) 'An examination of the impact of the Sarbanes-Oxley Act on the attractiveness of US capital markets for foreign firms', *Working Paper*, Northwestern University, June.

Howe, J. and Madura, J. (1990) 'The impact of international listings on risk: implications for capital market integration', *Journal of Banking and Finance*, 14: 1133–1142.

Karolyi, G.A. (2006) 'The world of cross-listings and cross-listings of the world: challenging conventional wisdom', *Review of Finance*, 10: 99–152.

Khanna, T., Palepu, K.G. and Srinivasan, S. (2004) 'Disclosure practices of companies interacting with US markets', *Journal of Accounting Research*, 42(2): 475–525.

Lane, P.R. and Milesi-Ferretti, G.M. (2004) 'International investment patterns', *IMF Working Paper*, WP/04/134, July.

Lang, M., Lins, K.V. and Miller, D.P. (2003a) 'ADRs, analysts, and accuracy: does cross listing in the United States improve a firm's information environment and increase market value?', *Journal of Accounting Research*, 41(2): 317–345.

Lang, M., Raedy, J.S. and Yetman, M.H. (2003b) 'How representative are firms that are cross-listed in the United States? An analysis of accounting quality', *Journal of Accounting Research*, 41(2): 363–386.

Lau, S., Diltz, D. and Apilado, V.P. (1994) 'Valuation effects of international stock exchange listings', *Journal of Banking and Finance*, 18: 743–755.

Leuz, C. (2003) 'IAS versus US GAAP: information asymmetry-based evidence from the German new market', *Journal of Accounting Research*, 41(3): 445–472.

Leuz, C., Triantis, A. and Wang, T. (2006) 'Why do firms go dark? Causes and economic consequences of voluntary SEC deregistrations', *Journal of Accounting and Economics Conference*, October.

Leventis, S. and Weetman, P. (2004) 'Impression management: dual language reporting and voluntary disclosure', *Accounting Forum*, 28: 307–328.

Melton, P. (1996) *The Investor's Guide to Going Global with Equities*. London: FT/Pitman Publishing.

Miles, S. and Nobes, C. (1998) 'The use of foreign accounting data in UK financial institutions', *Journal of Business Finance and Accounting*, 25(3–4): 309–328.

Ndubizu, G.A. (2007) 'Do cross-border listing firms manage earnings or seize a window of opportunity?', *Accounting Review*, 82(4), July: 1009–1030.

Olibe, K.O. (2002) 'The information content of annual general meetings. A price and trading volume analysis', *Journal of International Accounting, Auditing and Taxation*, 11(1): 19–37.

Olibe, K.O. (2006) 'The incremental information content of non-US GAAP earnings disclosures: evidence from UK firms', *Journal of International Accounting, Auditing and Taxation*, 15(2): 197–214.

Pagano, M., Randl, O., Roell, A.A. and Zechner, J. (2001) 'What makes stock exchanges succeed? Evidence from cross-listing decisions', *European Economic Review*, 45: 770–782.

Pagano, M., Roell, A.A. and Zechner, J. (2002) 'The geography of equity listing? Why do companies list abroad?', *Journal of Finance*, 57: 2651–2694.

Radebaugh, L.H., Gebhart, G. and Gray, S.J. (1995) 'Foreign stock exchange listings: a case study of Daimler–Benz', *Journal of International Financial Management and Accounting*, 6(2): 158–192.

Reckitt, E. (1953) 'Reminiscences of early days of the accounting profession in Illinois: Illinois Society of Certified Public Accountants', reprinted in Zeff, S.A. (ed.) *The US Accounting Profession in the 1890s and Early 1900s*, pp. 165–314. New York: Garland Publishing.

Rees, L. (1995) 'The information contained in reconciliations to earnings based on US accounting principles by non-US companies', *Accounting and Business Research*, 25(100): 301–310.

Rees, L. and Elgers, P. (1997) 'The market's valuation of nonreported accounting measures: reconciliations of Non-US and US GAAP', *Journal of Accounting Research*, 35(1): 115–127.

Sarkissian, S. and Schill, M. (2005) 'The cost of capital effects of overseas listings: market sequencing and selection', *Working Paper*, University of Virginia.

Saudagaran, S.M. (1988) 'An empirical study of selected factors influencing the decision to list in foreign stock exchanges', *Journal of International Business Studies*, Spring: 101–127.

Saudagaran, S.M. and Biddle, G.C. (1995) 'Foreign listing location: a study of MNCs and stock exchanges in eight countries', *Journal of International Business Studies*, 26(2): 319–342.

Scott-Quinn, B. (1994) 'EC securities markets regulation', in Steil, B. (ed.) *International Financial Market Regulation*, pp. 121–166. Chichester: John Wiley & Sons.

Smith, K.L. (1999) 'Major world equity market interdependence a decade after the 1987 crash: evidence from cross spectral analysis', *Journal of Business Finance and Accounting*, April/May: 365–392.

Solnik, B. (1974) 'Why not diversify internationally?', *Financial Analysts Journal*, July/August: 48–54.

Street, D.L. and Bryant, S.M. (2000) 'Disclosure levels and compliance with IASs: a comparison of companies with and without US listing and filings', *International Journal of Accounting*, 35(3): 305–329.

Street, D.L., Gray, S.J. and Bryant, S.M. (1999) 'Acceptance and observance of International Accounting Standards: an empirical study of companies claiming to comply with IASs', *International Journal of Accounting*, 34(1): 11–48.

Street, D.L., Nichols, N.B. and Gray, S.J. (2000) 'Assessing the acceptability of international accounting standards in the US: an empirical study of the materiality of US GAAP reconciliations by non-US companies complying with IASC standards', *International Journal of Accounting*, 35(1): 27–63.

Stulz, R.M. (1999) 'Globalization, corporate finance, and the cost of capital', *Journal of Applied Corporate Finance*, 12: 8–25.

Taylor, M.E. and Jones, R.A. (1999) 'The use of International Accounting Standards: a survey of IAS compliance disclosure', *International Journal of Accountancy*, 34(4): 447–570.

Taylor, M.P. and Tonks, I. (1989) 'The internationalization of stock markets and the abolition of UK exchange controls', *Review of Economics and Statistics*, 71: 332–336.

Tondkar, R.H., Adhikari, A. and Coffman, E.N. (1989) 'The internationalisation of equity markets: motivations for foreign corporate listing and filing and listing requirements of five major stock markets', *International Journal of Accounting*, Fall: 143–163.

Yamori, N. and Baba, T. (2001) 'Japanese management views on overseas exchange listings: survey results', *Journal of International Financial Management and Accounting*, 12(3): 286–316.

3 Confidence and assurance

Learning outcomes

After reading this chapter you should be able to:

- Explain and evaluate the steps taken around the world to improve the credibility of financial reporting.
- Explain and evaluate developments in audit and assurance.
- Explain how the development of corporate governance has affected financial reporting.
- Explain how developments in corporate social responsibility are reflected in financial reporting.
- Explain and evaluate the effectiveness of regulation in ensuring compliance with requirements for financial reporting.
- Explain how research into credibility and assurance is developing.

3.1 Introduction

It has become apparent that developing high-quality international accounting standards is necessary, but not sufficient, to give capital markets adequate confidence in the reliability of financial reporting. Mechanisms have emerged for encouraging, or enforcing, compliance and for identifying good practice. Chapter 10 explains that the IASB has no direct powers of enforcement of IFRS. It relies on national governments and regulators to support the adoption of these standards and set a system of penalties on those who fail to comply. This chapter explains how national and international authorities have been working towards supporting high-quality financial reporting. These authorities may be:

- departments of national governments;
- independent bodies supported by governments;
- independent bodies supported by capital market regulators;
- transnational bodies with an interest in the orderly conduct of capital markets;
- transnational bodies with an interest in improving corporate governance;
- transnational bodies with an interest in improving auditing and ethical standards.

The chapter begins with an overview of frameworks proposed for improving the credibility of financial reporting. These frameworks, in seeking to reduce or eliminate the prospect of repeating some of the major crises of recent years, range beyond financial reporting. However, high-quality financial reporting is an essential aspect of the proposals. The chapter describes in more detail the initiatives that have developed in auditing and assurance, corporate governance and corporate social responsibility. It then discusses ways in which these initiatives help those who need to have confidence in corporate financial reports. It concludes with an overview of research directions in this area of study.

3.2 Improving the credibility of financial reporting

The effectiveness of accounting in emerging markets was called into question as a result of the East Asian financial crisis of 1997. The 'financial meltdown', which directly affected Thailand, Malaysia, South Korea, Indonesia, Hong Kong, Singapore and Taiwan,[1] led to questions about the reliability of the financial statements of companies in those countries. The word 'transparency' was linked to calls for internationally recognized standards of accounting and auditing for the private sector. The Chairman of the Securities and Exchange Commission (SEC) in the USA gave a much publicized speech entitled 'The Numbers Game'. In that speech, where he called for greater transparency and comparability, he said:

> the significance of transparent, timely and reliable financial statements and its importance to investor protection has never been more apparent. The current financial situations in Asia and Russia are stark examples of this new reality. These markets are learning a painful lesson taught many times before: investors panic as a result of unexpected or unquantifiable news.[2]

At that stage the problems of transparency were seen primarily as an issue for emerging markets where the experience and expertise of the long-established markets could be of benefit. It was assumed that supplying international standards for accounting and auditing would bring this expertise to an international stage, to the benefit of all participants. The main focus of the debate was on whether international accounting standards or US accounting standards would give the stronger basis from which to achieve this aim.

It was therefore a much greater shock in November 2001 when a very large US company called Enron announced that it was restating its financial statements for the period from 1997 to 2001 because of 'accounting errors'. As the details of the 'errors' emerged, there was a rapid fall in market confidence and investor trust. By the end of 2001 Enron had filed for bankruptcy.[3] The effects of the collapse of Enron rippled across the world throughout 2002. Questions were asked about the reliability of accounting information, the reliability of audit, the effectiveness of monitoring by major shareholders and the

---

[1] Pilbeam (2001); *Business America* (1998).

[2] Quoted in *IASC Insight*, October 1998, p. 3. Also available on the SEC website at www.sec.gov/news/speech/speecharchive/1998/spch220.txt.

[3] There is a 'links' page on the library section of the Institute of Chartered Accountants in England and Wales that provides a useful guide to Enron sources. The link was archived in May 2004 but may still be effective: http://www.icaew.co.uk/librarylinks/index.cfm?AUB=TB2I_29490|MNXI_29553.

effectiveness of bodies intended to safeguard the rights of employees and investors. In the USA there were Congressional inquiries.[4] In July 2002 the US President signed the Sarbanes–Oxley Act which set out a significant expansion of US securities law, regulation of corporate governance, disclosure, reporting and accounting requirements and penalties.[5] The Sarbanes–Oxley Act is very wide ranging and has an effect on companies and audit firms around the world that have activities in the USA (see section 3.2.3).

This section explains how finance ministers and professional accountancy bodies have responded in their respective collective organizations by setting frameworks for action to restore confidence.

3.2.1 The Financial Stability Forum (FSF)[6]

The FSF was established by the finance ministers of the G7 countries[7] in 1999 to identify ways of avoiding or minimizing the effects of crises such as the East Asian financial crisis of 1997–98. The FSF wanted to see strong regulation of capital markets, banking and insurance. It identified 12 'standards' that would be particularly important in achieving this aim.[8] The word 'standard' is used here in a very broad sense of 'regulations or guidelines' that have an international impact. The key standards, which focus on creating sound financial systems, are listed in Exhibit 3.1. Some have a direct impact on financial reporting while others create a basis of assurance around the financial information. Chapter 10 deals with the first item listed; this chapter explains more on items 2, 3 and 8. Other items relate to the market structure and macroeconomic stability within which financial reporting is used.

3.2.2 The International Federation of Accountants (IFAC)[9]

Professional accountancy bodies around the world are members of IFAC. Its secretariat work is funded by membership subscriptions but much of its activity relies on voluntary service from organizations and individuals (see also section 13.2). IFAC develops pronouncements on auditing and assurance, ethics, education and public sector accounting.

In October 2002 a Task Force on Rebuilding Public Confidence in Financial Reporting came together at the request of IFAC to consider ways of restoring the credibility of financial reporting and corporate disclosure from an international perspective. The Task Force had to face the loss of credibility caused by high-profile corporate failures, such as Enron, and by the increased frequency of restated financial statements.[10] It also encountered the perception of unfairness in situations where business losses had caused hardship for shareholders, employees and those expecting pensions from private pension schemes, while those running companies had apparently made themselves richer despite the losses.[11]

---

[4] Congressional Committee (2002).

[5] Hermsen *et al.* (2002).

[6] www.fsforum.org/home/home.html.

[7] USA, Japan, Germany, France, UK, Italy and Canada.

[8] www.fsforum.org/compendium/key_standards_for_sound_financial_system.html.

[9] www.ifac.org.

[10] 'Restatement' means that a company has submitted revised financial statements to the regulator, usually with a lower profit than was first reported.

[11] IFAC (2003), p. 5.

Exhibit 3.1	The 12 key standards for sound financial systems

Institutional and market infrastructure			
1	Accounting	International Accounting Standards (IAS)	IASB
2	Auditing	International Standards on Auditing (ISA)	IFAC
3	Corporate governance	Principles of Corporate Governance	OECD
4	Insolvency	(Principles under development)	World Bank
5	Market integrity	The Forty Recommendations of the Financial Action Task Force/9 Special Recommendations Against Terrorist Financing	FATF
6	Payment and settlement	Core Principles for Systemically Important Payment Systems Recommendations for Securities Settlement Systems	CPSS CPSS/IOSCO
Financial regulation and supervision			
7	Banking supervision	Core Principles for Effective Banking Supervision	BCBS
8	Securities regulation	Objectives and Principles of Securities Regulation	IOSCO
9	Insurance supervision	Insurance Core Principles	IAIS
Macroeconomic policy and data transparency			
10	Monetary and financial policy transparency	Code of Good Practices on Transparency in Monetary and Financial Policies	IMF
11	Fiscal policy transparency	Code of Good Practices on Fiscal Transparency	IMF
12	Data dissemination	Special Data Dissemination Standard/General Data Dissemination System	IMF

BCBS = Basel Committee on Banking Supervision
CPSS = Committee on Payment Settlement Systems (Bank for International Settlements)
FATF = Financial Action Task Force
IAIS = International Association of Insurance Supervisors
IASB = International Accounting Standards Board
IFAC = International Federation of Accountants
IMF = International Monetary Fund
IOSCO = International Organization of Securities Commissions
OECD = Organization for Economic Cooperation and Development

Source: Financial Stability Forum (2007), www.fsforum.org.

The Task Force made ten recommendations, shown in Exhibit 3.2. The Task Force said that these ten recommendations would need to be taken up at national and international level, to influence legislation and other forms of regulation.

3.2.3 The Sarbanes–Oxley Act 2002

The Sarbanes–Oxley Act was the reaction of US legislators to the crisis of confidence following Enron. It has an international impact because its terms are drawn very widely. It applies to all companies that are registered with the SEC and listed on a US stock

Exhibit 3.2	Task Force on Rebuilding Public Confidence in Financial Reporting

Recommendations of the Task Force:

1 Effective corporate ethics codes, in place and monitored.

2 Effective financial management and controls from corporate management.

3 Reduce incentives to misstate financial information (e.g. pressures to meet analysts' forecasts, or to satisfy management reward schemes).

4 Improved oversight of management, carried out by independent directors.

5 Give attention to the threats to auditor independence.

6 Give greater attention to audit quality control procedures.

7 Codes of conduct for other market participants, such as analysts and credit-rating agencies.

8 Strengthen auditing standards and regulations.

9 Strengthen accounting and reporting practices.

10 Raise the standard of regulation of companies issuing equity in the market.

exchange and to the auditors of those companies. This section lists the main recommendations of the Act as they affect auditing and the regulation of corporate reporting. An impression of the impact of Sarbanes–Oxley in the USA may be gained from the web page devoted to listing the extensive rulemaking and reports that have emerged as a result.[12]

3.2.3.1 Auditing

The Act establishes a Public Company Accounting Oversight Board (PCAOB)[13] as a non-profit corporation subject to administration and oversight by the SEC of the USA. The PCAOB oversees the audits of public companies and related matters. All auditors of public companies must register with the PCAOB. This includes audit firms in other countries where those firms audit parent companies or subsidiaries of companies listed on US stock exchanges. The audit firm must identify public audit clients, all accountants associated with those clients, list fees earned for audit and non-audit services, explain its audit quality procedures and identify all legal proceedings against the firm in connection with an audit. The PCAOB is required to inspect all professional accountancy firms that audit public companies. All audit committees in companies must consist of independent directors (see section 3.3.3 and section 11.4.3.1). Audit firms are appointed by, and report to, the audit committee. The PCAOB is required to adopt standards for auditing, quality control, ethics and independence. It may look to standards established by recognized professional organizations such as the AICPA.[14] The Act restricts consulting work that auditors may undertake for their clients. There is a list of prohibited work. Tax services are not on this list but must be approved by the company's audit committee.

---

[12] *Spotlight on Sarbanes–Oxley Rulemaking and Reports,* www.sec.gov/spotlight/sarbanes-oxley.htm.

[13] www.pcaob.org.

[14] www.aicpa.org/.

The Act requires five-year rotation of the audit partner. An audit firm may not audit a public company whose officers worked for the audit firm within the previous year.[15]

The European Commission objected to the PCAOB's intention to apply its rules to auditors working for any EU company listed on the US stock exchanges. Under the rules of the PCAOB, approved by the SEC, registration with the PCAOB is required of European audit firms engaged by US subsidiaries in Europe if the US subsidiary has assets or revenues that are 20 per cent or more of the group total.[16] Discussions between the PCAOB and the European Commission led to an agreement to postpone the implementation of these rules until July 2004.[17] Subsequently the PCAOB's rules have permitted a degree of reliance on home country inspections, based on the independence and rigour of the home country system of oversight and agreement between the PCAOB and the home country regulator on the inspection work programme for individual firms. An example of movement in this direction is the cooperative agreement signed with the Australian Securities and Exchange Commission in 2007.

The more independent and rigorous the home country system, the more the PCAOB can rely on its counterpart to conduct an inspection of a PCAOB-registered firm. The PCAOB has been particularly encouraged by the revision of the Eighth Directive which strengthens auditor registration across member states.[18]

3.2.3.2 Executives of a company

The Act requires the company's chief executive officer and chief financial officer to certify the financial statements.[19] This is a formal process involving personal certification of the financial statements (see Exhibit 3.3) with serious penalties if the personal certification is later found to be untrue. The Act prohibits improper influences on auditors and requires executives to forfeit their bonuses and equity gains if financial statements are restated after they have been issued. This condition reflects the growing frequency of such restatement occurring with US companies.

3.2.3.3 Accounting standards and disclosure

The Act requires specific disclosures in financial reports, including information about internal control systems[20] and about off-balance-sheet transactions (which were part of the Enron problem),[21] and it requires the SEC to develop rules on 'pro-forma' disclosures.[22] This reflects concern over the growing practice of presenting financial statements, as supplementary information, that do not conform to US GAAP. They are used by companies as a preferred form of presentation but users of financial statements have no assurance about the comparability or reliability of such presentations.[23]

---

[15] *Commission Adopts Rules Strengthening Auditor Independence*, www.sec.gov/news/press/2003-9.htm.

[16] PCAOB Rule 1001(p).

[17] PCAOB (2004).

[18] PCAOB (2006).

[19] www.sec.gov/rules/final/33-8124.htm.

[20] *Final Rule: Management's Reports on Internal Control Over Financial Reporting and Certification of Disclosure in Exchange Act Periodic Reports*, http://www.sec.gov/rules/final/33-8238.htm.

[21] *Final Rule: Disclosure in Management's Discussion and Analysis about Off-Balance Sheet Arrangements and Aggregate Contractual Obligations*, www.sec.gov/rules/final/33-8182.htm.

[22] *Final Rule: Conditions for Use of Non-GAAP Financial Measures*, www.sec.gov/rules/final/33-8176.htm.

[23] *Cautionary Advice Regarding the Use of 'Pro Forma' Financial Information in Earnings Releases*, www.sec.gov/rules/other/33-8039.htm.

Exhibit 3.3	Certification by chief executive officer

CERTIFICATION

I, A.N. Other, certify that:

1. I have reviewed this annual report on Form 10-K of X Inc.;

2. Based on my knowledge, this report does not contain any untrue statement of a material fact or omit to state a material fact necessary to make the statements made, in light of the circumstances under which such statements were made, not misleading with respect to the period covered by this report;

3. Based on my knowledge, the financial statements, and other financial information included in this annual report, fairly present in all material respects the financial condition, results of operations and cash flows of the registrant as of, and for, the periods presented in this report;

4. The registrant's other certifying officer and I are responsible for establishing and maintaining disclosure controls and procedures (as defined in Exchange Act Rules 13a-15(e) and 15d-15(e)) and internal control over financial reporting (as defined in Exchange Act Rules 13a-15(f) and 15d-15(f)) for the registrant and have:

a) Designed such disclosure controls and procedures, or caused such disclosure controls and procedures to be designed under our supervision, to ensure that material information relating to the registrant, including its consolidated subsidiaries, is made known to us by others within those entities, particularly during the period in which this report is being prepared;

b) Designed such internal control over financial reporting, or caused such internal control over financial reporting to be designed under our supervision, to provide reasonable assurance regarding the reliability of financial reporting and the preparation of financial statements for external purposes in accordance with generally accepted accounting principles;

c) Evaluated the effectiveness of the registrant's disclosure controls and procedures and presented in this report our conclusions about the effectiveness of the disclosure controls and procedures, as of the end of the period covered by this report based on such evaluation; and

d) Disclosed in this report any change in the registrant's internal control over financial reporting that occurred during the registrant's most recent fiscal quarter (the registrant's fourth fiscal quarter in the case of an annual report) that has materially affected, or is reasonably likely to materially affect, the registrant's internal control over financial reporting; and

5. The registrant's other certifying officer and I have disclosed, based on our most recent evaluation of internal control over financial reporting, to the registrant's auditors and the audit committee of registrant's board of directors (or persons performing the equivalent functions):

a) All significant deficiencies and material weaknesses in the design or operation of internal control over financial reporting which are reasonably likely to adversely affect the registrant's ability to record, process, summarize and report financial information; and

b) Any fraud, whether or not material, that involves management or other employees who have a significant role in the registrant's internal control over financial reporting.

/s/ A.N. Other

Name: A.N. Other

Title: President and Chief Executive Officer

Date: 2007

The SEC was also required to study the adoption by the US financial reporting system of a 'principles-based accounting system', reporting back within one year of the legislation (see section 11.3.3). This reflects a concern that in Enron the detail of accounting rules was used to justify inappropriate accounting treatments which would have been less acceptable in a system focusing on the principles of fair presentation.

The Act permits the SEC to recognize standards established by a private sector standard setter provided the standard setter is acceptable to the SEC and 'considers' international convergence in developing standards. FASB meets those conditions. Section 10.3.3 describes the work of the FASB in discussing convergence with the IASB.

3.2.3.4 Protection, penalties and funding

The Act provides legal protection to any employee who assists a federal agency, a member or committee of Congress, or a supervisory employee (this is sometimes described as 'whistleblowing'). This reflects concern that in Enron some employees may have been aware of problems with the company's accounting practices, but were in fear of action against them or loss of employment. It sets criminal penalties for corporate fraud and for shredding documents. This is because documents were allegedly shredded relating to Enron, thus impeding investigation. The cost of this regulatory activity is significant. Some of the costs are carried by registration fees and annual fees paid by accounting firms, while the remaining costs are carried by a fee charged to public companies in proportion to their market capitalization.

3.2.4 The World Bank[24]

The World Bank and the International Monetary Fund (IMF) have together developed a system of benchmarks as an early-warning mechanism, based on such international best practices as the World Bank's Principles and Guidelines for Effective Insolvency and Creditor Rights Systems (April 2001, revised 2004).

At the global level, these benchmarks set minimum international standards for transparency, market efficiency and financial discipline. At the national level, they guide policy reform by identifying economic and financial vulnerability.

Countries are then evaluated against the benchmarks in Reports on the Observance of Standards and Codes (ROSCs).[25] This is a wide-ranging evaluation which includes a Program on Accounting and Auditing.[26] It aims to assess the comparability of national accounting and auditing standards with international accounting and auditing standards and to assist the country in developing and implementing a 'country action plan' for improving the institutional framework that underpins the corporate financial reporting regime in the country. Exhibit 3.4 lists the countries for which ROSC accounting and auditing modules have been published. One of the limitations of the process is that the World Bank only reviews countries that are borrowing money (creditor countries). Donor countries are not scrutinized.

---

[24] www.worldbank.org.

[25] www.worldbank.org/ifa/rosc.html.

[26] *Overview of the ROSC Accounting and Auditing Program, January 2004,* www.worldbank.org/ifa/rosc_aa.html.

| Exhibit 3.4 | ROSC Accounting and Auditing modules |

Albania	Azerbaijan	Bangladesh	Bosnia & Herzegovina
Botswana	Bulgaria	Chile	Colombia
Croatia	Czech Republic	Dominican Republic	Ecuador
Egypt	El Salvador	Estonia	Georgia
Ghana	Hungary	India	Indonesia
Jamaica	Jordan	Kazakhstan	Kenya
Korea	Kosovo	Latvia	Lebanon
Lithuania	FYR Macedonia	Mauritius	Mexico
Moldova	Morocco	Nigeria	Pakistan
Paraguay	Peru	Philippines	Poland
Romania	Senegal	Serbia	Slovakia
Slovenia	Sri Lanka	South Africa	Tanzania
Tunisia	Turkey	Uganda	Ukraine
Uruguay			

Source: www.worldbank.org/ifa/rosc_aa.html at June 2007.

3.3 Auditing and assurance

Regulation of audit and assurance is a national activity because it relies on national law and enforcement mechanisms. We have also explained in section 3.2 that the East Asian financial crisis and the collapse of Enron in the USA both led to questions about the reliability of the assurance process. Assurance comes primarily from independent audit but it comes also from the directors of the company explaining the controls that they have put in place. This section explains international activity to strengthen the quality and reliability of independent audit and also explains how the board of directors gives assurance through an audit committee.

3.3.1 International Auditing and Assurance Standards Board[27]

In 2002 IFAC established the International Auditing and Assurance Standards Board (IAASB). The IAASB is an independent standard-setting body which aims to serve the public interest by setting high-quality auditing standards. It encourages convergence of national and international standards to strengthen public confidence in the global auditing and accounting profession. It was created to accelerate and improve transparency of standard-setting activities in international auditing and assurance.

The IAASB has 18 volunteer members. Most of these are experts from around the world who have significant experience in auditing. There are also 'public members' who may be members of IFAC member bodies but are not engaged in the public practice of auditing. Members were initially appointed by the IFAC Board, with future nominations coming from the Public Interest Oversight Board (see section 3.3.2). Financial support comes from IFAC membership subscriptions and the Forum of Firms. This forum consists of accounting firms which share the aim of promoting high standards of financial

---

[27] http://www.ifac.org/IAASB/.

reporting and auditing worldwide. A Consultative Advisory Group to the IAASB consists of organizations with an interest in the development of international auditing standards.

3.3.1.1 Widening acceptance of ISAs

In 2002 the IAASB staff began working towards revision of the auditing standards in anticipation that the EU would adopt International Standards on Auditing (ISAs) for 2005 audits.[28] In its 2006 annual report the IAASB stated that more than 100 countries use auditing standards that are ISAs, either adopted as written or locally adapted, or national standards that are compared with ISAs to eliminate differences.[29] ISAs have been translated by member bodies into more than 20 languages, including French, German, Russian and Spanish. The 2006 annual report included a hope that the emergence of the EU's new Directive on Statutory Audit in 2006 would further encourage the application of ISAs. In 2004 IFAC issued guidance on translation, including practical advice on the approach to be taken.[30]

There is no consistent manner in which countries explain how they are harmonizing with ISAs. Exhibit 3.5 gives information on Australia, where the Auditing and Assurance Standards Board (AUASB) is an independent statutory body under section 227A of the *Australian Securities and Investments Commission Act 2001*, as from 1 July 2004.

Exhibit 3.6 gives information on China, where the Ministry of Finance publishes auditing standards using the principles of ISAs.

Exhibit 3.7 gives information from Hong Kong on full convergence with ISAs.

3.3.1.2 Obstacles to progress[31]

Progress in harmonizing national auditing standards with ISAs is not as fast as that of harmonizing national accounting standards with IFRS. One reason is that effective regulation of audit requires government backing. Effective auditing standards require

---

Exhibit 3.5	Australia

Extract from 'The AUASB Strategic Direction'

(a) The AUASB should develop Australian Auditing Standards that have a clear public interest focus and are of the highest quality.

(b) The AUASB should use, as appropriate, International Standards on Auditing (ISAs) of the International Auditing and Assurance Standards Board (IAASB) as a base from which to develop Australian Auditing Standards.

(c) The AUASB should make such amendments to ISAs as necessary to accommodate and ensure that Auditing Standards both exhibit and conform with the Australian regulatory environment and statutory requirements, including amendments as necessary for Australian Auditing Standards to have the force of law and be capable of enforcement under the requirements of the *Corporations Act 2001* by 30 June 2006.

Source: *Foreword to AUASB Pronouncements* Issued by the Auditing and Assurance Standards Board, April 2006.

---

[28] *IAASB Action Plan 2003–04*, January 2003, www.iaasb.org.

[29] IAASB Annual Report (2006), p. 2.

[30] IFAC (2004) *Translation of Standards and Guidance Issued by the International Federation of Accountants*, http://www.ifac.org/Downloads/TranslationOfStandards.pdf.

[31] Street and Needles (2002).

Exhibit 3.6 China

> Press release issued 15 February 2006
>
> ## Release Ceremony for Chinese Accounting Standards System and Auditing Standards System held in Beijing
>
> On the afternoon of February 15, the Ministry of Finance (MOF) held a ceremony to release 39 Chinese Accounting Standards for Business Enterprises and 48 Auditing Standards for Certified Public Accountants, marking the establishment of an accounting standards system for business enterprises and an auditing standards system for certified public accountants that suit the development of China's market economy and convergence with the international practices.
>
> …
>
> Liu Zhongli, President of Chinese Institute of Certified Public Accountants (CICPA), gave an introduction to the auditing standards system for certified public accountants. China's Auditing Standards system consists of standards on assurance, related services and quality control of accounting firms. The newly released system reflects requirement for convergence with the international auditing standards, meets the need of certified public accountants for practising under the new situation, highlights the purpose of the profession to safeguard public interests, makes the auditing standards more reader-friendly and easier to apply, and represents a historic breakthrough.

Source: http://www.iasplus.com/china/0602mofpr.pdf.

regulation, an effective auditing profession, a culture of compliance and a sound base of corporate governance. Some governments may not be able to cope with the magnitude of the changes required; others may have vested interests not to make the changes required.

The World Bank in its ROSC process (see section 3.2.4) reviews accounting and auditing standards against IFRS and ISAs as benchmarks. However, while a country is matching

Exhibit 3.7 Hong Kong

> **Hong Kong Institute of Certified Public Accountants**
> **Fifth Long Range Plan 2007–2011 [extract]**
>
> Today the Institute is fully converged with international standards and was among the first jurisdictions to do so. In parallel, the Institute created and launched a differential financial reporting framework and standard for small and medium-sized companies in 2005. These frameworks and standards have been widely accepted by the main stakeholders, including the business community, tax and government authorities and creditors and banks. Many institutes throughout the world have given up their standard setting role: The Hong Kong Institute of CPAs considers standard setting one of its core responsibilities.
>
> In the next five years, the Institute will consolidate its stance in financial reporting standards, auditing and assurance standards and standards of professional ethics in Hong Kong. This will require steady work with international bodies to ensure the Institute retains its authority and responsibility. It requires work from our members and the business community to develop understanding about the standards. The most work, however, will be devoted to our collaboration with our mainland counterparts as they fulfill their agreement to converge with international standards.

Source: http://www.hkicpa.org.hk/publications/Fifth_Long_Range_Plan.pdf.

its auditing standards to ISAs on paper, this is no guarantee that there is adequate education for professional accountants to know the ISAs or understand how to apply them. The World Bank produces the report but it is for the national government to implement change.

3.3.1.3 Issuing ISAs

IAASB operates 'due process' in developing ISAs. Draft standards and statements are issued as exposure drafts for public review and comment. Comments received are considered prior to finalization of the standard. IAASB meetings are open to the public, with agenda materials being publicly available. The IAASB includes three 'public members' who bring a broader interest to the discussions. All IAASB exposure drafts and standards are available free of charge on the website (see Exhibit 3.8).

ISA 700, *The Independent Auditor's Report on a Complete Set of General Purpose Financial Statements*, requires that when IFRS or International Public Sector Accounting Standards

---

Exhibit 3.8   International Standards on Auditing and other IAASB documents, 2007

AUDITS AND REVIEWS OF HISTORICAL FINANCIAL INFORMATION

100–999 International Standards on Auditing (ISAs)

100–199 INTRODUCTORY MATTERS

200–299 GENERAL PRINCIPLES AND RESPONSIBILITIES
200 Objective and General Principles Governing an Audit of Financial Statements
210 Terms of Audit Engagements
220 Quality Control for Audits of Historical Financial Information
230 Audit Documentation
240 The Auditor's Responsibility to Consider Fraud in an Audit of Financial Statements
250 Consideration of Laws and Regulations in an Audit of Financial Statements
260 Communications of Audit Matters with Those Charged with Governance

300–499 RISK ASSESSMENT AND RESPONSE TO ASSESSED RISKS
300 Planning an Audit of Financial Statements
315 Understanding the Entity and Its Environment and Assessing the Risks of Material Misstatement
320 Audit Materiality
330 The Auditor's Procedures in Response to Assessed Risks
402 Audit Considerations Relating to Entities Using Service Organizations

500–599 AUDIT EVIDENCE
500 Audit Evidence
501 Audit Evidence—Additional Considerations for Specific Items
505 External Confirmations
510 Initial Engagements—Opening Balances
520 Analytical Procedures
530 Audit Sampling and Other Means of Testing
540 Audit of Accounting Estimates
545 Auditing Fair Value Measurements and Disclosures
550 Related Parties
560 Subsequent Events
570 Going Concern
580 Management Representations

▶

| Exhibit 3.8 | *(Continued)* |

600–699 USING WORK OF OTHERS
600 Using the Work of Another Auditor
610 Considering the Work of Internal Auditing
620 Using the Work of an Expert

700–799 AUDIT CONCLUSIONS AND REPORTING
700 The Independent Auditor's Report on a Complete Set of General Purpose Financial
     Statements
701 Modifications to the Independent Auditor's Report
710 Comparatives
720 Other Information in Documents Containing Audited Financial Statements

800–899 SPECIALIZED AREAS
800 The Independent Auditor's Report on Special Purpose Audit Engagements

1000–1100 International Auditing Practice Statements (IAPSs)

2000–2699 International Standards on Review Engagements (ISREs)

ASSURANCE ENGAGEMENTS OTHER THAN AUDITS OR REVIEWS OF HISTORICAL FINANCIAL INFORMATION

3000–3699 International Standards on Assurance Engagements (ISAEs)

RELATED SERVICES

4000–4699 International Standards on Related Services (ISRSs)

STUDIES

Source: IAASB website, August 2007. The full text of all publications, together with additional information on the IAASB, recent developments and outstanding exposure drafts, are to be found on the IAASB's website at www.ifac.org/iaasb.

are not used as the financial reporting framework, the reference to the financial reporting framework in the wording of the opinion should identify the jurisdiction or country of origin of the financial reporting framework. Unless required by law or regulation to use different wording, the auditor's opinion on the financial statements states whether the financial statements 'give a true and fair view' or 'are presented fairly, in all material respects', in accordance with the applicable financial reporting framework. ISA 700 asserts that the phrases 'give a true and fair view' and 'are presented fairly, in all material respects', are equivalent. Which of these phrases is used in any particular jurisdiction is determined by the law or regulations governing the audit of financial statements in that jurisdiction, or by established practice in that jurisdiction.

3.3.2 Public Interest Oversight Board[32]

In November 2003 IFAC announced further reforms to increase confidence in the work of IFAC. In particular it set up the mechanism for establishing a Public Interest Oversight

---

[32] http://www.ipiob.org/.

Board (PIOB) which was formally established in February 2005 to oversee IFAC's auditing and assurance, ethics and education standard-setting activities as well as its Member Body Compliance Program. The PIOB takes over the role of nominating members of the IAASB and gives assurance on the procedures of the IAASB.

3.3.3 Audit committees

Forming an audit committee is part of good corporate governance (see section 3.4). However, the presence of an audit committee has not prevented major corporate collapses and questionable conduct by executive directors. Attention has therefore been given in more than one country since 2001 to make audit committees more effective. Exhibit 3.9 summarizes some international initiatives on audit committees since 2000. Chapters 11, 14 and 15 describe in more details the initiatives in the USA, EU and UK to improve the effectiveness of audit committees. In the USA there have been several initiatives on audit committees, the most recent coming from Sarbanes–Oxley (see section 11.4.3.1). In the UK the report chaired by Sir Robert Smith set out in detail what is expected of an audit committee (see section 15.6.4).

Exhibit 3.9	Initiatives on audit committees

European Union
The High Level Group of Company Law experts (2002) included in their report some recommendations on the nature and role of the audit committee.

USA
Sarbanes–Oxley (2002) contained legislation on the role and composition of audit committees.

The New York Stock Exchange (2002) issued new rules on the composition and conduct of audit committees.

Ireland
The Review Group on Auditing made recommendations that were incorporated into the Companies (Audit and Accountancy) (Amendment) Bill 2001.

France
The Bouton Report (2002) 'Promoting better corporate governance in listed companies' set out rules for audit committees.

Canada
There is a mandatory requirement for companies to establish audit committees under the Canada Business Corporations Act.

The Toronto Stock Exchange amended its rules in April 2002 to give guidance on the independence of the external auditor.

Australia
The Corporations Act does not require Australian companies to establish audit committees. However, CLERP 9 (2002) recommended mandatory regulation to impose audit committees on the top 500 listed companies, leaving the ASX Corporate Governance Council to develop best practice standards.

Source: Summarized from Appendix III, Smith Report (2003).

3.4 Corporate governance and financial reporting

It appears that equity investors have a keen interest in seeing good-quality corporate governance in companies in which they invest. A survey by McKinsey[33] found that investors are willing to pay more for a company that is well governed. This lowers the cost of capital for the company and so it is in the interests of the company to show good practice in corporate governance.

3.4.1 What is corporate governance?[34]

There is no unique definition of the term 'corporate governance'. Some writers do not attempt to define it. A very simple definition is found in the report of the Cadbury Committee in the UK:

Corporate governance is the system by which companies are directed and controlled.[35]

For some countries the 'system' may involve laws or regulations imposed by government; for other countries the 'system' may depend largely on private sector market forces in a strong equity market. Corporate governance describes the interaction of shareholders, managers and those who supervise managers in a company, but it also describes the assurance needed to satisfy a wider public interest about the proper conduct of business.

3.4.2 Corporate governance codes

From the late 1990s onwards there has been an explosion in codes of corporate governance. Some are established under the authority of national governments, some are imposed by national securities regulators on listed companies, and many are voluntary codes proposed by institutions or bodies with an interest in improving the way in which companies are managed. In countries where there are competitive capital markets the investment community has shown interest in offering codes of good practice for corporate governance.

Ownership concentration affects the type of corporate governance. Where the ownership of companies is widely spread, there is a wider gap between the shareholders who own the company and the managers who run the company. Some form of supervisory body is required to ensure that the managers act in the interests of the shareholders. In some countries a separate supervisory board oversees the activities of the executive board of directors who carry out the day-to-day management; in other countries there is a single board of directors with a strong representation of independent directors ('non-executives') to balance the activities of the executive directors.

Business practice also affects the approach to corporate governance. One approach to managing a business may involve a strong emphasis on cooperative relationships and consensus, with inclusion of employees in the running of the business. A different approach may rely on competition and market forces, with a focus on those who own the business.

---

[33] *McKinsey Investor Opinion Survey,* 2002, http://www.mckinsey.com/.

[34] *Comparative Study of Corporate Governance Codes Relevant to the European Union and Its Member States,* Section III.A.

[35] Cadbury Report (1992), paragraph 2.5.

The legal system of the country will influence the nature of corporate governance. A country with strong code law will probably have corporate governance regulations based in law. A country with a common law tradition will probably develop corporate governance through private sector self-regulation. (See section 6.4 for further discussion of code law and common law systems.)

3.4.3 What to look for in corporate governance codes

Whatever the form of the regulations for corporate governance, particular features to look for in codes of corporate governance are:

- stakeholder and shareholder interests
- supervisory and managerial bodies
- code enforcement and compliance.

This section describes each feature in more detail and then summarizes general guidance provided by the OECD. Case studies on specific codes, analyzing them in the OECD framework, are provided at the end of this chapter.

3.4.3.1 Stakeholder and shareholder interests

Shareholders are the owners of a company. Good corporate governance will ensure that managers act in the best interests of shareholders (see the research perspectives in section 3.7). It will also require that shareholders take an active interest in how the company is managed. A fair voting system is 'one share, one vote'. Shareholders should then use their votes in general meetings to indicate approval or disapproval of the acts of managers. In practice the voting arrangements, conduct of meetings and activity of shareholders are all very variable between countries and within countries.

The wider stakeholder interest extends to creditors, employees and the public interest in general. Most legislative systems have some protection for creditors but codes of governance may encourage transparency of information for them. In some countries employees have a formal involvement in the management of a company. Accountability to the public interest and the needs of society has become increasingly important.

3.4.3.2 Supervisory and managerial bodies

The first question here is to ask how the managers of the company meet to run the business. In some countries the regulation requires a two-tier board structure. There is an executive board of the managers or directors who run the business on a day-to-day basis. There is a supervisory board of experienced business persons who can oversee and guide the executives. This supervisory board may include representatives of employees or lenders as well as shareholders. In other countries the regulation requires a single board structure. In this case the rules of corporate governance usually expect to find a strong representation of independent (non-executive) directors, with wide experience in business, to exercise control over the activities of the executive directors. Corporate governance codes set limits on the number or proportion of each type of director or manager.

The next question to ask is how the roles of the executive and non-executive directors are defined. The non-executives may form the audit committee, and they may set the remuneration of the executive directors. Corporate governance codes define these roles for the non-executive directors and set out the powers they should have to allow them to exercise independence.

The third question is to ask how the directors are accountable for their actions. How do we know that they have carried out the duties expected? Corporate governance codes set out guidance on how frequently, and in how much detail, the directors should report on their activities.

3.4.3.3 Code enforcement and compliance

Codes of governance may rely, partly or totally, on market forces to enforce compliance. Shareholders will vote against the reappointment of directors who do not demonstrate high standards of governance. Other stakeholders may also monitor compliance with codes. There is a growing body of 'watchdog' organizations which monitor, compare and evaluate the corporate governance reports of companies. Evidence of compliance is found in corporate governance reports, usually included in the company's annual report. There may be a requirement for such reports to be audited. However, in general the auditor gives an opinion on the process of creating the corporate governance report, not on its content.

3.4.4 Organization for Economic Cooperation and Development[36]

In April 2004 the governments of the 30 OECD countries approved a revised version of the OECD's Principles of Corporate Governance. These Principles were first published in 1999. They give a benchmark to the member governments, mainly from developed countries, but are also used by the World Bank in working to improve corporate governance in emerging markets. The Principles emphasize the importance of a regulatory framework in corporate governance that promotes efficient markets, facilitates effective enforcement and defines the responsibilities of the regulatory and enforcement authorities. The Principles cover the following headings:

- Ensuring the basis for an effective corporate governance framework
- The rights of shareholders and key ownership functions
- The equitable treatment of shareholders
- The role of stakeholders in corporate governance
- Disclosure and transparency
- The responsibilities of the board.

These headings are used to analyze specific corporate governance codes in the case studies at the end of this chapter.

3.4.4.1 Ensuring the basis for an effective corporate governance framework

This section of the OECD framework is directed at ensuring an effective regulatory framework. It recommends that the corporate governance framework should promote transparent and efficient markets, be consistent with the rule of law and clearly articulate the divisions of responsibilities among different supervisory, regulatory and enforcement authorities.

3.4.4.2 The rights of shareholders and key ownership functions

This section sets out basic rights for shareholders. These basic rights should allow shareholders to have their ownership registered and to be able to buy and sell shares. The

---

[36] OECD (2004).

shareholders should be able to obtain relevant and material information about the company on a regular and timely basis. They should be able to participate effectively in the key corporate governance decisions and to vote in general meetings of shareholders. They should be able to use that vote to elect and remove members of the board of directors and to make their views known on the remuneration of directors. Institutional investors, who act on a 'good faith' (fiduciary) basis on behalf of their investments, should make clear their attitudes to corporate governance and their voting policies. Shareholders should have the rights to share in the profits of the company. All these rights and obligations may be well established in developed capital markets, where they are usually contained in company law rather than a voluntary code. Nevertheless they are important points to emphasize in emerging markets.

3.4.4.3 The equitable treatment of shareholders

Equitable treatment means that all shareholders of the same class of shares should be treated equally. All investors should have the same access to information. Minority shareholders should be protected against abusive actions by controlling shareholders. Insider trading should be prohibited. Members of the board of directors should declare their interest in any transaction affecting the company.

3.4.4.4 The role of stakeholders in corporate governance

The corporate governance framework should respect the rights of stakeholders established by law or through mutual agreements. Such stakeholders will include individual employees and their representative bodies. They should be able to communicate their concerns about illegal or unethical practices to the board without risking their rights as employees. Stakeholders will also include creditors. The corporate governance framework should be matched by an efficient insolvency framework and by effective enforcement of the rights of creditors.

3.4.4.5 Disclosure and transparency

This section is particularly relevant to corporate financial reporting and so it describes the OECD recommendations in detail.[37] The corporate governance framework should ensure that timely and accurate disclosure is made on all material matters regarding the company, including the financial situation, performance, ownership and governance of the company. Disclosure should include, but not be limited to, matters relating to:

1 The financial and operating results of the company
2 Company objectives
3 Major share ownership and voting rights
4 Remuneration policy for members of the board and key executives, with information about board members including their qualifications, selection process, other directorships and whether they are regarded as independent directors
5 Related party transactions
6 Foreseeable risk factors
7 Issues regarding employees and other stakeholders
8 Governance structures and policies, particularly the implementation of any code of corporate governance.

---

[37] OECD (2004), section V.

From the above list, only item 5, related party transactions, is covered by IFRS (IAS 24). The remainder of this list indicates the importance of descriptive disclosures that are still largely a matter of national regulation rather than international standards. (See Chapter 4 for further discussion of narrative disclosures.)

The OECD continues by recommending that information should be prepared and disclosed in accordance with high-quality standards of financial and non-financial disclosure. An annual audit should be conducted by an independent, competent and qualified auditor, in order to provide an external and objective assurance to the board and shareholders that the financial statements fairly represent the financial position and performance of the company in all material respects. External auditors should be accountable to the shareholders and owe a duty to the company to exercise due professional care in the conduct of the audit. Channels for disseminating information should provide for equal, timely and cost-efficient access to relevant information by users. The corporate governance framework should be complemented by an effective approach that addresses and promotes the provision of analysis or advice by analysts, brokers, rating agencies and others that is relevant to decisions by investors, free from material conflicts of interest that might compromise the integrity of their analysis or advice.

These recommendations from the OECD are designed to encourage national regulators to incorporate rules for disclosure and transparency in their national frameworks and codes. They also provide a useful starting point for evaluating the extent to which the annual reports of companies appear to be meeting these expectations on disclosure and transparency.

3.4.4.6 The responsibilities of the board

The OECD's final set of recommendations relates to the board of directors. The corporate governance framework should ensure the strategic guidance of the company, the effective monitoring of management by the board, and the board's accountability to the company and the shareholders. In this section the OECD does not specify the details of the structure of the board but it sets out key features of ethical conduct and effective management as follows. Board members should:

- act in the best interests of the company and the shareholders;
- treat all shareholders fairly;
- apply high ethical standards;
- fulfil certain key functions (listed in the report) including ensuring the integrity of the accounting and financial reporting system, including independent audit, and ensuring that appropriate systems of control are in place for risk management, financial and operational control and compliance with law and standards;
- exercise objective independent judgement;
- have access to accurate, relevant and timely information.

3.4.5 National codes of corporate governance

Many countries now have codes of corporate governance. Some are issued by government, others by committees representing key stakeholders having an interest in matters of governance. Exhibit 3.10 lists examples of codes in various countries, showing the name of the body issuing the code. The exhibit also gives the website reference for the body issuing the code, where this is available. The ECGI website gives a link to each code in English as well as in the national language.

Exhibit 3.10 National codes of corporate governance

Australia
Revised Corporate Governance Principles and Recommendations
Second edition August 2007
ASX Corporate Governance Council
www.asx.com.au/supervision/governance/
Revised_Corporate_Governance_Principles_and_Recommendations.htm

Brazil
Código das Melhores Práticas de Governança Corporativa
Instituto Brasileiro de Governança Corporativa www.cvm.gov.br/
http://www.ibgc.org.br/home.asp
http://www.ecgi.org/codes/documents/ibgc_may2004.pdf (In English)

China
Provisional Code of Corporate Governance for Securities Companies
Issued by: China Securities Regulatory Commission, 2004
www.csrc.gov.cn
http://www.ecgi.org/codes/documents/provisional_cgcode_csrc.pdf (In English)

France
The Corporate Governance of Listed Corporations: Principles for corporate governance
Based on consolidation of the 1995, 1999 and 2002 AFEP and MEDEF's reports, Association Française des Entreprises Privées (AFEP) and MEDEF (French Business Confederation), October 2003
www.medef.fr/staging/site/page.php

Germany
German Corporate Governance Code as amended 14 June 2007
Government Commission, 2007
www.corporate-governance-code.de/index-e.html

Hong Kong
Hong Kong Code on Corporate Governance. Appendix 14 to Main Board rules.
Hong Kong Stock Exchange 2004
www.hkex.com.hk/index.htm

Japan
Principles of Corporate Governance for Listed Companies
Tokyo Stock Exchange 2004
http://www.tse.or.jp/english/index.html

Kenya
Principles for Corporate Governance in Kenya 2002
Private Sector Initiative for Corporate Governance
http://www.ecgi.org/codes/documents/principles_2.pdf [local website not found]

▶

Exhibit 3.10	*(Continued)*

Malaysia
Malaysian Code on Corporate Governance (revised 2007)
Securities Commission Malaysia
www.sc.com.my

The Netherlands
The Dutch corporate governance code
Corporate Governance Committee, December 2003
www.commissiecorporategovernance.nl/

Poland
Best Practices in Public Companies 2005 29 October 2004
http://www.ecgi.org/codes/documents/pol_best_practice_2005_final.pdf

Sweden
Swedish Code of Corporate Governance *Report of the Code Group 2004*
http://www.ecgi.org/codes/documents/swe_codes_group_en_mar2005.pdf

UK
The Combined Code on Corporate Governance
The Financial Reporting Council (FRC), 2006
http://www.frc.org.uk/corporate/
Audit Committees – Combined Code Guidance (the Smith Report)
A report and proposed guidance by a Financial Reporting Council appointed group chaired by Sir Robert Smith, 2003
www.frc.org.uk/corporate/
Review of the role and effectiveness of non-executive directors (the Higgs Report),
Department of Trade and Industry, January 2003
http://www.dti.gov.uk/files/file23346.pdf

USA
Final NYSE Corporate Governance Rules
New York Stock Exchange, November 4, 2003
www.nyse.com
Restoring Trust – The Breeden Report on Corporate Governance for the future of MCI, Inc.
The United States District Court for the Southern District of New York, August 2003
www.nysd.uscourts.gov/

This table contains examples of the codes that exist in a selection of countries. Access to all the codes listed above, and to a more extensive list, is possible through the website of the European Corporate Governance Institute Index of Codes, http://www.ecgi.org/codes/all_codes.php.

As an additional source of information the home page for the specific codes in this table is shown under each entry. These all have an English-language version.

3.4.6 Researching international corporate governance

Denis and McConnell (2003) survey research into corporate governance systems around the world. They categorize this research into two 'generations'. The first 'generation' of research investigated corporate governance in US companies and then applied the same research methods to study companies in other major world economies, primarily Japan, Germany and the UK. The second 'generation' begins with the work of La Porta *et al.* (1998) in which they present empirical evidence to show that there are significant differences across countries in the degree of investor protection. Countries with low investor protection are generally characterized by a high concentration of equity ownership within firms and a lack of significant public equity markets. La Porta *et al.* (1998) provide valuable data for other researchers by developing objective measures of investor protection across 49 countries. The measures are constructed from variables related to shareholder and creditor rights, and variables related to the rule of law.

3.5 Corporate social responsibility

The European Commission has defined corporate social responsibility (CSR) as 'a concept whereby companies integrate social and environmental concerns in their business operations and in their interaction with their stakeholders on a voluntary basis'.[38] This definition was the basis of a Green Paper (a discussion paper) that was intended to launch a debate about the concept of CSR and the development of a European framework to promote CSR. It might seem strange to use the word 'voluntary' in the definition and then initiate a debate on a process that is likely to increase compulsion, but the Commission was probably reflecting the momentum already gathering pace from other quarters.

3.5.1 'Triple bottom line' reporting

In its communication on the EU Strategy for Sustainable Development (May 2001) the European Commission invited all publicly quoted companies with at least 500 staff to publish a 'triple bottom line' in their annual report to shareholders that measures their performance against economic, environmental and social criteria. The three aspects of economic performance, environmental performance and social performance are collectively described as 'the triple bottom line' of CSR reporting. The phrase 'bottom line' is used to link this idea with the traditional financial reporting of earnings for shareholders, often called 'the bottom line' of the statement of profit or loss.

In its communication of July 2002 on CSR,[39] the Commission proposed establishing a Multistakeholder Forum on CSR and then inviting the Forum to develop commonly agreed guidelines and criteria for measurement, reporting and assurance. The Final Report of the Forum (2004)[40] is in the nature of a review of continuing global initiatives

---

[38] COM (2001) 366.

[39] COM (2002) 347.

[40] *European Multistakeholder Forum on CSR, Final results and recommendations*, June 2004, http://ec.europa.eu/employment_social/soc-dial/csr/.

and provides some case studies. Its recommendations focus on raising awareness of current developments, including the Global Reporting Initiative (see section 3.5.3).

3.5.2 Sustainability

The idea of 'sustainability' is drawn from the study of ecology, where it represents the degree to which the earth's resources may be exploited without damaging the environment. Sustainable development means planning the long-term use of resources that do not damage the environment. This initial focus on physical resources has been extended to thinking about satisfying present needs of society without sacrificing future needs of society. The Global Reporting Initiative (see next section) gives the following explanation:

> The goal of sustainable development is to 'meet the needs of the present without compromising the ability of future generations to meet their own needs'.[41]

3.5.3 Global Reporting Initiative (GRI)[42]

The GRI was launched in 1997 as a joint initiative of the US NGO Coalition for Environmentally Responsible Economies (CERES) and the United Nations Environmental Programme with the goal of enhancing the quality, rigour and utility of sustainability reporting. Guidelines were published in 2000 and have been updated regularly. The GRI has developed into a new permanent global institution, creating an accepted disclosure framework for sustainability reporting.

The GRI has identified the trends that have caused this rapid movement:

- the search for new forms of global governance;
- reform of corporate governance;
- the global role of emerging economies;
- rising visibility of and expectations for organizations;
- measurement of progress towards sustainable development;
- governments' interest in sustainability reporting;
- financial markets' interest in sustainability reporting;
- emergence of next-generation accounting, such as 'business reporting', 'intangible assets analysis', 'value reporting'.

The Reporting Framework contains the core product of the *Sustainability Reporting Guidelines*, as well as *Protocols* and *Sector Supplements*.[43]

The base content of the GRI Report produced by a company will have three different types of disclosure[44] (organizations are encouraged to use this structure but other formats may be chosen):

1 *Strategy and profile*. This section contains disclosures that set the overall context for understanding organizational performance such as its strategy, profile and governance.
2 *Management approach*. This section contains disclosures that cover how an organization addresses a given set of topics in order to provide context for understanding performance in a specific area.

---

[41] GRI (2006), p. 2, quoting the World Commission on Environment and Development, *Our Common Future*. Oxford University Press, 1987, p. 43.

[42] www.globalreporting.org.

[43] http://www.globalreporting.org/ReportingFramework/ReportingFrameworkOverview/.

[44] GRI (2006), p. 19.

Exhibit 3.11	Headings and examples for CSR performance indicators

Economic performance indicators

Aspects

- Economic performance, e.g. risks for the organization's activities due to climate change
- Market presence, e.g. entry level wages compared to local minimum pay agreements
- Indirect economic impacts, e.g. developing infrastructure for public benefit

Environmental performance indicators

Aspects

- Materials, e.g. percentage of recycled materials used
- Energy, e.g. energy saved due to efficiency improvements
- Water, e.g. percentage and total volume recycled and reused
- Biodiversity, e.g. habitats protected or restored
- Emissions, effluents and waste, e.g. greenhouse gas emissions
- Products and services, e.g. packaging materials reclaimed
- Compliance, e.g. fines and sanctions for non-compliance with environmental regulations
- Transport, e.g. environmental impact of transporting employees
- Overall, e.g. total environmental protection expenditures and investments

Social performance indicators

- Labour practices and decent work, e.g. labour relations, health and safety
- Human rights, e.g. policies and practices related to international conventions
- Society, e.g. policies to manage impact on community
- Product responsibility, e.g. policies regarding customer health and safety

Source: Examples based on Section 5 Performance Indicators, GRI *Sustainability Reporting Guidelines* (2006).

3 *Performance indicators*. These are indicators that bring out comparable information on the economic, environmental and social performance of the organization. The main headings, and some examples, are set out in Exhibit 3.11.

The *Sustainability Reporting Guidelines* set out principles for reporting. These are: materiality, stakeholder inclusiveness, sustainability context and completeness. 'Sustainability context' means that the reporting company should seek to place its performance in the larger picture of ecological, social or other constraints, where this larger picture adds significant meaning to the reported information.

The GRI website lists companies that confirm the use of the GRI Guidelines.[45] Exhibit 3.12 is taken from the annual report of BASF, a German company in the chemicals sector. The Introduction to the annual report explains how sustainability reporting has been combined with other information to give a single corporate report rather than

---

[45] http://www.corporateregister.com/gri/.

| Exhibit 3.12 | Reference in annual report to GRI Guidelines, BASF |

About this report

Our Corporate Report provides an appropriate picture of the aspects of sustainability that are important to the BASF Group. It contains information on the three dimensions of sustainable development: economy, the environment and society. We have developed key contents of this report based on our dialogue with stakeholders and in the light of internal processes.

Our reporting is based on the international G2 recommendations of the Global Reporting Initiative (GRI). We are actively involved in the discussions to develop this initiative (page 83). All data and calculations are based on international standards. The report was developed by our Corporate Communications department, our Sustainability Center and further specialist units.

GRI Index

Since 2003, BASF has been participating in the feedback meetings of the Global Reporting Initiative (GRI) and has been working to further develop the guidelines together with experts from industry, nongovernmental organizations, analysts and financial auditors. We reported on the basis of the GRI for the first time in our Corporate Report 2003. The GRI aims to make international reporting comparable.

The G2 Guidelines provided us with valuable orientation when producing our Corporate Report 2006. In our reporting, however, we do not completely adopt the structure proposed by the GRI because it does not always show aspects relevant to sustainability and key issues at our company in a suitable manner. We consider it crucial to set our own priorities in corporate reporting and thus foster a constructive and critical dialogue with our partners and stakeholders.

This index shows where you can find information on the core elements and indicators of the GRI in this report and in our Financial Report. Our online reporting provides additional information on some indicators at corporate.basf.com/gri-index_e. An extended overview is available on the internet. The online index contains all GRI reporting elements, all GRI core and additional indicators and shows where details are to be found in our online reporting. We also give a brief explanation if no data are available for a given indicator.

Source: BASF Corporate Report (2006), p. 2, Introduction 'About this report'; GRI Index starts p. 83, following 'Assurance' information.

three separate documents. The heading to the GRI Index shows that a further recommendation of the GRI Guidelines has been implemented, with the detail of the index covering more than one page.

3.5.4 The Accountability Rating[46]

The Accountability Rating™ has been developed by AccountAbility and csrnetwork™.[47] AccountAbility is a professional institute whose mission is to promote accountability for sustainable development. It develops innovative and effective accountability tools and standards, called the AA1000 Series. The partner organization, csrnetwork, is one of the UK's leading CSR consultancies. Six areas are scored: stakeholder engagement, governance, strategy, performance management, assurance and public disclosure.[48]

---

[46] http://www.accountabilityrating.com.

[47] www.accountability.org.uk and www.csrnetwork.com.

[48] Accountability Rating 2006, http://www.accountabilityrating.com/files/AR_benchmarking_services.pdf.

3.5.5 Dow Jones sustainability indexes

The Dow Jones sustainability indexes track the performance of market leaders in sustainability. Companies apply to be included in the indexes and are assessed. The sustainability assessment of each company is based on responses to a questionnaire and the contents of documents provided by the company, including the annual report. Five corporate sustainability principles are applied, covering strategy, innovation, governance, the needs of shareholders and the well-being of employees and other stakeholders.

There is a range of indexes, including

- Dow Jones EURO STOXX^{SM} Sustainability Index (DJSI EURO STOXX). This consists of the leading 20 per cent of Eurozone companies, evaluated for sustainability, from the Dow Jones STOXX^{SM} 600 Index.
- Dow Jones STOXX^{SM} Sustainability Index (DJSI STOXX). This consists of the leading 20 per cent of all companies, evaluated for sustainability, from the Dow Jones STOXX^{SM} 600 Index.
- Dow Jones Sustainability World Index (DJSI World). This consists of the top 10 per cent of the leading 2,500 companies, evaluated for sustainability, from the Dow Jones World Index.

These indexes are defined, and the constituent companies are listed, on the website.[49] These lists give a useful source for planning a research project into companies whose annual report is likely to reflect high standards of sustainability.

3.5.6 FTSE4Good[50]

The FTSE4Good Index Series is designed to create a family of benchmark and tradable indices in response to the growing interest in socially responsible investment around the world. Companies that are included in one of the indices must pass the eligibility criteria detailed in the FTSE4Good Philosophy and Criteria document. There are four main benchmark indices:

- FTSE4Good Global Index
- FTSE4Good USA Index
- FTSE4Good Europe Index
- FTSE4Good UK Index.

To be eligible, companies must meet criteria requirements in five areas:[51]

- Working towards environmental sustainability
- Developing positive relationships with stakeholders
- Upholding and supporting universal human rights
- Ensuring good supply chain labour standards
- Countering bribery.

---

[49] www.sustainability-indexes.com.

[50] http://www.ftse.com/Indices/FTSE4Good_Index_Series/index.jsp.

[51] *FTSE4Good Index Series*: *Inclusion Criteria* (2006), FTSE International Limited.

3.5.7 Fédération des Experts Comptables Européens (FEE)[52]

In June 2004 FEE called on the Multistakeholder Forum to recognize CSR at a level similar to financial reporting. FEE launched an issues paper calling for action. The actions proposed were:

- *Companies* should seek independent assurance on their CSR reports.
- *Companies* and *those providing assurance* should disclose information to stakeholders regarding the independence of those providing assurance.
- *Global Reporting Initiative (GRI)*, as the global standard setter for sustainability reporting, should ensure that indicators and other disclosures do not preclude assurance. The GRI should also encourage disclosures about internal and external assurance.
- *Sustainability indexes*, such as FTSE4Good or the Dow Jones Sustainability Index, when rating a company, should consider whether CSR reports have received assurance.
- *Stakeholder organizations* should increase their members' awareness of the issue of assurance and engage with standard setters.
- The *European Commission* and national governments should monitor reaction to CSR legislation in France, Denmark and Sweden.
- *IAASB* should develop a specific standard on assurance for sustainability within its assurance framework.

3.5.8 The Carbon Disclosure Project[53]

The Carbon Disclosure Project (CDP) is an independent not-for-profit organization aiming to create a lasting relationship between shareholders and corporations regarding the implications for shareholder value and commercial operations presented by climate change. Its goal is to facilitate a dialogue, supported by quality information, from which a rational response to climate change will emerge.

The CDP website claims to be the largest repository of corporate greenhouse gas emissions data in the world. It works on behalf of large institutional investors to seek information on the business risks and opportunities presented by climate change and greenhouse gas emissions data from the world's largest companies. The website provides reports based on submissions of FT 500 and S&P 500 companies in response to information requests sent out by CDP. It claims that CDP has become the gold standard for carbon disclosure methodology and process. This is an example of information gathering and dissemination which is occurring beyond the traditional corporate annual report and illustrates the importance of studying a wide range of source material to discover all the information that is available about a company which is likely to be of interest to investors.

3.5.9 Monitoring for effective reporting

Standard & Poor's[54] is an organization that provides independent financial information, analytical services and credit ratings to the world's financial markets. In 2002 it developed

---

[52] www.fee.be.

[53] http://www.cdproject.net/.

[54] www.standardandpoors.com.

a *Corporate Governance Score* that provided a detailed analysis of a company's corporate governance standards by reference to global practices. Scores were available briefly but subsequently were discontinued. S&P now considers corporate governance practices as part of its normal credit-rating surveillance. S&P continues to provide periodic surveys of transparency but uses only information available in the public domain and points out that transparency is not to be equated with corporate governance.

Laufer (2003) comments on the limitations of retaining a voluntary approach to social accounting. There are those who complain of poor quality and lack of reliability in voluntary reporting; there are others who worry that regulatory intervention would destroy initiative and development. He regrets that the GRI Guidelines do not press for external audit and concludes that decisions to defer third-party auditing undermined an appearance of legitimacy. The term 'greenwashing' refers to the idea of using disclosure tactics that appear to meet expectations, because they are supported by reputable bodies, but without in reality making any meaningful disclosures.

3.6 Regulating compliance

This section contrasts the direct statutory control imposed by the SEC in the USA with the private sector regulation of the UK where there is statutory support for the work of the Financial Reporting Review Panel in taking action on defective accounts and for the work of the Financial Services Authority in maintaining a fair market. The USA and the UK present two different approaches to government monitoring of financial reporting by listed companies. The section then explains the initiatives taken by stock market regulators to improve financial reporting across markets.

3.6.1 The US Securities and Exchange Commission[55]

The primary mission of the US SEC is to protect investors and maintain the integrity of the securities markets. It applies a basic principle that all investors, whether large institutions or private individuals, should have access to certain basic facts about an investment prior to buying it. To achieve this, the SEC requires public companies to disclose meaningful financial and other information to the public, which provides a common pool of knowledge for all investors to use to judge for themselves if a company's securities are a good investment. A steady flow of timely, comprehensive and accurate information enables people to make sound investment decisions.

The SEC also oversees other key participants in the securities world, including stock exchanges, broker–dealers, investment advisors, mutual funds, and public utility holding companies. Here again, the SEC is concerned primarily with promoting disclosure of important information, enforcing the securities laws, and protecting investors who interact with these various organizations and individuals.

3.6.1.1 Enforcement

An important feature of the SEC's effectiveness is its enforcement authority. Each year the SEC brings between 400 and 500 civil enforcement actions against individuals and

---

[55] www.sec.gov.

companies that break the securities laws. Typical infractions include insider trading, accounting fraud, and providing false or misleading information about securities and the companies that issue them.

The Enforcement Division obtains evidence of possible violations of the securities laws from many sources, including its own surveillance activities, other divisions of the SEC, the self-regulatory organizations and other securities industry sources, press reports and investor complaints.

All SEC investigations are conducted privately. Facts are developed to the fullest extent possible through informal enquiry, interviewing witnesses, examining brokerage records, reviewing trading data, and other methods. Once the SEC issues a formal order of investigation, the Division's staff may compel witnesses by subpoena to testify and produce books, records and other relevant documents. Following an investigation, SEC staff present their findings to the SEC for its review. The SEC can authorize the staff to file a case in a federal court or bring an administrative action. Individuals and companies charged sometimes choose to settle the case, while others contest the charges.

The Chief Accountant is the principal advisor to the SEC on accounting and auditing matters. The Office of the Chief Accountant also works closely with domestic and international private sector accounting and auditing standards-setting bodies (e.g. the FASB, the IASB, the AICPA and the PCAOB); consults with registrants, auditors and other SEC staff regarding the application of accounting standards and financial disclosure requirements; and assists in addressing problems that may warrant enforcement actions.

3.6.1.2 Regulation FD[56]

In 2000, the SEC adopted Regulation FD (Fair Disclosure) to address the selective disclosure of information by companies and other issuers. Regulation FD provides that when an issuer discloses material non-public information to certain individuals or entities – generally, securities market professionals, such as stock analysts, or holders of the issuer's securities who may well trade on the basis of the information – the issuer must make public disclosure of that information. In this way, the new rule aims to promote full and fair disclosure.

Whenever an issuer, or any person acting on its behalf, discloses any material non-public information regarding that issuer or its securities to any person in a defined class (such as investors or market participants), the issuer shall make public disclosure of that information:

- simultaneously, in the case of an intentional disclosure; and
- promptly, in the case of a non-intentional disclosure.

3.6.2 UK: FRRP and UKLA

3.6.2.1 The Financial Reporting Review Panel[57]

The Financial Reporting Review Panel (FRRP) is authorized by the Secretary of State to examine departures from the accounting requirements of the Companies Act 1985 and accounting standards. It has the power to appeal to a court of law to require directors to correct and reissue accounts that do not comply. The FRRP covers the accounts of all

---

[56] *Regulation FD – Fair Disclosure,* www.sec.gov/divisions/corpfin/forms/regfd.htm.

[57] www.frc.org.uk/frrp/.

public limited companies, whether listed or not, and some large private companies. Its powers are much more limited than those of the SEC but it appears to have influenced financial reporting compliance in the UK.[58]

The FRRP considers any matter drawn to its attention from a review of accounts selected by the FRRP, or by complainants or press comment. It initially considers whether there is a case to answer. When there is such a case, the Chair appoints a Group to conduct the inquiry, normally made up of five members including the Chair and the Deputy Chair. Other members are chosen from the FRRP to provide a balance of experience relevant to the enquiry, excluding any potential conflicts of interest. The Group's discussions with the company are confidential.

The Group puts its concerns to the directors and may discuss them in correspondence and at meetings. The FRRP encourages directors to consult with their auditors and to take any other advice they feel they need. The process is informal but is intended to combine efficiency with fairness. As defective accounts could mislead the public, the procedures need to allow for speedy rectification. The Group aims to reach agreement with the directors of the company by persuasion. If the Group is satisfied by the company's explanations, the case is closed and the fact that an enquiry was made remains confidential. Where the directors do agree to take some form of remedial action, the FRRP issues a Press Notice. The FRRP does not comment on or discuss its conclusions.

3.6.2.2 The UK Listing Authority[59]

The Financial Services Authority (FSA) is another private sector body operating under the authority of legislation. When it acts as the competent authority for listing, it is referred to as the UK Listing Authority (UKLA), and maintains the Official List. The Financial Services and Markets Act 2000 imposes this requirement on the FSA and gives the necessary powers to the competent authority. By this means the relevant European Community Directives are implemented.

The UKLA has a set of rules known collectively as the 'Disclosure and Transparency Rules' (DTR) of which Periodic Financial Reporting (DTR 4) has most relevance to annual and interim reporting. The DTR reflect disclosure requirements that are compulsory under the relevant European Community Directives, and additional requirements of the Financial Services and Markets Act. Further requirements are set out in the Listing Rules (LR) at LR section 9. In particular the Listing Rules require a statement of how the listed company has applied the principles set out in Section 1 of the Combined Code (see Exhibit 3.10), in a manner that would enable shareholders to evaluate how the principles have been applied.

3.6.3 Associations of stock market regulators

3.6.3.1 International Organization of Securities Commissions (IOSCO)[60]

IOSCO is an international association of securities regulators that was created in 1983. The members of IOSCO are the securities regulators of more than 100 jurisdictions. The SEC in the USA is a member of IOSCO. The three core objectives of IOSCO are the protection of investors; ensuring that markets are fair, efficient and transparent; and the

---

[58] Fearnley *et al.* (2000).

[59] http://www.fsa.gov.uk/Pages/Doing/UKLA/index.shtml.

[60] www.iosco.org.

reduction of systemic risk. IOSCO sets international standards, called Principles, for securities markets. It claims to be the world's primary forum of international cooperation for securities regulatory agencies. One of the key themes of its technical committee work is 'Disclosure and Accounting', focusing both on multinationals in established markets and on emerging markets.

After the Asian crisis of 1997, IOSCO consolidated its work to that date in a set of Principles of Securities Regulations that were recognized as key standards by the Financial Stability Forum. Following the Enron collapse, three further sets of IOSCO Principles were issued in 2002 to strengthen ongoing disclosure and reporting of material developments by listed companies. The current Objectives and Principles of Securities Regulations are available on the IOSCO website.

3.6.3.2 The Committee of European Securities Regulators (CESR)[61]

CESR was established by a European Commission Decision of June 2001. This Decision was taken in the light of the recommendation of the Report of the Committee of Wise Men on the Regulation of European Securities Markets (the Lamfalussy Report) as endorsed by the European Council and the European Parliament. CESR is an independent committee bringing together senior representatives from national public authorities that act in the field of securities. It adopted the previous work of the Forum of European Securities Commissions (FESCO). CESR reports annually to the European Commission.

The work of CESR is prepared by Expert Groups formed specifically for each project. One of its first actions was to issue, in 2003, a recommendation for additional guidance regarding the transition to IFRS in 2005.[62] It was effectively a recommendation from the CESR members to themselves to encourage listed companies to prepare thoroughly for 2005 and communicate the process of preparation. The recommendation covered the information that might be published in the year of transition to IFRS implementation, the accounting framework to be used in interim financial reporting, and achieving comparability in the presentation of comparative figures for previous periods.

CESR has held discussions with the US SEC as part of an ongoing dialogue. A joint work programme was agreed between CESR and the US SEC in August 2006. By April 2007 there had been good progress. The possibility of the SEC eliminating the reconciliation requirement was becoming more likely. There was cooperation between CESR members and staff of the SEC on the application of US GAAP and IFRS in the EU and the USA.[63]

3.6.3.3 EU and US cooperation

CESR and the SEC announced in 2004[64] that they intended to increase cooperation and collaboration so as to identify emerging risks and engage in early discussion of potential regulatory projects. One of their projects for 2004 was to explore an effective infrastructure to support the use of IFRS. The aim was to ensure consistent application, interpretation and enforcement of IFRS, with the objective of avoiding reconciliation from IFRS to national GAAP.

---

[61] www.cesr-eu.org/.

[62] CESR (2003).

[63] CESR Press Release 07-274, April 2007.

[64] *Accountancy*, July 2004, p. 75, www.sec.gov/news/press/2004-75.htm.

3.7 | A research perspective

We have seen from the previous sections that good corporate governance is required to give confidence in financial accounting information, and that reliable disclosure of financial accounting information is an essential aspect of effective corporate governance. This means there are two directions to take in identifying research questions that link corporate governance and financial reporting.

A large body of research starts with an agency theory[65] perspective that the separation of managers from those who own the company can create a potential conflict for the agent (manager). There is a legal duty on the manager, as agent, to serve the needs of the principal (the shareholders) but this legal duty may conflict with self-interested motives where the manager seeks to protect personal remuneration, reputation or job security. The most frequent subject of research concerns the relationship between accounting information and management compensation (remuneration) contracts. That is because a great deal of this kind of research is produced in the USA where it is common for managers to receive rewards based on accounting targets and the information is published in the annual report.

Reflecting the two directions identified at the start of this section, there are two different 'schools' of research into governance and financial reporting. One is governance research,[66] which takes the accounting information as given and asks how financial accounting information is used in control mechanisms, mainly management compensation contracts, that promote the efficient governance of companies. The other is contracting research,[67] which takes the contract as given and asks how the nature of the contract affects managerial attitudes to accounting information.

Examples of research questions are set out in the next two sections.

3.7.1 Governance research

This section gives examples of research questions that ask how accounting information is used to control managerial behaviour:

1 How frequently is accounting information used to determine the amount of management compensation in reward schemes? Research shows that accounting numbers have featured strongly in cash-based bonus schemes but in more recent years there has been a rise in reward schemes based on stock price performance (Sloan, 2001, p. 342).

2 How is accounting information used in the decision to change the chief executive officer? Research finds an inverse relationship between earnings performance and the rate of turnover of chief executives (Conyon and Flourou, 2002).

3 How is accounting information used in debt covenant contracts (Day and Taylor, 1995)? How is accounting information used in other forms of financial contracting, such as using accounting information to restrict a company's ability to pay dividends (Leuz *et al.*, 1998)?

---

[65] Jensen and Meckling (1976).
[66] Bushman and Smith (2001).
[67] Watts and Zimmerman (1986).

4 How is accounting information used by management to reduce the risk of stockholder litigation caused by accounting disclosure omissions or misstatements? Skinner (1994) suggests that companies will voluntarily disclose bad news rather than cause suspicion in the minds of investors by withholding information.

The academic literature in this area is dominated by papers in the USA based on US data. Bushman and Smith (2001), in noting this US dominance, suggest (p. 297) that cross-country analyses are a promising way to assess the effects of financial accounting information on economic performance. One of their reasons is the possibility of observing 'grossly inefficient financial accounting and other regimes' in the sample, which they deem to be unlikely in the US context. That perhaps reflects a pre-Enron perception of US accounting.

3.7.2 Contracting and earnings management

How does the use of accounting information in management compensation contracts affect managerial choices of accounting policies? Watts and Zimmerman (1986, p. 208) offered the 'bonus plan hypothesis'. This says that, other things being equal, managers of firms with bonus plans are more likely to choose accounting procedures that shift reported earnings from future periods to the current period. One form of this process involves making choices that will not be challenged by the auditors. The accounting policies must conform to acceptable accounting standards and the choice is then exercised within the bounds of the accounting policy. This type of earnings management does not breach accounting standards and so does not attract a qualified audit report. It is not illegal but may be misleading for those who attempt to make forecasts of future accounting figures based on the reported results. It is difficult to research because there is no disclosure. A more extreme form of earnings management involves some form of deception, such as entering dates on sales invoices that are earlier than the date of despatch of goods, in order to increase reported revenue of the period. This type of earnings management leads to headlines in the newspapers when the story emerges. It is difficult to research prior to discovery because it is kept secret. There is therefore a challenge to researchers to find indirect methods of identifying earnings management.

Most of the earnings management literature[68] focuses on identifying whether it exists and, if so, what the causes are. The reasons identified are a desire to influence market perceptions, to increase management's compensation, to reduce the likelihood of violating lending agreements (debt covenants) and to avoid regulatory intervention. The literature does not evaluate the extent of earnings management in the population as a whole, and does not identify which accounting standards are most likely to be associated with earnings management.

The models used to test for earnings management are based on the presumption that those who seek to distort reported profits will do so either through working capital adjustments (called 'accruals' in the earnings management literature) or through depreciation adjustments. To overstate profit a company might overstate inventory or receivables, or understate payables. It might also lengthen the life of fixed assets to reduce the depreciation charge. Papers investigating earnings management[69] establish a 'normal'

---

[68] Healy and Wahlen (1999).

[69] Jones (1991); Dechow et al. (1995); Peasnell et al. (2000).

expectation of accruals based on a control group and then compare this outcome with the level of accruals in a set of companies that are believed to be indulging in earnings management.

3.7.3 Other aspects of managerial choice

How do changes in corporate governance regulations affect the voluntary disclosures made by management? In a study of listed firms in Hong Kong, Ho and Wong (2001) found that the existence of an audit committee was significantly and positively associated with greater voluntary disclosure, while the percentage of family members on the board was negatively related to the extent of voluntary disclosure.

3.7.4 Effectiveness of audit committees

A paper by DeZoort *et al.* (2002) provides a useful review of the empirical literature on the effectiveness of audit committees and also gives suggestions for future directions of research. They set out four areas of research investigation:

1 *How does the composition of the audit committee give it adequate independence?* This area of research generally requires the use of survey research methods to discover the independence issues, linked to the information available in the public domain about the composition of the audit committee. It is also possible to observe extreme events such as corporate failure or high levels of earnings management, and attempt to link these to the composition of the audit committee.
2 *How does the audit committee exercise its authority?* This also requires survey research to find out how the audit committees carry out their work. As the corporate governance codes are extended, there may be more information in the public domain describing the work of the audit committee but it is likely that surveys will continue to be important for deeper insight.
3 *Are adequate resources made available to the audit committee?* Resources available include the size of the committee and the support from external and internal auditors. The flow of information to the committee and its access to external advisors are also important resources. Research relates the effectiveness of the audit committee to the resources available to it.
4 *How diligent is the audit committee in its work?* Measuring diligence generally involves measuring the attendance record of committee members. This could be linked to discovery of fraudulent reporting or some other extreme event, but linking to the general efficiency of the company is less easy to quantify.

Summary and conclusions

This chapter has presented a range of the ways in which regulators and voluntary bodies have sought to improve the credibility of corporate reporting through giving more assurance and through encouraging relevant and reliable disclosures. What are the implications of this explosion of assurance and monitoring activity for the person who seeks to analyze the financial statements of companies? The question to ask is 'how much assurance is available for this particular set of financial statements?' The clues will be found in the annual report and other published documents, or on the company's website. The following list is a suggested system for establishing the assurance underlying an annual report:

- Read the audit report. What are the audit regulations, accounting principles, company law and codes of corporate governance that have been applied?
- Read the report of the directors. What sources of authority do they mention?
- Look for the certification by the directors. What is the wording? Who has signed it personally?
- Read the report of the supervisory board or the independent directors. What level of authority and control have they exercised?
- Read the corporate governance report. Which code has been applied? Is it full or partial application? Is there an audit view on this report?
- Read the corporate social responsibility report. Which guidance has been applied? Is there an audit view on this report?
- Look beyond the annual report to the websites listed in this chapter. Is the company listed as meeting the criteria of any of these evaluations?

Key points from the chapter:

There is a great deal of detail in this chapter and a wide range of bodies either setting regulations or issuing guidance. For revision you will need to bring the detail down to a manageable level. The following list may be helpful in collecting the detail under three themes of auditing, reporting and regulatory control.

Auditing

- International Standards for Auditing are issued by the IAASB.
- Sarbanes–Oxley has set new conditions on the independence and regulation of audit firms that affects audit firms.
- Audit committees show the commitment of independent directors in strengthening the internal controls and the relationship with the external auditor.

Reporting

- Corporate governance initiatives include requirements for companies to report how they are complying with corporate governance codes.
- Corporate social responsibility initiatives require companies to report their policies and practices, with a focus on three themes of economic, environmental and social performance.

Regulatory control

- The Sarbanes–Oxley Act (2002) has set an example that is being imitated in other countries.
- Stock market regulators have taken a strong lead in supporting corporate governance initiatives and supporting global initiatives in accounting and auditing standards.
- Public Company Oversight has become an activity with statutory backing, even in countries that would be regarded as having more of a professional tradition in accounting values.

Case study 3.1 | Corporate governance: Germany

The German Corporate Governance Code, revised in 2007, is issued by the Government Commission for the German Corporate Governance Code. It sets statutory regulations for the management and supervision of German listed companies.

Ensuring the basis for an effective corporate governance framework

The code presents statutory regulation. Recommendations are presented using the verb 'shall'. Companies can deviate from recommendations but must disclose this in the annual report. Suggestions are presented using the verbs 'should' or 'can'. Companies can deviate from suggestions without disclosing this. The remaining passages of the Code require compliance under law.

The rights of shareholders and key ownership functions

Shareholders vote at meetings with one vote per share (2.1). The Code sets a procedure for the general meeting (2.2) and the exercise of proxy votes (2.3).

The equitable treatment of shareholders

This is not covered explicitly in the Code, but is implied in the conditions set out. In particular the treatment of all shareholders in terms of information must be equal (6.3).

The role of stakeholders in corporate governance

In enterprises having more than 500 employees, the Supervisory Board is one-third employee representatives. Where there are more than 2,000 employees the fraction is one-half.

Disclosure and transparency

The Management Board and the Supervisory Board shall report each year on the enterprise's corporate governance in the annual report (3.10). Transparency is achieved by prompt disclosure of any new facts ('insider information') that could influence the price of the company's securities (6.1) and of specific levels of shareholding (6.2). All information made known to financial analysts shall be disclosed to shareholders without delay (6.3). Information shall be accessible on the company's Internet site and publications shall also be in English (6.8).

The Code asserts (7.1) that shareholders and third parties are mainly informed by the consolidated financial statements, using internationally recognized accounting principles. They shall also be informed by interim reports, also using internationally recognized accounting principles. For corporate law purposes of calculating dividends, for shareholder protection, and for taxation, annual financial statements will be prepared according to the applicable accounting regulations. The consolidated financial statements shall be prepared by the Management Board and examined by the auditor and the Supervisory Board, to be publicly accessible within 90 days of the end of the financial year. Interim reports shall be published within 45 days of the end of the reporting period. The consolidated financial statements shall contain information on stock option programmes and on relationships with shareholders as 'related parties'. Compensation of directors must be reported individually (5.4.7).

▶

Case study 3.1 *(Continued)*

The responsibilities of the board

German companies have a dual board system. The Management Board manages the enterprise. The Supervisory Board appoints and advises the members of the Management Board and is involved in decisions of fundamental importance. The Supervisory Board members are elected by shareholders at the annual general meeting. The Management Board and Supervisory Board cooperate closely (3.1 to 3.10). The Management Board has specific tasks and responsibilities (4.1). Its composition, and the remuneration of members, are defined by the Supervisory Board (4.2). There are strict rules applied to the Management Board to prevent conflicts of interest (4.3). The tasks and responsibilities of the Supervisory Board are defined (5.1) as are those of the Chair of the Supervisory Board (5.2). The Supervisory Board shall set up an Audit Committee (5.3.2) and any other committees that increase the efficiency of the Supervisory Board. There are rules for the composition and compensation of the Supervisory Board (5.4) and for the avoidance of conflicts of interest (5.5). It must examine its efficiency on a regular basis (5.6). The Supervisory Board appoints the auditor and determines the audit fee (7.2). It receives the auditor's report and includes the auditor in its discussions on the annual financial statements.

Case study 3.2   Corporate governance: Japan

Principles of Corporate Governance for Listed Companies were issued by the Tokyo Stock Exchange in 2004. The format is to make a general statement of principle and then list 'issues requiring attention'. There are five main sections of Principles, followed by an Appendix which describes the mechanisms of corporate governance (see Chapter 16).

Ensuring the basis for an effective corporate governance framework

The Appendix to the Principles describes two types of corporate governance framework which may be used in listed companies (see Chapter 16).

The rights of shareholders and key ownership functions

Corporate governance for listed companies should protect the rights of shareholders. Issues for attention are: (1) Respect of shareholders' basic rights; and (2) Due consideration to the infringement of rights of existing shareholders.

The equitable treatment of shareholders

Corporate governance for listed companies should ensure the equitable treatment of all shareholders, including minority and foreign shareholders. Issues for attention are: (1) Development and improvement of a system to prohibit transactions against the primary interests of the company or shareholders through the abuse of concerned parties' positions such as officers, employees and controlling shareholders; (2) Enhanced disclosure of information to shareholders in cases where concerned parties conduct actions that are likely to damage the primary interests of the company or shareholders; (3) Prohibition of special benefits provided to specified shareholders.

The role of stakeholders in corporate governance

Corporate governance for listed companies should help create corporate value and jobs through the establishment of smooth relationships between the company and its stakeholders and encourage further sound management of the enterprise. Issues for attention are: (1) Cultivation of a corporate culture that respects the positions of stakeholders, and development of internal systems to that end; (2) Timely and accurate disclosure to stakeholders of material information relating to stakeholders, and development of internal systems to that end.

Disclosure and transparency

Corporate governance for listed companies should ensure that timely and accurate disclosure is provided on all material matters including the financial condition, performance results and ownership distribution. Issues for attention are: (1) Enhanced disclosure of quantitative information on financial conditions and operating results and enhanced disclosure of qualitative information that deepens the understanding of the management conditions of companies by investors; (2) Securing opportunities for investors to access information equally and easily; (3) Development and improvement of internal systems to secure the accuracy and promptness of disclosure.

The responsibilities of the board

Corporate governance for listed companies should enhance the supervision of management by the board of directors, auditors, board of corporate auditors and other relevant group(s) and ensure their accountability to shareholders. The list of issues for attention in this section is longer than those of the previous sections. In summary the issues are: (1) Monitoring of the management by the board of directors and auditors or board of corporate auditors and other relevant group(s); (2) Motivation for the management to maximize corporate value through positive convergence of management and company interests by appropriate means; and (3) Development and improvement of a mutual monitoring system by directors under which fulfilment of duty and integrity as prudent managers should be secured and under which illegal activities and inappropriate activities from the perspective of generally accepted views are prevented.

Case study 3.3   Corporate governance: UK

The Combined Code on Corporate Governance was issued by the Financial Reporting Council (FRC) in 2006. The first version was issued in 1998 based on the Cadbury[70] and Hampel[71] Reviews of Corporate Governance. The 2003 revision took in the recommendations of the Higgs[72] and Smith[73] Reports.

---

[70] Cadbury Report (1992).
[71] Hampel (1998).
[72] Higgs (2003).
[73] Smith (2003).

Case study 3.3 *(Continued)*

Ensuring the basis for an effective corporate governance framework

The Code is prepared by the Financial Reporting Council which has oversight of the process of setting accounting standards. It is enforced by the requirement of the Financial Services Authority that all listed companies apply the Code as part of the Listing Rules.

The rights of shareholders and key ownership functions

There should be a dialogue with shareholders based on the mutual understanding of objectives (D.1). The board should use the annual general meeting to communicate with investors and encourage their participation (D.2). Proxy votes should be counted and reported. The Chairs of the audit, remuneration and nomination committees should attend the meeting to answer questions.

The equitable treatment of shareholders

In the UK this is an area covered by company law and the takeover code.

The role of stakeholders in corporate governance

Institutional shareholders should enter into a dialogue with companies based on the mutual understanding of objectives (E.1). When evaluating corporate governance, institutional shareholders should give due weight to all relevant factors (E2). Institutional shareholders have a responsibility to make considered use of their votes (E.3). The Code does not refer to other stakeholders.

Disclosure and transparency

The Code refers to accountability and audit. The board should present a balanced and understandable assessment of the company's position and prospects (C.1). It should maintain a sound system of internal control to safeguard shareholders' investment and the company's assets (C.2). An audit committee should be established to monitor the integrity of the financial statements and to maintain an appropriate relationship with the company's auditors (C.3).

The Listing Rules of the Financial Services Authority require companies to include in the annual report a statement on compliance with the Code. Schedule C of the Code sets out detailed guidance on disclosure in this statement. In the first part of the statement the company should explain its governance policies. In the second part it either confirms that it complies with the Code or explains why it does not comply. This is described as a 'comply or explain' approach.

The responsibilities of the board

Every company should be headed by an effective board, which is collectively responsible for the success of the company (A.1). The annual report should include a statement of how the board operates, including a high-level statement of which types of decisions are to be taken by the board and which are delegated to management (A.1.1). There should be a clear division of responsibilities between the running of the board (the Chair) and the executive responsibility for the running of the company's business (the chief executive). The board should include a balance of executive and non-executive directors so that no individual dominates decisions of the board (A.3). Independence of non-executive directors is defined in the Code. Except for smaller companies, at least half the board should be independent non-executive directors. The Chair should be independent at the point of appointment. There should be a transparent procedure for appointing new directors, based on a nominating committee (A.4). The board should receive timely information for its work and should undergo regular training (A.5). It should evaluate its own performance annually (A.6). Regular re-election and refreshing of the board should be planned (A.7).

Case study 3.4 Corporate governance: USA

The corporate governance rules of the New York Stock Exchange (NYSE) were approved by the SEC in November 2003. They are codified in Section 303A of the NYSE's Listed Company Manual.

Ensuring the basis for an effective corporate governance framework

Companies listed on the NYSE must comply with these standards of corporate governance. There are penalties for failing to follow a listing standard. The first level of penalty is a public reprimand letter. The ultimate sanction is to suspend trading or delist the company (Rule 13).

The rights of shareholders and key ownership functions

Matters such as voting rights and protection of minority interests are not covered in this guidance.

The equitable treatment of shareholders

These issues are not covered in this guidance.

The role of stakeholders in corporate governance

There is no mention of stakeholders other than shareholders.

Disclosure and transparency

Listed companies must adopt and disclose corporate governance guidelines relating to the responsibilities of directors (Rule 9). The website of each listed company must include its corporate governance guidelines and the charters of its most important committees. The information must be made available in print to any shareholder who requests it. Listed companies must also adopt and disclose a code of business conduct and ethics for directors, officers and employees (Rule 10). Listed foreign private issuers must disclose any significant ways in which their corporate governance practices differ from those followed by domestic companies under NYSE listing standards (Rule 11). This disclosure may be provided on the website or in the annual report. It must be in English and accessible from the USA.

▶

| Case study 3.4 | (Continued) |

The responsibilities of the board

Listed companies must have a majority of independent directors (Rule 1) who must have no material relationship with the listed company (Rule 2). The non-management directors must meet regularly without the managing directors being present (Rule 3). Some non-management directors may not meet the conditions for being regarded as independent. If so the independent directors should meet separately at least once per year. There must be a nominating committee (Rule 4) and a compensation committee (Rule 5) each consisting entirely of independent directors. There must be an audit committee that meets the standards of the SEC regulations (Rule 6) and this audit committee must have at least three members who must be financially literate and independent (Rule 7). The chief executive officer of each listed company must certify to the NYSE each year that he or she is not aware of any violation by the company of the NYSE corporate governance listing standards (Rule 12).

| Case study 3.5 | Corporate governance: Kenya |

In October 1999, the corporate sector, at a seminar organized by the Private Sector Initiative for Corporate Governance, formally adopted a national code of best practice for corporate governance to guide corporate governance in Kenya. The sample code was updated in 2002.

Ensuring the basis for an effective corporate governance framework

The code has no statutory power of enforcement. The principles are designed to assist companies formulate their own specific and detailed codes of best practice. The Private Sector Corporate Governance Trust works towards helping corporate organizations develop and improve their corporate governance practices.

The rights of shareholders and key ownership functions

The code describes the duties of shareholders to exercise authority in appointing and overseeing the Board of Directors. Shareholders rights are specified, including the right to obtain relevant information about the company on a timely and regular basis.

The equitable treatment of shareholders

There is specific guidance to the Board of Directors on equitable treatment of shareholders, including minority and foreign shareholders. Members of the Board must disclose material interests in transactions. Self-dealing and insider trading are prohibited.

The role of stakeholders in corporate governance

The directors are required to recognize the rights of stakeholders as established by law, to develop a code of ethics and monitor the social responsibilities of the company.

Disclosure and transparency

The section of the code on Accounts: Audit and Disclosure reminds directors of their statutory duties, requires an independent audit, and recommends an audit committee be established to review the annual and half-year financial statements before sub-mission to the Board. The audit committee should focus particularly on changes in accounting policy, significant adjustments arising from the audit, and major judge-mental areas.

The responsibilities of the board

The code covers the composition of the Board, recommending at least one-third non-executives. It recommends a separate Chair and chief executive and also a competent company secretary. Re-election to the Board should take place at least every three years. Service contracts for directors should not exceed three years. There should be an independent remuneration committee. Potential conflicts of interest should be reported to the Board and to the external auditors. Directors should receive formal training. The code also sets out a detailed schedule for board meeting management and procedures.

Case study 3.6 | Corporate governance: Poland

A document 'Best Practices in Public Companies 2005', issued by the Best Practices Committee of the Corporate Governance Forum, describes rules of conduct for all parties involved in the company. The World Bank reported[74] that all publicly traded companies fulfilled their duties to submit compliance statements in 2005 but 68 per cent of companies were unable to meet the principles concerning independent members of the supervisory board. Nevertheless the World Bank regarded this as a significant improvement from the previous year.

Ensuring the basis for an effective corporate governance framework

The Warsaw Stock Exchange is empowered to make this a formal obligation of listing. The Polish Corporate Governance Forum publishes a corporate governance rating based on the Code.

The rights of shareholders and key ownership functions

The main objective of the company should be to operate in the common interests of all the shareholders, which is to create shareholder value (General rule I).

The equitable treatment of shareholders

The shareholders' meeting should be convened and organized so as not to violate the interests and rights of shareholders. The principle of majority rule should be respected but a majority shareholder should take into account the interests of the minority (General rule II). There should be no abuse of the rights of the majority or the minority and no abuse of law (General rule III). The company's authorities and those chairing

▶

---

[74] *Corporate Governance Country Assessment: Poland.* World Bank Report on the Observance of Standards and Codes (ROSC), June 2005.

> **Case study 3.6** *(Continued)*
>
> general meetings cannot decide on issues that should be resolved by judgment of a court of law (General rule IV).
>
> ### The role of stakeholders in corporate governance
>
> The standards of good behaviour expected of all shareholders are described in detail in two sections, 'Best practices of general meetings' and 'Best practices in relations with third parties and third party institutions'. There is no explicit recognition of wider stakeholder interests.
>
> ### Disclosure and transparency
>
> When choosing an entity to provide expert services, including audit, the company should consider whether there are circumstances that may limit the independence of that entity (General rule V). The detailed relationship with the auditor is described in 'Best practices in relations with third parties and third party institutions'. The supervisory board submits its evaluation of the company to shareholders in advance of the general meeting.
>
> ### The responsibilities of the board
>
> There are detailed statements of Best Practice for the conduct of general meetings, the work of the Supervisory Boards and the work of the Management Boards.

Questions

The following questions test your understanding of the material contained in the chapter and allow you to relate your understanding to the learning outcomes specified at the start of this chapter. The learning outcomes are repeated here. Each question is cross-referenced to the relevant section of the chapter.

Explain and evaluate the steps taken around the world to improve the credibility of financial reporting

1 What were the standards identified by the Financial Stability Forum? (section 3.2.1)

2 What were the recommendations of the IFAC Task Force? (section 3.2.2)

3 What were the main recommendations of Sarbanes–Oxley on auditing and assurance? (section 3.2.3)

4 How does the World Bank contribute to developing accounting practices through ROSCs? (section 3.2.4)

Explain and evaluate developments in audit and assurance

5 What is the role of the IAASB? (section 3.3.1)

6 To what extent are ISAs gaining international acceptance? (section 3.3.1.1)

7 What is the role of the Public Interest Oversight Board of IFAC? (section 3.3.2)

Explain how the development of corporate governance has affected financial reporting

8 What is meant by 'corporate governance'? (section 3.4.1)

9 What is the purpose of corporate governance codes? (section 3.4.2)

10 What are the main features of corporate governance codes? (section 3.4.3)

11 What guidance is provided by the OECD on principles of corporate governance? (section 3.4.4)

12 What is the range of bodies issuing national codes of corporate governance? (section 3.4.5)

Explain how developments in corporate social responsibility are reflected in financial reporting

13 What is meant by 'triple bottom line' reporting? (section 3.5.1)

14 How does the GRI define 'sustainability'? (section 3.5.2)

15 What is the Global Reporting Initiative? (section 3.5.3)

16 What is the Accountability Rating™? (section 3.5.4)

17 How are the Dow Jones sustainability ratings compiled? (section 3.5.5)

18 How is the FTSE4Good Index Series compiled? (section 3.5.6)

19 What are the proposals of FEE in relation to CSR? (section 3.5.7)

20 Does the requirement to report CSR ensure that the reporting is effective? (section 3.5.8)

Explain and evaluate the effectiveness of regulation in ensuring compliance with requirements for financial reporting

21 How does the SEC regulate compliance in financial reporting by US listed companies? (section 3.6.1)

22 How does the UK regulate compliance with accounting standards? (section 3.6.2)

23 How do stock market regulators control standards of reporting by listed companies? (section 3.6.3)

Explain how research into credibility and assurance is developing

24 How does governance research contribute to an understanding of the relationship between accounting information and managerial actions? (section 3.7.1)

25 How does research into contracting and earnings management contribute to an understanding of the relationship between accounting information and managerial actions? (section 3.7.2)

26 How does research evaluate the effectiveness of audit committees? (section 3.7.4)

References and further reading

Bushman, R.M. and Smith, A.J. (2001) 'Financial accounting information and corporate governance', *Journal of Accounting and Economics*, 32: 237–333.

Business America (1998) 'The Asian financial crisis: how did it happen?', 119(7), July: 30–32.

Cadbury Report (1992) Report of the Committee on the Financial Aspects of Corporate Governance (Cadbury Committee), December 1992, available on www.ecgn.org.

CESR (2003) European regulation on the application of IFRS in 2005: Recommendation for additional guidance regarding the transition to IFRS. Ref. CESR/03–323e.

COM (2001) 366 *European Commission Green Paper 'Promoting a European Framework for Corporate Social Responsibility'*, www.europa.eu.int/comm/employment_social/soc-dial/csr/csr_index.htm.

COM (2002) 347 *Communication from the Commission concerning Corporate Social Responsibility: A business contribution to Sustainable Development*, www.europa.eu.int/comm/employment_social/soc-dial/csr/csr_index.htm.

Comparative Study of Corporate Governance Codes Relevant to the European Union and Its Member States. Report by Weil, Gotshal & Manges, LLP in conjunction with EASD (European Association of Securities Dealers) and ECGN (European Corporate Governance Network), January 2002. Published by the European Commission, Internal Market Directorate General, www.europa.eu.int/comm/internal_market/en/company/company/news/corp-gov-codes-rpt_en.htm.

Congressional Committee (2002) Committee Report 107–70. *The role of the board of directors in Enron's collapse*. Report prepared by the Permanent Subcommittee on Investigations of the Committee on Governmental Affairs, United States Senate, 107th Congress, 2nd Session, July 8, 2002.

Conyon, M.J. and Flourou, A. (2002) 'Top executive dismissal, ownership and corporate performance', *Accounting and Business Research*, 32(4): 209–244.

Day, J.F.S. and Taylor, P.J. (1995) 'Evidence on the practices of UK bankers in contracting for medium-term debt', *Journal of International Banking Law*, September: 394–401.

Dechow, P.M., Sloan, R.G. and Sweeney, A.P. (1995) 'Detecting earnings management', *Accounting Review*, 70(2): 193–225.

Denis, D.K. and McConnell, J.J. (2003) 'International corporate governance', *Journal of Financial and Quantitative Analysis*, 38(1): 1–45.

DeZoort, F.T., Hermanson, D.R., Archambault, D.S. and Reed, S.A. (2002) 'Audit committee effectiveness: a synthesis of the empirical audit committee literature', *Journal of Accounting Literature*, 21: 38–75.

Fearnley, S., Hines, T., McBride, K. and Brandt, R. (2000) *A peculiarly British institution*. London: Centre for Business Performance, The Institute of Chartered Accountants in England and Wales.

GRI (2002) *GRI Sustainability Reporting Guidelines* (First version), www.globalreporting.org.

GRI (2006) *GRI Sustainability Reporting Guidelines* (Version 3.0), www.globalreporting.org.

Hampel, R. (1998) *Committee on Corporate Governance: The Final Report*, chaired by Sir Ronald Hampel. London: Gee Publishing.

Healy, P.M. and Wahlen, J.M. (1999) 'A review of the earnings management literature and its implications for standard-setting', *Accounting Horizons*, 13(4): 365–383.

Hermsen, M.L., Niehoff, P.J. and Uhrynuk, M.R. (2002) 'An extraordinary expansion', *Accountancy*, October: 110–112.

Higgs, D. (2003) *Review of the role and effectiveness of non-executive directors*, Department of Trade and Industry, www.dti.gov.uk/cld/non_exec_review.

Ho, S.S.M. and Wong, K.S. (2001) 'A study of the relationship between corporate governance structures and the extent of voluntary disclosure', *Journal of International Accounting, Auditing and Taxation*, 10: 139–156.

IFAC (2003) *Rebuilding Public Confidence in Financial Reporting: An International Perspective*, www.ifac.org.

Jensen, M.C. and Meckling, W.H. (1976) 'Theory of the firm: managerial behaviour, agency costs and ownership structure', *Journal of Financial Economics*, 3: 305–360.

Jones, J. (1991) 'Earnings management during import relief investigations', *Journal of Accounting Research*, 29(2): 193–228.

La Porta, R., Lopez-de-Silanes, F. and Shleifer, A. (1998) 'Law and finance', *Journal of Political Economy*, 106(6): 1113–1155.

Laufer, W.S. (2003) 'Social accountability and corporate greenwashing', *Journal of Business Ethics*, 43(3): 253–261.

Leuz, C., Deller, D. and Stabenrath, M. (1998) 'An international comparison of accounting-based payout restrictions in the United States, United Kingdom and Germany', *Accounting and Business Research*, 28(2): 111–129.

OECD (2004) *New OECD Principles of Corporate Governance*, Organisation for Economic Cooperation and Development, 22 April 2004, www.oecd.org/daf/corporate/principles.

PCAOB (2004) Testimony – The Regulatory Dialogue Between the PCAOB & the European Commission, by Samantha Ross, Chief of Staff Public Company Accounting Oversight Board, Before the Committee on Financial Services, United States House of Representatives, May 13, 2004.

PCAOB (2006) Speech Text – Auditor Oversight and its Implications on the Resilience of our Capital Markets by Chairman Mark W. Olson, at the FEE Conference on Audit Regulation in Brussels, Belgium, October 12, 2006.

Peasnell, K.V., Pope, P.F. and Young, S. (2000) 'Detecting earnings management using cross-sectional abnormal accruals models', *Accounting and Business Research*, 30(4): 313–326.

Pilbeam, K. (2001) 'The East Asian financial crisis: getting to the heart of the issues', *Managerial Finance*, 27(1/2): 111–133.

Skinner, D. (1994) 'Why firms voluntarily disclose bad news', *Journal of Accounting Research*, 32: 38–60.

Sloan, R.G. (2001) 'Financial accounting and corporate governance: a discussion', *Journal of Accounting and Economics*, 32: 335–347.

Smith, R. (2003) *Audit Committees: Combined Code Guidance*. A report and proposed guidance by an FRC-appointed group chaired by Sir Robert Smith. Financial Reporting Council, www.frc.org.uk/publications.

Street, D.L. and Needles, B.E. (2002) 'An interview with Brian Smith of the International Forum on Accountancy Development (IFAD)', *Journal of International Financial Management and Accounting*, 13(3): 254–273.

Watts, R.L. and Zimmerman, J.L. (1986) 'Compensation plans, debt contracts and accounting procedures', Chapter 9 in *Positive Accounting Theory*. Englewood Cliffs, NJ: Prentice Hall International.

4 Transparency and disclosure

Learning outcomes

After reading this chapter you should be able to:

- Explain the problems of defining 'transparency' in disclosure.
- Explain the requirements of narrative reporting in the USA.
- Explain how management reports are produced outside the USA.
- Explain and evaluate the initiatives being taken on developing CSR reports.
- Explain the nature and evaluate the usefulness of remuneration reports.
- Explain and contrast methods used to carry out research into disclosure.

4.1 Introduction

The purpose of this chapter is to explain and illustrate the steps that have been taken in many countries to respond to calls for transparency of corporate disclosure. Those calls, which originated in the USA, particularly following the Asian economic crisis of 1997, took on greater significance following the failure of Enron. We have explained in Chapter 3 the range of regulations on governance which affected corporate reporting after Enron and how this rippled around the world from the Sarbanes–Oxley Act. In this chapter we give more detail on the nature of the resulting corporate disclosures and the work done by market participants and by academic researchers in assessing the relative achievement of transparency in disclosure. In particular we give examples of corporate social responsibility reports and we discuss remuneration reports. We finish with a description of the methods being used by academic researchers to investigate disclosure.

4.2 The meaning of 'transparency'

In section 3.2 we explained how 'transparency' came to the fore as a criterion of the SEC in the USA, following the Asian financial crisis. It became widely used by policy makers in comments on questionable accounting practices. Being a policy-related issue made it a useful motivation for accounting research. There has been an explosion of documents using the word 'transparency'. Unfortunately it is one of those words that is assumed to have a common basis of understanding but in fact is used in different ways by different people. Even more unfortunately, some omit to explain what they think transparency means.

4.2.1 Some definitions and explanations

A policy-oriented definition is provided by the Global Reporting Initiative (GRI):

> Together, the Principles are intended to help achieve transparency – a value and a goal that underlies all aspects of sustainability reporting.
>
> Transparency can be defined as the complete disclosure of information on the topics and Indicators required to reflect impacts and enable stakeholders to make decisions, and the processes, procedures, and assumptions used to prepare those disclosures
>
> (*GRI Sustainability Reporting Guidelines*, Version 3.0, 2006, p. 6)

A research-oriented definition is applied by Bushman *et al.* (2004) as 'the availability of firm-specific information to those outside publicly traded firms'. They acknowledge 'the multifaceted nature of corporate transparency' and then define two facets for their investigation. They describe 'financial transparency' as the intensity and timeliness of financial disclosures, and their interpretation and dissemination by analysts and the media. They further describe 'governance transparency' as the intensity of governance disclosures used by outside investors to hold officers and directors accountable. Their descriptions are based on data which is available to researchers using large data sets. We describe the method of their research in section 4.7.1.1. At the research conference where the paper was discussed, there were comments on the lack of a theoretical basis to support the view of 'transparency' taken by the paper (Miller, 2004). The authors claimed that they were examining relationships without making predictions based on theory.

In the immediate aftermath of Sarbanes–Oxley, the word was in wide use. IFAC's annual report 2002 was entitled 'Promoting transparency and the public interest'. Page 8 indicated that 'transparency' referred to the openness of the processes used by IFAC in holding public meetings, permitting public access to documents and carrying out due process of consultation. The 2003 annual report of the IAASB was entitled 'Transparency, quality and the public interest'. This referred to the transparency of the process for setting international auditing standards.

In Canada, as in the USA, chief executive officers and chief finance officers are required to certify that the financial statements, together with other financial information included in their company's filings, 'fairly present' in all material respects the financial condition, results of operations and cash flows of the issuer. The Canadian Performance Reporting (CPR) Board of the Canadian Institute of Chartered Accountants published a discussion document[1] inviting comment on the proposals. It defined 'transparency' and 'accountability':

> **Transparency** refers to the degree to which the information contained in the filings being certified by the CEO and CFO enables a reader to reliably assess and interpret the financial condition, results of operations and cash flows of the issuer.
>
> For the CEO and CFO certification, the 'fairly present' assessment and the attestation that the filings do not contain any untrue statement of a material fact or omit to state a material fact is the mechanism used to achieve transparency.
>
> **Accountability** refers to the public acknowledgement by the CEO and CFO of their responsibility for the completeness, accuracy, timeliness and reliability of the information contained in the fillings being certified.

The Discussion Paper on the revision of the IASB's conceptual framework[2] analyzes the case for including 'transparency' as a qualitative characteristic of financial statements. It points to the use of the word in the FASB's mission statement and the constitution of the IASB.[3] It notes that accountants, regulators and others have used the word 'transparency' in different ways. Some see it as a quality of financial reporting information while others see it as quality of accounting standards.[4] The Discussion Paper offers several ideas from other sources such as '*clear, candid,* or *easily seen through*', consistent with the term's meaning in general use such as 'easily seen through, recognized, understood, or detected; manifest, evident, obvious, clear' and 'frank, open, candid, ingenuous'.[5] The IASB concluded

---

[1] CICA (2004).

[2] IASB (2006).

[3] IASB (2006) BC42.

[4] IASB (2006) BC43.

[5] IASB (2006) BC44.

that transparent information results from applying qualitative characteristics already identified in the framework, such as faithful representation, neutrality, completeness and understandability.[6]

4.2.2 Standard & Poor's studies[7]

Standard & Poor's (S&P) publishes periodic studies on relative transparency and disclosure in global markets. The transparency surveys were part of an S&P initiative to introduce new governance information and analytical services. In the S&P methodology, greater transparency is associated with covering greater amounts of information from a checklist of items defined by S&P as being useful to decision makers.

In 2002–03 S&P published studies on Asia, Latin America, Asia–Pacific, Japan and USA. There has been a series of Russian surveys, reflecting interest in accounting in that country. Three surveys in Turkey have been based on research conducted by Corporate Governance Forum researchers at Sabanci University, analyzing the disclosure practices of 52 Turkish companies. In the 2007 survey of transparency in Turkey,[8] S&P reported that the pace of improvement had slowed in relation to that of previous surveys.

In the study on Turkey, transparency and disclosure are evaluated by assessing the inclusion of 106 possible information items ('attributes') in companies' disclosure. The 106 attributes were selected after examination of the annual report and accounts, regulatory filings and websites of leading companies around the world, and identification of the most common disclosure items. A list is provided on the S&P website. The attributes are grouped into three subcategories:

● Ownership structure and investor relations
● Financial transparency and information disclosure
● Board and management structure and process.

The inclusion of each attribute is scored as either 'yes' (included) or 'no' (not included). S&P claims that this simple 'yes/no' scoring ensures objectivity.

Exhibit 4.1 shows the S&P scores for companies across a range of global markets from the 2002 and 2003 studies. The S&P analysis brings out the importance of reading all regulatory filings in countries where the annual report gives an incomplete picture. For US companies in particular it is essential to read the annual report, Form 10-K and the proxy statement because the annual report alone gives incomplete disclosure in many cases. S&P also uses additional regulatory filings for its evaluation of companies in Japan and France.

4.2.3 The language of account

The language in which accounting information is reported is an issue that is not discussed in papers that originate in the USA. However it is an important aspect of transparency for global investment generally. Parker (2001) discusses the problems of choosing a 'language of account' for European companies. The number of official languages

---

[6] IASB (2006) BC45.

[7] http://www2.standardandpoors.com, Transparency and Disclosure: overview of methodology and study results – United States (October 2002); http://pages.stern.nyu.edu/~adamodar/pdfiles/articles/S&Pdisclosure.pdf, Transparency and Disclosure Study: Europe (April 2003).

[8] http://www2.standardandpoors.com/.

Exhibit 4.1	Distribution of transparency and disclosure rankings based on annual reports and other regulatory filings for global markets

Country/region	Composite	Ownership structure and investor rights	Financial transparency	Board process and structure	No. of companies
France	68	63	73	66	45
Germany	56	44	76	44	32
Italy	55	43	68	50	26
The Netherlands	65	58	69	65	23
Spain	55	44	68	49	17
Sweden	62	53	73	57	18
Switzerland	59	44	74	54	16
UK	71	57	79	73	127
US (annual report only)	42	25	66	31	500
US (combined)	70	52	77	78	50
Japan	61	70	76	37	150
Asia–Pacific	48	41	60	42	99
Latin America	31	28	58	18	89
Emerging Asia	40	39	54	27	253

Source: *Transparency and Disclosure Study*: Europe, April 2003, Table 2, p. 9 of 16.

of member states is considerably greater than the number of member states themselves. English is the dominant language of account of the early twenty-first century – but whose English should be used? Parker illustrates the European divide between preferences for 'British' English and preference for 'American' English. He also discusses the moves to resist English, and particularly the efforts in past years to find French descriptions that would avoid the 'anglicization' of the national language. Translation of regulations into the language of member states will not be an easy task. The difficulties of translating 'true and fair view' are already well researched but the IFRS have their own language of instruction – 'may' and 'should' as well as many shades of uncertainty phrases. The problems of understanding accounting in UK English and US English are well illustrated in the Glossary provided by BT in its 'US information package' within the annual report and Form 20-F. Compare Exhibit 4.2 and Exhibit 4.3 and look for the changes between 2004 and 2007. The items that have disappeared between the two dates are examples of how US terminology has become incorporated in financial reporting by UK listed companies following the European conversion to IFRS in 2005.

4.3 Narrative reporting in the USA

Every US company listed on a national stock exchange must comply with the regulations of the Securities and Exchange Commission (SEC). The SEC requires companies to produce an annual report on Form 10-K. This is a public document and is available free of charge on EDGAR.[9] However, if you try to download a Form 10-K from EDGAR you

---

[9] www.sec.gov and select link to EDGAR.

| Exhibit 4.2 | Glossary of UK and US accounting terms, BT 2004 |

Term used in UK annual report	US equivalent or definition
Accounts	Financial statements
Associates	Equity investees
Capital allowances	Tax depreciation
Capital redemption reserve	Other additional capital
Creditors	Accounts payable and accrued liabilities
Creditors: amounts falling due within one year	Current liabilities
Creditors: amounts falling due after more than one year	Long-term liabilities
Debtors: amounts falling due after more than one year	Other non-current assets
Employee share schemes	Employee stock benefit plans
Finance lease	Capital lease
Financial year	Fiscal year
Fixed asset investments	Non-current investments
Freehold	Ownership with absolute rights in perpetuity
Gearing	Leverage
Interests in associates and joint ventures	Securities of equity investees
Investment in own shares	Treasury shares
Loans to associates and joint ventures	Indebtedness of equity investees not current
Net book value	Book value
Operating profit	Net operating income
Other debtors	Other current assets
Own work capitalized	Costs of group's employees engaged in the construction of plant and equipment for internal use
Profit	Income
Profit and loss account (statement)	Income statement
Profit and loss account (under 'capital and reserves' in balance sheet)	Retained earnings
Profit for the financial year	Net income
Profit on sale of fixed assets	Gain on disposal of non-current assets
Provision for doubtful debts	Allowance for bad and doubtful accounts receivable
Provisions	Long-term liabilities other than debt and specific accounts payable
Recognized gains and losses (statement)	Comprehensive income
Reserves	Shareholders' equity other than paid-up capital
Share based payment	Stock compensation
Share premium account	Additional paid-in capital or paid-in surplus (not distributable)
Shareholders' funds	Shareholders' equity
Stocks	Inventories
Tangible fixed assets	Property, plant and equipment
Trade debtors	Accounts receivable (net)
Turnover	Revenues

Source: BT Annual Report and Form 20-F (2004), p. 154.

Exhibit 4.3	Glossary of UK and US accounting terms, BT 2007

Term used in UK annual report	US equivalent or definition
Accounts	Financial statements
Associates	Equity investees
Capital allowances	Tax depreciation
Capital redemption reserve	Other additional capital
Finance lease	Capital lease
Financial year	Fiscal year
Freehold	Ownership with absolute rights in perpetuity
Gearing	Leverage
Inland calls	Local and long-distance calls
Interests in associates and joint ventures	Securities of equity investees
Leaver costs	Termination benefits
Loans to associates and joint ventures	Indebtedness of equity investees not current
Own work capitalised	Costs of labour engaged in the construction of plant and equipment for internal use
Provision for doubtful debts	Allowance for bad and doubtful accounts receivable
Provisions	Long-term liabilities other than debt and specific accounts payable
Statement of recognised income and expense	Comprehensive income
Reserves	Shareholders' equity other than paid-up capital
Share premium account	Additional paid-in capital or paid-in surplus (not distributable)

Source: BT Annual Report and Form 20-F (2007), p. 143.

may find it takes up considerable storage space on your computer. The narrative reporting required in Form 10-K is extensive in detail and the Form 10-K report may contain several hundred pages. The requirements for Form 10-K are set out in Regulation S-K.[10] An extract from the table of contents of Regulation S-K is set out in Exhibit 4.4. One complication of the SEC regulation for Form 10-K is that the requirements may be met by cross-referencing. Accordingly you may find that one company produces a Form 10-K containing all this information in full, while another company gives only the headings and then makes a cross-reference to the published annual report or the 'proxy statement' (a document issued to shareholders prior to the annual general meeting).

4.3.1 Management discussion and analysis

You will see from Exhibit 4.4 that 'Management's Discussion and Analysis' is one of the items of disclosure required by Regulation S-K. This disclosure is frequently abbreviated as 'MD&A'. The requirement for US companies to produce an MD&A has existed since 1980 and it has given a basis for development of similar discussions in other countries. The benefit of having a Regulation to define the content of the MD&A is that all companies

---

[10] www.sec.gov/investor/pubs/securitieslaws.htm.

Exhibit 4.4   **Extract from Table of Contents of Regulation S-K**

Subpart 229.100 — Business
229.101 (Item 101) Description of Business
229.102 (Item 102) Description of Property
229.103 (Item 103) Legal Proceedings

Subpart 229.200 — Securities of the Registrant
229.201 (Item 201) Market Price of and Dividends on the Registrant's Common Equity
and Related Stockholder matters
229.202 (Item 202) Description of Registrant's Securities

Subpart 229.300 — Financial Information
229.301 (Item 301) Selected Financial Data
229.302 (Item 302) Supplementary Financial Information
229.303 (Item 303) Management's Discussion and Analysis of Financial Condition
and Results of Operations
229.304 (Item 304) Changes in and Disagreements with Accountants on Accounting
and Financial Disclosure
229.305 (Item 305) Quantitative and Qualitative Disclosures About Market Risk
229.306 (Item 306) Audit Committee Report
229.307 (Item 307) Disclosure Controls and Procedure
229.308 (Item 308 and 308T) Internal Controls Over Financial Reporting

Subpart 229.400 — Management and Certain Security Holders
229.401 (Item 401) Directors, Executive Officers, Promoters and Control Persons
229.402 (Item 402) Executive Compensation
229.403 (Item 403) Security Ownership of Certain Beneficial Owners and Management
229.404 (Item 404) Transactions with Related Persons, Promoters and Certain Control
Persons
229.405 (Item 405) Compliance With Section 16(a) of the Exchange Act
229.406 (Item 406) Code of Ethics
229.407 (Item 407) Corporate Governance

Source: Extracted from SEC Regulation S-K at August 2007.

must comply and all use the same headings, so comparison is relatively straightforward. The limitation is that companies may be tempted to 'boilerplate', which means that over a period of time they develop a standard form of wording that is used regardless of circumstances. The section of Regulation S-K setting out the MD&A requirements is very detailed. A summary of the main requirements is set out in Exhibit 4.5. The section dealing with 'off-balance-sheet finance' reflects concerns arising from Enron (see section 3.2). The Sarbanes–Oxley Act of 2002 instructed the SEC to add rules for disclosing off-balance-sheet arrangements.[11]

In December 2003 the SEC issued interpretive guidance on the MD&A, intended to encourage more meaningful disclosures in the MD&A in a number of areas, with general emphasis on the discussion and analysis of known trends, demands, commitments,

---

[11] Release No. 33-8182, 'Disclosure in Management's Discussion and Analysis about off-balance-sheet arrangements and aggregate contractual obligations', www.sec.gov/rules/final/33-8182.htm.

| Exhibit 4.5 | Summary of contents of the MD&A report |

(a) *Full fiscal years. For each of the three years covered by the annual report*, discuss registrant's financial condition, changes in financial condition and results of operations.

(1) *Liquidity*

Describe known trends or events that are likely to increase or decrease liquidity materially; course of action taken or proposed to remedy any deficiency; internal and external sources of liquidity, and any material unused sources of liquid assets.

(2) *Capital resources*

　(i) material commitments for capital expenditures
　(ii) any known material trends, favorable or unfavorable, in the registrant's capital resources; changes between equity, debt and any off-balance-sheet financing arrangements.

(3) *Results of operations*

Discuss:

　(i) unusual or infrequent events or transactions or any significant economic changes that materially affected the amount of reported income from continuing operations; the extent to which income was affected; any other significant components of revenues or expenses.
　(ii) known trends or uncertainties that have had or will have a material favorable or unfavorable impact on net sales or revenues or income from continuing operations known events that will cause a material change in the relationship between costs and revenues.
　(iii) narrative discussion of the extent to which material increases in net sales or revenues are attributable to increases in prices or to increases in the volume or amount of goods or services being sold or to the introduction of new products or services.
　(iv) impact of inflation and changing prices on the registrant's net sales and revenues and on income from continuing operations for the three most recent fiscal years.

(4) *Off-balance-sheet arrangements*

　(i) In a separately-captioned section, discuss
　　(A) nature and business purpose of off-balance-sheet arrangements
　　(B) importance to the registrant of such off-balance-sheet arrangements in respect of its liquidity, capital resources, market risk support, credit risk support or other benefits
　　(C) amounts of revenues, expenses and cash flows of the registrant arising from such arrangements; nature and amounts of any interests retained; nature and amounts of any other obligations or liabilities (including contingent obligations or liabilities)
　　(D) likely termination of off-balance-sheet arrangements
　(ii) This section defines the term 'off-balance-sheet arrangement'.

(5) *Tabular disclosure of contractual obligations*

This section sets out a table for disclosing contractual obligations payments due by period, separated as: less than one year, 1–3 years, 3–5 years, and more than five years.

The contractual obligations listed are: long-term debt obligations, capital (finance) lease obligations, operating lease obligations, purchase obligations, and other long-term liabilities reflected on the company's balance sheet.

Source: The above summary is based on Regulation S-K, §229.303, Item 303, August 2007.

events and uncertainties, and specific guidance on disclosures about liquidity, capital resources and accounting estimates.[12] It gave some general guidance on good presentation, including starting with an executive-level overview and making the most important information the most prominent. It pointed to a focus on:

- key indicators of financial condition and operating performance
- materiality
- material trends and uncertainties
- analysis.

It also gave specific guidance on reporting liquidity and capital resources, as being essential to the survival of a business, and on disclosing critical accounting estimates or assumptions (see Exhibit 11.16).

4.3.2 Market risk disclosure

There is a further disclosure requirement of Regulation S-K that extends the contents of the MD&A. Item 305 requires quantitative and qualitative disclosures about market risk (see Exhibit 4.6). Some companies incorporate this disclosure within the MD&A report,

| Exhibit 4.6 | Quantitative and qualitative disclosures about market risk |

(a) *Quantitative information about market risk*

Give quantitative information for each category of market risk exposure (i.e., interest rate risk, foreign currency exchange rate risk, commodity price risk, and other relevant market risks, such as equity price risk). Use one of three alternatives:

(i) Tabular presentation of information related to market risk sensitive instruments, including fair values, contract terms that indicate future cash flows, and expected maturity dates.

(ii) Sensitivity analysis disclosures that express the potential loss in future earnings, fair values, or cash flows of market risk sensitive instruments resulting from one or more selected hypothetical changes in interest rates, foreign currency exchange rates, commodity prices, and other relevant market rates or prices over a selected period of time.

(iii) Value at risk disclosures that express the potential loss in future earnings, fair values, or cash flows of market risk sensitive instruments over a selected period of time, with a selected likelihood of occurrence, from changes in interest rates, foreign currency exchange rates, commodity prices, and other relevant market rates or prices.

Explain any limitations in the information, make comparisons with preceding year and explain any changes in models or assumptions used.

(b) *Qualitative information about market risk*

(i) Primary market risk exposures.

(ii) How those exposures are managed.

(iii) Changes in either of the above.

Source: Summarized from Regulation S-K, §229.305, Item 305, August 2007.

---

[12] Release No. 33-8350, 'Interpretation: Commission guidance regarding management's discussion and analysis of financial condition and results of operations', www.sec.gov/rules/interp/33-8350.htm.

while others have a separate section in the Form 10-K. It is an example of the way in which the SEC adds disclosure detail, both quantitative and qualitative, beyond the requirements of financial reporting standards.

4.3.3 Forward-looking information

Those who use narrative information are looking for indications of the future prospects of the company. Financial statements are mainly concerned with stewardship and are backward looking. The narrative reports provide an opportunity for looking forward. However, those managing companies face a risk in making projections or forecasts because legal action may be taken by investors if the projections or forecasts are not met. This risk of legal action is particularly high in the USA, where shareholders may decide to bring 'class actions' in which all shareholders of the same class take action together against the management.

To protect management, the Private Securities Litigation Reform Act of 1995 extended the basic legislation of the Securities Act of 1933 and the Securities Exchange Act of 1934, allowing the SEC to clarify what is called a 'safe harbor' of protection against legal action in respect of forward-looking statements. To benefit from this protection the forward-looking statements must be made outside the financial statements and notes. Companies must state the factors that could affect the financial performance or cause actual results to differ from any estimates made in forward-looking statements. Because this statement provides warnings, it is given the title 'Cautionary statement'. It must be a meaningful cautionary statement with relevance to the company. Companies give the cautionary statement in the Form 10-K. They usually repeat it in the published annual report. Exhibit 4.7 shows typical wording of a cautionary note on forward-looking information.

4.3.4 Pro-forma ('non-GAAP') financial statements

In 2001 the SEC expressed concern about the growing frequency of presenting earnings information using accounting methods that were not based on Generally Accepted Accounting Principles (GAAP).[13] This type of presentation is often referred to as 'pro-forma' information. The SEC explained that some 'pro-forma' financial information serves useful purposes. Companies may wish to focus the attention of investors on some particular aspect of the interim or annual results to give comparisons or to emphasize particular activities. One purpose of the MD&A is to focus attention in this way, so it seems reasonable to use pro-forma figures to achieve the same outcome. However, it could also be the case that pro-forma information confuses investors, who do not realize that it fails to comply with official GAAP. The SEC was therefore warning investors to be cautious in reading pro-forma information.

The concern expressed in 2001 increased after the collapse of Enron. The Sarbanes–Oxley Act of 2002 (see section 3.2.3) required the SEC to adopt new rules to address public companies' disclosure of financial information that is calculated and presented on the basis of methodologies other than GAAP. In consequence a new disclosure

---

[13] Release No. 33-8039, 'Cautionary advice regarding the use of "pro-forma" financial information in earnings releases', www.sec.gov/rules/other/33-8039.htm.

Exhibit 4.7   Cautionary statement regarding forward-looking statements

This Annual Report on Form 10-K may include or incorporate by reference certain statements that may be deemed to be "forward-looking statements" within the meaning of the Private Securities Litigation Reform Act of 1995 and are intended to enjoy the protection of the safe harbor for forward-looking statements provided by that Act. The forward-looking statements may relate, for example, to the amount and nature of future capital expenditures, opening of additional sales outlets, expansion of the size of operating units, special projects at existing units, anticipated levels of change in comparable sales from one period to another period, expansion and other development trends of the industry, our ability to integrate newly acquired operations into our existing operations, our business strategy, our financing strategy, expansion and growth of our business, our liquidity and ability to access the capital markets and other similar matters. Forward-looking statements are often identified by the use of words or phrases such as "anticipate," "believe," "could occur," "could result," "estimate," "expect," "forecast," "plan," "will be," and "will continue." Although we believe the expectations expressed in the forward-looking statements included in this Form 10-K are based on reasonable assumptions within the bounds of our knowledge of our business, a number of factors could cause our actual results to differ materially from those expressed or implied in any forward-looking statements made by us or on our behalf.

These factors include, but are not limited to; the cost of goods, information security costs, labor costs, the cost of fuel and electricity, the cost of healthcare benefits, insurance costs, the cost of construction materials, competitive pressures, inflation, accident-related costs, consumer buying patterns and debt levels, weather patterns, catastrophic events, transport of goods from foreign suppliers, currency exchange fluctuations, trade restrictions, changes in tariff and freight rates, adoption of or changes in tax and other laws and regulations that affect our business, the outcome of legal proceedings to which we are a party, unemployment levels, interest rate fluctuations, changes in employment legislation and other capital market, economic and geo-political conditions and events. The foregoing list of factors that may affect our performance is not exclusive. Readers are urged to consider all of these risks, uncertainties and other factors carefully in evaluating the forward-looking statements. Because of the factors described and listed above, as well as other factors, or as a result of changes in facts, assumptions not being realized or other circumstances, actual results may differ materially from those contemplated in the forward-looking statements. Consequently, this cautionary statement qualifies all of the forward-looking statements we make herein and that are incorporated by reference herein. We cannot assure the reader that the results or developments expected or anticipated by us will be realized or, even if substantially realized, that those results or developments will result in the expected consequences for us or affect us, our business or our operations in the way we expect. We caution readers not to place undue reliance on such forward-looking statements, which speak only as of their dates. We undertake no obligation to update any of the forward-looking statements to reflect subsequent events or circumstances except to the extent required by applicable law. Item IA 'Risk factors' below gives further information.

regulation, Regulation G,[14] was introduced and also Regulation S-K was amended to set rules for such pro-forma information.[15] The detail is extensive but the essence of the requirements is as follows:

- Present, with equal or greater prominence, the most directly comparable financial measure or measures calculated and presented in accordance with GAAP, together with a reconciliation of the non-GAAP measure to the GAAP measure.
- Explain why the registrant's management believe that presentation of the non-GAAP financial measure provides useful information to investors regarding the registrant's financial condition and results of operations.

Motorola (Exhibit 4.8) provides an example of a pro-forma statement that meets the conditions. It has an introductory paragraph of explanation and columns that compare GAAP and non-GAAP results.

4.3.5 Internal control over financial reporting

The Sarbanes–Oxley Act of 2002 required the SEC to write new rules requiring companies to include in their annual reports a report of management on the company's internal control over financial reporting.[16] The report must include:

- a statement of management's responsibility for establishing and maintaining adequate internal control over financial reporting for the company;
- management's assessment of the effectiveness of the company's internal control over financial reporting at the end of the most recent fiscal year;
- a statement identifying the framework used by management to evaluate the effectiveness of the company's internal control over financial reporting;
- a statement that the registered public accounting firm that audited the company's financial statements has issued an attestation report on management's assessment of the company's internal control over financial reporting.

The new items 307 and 308 in Regulation S-K reflect this requirement for reporting on internal control. The wording is relatively narrow, confining attention to internal control over financial reporting. Internal control has a much wider remit in many countries, covering organizational and operational controls as well as financial controls.

4.4 Management reports in other countries

4.4.1 The EU Modernisation Directive[17]

In June 2003 the EU adopted the Accounts Modernisation Directive (see section 12.9). For company financial years starting on or after 1 January 2005, large and medium-sized companies are required by this Directive to provide a balanced and comprehensive

---

[14] Release No. 33-8176, 'Final Rule: Conditions for use of non-GAAP financial measures', http://www.sec.gov/rules/final/33-8176.htm.

[15] Reg. §229.10 (e) Use of non-GAAP financial measures in Commission filings.

[16] Release No. 33-8238, 'Final Rule: Management's report on internal control over financial reporting and certification of disclosure in Exchange Act periodic reports', www.sec.gov/rules/final/33-8238.htm.

[17] EC (2003).

Exhibit 4.8 Pro-forma financial statement, Motorola

NON-GAAP MEASUREMENTS: RESULTS OF OPERATIONS EXCLUDING SPECIAL ITEMS AND CERTAIN EXITED BUSINESSES

The tabular presentation below and as found on pages 28–30 reflects non-GAAP measurements of Motorola's results of operations presented on a basis excluding special items and certain exited businesses. The non-GAAP measurements used throughout this report do not replace the presentation of Motorola's GAAP financial results. These measurements provide supplemental information to assist the reader in analyzing the Company's financial condition and results of operations. Items that the Company considers to be special items generally relate to restructuring activities and asset revaluations.

The Company is providing this information to enable comparisons of current operating results to prior years and show the results of core ongoing operations. These ongoing results of operations are used by investors and management to measure the Company's current and future performance.

CONSOLIDATED STATEMENTS OF OPERATIONS EXCLUDING SPECIAL ITEMS

(In million, except per share amounts) Year Ended December 31, 2002	GAAP Results	Special Items Inc/(Exp)	Excluding Special Items
Net sales	$ 26,679	$ –	$ 26,679
Costs of sales	17,938	(56)	17,882
Gross margin	8,741	(56)	8,797
Selling, general and administrative expenses	4,203	(44)	4,159
Research and development expenditures	3,754	–	3,754
Reorganization of businesses	1,764	(1,764)	–
Other charges	883	(833)	–
Operating earnings (loss)	(1,813)	(2,697)	884
Other income (expense):			
Interest expense, net	(356)	–	(356)
Gains on sales of investments and businesses, net	96	96	–
Other	(1,373)	(1,351)	(22)
Total other income (expense)	(1,633)	(1,255)	(378)
Earnings (loss) before income taxes	(3,446)	(3,952)	(506)
Income tax provision	(961)	1,153	192
Net earnings (loss)	$ (2,485)	$ (2,799)	$ 314
Earnings (loss) per common share			
Basic	$ (1.09)		$ 0.14
Diluted	$ (1.09)		$ 0.14

Source: Motorola Annual Report (2002), p. 27, www.motorola.com.

analysis of the development and performance of the company's business. This analysis shall include both financial and non-financial key performance indicators, including information relating to environmental and employee matters. The requirements of the Directive are very general, so that member states have the opportunity to add more specific requirements to match national circumstances.

4.4.2 France[18]

By law, commercial companies must publish each year a management report on the group. It may be combined with the management report on the parent company. For a *société anonyme* the content of the management report is based on brief legal requirements augmented by advice from the *Autorité des marchés financiers* (AMF) (see section 10.4.3.1). Information that might be found in a management report includes: the structure of the group and its evolution, identities of major shareholders, employees and their training, the situation of the entity (without defining 'situation'), important events following the balance sheet date, research and development, probable evolution of the situation, the activity of the company and its subsidiaries and information on branches.

Richard [19] commented that French companies did not yet appear to give high importance to this report. Its location in the annual report may vary, even to the extent of being spread across different sections. There appeared to be deficiencies in matters of provisions, events after the balance sheet date, research and development and segmental information.

Under the *loi de sécurité financière* (LSF), issuers of securities are subject to new disclosure requirements for corporate governance and internal control. From 2003, the Chairs of the board of directors or the supervisory board of limited liability companies (*sociétés anonymes*) are required to report to shareholders annually, in a document appended to the management report issued by the board of directors, regarding the way in which the board prepares and organizes its work ('corporate governance'), as well as on the internal control procedures implemented by the company. For limited companies with a board of directors, the report must also specify whether the powers of the chief executive have been restricted in any way. Statutory auditors are required to submit their observations concerning the section of the Chair's report dealing with the internal control procedures for preparing and handling financial and accounting information. These observations are contained in a special report appended to the auditors' report. Exhibit 4.9 is an example of such a report. The company, Alcatel Lucent, is listed on stock exchanges in France and the USA. This means that the auditors of the company have to satisfy the reporting requirements of French law and also the Sarbanes–Oxley Act.

Companies that have more than 300 employees and that are required to establish a staff committee are required by French employment law to produce a social report (*bilan social*).[20] The social report contains seven sections covering: employment policy, remuneration and social security costs, health and safety at work, other working conditions, training policy, professional relations, and facilities available to employees and their families. The social report is given to the staff committee and the trade union representatives, who make comments prior to publication. It is then sent to the Employment

---

[18] Richard, J., 'France: Group Accounts', in Ordelheide and KPMG (2001), Vol. 2: 1197–1204.

[19] Richard, J., 'France: Group Accounts', in Ordelheide and KPMG (2001), Vol. 2: 1203.

[20] Gelard, G., 'France: Individual Accounts', in Ordelheide and KPMG (2001), Vol. 2, p. 1110.

Exhibit 4.9 Auditors' report on internal control

This is a free translation into English of a report issued in the French language and is provided solely for the convenience of English-speaking readers. This report should be read in conjunction with, and construed in accordance with, French law and professional auditing standards applicable in France.

Statutory auditors' report on the internal control

Statutory auditors' report, prepared in accordance with article L. 225-235 of the French Commercial Code (Code de Commerce), on the report prepared by the Chairman of the Board of Alcatel Lucent Company (formerly Alcatel), on the internal control procedures relating to the preparation and treatment of financial and accounting information.

To the shareholders,

In our capacity as statutory auditors of Alcatel Lucent Company, and in accordance with article L.225-235 of the French Commercial Code (Code de Commerce), we report to you on the report prepared by the Chairman of your company in accordance with article L.225-37 of the French Commercial Code (Code de Commerce) for the year ended December 31, 2006.

In his report, the Chairman reports, in particular, on the conditions for the preparation and organization of the Board of Directors' work and the internal control procedures implemented by the company.

It is our responsibility to report to you our observations on the information set out in the Chairman's report on the internal control procedures relating to the preparation and treatment of financial and accounting information.

We performed our procedures in accordance with professional standards applicable in France. These require us to perform procedures to assess the fairness of the information set out in the Chairman's report on the internal control procedures relating to the preparation and treatment of financial and accounting information. These procedures notably consisted of:

- obtaining an understanding of the objectives and general organization of internal control, as well as the internal control procedures relating to the preparation and processing of financial and accounting information, as set out in the Chairman's report;
- obtaining an understanding of the work performed to support the information given in the report.

On the basis of these procedures, we have no matters to report in connection with the information given on the internal control procedures relating to the preparation and treatment of financial and accounting information, contained in the Chairman's report, prepared in accordance with article L.225-37 of the French Commercial Code (Code de Commerce).

Furthermore, in the context of our diligences on the annual report filed with the SEC ('Form 20-F'), we have, in accordance with section 404 of the Sarbanes Oxley Act, issued a report concluding, based on the criteria established in the framework on internal control issued by the Committee of Sponsoring Organizations of the Treadway Commission, on the effectiveness of the Chief Executive Officer and Chief Finance Officer's assessment of the internal control over financial reporting and on the effectiveness of the internal control over financial reporting at December 31, 2006. In accordance with section 404 of the Sarbanes Oxley Act, Alcatel Lucent has excluded from the scope of its report Lucent Technologies Inc. and certain assets from Nortel Networks which were acquired at the end of 2006.

Neuilly-sur-Seine, April 6, 2007

The Statutory Auditors
DELOITTE & ASSOCIES
Antoine de Riedmatten

ERNST & YOUNG et Autres
Jean-Yves Jégourel

Source: Reference Document 2006, Alcatel-Lucent, p. 63.

Inspectorate and is made available to employees and to shareholders, together with any comments from the staff committee.

An illustration of the complexity of national legislation is provided by Combes-Thuélin *et al.* (2006) in their investigation of communication of risk disclosures in the corporate reports of French companies. Disclosures of risks are required by the *Loi sur les nouvelles régulations économiques* (2001), *L'autorité des marchés financiers* (formerly the *Commission des opérations de bourse*), the *Loi de sécurité financière* and IFRS or French accounting standards (which are similar to IFRS in the area of risk disclosures). Disclosure requirements focus on risk management as well as risk disclosure. The different sources of regulation and differences in terminology lead to a lack of harmonization between different companies.

4.4.3 Germany[21]

Corporations that are of medium or large size are required by the HGB to present an annual management report. The management report must be audited and published. The nature of the report is defined in law (the HGB). It must include a description of the development of the business and the situation of the business, so as to give a true and fair view. The risks of future developments must be mentioned. The report must also comment on post-balance-sheet events of special importance, anticipated development of the company, and research and development. The words 'development' and 'situation' are equivalent to 'past' and 'present' respectively.

In describing the present situation the report will give information about factors affecting employees and structural changes in the business. The discussion of research and development requires a description of the activities but there is no necessity to quantify details. Important post-balance-sheet events might include changes in capacity, closure or start-up of new plant, new agreements, or significant changes in ownership. The requirement to provide information about risks was added in 1998 but there is no clear agreement on how such information should be conveyed in the public domain.

4.4.4 Japan[22]

The Commercial Code (law) in Japan requires a business report to be filed with the balance sheet and income statement for reporting to shareholders. The business report must be audited. The financial statements issued under the Securities and Exchange Law do not contain a business report. However similar information is provided in a Registration statement filed with the stock exchange.[23] The information that must be reported includes: a description of the principal business activities, location of factories and offices, description of the capital of the business, operating results by division, relationship with the parent company and status of significant subsidiaries, results of operations and financial position for the past three years, significant problems facing the corporation, name of directors and statutory auditors, the top seven shareholders and their holdings, major lenders with the amount of borrowings and the number of shares owned by these major lenders, treasury stocks acquired or disposed of in the period, and post-balance-sheet events.

---

[21] Ballwieser, W., 'Germany: Individual Accounts', in Ordelheide and KPMG (2001), Vol. 2, pp. 1331–1332.

[22] Sakurai, H., 'Japan: Individual Accounts', in Ordelheide and KPMG (2001), Vol. 2, p. 1778.

[23] Sakurai, H., 'Japan: Individual Accounts', in Ordelheide and KPMG (2001), Vol. 2, pp. 1796–1797.

4.4.5 Sweden[24]

The law requires a management report that provides sufficient information on facts not available in the financial statements, to allow the user to form an opinion on the profitability and financial position of the company. There should also be information on: important transactions or events that occurred during the year or since the balance sheet date; expectations for future years; ongoing research and development work; and foreign branches. Rundfelt indicates that in practice the management report has become a formal document with little information value. Most companies publish a overview based on the US MD&A, but it is not a mandatory part of the annual report.

Some companies are required to report on how their operations affect the environment. These are companies which operate under a special licence because their activities may be harmful to the environment. The report only covers their activities in Sweden. An example is Holmen, a forest industry group (Exhibit 4.10).

Exhibit 4.10 **Environmental disclosure, Holmen AB**

Extract from Report of the Directors

Environmental information

The environmental aspects of Holmen's business are regulated by laws and permits in each country. The allocation of environmental responsibility and the organisation and management of its environmental activities are based on the Group's environmental policy. At the production units various types of rules are integrated as key elements in the planning of production and investments.

The environmental status of Holmen's mills is high as a result of investments in process and treatment equipment and the continuous process of improvement within the frame of the environmental and energy management systems at the mills and the statutory, official supervision.

Activities in Sweden. At the end of 2006 Holmen was engaged in environmentally hazardous activities at seven production units, three of which had environmental permits pursuant to the Environment Protection Act and another three had permits pursuant to the Code of Environmental Statutes. The seventh facility, the processing unit at

Strömsbruk, is expected to be reclassified in 2007 as a business required to submit an environmental report. This unit is supervised in the same way as before, with the municipality being the supervisory authority. With effect from the end of 2005, the processing unit at Strömsbruk has been incorporated into Iggesunds Bruk.

Sales of these seven units accounted for 63% of the Group's net turnover.

Environmental activities are largely a matter of planning issues pertaining to environmental permits. Most of the environmental impact of these facilities takes the form of emissions into air and water, noise, and the production of waste. Much attention is nowadays being given to issues relating to fossil fuels and biofuel.

Numerous environmental projects, investigations and measures were carried out in 2006, of which those mentioned below are just a few.

- Projects to reduce water consumption were carried out at several mills.
- Measures were taken at several mills to treat emissions into water and air more effectively.
- Certificated energy management systems were introduced at Braviken, Wargön and Iggesund Sawmill, which means that all the Group's mills in

Sweden now have such systems and are certificated in accordance with SS 627750.

- Actions are being taken to make more effective use of energy at Holmen's mills. The Swedish mills are participating in the Energy Agency's Programme for Energy Efficiency.
- Several projects were concerned with exploring the potential to find external, environmentally sound ways of using waste.
- Several investigations were carried out in consultation with the environmental authorities at industrial sites that had been contaminated by discontinued commercial activities that were once part of Holmen.
- On the forestry side several projects are underway in association with external forest researchers into ways of making nature conservation measures more effective.

The Braviken and Wargön pulp and paper mills underwent environmental audits pursuant to the Code of Environmental Statutes in 2002 for their permits. Skärnäs Port Terminal has had an environmental permit pursuant to the Code since 1999. Hallsta has had a permit pursuant to the Environment Protection

▶

---

24 Rundfelt, R., 'Sweden: Individual Accounts', in Ordelheide and KPMG (2001), Vol. 3, pp. 2408–2411.

Exhibit 4.10 *(Continued)*

Act since 2000. Iggesunds Bruk had its permit pursuant to the same act renewed in 2003. The Iggesund Sawmill has had its permit pursuant to the Act since 1994.

Hallsta, Iggesunds Bruk and the Iggesund Sawmill have submitted to the supervisory authority an account of how they intend to comply with the requirements of the EU's IPPC Directive by 30 October 2007.

No permits of significance need to be renewed or reviewed in 2007.

Holmen Energi produces electricity at Holmen's wholly and partly owned hydro power stations. The permits that all of these units have pursuant to the Water Rights Act include environmental conditions. In 2006 a decision by the Environmental Court granted a permit to construct a new power station on the river Iggesund, which will replace three existing power stations on the site.

Review of past water rights decisions may be called for on the basis of the Code of Environmental Statutes. In the case of the river Ljusnan, on which Holmen Energi has power stations, such a review is in process.

The Group's mills are participating in the EU trading in carbon dioxide emission rights. The Swedish mills are also active in the trade in electricity certificates.

The activities in group forests, and the activities at the mills, were certified at the end of 2006 in accordance with ISO 14001. The forestry activities were also certified in accordance with FSC and PEFC.

During the year there were a few cases in which threshold values were exceeded, incidents, and complaints relating to mill and forestry activities. They did not have any effect on the result and were resolved by means of corrective measures within the environmental management systems.

Activities outside Sweden. The mills in Workington in England, and Madrid, are engaged in activities having some kind of environmental impact. Their sales represented 20% of the Group's net turnover.

In 2002, Workington received an environmental permit for its activities pursuant to the EU's IPPC Directive. At the beginning of 2006, Madrid received an environmental permit for its activities pursuant to the same Directive. The mills in Workington and Madrid are certificated in accordance with ISO 14001.

Environmental report. Holmen's environmental activities in 2006 are described in 'Holmen and its World 2006', which will be published at the end of March 2007. It will also be published on Holmen's website, www.holmen.com, which will also provide links to complementary information on the environment. Taken together this constitutes Holmen's complete environmental report for 2006.

Source: Holmen Annual Report 2006, p. 31.

4.4.6 UK

Narrative reporting in the annual reports of UK companies consists of all the information within the annual report but outside the statutory financial statements. Typically the narrative reporting includes the Chair's statement, the directors' report, incorporating a Business Review, the statement on corporate governance, the remuneration report, social and environmental reports, and the Operating and Financial Review (OFR).[25] For UK companies the OFR is the closest equivalent of the US MD&A.

The OFR in the UK has been encouraged since 1993 by non-mandatory guidance from the ASB. A survey of users' needs[26] asked expert users, private shareholders, audit partners and finance directors to rank the relative importance of 130 items of information that might appear in a narrative report. Financial information, objectives and strategy ranked highly, followed by management discussion and analysis, background, innovation value drivers, risks and opportunities, customer, process and employee value drivers, and intellectual capital. Environmental, social and community information trailed behind.

---

[25] ASB (1993); ASB (2003); ASB (2005); ASB (2006).

[26] Beattie and Pratt (2002).

Exhibit 4.11	Summary of ASB's Operating and Financial Review (2006)

Principles

- Analysis of the business through the eyes of the directors.
- Focus on matters relevant to investors, consider matters of interest to other users where also of signficance to members.
- Forward-looking orientation, trends and factors relevant to assessing future performance, progress towards achieving long-term business objectives.
- Complement and supplement financial statements, to enhance overall corporate disclosure.
- Comprehensive and understandable.
- Balanced and neutral.
- Comparable over time.

Guidance

DISCLOSURE FRAMEWORK

The Statement lists key content elements that should be addressed. These are not to be considered as formal headings for a report. The nature of the report will depend on the circumstances of the business, the industry and the markets in which it operates.

(a) *Nature of the business, including a description of the market, competitive and regulatory environment of operations, the entity's objectives and strategies and the key performance indicators used by management to assess performance against targets.*

(b) *Development and performance of the business, both in the year under review and in the future.*

(c) *Resources, principal risks and uncertainties and relationships that may affect the entity's long-term value.*

(d) *Position of the business including a description of the capital structure, treasury policies and objectives and liquidity of the entity, both in the financial year and in future.*

KEY PERFORMANCE INDICATORS

For each KPI disclosed, the OFR should provide the definition and method of calculation, the purpose, the source of underlying data, underlying assumptions and an explanation of future targets.

OTHER PERFORMANCE INDICATORS

Where a quantified measure other than a KPI is included, the OFR should explain the definition and method of calculation, giving the corresponding amount for the previous year.

STATEMENT OF COMPLIANCE

The Reporting Statement sets out for voluntary best practice. Directors who choose to comply with it should, as a matter of best practice, state whether their report is prepared in accordance with the Reporting Statement.

Source: Summarized from Reporting Statement: Operating and Financial Review, Accounting Standards Board, January 2006.

The development of the OFR is explained in section 15.7.4.2 and the Business Review is described in section 15.7.4.3. The contents of the OFR are outlined in Exhibit 4.11.

The complexity of regulation and guidance which creates the annual report of a UK listed company may be seen in Exhibit 4.12. The harmonization of financial statements and notes that has been achieved with IFRS leaves considerable amounts of the annual report still subject to national influences and company choice.

Exhibit 4.12 Some elements of the annual report of a UK listed company

Chair's Statement	Voluntary statement, entirely at the discretion of the Chair
Directors' Report	Contents specified by company law
Business Review	Contents specified by company law, may be provided by cross-reference to other parts of annual report
Statement on Corporate Governance	Combined Code compliance required by Stock Exchange Listing Rules
Directors' Remuneration Report	Contents specified by company law and by the Stock Exchange Disclosure and Transparency Rules. Remuneration Committee required by the Combined Code
Social and Environmental Reports	Voluntary but may be applying the GRI Guidelines
Financial Statements and Notes	IFRS requirements
Operating and Financial Review	Non-mandatory guidance available from ASB Reporting Statement RS1

4.5 Corporate social responsibility (CSR) reports

Section 3.5 explains the sources of encouragement and pressure on companies to produce CSR reports, either with the annual financial report or as a separate document. Look back at that section which describes how those activities have led to action in various countries.

4.5.1 Flexibility in contents

We have already noted in Chapter 3 (see Exhibit 3.12) that the German company BASF has redesigned its entire annual report to comply with the GRI Guidelines. In Exhibit 4.13 we set out a section from the OFR of a UK company, BT, which deals with CSR reporting partly in the OFR and partly in a separate social and environmental report.

In France, the Law on New Economic Regulations requires a social and environmental report (see section 14.7.5.1). In its 2006 annual report, Michelin provides 12 pages of detail on company and environmental information, with the majority relating to employment issues. An example of the detail available is shown in Exhibit 4.14 which provides quantitative evidence on equal opportunities.

4.5.2 Comparative research studies

Bebbington *et al*. (2000) point out that although there have been developments in social and environmental reporting across Europe, the English-language research literature says relatively little about activities outside English-speaking countries. An attempt was

Exhibit 4.13 CSR Report, BT

OUR COMMITMENT TO SOCIETY

Corporate social responsibility

Managing social, ethical and environmental issues in a way that grows shareholder value, builds our brand and helps us and our customers become more sustainable is very important to us.

This section, together with the broad statement on social, environmental and ethical matters on page 69, conforms to the Association of British Insurers' disclosure guidelines on social responsibility. More detailed information about our social, ethical and environmental performance is available in our independently verified 2007 Sustainability Report at **www.bt.com/betterworld**

We invest significant resources in our CSR programmes and it is vital that we continue to be forward looking and responsible in our everyday operations and maintain our reputation for excellence. For a number of years we have measured the link between customer satisfaction and CSR performance. Customers who believe that BT takes its responsibility to society seriously are 49% more likely to be 'very' or 'extremely' satisfied with BT.

During the 2007 financial year, BT was ranked as the top telecommunications company in the Dow Jones Sustainability Index for the sixth year in a row. (The Dow Jones Sustainability Indexes rank companies for their success in managing social, ethical and environmental issues for competitive advantage.) We also hold the Queen's Award for Enterprise in recognition of our contribution to sustainable development, and in the 2006/07 Business in the Community Corporate Responsibility, Environment and Community indexes, BT is one of only four companies out of 100 to score over 95% on all six dimensions. We were also named for the first time as the leading corporate organisation for sustainability reporting in a survey published by SustainAbility, in association with UNEP (United Nations Environment Programme) and Standard & Poor's.

CSR Strategy

During the 2007 financial year, the implementation of our revised CSR strategy, which was discussed and agreed by the Board, was a top priority. There are four key strands to this strategy: maintaining current momentum, tackling climate change, enabling sustainable economic growth and enabling a more inclusive society – all issues to which we believe we can make a positive contribution.

Maintaining current momentum

CSR touches every part of our business – from the way we interact with our customers, suppliers and partners, look after our people, give back to communities and support charities such as ChildLine and UNICEF, right through to our practical concern for the environment.

We commit a minimum of 1% of our UK pre-tax profits to activities which support society. We provided a total of £22 million designed to benefit society in the 2007 financial year, of which £3 million was charitable donations. Our key

performance indicator for a number of years has been based on our contribution. In the 2007 financial year, we added a new indicator to measure the effectiveness of our investment.

Our community investment strategy aims to help individuals and communities make a better world through improved communications skills and technology. A key strand of this is our Better World campaign which has brought together our education programme (which provides free resources for teachers, pupils and parents and in-school activities with drama groups and BT volunteers, both in the UK and internationally) and other activities for young people. To date, we have involved over three million pupils at more than 12,000 schools.

ChildLine, a UK charity, receives 4,500 calls every day but lack of funds means that many hundreds go unanswered. We are working with ChildLine on a campaign to ensure that every child's call for help is answered. In the 2007 financial year, we raised £2 million for ChildLine and also raised money for There4Me, an online counselling service for children run by the NSPCC. We also helped Comic Relief, Sport Relief and Children in Need run successful telethons which raised over £80 million for good causes around the globe.

In the 2007 financial year, as part of our Better World campaign, we launched our first global development partnership with UNICEF. Community projects to bring education, ICT (information and communications technology) and communications skills to disadvantaged children will initially focus on South Africa, to be followed by Brazil and China in subsequent years. BT is investing £1.5 million over three years and this will be enhanced by fundraising activities by our employees around the world.

We recognise that we have a responsibility to the environment and we continue actively to manage our waste reduction and recycling. During the 2007 financial year, we received an income of £4.5 million from our recycling activities, offset against the £5.2 million we spent managing our waste contracts, recycling our waste and sending waste to landfill.

Waste

	2004	2005	2006	2007
Total waste (tonnes)	107,303	110,622	102,005	94,928
Total waste recycled (tonnes)	27,626	37,421	42,340	40,007
% recycled	26%	34%	42%	42%

Tackling climate change

BT is currently responsible for over 0.7% of the UK's total electricity consumption so we are well placed to make a significant contribution by actively reducing our carbon emissions. In fact, we have been actively managing our UK CO_2 emissions for a number of years – they are currently 60% below their 1996 levels. However, given the scale of the climate change challenge we face, we have committed to achieving an 80% reduction in CO_2 emissions from our 1996 baseline by 2016.

▶

Exhibit 4.13   *(Continued)*

As we transform our business and increasingly provide innovative new wave services, our energy consumption could increase as a result, for example, of the growth in our data centres. Consequently, we have conducted an audit of the energy consumption of these data centres and are implementing energy saving recommendations. We will also be helping and encouraging our customers, employees and suppliers to play their part and this includes encouraging our suppliers to develop products that emit lower levels of carbon. And we have launched a website to enable people to calculate their carbon footprint – **www.bt.com/climatechange**

The renewal of our green energy contract until 2010 means that approximately 50% of our electricity needs in the UK will be met by renewable sources and 50% from combined heat and power.

The following table shows BT's CO_2 emissions as defined in the Greenhouse Gas Protocol and therefore includes not only the CO_2 emitted directly by BT, but also that emitted in the production of the electricity purchased by us.

CO_2 emissions

	2004	2005	2006	2007
Total (UK only – million tonnes)	0.94	0.76	0.64	0.64
% below 1996	42%	53%	60%	60%
Tonnes per £1m turnover	50	41	33	31

Our Chief Executive, Ben Verwaayen, chairs the CBI's climate change task force, which has been established to set the agenda for business's approach to climate change and will make wideranging recommendations to the UK Government, the CBI and businesses later in 2007.

Enabling sustainable economic growth

Enabling growth that benefits society – in both the developed and developing worlds – within environmental limits is a new area of focus for BT. In the 2008 financial year, we will be integrating sustainability into our business processes such as product and proposition development. As part of this programme, we are also looking at the issue of obsolescence in the ICT industry.

Enabling a more inclusive society

We believe that ICT has a role to play in creating a more inclusive society, helping everyone get a fair chance. Work on this part of our CSR strategy is at an early stage, but we are looking at:

- what we need to do to build up our digital inclusion activities in the UK to help even more people get online. For a number of years, our key performance indicator for digital inclusion related to levels of broadband penetration. As these now stand at more than 99.9%, we have introduced a new target: to reduce the number of digitally excluded people in the UK from 36% to 32.4% (a reduction of 10%) in three years.
- involving less advantaged and minority groups in ICT-enabled work

- which new markets/services give all members of society the same freedom and opportunities to communicate
- helping the voluntary and charity sectors to become more effective through the application of ICT
- working with partners and customers to release the power of diversity within our supply chain.
- We believe that an inclusive approach to product design is good for customers and good for business. We are proud, for example, of our reputation for developing products that can be used by all our customers, regardless of age or ability. For example, we offer a wide range of phones with accessible features. Our Age and Disability Action team works to raise awareness within BT of the importance of inclusive design in services ranging from billing to broadband and has been working with The Centre for Inclusive Technology and Design on the development of a toolkit to help designers and others involved in product development, and to produce a general guide for inclusive design for businesses.

CSR Risks

For a number of years we have maintained a CSR risk register. During the 2007 financial year, we continued to develop our knowledge and understanding of our CSR risks. Our most significant CSR risks continue to be:

- breach of the code of business ethics
- climate change
- diversity
- health and safety
- outsourcing
- privacy
- supply chain working conditions.

Each of these risks has an owner and a mitigation strategy in place. These risks are not regarded as material in relation to the group and consequently are not included in Group risk factors.

CSR opportunities

The increasing importance of sustainability issues both inside and outside BT is leading to a much greater focus on the opportunities that CSR provides as well as the risks that need to be managed. This is not only in relation to building competitive advantage by growing our brand and reputation for CSR, but also in terms of commercial marketplace opportunities.

We believe that ICT has a positive role to play as part of the solution as individuals and organisations look for more sustainable ways of communicating, working and living.

We are planning to offer our business customers a carbon audit which will measure their carbon footprint and explore ways in which the use of ICT can reduce greenhouse gas emissions. Products such as remote working and teleconferencing, for example, play an important part in creating sustainable businesses.

Source: BT Group plc Annual Report & Form 20-F, 2007, Business review, pp. 24–26, www.bt.com.

Exhibit 4.14	Equal opportunities, CSR report, Michelin

Equal opportunities for men and women

In each country, the average wage differential between men and women is calculated for each employee category, for the three levels of responsibility where women are most represented. A weighted average based on country's headcount is then calculated for the Group.

Group average pay differential between women and men employees:

Status	Differential
Production workers	0.21%
Administrative and technical staff	−4.06%
Management	−7.14%

The differential can be attributed to company seniority, or experience and responsibility, generally lower among women. Pay policy is strictly identical for men and women in each personnel category and country.

Source: Michelin Annual Report (2006), p. 156, www.michelin.com.

made to address this defect by devoting an entire issue of *The European Accounting Review* (2000, Vol. 9(1)) to environmental and social accounting in Europe. One concern for the editors was the lack of pan-European and nation-specific studies across the range of European countries that emerged from their call for papers. The largest number of submissions came from Spain and the UK. The journal issue gives a range of perspectives on environmental and social issues across Europe but there is no single article giving a comprehensive comparative evaluation.

4.5.3 Questioning CSR[27]

Goyder (2003) comments on the growing enthusiasm for CSR in all quarters and asks whether it is a victory to celebrate. He distinguishes two types of CSR. In the first type, CSR expresses a company's purpose and values in all its relationships. Some companies will have higher levels of commitments to society, others will have less, but in all cases the CSR report will faithfully reflect the values and commitment of the company. Goyder calls this 'conviction' or 'values-led' CSR. In the second type, companies are required by social pressures to comply with a widening range of social expectations. CSR becomes a kind of fashion parade in which companies are applauded for saying the right things in their annual report, without anyone questioning whether they actually mean what they say. He calls this 'compliance' CSR. He is concerned that the CSR which is emerging from the current intensive activity around the world looks more like compliance CSR than conviction CSR. His concern is that communications from companies should reinforce the unique personality of the company, rather than bury it in meaningless forms of words.

---

[27] Goyder (2003).

4.6 Remuneration reports

The discussion of corporate governance codes in previous sections of this chapter and also in Chapter 3 has shown the emphasis that is placed on remuneration reports. The managers of a company must be accountable for their actions in the accounting information they present, but they must also be transparent in the rewards that they are taking for their actions as managers. Remuneration reports now cover many pages in the annual reports of some companies and provide a useful starting point for research into the agency relationship between managers and shareholders. For US companies the detailed information about management compensation arrangements is often found in the proxy statement published in preparation for the annual general meeting. For UK companies the information is found in the report of the remuneration committee. Exhibit 4.15 shows the contents table of the remuneration report of GlaxoSmithKline, a

| Exhibit 4.15 | Remuneration report, contents, GlaxoSmithKline |

Remuneration Report

The Remuneration Report sets out the remuneration policies operated by GSK in respect of the Directors and Corporate Executive Team (CET) members, together with disclosures on Directors' remuneration including those required by The Directors' Remuneration Report Regulations 2002 (the Regulations). In accordance with the Regulations, the following sections of the Remuneration Report are subject to audit: Annual remuneration; Non-Executive Directors' remuneration; Share options; Incentive plans; performance criteria on Performance Share Plans and share options; and Pensions for which the opinion thereon is expressed on page 166. The remaining sections are not subject to audit nor are the pages referred to from within the audited sections.

This Report is submitted to shareholders by the Board for approval at the Annual General Meeting, as referenced in the notice of Annual General Meeting.

Throughout the Remuneration Report the Executive Directors and CET members are referred to as the 'Executives'.

References to GlaxoSmithKline shares and ADSs mean, respectively, Ordinary Shares of GlaxoSmithKline plc of 25p and American Depository Shares of GlaxoSmithKline plc. Each ADS represents two GlaxoSmithKline shares.

Contents

Introduction	66
Remuneration policy	66
Executive Director terms, conditions and remuneration	71
Non-Executive Director terms, conditions and fees	72
Directors and Senior Management remuneration	72
Annual remuneration	73
Non-Executive Directors' remuneration	74
Directors' interests	76
Share options	76
Incentive plans	79
Pensions	81
Directors and Senior Management	82
Directors' interests in contracts	82

Source: GlaxoSmithKline Annual Report (2006), p. 65, www.gsk.com.

| Exhibit 4.16 | Remuneration report, policy, GlaxoSmithKline |

Remuneration policy

Principles

The remuneration policy for GlaxoSmithKline is designed to secure outstanding executive talent, and to provide pay for performance and only for performance, within a transparent and robust governance structure.

The Committee determined that GSK's remuneration policy would be based on the following key principles:

- the remuneration structure must support the needs of the business in a very competitive market place
- UK shareholder guidelines will be followed to the maximum extent consistent with the needs of the business and the company would maintain a regular dialogue with shareholders
- global pharmaceutical companies are the primary pay comparator group
- performance conditions would be based on the measurable delivery of strong financial performance and the delivery of superior returns to shareholders as compared with other pharmaceutical companies
- a high proportion of the total remuneration opportunity will be based on performance-related remuneration which will be delivered over the medium to long term
- remuneration would be determined using the projected value method (see 'Benchmarking' below)
- there would be one remuneration structure for Executive Directors and the CET with the same performance conditions applying equally to their long-term incentive awards
- no ex-gratia payments will be made
- pay structures would be as simple as is consistent with the business needs.

Overall, the policy is intended to provide median total remuneration for median performance, with the opportunity to earn upper quartile total remuneration for exceptional performance. Poor performance will result in total remuneration significantly below the pay comparator group median.

This strong alignment with performance is demonstrably in the interests of shareholders and provides the Executives with unambiguous signals about the importance of delivering success to the company's shareholders.

Source: GlaxoSmithKline Annual Report (2006), p. 66, www.gsk.com.

UK company having a US listing, while Exhibit 4.16 presents an extract from the remuneration report stating the remuneration policy for rewarding performance. The full report contains a great deal of detail, covering several pages, with information about each director separately.

In contrast, Fiat (Exhibit 4.17) applies the 'comply or explain' approach by giving minimal description of the work of the compensation committee (see extract from corporate governance report). The group provides very detailed information, in the notes to the financial statements, about the actual amounts of compensation paid. There is a short reference to policy in the agenda of the annual general meeting.

Exhibit 4.17	Executive remuneration, Fiat

> **Nominating and Compensation Committee**
>
> [*extract from Corporate Governance section of Report on Operations*]
>
> The Board of Directors established the Internal Control Committee and the Nominating and Compensation Committee. The Board also entrusted the Nominating and Compensation Committee with the task of selecting and proposing nominees for the post of Director and it also established the Strategic Committee, on which it relies for the preparation of Company and Group strategies.
>
> Source: Fiat annual report (2006), p. 51, www.fiatgroup.com.
>
> **Incentive Plan pursuant to Article 114 bis of Legislative Decree 58/98**
>
> *332 Items on the Agenda and Related Reports and Motions*
>
> Stockholders,
> The May 3, 2006 Stockholders Meeting resolution approved the motions submitted by the Board of Directors and authorised an incentive plan with 20 million underlying Fiat ordinary shares based on financial instruments issued by leading financial institutions and linked to Fiat shares. On November 3, 2006, the Board of Directors examined the above mentioned plan in light of the changed market conditions and, after receiving the opinion and proposals of the Nominating and Compensation Committee, resolved that, subject to authorisation by today's Stockholders Meeting pursuant to Article 114 bis of the Consolidated Law on Financial Intermediation, an incentive plan based on stock options was a more convenient technical solution.

Source: Fiat Annual Report (2006), p. 333, www.fiatgroup.com.

4.7 Comparative research into disclosure

Much of the research into disclosure is based on single country studies. A comprehensive review of research methods and issues in disclosure studies is provided by Healy and Palepu (2001) with discussion by Core (2001). The review is confined to US studies and calls for extension to other countries. Any research into narrative disclosures runs into two significant problems. The first problem is obtaining the data and the second is the time required to analyze it manually. This section gives examples of comparative studies and in each case explains how the authors dealt with the problems of obtaining and analyzing data.

One feature to note is that in many papers the year of publication is several years later than the period of the data under investigation. This means that considerable caution is needed before drawing any conclusions about the relevance of the findings to current-day practice. For researchers the interest lies in the method of research and the potential to replicate the research with more recent data.

4.7.1 Making use of surveys

One way of avoiding the time taken to measure disclosure in annual reports is to use scores created for some other purpose.

4.7.1.1 CIFAR database

A source that has been used repeatedly in comparative studies is the CIFAR database, created by CIFAR, the Center for International Financial Analysis and Research at Princeton, New Jersey. The data provides scores for disclosures measured for companies in 42 countries in the first half of the 1990s. Researchers use this database as their source of information and test hypotheses about the factors that are associated with different types and amounts of disclosure.

Hope (2003) uses legal origin (common law or code law) to represent institutional differences between countries. It uses Hofstede's culture measures to represent country cultures. Using regression analysis the paper finds that both culture and legal system are significant in explaining the CIFAR disclosure scores. It is not possible to say which of these is dominant. Companies in common law countries have significantly higher disclosure scores than companies in code law countries. However, the number of stock exchange listings and the number of analysts following the company's performance are also positively related to disclosure, so Hope suggests an explanation that companies in common law countries are more active in capital markets. Of the culture variables, individualism is significantly positively associated with disclosure and masculinity (low nurture) is significantly negatively associated with disclosure. The author concludes that 'it may be prudent to consider cultural variations when attempting to change a country's accounting infrastructure'.

Archambault and Archambault (2003) used the CIFAR scores to test a model of cultural, national and corporate factors that influence the financial disclosure of companies. They found that each factor contributed significantly to the disclosure model and concluded that disclosure is a complex process influenced by a broad set of factors. As the signs and significance of some relationships changed with the model used, they were not able to draw firmer conclusions but felt that nevertheless they had extended the literature by simultaneous testing of a range of factors.

Bushman et al. (2004) investigated corporate transparency by specifying their own perception of transparency and then quantifying it. We explained in section 4.2 that they offered a definition of transparency as 'the availability of firm-specific information to those outside publicly traded firms'. They then collected a range of measures from the CIFAR database that captured the information environments of different countries. Using the analytical technique of factor analysis, which applies statistical analysis to group the measures that seem to relate closely to each other, they identified two main factors, each representing a group of measures. One was 'financial transparency', describing the intensity and timeliness of financial disclosures, and their interpretation and dissemination by analysts and the media. The other was 'governance transparency', describing the intensity of governance disclosures used by outside investors to hold officers and directors accountable. They found that the governance transparency factor was primarily related to a country's legal/judicial regime, whereas the financial transparency factor was primarily related to political economy. The legal/judicial regime was represented by protection of investor rights and efficiency of the judicial system, both evaluated in La Porta et al. (1998), and patent protection levels taken from an economic survey. Political economy was represented by autocracy, state-owned enterprises, cost of entry (all from political and economic data sources) and state-owned banks and risk of expropriation (both from La Porta et al., 1998).

Bushman et al. (2004) is interesting for its use of a wide range of date sets. Reporting conference discussion and comments on the paper, Miller (2004) focuses on the lack of theory and therefore lack of expectations against which to judge the empirical findings. Bushman *et al.* would say that their paper is an example of 'let the data speak'. There are also comments on the detail of the statistical analysis and the problems of using data sets relating to different periods of time. However, the most interesting comment from the perspective of comparative study is Miller's concern (p. 265) that we run the risk of creating a standard that is accepted without being critically examined. The classification of regimes as code law or common law is quite crucial and Miller points out that other research papers have used different classifications. This may not affect the results in a broadly based paper such as Bushman *et al.* but could become significant if applied uncritically in a different combination of countries.

Using a data set such as the CIFAR survey has the benefit of speed of working and provides a relatively large amount of data for comparison, but it has the limitation of freezing research at a point in time. Salter and Niswander (1995) (see section 5.4.4) used the CIFAR data. Thus a range of research papers spanning almost ten years of publication dates are all based on the same data collection from the early 1990s. Also these papers tend to use the common law/code law distinction as a representation of institutional differences. The distinction is convenient as a variable for regression analysis but tells us little about disclosure differences within those broad categories. The papers that use the distinction do not add a discussion of limitations such as that found in Ball *et al.* (2000) (see section 7.7.3).

4.7.1.2 Standard & Poor's ratings

Section 4.2.1 explains Standard & Poor's major initiative to measure transparency through identifying and scoring 98 disclosure items covering accounting and corporate governance information.

Khanna *et al.* (2004) used the transparency and disclosure scores developed by Standard & Poor's. The data in their investigation covered 794 companies in 24 countries from the 2002 S&P survey. Country representation is uneven (e.g. Japan 150, UK 127, down to Portugal 7 and Denmark 6). The researchers found a positive association between the disclosure scores and a variety of market interaction measures, including US listing, US investment flows, exports to, and operations in, the USA. They acknowledge that correlation evidence does not allow conclusions about the direction of causes. It does not show whether interacting with US markets causes the sample companies to adopt US practices, or whether adopting US practices allows the companies to become more active in US markets.

4.7.1.3 World Federation of Exchanges (WFE) 2003[28]

The 2003 WFE Disclosure Survey, carried out by Carol Ann Frost, examines systems for disclosure of information about listed companies at 52 members of the WFE. It has three aims:

- to describe noteworthy features of the disclosure systems;
- to identify recent changes in these disclosure systems;
- to identify and interpret recent trends and emerging issues relevant to the regulated financial exchanges industry.

The reported results of the survey are based on evidence from a questionnaire to WFE members. The value of the survey to researchers lies in helping them to plan comparative

---

[28] Frost (2003).

disclosure studies by being aware of the potential range of disclosures available and the possible restrictions on availability.

4.7.2 Using a disclosure checklist

We explain in Chapter 9 the general principles of measuring disclosure practices and we give examples of disclosure checklists from research papers that have been applied widely in subsequent research. This section describes research on the developments that have taken place in various aspects of disclosure studies.

4.7.2.1 Scoring to an independent checklist

One method of carrying out comparative research is to find a suitable checklist and then apply it to a range of company reports. Robb *et al*. (2001) studied non-financial disclo-sures as recommended by US financial analysts to the Jenkins Committee in 1994. They compared corporate annual reports of companies in Australia, Canada and the USA, sampled in 1995. In comparisons of the disclosure scores the US companies scored highest on average, both in forward-looking disclosures and in historical disclosures. However, the Canadian and Australian companies were not significantly different from the US ones in historical disclosures. The Australian companies were significantly lower in forward-looking scores than the US companies, with the Canadian companies in between. The authors concluded that similar cultures provide similar levels of historical disclosures, but dissimilar levels of forward-looking disclosures that are non-financial in nature. In regression analysis the authors found that the disclosure scores were positively related with size of company and with listing on foreign stock exchanges.

The benefit of creating a checklist from an independent source, such as the Jenkins Report, lies in avoiding researcher bias in creating the list. The disadvantage is that it biases the research towards the USA as the country in which Jenkins reported. It is per-haps not surprising that the US companies had more feeling for what US analysts are expecting in corporate reports. In its conclusions on cultural influence, the paper assumes that Australia, Canada and the USA share an 'Anglo-Saxon' or 'Anglo-American' culture, an assumption that has been questioned by Alexander and Archer (2000) (see section 15.5.1).

4.7.2.2 Comparing disclosure scores to analysts' forecasts

Researchers may try to link disclosure studies to the uses of disclosed information. Vanstraelen *et al*. (2003) asked whether there was an association between non-financial disclosures, as recommended by the Jenkins Committee, and the accuracy of financial ana-lysts' earnings forecasts. They used the same checklist as did Robb *et al*. (2001), applied to annual reports in Belgium, Germany and The Netherlands. The analysis was based on the manual analysis of the contents of the annual reports of 120 companies across these three countries in 1999. The disclosure scores were compared with accuracy of analysts' forecasts as reported by IBES, the International Brokers' Estimate System. The research found that voluntary disclosure of forward-looking non-financial information was significantly asso-ciated with higher levels of accuracy in analysts' earnings forecasts. The paper concludes that increased disclosure of non-financial information may help to level the playing field for analysts and investors. There could be another explanation, which is that companies providing more information in their annual reports are also more open in their discussions with analysts, in helping them to understand the information provided.

4.7.2.3 Creating a checklist tailored to the project

Creating a tailored checklist has the benefit of matching the research design to the purpose of the investigation. It has the limitation that the checklist is less readily verifiable as independent and so is open to suggestions of researcher bias. It also lacks comparability with previous work. One approach to providing a degree of comparability is to build on previous work. We explain in section 9.6.2 that the work of Meek *et al.* (1995) and Gray *et al.* (1995) has been widely cited and built upon in subsequent research. One example is Chau and Gray (2002) who found a significant positive relationship between the extent of voluntary disclosure and the proportion of outsiders' interests in Hong Kong and Singapore listed company annual reports. They defined 'outside owners' by the total proportion of shares not held by directors and dominant shareholders (treating both of these groups as 'insiders'). They explain their choice of checklist in terms of the advantages of benchmarking against previous work.

Researchers who design their own checklist have to explain carefully how they have used prior literature to give some basis of validity and comparability, and must justify the modifications they make. Newson and Deegan (2002) used this approach in comparing social disclosure practices in Australia, Singapore and South Korea. They examined the annual reports of the 50 largest companies by market capitalization in each country. The size of each disclosure was measured to the nearest hundredth of a page using a transparent plastic A4 sheet. This is an alternative to counting sentences. The findings were compared with 'global expectations' derived from previous surveys in other research works. Australian companies had higher mean disclosure (in number of pages) than Singaporean or South Korean companies. Detailed analysis of the nature of disclosures showed variations in country differences – Singaporean companies gave the most disclosure about training and empowering employees.

4.7.3 Choosing a specific aspect of disclosure

Some researchers choose a specific aspect of disclosure and make comparisons over a range of countries.

4.7.3.1 Going-concern uncertainties

Narrative disclosures cover a wide area of subject matter. One way of making comparisons more manageable is to focus on a specific aspect of disclosure. Martin (2000) chose going-concern uncertainty disclosures in French, German and US practices. The sample size was not large. It compared 61 French and German companies with 61 US companies in the period 1987–91. The research found that going-concern uncertainty disclosures, whether in the audit report or the management discussion, occurred more frequently in the US companies than in the French and German companies. It also analyzed the different causes of going-concern qualifications in these countries. The data was taken from annual reports in electronic form, paper form on request to the companies, or purchased from CIFAR.

4.7.3.2 Financial graphs

Financial graphs appear in many corporate annual reports. They are placed in a prominent position and are intended to create an impression on the reader. If the scale of the graphs is distorted (measurement distortion) or the graph shows only the good news (selectivity distortion) the financial graphs may mislead the readers. This is called 'impression management'. Beattie and Jones (2000) compared financial graphs in the corporate annual reports of 300 companies in Australia, France, Germany, The Netherlands, UK and USA. They found evidence of selectivity, particularly in the USA and Australia, and of measurement distortion, particularly in the USA and The Netherlands, and concluded that there was some evidence that impression management was greater in the countries with strong capital markets.

The data for the paper was taken from the largest companies in each country having only a domestic listing. Annual reports for 1992 were obtained from the companies, in the English language where possible. Analyzing the data required a manual exercise, finding and evaluating financial graphs for sales, earnings and earnings per share.

4.7.3.3 Ethical issues

A comparative study of corporate reporting on ethical issues by UK and German chemical and pharmaceutical companies was reported by Adams and Kuasirikun (2000). They analyzed the annual reports of UK and German companies in *The Times 1000* companies in 1995. This method of sampling has the benefit of selecting the largest, and so probably the most influential, companies in the stock market for those industries. It has the limitation that the German companies in particular would be looking towards reaching international investors and therefore might be expected to be willing to give disclosures to reassure English-speaking investors who were unfamiliar with the German market. The checklist used for scoring is one developed by Adams in previous research, which gives the benefit of comparability. The results show that the German companies scored higher than the UK companies in reporting environmental information and in reporting on other ethical issues. The higher level of environmental reporting is explained by the authors in terms of the greater amount of environmental legislation in Germany at the time of the study. They also pointed out that the German companies did not show the secrecy that might be expected from Gray (1988) as outlined in Chapter 7.

4.7.3.4 Environmental disclosures

A comparative study of environmental reporting in the UK and USA (Holland and Boon Foo, 2003) analyzed the annual reports of 37 companies across five environmentally sensitive industries at the end of 2000. They found that the most frequently occurring disclosures by the UK companies in the sample were the environmental policy and environmental awards. The most frequently occurring disclosures by the US companies were environmental expenditure and a discussion of environmental issues or risks. In general the US reporting appeared to reflect the requirements of legislation while the UK disclosure appeared to be driven by management and reporting initiatives. The authors concluded that the voluntary approach in the UK was preferable to the stronger regulatory hand in the USA.

Summary and conclusions

Corporate financial reporting no longer stops with the financial statements and notes to the accounts. The need to be assured about the reliability and quality of the financial statements has created a framework of assurance (see Chapter 3) which in turn has led to an explosion of disclosures, outlined in Chapter 3 and expanded upon in this chapter. Some are mandatory regulation under law and accounting standards; others are voluntary but with strong guidance. The new disclosures also reflect the need for accountability regarding the non-financial aspects of business operations. Under the broad heading of corporate social responsibility (CSR) there are sources of guidance on disclosure that are increasingly being endorsed by market regulators and are being applied by companies which seek to maintain the best standards of communication with stakeholders. Information on the remuneration of those managing a company, and the conditions applied to their rewards, is seen as an essential element of corporate governance in which those who own the company can see how their agents (the directors) are rewarded for their stewardship of the business.

Research into transparency of disclosures is mainly of the kind that explains which types of company show high scores and which type show low scores. It is an area of comparative international research that seems likely to continue while independent bodies are measuring disclosure scores across countries to evaluate the success of new regulations and recommendations.

Key points from the chapter:

- Transparency is a criterion applied in many commentaries on the quality of accounting disclosure, but there is no agreement on how it is defined or evaluated.

- Narrative reporting in the USA is highly regulated through SEC requirements but this sets a benchmark against which other countries are evaluated.

- Management reports have an established tradition in some countries; in others they are recent additions to the disclosure package. Regulation varies from statutory control, with flexible interpretation, to voluntary disclosure under guidance or codes.

- Corporate social responsibility reports have become increasingly common sections within the annual report, rather than being stand-alone documents available to interested parties. At the extreme, companies are beginning to restructure the entire annual report in the framework of CSR reporting.

- Remuneration reports, as part of corporate governance reporting, provide information that allows users to evaluate the effectiveness of company managers. They also provide researchers with information on management compensation that can be used in investigations linking accounting information to managerial performance (and vice versa).

- Comparative research into disclosure continues to be an active area of investigation, with more emphasis on the narrative disclosures. Some papers focus on using transparency scores created by organizations monitoring corporate reports, while others apply or create tailored scores to meet specific research aims.

Questions

The following questions test your understanding of the material contained in the chapter and allow you to relate your understanding to the learning outcomes specified at the start of this chapter. The learning outcomes are repeated here. Each question is cross-referenced to the relevant section of the chapter.

Explain the problems of defining 'transparency' in disclosure

1 What does 'transparency' mean? (section 4.2)

2 Why might a regulator's definition of 'transparency' differ from that of (a) a preparer of accounts; (b) an academic researcher? (section 4.2)

Explain the requirements of narrative reporting in the USA

3 What is the purpose of the MD&A in US annual reporting? (section 4.3.1)

4 What are the main contents of the MD&A? (section 4.3.1)

5 Why is market risk disclosure regarded as important by the SEC? (section 4.3.2)

6 What are the problems for companies in reporting forward-looking information? (section 4.3.3)

7 What are the benefits and problems of 'non-GAAP' pro-forma financial statements? (section 4.3.4)

8 How is internal control over financial reporting achieved and described to shareholders? (section 4.3.5)

Explain how management reports are produced outside the USA

9 What does the EU Modernisation Directive recommend about management reports? (section 4.4.1)

10 What is the evidence from specific countries that suggests diversity in reporting will continue to be seen in management reports? (sections 4.4.2 to 4.4.6)

Explain and evaluate the initiatives being taken on developing CSR reports

11 Why are different forms of CSR found in the annual reports of different companies? (section 4.5.1)

12 What has been shown by comparative research studies of economic and social disclosures? (section 4.5.2)

13 Is CSR reporting likely to be effective in achieving the aim of improving CSR? (section 4.5.3)

Explain the nature and evaluate the usefulness of remuneration reports

14 Why are remuneration reports seen as an important item for inclusion in corporate annual reports? (section 4.6)

15 What kind of information is contained in remuneration reports? (section 4.6)

Explain and contrast methods used to carry out research into disclosure

16 How do published surveys help in the design of academic research into transparency and disclosure? (section 4.7.1)

17 What are the limitations of using published surveys in academic research? (section 4.7.1)

18 What are the benefits and limitations of using a purpose-designed disclosure checklist in academic research? (section 4.7.2)

19 What are the benefits and limitations of selecting a specific item of disclosure for comparative study in academic research? (section 4.7.3)

References and further reading

Adams, C.A.A. and Kuasirikun, N. (2000) 'A comparative analysis of corporate reporting on ethical issues by UK and German chemical and pharmaceutical companies', *European Accounting Review*, 9(1): 53–79.

Alexander, D. and Archer, S. (2000) 'On the myth of Anglo-Saxon financial accounting', *International Journal of Accounting*, 33(4): 539–557.

Archambault, J.J. and Archambault, M.E. (2003) 'A multinational test of determinants of corporate disclosure', *International Journal of Accounting*, 38: 173–194.

ASB (1993) *Operating and Financial Review*, Statement issued by the Accounting Standards Board, UK.

ASB (2003) *Operating and Financial Review*, Statement issued by the Accounting Standards Board, UK.

ASB (2005) *Reporting Standard 1: Operating and Financial Review*, Accounting Standards Board, UK. Issued May 2005, withdrawn January 2006.

ASB (2006) *Reporting statement: Operating and Financial Review*, Accounting Standards Board, UK. Issued January 2006.

Ball, R., Kothari, S.P. and Robin, A. (2000) 'The effect of international institutional factors on properties of accounting earnings', *Journal of Accounting and Economics*, 29: 1–52.

Beattie, V.A. and Jones, M.J. (2000) 'Impression management: the case of inter-country financial graphs', *Journal of International Accounting, Auditing and Taxation*, 9(2): 159–183.

Beattie, V. and Pratt, K. (2002) *Voluntary annual report disclosures: what users want*. The Institute of Chartered Accountants of Scotland, 107 pp., www.icas.org.uk.

Bebbington, J., Gray, R. and Larrinaga, C. (2000) 'Editorial: environmental and social accounting in Europe', *European Accounting Review*, 9(1): 3–6.

Bushman, R.M., Piotroski, J.D. and Smith, A.J. (2004) 'What determines corporate transparency?', *Journal of Accounting Research*, 42(2): 207–251.

Chau, G.K. and Gray, S.J. (2002) 'Ownership structure and corporate voluntary disclosure in Hong Kong and Singapore', *International Journal of Accounting*, 37: 247–265.

CICA (2004) *Improving Transparency and Accountability: CEO and CFO Certification*, A Canadian Performance Reporting Board Discussion Brief, The Canadian Performance Reporting (CPR) Board of the Canadian Institute of Chartered Accountants.

Combes-Thuélin, E., Henneron, S. and Touron, P. (2006) 'Risk regulations and financial disclosure: an investigation based on corporate communication in French traded companies', *Corporate Communications: An International Journal*, 11(3): 303–326.

Core, J.E. (2001) 'A review of the empirical disclosure literature: discussion', *Journal of Accounting and Economics*, 31: 441–456.

EC (2003) Directive 2003/51/EC of the European Parliament and of the Council of 18 June 2003.

Frost, C.A. (2003) *Disclosure Survey 2003*, World Federation of Exchanges, www.world-exchanges.org.

Goyder, M. (2003) *Redefining CSR: From the rhetoric of accountability to the reality of earning trust*, Tomorrow's Company, www.tomorrowscompany.com.

Gray, S.J. (1988) 'Towards a theory of cultural influence on the development of accounting systems internationally', *Abacus*, 24(1): 1–15.

Gray, S.J., Meek, G.K. and Roberts, C.B. (1995) 'International capital market pressures and voluntary annual report disclosures by US and UK multinationals', *Journal of International Financial Management and Accounting*, 6(1): 43–68.

Healy, P.M. and Palepu, K.G. (2001) 'Information asymmetry, corporate disclosure, and the capital markets: a review of the empirical disclosure literature', *Journal of Accounting and Economics*, 31: 405–440.

Holland, L. and Boon Foo, Y. (2003) 'Differences in environmental reporting practices in the UK and the US: the legal and regulatory context', *British Accounting Review*, 35(1): 1–18.

Hope, O.-K. (2003) 'Firm-level disclosures and the relative roles of culture and legal origin', *Journal of International Financial Management and Accounting*, 14(3): 218–248.

IASB (2006) *Discussion Paper Preliminary Views on an improved Conceptual Framework for Financial Reporting: The Objective of Financial Reporting and Qualitative Characteristics of Decision-useful Financial Reporting Information*. International Accounting Standards Board/Financial Accounting Standards Board.

Khanna, T., Palepu, K.G. and Srinivasan, S. (2004) 'Disclosure practices of foreign companies interacting with US markets', *Journal of Accounting Research*, 42(2): 475–508.

La Porta, R., Lopez-de-Silanes, F. and Shleifer, A. (1998) 'Law and finance', *Journal of Political Economy*, 106(6): 1113–1155.

Martin, R.D. (2000) 'Going-concern uncertainty disclosures and conditions: a comparison of French, German and US practices', *Journal of International Accounting, Auditing and Taxation*, 9(2): 137–158.

Meek, G.K., Roberts, C.B. and Gray, S.J. (1995) 'Factors influencing voluntary annual report disclosures by US, UK and continental European multinational corporations', *Journal of International Business Studies*, Third Quarter: 555–572.

Miller, G.S. (2004) 'Discussion of "What determines corporate transparency?"', *Journal of Accounting Research*, 42(2): 253–268.

Newson, M. and Deegan, C. (2002) 'Global expectations and their association with corporate social disclosure practices in Australia, Singapore and South Korea', *International Journal of Accounting*, 37: 183–213.

Ordelheide, D. and KPMG (eds) (2001) *Transnational Accounting*, 2nd edn. Basingstoke: Palgrave.

Parker, R.H. (2001) 'European languages of account', *European Accounting Review*, 10(1): 133–147.

Robb, S.W.G., Single, L.E. and Zarzeski, M.T. (2001) 'Nonfinancial disclosures across Anglo-American countries', *Journal of International Accounting, Auditing and Taxation*, 10: 71–83.

Rutherford, B.A. (2003) *Half the Story: Progress and Prospects for the Operating and Financial Review*. ACCA Research Report No. 80, Association of Chartered Certified Accountants, www.accaglobal.com.

S&P (2002) Transparency and Disclosure: overview of methodology and study results – United States, http://pages.stern.nyu.edu/~adamodar/pdfiles/articles/S&Pdisclosure.pdf.

S&P (2003) Transparency and Disclosure Study: Europe (April 2003).

S&P (2007) Corporate Governance: Turkish *Transparency* and Disclosure Survey 2007, http://www2.standardandpoors.com/.

Salter, S.B. and Niswander, F. (1995) 'Cultural influence on the development of accounting systems internationally: a test of Gray's [1988] theory', *Journal of International Business Studies*, 26(2): 379–398.

Vanstraelen, A., Zarzeski, M. and Robb, S.W.G. (2003) 'Corporate nonfinancial disclosure practices and financial analyst forecast abilities across three European countries', *Journal of International Management and Accounting*, 14(3): 249–278.

5 Choices in global accounting

Learning outcomes

After reading this chapter you should be able to discuss the scope for choice within IFRS and the likely effect of the IFRS/US GAAP convergence process in each of the following topics:

● Presentation of financial statements

● Fair value measurement

● Defining a group

● Acquisitions and uniting of interests

● Goodwill on acquisition

● Associates and joint ventures

● Segmental reporting

● Foreign currency translation.

5.1 Introduction

The increasing adoption of IFRS as the global basis for harmonized accounting practices does not remove all scope for choice in the preparation of financial statements. The apparent standardization of the accounting rules may give a false sense of comparability when the underlying economic stories are different. In particular the interpretation of financial statements of multinational companies may require careful attention to potential underlying differences. Multinational means 'many countries', reflecting the wide geographical spread of companies within a group entity. When reading consolidated financial statements it is important to be aware of the benefits and limitations of the apparent harmonization of accounting information under IFRS.

This chapter considers particular challenges to users in making cross-country comparisons and to preparers in multinational groups of companies in making choices where there may be underlying differences in institutional characteristics and accounting cultures. These aspects of continuing choice within IFRS reflect areas of accounting which have been the matter of much debate over many years. The chapter also describes some of the initiatives recently completed or in process to achieve convergence of IFRS and US GAAP in the short term and in the longer term.

We discuss first the general issues of choice in presentation (section 5.2) and fair value measurement (5.3). We then explain some of the particular problems in business combinations – the definition of a group (section 5.4), acquisition and uniting of interests (section 5.5), goodwill on acquisition (section 5.6) and associates and joint ventures (section 5.7). Segmental reporting (section 5.8) and foreign currency translation (section 5.9) follow and we conclude with research into accounting choices (section 5.10).

5.2 Presentation of financial statements

5.2.1 Flexibility with IAS 1[1]

IAS 1 *Presentation of Financial Statements* was revised for the convergence project at the end of 2003 and was subsequently revised further in 2007 with the changes to take effect from 2009. IAS 1 sets out a framework for presentation but does not give the detailed guidance found in some national accounting codes (see for example the Appendix to Chapter 12). IAS 1 therefore allows considerable flexibility of presentation. Flexibility is helpful to reporting entities in making their financial statements relevant to the needs of users but may be unhelpful to users in reducing comparability. There has been particular criticism of the failure of IAS 1 to insist on companies reporting their profit on operating activities as a line item in the income statement. The IASB's explanation[2] is that 'operating activities' are not defined in the standard and the IASB decided not to require disclosure of an undefined item.

5.2.2 Convergence

The revision of IAS 1 in December 2003 brought to wider usage some terminology previously identified with US financial statements. However, some aspects of financial statements prepared in compliance with IAS 1 still looked unfamiliar to a US-oriented readership. As part of the short-term convergence project 2006–08 the FASB and IASB jointly undertook a project to establish a common, high-quality standard for presentation of information in the financial statements. Specific issues considered were:

- identifying what constitutes a complete set of financial statements;
- the use of totals and subtotals, particularly in relation to reporting net income/profit and loss but also in relation to categories such as business and financing;
- the use of disclosure in notes to the financial statements where an objective cannot be achieved on the face of the financial statement;
- developing principles for aggregating and disaggregating information in each financial statement;
- deciding whether components of other comprehensive income/other recognized income and expense should be recycled to profit or loss and, if so, the characteristics of the transactions and events that should be recycled and when recycling should occur;
- considering FASB Statement No. 95, *Statement of Cash Flows*, and IAS 7, *Cash Flow Statements*, including whether to require the use of the direct or indirect method.

---

[1] IAS 1 (2007) *Presentation of Financial Statements*.

[2] IAS 1 (2003) para. BC 12; IAS 1 (2007 revision) para. BC55.

'Recycling' occurs when a previously unrealized gain or loss which has been reported in the statement of changes in equity becomes realized. For example, a property asset has been revalued each year and the gain recorded in the statement of changes in equity. The asset is sold and management calculate the gain by comparing the selling price with the historical cost book value. In some countries it has been the practice to report the full gain in the income statement, thus recycling the unrealized gains through the income statement. In other countries it has been argued that if the gain was reported as unrealized, it cannot be reported again as realized.

The revised IAS 1 was issued in 2007 to take effect for accounting periods starting on or after 1 January 2009. Key changes were:

- The title 'balance sheet' is replaced by 'statement of financial position'.
- The title 'cash flow statement' is replaced by 'statement of cash flows'.

These titles are seen as more closely representing the function of the respective financial statements:

- Comparative information is required in respect of the previous period but a statement of financial position at the start of the comparative period is only required when there is a retrospective change of accounting policy, restatement or reclassification.

This was a compromise from the exposure draft, which proposed an opening statement of financial position at the start of the previous year on every occasion (i.e. three 'balance sheet' columns on one financial statement):

- All changes in equity arising from transactions with owners in their capacity as owners to be presented separately from non-owner changes in equity.
- Income and expenses to be presented in one statement (a statement of comprehensive income) or in two statements (a separate income statement and a statement of comprehensive income).
- Components of other comprehensive income to be displayed in the statement of comprehensive income.
- Total comprehensive income to be presented in the financial statements.

This specification of the reporting of comprehensive income reflects the balance of a desire to reduce the flexibility of the previous version of IAS 1 and the strong preference of respondents in the consultation to retain the income statement as a means of reporting 'profit'. The IASB would prefer a single statement of comprehensive income and four members of the IASB explicitly disagreed with permitting a separate income statement. IAS 1 does not define 'profit'. It seems likely that the IASB will try again for a single statement of comprehensive income when it takes its project on financial statement presentation to a further stage.

As an example of the detail of convergence between 2003 and 2007, under IAS 1 (2003) the IASB used the title 'statement of recognized income and expense' to describe changes in equity other than those arising from transactions with equity holders. The IASB has decided to change this description to 'statement of comprehensive income' to converge with the US terminology. However, the IASB also emphasizes that no titles are prescribed.[3] Entities may still make choices.

---

[3] IAS 1 (2007) para. 8.

5.2.3 Continuing variation

The plan for the convergence project on financial statement presentation acknowledged that there are aspects of financial reporting that were not addressed in the project. These include:

- Management discussion and analysis or management commentary
- Pro-forma measures
- Segment reporting requirements
- Financial ratios (except earnings per share (EPS) and other per-share amounts)
- Forecasts of information
- Non-financial ratios or other non-financial information
- Financial statements for specific industries

In all the items listed there remains considerable scope for international differences, as discussed in Chapter 4.

5.3 Fair value measurement

5.3.1 Debate over definition

Two definitions of 'fair value' are set out in Exhibit 5.1. The first is a definition that has been used for some years in international financial reporting standards. The second is a definition produced relatively recently by the FASB in the USA. What do you see as the differences between them?

There are differences in the detail of the wording but from a measurement perspective the most interesting difference is that the focus of the US definition is on the position of the *seller* and therefore fair value is equated with the theoretical idea of 'exit value'.[4] Debates on accounting valuation methods go back a long way. Some have said that exit value is useful because it links to the idea of opportunities foregone – 'if we sold this asset, what could we do with the proceeds?' It is also a current value and so takes account of price inflation. Others have said that exit value is not useful because most businesses hold assets for use rather than for sale. The FASB claims that its definition removes subjectivity and takes the viewpoint of independent market participants.

Exhibit 5.1 Definitions of fair value

> **IASB definition of fair value**
> Fair value is the amount for which an asset could be exchanged, or a liability settled, between knowledgeable, willing parties in an arm's length transaction.
>
> (para. 9, IAS 39 *Financial Instruments: Recognition and Measurement* (IASB, 2007))
>
> **FASB definition of fair value**
> Fair value is the price that would be received to sell an asset or paid to transfer a liability in an orderly transaction between market participants at the measurement date.
>
> (para. 5, SFAS 157 *Fair Value Measurements*, No. 284-A, September 2006, http://fasb.org)

---

[4] King, A.M. (2007) 'What SFAS 157 does and does not accomplish', in Walton (2007).

The focus of the IASB definition is broader and could include 'entry price' (such as replacement cost) as well as 'exit price'. It gives the reporting entity more involvement in deciding what value it places on an asset or liability. However, it uses the complex notion of 'an arm's length transaction' which means that a willing buyer and willing seller, acting independently and not being in any close relationship, are able to meet together to agree a price.

5.3.2 Issues in international comparison

In some cultures the concept of an 'arm's length transaction' used in the IASB definition is not easy to put into practice. This is a problem that the FASB claims is removed in its focus on participants in a market.

However, the FASB definition does not suit all countries or economies because sometimes there is no market in existence. The FASB provides a list of steps to take (a 'hierarchy') in which the likely outcome of a market transaction may be estimated. These steps effectively reintroduce the idea of guessing at what is in the minds of hypothetical buyers and sellers.

The UK Accounting Standards Board (ASB) has expressed reservation about a total reliance on market-derived exit values as the representation of 'fair' value. The ASB is concerned about assets and liabilities for which no market exists. The ASB also questions the emphasis on the perspective of a market participant rather than that of the entity. It prefers to see the appropriate basis of fair value to be assessed for each accounting standard separately and that more prominence should be given to entity-specific measures.[5]

Issues to consider in making international comparisons of fair value measurements are:

- How has the reporting entity identified the market participants?
- How has the reporting entity selected a fair value from the options available? Is there a well-established market?
- If there is no market, what principles have been applied in determining a fair value?
- Has fair value been chosen where allowed for remeasurement?

5.3.3 Convergence

Fair value was one of the projects included in the *Roadmap for Convergence 2006–08*. In November 2006 the IASB issued a Discussion Paper, *Fair Value Measurements*, inviting comments to be submitted. The Discussion Paper included the text of SFAS 157 *Fair Value Measurement* as the basis for convergence of the definitions used in IFRS and SFAS. The IASB's intention was to establish a single source of guidance for all fair value measurements required by IFRS. It also wanted to clarify the definition of fair value and related guidance in order to communicate more clearly the measurement objective and enhance disclosures about fair value. Although the IASB repeatedly stated that it was not intending to change the meaning of 'fair value' or extend its application, some commentators felt that taking SFAS 157 as the starting point for discussion would impose the US preference for an exit value approach on a much wider international field.

---

[5] Macintosh, I. (2007) 'Standards board wary of total reliance on exit values', *Financial Times*, 10 May, p. 30.

Exhibit 5.2	Choice in the use of fair values

IAS 16 Property, Plant and Equipment. Initial recognition must be at cost (para. 15). Subsequent remeasurement may use the cost model (para. 30) or the revaluation model (para. 31). The model chosen must be applied to an entire class of property, plant and equipment. The revalued amount is the fair value at the date of the revaluation less any subsequent accumulated depreciation and subsequent accumulated impairment losses (para. 31).

IAS 38 Intangible Assets. An intangible asset must be measured initially at cost (para. 24). If an intangible asset is acquired in a business combination, the cost of that intangible asset is its fair value at the acquisition date (para. 33). Subsequent remeasurement may use the cost model (para. 74) or the revaluation model (para. 75), similar to IAS 16.

IAS 40 Investment Property. An investment property must be measured initially at its cost (para. 20). Subsequently the entity may choose either the fair value model (paras 33–55) or the the cost model (para. 56) and must apply that choice to all of its investment property.

IAS 41 Agriculture. A biological asset is measured on initial recognition and at each balance sheet date at its fair value less estimated point-of-sale costs (para. 10), except where the fair value cannot be measured reliably, when depreciated cost may be used (para. 30).

5.3.4 Continuing variation

Cairns (2007)[6] shows that while the use of fair value is required for initial measurement in some standards (such as IAS 39 and IAS 41), it is an option for subsequent remeasurement in most IFRS where it is used. The mandatory remeasurements are confined to financial assets and liabilities under IAS 39 and agricultural produce at the time of harvest under IAS 41. Fair value is also important in impairment testing. Cairns concludes that the use of fair value in IFRS financial statements is nowhere near as extensive as some critics imply. Exhibit 5.2 gives examples of choice in fair value, either at initial measurement or subsequent remeasurement.

Even when fair value must be used, there is judgement needed in arriving at a value. Exhibit 5.3 summarizes the guidance provided within IAS 41. In annual reports companies may decide to say relatively little about how they have made their choices.

5.4 Defining a group

5.4.1 Issues of definition

An economic entity is formed when a group of companies is brought together under arrangements involving ownership and control, in order to provide future benefits to the owners of the group. The arrangements usually mean that risks that are shared across all, or parts of, the group are ultimately borne by the owners of the group. Defining the membership of such an economic entity is not an easy task. Accordingly accounting resorts to identifying the economic entity through legal relationships. These legal relationships may define ownership, or they may establish contractual control. Further

---

[6] Cairns, D. (2007) 'The use of fair value in IFRS', in Walton (2007).

Exhibit 5.3 | **IAS 41 guidance on determining fair value**

> If an active market exists for a biological asset or agricultural produce, the quoted price in that market is the appropriate basis for determining the fair value of that asset. If an entity has access to different active markets, the entity uses the most relevant one. For example, if an entity has access to two active markets, it would use the price existing in the market expected to be used.[7]
>
> If an active market does not exist, an entity uses one or more of the following, when available, in determining fair value:
>
> - the most recent market transaction price, provided that there has not been a significant change in economic circumstances between the date of that transaction and the balance sheet date;
> - market prices for similar assets with adjustment to reflect differences; and
> - sector benchmarks such as the value of an orchard expressed per export tray, bushel or hectare, and the value of cattle expressed per kilogram of meat.[8]

problems follow where the law defines some of the relationships within an economic entity but is not designed to match the economic relationships precisely. The result is that some entities that ought to be included within the economic group are excluded by legal definitions, while some entities that are included by legal definition are not part of the economic substance and should possibly be excluded from the accounting procedures. Accounting standard setters then step in to propose a solution to such problems in order to establish comparability of treatment. The accounting standards seek to represent the economic entity but also want to maintain the objectivity that comes from using definitions based in law. Accounting standard setters are also aware of the problems that have arisen where company managers have used the precise wording of legal definitions to create or eliminate relationships in order to avoid reporting some part of the economic entity, perhaps because it would portray 'bad news' to investors or lenders.

5.4.2 IFRS

5.4.2.1 Parent and subsidiaries

A group of companies usually has a parent and subsidiaries. IFRS definitions of 'parent' and 'subsidiary' are given in Exhibit 5.4 which also defines the relationship of control that links the parent to the subsidiary. The definitions of control are built on a combination of 'power' and 'benefit'.

5.4.2.2 Special purpose entities

The 'special purpose entity' (SPE) is a particularly important aspect of defining a group because these SPEs have in previous times been created in some countries in order to avoid consolidation (sometimes referred to as 'off-balance-sheet finance', OBSF). Managerial motives for avoiding consolidation include concealing borrowing from shareholders and intending investors in order to give a better impression of gearing (leverage); concealing

---

[7] IAS 41 (2007) para. 17.
[8] IAS 41 (2007) para. 18.

| Exhibit 5.4 | Defining a group in IFRS |

A *group* is a parent and all its subsidiaries.[9]

Control is the power to govern the financial and operating policies of an entity so as to obtain benefits from its activities.[10]

A *parent* is an entity that has one or more subsidiaries.[11]

A *subsidiary* is an entity, including an unincorporated entity such as a partnership, that is controlled by another entity (known as the parent).[12]

Consolidated financial statements shall include *all subsidiaries* of the parent.[13]

Control is presumed to exist when the parent owns, directly or indirectly, more than half of the voting power of an entity.

Control also exists where the parent owns half or less than half of the voting power of an entity where there is:[14]

(a) power over more than half of the voting rights by virtue of an agreement with other investors;

(b) power to govern the financial and operating policies of the entity under a statute or an agreement;

(c) power to appoint or remove the majority of the members of the board of directors or equivalent governing body;

(d) power to cast the majority of votes at a meeting of the board of directors or equivalent governing body.

In addition to the situations described in IAS 27 (para. 13) the following circumstances may indicate a relationship in which an entity controls an *SPE (Special Purpose Entity)*:[15]

(a) in substance, the activities of the SPE are being conducted on behalf of the entity according to its specific business needs so that the entity obtains benefits from the SPE's operations; or

(b) in substance, the entity has the decision-making powers to obtain the majority of the benefits of the activities of the SPE; or

(c) in substance, the entity has the right to obtain the majority of the benefits of the SPE and therefore may be exposed to risks of the activities of the entity; or

(d) in substance, the entity retains the majority of the residual or ownership risks relating to the SPE.

losses in order to give a better impression of performance; concealing non-performing assets in order to give a better impression of performance; and avoiding reporting expenditure such as research and development in the group profit or loss. The benefits claimed by managers who create SPEs are that they package risks and rewards in a way that meets the requirements of particular investors or lenders and so reduce the cost of capital for the

---

[9] IAS 27 (2007) para. 4.

[10] Ibid.

[11] Ibid.

[12] Ibid.

[13] IAS 27 (2007) para. 12.

[14] IAS 27 (2007) para. 13.

[15] SIC-12 (2007) para. 10.

activity within the SPE. The essential message of SIC-12 is that if the parent obtains the benefits and carries the risks of the SPE, then the SPE should be consolidated.

5.4.2.3 Exclusions and exemptions

'Exclusion' means that some subsidiaries are omitted from the consolidated financial statements. 'Exemption' means that under specific conditions the parent company does not produce consolidated financial statements.

Exclusion from consolidation is a subject of debate in situations where the legal entity appears not to be a good representation of the economic entity. Managers tend to want to omit loss-making subsidiaries, or any subsidiary that reflects poorly on economic performance. That distorts the reported performance and position of the group. The IASB has gradually tightened up on exclusions, with its decision in March 2004 to remove from IAS 27 the previously permitted exclusion for temporary control. In most countries the law has allowed exclusions from consolidation on grounds such as:

- the activities of the subsidiary are sufficiently different from those of the rest of the group;
- there are severe long-term restrictions over the parent's rights;
- the subsidiary is held with a view to subsequent resale;
- obtaining the information required would involve disproportionate expense or undue delay;
- the subsidiaries are immaterial (separately or in aggregate).

When you read the accounting policies in consolidated financial statements you should look for the definition of the group to be sure that it is fully represented. If there are exclusions, look for the reasons given and consider the implications for the full accounting picture of performance and position.

Exemption is allowed by IFRS where the parent is wholly owned by another company or else the owners of the minority interest have been informed and do not object to the parent not presenting consolidated financial statements and the securities are not publicly traded. In all cases the exemption only applies if the ultimate parent publishes consolidated financial statements that comply with IFRS.[16]

5.4.2.4 Disclosures

IFRS 3 *Business Combinations* substantially increased the disclosures required about a business combination. The full list (paras 66 to 77) is too long to reproduce here but the principles provide a useful starting point. An acquirer must disclose information that enables users of its financial statements to evaluate the nature and financial effect of business combinations that took place during the period, or after the balance sheet date but before the financial statements were authorized for issue.[17] The acquirer must disclose information that enables users of its financial statements to evaluate the financial effects of gains, losses, error corrections and other adjustments recognized in the current period that relate to business combinations put in place in previous periods.[18] An entity must disclose information that enables users of its financial statements to evaluate changes in the carrying amount of goodwill during the period.[19]

---

[16] IAS 27 (2007) para. 10.
[17] IFRS 3 (2007) para. 66.
[18] IFRS 3 (2007) para. 72.
[19] IFRS 3 (2007) para. 74.

IAS 27 (paras 40–42) set out disclosure requirements for consolidated financial statements. These are primarily concerned with explaining the exceptions, such as reasons for not consolidating a subsidiary, and exclusions, such as the information expected when the parent elects not to prepare consolidated financial statements.

5.4.3 USA

We describe in Chapter 11 the history and current state of US definitions of a group. The approach to definition of a subsidiary differs from that of IFRS. In the USA a dual decision model is applied. All consolidation decisions should be evaluated under traditional consolidation models, focusing on majority voting interests, and under the relatively new 'variable interest' model. Variable interest entities (VIEs) are those in which the parent does not have a controlling voting interest but the parent absorbs the majority of the VIE's expected losses or returns. SPEs are tested for consolidation using the VIE tests. This idea of identifying VIEs emerged in the Sarbanes–Oxley Act, following the collapse of Enron, as explained in Chapter 11. However, even with the VIEs percentage-based tests of ownership continued to be applied to establish 'at risk' equity. An example of the impact of the Sarbanes–Oxley requirement for VIEs is seen in Sara Lee (Exhibit 5.5).

A description of FIN 46 (see 11.7.3.10) was shown by the Walt Disney Company in its annual report for 2003 (Exhibit 5.6). The company indicated that FIN 46 would change the balance sheet by fully consolidating two companies for which equity accounting was previously applied. It explained the change and gave a pro-forma balance sheet in the 'as adjusted' column.

| Exhibit 5.5 | Variable interest entities, Sara Lee |

Issued But Not Yet Effective Accounting Standards
Following is a discussion of recently issued accounting standards that the corporation will be required to adopt in a future period.

Consolidation of Variable Interest Entities
In January 2003, the FASB issued Interpretation No. 46, 'Consolidation of Variable Interest Entities, an Interpretation of Accounting Research Bulletin No. 51' (FIN 46). Prior to the effective date of FIN 46, an entity was generally included in the Consolidated Financial Statements if it was controlled through ownership of a majority voting interest. In FIN 46, the FASB concluded that the voting interest approach is not always effective in identifying controlling financial interest. In some arrangements, equity investors may not bear the residual economic risks, and in others, control is not exercised through voting shares.

FIN 46 provides guidance for determining whether an entity lacks sufficient equity or its equity holders lack adequate decision-making ability. These entities – variable interest entities (VIEs) – are evaluated for consolidation. Variable interests are ownership, contractual or other interests in a VIE that change with changes in the VIE's net assets. The party with the majority of the variability in gains or losses of the VIE is the VIE's primary beneficiary, and is required to consolidate the VIE.

The corporation was required to apply the provisions of FIN 46 to variable interests in VIEs created after January 31, 2003. Beginning in 2004, the corporation will be required to apply the provisions of FIN 46 to variable interests in VIEs created before February 1, 2003. The corporation does not believe that the provisions of FIN 46, when fully adopted in 2004, will have a material impact on its financial statements.

Source: Sara Lee Annual Report (2003), pp. 45–46, www.saralee.com.

| Exhibit 5.6 | Effect of FIN 46, Walt Disney Company |

Impact of FIN 46 on Equity Investments As discussed in Note 2, the implementation of FIN 46 will likely require the Company to consolidate both Euro Disney and Hong Kong Disneyland for financial reporting purposes in the first quarter of fiscal 2004. The following tables present consolidated results of operations and financial position for the Company as of and for the year ended September 30, 2003 as if Euro Disney and Hong Kong Disneyland had been consolidated based on our current analysis and understanding of FIN 46.

(all in million dollars)	As Reported	Euro Disney	Hong Kong Disneyland	Adjustments	As Adjusted
Results of Operations:					
Revenues	$ 27,061	$ 1,077	$ 5	$ (10)	$ 28,133
Cost and expenses	(24,330)	(1,032)	(7)	9	(25,360)
Amortization of intangibles assets	(18)	–	–	–	(18)
Gain on sale of business	16	–	–	–	16
Net interest expense	(793)	(101)	–	–	(894)
Equity in the income of investees	334	–	–	24	358
Restructuring and impairment charges	(16)	–	–	–	(16)
Income before income taxes, minority interest and the cumulative effect of accounting change	2,254	(56)	(2)	23	2,219
Income taxes	(789)	–	–	13	(776)
Minority interests	(127)	–	–	22	(105)
Cumulative effect of accounting change	(71)	–	–	–	(71)
Net income/(loss)	$ 1,267	$ (56)	$ (2)	$ 58	$ 1,267
Balance Sheet:					
Cash and cash equivalents	$ 1,583	$ 103	$ 76	$ –	$ 1,762
Other current assets	6,731	191	9	(9)	6,922
Total current assets	8,314	294	85	(9)	8,684
Investments	1,849	–	–	(623)	1,226
Fixed assets	12,678	2,951	524	–	16,153
Intangible assets	2,786	–	–	–	2,786
Goodwill	16,966	–	–	–	16,966
Other assets	7,395	128	9	–	7,532
Total assets	$ 49,988	$ 3,373	$618	$(632)	$ 53,347
Current portion of borrowings[1]	$ 2,457	$ 2,528	$ –	$(388)	$ 4,597
Other current liabilities	6,212	487	61	(35)	6,675
Total current liabilities	8,669	3,015	61	(473)	11,272
Borrowings	10,643	–	237	–	10,880
Deferred income taxes	2,712	–	–	–	2,712
Other long-term liabilities	3,745	289	–	(71)	3,963
Minority interests	428	–	–	301	729
Shareholders' equity	23,791	69	320	(389)	23,791
Total liabilities and shareholders' equity	$ 49,988	$ 3,373	$618	$(632)	$ 53,347

[1]All of Euro Disney's borrowings are classified as current as they are subject to acceleration if a long-term solution to Euro Disney's financing needs is not achieved by March 31, 2004.

Source: Walt Disney Annual Report (2003), www.disney.com/investors.

5.5 Acquisition and uniting of interests

The general term **business combination** may be applied to any transaction whereby one company becomes a subsidiary of another. The most common form of business combination is an **acquisition** (also called a **purchase**) where one of the combining entities obtains control over the other, enabling an acquirer to be identified. A **uniting of interests** occurs where it is not possible to identify an acquirer; instead the shareholders of the combining entities join in substantially equal arrangements to share control. A uniting of interests is called 'pooling of interests' in some countries and 'merger' in others.

The identification of a 'uniting of interests' has in the past allowed special accounting treatment. In particular the profit of both parties for the full year of a merger may be added together in the consolidated financial statements despite the merger taking place partway through the year. This special treatment has led groups to claim a uniting of interests when in reality there has been an acquisition. In some countries the accounting rules have allowed this ambiguity of treatment. Recent trends have been moving towards tightening the accounting rules for uniting of interests or else eliminating them entirely. However, there has been a longer debate over the treatment of 'entities under common control'.

5.5.1 Comparing acquisition with uniting of interests

This section gives a simplified comparison of the purchase (acquisition) method of accounting and uniting of interests accounting in order to bring out the key differences. A specialist textbook or manual should be consulted for further detail.

The examples are based on two companies, A and B, consolidating their separate balance sheets at the date of acquisition. Both cases involve an acquisition of A by B where the shareholders in B accept shares of A in exchange for their shares in B on a one-for-one basis. The share price of A is $2 and the share price of B is $2. The directors of A examine the fixed assets of B at the date of acquisition and decide that the fair value of these fixed assets is $10m greater than their recorded book value.

The acquisition method is shown in Exhibit 5.7. Column 1 records the cost of the investment to A as $120m, consisting of $60m nominal value and $60m share premium. Column 2 shows the recorded balance sheet of B. Column 3 shows the fair value adjustment increasing the fixed assets of B and the reserves of B. Column 4 shows the adjusted balance sheet of B. Column 5 shows the consolidation adjustment where the goodwill is calculated as the excess of the fair value of the consideration given, $120m, over the fair value of the net assets acquired, $100m. Column 6 shows the consolidated balance sheet of the group.

The consolidation worksheet for the uniting of interests method is shown in Exhibit 5.8. The principle applied in this approach is to create a balance sheet as it would appear if these two companies had always been united. In column A the cost of the investment in B is shown as $60m which is the nominal value of the shares issued. The share premium is not recorded because there would not be a share premium if they had always been united. The second column shows the recorded balance sheet of B. There is no fair value adjustment, again because there would not be such an adjustment if they had always been united. The consolidated balance sheet is therefore a direct addition of the two separate balance sheets, as if they had always been united.

Comparing Exhibit 5.7 and Exhibit 5.8 allows us to draw the following conclusions about acquisition accounting and uniting of interests accounting.

Exhibit 5.7 Illustrating the purchase (acquisition) method

	A $m	B $m	Fair value adjusted $m	B adjusted $m	Consol adjusted $m	Consolidated $m
	(1)	(2)	(3)	(4)	(5)	(6)
Goodwill					+20	20
Fixed assets	100	60	10	70		170
Investment in B	120				−120	–
Net current assets	20	30		30		50
Net assets	240	90	10	100	−100	240
Ordinary share capital	140	60		60	−60	140
Share premium	60					60
Fair value adjustment	–		10	10	−10	
Reserves of retained profit	40	30		30	−30	40
	240	90	10	100	−100	240

If the purchase method (acquisition accounting) has been used:

- There will probably be goodwill on consolidation which is recorded as an asset and subsequently amortized through the profit and loss account or subjected to an impairment test.
- There may be negative goodwill on consolidation which is immediately or subsequently released to the profit and loss account.
- Assets and liabilities of the subsidiary will be consolidated at their fair value at the date of acquisition.
- Where the acquisition takes place partway through an accounting period, a proportion of the subsidiary's profit or loss for the period will be included in the profit and loss account, representing only the period after the date of acquisition.

Exhibit 5.8 Illustrating the uniting of interests method

	A £m	B £m	Consol adjusted £m	Consolidated £m
Fixed assets	100	60		160
Investment in B	60		260	–
Net current assets	20	30	–	50
Net assets	180	90	260	210
Ordinary share capital	140	60	260	140
Reserves of retained profit	40	30	–	70
	180	90	260	210

If uniting of interests accounting has been used:

- There will be no goodwill or negative goodwill, and no subsequent impact on the profit and loss account.
- The assets and liabilities of the merging companies will be combined at recorded book value, not fair value.
- Where the acquisition takes place partway through an accounting period, the full amount of the subsidiary's profit or loss for the period will be included in the profit and loss account, regardless of the date of acquisition.

This comparison shows why some companies try to create the circumstances that allow uniting of interests accounting. It tends to produce higher profit and lower net assets in the year of acquisition, giving an apparently higher return on capital employed. In the longer term there is no amortization or impairment of goodwill, which continues the appearance of better performance.

5.5.2 IFRS

The IASB made significant changes to its previous standards when it issued IFRS 3 *Business Combinations* in March 2004.

5.5.2.1 Prohibiting 'uniting of interests' accounting

Previously IAS 22 had permitted both the purchase method and the pooling of interests method. Although it restricted the pooling of interests method to combinations that met the test of 'uniting of interests', there was a lack of comparability because transactions were deliberately structured to match the accounting rules and the methods produced quite different results. Once the USA and Canada had changed their rules to prohibit pooling of interests accounting, joining Australia which already prohibited it, the IASB decided to converge with the standards in these countries.[20]

Basic definitions from IFRS 3 are set out in Exhibit 5.9.

Exhibit 5.9   Business combination definitions[21]

- *Business combination*. Bringing together separate entities or businesses into one reporting entity.
- *Acquisition date*. The date on which an acquirer effectively obtains control of the acquiree.
- *Fair value*. The amount for which an asset could be exchanged, or a liability settled, between knowledgeable, willing parties in an arm's length transaction.
- *Goodwill*. Future economic benefits arising from assets that are not capable of being individually identified and separately recognized.
- Where shares are issued as 'consideration' (the price paid) for the acquisition, they are recorded at their fair value at the date of the exchange. In an active market the published price of a share at the date of exchange is the best evidence of fair value.[22]

---

[20] IFRS 3 (2007) IN3.

[21] IFRS 3 (2007) Appendix A.

[22] IFRS 3 (2007) para. 24.

5.5.2.2 Provisions for restructuring

In allocating the cost of the combination, the acquirer recognizes only the identifiable assets, liabilities and contingent liabilities of the acquiree that existed at the date of acquisition. If the acquiree has a liability for restructuring which already exists at the date of acquisition, that is recognized in allocating the cost of acquisition. The acquirer must not recognize liabilities for future losses or other costs expected to be incurred as a result of the business combination.

This was a significant change in IFRS 3, compared with previous international accounting standards. It is discussed in the 'Basis of Conclusions' to IFRS 3, paras BC 74–87. In particular, para. BC 80 notes that the price paid by the acquirer will take account of future costs arising from the acquisition. To make a provision for such costs at the date of acquisition would be double counting. Paragraph BC 87 confirms that there was majority support for this change among the respondents to the exposure draft ED3.

The scenario set out in Exhibit 5.10 shows the potential for creative accounting and income smoothing by the use of provisions at the date of acquisition where these provisions take 'the acquirer's perspective'. This type of flexibility has been curtailed by IFRS 3. In this particular case the acquirer, Over, would not be permitted under IFRS 3 to make the provision because it was not a liability of the acquiree at the date of the acquisition.

5.5.2.3 Minority interests on acquisition

Because the acquirer recognizes the acquiree's identifiable assets, liabilities and contingent liabilities at their fair values at the date of acquisition, any minority interest in the acquiree is stated at the minority's portion of the net fair value of those items.[23] Practical examples are relatively rare because many acquisitions involve 100 per cent of the target company's shares. Exhibit 5.11 shows how a South African company, SABMiller, reported the acquisition of 60 per cent of an Italian subsidiary, reporting the minority interest at 40 per cent of fair value.

5.5.2.4 Businesses under common control

The IASB decided to defer the treatment of businesses under common control to Phase II of the Business Combinations project, along with mutual entities and entities brought together by contract alone. These appear to be the kinds of organization for which 'uniting of interests' would be an appropriate treatment. However, the IASB felt that if this were allowed there would be cases where acquisitions would be restructured to appear to be combinations under common control to avoid purchase method accounting. There is an argument for applying 'fresh start' accounting to such 'true mergers'. Fresh start requires the revaluation of all the assets of the combining entities at the date of the combination. It has also been called the 'new entity method' in the debate leading to IFRS 3. In a dissenting view on IFRS 3 one member of the IASB felt that the 'fresh start' method should have been available for some of the former 'uniting of interests' cases rather than forcing the identification of an acquirer.[24]

---

[23] IFRS 3 (2007) para. 40.
[24] IFRS 3 (2007) BC 24–8, DO 1–6.

Exhibit 5.10	Provision for restructuring

Provision for restructuring

At the start of Year 1 the entire share capital of Under Inc. was acquired by Over Inc. The recorded net assets of Under were £260m and the price paid for the acquisition was £320m.

The directors of Over were satisfied that the recorded book values of fixed and current assets were equivalent to fair values, but they decided, prior to acquisition, that restructuring would probably be necessary. On the date of acquisition they held a board meeting to confirm their plans. During the following week they signed contracts for building work and issued the necessary warnings to staff where relocation would take place. There was no doubt about the commitment of Over to carry out the reorganization but there was a long debate about the likely cost. The finance director asked for a conservative approach and estimated a total cost of £30m over three years. The personnel director was optimistic about staff flexibility and suggested that £21m over three years would be sufficient. The board decided to take the advice of the finance director on grounds of prudence.

At the date of acquisition the goodwill was calculated as follows:

	£m	£m
Price paid for subsidiary		320
Recorded net assets acquired, at fair value	260	
Less provision for reorganization	(30)	
Net fair value		230
Consolidation adjustment: goodwill		90

Note that the provision caused the goodwill figure to be higher than it would have been based on recorded net assets alone.

If the finance director has estimated correctly, then in each of the three subsequent years there will be a cost of £10m for reorganization. This can be matched against the provision of £30m which will reduce to £20m at the end of Year 1, £10m at the end of Year 2 and nil at the end of Year 3. The profit and loss account in those years will not be encumbered by costs of reorganization.

However, supposing the personnel director estimated correctly, each year there will be a cost of £7m rather than the expected cost of £10m. This means that each year there is an unused provision of £3m which could be returned to enhance the appearance of the profit and loss account. IFRS 3 does not permit this creative accounting.

5.5.3 USA

The USA is in agreement with IFRS on prohibiting 'uniting of interests' accounting but differs in the treatment of provisions for restructuring and in the method of measuring and reporting minority interests.

5.5.3.1 Prohibiting 'uniting of interests' accounting

We will explain in section 11.3.4 the controversy in the USA that surrounded the FASB's decision to prohibit the 'pooling of interests' method of accounting (called 'uniting of interests' in IFRS). SFAS 141 *Business Combinations* allows only the purchase method of accounting. One aspect of the objections lay in the concern that the purchase method involves applying fair values to the acquiree's assets and liabilities and then charging

Exhibit 5.11	Fair value and minority interest, SABMiller

29. Acquisitions and disposals

Birra Peroni SpA

The acquisition of a 60 per cent interest in Birra Peroni SpA (Peroni), the number two brewer in Italy, with options to increase the holding in the future, was completed on 4 June 2003, although control passed to SAB-Miller on 21 May 2003 when the SABMiller appointed directors assumed control of the business. Consequently, the business has been accounted for from 21 May 2003. The acquisition was funded in cash from existing resources.

Put and call option arrangements exist between the group and the remaining Birra Peroni minority share-holders which, if exercised, will result in the group's interest increasing to 99.36 per cent over a three to six-year period. The price payable in relation to these options is based on the equity value of Birra Peroni together with earn-out arrangements dependent on the future domestic and international performance of Birra Peroni.

The fair values of the assets and liabilities acquired, which are considered to be provisional as a number of matters are still under consideration, were as follows:

	Book value US$m	Fair value adjustments US$m	Provisional fair value US$m
Tangible fixed assets	224	(10)[1]	214
Intangible assets	33	(33)[2]	–
Investments in associates	2	(2)[3]	–
Other fixed asset investments	17	(1)[4]	16
Stock	71	(4)[6]	67
Debtors	217	(25)[6]	192
Cash and cash equivalents	14	–	14
Creditors – amount falling due within one year	(348)	(3)[7]	(351)
Creditors – amounts falling due after one year	(95)	–	(95)
Provisions for liabilities and charges	(22)	(6)[8]	(28)
	113	(84)	29
Equity minority interests	(49)	36[9]	(13)
Net assets acquired	6	(48)	16
Goodwill			283
Consideration – all cash			299

In accordance with the group's accounting policy, the goodwill of US$283 million arising on consolidation has been stated in the group's balance sheet as an intangible asset.

Source: SABMiller Annual Report (2004), p. 95, www.sabmiller.com.

amortization of the asset of goodwill. Fair values and goodwill do not appear in uniting of interests. The parallel development of SFAS 142 allowed companies to use an impairment test on goodwill rather than amortize for up to 40 years. This softened the blow to the reported profit of implementing SFAS 141.

5.5.3.2 Provisions for restructuring

At the date of the acquisition, management must begin to assess and formulate a plan to close down or reorganize a part of the acquired entity. The plan must be completed as soon as possible, but no longer than 12 months from the date of the acquisition. Management must then communicate the termination or relocation plans to the employees of the acquired company. The restructuring provision can then be recorded in fair value at the date of acquisition, if it meets the definition of a liability. In the case study of Exhibit 5.10, the provision would probably be allowed. The guidance would not necessarily help in choosing between the two different proposals for the amount of the provision.

5.5.3.3 Minority interest

The US treatment of minority interest was not prescribed in the standards but the usual treatment was to calculate the minority's percentage of share capital and reserves at the book value of the acquiree, without including any fair value adjustment. There was no clear position in the balance sheet for reporting minority interest. Some companies did not regard it as part of the equity interest and reported it between the liability section and the stockholders' equity section. This is described as the **parent company theory**. Other companies reported minority interest as part of the stockholders' equity section. This is described as the **entity theory**. The treatment of minority interests was a topic for Phase II of the Business Combinations project for convergence between IFRS and FASB on purchase accounting, leading to revision of IFRS 3 and IAS 27 by the end of 2007.

The outcome of the discussion in Phase II was that 'minority interests' in IAS 27 became renamed 'controlling interests'. The FASB decided to report non-controlling interests within equity. IAS 27 already reported minority interests within equity.

To achieve convergence on non-controlling interests, the FASB has undertaken a project to review and revise the contents of Accounting Research Bulletin No. 51, *Consolidated Financial Statements*. The IASB has undertaken a project to amend IAS 27.

5.6 Goodwill

5.6.1 Questions about goodwill

Goodwill arising on acquisition is essentially an arithmetic difference. It is the description given to the difference between the fair value of the payment for a subsidiary and the fair value of the net assets acquired. The directors of an acquirer which offers more than the fair value of the net assets acquired must be seeing some value in the target in terms of future earnings potential and growth. It is described in IFRS 3 as 'future economic benefits arising from assets that are not capable of being individually identified and separately recognized'. Goodwill has the characteristic of an asset in the expectation of future benefit but it is different from any other asset because it is not separable from the business. The term 'goodwill' has been applied in Anglo-American terminology. In some countries it is described as a 'difference on consolidation'. Questions about the measurement of goodwill include the following:

● How is goodwill measured at the date of acquisition?
● How is goodwill measured subsequent to the date of acquisition?
● How is negative goodwill treated?

5.6.2 IFRS

The answers to the three questions about goodwill measurement are given in Exhibit 5.12.

Exhibit 5.12	Treatment of goodwill and negative goodwill, IFRS

How is goodwill measured at the date of acquisition?

The acquirer initially measures goodwill at its cost, being the excess of the cost of the business combination over the acquirer's interest in the net fair value of the identifiable assets, liabilities and contingent liabilities recognized according to the procedures set out in IFRS 3.[25]

How is goodwill measured subsequent to the date of acquisition?

After initial recognition the acquirer shall measure goodwill acquired in a business combination at cost less any accumulated losses.[26] Goodwill acquired in a business combination is not amortized. It is tested annually for impairment in accordance with IAS 36 *Impairment of Assets*.[27]

How is negative goodwill treated?

If the goodwill is negative then the acquirer shall:

(a) reassess the identification and measurement of the acquiree's identifiable assets, liabilities and contingent liabilities and the measurement of the cost of the combination; and

(b) recognize immediately in profit or loss any excess remaining after that assessment.[28]

5.6.3 USA

The initial measurement of goodwill and the subsequent annual impairment test are applied in the USA under FAS 141 and 142 in a manner consistent with that required by IFRS 3.

Negative goodwill is initially allocated on a 'pro rata' basis against the carrying amounts of certain acquired non-financial assets. If, after reducing these assets to zero, an excess of negative goodwill remains, the excess is recognized as an extraordinary gain.[29] Under the convergence project, FASB is considering whether to move to the IASB model for negative goodwill.

5.7 Associates and joint ventures

The issues of interest here are the definition of associates and joint ventures, and the arguments for and against equity accounting, proportionate consolidation and full consolidation. This section first compares equity accounting and proportionate consolidation before moving to the IFRS definitions and some international comparisons. (Some national legislation uses the term 'proportional consolidation'; we use 'proportionate' throughout for consistency.)

---

[25] IFRS 3 (2007) para. 51.

[26] IFRS 3 (2007) para. 54.

[27] IFRS 3 (2007) para. 55.

[28] IFRS 3 (2007) para. 56.

[29] Williams and Carcello (2007), p. 4.08.

| Exhibit 5.13 | Balance sheets (Q Ltd treated as a trade investment) |

	P Co. $m	Q Ltd $m
Assets less current liabilities	45	120
Investment in Q Ltd	5	
Long-term loan	(20)	(80)
	30	40
Share capital	10	20
Retained profits (all post acquisition)	20	20
	30	40

5.7.1 Comparing equity accounting and proportionate consolidation

This section presents a simple example to show the difference between equity accounting and proportionate consolidation of the balance sheet. For more information it is necessary to consult a specialist text.

In the following example, P Co. owns 25 per cent of the ordinary share capital of Q Ltd. The investment cost $5m some years ago when the retained profits of Q Ltd were zero. Three other companies each own 25 per cent of Q Ltd. This is effectively a partnership of the four shareholders in owning Q Ltd. Exhibit 5.13 shows the balance sheet of P Co. reporting its investment in Q Ltd as a trade investment (i.e. applying the cost method). The balance sheet of Q Ltd is shown alongside.

We now compare the balance sheet of P Co. using equity accounting with its balance sheet using proportionate consolidation. Both are set out in Exhibit 5.14.

For the equity method of accounting the investment in Q Ltd is reported at the cost of the equity investment ($5m) plus the parent's share of reserves of retained profit accumulated since the date of acquisition (25 per cent of $20m). This is the reason for the description 'equity accounting'; in one line it shows the amount of the equity investment for the 25 per cent holding.

| Exhibit 5.14 | Group accounts, P Co. |

	Equity method Calculation	$m	$m	Proportionate consolidation Calculation
Assets less current liabilities		45	75	45 + (0.25% × 120)
Investment in Q Ltd	5 + 5	10		
Long-term loan		(20)	(40)	20 + (0.25% × 80)
		35	35	
Share capital		10	10	
Retained profits	(20 + 5)	25	25	
		35	35	
Debt/equity ratio		20/35	40/35	
		57%	114%	

Proportionate consolidation takes a totally different approach. It consolidates the parent's proportionate interest on each line of assets and liabilities on each. The usual consolidation adjustments are made to set the cost of the investment against the equity interest acquired.

The overall effect on equity is the same but it may be seen from the calculation of gearing (leverage) that proportionate consolidation reports a higher ratio and therefore gives a higher perception of financial risk. Equity accounting produces a single-line figure for net investment that sets assets against liabilities.

Equity accounting might be viewed as a means of keeping liabilities off the balance sheet. Imagine the situation where a group has a highly geared subsidiary. The group might reduce its reported gearing by setting up a company that avoids the legal definition of a subsidiary, while retaining significant influence. It could then move the trading activity of the former subsidiary to this new company. Application of equity accounting would allow the benefit of reporting a share of profit without the disadvantage of reporting the full extent of gearing.

5.7.2 IFRS

The relevant standards are IAS 28 *Investments in Associates* and IAS 31 *Interests in Joint Ventures*. Basic definitions are set out in Exhibit 5.15.

An investment in an associate must be accounted for using the equity method except where the investment is held for sale (see IFRS 5), or special conditions apply where the

| Exhibit 5.15 | Definitions of associate and joint venture |

- An *associate* is an entity, including an unincorporated entity such as a partnership, over which the investor has significant influence and that is neither a subsidiary nor an interest in a joint venture.[30]

- *Significant influence* is the power to participate in the financial and operating policy decisions of the investee but is not control or joint control over those policies.[31]

- The *equity method* is a method of accounting whereby the investment is initially recognized at cost and adjusted thereafter for the post-acquisition change in the investor's share of the net assets of the investee. The profit or loss of the investor includes the investor's share of the profit or loss of the investee.[32]

- A *joint venture* is a contractual arrangement whereby two or more parties undertake an economic activity that is subject to joint control.[33]

- *Joint control* is the contractually agreed sharing of control over an economic activity, and exists only when the strategic financial and operating decisions relating to the activity require the unanimous consent of the parties sharing control (the venturers).[34]

- A *venturer* is a party to a joint venture and has joint control over that joint venture.[35]

[30] IAS 28 (2007) para. 2.
[31] Ibid.
[32] Ibid.
[33] IAS 31 (2007) para. 3.
[34] Ibid.
[35] Ibid.

investing company has an ultimate parent company that is publishing financial statements that comply with IFRS.[36]

Joint control may apply to operations, assets or entities. In respect of its interests in jointly controlled operations, a venturer shall recognize in its financial statements the assets it controls and the liabilities that it incurs, the expenses that it incurs and its share of the income that it earns.[37] Similar treatment is applied to jointly controlled assets.[38] For a jointly controlled entity the venturer shall use proportionate consolidation[39] or the equity method.[40] Where proportionate consolidation is used the venturer may either combine the items line by line or have separate lines under each category of asset and liability.[41] It must not offset assets and liabilities.[42]

While the UK and USA have not permitted proportionate consolidation for joint ventures, it has been commonly used in some EU countries. Under the EU Seventh Directive (see Chapter 13), member states had the option to allow to use either approach. In some countries proportionate consolidation was widely used.[43] In France proportionate consolidation was compulsory for joint ventures prior to the move to IFRS.[44] The Netherlands allowed joint ventures the choice but most used proportionate consolidation.[45] Preserving this flexibility under IAS 31 was therefore a significant concession to established differences in accounting practices.

5.7.3 Convergence

The USA does not permit proportionate consolidation. Equity accounting is applied to associates and joint ventures.

At the end of 2005 the IASB agreed to consider accounting for interests in joint ventures within the short-term convergence project. The major difference between IAS 31 *Interests in Joint Ventures* and US GAAP was the option in IAS 31 of accounting for joint venture entities using proportionate consolidation. The IASB decided to remove the option of accounting for jointly controlled entities using proportionate consolidation. The change is expected to be introduced by IFRS in 2008.

5.8 | Segment reporting

Consolidated accounts are often the only sets of financial statements presented to users. The financial statements of the individual companies within a group may be available through a registration system but they are not readily accessible and are not publicized by companies. Consolidated financial statements have the benefit of bringing a large group down to a manageable size for reporting as a single entity. They have the disadvantage that

---

[36] IAS 28 (2007) para. 13.

[37] IAS 31 (2007) para. 15.

[38] IAS 31 (2007) para. 21.

[39] IAS 31 (2007) para. 30.

[40] IAS 31 (2007) para. 38.

[41] IAS 31 (2007) para. 34.

[42] IAS 31 (2007) para. 35.

[43] Ordelheide (2001), pp. 1383, 1409.

[44] Richard (2001), p. 1176.

[45] Klaassen (2001), pp. 2036–2037.

they lose the detail of the separate component parts of the group. An enthusiastic investor might decide to seek out and read the financial statements of all the companies in a group. However, that would be time consuming and there could be problems of gaining access to information about subsidiaries overseas from the parent. Segmental reporting is a half-way house in restoring the detail available in the separate financial statements, but with a selective approach that focuses on what users need.

5.8.1 What to look for in segment reporting

5.8.1.1 Evaluating performance

Obviously, there is no point in making companies disclose additional information if it does not tell users something new and of interest. One test therefore is to ask, 'Does segment information tell the user something that is not obvious from the group accounts?' The answer will depend upon the degree of diversification of the company. There would be little benefit in requiring a company to report line of industry data if it operated only in one industry or to report geographical data if it operated in only one country. But there would also be little point if it operated in several industries or countries that were very similar to each other so each segment resembles the other, or if it was so diversified that it resembled the entire world, so that it could not reduce its risk by changing its mix of operations. However, most companies fall somewhere between these two extremes, operating in a relatively small number of industries or countries with each industry or country varying in some important way(s) from the others. Different industries and countries are usually expected to perform differently. They have different profit potentials, growth opportunities and degrees of and types of risk, different rates of return on investment and different capital needs. For example, a company that operates in a fairly stable market with well-understood and relatively simple technology, such as food processing, would face relatively little risk and so should have lower but more stable profits than, for example, a biotechnology company which is dependent upon high levels of risky research and constantly changing, extremely complex and expensive technology. Therefore, the past performance of a company and its future prospects can usually only be understood in the context of information on the importance of each class of business and geographical area that the company operates in.

5.8.1.2 Relevance to stakeholders

The second test is to ask, 'Is this extra information of use?' Many users of financial accounts will be interested in the performance and prospects of one particular part of the company. For example, employees' security of employment, pay and conditions will generally be more directly dependent upon the performance of the specific division they work for than the performance of the whole group. Similarly, host governments will be primarily interested in the performance of that part of the group that is located in their countries. Customers, suppliers and creditors will be most interested in the subsidiary that they have contracted with. All of these users will therefore want disaggregated information. Segment information, while far from perfect, goes some way towards meeting these needs. Such information will be especially important for users such as trade unions and developing country host governments, which lack the power to demand the information they want.

Shareholders, in contrast, invest in a company as a whole and it is therefore the performance and prospects of the entire company that interest them. Investing in a diversified company is similar to investing in a unit trust (mutual fund) which in turns invests in a number of individual companies. Here, the investor is directly affected by the returns of the portfolio as a whole. However, knowledge of the individual stocks is important as it helps the investor assess the risks and likely returns of the portfolio as a whole and helps the investor judge whether or not that particular portfolio is suitable. Similarly, a single company may be thought of as a portfolio of segments. While the shareholder cannot invest in the individual segments, knowledge of the performance and prospects of the constituent parts helps the shareholder to understand the risk and returns of the group.

An investor will want to know many things about a company. One obvious question of interest to all investors should be the question of whether or not its past performance is satisfactory. There are many ways of tackling this question, but one place to start is to compare the company's performance with that of similar companies. Segment data may allow the user to compare the performance of individual segments with non-diversified companies or with segments of other diversified companies. An idea of the success of the entire company can then be built up from these individual segment assessments. Users may also be able to combine company-specific information with external information. This should help them to assess the future prospects of the company. For example, knowledge regarding the geographical sales of a company can be combined with knowledge of the growth prospects of particular countries or regions to aid in the more accurate prediction of future sales.[46]

5.8.1.3 Defining segments

To create segment reports, a company can break down its operations in any number of ways, although there should be some logical reason for the choices made. The two most common categories are segmentation by industry or type of business (often called line of business or LoB) and by geographical area (in terms of either location of operations or location of customers). If both categories are used then either two separate tables are required or a large table is used (a 'matrix') with one category running vertically and the other running horizontally. This requires very small print and soon overflows a page and so most groups have separate tables for each category of segmentation.

5.8.2 From IAS 14 to IFRS 8

This section describes the development of IAS 14 from an encouraging but somewhat flexible original version to a more precisely defined and extensive revision issued in 1997. It then describes the change to IFRS 8, to be applied to annual financial statements for periods beginning on or after 1 January 2009.

5.8.2.1 History of IAS 14[47]

The original version of IAS 14, issued in 1981, used geographical segments and industry segments but called for relatively little information on each. It required only segment sales (with internal and external sales shown separately), operating results and identifiable assets. This was supplemented by a reconciliation statement explaining the difference between the group results reported and the sum of the segment results when these

---

[46] See, for example, Herrmann (1996); Roberts (1989).
[47] See Introduction to IAS 14 (1997) IN1 to IN 14.

differed, plus information on the composition of each segment and the basis for determining the value of any inter-segment transfers.

The original IAS 14 received increasing amounts of criticisms over the years for three reasons. Firstly, the number of items of information disclosed was thought to be inadequate. Secondly, and more importantly, it contained relatively little guidance on either identifying a segment or measuring the items reported. In consequence, identical companies could have used discretion to produce very difference segments and very different numbers of segments.[48] Finally, it also ignored the internal structure of an enterprise. If the internal structure is not organized along a geographical and a line-of-business basis, it can sometimes be very expensive to produce the required information. Companies may even have to redesign information systems to the extent that the costs may outweigh the benefits. Indeed, it is not even clear that in all cases line-of-business and geographical segment information is going to be particularly useful. It might be that the enterprise is organized in a different way for very good and logical reasons and that reporting on this basis would also be more logical and useful.

These types of consideration led the IASC, in consultation with North American standard setters, to review its standard. The revised IAS 14 was issued in 1997. While it did not go as far as those of either the USA or Canada, it involved some substantial changes which changed both the method of identification of segments and the disclosure requirements. In particular it focused on the internal reporting system and the relative risks and returns as being the key features that distinguish segments.

5.8.2.2 Main requirements of IAS 14 (1997)

A **reportable segment** was defined as a business segment or a geographical segment.[49] One of these was the **primary segment** and the other was the **secondary segment**. The dominant source and nature of an entity's *risks and rewards* would determine which was primary and which was secondary.[50] The internal organization and management structure and the system of reporting to the board of directors and the chief executive officer were normally the basis for identifying the dominant source and nature of risks and rewards.[51] If the company's risks and returns were strongly affected by differences in both geographical areas and industries, then both types of segments were regarded as primary segments.[52]

A **business segment** was a distinguishable component of an entity engaged in providing an individual product or service or a group of related products or services. A **geographical segment** was a distinguishable component of an entity engaged in providing products or services within a particular economic environment. In both cases the segment was distinguished by risks and returns that were different from those of other business segments.[53] IAS 14 prescribed a series of disclosures for each primary segment and each secondary segment. The standard also prescribed that the *accounting policies* used for all items should be the same across all segments and should be the same as those used for external reporting.[54]

---

[48] See, for example, Gray and Radebaugh (1984); Street *et al.* (2000).

[49] IAS 14 (1997) para. 9.

[50] IAS 14 (1997) para. 26.

[51] Ibid.

[52] IAS 14 (1997) para. 29.

[53] IAS 14 (1997) para. 9.

[54] IAS 14 (1997) para. 44.

5.8.2.3 Problems of segment identification under IAS 14

If the operating divisions of a company were not suitable for segment reporting purposes it could often be difficult to decide exactly what the segments should be. Although IAS 14 set out fairly unambiguous disclosure rules, this was of little use if the company was left free to decide for itself if it had any reportable segments and, if so, how many and of what type. This problem could be compounded by the unwillingness of companies to disclose segment information for a variety of reasons. If the segments reported did not reflect the operating structure of the company and the information was not collected for internal purposes, it could be expensive to collect, collate, audit and disseminate. Alternatively, segment data might highlight particularly poor or good performance. Indeed, this question of the competitive disadvantage of reporting segment information has in the past been claimed to be a major problem by a significant number of companies.[55]

To limit the freedom of choice, IAS 14 gave detailed guidance on the identification of segments and also specified thresholds that triggered requirement for disclosure.

While IAS 14 provided what appeared to be quite specific guidance it was clear that segment identification was still very much left to the discretion of companies and the guidance offered was simply that – guidance and not rules. This meant that, perhaps inevitably, a company which wished to provide minimal disclosures, or 'good news' only, might manipulate its segment disclosures to achieve these objectives. However, the scope to manipulate disclosure was reduced as the standard also required the disclosure of the changes made, explaining the nature of the changes, the reasons for them and their effect[56] and revised comparative figures should be restated to reflect the changes.[57]

5.8.2.4 IFRS 8

It might be asked why a further revision was needed when IAS 14 had become so detailed and had improved the quality and amount of segmental reporting. The Basis for Conclusions to IFRS 8 explains that this was part of the short-term convergence project to reduce the differences between IFRS and US GAAP. The relevant US FASB standard is SFAS 131. The requirements of SFAS 131 are based on the way that management regard the entity. It is argued that the provision of information based on the structure of an entity's internal organization could enhance the user's ability to predict how management's actions would affect future cash flows.[58]

IFRS 8 is more relaxed than IAS 14 in the requirements for disclosure of information about segments. This led to a dissenting opinion from two members of the IASB. They felt that IFRS 8 should retain the rigorous requirements to disclose segment revenue, expense, assets and liabilities as required in IAS 14. The difference between IFRS 8 and IAS 14 is that under IFRS 8 the information reported for each segment is the measure reported to the chief operating decision maker for internal decision-making purposes. Thus information is only disclosed if the management system uses that information. A secretive approach to internal management will reduce the relative disclosure to external users. The role of risk and return as criteria for identifying segments does not appear in IFRS 8. Another concern with IFRS 8 is potential inconsistency in measurement. The basis of accounting will not necessarily be the same as that required by IFRS for external reporting.[59]

---

[55] Edwards and Smith (1996).

[56] IAS 14 (1997) paras 77–78.

[57] IAS 14 (1997) para. 79.

[58] IFRS 8 (2007) BC4–BC5.

[59] IFRS 8 (2007) paras 25–27.

The process of EU endorsement of IFRS 8 raised unexpected political problems which are discussed further in Chapter 13 (section 13.4.4).

5.8.3 USA

SFAS 131 also uses the 'management structure' approach for determining the primary segments. The primary segments may be defined by a combination of both geographical spread and line of business, or they may be defined on any other basis employed by the enterprise. SFAS 131 does not require consistent earnings or assets definitions or accounting methods across the primary segments. Instead, they must be based upon the accounting rules and definitions used for internal management purposes. However, the problem of lack of comparability within any one enterprise is reduced by the additional requirements to explain both differences in the measurement of segments and total profits or losses and assets, and differences in the allocations across segments. Companies must also disclose, where relevant, a reconciliation statement explaining the differences between segment and consolidated figures. The impact of using the management perspective is seen in Exhibit 5.16 where a change in the management structure brought together Eastern Europe and Greater Asia and combined Australia with the rest of Europe. It seems unlikely that a risk-based focus, such as that of IAS 14, would combine countries and subcontinents with significantly different economic risk profiles.

Appendix A to IFRS 8 contains information on how the FASB chose the approach taken in SFAS 131 and traces the discussions over several years on issues of segment definition and reporting.

5.8.4 Presentation of segment information

Nestlé in 2006, in a large table ('matrix presentation') spreading across two pages of the annual report, applies IAS 14, providing primary and secondary segments, but also indicates awareness of the US view by confirming that the primary segments reflect the

---

Exhibit 5.16 **Management perspective, Colgate-Palmolive**

Segment Results

Effective January 1, 2006, the Company modified the geographic reporting structure of its Oral, Personal and Home Care segment in order to address evolving markets and more closely align countries with similar consumer needs and retail trade structures. Management responsibility for Eastern European operations, including Russia, Turkey, Ukraine and Belarus, was transferred to Greater Asia management and responsibility for operations in the South Pacific, including Australia, was transferred to European management. The financial information for 2005 and 2004 has been reclassified to conform to the new reporting structure.

The Company markets its products in over 200 countries and territories throughout the world in two distinct business segments: Oral, Personal and Home Care; and Pet Nutrition. Management evaluates segment performance based on several factors, including Operating profit. The Company uses Operating profit as a measure of operating segment performance because it excludes the impact of corporate-driven decisions related to interest expense and income taxes.

Source: Annual Report (2006) Colgate-Palmolive, p. 21.

Exhibit 5.17 Segment disclosures, Nestlé

Segmental information

Segmental information is based on two segment formats: The primary segment format – by management responsibility and geographic area – reflects the Group's management structure. The Group manages its Food and Beverages business through three geographic Zones and globally for Nestlé Waters and Nestlé Nutrition. The Group's pharmaceuticals activities are also managed on a worldwide basis and are presented separately from Food and Beverages. The secondary segment format – by product group – is divided into six product groups (segments).

Source: Nestlé Annual Report (2006), Accounting Policies section, p. 13.

Primary Segments
Zone Europe
Zone Americas
Zone Asia, Oceania and Africa
Nestlé Waters
Nestlé Nutrition
Other Food and Beverages
Pharmaceuticals

Secondary Segments
Beverages
Milk products, Nutrition and Ice Cream
Prepared dishes and cooking aids
Chocolate, confectionery and biscuits
PetCare
Pharmaceutical products

Source: Nestlé Annual Report (2006), pp. 24–27, www.ir.nestle.com.

Group's management structure as well as geographic area (Exhibit 5.17). In the segment reporting tables, covering four pages, the reporting line items required by IAS 14 are listed vertically and the segments are listed across the page.

The Swiss company, Roche, also provides extensive IAS 14 disclosures in its 2006 annual report. The information on primary segments is provided by listing the line items down the table and the segments across two pages of the report. The information on secondary segments is provided by listing the geographical areas down the table and the items required by IAS 14 across the top. The accounting policy note for defining segments (Exhibit 5.18) refers first to risk and return and then explains that the management structure reflects the risk/return profile of the parts of the business.

5.8.5 Research into segment reporting

Segmental data has provided an interesting motivation for research projects over many years. The main research interest lies in the identification of segments and the disclosures relating to segments. An example of this research is provided in Emmanuel and Garrod (2002) using data from UK companies in 1995. They linked their investigation of segment data to the concepts of 'relevance' and 'comparability' used in conceptual

Exhibit 5.18 Segment information, Roche

Segment reporting [extract from accounting policies]

The Group's primary format for segment reporting is business segments and the secondary format is geographical segments. The risks and returns of the Group's operations are primarily determined by the different products that the Group produces rather than the geographical location of the Group's operations. This is reflected by the Group's management and organisational structure and internal financial reporting systems.

The determination of the Group's business and geographical segments is based on the organisation units for which information is reported to the Group's management. The Group has two divisions, Pharmaceuticals and Diagnostics. Within the Pharmaceuticals Division there are three sub-divisions, Roche Pharmaceuticals, Genentech and Chugai. The three sub-divisions have separate management and reporting structures within the Pharmaceuticals Division and are considered separately reportable business segments. The Vitamins and Fine Chemicals business and the Consumer Health (OTC) business were previously separately reportable business segments. These have been divested and are presented as discontinued businesses. Certain headquarter activities are reported as 'Corporate'. These consist of corporate headquarters, including the corporate executive committee, corporate communications, corporate human resources, corporate finance, including treasury, taxes and pension fund management, corporate legal and corporate safety and environmental services. The Group's geographical segments are determined by geographical location and similarity of economic environments.

Transfer prices between business segments are set on an arm's length basis. Divisional assets and liabilities consist of property, plant and equipment, goodwill and intangible assets, trade receivables/payables and inventories. Other segment liabilities consist of other liabilities, such as provisions, which can be reasonably attributed to the reported business segments. Non-segment assets and liabilities mainly include current and deferred income tax balances, post-employment benefit assets/liabilities and financial assets/liabilities. These are principally cash, marketable securities, other investments and debt. Capital expenditure comprises additions to goodwill, intangible assets and property, plant and equipment, including those arising from business combinations.

Source: Roche (2006) Annual Report – Finance Report, pp. 28–29.

Segmental reporting: Notes to the financial statements:

- [Note: The segment report covers three pages. The primary segment information is reported over two pages and the secondary segment information is reported over one page. The outlines below show the line items and headings of each table.]

Segment reporting (pp. 42–44)

Primary segments

Roche Pharmaceuticals, Genentech, Chugai, Pharmaceutials division, Diagnostics division
Divisional information *in millions of CHF*

[Note that in the full report there are five segment columns, representing Roche Pharmaceuticals, Genentech, Chugai, Pharmaceutials division, and the Diagnostics division]

Exhibit 5.18 *(Continued)*

	Segment A		Segment B			Total	
	Current	Previous	Current	Previous	...	Current	Previous
Segment revenues							
Segment revenues/divisional sales	xx	xx	xx	xx	...	xx	xx
Less inter-divisional sales	(xx)	(xx)	(xx)	(xx)	...	(xx)	(xx)
Divisional sales to third parties	xx	xx	xx	xx	...	xx	xx
Segment results							
Operating profit before exceptional items	xx	xx	xx	xx	...	xx	xx
Major legal cases- - - -		(xx)			...		(xx)
Segment results/operating profit	xx	xx	xx	xx	...	xx	xx
Segment assets and liabilities							
Divisional/segment assets	xx	xx	xx	xx	...	xx	xx
Non-segment assets					...		xx
Total assets					...		xx
Divisional liabilities	(xx)	(xx)	(xx)	(xx)	...	(xx)	(xx)
Other segment liabilities	(xx)	(xx)	(xx)	(xx)	...	(xx)	(xx)
Segment liabilities	(xx)	(xx)	(xx)	(xx)	...	(xx)	(xx)
Non-segment liabilities					...		(xx)
Total liabilities					...		
Segmental expense information							
Research and development costs	xx	xx	xx	xx	...	xx	xx
Equity compensation plan expenses	xx	xx	xx	xx	...	xx	xx
Restructuring expenses	xx	xx			...	xx	xx
Capital expenditure							
Business combinations		xx			...		xx
Additions to property, plant and equipment	xx	xx	xx	xx	...	xx	xx
Additions to intangible assets	xx	xx	xx	xx	...	xx	xx
Total capital expenditure	xx	xx	xx	xx	...	xx	xx
Other segment information							
Depreciation of property, plant and equipment	xx	xx	xx	xx	...	xx	xx
Amortisation of intangible assets	xx	xx	xx	xx	...	xx	xx
Impairment of property, plant and equipment	xx	xx			...		xx
Impairment of goodwill					...		–
Impairment of intangible assets					...		–
Income from associated companies	(xx)	(xx)			...		(xx)
Investments in associated companies		xx			...		xx

Secondary segments
Information by geographical segment *in millions of CHF*

Current year	Sales to third parties (by destination)	Segment assets	Capital expenditure
Switzerland	xx	xx	xx
European Union	xx	xx	xx
Rest of Europe	xx	xx	xx
Europe	xx	xx	xx
North America	xx	xx	xx
Latin America	xx	xx	xx
Japan	xx	xx	xx
Rest of Asia	xx	xx	xx
Asia	xx	xx	xx
Africa, Australia and Oceania	xx	xx	xx
Segment total	xx	xx	xx
Non-segment assets	xx	xx	xx
Consolidated total	xx	xx	xx

Previous year [similar table]

Source: Based on Roche Annual Report – Finance Report, pp. 42–45.

frameworks. They suggested that segmental data is relevant if it confirms the consolidated results. It is comparable if it provides data that is comparable within industry norms. They then calculated return on assets for the industry, the group and the segments. They found that for a significant portion of the sample, the levels of both relevance and comparability were low because of the choices made in identifying segments. They suggested that this might indicate a problem in allowing the management of companies to have discretion in identifying segments.

5.9 Foreign currency translation

Most companies will be affected in some way by changes in exchange rates. If they import goods or services, their costs will change because the prices paid in domestic currency will change. If they export goods or services, their revenues will change in one of two ways. If companies price goods in their domestic currency, the volume of sales will decrease if the domestic currency strengthens (becomes more expensive). If companies price goods in foreign currency then the amount received in domestic currency will fluctuate. Companies may face risk through borrowing or lending money in other currencies. They may have foreign currency investments or may trade in foreign currency contracts. The parent company must then decide how to use those figures for internal or management purposes and how to incorporate them in group accounts for external reporting purposes.

5.9.1 Issues in translation

The financial statements of overseas subsidiaries need to be restated in terms of the currency of the parent company before they can be consolidated as part of the group. Two questions arise:

- What rate of exchange should be used when translating accounting statements?
- How do we report gains and losses resulting from the process of translation?

5.9.1.1 Relationship between parent and subsidiary

One factor relevant to answering both questions is the nature of the relationship between the parent and its foreign subsidiary. In some cases the subsidiary is quite independent in its day-to-day operations, having a local management structure in which operating decisions are taken. The subsidiary raises finance on its own initiative and retains profit for reinvestment after paying a dividend to the parent. Such a subsidiary is seen by the parent company as an investment in equity, with the emphasis on growth of the ownership interest through generation of profit. In other cases the subsidiary is closely controlled from the parent, having a local management which operate under direction from the parent company. Such a subsidiary is seen by the parent company as a branch activity where monetary resources (cash and loans) are provided to the subsidiary as needed and surplus monetary resources are returned to the parent on a regular basis.

Both of these types of relationship leave the parent exposed to fluctuations in foreign exchange rates, but there is a different type of exposure. In the first case the parent has regard for the investment in equity and whether it is increasing or decreasing in terms of the home currency. It may also arrange the timing of dividend payments to avoid temporary weaknesses in the home currency. In the second case there is a constant flow of monetary resources to and from the parent and so there is exposure in terms of the balance of monetary assets and monetary liabilities held in the subsidiary at any point in time. These different views of exposure to foreign currency fluctuations have led to different views of the process of translation, as explained in the rest of this section.

The parent company's view of the translation process is also affected by the relative strength of the currency of the parent company compared with that of the subsidiary. Parent companies do not like to report losses, particularly where they feel that the losses are caused by factors beyond their control. If a choice exists they may prefer to use a method of translation which avoids giving an impression of loss. Recognizing this characteristic of multinationals helps us to understand the positions taken by them when an accounting standard is in the course of preparation.

In the absence of a standard, companies could in practice choose between two exchange rates, the **historic rate**, being the rate of exchange when the transaction took place, and the **closing rate**, being the rate of exchange at the balance sheet date. In theory, it might be reasonable to consider **future exchange rates**, defined as the expected rate of exchange when the obligation will be met. In practice the high degree of uncertainty about future exchange rates is regarded as too great for these to be used, so that the choice lies between the historic rate and the closing rate method.

5.9.1.2 Translating the balance sheet

Before accounting standards were developed, various systems were developed and applied at different times and in different countries. Two which caused particularly intensive debate about their relative merits and limitations were:

- the temporal method
- the closing rate (net investment) method.

Each one makes a different assumption about exposure to the risk of a movement in exchange rates. This section explains the assumption made under each system, and the rate of exchange to be applied.

Temporal method

There are cases in which the affairs of a foreign enterprise are so closely interlinked with those of the investing company that its results may be regarded as being more dependent on the economic environment of the investing company's currency than on that of its own reporting currency. In such a case the financial statements of the foreign enterprise should be included in the consolidated financial statements as if all its transactions had been entered into by the investing company itself in its own currency. For this purpose the temporal method of translation should be used; the mechanics of this method are identical with those used in preparing the accounts of an individual company.

All the available evidence should be considered in determining whether the currency of the investing company is the dominant currency in the economic environment in which the foreign enterprise operates. Among the factors to be taken into account will be:

- the extent to which the cash flows of the enterprise have a direct impact upon those of the investigating company;
- the extent to which the functioning of the enterprise is dependent directly upon the investing company;
- the currency in which the majority of the trading transactions are denominated;
- the major currency to which the operation is exposed in its financing structure.

Examples of situations where the temporal method may be appropriate are where the foreign enterprise:

- acts as a selling agency receiving stocks of goods from the investing company and remitting the proceeds back to the company; or
- produces a raw material or manufactures parts of sub-assemblies which are then shipped to the investing company for inclusion in its own products; or
- is located overseas for tax, exchange control or similar reasons to act as a means of raising finance for other companies in the group.

Rate of exchange to be applied

The rate of exchange to be used will be the one that is appropriate with regards to when the transaction was undertaken or when the valuation process being used in the financial reports took place:

- Cash, short-term debtors and short-term creditors are translated at the closing rate.
- Other assets and liabilities may be translated at current or historic rates depending on how the item has been valued in the original financial statements. If they are valued

at historic cost then the historic rate will be used. If they are valued at current (or expected future) market price the closing rate of exchange will be used. The rate of exchange is sensitive to the underlying basis of valuation of non-monetary items.

Closing rate/net investment method

The closing rate method recognizes that the investment of a company is in the net worth of its foreign enterprise rather than a direct investment in the individual assets and liabilities of that enterprise. The foreign enterprise will normally have net current assets and fixed assets which may be financed partly by local currency borrowings. In its day-to-day operations the foreign enterprise is not normally dependent on the reporting currency of the parent company. The parent company may look forward to a stream of dividends but the net investment will remain until the business is liquidated or the investment is sold.

Rate of exchange to be applied

All assets and liabilities are translated at the closing rate of exchange. Exchange differences will arise if this rate differs from that ruling at the previous balance sheet date or at the date of any subsequent capital injection (or reduction).

Exhibit 5.19 compares the temporal and closing rate methods of translating the balance sheet of a subsidiary into the currency of the parent company.

Exhibit 5.19	Temporal and closing rate compared

Hill plc ('Hill'), a company based in Home country, set up a wholly owned subsidiary, Valley Inc. ('Valley'), in Away country on 1 January Year 1. The share capital of Valley Inc. is A$3,000,000. Initial information about Hill and Valley is provided in Step 1.

Step 1   Initial information about Hill and Valley on 1 January Year 1
The rate of exchange on 1 January Year 1 was H$15 = A$12. Hill plc subscribed H$250,000 for the share capital of Valley Inc.

On 1 January Year 1, Valley carried out two transactions:

(a) raised a long-term loan amounting to A$1,000,000;
(b) bought plant and machinery costing A$3,500,000 and having a useful life of ten years, to be depreciated on a straight-line basis.

The balance sheet of Valley on 1 January Year 1 is translated as shown in Step 2. The rate of exchange used is the same for both systems of translation because the historical rate equals the current rate at the date on which the transaction takes place.

Step 2   Valley: Balance sheet at 1 January Year 1

	A$000s	Conversion factor	H$000s
Plant and machinery	3,500	1/12	292
Cash	500	1/12	42
	4,000		334
Long-term loan	(1,000)	1/12	(84)
	3,000		250
Share capital	3,000	1/12	250

The investment in share capital of Valley is included in the balance sheet of Hill at the amount of H$250,000.

The business of Valley operates during Year 1. The rates of exchange between the H$ and the A$ vary during the year as shown in Step 3.

Step 3   Rates of exchange rate between the H$ and the A$ during Year 1

Date	Exchange rate	Comment
1 January Year 1	H$1 = A$12	This is the historic rate (hr) for fixed assets and the long-term loan
Purchase of goods held as closing stock	H$1 = A$10.5	This is the historic rate (hr) for the closing stock
31 December Year 1	H$1 = A$10	This is the closing rate.

The balance sheet of Valley in A$ is shown in the first column of Step 4. It is then translated into H$ using each of the two systems of translation described earlier.

Step 4   Balance sheet of Valley at 31 December Year 1 in its own currency and translated using closing rate and temporal systems of translation

Balance sheet at 31 December Year 1	Own currency A$000s	Calculation	Translations to parent's currency Closing rate H$000s	Calculation	Temporal H$000s
Fixed assets	3,150	/10	315	/12	263
Stock	1,050	/10	105	/10.5	100
Cash and net current monetary items (creditors and debtors)	200	/10	20	/10	20
Long-term loan	(1,000)		(100)		(100)
	3,400		340		283
Share capital at 1 Jan Year 1	3,000	/12	250	/12	250
Reserves (profit for year to 31 December Year 1)	400	Balancing figure	90	Balancing figure	33
	3,400		340		283

Each system of translation uses a different combination of rate of exchange for various elements of financial statements.

Both these translation methods will leave the resulting financial statement out of balance. This creates a need for a 'balancing figure' to be given a suitable description. It is normally reported in reserves and described as *Reserves at the balance sheet date*.

The rates of exchange used in each method are summarized in Step 5.

Step 5 Translation rates of exchange and treatment of gain or loss on exchange

Balance sheet item	Translation methods Closing rate	Temporal
Cash and net current monetary items (creditors and debtors)	cr	cr
Stock and work in progress	cr	hr or cr*
Fixed assets	cr	hr or cr*
Long-term monetary items (creditors and debtors)	cr	cr
Ownership equity (share capital and reserves) when subsidiary acquired	hr	hr
Increase in reserves since acquisition	Balancing figure	Balancing figure

*In the temporal method when stocks and fixed assets are valued on historic cost terms, the historic rate (hr) will be used. When current market value is used (replacement/current cost/net realizable value) the closing rate (cr) will be applied.

If the sum of opening reserves plus profit for the year does not equal this balancing figure an adjustment is needed in the form of a *gain on exchange* or *loss on exchange*.

The example ends with a gain or loss on translation shown in the reserves of shareholders' equity as a balancing figure in the balance sheet. The key accounting question arising at this point is 'should this gain or loss on exchange be treated as part of current year's profit or as a movement on reserve?' The argument in favour of reporting in profit or loss is that the gain or loss relates to the current period and so should be reported as part of the profit. The argument against reporting in profit or loss is that the foreign exchange effects can distort the underlying trends of business activity. The treatment of the translation gain or loss depends on other assumptions about the business and so varies according to the model chosen. In the previous version of IAS 21, and in US and UK standards, the gain or loss on translation has been reported as a movement on reserves under the closing rate method and as part of the current year's profit or loss under the temporal method. This increased the non-comparability of the outcome of foreign currency translations and gave further opportunities for earnings management.

5.9.2 IAS 21

IAS 21 *The Effects of Changes in Foreign Exchange Rates* was first issued in 1983. For many years IAS 21 allowed both the temporal method and the closing rate method of translation of the financial statements of foreign subsidiaries, reflecting the diversity of national practices. It tried to achieve comparability by setting conditions on the circumstances in which each could be applied. This reflected the US and UK standards, both of which set circumstances in which the temporal method should be used, and circumstances in which the closing rate method should be used. However, in the USA in particular the SEC was aware that companies tended to change their use of accounting method whenever exchange rates strengthened or weakened, and there appeared to be a great deal of flexibility in the choices available to each company.

5.9.2.1 Definitions

The revision of IAS 21 in 2003 cut through all the problems of flexibility and made the process of translation much more straightforward, without destroying the underlying concepts of the previous versions.

One key to the simplicity of the standard lies in the ideas of 'functional currency' and 'presentation currency' which replace the previous idea of 'reporting currency'. The other key to simplicity lies in the focus on the underlying economy that determines the pricing of transactions. IAS 21 now takes the view that an 'integral' foreign subsidiary could not have a functional currency that differs from that of the parent. This eliminates another source of variability in translation of the results of foreign subsidiaries for consolidation with the parent's financial statements. It allows the basic principle of the temporal method to be preserved without allowing companies the scope for creative accounting through redefining the functional currency of a subsidiary. The economic facts drive the accounting.

The **functional currency** is the currency of the primary economic environment in which the entity operates.[60]

---

[60] IAS 21 (2007) para. 8

Exhibit 5.20 **Illustration of definitions**

> **Functional currency of a dependent subsidiary**
>
> A multinational parent company based in the USA sets up a manufacturing subsidiary in an export zone in Malaysia. The parent company supplies the capital, debt, management expertise and the raw materials and then exports the goods out of the country when manufacture is completed. The subsidiary controls neither its inputs nor its outputs. In this case, any exchange rate changes between Malaysian currency and the US dollar will have an immediate effect upon the subsidiary's cash flows and will also affect the subsidiary's monetary assets and liabilities (cash, accounts receivable and payable, and loans). In this case the functional currency would be the currency of the parent, which is the US dollar.
>
> **Functional currency and economic market**
>
> A parent company based in France sets up a subsidiary in India to produce oil from an oil field and then supply the amount demanded by the parent at current market prices. Given that world oil prices are stated in US dollars, this subsidiary may be more dependent upon US dollar exchange rates than it is on the Indian rupee. Any change in the value of the dollar would have an immediate effect upon the subsidiary's cash flows and the US dollar is the functional currency of the subsidiary even if neither it nor its parent company is in the USA.
>
> **Presentation currency**
>
> Gamma is based in Italy. Gamma has a US parent and is dependent on the US parent. Gamma buys and sells goods using US dollars and regards the US dollar as its *functional currency*. The day-to-day accounting records are maintained in dollars. However, Gamma reports to its own shareholders in euros. In the terminology of IAS 21, the euro is the *presentation currency* for the financial statements of Gamma. The US dollar is the currency of the economic environment in which Gamma operates. The parent cannot choose to change the definition of Gamma's functional currency to the euro. This eliminates one possibility for 'earnings management' that some parent companies have used previously.

The **presentation currency** is the currency in which the financial statements are presented. The company is allowed to choose whatever presentation currency it wishes.[61]

Exhibit 5.20 illustrates these definitions by way of examples.

IAS 21 sets procedures for reporting foreign currency transactions in the functional currency. It also sets procedures for translating the financial statements of a foreign operation for inclusion in the financial statements of the reporting entity. The same procedures must be used for translating the results and financial position from the entity's functional currency to its presentation currency.

5.9.2.2 Transactions

The accounting treatment for transactions under IAS 21 is relatively straightforward. This section gives three examples of transactions:

- a foreign currency monetary item (Exhibit 5.21);
- a non-monetary item measured in historical cost (Exhibit 5.22); and
- a long-term loan made to a foreign subsidiary (Exhibit 5.23).

---

[61] Ibid.

Exhibit 5.21	Foreign currency, monetary item

AB Inc. is based in the USA and its functional currency is the dollar. The company borrowed €2m on a three-year loan from a bank in a European country on 1 July Year 1. The rate of exchange on that date was $1.22 = €1. At the balance sheet date, 31 December Year 1, the rate of exchange is $1.20 = €1.

On initial recognition the liability is recorded by AB Inc. using the spot rate at the date of the transaction. The loan is recorded at $2.44m.

At the balance sheet date the liability is translated using the closing rate of $1.20 = €1.[62] It is shown in the balance sheet as $2.40m. This means that AB Inc. has benefited from the stronger dollar at the end of the year. It would require fewer dollars to repay the loan which is fixed in euros. However, the loan has not actually been repaid. There is an unrealized gain of $40,000. This is reported in the profit or loss of AB Inc.

Exhibit 5.22	Foreign currency, non-monetary item at historical cost

AB Inc. is based in the USA and its functional currency is the dollar. The company purchased a fixed asset from a European country on 1 July Year 1. The price is €2m. The rate of exchange on the date of purchase is $1.22 = €1. At the balance sheet date, 31 December Year 1, the rate of exchange is $1.20 = €1.

On initial recognition the transaction is recorded by AB Inc. using the spot exchange rate at the date of the transaction. The asset is recorded at $2.44m. This is the cost base that is used for depreciation calculations.[63]

At each balance sheet date the fixed asset is translated using the exchange rate at the date of the transaction, which is $1.22 = €1 in our example. The rate of exchange at the balance sheet date has no relevance.[64]

The explanation of the treatment of the unrealized gain or loss in the consolidated financial statements, as in Exhibit 5.23, is based on the special relationships within a group. Exhibits 5.21 and 5.22 show that there are different treatments for a monetary item and a non-monetary item. A gain or loss on a monetary item is recognized but no loss or gain on a non-monetary item is recognized. This unsymmetrical treatment of monetary and non-monetary transactions can have a significant and potentially mis-leading effect on the group's reported figures if the monetary item is being used to fund part of the net investment in a foreign entity. For example, a group will often purchase a foreign subsidiary with a combination of equity and locally raised long-term debt, raised by the parent company. The interest on the long-term debt and the repayment of the debt are all based on the foreign subsidiary's local currency cash flows. No monies are ever transferred to or from the parent from the initial loan or to pay interest or repay the loan. As such, the loan is effectively cushioned from and unaffected by subsequent exchange rate changes. Yet, if the monetary item were treated using the approach in

---

[62] IAS 21 (2007) para. 23(a).

[63] IAS 21 (2007) para. 21.

[64] IAS 21 (2007) paras 23(c) and 24.

| Exhibit 5.23 | Long-term loan to a foreign subsidiary |

> AB Inc. is based in the USA and its functional currency is the dollar. The company has a sub-sidiary, MN SA, located in a European country. MN SA owes €2m to AB Inc. for management advice on capital projects. AB Inc. has allowed MN SA to regard this as a long-term loan which will not be repaid until MN SA ceases to be a subsidiary of AB Inc. The rate of exchange on 1 July Year 1, when the long-term loan agreement started, was $1.22 = €1. At the balance sheet date, 31 December Year 1, the rate of exchange is $1.20 = €1.
>
> On initial recognition the long-term asset is recorded by AB Inc. using the spot exchange rate at the date of the transaction. The amount of the asset is $2.44m. At the balance sheet date the asset is measured at the closing rate $1.20 = €1. The amount of the asset is now $2.40m. There is an unrealized loss of $40,000. It is recorded as a loss in the separate profit and loss statement of AB Inc. but is recorded as a separate component of equity in the con-solidated financial statements of the AB Group. It is recognized in profit or loss of the group when the subsidiary is disposed of.[65]

Exhibit 5.20, the group would report a profit or loss in the consolidated account. This would be misleading as a loss implies a fall in the wealth of the group's shareholders and a profit implies an increase in its wealth, while, in this case, the group's shareholders are unaffected by the change in the reported value of the foreign debt. Therefore IAS 21 requires that, in this situation, any gain or loss on the long-term monetary item should be recognized as a separate component of equity in the balance sheet rather than as income or expense in the income statement.

It is important to note that these three examples are discussed separately. If the trans-actions were combined in some way, perhaps to hedge against the risks of foreign cur-rency fluctuations, they would come within the scope of IAS 39. There would then be a series of tests to examine whether the transactions could be matched as hedges rather than being accounted for separately.

5.9.2.3 Translation of a foreign operation[66]

When a group contains individual entities with different functional currencies, the results and financial position of each entity are expressed in common currency so that consolidated financial statements may be presented.[67] This process is called **translation**.

The results and financial position of the foreign operation are translated as follows:[68]

- assets and liabilities in each balance sheet presented shall be translated at the closing rate at the date of that balance sheet;
- income and expenses for each income statement presented shall be translated at exchange rates ruling at the date of the transaction (the average rate for the period may be used as a practical approximation provided the exchange rates do not fluctu-ate significantly);[69]
- all resulting exchange differences shall be recognized as a separate component of equity.

---

[65] IAS 21 (2007) para. 32.

[66] IAS 21 (2007) paras 44–47.

[67] IAS 21 (2007) para. 38.

[68] IAS 21 (2007) para. 39.

[69] IAS 21 (2007) para. 40.

These exchange differences will result from:[70]

- translating income and expenses at the exchange rates at the date of the transactions, while translating assets and liabilities at the closing rate;
- translating the opening net assets at a closing rate that differs from the previous closing rate.

5.9.2.4 Hyperinflation

IAS 21 (2003) was used to clarify ambiguity between the previous version of IAS 21 and IAS 29 on the treatment of hyperinflation where translation is also required.

The term 'hyperinflation' is used to describe a situation of very high rates of inflation where the purchasing power of money is diminishing rapidly during an accounting period. Because exchange rates tend to reflect the relative inflation of different countries, the exchange rate of the hyperinflationary country will weaken in relation to low-inflation countries.

There is no ready definition of hyperinflation but some characteristics of hyperinflationary economies are set out in IAS 29:[71]

- The general population prefers to hold its wealth in the form of non-monetary assets or in a more stable foreign currency.
- Sales and purchases on credit take place on terms that allow for an expected loss of purchasing power in the short term.
- Interest rates, wages and prices are linked to a price index.
- The cumulative inflation rate over three years is approaching, or exceeds, 100 per cent.

IAS 29 requires adjustment for inflation. It has been interpreted flexibly by companies so that some have adjusted for inflation and then translated, while others have translated and then adjusted for inflation. This has led to some earnings management and non-comparable results. IAS 21 gives the clarification that when an entity's functional currency is the currency of a hyperinflationary economy, the entity shall restate its financial statements in accordance with IAS 29 before applying the translation process.[72] IAS 21 explains the process of translation to be used.[73] The results and financial position of an entity whose functional currency is the currency of a hyperinflationary economy shall be translated into a different presentation currency using the following procedures:

- all amounts shall be translated at the closing rate at the date of the most recent balance sheet, except that
- when amounts are translated into the currency of a non-hyperinflationary economy, comparative amounts shall be those that were presented as current year amounts in the relevant prior year statements (i.e. not adjusted for subsequent changes in the price level or subsequent changes in exchange rates).

5.9.3 USA

The US standard on foreign currency translation is FAS 52. It is substantially similar in approach to IAS 21 although the detailed terminology and guidance differ. The creation

---

[70] IAS 21 (2007) para. 41.
[71] IAS 29 (2007) *Financial Reporting in Hyperinflationary Economies*.
[72] IAS 21 (2007) para. 43.
[73] IAS 21 (2007) paras 42–43.

of FAS 52 in the US, SSAP 20 in the UK and the original version of IAS 21 in the 1980s could be seen as an early example of the convergence process at work,[74] or it could be taken as an example of Anglo-American dominance of IFRS.

5.10 Researching accounting choices

The growing acceptance of IFRS as a global set of accounting standards will not eliminate the scope for researching accounting choice. However, the methods of investigation may need to change. Nobes (2006) lists examples of accounting choices, or options, that will continue for the following three reasons:

1 In some IFRS there are overt (openly stated) options such as choice of formats (in IAS 1), choice of FIFO or average cost to value inventories (in IAS 2), choice of historical cost or fair value for property, plant and equipment (in IAS 16).

2 In some IFRS there are covert options (broad definitions allow choice in interpretation) or vague criteria, such as using the percentage of completion method where the outcome of a contract can be estimated reliably (in IAS 11).

3 In some IFRS there are estimations of value to be carried out, requiring judgement (such as fair value estimates in IAS 39 or IAS 41).

Nobes predicts that future research will need to investigate the extent of such choices and of the factors associated with making choices.

Summary and conclusions

The application of IFRS has brought greater harmonization of accounting practices to multinational groups in the areas of business combinations, segmental reporting and foreign currency translation. This has been particularly true of groups based in Europe where these areas of accounting were previously flexible through the choices offered by the Seventh Directive and the silences of the Seventh Directive. US multinationals, and those based in other countries that have followed US GAAP, have applied the standards of one regulatory body, the FASB, but within those standards there has again been flexibility of choice. The FASB has removed some of the flexibility surrounding business combinations and is working with the IASB on the convergence of accounting for business combinations. Similar convergence has taken place in respect of segmental reporting and foreign currency translation.

In all these accounting matters it is important to be aware that flexibility of choice still exists within the IFRS. It is necessary to read the accounting policies and notes to the accounts to understand how particular companies have used that flexibility of choice and to consider its relevance to the company. A fundamental concern is that this harmonization of accounting rules may create underlying disharmony if the economic situation of a particular group of companies is not well represented by the accounting practices applied. This leads to the question of whether accounting reports reality or creates reality.[75]

---

[74] Bonham *et al.* (2006), p. 702.

[75] Hines (1988).

Key points from the chapter:

In reading the annual report of a multinational group and considering its comparability with other groups, ask the following questions, each of which may potentially affect the reported profit or loss and net assets:

● Which forms of presentation has the company chosen for its financial statements?

● Which assets and liabilities are recorded at fair value and how is it determined?

● How is the group defined, and are there any exclusions?

● Has the focus on the purchase method and elimination of pooling of interests improved international comparability of group financial statements?

● How has the group calculated goodwill on acquisition and how is it tested for impairment?

● How does the group identify associates and joint ventures and how are these reported – equity method or proportionate consolidation?

● What is the basis of defining segments and what does the segment information reveal about segment performance?

● How has the group chosen its functional currency and presentation currency? How have changes in rates of exchange affected the shareholders' equity?

Questions

The following questions test your understanding of the material contained in the chapter and allow you to relate your understanding to the learning outcomes specified at the start of this chapter. The learning outcomes are repeated here. Each question is cross-referenced to the relevant section of the chapter.

Presentation of financial statements

1 What are the benefits and limitations of allowing flexibility in presentation of financial statements? (section 5.2.1)

2 What are the presentation issues resolved in the short-term convergence project? (section 5.2.2)

3 What are the aspects of financial reporting where continuing variation may be expected? (section 5.2.3)

Fair value measurement

4 What are the differences between the IASB and FASB definitions of fair value? (section 5.3.1)

5 What are the issues to consider in making international comparisons of fair value measurements? (section 5.3.2)

6 What areas of fair value measurement may cause continuing variation in financial reporting practice? (section 5.3.4)

Defining a group

7 What are the main problems in defining a group for consolidated financial statements? (section 5.4.1)

8 How do IFRS define a group? (section 5.4.2)

9 How have IFRS improved harmonization of definition of a group? (section 5.4)

Acquisitions and uniting of interests

10 What are the main problems in defining an acquisition and a uniting of interests? (section 5.5.1)

11 How do IFRS deal with the problem of defining an acquisition and a uniting of interests? (section 5.5.2)

12 Are there any problems with the IFRS approach to acquisitions and uniting of interests? (section 5.5)

Goodwill on acquisition

13 What are the main problems in defining and measuring goodwill? (section 5.6)

14 How do IFRS deal with the problem of defining and measuring goodwill? (section 5.6)

15 Are there any problems with the IFRS approach to accounting for goodwill? (section 5.6)

Associates and joint ventures

16 What are the main problems in defining and reporting associates and joint ventures? (section 5.7.1)

17 How do IFRS deal with the problem of defining and reporting associates and joint ventures? (section 5.7.2)

18 Are there any problems with the IFRS approach to associates and joint ventures? (section 5.7)

Segmental reporting

19 What are the main problems in defining and reporting segments? (section 5.8.1)

20 How do IFRS deal with the problem of defining and reporting segments? (section 5.8.2)

21 Are there any problems with the IFRS approach to segment reporting? (section 5.8)

Foreign currency translation

22 What are the main issues in foreign currency translation? (section 5.9.1)

23 How do IFRS deal with the problem of foreign currency translation? (section 5.9.2)

24 How have IFRS improved the accounting treatment of foreign currency translation? (section 5.9)

25 Are there any problems with the IFRS approach to foreign currency translation? (section 5.9)

References and further reading

IAS and IFRS

References to 2007 versions of IAS and IFRS are to the versions published in the Bound Volume of IFRS (including IAS and Interpretations) as at 1 January 2007, by the IASB.

Other reading

Bonham, M., Curtis, M., Davies, M., Dekker, P., Denton, T., Moore, R., Richards, H., Wilkinson-Riddle, G., Williams, M. and Wilson, A. (2006) *International GAAP® 2007*. London: Ernst & Young and Lexis Nexis.

Edwards, P. and Smith, R.A. (1996) 'Competitive disadvantage and voluntary disclosures', *British Accounting Review*, 28(2): 155–172.

Emmanuel, C.R. and Garrod, N. (2002) 'On the relevance and comparability of segmental data', *Abacus*, 38(2): 215–234.

FASB (1997) *Statement of Financial Accounting Standards 131: Reporting Disaggregated Information About a Business Enterprise.* Norwalk, CT: Financial Accounting Standards Board.

Gray, S.J. and Radebaugh, L. (1984) 'International segment disclosures by US and UK multinational enterprises: a descriptive study', *Journal of Accounting Research*: 351–360.

Herrmann, D. (1996) 'The predictive ability of geographic segment information at the country, continent and consolidated levels', *Journal of International Financial Management and Accounting*, 7(1): 50–73.

Hines, R. (1988) 'In communicating reality, we construct reality', *Accounting, Organizations and Society*, 13(3): 251–261.

IASC (1997) *IAS 14 Revised: Segment Reporting.* London: International Accounting Standards Committee.

Klaassen, J. (2001) 'The Netherlands – Group accounts', in Ordelheide, D. and KPMG (eds) *Transnational Accounting TRANSACC.* Basingstoke and New York: Palgrave.

Kuroda, M. (2001) 'Japan – Group accounts', in Ordelheide, D. and KPMG (eds) *Transnational Accounting TRANSACC.* Basingstoke and New York: Palgrave.

Nobes, C. (2006) 'The survival of international differences under IFRS: towards a research agenda', *Accounting and Business Research*, 36(3): 233–245.

Ordelheide, D. (2001) 'Germany – Group accounts', in Ordelheide, D. and KPMG (eds) *Transnational Accounting TRANSACC.* Basingstoke and New York: Palgrave.

Richard, J. (2001) 'France – Group accounts', in Ordelheide, D. and KPMG (eds) *Transnational Accounting TRANSACC.* Basingstoke and New York: Palgrave.

Roberts, C.B. (1989) 'Forecasting earnings using geographic segment data: some UK evidence', *Journal of International Financial Management and Accounting*, 1(2): 130–151.

Street, D.L., Nichols, N.B. and Gray, S.J. (2000) 'Segment disclosures under SFAS131: has business segment reporting improved?', *Accounting Horizons*, 14(3): 259–286.

Walton, P. (ed.) (2007) *The Routledge Companion to Fair Value and Financial Reporting.* Abingdon: Routledge.

Williams, J.R. and Carcello, J.V. (2007) *GAAP Guide Level A 2007.* Chicago: CCH.

PART 2

Contrasting harmonization and diversity across corporate reporting systems

Introduction to Part 2

Part 1 has discussed the pressures towards establishing one set of financial reporting standards. It has also shown the continuing diversity of corporate reporting where financial statements are only one aspect of a broader system of periodic reporting and accountability. The external pressures for accountability and assurance have been described and discussed. The limitations of applying one accounting system in all countries to all entities have also been considered.

For the remainder of this book we accept that at present there is a strong movement towards increasing acceptance of the international financial reporting standards (IFRS) of the International Accounting Standards Board (IASB). However, the corporate reporting cycle is critically dependent on the presentation of relevant and reliable financial statements based on accounting measures. It is also essential that a system of international standards is understandable to a wide range of preparers and users of corporate reports. In practice the accounting measures reported are servants of the influences under which they are created and the process by which are communicated. Part 2 focuses on the influences on corporate reporting rules and practices.

Framework for comparative study

This book uses two frameworks, established in Part 2, to explain why accounting across different countries may show signs of both diversity and harmony. The first framework is that of the institutional and external influences on accounting rules and practice, as explained in Chapter 6. In selecting the basis for a framework, Chapter 6 draws on academic research for justification. The headings used in Chapter 6 are:

- political and economic system
- legal system
- taxation system
- corporate financing system
- accounting profession
- other influences.

Chapter 6 describes general subdivisions within each of these categories and adds some illustrative material. Two case studies at the end of Chapter 6 give added insight relating to countries not covered in subsequent chapters.

The second framework used is that of cultural influences on accounting rules and practice. Chapter 7 leads you through general considerations of culture, discusses more specific links between culture and business, and finally addresses specific findings regarding culture and accounting. The chapter draws on the academic literature for its justification but also points to critical evaluation of the extent to which culture influences accounting values and practices.

The accounting values drawn as conclusions for Chapter 7 are:

- professionalism versus statutory control
- uniformity versus flexibility

- conservatism versus optimism
- secrecy versus transparency.

These are applied as a framework of discussion in the country chapters.

Classification of accounting systems

A considerable amount of effort from academics and practitioners has been devoted to classifying accounting systems. In some cases the characteristics of the accounting practices are used as the basis for classification. In other cases the characteristics of the political, economic and legal situations are used for classification. Deductive classification schemes rely strongly on the knowledge or beliefs of the observer who chooses a set of features which vary from one country to the next. Inductive classification systems look to a large body of data, such as that generated by an international survey, and painstakingly generate groups of data which seem to 'belong' together. From the clusters of data which relate closely, the researchers draw conclusions about countries which have accounting similarities and differences.

Chapter 8 describes and explains the research which has created a range of types of classifications of accounting systems.

Measuring the differences and similarities

A full understanding of the existing and potential impact of the international financial reporting standards requires the measurement of differences and similarities across accounting systems. Differences and similarities can be observed by practical persons but much of the systematic measurement and analysis has been undertaken in the academic sphere. Chapter 9 explains the methods used in academic research to measure international differences. The chapter discusses the importance of observed differences, and explains in simple terms how to measure differences in the figures reported and how to measure differences in the accounting methods used. Academic papers are cited and explained but simple illustrations are also provided so that there is guidance for you if you are considering such analysis in relation to a planned project or dissertation.

Purpose of Part 2

Part 2 is particularly useful as a module on which to base a study of analysis and research methods in comparative corporate reporting. It equips students with the analytical framework and research methods that may be used in research projects. It also helps them to understand and evaluate research papers in this field of study.

Learning outcomes

Specific learning outcomes are set out at the start of each chapter, but overall, on completion of Part 2, the student should be able to:

- set out a framework of institutional and external influences which could be applied to any country-specific study;
- set out a framework of cultural factors and accounting values to be applied to any country-specific study;
- explain the various approaches to accounting classification;
- carry out a simple measurement of international differences in accounting practices using data provided for the purpose.

6 Institutional and external influences on accounting rules and practices

Learning outcomes

After reading this chapter you should be able to:

● Understand how various aspects of a country's political and economic system have influenced its accounting system.

● Distinguish between common and code law systems and describe how the legal system typically influences the system of accounting regulation.

● Describe the ways in which the tax system can influence accounting rules and practices.

● Identify possible differences in the financing of companies internationally and describe how these differences may help to explain differences in accounting rules and practices.

● Understand how the way in which the accounting profession is organized can influence accounting rules and practices.

● Understand how a country might import or export accounting rules and practices.

6.1 Introduction

This chapter explores some of the reasons why financial accounting rules and practices have differed across countries. Many factors have influenced the development of accounting and there are many reasons why countries have developed different accounting systems.[1] This chapter explores some of the ways in which a society can organize itself and how this has affected the way in which accounting is undertaken. Six different features of a country are explored in this chapter, namely:

● the political and economic system
● the legal system
● the taxation system
● the corporate financing system
● the accounting profession
● religion.

Accounting rules and practices not only are developed inside a country, but also may have been imported into the country. This chapter therefore concludes by looking at the process of importing and exporting accounting rules and practices.

The chapter is primarily concerned with the position before the IASB began to wield a significant influence on practices internationally. It therefore seeks at least partially to answer the question of why moves towards increasing international harmonization became important. It also shows the factors that may continue to influence diversity in areas of accounting and accountability not regulated by the IASB where national influences remain stronger.

The chapter proceeds by introducing a general model that explains the types of factors that influence accounting. It then carries on to look at two of these, namely institutional factors and external factors. Chapter 7 then explores what is meant by 'culture', and looks at how the culture of a country can influence its accounting system.

---

[1] While accounting includes not only financial reporting but also management accounting, auditing and public sector accounting, the term 'accounting system' is used in this book, unless otherwise stated, to mean the financial reporting system. This includes both the rules or regulations and the actual practices of profit-orientated limited liability companies.

6.2 Factors influencing the development of accounting systems

As discussed in Chapter 1, before the work of the IASB started to have a major impact on accounting, accounting systems varied enormously around the world in terms of the systems of regulation, the measurement and disclosure rules in place and the voluntary measurement and disclosure decisions taken by companies. Many reasons have been given to explain why accounting systems varied so much. Exhibit 6.1 illustrates the range of possible influences.

The accounting system is the outcome of a complex process. It is influenced by and it also influences a number of factors. Governmental or political, economic, legal, tax, educational and financial systems are all important. Factors originating from outside a country can also be important, and its past trading and colonial links and current patterns of foreign investment can influence accounting. The culture of a country is also important. It can perhaps best be seen as a moderating influence that either reinforces or reduces the influence of these other factors. All of the following help to explain the accounting regulations of a country:

- the objectives of accounting regulation, whether the needs of investors, creditors, the government or other users are given precedence;
- the mode of regulation, whether by government, the profession or other group(s); and
- the extent and strictness of regulation.

Exhibit 6.1 The Influences on an accounting system

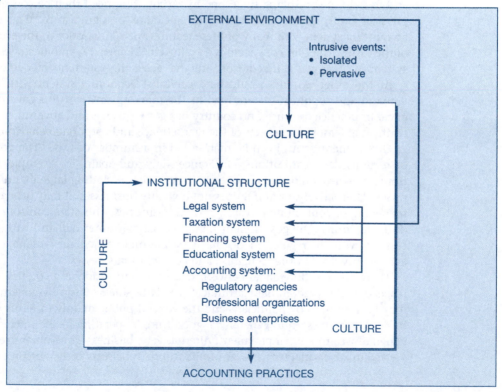

Source: Adapted from Doupnik and Salter (1995).

However, accounting practices are not simply the result of regulations. Voluntary practices are also important. As can be seen in Exhibit 6.1, voluntary practices are also the outcome of a complex process, being influenced by a wide range of factors.

While both internal and external factors are important, in most developed western countries the most important influences on the accounting system have been the institutions of that country – in particular how it organizes its political and economic, legal, financial and professional systems.[2] In contrast, as will be discussed later, factors external to the country have often been as or even more important for many developing countries. It is to the *internal or institutional* factors that we now turn our attention.

6.3 The political and economic system

6.3.1 Types of systems

One of the most important determinants of accounting regulations and practices is the political and economic system of a country. Differences in political systems will be reflected in differences in how the economy is organized and controlled. This will in turn influence the objectives or role of accounting.

What is particularly important to accounting is how a country organizes economic relations. At one extreme, all the processes of production could be jointly owned and controlled by society; prices, outputs, demand and supply would all be determined by centralized plans. Accounting would then serve two roles – to help in centralized planning and to help in controlling the economy. Accounting need then be concerned only with physical units; 'profit' would have no meaning or significance. One example of an accounting system with many of these features was China prior to the economic reforms of the 1980s. The Chinese system is described in Chapter 17, and illustrates an accounting system that was very different from any that exists in western liberal-democratic societies.

At the other extreme would be a capitalist economic system with prices, output, demand and supply all determined in the marketplace, with no government interference. In practice of course, no country has gone this far, and government regulates and controls at least some aspects of the marketplace and corporate behaviour.

Government control can be manifested in a number of ways. The government may own industrial organizations – in France, Italy and Spain, for example, the state traditionally owned a range of commercial companies, including large manufacturing enterprises. Alternatively, even if it does not own any businesses, it may play an active role in managing or controlling privately owned businesses. This state control can take several different forms. The government may manage consumer demand with relatively little contact with, or regulation of, business; alternatively, it may manage supply, being actively involved in the regulation and control of businesses.

There are also differences between countries and inside any country over time with respect to the predominant attitude towards business. Business–government relations may be seen both by politicians and the general public mainly in terms of cooperation: business may be seen as generally a 'good thing', operating in the interests of society to generate wealth and employment. Alternatively, business–government relations may be viewed in adversarial terms: large profits will then be seen as the outcome of exploitation

---

[2] Puxty *et al.* (1987).

of workers, customers or other groups. Government will then regulate more to protect these less powerful groups, whether labour, customers or society in general.

6.3.2 The regulation of accounting

The extent to which the government actively controls the economy, and the means it uses, will influence its willingness to control or regulate accounting, the regulatory structures used and the types of regulation.

If the government believes in a 'hands-off' approach with minimal regulation of companies, accounting is also less likely to be heavily regulated by the state. Companies will tend to be left to decide what to report and how to report it. Uniform accounting methods and the reporting of strictly comparable information will be relatively unimportant and accounting regulation will probably be delegated to the profession or other independent bodies.

If, instead, the government believes in a 'hands-on' approach to controlling the economy, it will tend to be much more likely to regulate accounting. Accounting information will now be needed by the government so that it can actively plan and manage corporate behaviour. There is more likely to be a uniform or rigid system of financial reporting imposed upon all companies.

6.3.3 Corporate attitudes towards accounting

The ways in which government–business relations are organized and the government's attitude towards business will affect the attitudes of business managers. If big business is viewed with suspicion, managers are more likely to use financial statements to manage business–society and business–government relationships. Extra disclosures may be seen as a way of demonstrating that the company is acting in socially desirable ways – disclosure may thus be seen as a way of legitimating the actions and activities of business. For example, there has been a significant amount of empirical and theoretical work using legitimacy theory to try to explain social and environmental disclosures by companies.[3] Managers may also be more likely to favour measurement rules and practices that reduce reported earnings.

If, on the other hand, business–government relations are generally cooperative and profits are seen as a measure of success, companies will generally be less concerned with trying to justify themselves. There may be less voluntary disclosure of information, especially social and environmental information. Companies may also be less likely to favour conservative income measurement rules and will instead tend to attempt to maximize rather than minimize their reported earnings (this assumes, of course, that there is no adverse impact on the company's tax bill).

6.3.4 Types of business organization

An important economic feature influencing accounting is the type of business organization that dominates the economy. Two features of business organizations are particularly important in helping to explain accounting rules and practices:

- the complexity of business organizations
- the industrial structure of the country.

---

[3] See, for example, the special issue of *Accounting, Accountability and Auditing Journal*, No. 15.3, 2002.

6.3.4.1 The complexity of business organizations

The way in which businesses are organized obviously has a major impact on the internal accounting information system and management accounting in general. As a company increases in size and complexity, the need for sophisticated management accounting systems increases – problems of control, performance evaluation and decision making all increase. While less obvious, differences in business complexity also affect the financial accounting system. If companies are generally small or family owned there is little need for external reporting and there should be relatively few accounting regulations. As companies increase in size, both their impact upon society and their need for external finance, whether by debt or equity, will increase. This means that there is a greater need for external information and the amount of accounting regulation will increase in response. As companies increase in size they are also likely to become more complex and more international. Typically, companies will start to arrange themselves into groups, with subsidiaries, associates and/or joint ventures all becoming more important. Again, accounting regulations will tend to reflect these changes. For example, greater emphasis will be placed upon the regulation of group financial statements and extra disclosure requirements in areas such as segment reporting will be more likely. As size increases, the need for more sophisticated accounting also increases. For example, regulations in the areas of off-balance-sheet finance, hedge accounting, financial instruments and share options should all become increasingly important.

6.3.4.2 The industrial structure of a country

Some accounting issues are industry specific. Whether or not a country regulates a particular industry-specific issue will obviously depend upon the relative importance of that industry to the economy. For example, if a country is highly dependent upon foreign trade and investment, with many of its companies being multinational, it is more likely to be concerned with the issue of foreign currency transactions and translation and is more likely to issue accounting regulations in this area. Other issues are even more industry specific. For example, accounting for the oil and gas industry has been an important and contentious issue in the USA. Issues of how to account for other extractive industries and agriculture are generally more important in developing countries than in developed countries. Thus, IAS 41 *Agriculture* was a result of pressure from a number of developing countries.

The importance of certain types of industry may also influence wider accounting regulations. For example, the UK standard on research and development was strongly influenced by the potential impact of alternative accounting methods on the behaviour of companies in the aeroengineering and other R&D-dependent industries.[4] Likewise, one of the very few times when the US Congress directly regulated accounting was over the issue of investment tax credits: Congress was concerned that the accounting rules should not adversely affect the investment behaviour of capital-intensive businesses and so impede the economic recovery of the USA.[5]

The importance or relevance of other accounting issues depends upon how the economy of a country is structured. For example, accounting for pensions is an important issue in the USA, which has a very complex and detailed pension standard. This reflects

---

[4] Hope and Gray (1982).
[5] Zeff (1972).

the particular institutional arrangements of the USA, where many companies run employee pension schemes. In other countries, pensions are run entirely by the state or through private arrangements, and accounting for pensions is less important. Likewise, the importance of issues such as leases and financial instruments depends upon the ways in which banks and other financial institutions work and the types of financing they provide.

6.3.5 The importance of inflation

Another important economic influence on accounting is inflation. As inflation rates increase, the problems of historical cost accounting also increase. Developed western countries have seldom suffered from high inflation and have tended to view inflation accounting with suspicion, and as a result a system of strict historical accounting is found in much of continental Europe and North America.

Inflation continues to be a serious problem in some countries, though. Many South American countries, for example, have had annual inflation rates of over 100 per cent in the past. Obviously, when inflation is running at such levels, the historical cost of an asset soon becomes irrelevant. Thus, various forms of inflation accounting are or have been found in these countries. One interesting example of this is Brazil.[6] A new corporation law was introduced in 1976 which was designed to strengthen the stock market. One of its major concerns was the protection of minority shareholders, so it introduced rules making the payment of dividends obligatory. Therefore, income had to be clearly defined and this was done using a system of monetary corrections: official monthly price indexes were used to update the values of assets, depreciation, cost of sales and owners' equity. These regulations were withdrawn in 1986 as part of a series of anti-inflationary economic measures. Other Central and South American countries have also used various forms of current cost accounting at various times. A description of one such method can be seen in Exhibit 6.2 which reproduces part of the accounting policy statement of the Chilean electricity generation company, Empresa Nacional de Electricidad SA (Endesa Chile).

6.4 The legal system

6.4.1 Types of legal system

Commercial law is generally based upon one or other of two types of legal systems, namely Romano-Germanic or code law which can be further subdivided into three families: French, German and Scandinavian code law and common law legal systems.

The countries of continental Europe, Latin America and much of Asia have various forms of code law. Laws are generally codified (often using a similar organizational framework to that of the French Napoleonic codes of 1804–11). The philosophy behind the laws in these countries may be described as one where the role of law is to describe and mandate acceptable behaviour. Laws consist of rules and procedures that have to be followed. Typically, commercial codes regulate the behaviour of all commercial organizations, including the regulation of accounting.

---

[6] Doupnik (1987).

| Exhibit 6.2 | Endesa Chile: price-level statements and accounting policy |

Constant currency restatement:

The cumulative inflation rate in Chile as measured by the Chilean Consumer Price Index ('CPI') for the three year period ended December 31, 2006 was approximately 8.2%.

Chilean GAAP requires that the financial statements be restated to reflect the full effect of loss in the purchasing power of the Chilean peso on the financial position and results of operations of reporting entities. The method described below is based on a model that enables calculation of net inflation gains or losses caused by monetary assets and liabilities exposed to changes in the purchasing power of local currency. The model prescribes that the historical cost of all non-monetary accounts be restated for general price-level changes between the date of origin of each item and the year end.

The financial statements of the Company have been price-level restated in order to reflect the effects of the changes in the purchasing power of the Chilean currency during each year. All non-monetary assets and liabilities, all equity accounts and income statement accounts have been restated to reflect the changes in the CPI from the date they were acquired or incurred to year end.

The resulting gain or loss included in net income reflects the effects of Chilean inflation on the monetary assets and liabilities held by the Company.

The restatements were calculated using the official consumer price index of the National Institute of Statistics and . . .

The above-mentioned price-level restatements do not purport to represent appraisal or replacement values and are only intended to restate all non-monetary financial statement components in terms of local currency of a single purchasing power and to include in net income or loss for each year the gain or loss in purchasing power arising from the holding of monetary assets and liabilities exposed to the effects of inflation.

Source: Taken from the financial statements, year ended 31 December 2006, p. 126, www.endesa.cl.

The alternative to code law is common law. Here, the philosophy is one where the role of law is to prohibit undesirable behaviour rather than to prescribe or codify desirable behaviour. This system has its origin in England from where it was exported to the USA and the Commonwealth, where it takes various forms. In common law countries much of the law is developed by judges or the courts who set case law during the resolution of specific disputes. Statute law does exist, but it tends to be less detailed and more flexible than its equivalent in code law countries.

La Porta *et al.* (1998) explain how these legal systems have been exported to other countries and it is worth quoting them on this:

> The French Commercial Code was written under Napoleon in 1807 and brought by his armies to Belgium, the Netherlands, part of Poland, Italy and western regions of Germany. In the colonial era, France extended its legal influence to the Near East and Northern and sub-Saharan Africa, Indochina, Oceania and French Caribbean countries. . . .
>
> The German Commercial Code was written in 1897 after Bismarck's unification of Germany, and perhaps because it was produced several decades later, was not as widely adopted as the French code. It had an important influence on legal theory and doctrine in Austria, Czechoslovakia, Greece, Hungary, Italy, Switzerland, Yugoslavia, Japan and Korea. Taiwan's laws come from China, which borrowed heavily from the German code during its modernization.

(pp. 1119–1120)

Writers often argue that the main difference between the two systems is that code law tends to favour the protection of creditors while common tends instead to place emphasis upon the protection of shareholders. However, this is too much of a simplification. La Porta *et al.* (1998) in a study of the legal rules and enforcement systems in 49 countries looked at the protection offered to both shareholders and creditors. They found instead that countries that had the highest protection for shareholders tended also to have the highest protection for creditors. Thus it was that, after controlling for income levels, common law countries tended to offer the highest protection for both groups while French code law countries offered the least protection. However, German code law countries tended to have strong creditor protection in some areas.

This does not mean that the legal system is unimportant, only that it is not correct to argue that code law equates with creditor protection and common law equates with shareholder protection. The legal system does, however, seem to affect how accounting is regulated.

6.4.2 Accounting and code law legal systems

In code law countries governments have generally regulated accounting as one part of their measures to ensure orderly business conduct. Accounting regulations are one part of a complete system of commercial regulations that apply to all business organizations. Regulations are designed to protect all the parties to any commercial transaction and to ensure orderly business conduct. The tax authorities are often also an important user, and accounting regulations have often been set with their needs in mind. Shareholders have generally not been seen as so important. (This is not surprising when it is realized that most businesses are not listed and do not have many external shareholders.) The financial statements of individual companies were usually more highly regulated than are consolidated statements. This is because the tax authorities are interested in the individual company, not the group, and most legal contracts with creditors, suppliers or customers also occur at the individual company level.

In most code law countries accounting is regulated primarily through an accounting code which is typically prescriptive, detailed and procedural. Thus, the accounting regulations include not only detailed disclosure rules but also measurement and bookkeeping rules. It is quite common for countries also to have industry-specific regulations or plans.

6.4.3 Accounting and common law legal systems

England is a good example of a common law country. Companies Acts have been concerned mainly with disclosure of information for the protection of the owners of limited liability companies, that is the shareholders. Not only have companies to follow the specific provisions of the Companies Acts but they also have a general duty to present financial statements that are 'true and fair'. The courts have interpreted this legal requirement to mean that, unless a company can demonstrate otherwise, it must also follow accounting standards as set by the private sector body, the Accounting Standards Board (ASB). The standards set by the ASB are an example of piecemeal regulations – each standard covers one particular issue. They have often been issued as a reaction to a particular business problem and so are ad hoc rather than part of a larger plan. From 2005 the courts have looked to the IFRS rather than ASB in judging listed companies, but they continue to apply common law principles in forming judgments.

The legislature has an even less important direct role in accounting regulation in some other common law countries. For example, in the USA while the legislature in the form of the Congress has ultimate authority for the federal regulation of accounting, it has used this in very few cases. Instead, it has delegated authority to the Securities and Exchange Commission (SEC) which in turn has delegated authority for accounting standard setting to an independent body, the Financial Accounting Standards Board (FASB) (see Chapter 12).

In contrast to code law countries, accounting regulations have tended to grow in a piecemeal fashion alongside the growth of limited liability companies and the separation of owners and managers, with an emphasis on accounting and reporting at the group level. Accounting has often been regulated because the free market system has been seen to break down and has not provided sufficient information of an adequate quality. Finally, because the emphasis is on finance providers rather than taxation authorities, the measurement rules often tend to be less conservative than those of code law countries.

6.5 The taxation system

6.5.1 The relationship between tax rules and financial reporting rules

In some countries, the taxation system is an important influence on accounting. In others it has little or no influence on reporting rules and practices. Code law countries tend to have common tax and financial reporting regulations, while common law countries tend instead to keep the tax and financial reporting regulations separate from each other. However, the precise relationship between the two varies across countries and there are always exceptions to these generalizations. (For example, The Netherlands is an important exception to this rule, as discussed in Chapter 14.)

Three types of tax systems can be identified. These are systems where:

- the tax rules and the financial reporting rules are kept entirely, or very largely, independent of each other;
- there is a common system, with many of the financial reporting rules also being used by the tax authorities;
- there is a common system, with many of the tax rules also being used for financial reporting purposes.

6.5.2 Independent tax and financial reporting regulations

One of the best examples of this type of system is the UK. Here, the tax and financial reporting rules are kept separate with the two being set by different bodies. For example, Financial Reporting Standard 15 (FRS 15) requires that the depreciation method used in the financial statements 'should reflect as fairly as possible the pattern in which the asset's economic benefits are consumed by the entity' (para. 77). In contrast, the tax charge is based upon a system of predetermined tax-depreciation allowances. Not only is tax depreciation uniform, but the rates often serve economic policy objectives providing investment incentives. For example, the first year capital allowance on fixed assets for small and medium-sized enterprises (SMEs) was increased from 40 per cent to 50 per cent for tax year 2004–05. (This is despite a 2001 discussion paper issued by the

Inland Revenue suggesting that small companies' taxation should be based upon reported profits.)[7] This means that deferred taxation is often of considerable importance in the UK and other countries with a similar corporate taxation system, but is relatively uncommon in many other countries.

While many other countries also have largely independent tax and reporting rules, there are often some issues where the tax and accounting rules are not independent of each other. For example, in the USA the tax rules do not generally affect the financial reporting rules or practices. However, an important exception is stock or inventory valuation. Thus, the 'last-in–first-out' (LIFO) system can be used for tax purposes only if it is also used for financial reporting.

6.5.3 The use of financial reporting rules by the tax authorities

Many of the countries of the Commonwealth follow the example of the UK with the financial reporting rules being set without direct control or influence of the taxation authorities. (Not only did the UK often export the English common law legal system, but it also exported its taxation system.) However, the tax system in many developing Commonwealth countries is not as sophisticated and the rules are not as well developed as they are in the UK. This has meant that the tax authorities have not set detailed and all-embracing rules for the calculation of taxable income. Instead, they have tended to rely wholly or largely upon reported earnings as the basis for calculating tax liabilities. The accounting regulations are therefore by default also the tax regulations.

This has important implications for accounting practice. It means that where there are no accounting regulations, or where the regulations permit some choice, there will be a very much stronger incentive for managers to choose methods that minimize their reported earnings and therefore also their tax liability. They will prefer not to choose the method that is most informative or the method that best reflects the 'true and fair' position of the company if it leads to a higher tax bill. It also means that companies will be more resistant to new accounting regulations that increase their tax liability, thus making it more difficult to introduce such regulations and, if they are introduced, increasing the problems of non-compliance.

6.5.4 The use of tax rules for financial reporting

The third alternative is where the tax authorities set detailed rules for the calculation of taxable earnings and these rules have to be followed not only in the tax returns but also in the external financial statements. There are variations in exactly how the system works, but this approach can be found in most of the countries of Western Europe. The systems in place in France and Germany will be discussed in Chapter 14. Another example is that of Austria.[8] Commercial law regulates financial reporting. Here, there are several tax allowances that can be claimed only if they are also disclosed in the financial reports; this applies even if the resultant values would not otherwise be allowed by the commercial law. For these items, the tax rules take precedence. Most companies attempt to provide information of most use to external report readers. They therefore show the tax allowances as a separate item in untaxed reserves in the balance sheet rather than treat them as changes in the value of the relevant assets.

---

[7] Inland Revenue Technical note, 12 March 2001.

[8] Wagenhofer (2001).

For example, Telekom Austria AG discloses in its Balance Sheet produced according to the Austrian Commercial Code, two types of untaxed reserves.[9] One of these is 'Reserves from special depreciation' which contains two items: 'Continuation of special depreciation as permitted by section 8 and 122 of the Austrian Income Tax Act 1972' and 'Transfer of hidden reserves as permitted by Section 12 of the Austrian Income Tax Act'. The second type of untaxed reserve is simply investment allowances as per section 10 of the Austrian Income Tax Act.

Commercial law may also allow companies to choose between alternative accounting treatments when the tax authorities do not prescribe a particular treatment (e.g. LIFO or FIFO for inventory). In these cases, whichever method is used for financial reporting purposes will also be used by the tax authorities.

Tax is calculated at the individual company rather than at the group level. This is one reason why accounting for the individual company has traditionally been considered more important than group accounting in much of Western Europe. It also means that companies were often far more restricted in their choice of methods of accounting at the individual company level than at the group level. Thus, the tax rules were largely responsible for a two-tier system of regulation and reporting in many EU countries, with accounting at the group level converging much more towards an international norm.

6.6 The corporate financing system

Companies can be financed in a variety of ways. Both debt and equity can take many different forms and can be provided by many different types of individuals and institutions. The way in which a company is financed affects accounting in a number of ways. For example, if equity finance is relatively more important than debt finance, accounting regulations are more likely to be designed to provide forward-looking information useful for investment decision-making purposes. If debt financing is relatively more important, accounting measurement rules should be relatively more conservative, being designed to protect creditors. The sophistication of finance providers and the extent to which they have to rely upon financial statements will also impact significantly upon accounting disclosures – both mandatory and voluntary.

6.6.1 Corporate financing patterns

Average debt–equity ratios provide an indication of differences in financing across countries.[10] One study of the relationship between culture and financing patterns in 22 countries[11] found some significant differences in debt–equity ratios even after controlling for differences in performance, legal system, GDP and financial institutions. The highest corporate debt ratios were found in Germany (71 per cent), Italy (65 per cent), The Netherlands (63 per cent), France (62 per cent) and Japan (61 per cent). In contrast, the lowest ratios were found in the USA (47 per cent), Australia (45 per cent), Greece (44 per cent) and Taiwan and China (both 42 per cent). Differences in corporate financing

---

[9] Telekom Austria AG, 2006. Available at http://www.telekomaustria.com.

[10] Average debt–equity ratios only provide an indication of differences. They will be affected by differences in the samples chosen and by differences in the accounting rules used in different countries.

[11] Chui *et al.* (2002).

| Exhibit 6.3 | Major equity markets, 2006 |

Exchange	Domestic market value ($bn)	Turnover value ($bn)		No. of companies listed		Domestic market capitalization as % of GDP	% capitalization by 10 largest cos
		Domestic	International	Domestic	International		
NYSE	15,421.2	19,916.1	1,795.4	1,829	451	109.2	16.1
Tokyo	4,614.1	5,791.3	1.3	2,391	25	107.4	20.1
NASDAQ	3,865.0	9,985.4	712.0	2,812	321	28.9	29.5
London	3,794.3	4,283.6	3,288.1	2,913	343	145.0	37.1
Euronext	3,708.2			954	256	86.4	29.0
Hong Kong	1,715.0	830.4	1.7	1,165	8	591.9	46.9
TSX (Toronto)	1,700.7	1,273.1	8.6	3,790	52	126.1	23.4
Deutsche Borse	1,637.6	2,483.4	253.8	656	104	46.1	40.9
BME Spanish	1,322.9	1,916.0	17.8	N/A	N/A	90.0	44.0
Swiss	1,212.3	1,284.6	109.4	256	92	269.1	66.3
Shanghai	917.5	726.6	0	842	0	12.7	56.6
Shenzhen	227.9	410.3	0	579	0	5.1	22.2

Source: World Federation of Stock Exchanges, 2006 Annual Report, www.world-exchanges.org.

patterns will also be reflected in differences in stock market activity. Exhibit 6.3 provides some information on some of the major stock markets.[12]

Reflecting the long history of foreign trading and financing in the UK, the London Stock Exchange (LSE) had, until very recently, more foreign listings than any other market. However, it has clearly been overtaken by New York (the NYSE) as the popular market for foreign listing. Slightly less popular than London is a second US exchange, NASDAQ,[13] which tends to attract rather smaller foreign companies or foreign companies requiring less financing than does the NYSE, and also Euronext, which tends to attract mainly companies from nearby European countries. Euronext was established in 2000 from the exchanges of Amsterdam, Paris and Brussels. In April 2007 the NYSE acquired Euronext N.V. In 2002 the London futures market and the Portuguese stock markets joined.

However, it is not just the number of companies listed that is important; the size of the companies listed is also relevant. One measure of size is the market value of a company's shares or its stock market capitalization. If we look at the stock market capitalization of domestic companies only, then a rather different picture emerges. The NYSE is now clearly the most important stock market. Indeed, its domestic capitalization is slightly more than the combined value of the next three exchanges (i.e. Tokyo, NASDAQ and London). An alternative measure of the significance of the equity market is the ratio of domestic market capitalization to GDP which relates the size of the equity market to the output of the domestic economy. This ratio is also shown in Exhibit 6.3, where some very large differences emerge.

---

[12] World Federation of Exchanges website www.world-exchanges.org. Again, a word of warning is in order. Differences in market structures and differences in the methods of data collection mean that these figures are not strictly comparable, although they do indicate important differences.

[13] NASDAQ or the National Association of Securities Dealers Automated Quotation system is a computerized quotation system which allows potential buyers and sellers of securities traded on the over-the-counter (OTC) market to locate the market makers who will buy and sell OTC securities.

Exhibit 6.4	Stock market capitalization, 1990–2006 (US$bn)								
	1990	**1992**	**1994**	**1996**	**1998**	**2000**	**2002**	**2004**	**2006**
Euronext	–	–	761.0	1,105.7	1,903.3	2,271.7	1,538.7	2,441.3	3,708.2
Germany	355.3	346.9	499.3	664.9	1,086.7	1,270.2	686.0	1,194.5	1,637.6
London	850.0	928.4	1,145.3	1,642.6	2,372.7	2,612.2	1,856.2	2,865.2	3,774.3
NASDAQ	310.8	618.8	793.7	1,511.8	2,243.7	3,597.1	1,994.5	3,532.9	3,865.0
NYSE	2,692.1	3,798.2	4,147.9	6,842.0	10,277.9	11,534.6	9,015.3	12,707.6	15,421.2
Tokyo	2,928.5	2,318.9	3,592.2	3,011.2	2,439.5	3,157.2	2,089.3	3,557.7	4,614.1
TSX (Canada)	241.9	241.9	315.1	487.0	543.4	766.2	570.2	1,177.5	1,700.7

Note: these figures are for domestic companies only.

Source: World Federation of Stock Markets, various Annual Reports.

Exhibit 6.4 provides details of the domestic capitalization of seven major equity markets in the period 1990–2006. From this, it can be seen that while the NYSE is now much larger than any other exchange, this is a relatively recent phenomenon. Indeed, it was briefly overtaken by Tokyo in the late 1980s and early 1990s. Exhibit 6.4 also shows some other interesting changes in relative capitalization since 1990. These suggest that Euronext has been a success so far. In contrast, Tokyo has shown only very moderate growth over this period.

6.6.2 Equity ownership patterns

From an accounting perspective, what is important is not only the size of the equity market but also its microstructure. The amount of active trading that occurs, and the types of traders that exist, affect the level of demand for both financial information in general and for particular types of information. For example, if individual small shareholders are active investors then there will be more demand for financial statements orientated to relatively unsophisticated shareholders. If most shares are owned by a small number of pension funds or investment trusts then more emphasis will probably be placed on investor–corporate relationships. Important concerns may then be the protection of private shareholders and the prevention of insider trading.

Exhibit 6.5 provides some information on the popularity of share ownership in eight countries.

The proportion of the population owning shares has tended to remain remarkably stable in most countries over the last few years, and there remain some significant differences across countries. Private share ownership appears particularly common in North America and Australia. In contrast, only approximately one in five of the population in the UK, Switzerland, Sweden or Hong Kong own shares while the figure is much lower in Germany despite its relatively high standard of living. While this table tells us something about the number of individuals owning shares, a more important determinant of the demand for accounting information is the relative importance of private shareholders and other types of shareholders as providers of finance. That is, not only is the number of shareholders important, but also important is the size of their shareholdings. Unfortunately, up-to-date information on this is far more difficult to obtain as it is not routinely collected by stock markets. To give some idea of the differences that can be

Exhibit 6.5	Percentage of individuals owning shares

	1980s	1990–96	1997	1998	1999	2000	2001	2002	2003	2004
Australia	'88 9	'94 16	20	32	41	40	N/A	37	39	44
Hong Kong	N/A	'94 10	16	N/A	16	21	20	20	18	24
Korea	N/A	'95 5	6	7	9	9	8	8	8	8
Germany	'88 7	'94 6	6	7	8	10	9	8	8	7
Switzerland	N/A	N/A	N/A	N/A	N/A	32	N/A	24	N/A	20
Sweden	N/A	N/A	N/A	N/A	N/A	22	22	21	23	N/A
UK	N/A	N/A	28	24	25	25	24	22	N/A	N/A
USA	N/A	N/A	N/A	N/A	36	N/A	N/A	34	N/A	N/A

Note: The 'results are not directly comparable because of different time periods in which the data were collected, definitions of shares/stocks, methodologies used to collect the data and sample criteria and sizes' (p. 2).

Source: 'International Share Ownership', Australian Stock Exchange, September 2005, p. 2.

found across countries, Exhibit 6.6 gives some data on four very different countries – Sweden, Japan, Australia and Thailand. What is most apparent here is simply the differences across the four countries coupled in all cases with the significance of foreign shareholders.

The most important differences lie in the relative importance of individuals, financial institutions and non-financial corporations. Thailand shows what is probably a fairly typical picture for a developing country, with most shares owned by individuals or foreigners, with non-financial enterprises holding a much smaller proportion of the stock market and financial institutions being a very minor player. The other countries are more typical of developed countries, although it is noticeable how much more important non-financial enterprises are in Japan than in Sweden or Australia. This reflects the fact that Japanese companies will often hold, on a long-term basis, relatively small shareholdings in companies in the same group of companies that they do business with to show their long-term commitment and shared interests in maintaining good relationships.

There are a number of reasons why the importance of, and the structure of, markets might consistently differ across countries. Cultural factors may affect individuals' saving habits and attitudes to stock market trading. Historical factors affecting the growth of stock

Exhibit 6.6	Share ownership in Sweden, Japan, Australia and Thailand

	Sweden (2002)	Japan (2003)	Australia (2003)	Thailand (2003)
Household	18.3	20.5	22	32.3
Non-financial enterprises	8.0	21.8	3	15.0
Financial enterprises	30.6	34.5	35	7.4
Public sector	8.8	0.2	–	3.6
Foreigners	33.7	21.8	40	24.8
Other	–	8.7	–	7.6
Total	100 %	100 %	100 %	100 %

Source: World Federation of Stock Exchanges web pages, www.world-exchanges.org.

markets and the relationships between banks and industrial companies are obviously also important, as are current institutional arrangements. Particularly important here are the costs and ease of trading, the ways in which pensions are organized and the range of financial intermediaries that exist. For example, pension premiums of current employees may be used to finance existing pension commitments; alternatively, they may be held and invested in the stock market until used to finance the future pensions of current employees. Investment trusts and unit trusts are important in some countries, both being designed to allow individuals to invest cheaply and efficiently in the stock market.

La Porta *et al.* (1997) examined the extent to which the legal system in a country affected the financing system of the country. They argued that the legal system and the effectiveness of creditor and shareholder protection would influence the savings and investment decisions they make. The extent that companies could access equity finance was proxied by three measures: the stock market capitalization as a percentage of GNP scaled by the proportion of the stock market held by outsiders, that is a measure of the extent of external shareholdings; the number of listed domestic companies scaled by the size of the population; and the number of initial public offerings again scaled by the size of the population. These measures were compared with the legal system and shareholder and investor protection. As expected, these authors found consistent differences across the 49 countries examined. On all the measures examined the common law countries provided better access to equity finance and the French code countries were generally the worst. However, debt availability was highest in the German code law countries. Later work by Frost *et al.* (2006) found that stock markets that are the most developed, that is those that are most liquid and largest in relative terms, also tend to be those with the strongest disclosure systems as measured by disclosure requirements and monitoring and enforcement mechanisms.

These results support the conclusion that two models may be identified. In the 'UK model' there is a long history of an active stock market. A wide range of financial intermediaries exists, with pensions being increasingly financed through insurance companies, and investment and unit trusts being important depositories of personal savings. Complementing this is the role of banks, which have traditionally provided only short-term or medium-term financing to industry. This contrasts sharply with what is often termed the 'German model'. Here, the financial system is dominated by banks. Often the banks also tend to be less specialized than in the UK, with no distinction between commercial and investment banks. While other types of financial institutions do exist, they are far less important than in the UK. The banks are the repository of most personal savings, increasingly offer pension and insurance products and have tended to have close relationships with industrial companies. They offer more long-term loans than do UK banks, and they often also hold shares in industrial companies as well as acting as proxy shareholders for their private customers. They are also more likely to have representatives on the boards of companies than do their equivalent in the UK. As illustrated in Exhibit 6.7, these two systems may also be termed 'control-oriented' and 'arm's length' financial systems.[14]

As with any simple categorization, the divide between the two systems is not always clear cut. Indeed, the two systems are converging. While UK and US capital markets can be characterized by the relatively greater importance of outside shareholders and by relatively greater interest in short-term financial results, many of the larger companies

---

[14] Berglof (1997).

Exhibit 6.7	Financial systems and capital structure	

	Type of financial system	
	Control-oriented	**Arm's length**
Share of control-oriented finance	High	Low
Financial markets	Small, less liquid	Large, highly liquid
Share of all firms listed on exchanges	Small	Large
Ownership of debt and equity	Concentrated	Dispersed
Investor orientation	Control-oriented	Portfolio-oriented
Use of mechanisms for separating control and capital base	Frequent	Limited (often by regulation)
Dominant agency conflicts	Controlling v minority shareholders	Shareholder v management
Role of board of directors	Limited	Important
Role of hostile takeovers	Very limited	Potentially important

Source: Berglof (1997).

are actively engaged in promoting and building long-term relationships with their various stakeholders, so reducing the differences between 'outsiders' and 'insiders'. Similarly, many companies in countries such as Germany, France or Japan, all members of the continental European group, are coming to rely more upon outside shareholders for finance and so are becoming more concerned with increasing shareholder value.

Later work by La Porta *et al.* (2002) shows how the valuation of firms is positively related to aspects of the protection of outside investors, while Hail and Leuz (2006) instead document how markets that offer better legal protection to shareholders also provide cheaper capital if the stock markets are also not well integrated. However, stock market integration, as seen for example in openness to foreign investors, reduces these impacts and has the effect of reducing international differences in the cost of capital.

6.7 The accounting profession

A further important influence on the regulation and practice of accounting may be the accounting profession itself. The size, role, organization and importance of the accounting profession all result from the interplay of the various factors discussed earlier in this chapter. For example, the role of the auditor and the way in which the profession is regulated (whether by government or self-regulation) both depend upon the type of legal system in place. Likewise, the importance of the profession – in terms of who it audits and how many audits are conducted – depends upon the types and numbers of companies that exist.

The profession in turn influences the institutions of a country and its accounting system. The way in which the profession is organized and society's attitude towards accountants and auditors will tend to affect auditors' ability to influence or control the behaviour of companies and their reporting systems. The extent to which auditors are independent and their power relative to the companies which they audit are important here. Whether auditors are seen as being independent, powerful professionals, or instead are seen as being under the control or influence of the companies they audit, will affect the perceived value of financial statements, and this will happen even if these perceptions are wrong.

6.7.1 Size of the accounting profession

Some idea of the size of the accounting profession in a range of countries can be seen from the data given in Exhibit 6.8. This illustrates some very large differences. The most extreme difference emerges between the UK and Germany: there are approximately

Exhibit 6.8 The accountancy profession in selected countries

Country	Professional body	Year start	Size	Students	Practising	Population (m) (2004)
Australia	Institute of Chartered Accountants of Australia (ICAA)	1885	40,650	10,950	16,260	19.9
	CPA Australia	1886	96,370	11,150	21,801	
China	Chinese Institute of Certified Public Accountants	1988	140,000	–	61,250	1,313
France	Ordre des Experts-Comptables	1952	17,460	4,750	17,460	60.4
Germany	Institut der Wirtschaftsprüfer (IdW)	1931	11,040	–	10,522	82.5
Hong Kong	HK Institute of Certified Public Accountants		22,800	18,000	6,250	7.1
India	Institute of Chartered Accountants of India	1949	110,250	79,900	75,400	1,082.2
Japan	Japanese Institute of Certified Public Accountants (JICPA)	1927	14,240	4,700	14,240	127.8
The Netherlands	Nederlands Instituut van Registeraccountants (NIvRA)	1895	13,510	–	4,390	16.2
UK and Ireland	Institute of Chartered Accountants in England & Wales (ICAEW)	1880	125,000	12,600	25,000	59.4
	Institute of CA of Scotland (ICAS)	1854	15,580	2,160	4,180	
	Institute of CA of Ireland (ICAI)	1888	13,810	3,640	4,600	4.0
	Association of Chartered Certified Accountants (ACCA)	1891	98,300	173,200	28,600	
USA	American Institute of Certified Public Accountants (AICPA)	1927	335,110	–	128,700	297.0

Sources: www.ifac.org (most are 2003 figures); Economist World in Figures 2007.

250,000 financial accountants with UK qualifications and only 11,000 with German. While this example is commonly discussed, it is somewhat misleading. The UK figures are overstated when compared with most other countries. It is common for people to retain membership of an accounting body even if they have moved into industry or commerce – or, indeed, even retired – and if the figures for practising accountants are compared the difference is significantly reduced. Movement from accounting into industry or commerce on qualification or relatively soon after gaining full membership of an accounting body is common in the UK. In contrast, the German figure is considerably understated compared with most other countries. There are many more tax experts (*Steuerberater*) than accountants (*Wirtschaftsprüfer*). Also excluded from these figures are a second tier of auditors who can audit only private companies. The typical role of the accountant is also smaller in countries such as Germany than in the UK. Many of the tasks undertaken by professional accountants in the UK are undertaken by engineers, lawyers or other professionals in much of Western Europe with the term 'accountant' being more synonymous with the role of the auditor in the UK. Finally, the UK figures and in particular the figures for ACCA membership include many people who qualified in and practise in other countries. However, while much of the differences in the size of the profession across countries are explicable by methods of definition, large differences still remain. In particular, it remains true that the profession tends to be relatively larger in the Commonwealth and the USA than it is in Western Europe or Japan.

Not only are there major variations in the size of the profession, but there are also a number of other important differences. There are differences in the degree of the profession's independence – in most of the common law countries the profession has traditionally been largely self-regulating, taking responsibility for the licensing of accountants or auditors, including setting entry requirements, training and examinations. (In recent years this self-regulation has been moderated by the establishment of Oversight Boards having statutory powers, for example the PCAOB in the USA, as described in Chapter 3.) In contrast, in the code law countries many of these roles are carried out by the state. Similar differences exist with respect to control of the audit – who determines auditing guidelines or standards, and under what authority auditors act.

6.7.2 Accountants' role in regulation

Accounting regulations may or may not be set by the profession. As discussed above, in code law countries accounting regulations are generally set by the government. However, even here the profession often plays a role. It may act as an advisor to the government, providing input into the regulatory process. It may issue standards or recommendations in areas where there are no legal regulations. It may issue pronouncements that explain or expand government regulations. The French profession in the form of the OEC and the CNCC provides a good example of this approach (as discussed in Chapter 14).

In common law countries, the regulation of accounting tends to be delegated by the government to an independent body. The Financial Accounting Standards Board (FASB) in the USA, the Australian Accounting Standards Board (AASB) and the UK Accounting Standards Board (ASB) are examples. However, these distinctions are becoming blurred with the establishment of standard-setting bodies such as the German Accounting Standards Board (see section 14.3.3) and the Accounting Standards Board of Japan (see section 16.3.5).

6.8 Other influences

There are a number of other factors which have affected various accounting rules and practices in one or more countries. Particularly important are:

- religion
- accidents of history
- the exporting or imposition of accounting rules or practices by more powerful societies
- the importing of accounting rules or practices from another country or countries.

6.8.1 Religion

The most obvious example of the influence of religion on accounting is with respect to Islam, and in particular Islamic banking. There has been a significant increase in Islamic banking since it started in the 1960s in Egypt. Now, several global western banks such as Deutsche Bank and Citibank offer Islamic banking services to their customers.

The most obvious difference from western or secular banks is that under Islamic law, riba or usury is considered to be wrong. This means that banks cannot charge interest. Instead, they have set up a range of alternatives that are designed to share both risks and returns between the borrower and the lender. Also, in a manner similar to western ethical funds, the banks will not invest in organizations that do not follow Quranic injunctions. In particular, they will not invest in or lend to non-Islamic banks and companies involved in alcohol, gambling or rearing pigs.

This obviously affects accounting as there will be no loans or interest, but instead 'participations' and 'investment accounts', and Islamic accounting including social accounting has been the subject of a significant amount of academic research.[15] Many Islamic financial institutions use the accounting standards issued by the Accounting and Auditing Organization for Islamic Financial Institutions rather than IFRS. This organization was set up in 1993 in Bahrain and has issued 16 standards to date.[16] Exhibit 6.9 shows the Shari'a Supervisory Board Report of the Bahrain Islamic Bank which includes a statement that the Bank is 'committed to the Shari'a standards issued by the Accounting & Auditing Organisation for Islamic Financial Institutions'.

Religion has been used in a number of studies of accounting and finance as an explanatory variable. However, in most of these studies it is not clear if it is religion and the dominant religious system in the country that is important, or whether religion is being used as a proxy for culture, as discussed in the next chapter. For example, Stulz and Williamson (2003), building upon the work of La Porta *et al.* (as described above in section 6.6.2), examine the factors that help explain the level of creditor protection across countries. They argue that creditor protection depends upon a society's attitude towards capital and interest payments, and therefore there will be higher levels of creditor protection in societies where borrowing and lending and the charging of interest are more socially acceptable. They then argue that the Calvinistic reformation that took place in Protestant countries led to a more supportive attitude towards interest payment than the attitude which continued to hold in predominantly Catholic countries. Looking at the predominant religion, openness to international trade, the per capita income

---

[15] See, for example, Baydoun and Willett (2000); Gambling and Karim (1986); Lewis (2001); Maali *et al.* (2006).
[16] Drummond (2001); Karim (2001).

Exhibit 6.9 Shari'a Supervisory Board's Report, Bahrain Islamic Bank

To the shareholders of
Bahrain Islamic Bank B.S.C.

In The Name of Allah, most Gracious, most Merciful
Peace and Blessings Be Upon His Messenger

Assalam Alaykum Wa Rahmatu Allah Wa Barakatoh

Pursuant to the powers entitled to the Shari'a Supervisory Board to supervise over the Bank's activities and investments, we hereby submit the following report:

The Shari'a Supervisory Board monitored the operations and transactions and contracts related to transactions carried out by the Bank throughout the year ended 31 December 2005, to express opinion on the Bank's commitment to the provisions and principles of Islamic Shari'a in its activities and investments in accordance to the guidelines and decisions issued by the Supervisory Board. The Shari'a Supervisory Board believes that ensuring the conformity of the Bank's activities and investments with provisions of Islamic Shari'a is the sole responsibility of the Bank's Management, while the Shari'a Supervisory Board is only responsible for expressing an independent opinion and preparing a report thereabout.

The Shari'a Supervisory Board's monitoring functions included the checking of the Bank's documents and procedures to scrutinize each single operation carried out by the Bank, whether directly or through Shari'a Internal Audit. We planned with Shari'a Internal Audit Department to carry out monitoring functions through the acquisition of all information and clarifications that are deemed necessary to confirm that the Bank did not violate the principles and provisions of Islamic Shari'a. The Shari'a Internal Audit Department carried out its functions of auditing the Bank's transactions and submitting a report to the Shari'a Supervisory Board, which indicated the Bank's commitment and conformity to the Shari'a Supervisory Board's opinions.

The Shari'a Supervisory Board obtained data and clarifications that it deemed necessary to confirm that the Bank did not violate the principles and provisions of Islamic Shari'a. The Shari'a Supervisory Board held several meetings throughout the year ended 31 December 2005 and replied to inquiries, in addition to approving a number of new products presented by the Management. The Shari'a Supervisory Board discussed with the Bank's officials all transactions and applications carried out by the Management throughout the year ending 31st December 2005, and reviewed the Bank's conformity with the provisions and principles of Islamic Shari'a, as well as the resolutions and guidelines of the Shari'a Supervisory Board.

The Shari'a Supervisory Board believes that:

1. Contracts, operations, and transactions conducted by the Bank throughout the year, ending 31 December 2005 were made in accordance to the standard contracts pre-approved by the Supervisory Board.

2. Distribution of profits and losses on investment accounts was in line with the basis approved by the Supervisory Board in accordance with the principles pre-approved by the Supervisory Board.

3. No gains resulted from sources or by means prohibited by the provisions and principles of Islamic Shari'a.

4. Zakah was calculated according to the provisions and principles of Islamic Shari'a. The Bank distributed Zakah on the statutory reserve, general reserve and retained earnings. The Shareholder should pay his proportion of Zakah on his/her shares as stated in the financial report.

5. The Bank was committed to the Shari'a standards issued by the Accounting & Auditing Organisation for Islamic Financial Institutions.

We pray that Allah may Grant all of us Further Success and Prosperity.

Shari'a Supervisory Board Members:

Dr. Shaikh A. Latif Mahmood Al Mahmood
Chairman of Shari'a Supervisory Board

Shaikh Mohammed Jaffar Al Jiffari
Vice Chairman of Shari'a Supervisory Board

Shaikh Adnan Abdullah Al Qattan
Member of Shari'a Supervisory Board

Shaikh Nedham M. Saleh Yacoubi
Member of Shari'a Supervisory Board

Source: Bahrain Islamic Bank, Annual Report 2005, p. 17.

and the legal system of 49 countries they found that religion was the variable that was the best predictor of the level of creditor rights in a society and, as they expected, creditor protection was higher in protestant countries.

6.8.2 Accidents of history

There are numerous examples of accounting rules or practices originating from shocks to the system or accidents of history. For example, much of the early UK company law legislation, including accounting regulations, was the result of financial crises or collapse of companies. Other more significant examples of major economic shocks include the collapse of the US and German stock markets in the 1920s. Similar events in the two countries resulted in very different institutions and regulations. In the USA the collapse of the stock market led to the creation of the SEC and increased accounting regulations to protect and encourage share ownership (see section 11.3.1). In Germany, the collapse of the stock market and the resulting increase in debt financing led to regulations which were focused upon creditor protection. The Asian economic crisis of 1997 was a major shock across several countries, but the most significant shock of recent years for accounting was the failure of the US company Enron which led to significant changes in corporate governance rules and the regulation of audit firms in many countries (see section 3.2 and Chapter 11).

6.8.3 The exporting/imposition of accounting

Accounting regulations and practices have always been exported and imported from the earliest days of double-entry bookkeeping. Exporting occurs for a number of reasons.[17] The profession itself has always been one source. For example, Price Waterhouse started in London in 1849, but then opened offices in New York and Chicago before it opened its second UK office in Liverpool in 1904. Several US accounting firms were set up by UK-trained accountants. This movement of accountants led to many early similarities between accounting in the UK and the USA. International trade in accountants and accounting firms continues to the present time, with the larger firms being active worldwide. This means that they often export their accounting and auditing standards and these are then used where there are no local regulations.

A second major factor in the export of accounting has been colonialism. The UK and France exported many of their legal and administrative structures and their educational systems to their colonies. Following independence, local factors have become more important and the influence of the former colonial powers has declined.[18] But many institutions have not changed very much. For example, all of the Caribbean Economic Community (CARICOM) members (which are English-speaking, former British colonies), with the one exception of Barbados, have Company Acts based upon various UK Companies Acts ranging from the 1829 Act to the 1948 Act.[19] Similar influences can also be seen in the former French colonies of Africa which use accounting codes based upon the French code.[20]

---

[17] See, for example, Parker (1989).

[18] Cooke and Wallace (1990); Chua and Poullaos (2002).

[19] Chaderton and Taylor (1993).

[20] United Nations (1991).

Countries have imported the legal system of other countries as well as the accounting system in the form of the accounting laws or regulations. They have also imported the system of regulation of the accounting profession[21] and increasingly the accounting education system and the accounting qualifications. For example, Uche (2007) documents the impacts of the increasing importance of the UK ACCA qualification in British West Africa and argues that while the ACCA has introduced regional differences in the exams, they are still not sufficiently focused on small and medium-sized companies and the specific development needs of these countries. Other studies have instead looked at the impact of supranational organizations arguing for example that the use of US GAAP-based accounting methods by the World Bank has also led to the exporting of such practices.[22]

Depending upon the history of a country, the accounting system may show evidence of many different influences. For example, as will be discussed in Chapter 16, Japanese accounting regulations reflect the exporting of both German and US regulations. One particularly interesting example of a country influenced by a large number of other countries is Turkey. (See Case study 6.1 for a description of the various external influences on the Turkish accounting system.) Another example of a group of countries that has been influenced by a variety of more developed systems is the ASEAN countries. (See Case study 6.2 for information on these.)

6.8.4 The importing of accounting

Countries may have sought to retain the exported accounting systems in the face of forces for indigenization of accounting.[23] Alternatively, they may instead have sought actively to import accounting regulations or practices. This may have been done because developing accounting rules is both expensive and time consuming. It is much less costly to see what other countries have done and to select those rules that most suit your own needs. Thus countries may import an entire set of rules, or specific rules only. The countries of Eastern Europe are a good example of the importation of accounting. Having overthrown communism they sought links with the EU and faced the task of completely overhauling their accounting systems. Most already had a chart of accounts in place from the previous regime, as a basis for bookkeeping, but their accounting regulations had to be rewritten. They tended to look to the countries of Western Europe and the EU for models of regulation. Consequently they imported aspects of EU accounting as well as IASB accounting.[24] In a similar way, individual companies have also imported accounting practices from other countries or from the IASB. Below are some examples of the accounting policies used by some European companies in the period prior to EU endorsement of IFRS:

Use of IFRS-compatible local rules and US rules by German companies: Allianz Group (2003):

In accordance with section 292a of the German Commercial Code (HGB) the consolidated financial statements have been prepared in conformity with International Financial Reporting Standards (IFRS). All standards currently in force for the years under review have been adopted in the presentation of the consolidated financial statements.

---

[21] Sian (2006).

[22] Neu and Ocampo (2007).

[23] Annisette (2000).

[24] See, for example, King *et al.* (2001) or Daniel *et al.* (2001).

IFRS do not provide specific guidance concerning the reporting of insurance transactions in annual financial statements. In such cases as envisioned in the IFRS Framework, the provisions embodied under accounting principles generally accepted in the United States of America (US GAAP) have been applied.

Use of IFRS and local rules by Finnish companies: Nokia (2003)
The consolidated financial statements of Nokia Corporation, a Finnish limited liability company with domicile in Helsinki, are prepared in accordance with International Accounting Standards (IAS). The consolidated financial statements are presented in millions of euro (EURm), except as noted, and are prepared under the historical cost convention except as disclosed in the accounting policies below. The notes to the consolidated financial statements also conform with Finnish Accounting legislation.

Use of US GAAP by Dutch companies: Royal Dutch Petroleum Company (2003)
Previously published Financial Statements were presented based on accounting policies which were in accordance with Netherlands and US in all material respects. With effect from 2003, the financial statements are presented in accordance with US GAAP, with separate financial statements presented under Netherlands GAAP.

Summary and conclusions

This chapter has provided an overview of many of the factors that influence accounting. It is always dangerous to generalize too much: there will always be exceptions to any generalizations, and there will always be countries that do not follow the typical pattern. As long as this is recognized, there are enough similarities across countries to make generalizations possible. Therefore, in this chapter we have seen how accounting rules and practices have been influenced by a large number of quite different factors. Particularly important are the following:

- the political and economic system
- the legal system
- the taxation system
- the corporate financing system
- the accounting profession.

Finally, we also saw how a country may import and export accounting rules and practices.

Key points from the chapter:

- There is no simple universal relationship between any particular institution and the accounting system. All the factors identified are important, as are their interactions.
- Accounting and accountants are influenced by the institutions of a country and by external influences and they in turn can also influence a country's institutions in many complex and changing ways.
- The political and economic system, the taxation system and the corporate financing system all tend to influence the demand for accounting information and the objectives served by the financial reporting system.

- The most important users of financial statements may be shareholders or they may be creditors or taxation authorities.

- The type of legal system a country has and the strength of the accounting profession tend to influence who regulates accounting, and the rigidity of the regulations.

- The regulatory structures and the users both tend in turn to influence the specific measurement rules adopted and the extent of disclosures made, whether mandatory or voluntary.

Case study 6.1 Accounting in Turkey: external influences

Legal requirements that affected accounting entered Turkish business life for the first time with the adoption of the Commercial Code (Law on Commerce) in 1850, which was a translation of the first and third books of the French Commercial Code. By 1864, translation of the whole of the French Commercial Code had been completed.

From 1850 until about 1925, the impact of French accounting on Turkish accounting practice was significant. This was because most of the instructors or authors on accounting and tax in Turkey had received their accounting education in France. Since Italian accounting principles were largely adopted by the French, the so-called Italian System of Accounting practised in Turkey was first introduced through French publications.

In 1926 a new Commercial Code was introduced based mainly on the Commercial Codes of Italy and Germany. However, sections of the new code were taken from the Commercial Codes of Belgium, France, Austria, Hungary, Chile, Argentina, Spain, Romania, Britain and Japan as well as Italy and Germany. The copying of elements of foreign law led to the Turkish Code being piecemeal, and it was therefore not as effective as planned.

During the period 1926–60, Turkish accounting practice was considerably influenced by German accounting. This influence became more pronounced after several well-known German management and accounting professionals emigrated to Turkey in the early 1930s, fleeing the Nazi regime in Germany. In this period, most of the students going abroad went to Germany for accounting education and many Turkish state economic enterprises employed German consultants for the reorganisation of their accounting systems. Another German influence on the Turkish accounting system was the introduction of income tax based on the 1950 German model.

After the defeat of Germany in the Second World War the USA emerged as the main influence. Of particular importance was the Marshall Plan of economic help which marked the beginning of US business involvement on Turkey. More and more students were sent to the USA for business education and special institutions and programmes were established in Turkey to introduce American management theories and practice. The impact of American accounting practice has been even more pronounced over the last three decades.

Source: Cooke and Curuk (1996), p. 341.

European Accounting Review, Taylor & Francis, www.tandf.co.uk/journals.

Case study 6.2 | Accounting in ASEAN: external influences

The comparative analysis of national corporate and companies law within ASEAN suggests four patterns of development: (1) A British approach (adopted by Brunei, Malaysia and Singapore); (2) A Dutch approach (adopted by Indonesia); (3) A US approach (adopted by the Philippines); and (4) A mixed-country approach (adopted by Thailand). Accordingly, Brunei, Malaysia and Singapore (all former British colonies) have each adopted a Companies Act modelled on the UK Companies Act 1948 and the Australian Uniform Companies Act 1961. However, the Companies Act of Singapore has undergone considerable changes since first enacted in 1967. Indonesian Commercial Code, 1848, was patterned on the early Dutch Commercial Code with some minor amendments. Under this system, law is codified, and company legislation prescribes rules in details for accounting and financial reporting. Unfortunately, many of the amendments that have been made in The Netherlands since 1848 were not incorporated in the commercial code in Indonesia. As a result, Indonesia is operating an out of date commercial code adopted in the nineteenth century that is incompatible with today's commercial environment. . . . It is therefore obvious that company laws in ASEAN have been affected strongly by each country's former colonial links despite the appropriateness of such legislation to its environment. [The] British group (Brunei, Malaysia, Singapore) was mainly influenced by [the] British, and [the] non-British group (mainly the Philippines, Thailand and Indonesia) was influenced by [the] US, Japan, The Netherlands and Germany, reflecting its important trading links with these major economic powers during the late 1800s and early 1900s. With this backdrop, it is obvious that accounting practice which is a product of accounting education and training in ASEAN has been structured based on the corporate legal environment created by colonial powers during their administration without due regard to local needs and conditions.

Source: Yapa (2003), p. 270 (references excluded from quote).

Questions

The following questions test your understanding of the material contained in the chapter and allow you to relate your understanding to the learning outcomes specified at the start of this chapter. The learning outcomes are repeated here. Each question is cross-referenced to the relevant section of the chapter.

Understand how various aspects of a country's political and economic system have influenced its accounting system

1 What are the main institutional influences on accounting practices in general? (section 6.2)

2 Which of the influences identified above are most important in your country? (section 6.2)

3 Why might the importance of the various influences identified differ across countries and over time? (section 6.2)

4 To what extent has the importance of the influences identified above varied over time in your country? (section 6.2)

5 How does the political and economic system of your country fit into the classifications described? (section 6.3)

6 How might the type of political and economic system of a country influence the accounting regulatory system? (section 6.3)

7 How might the type of political and economic system of a country influence the types of accounting measurement rules adopted? (section 6.3)

8 How might the type of political and economic system of a country influence the type of accounting disclosure rules adopted? (section 6.3)

9 How might the type of political and economic system of a country influence the type of accounting measurement and disclosure practices voluntarily adopted by companies? (section 6.3)

Distinguish between common and code law systems and describe how the legal system typically influences the system of accounting regulation

10 How does the legal system of your country fit into the classifications described? (section 6.4)

11 How might the type of legal system of a country influence the accounting regulatory system? (section 6.4)

12 How might the type of legal system of a country influence the types of accounting measurement rules adopted? (section 6.4)

13 How might the type of legal system of a country influence the type of accounting disclosure rules adopted? (section 6.4)

14 How might the type of legal system of a country influence the type of accounting measurement and disclosure practices voluntarily adopted by companies? (section 6.4)

Describe the ways in which the tax system can influence accounting rules and practices

15 How does the taxation system of your country compare with the descriptions given? (section 6.5)

16 How might the type of taxation system of a country influence the accounting regulatory system? (section 6.5)

17 How might the type of taxation system of a country influence the types of accounting measurement rules adopted? (section 6.5)

18 How might the type of taxation system of a country influence the type of accounting disclosure rules adopted? (section 6.5)

Identify possible differences in the financing of companies internationally and describe how these differences may help to explain differences in accounting rules and practices

19 How does the corporate financing system of your country compare with the descriptions given? (section 6.6)

20 How might the type of corporate financing system of a country influence the accounting regulatory system? (section 6.6)

21 How might the type of corporate financing system of a country influence the types of accounting measurement rules adopted? (section 6.6)

22 How might the type of corporate financing system of a country influence the type of accounting disclosure rules adopted? (section 6.6)

23 How might the type of corporate financing system of a country influence the type of accounting measurement and disclosure practices voluntarily adopted by companies? (section 6.6)

Understand how the way in which the accounting profession is organized can influence accounting rules and practices

24 How does the accounting profession in your country compare with the descriptions given? (section 6.7)

25 How might the type of accounting profession of a country influence the accounting regulatory system? (section 6.7)

26 How might the type of accounting profession of a country influence the types of accounting measurement rules adopted? (section 6.7)

27 How might the type of accounting profession of a country influence the type of accounting disclosure rules adopted? (section 6.7)

Understand how a country might import or export accounting rules and practices

28 How do the external influences on accounting practice in your country compare with those described? (section 6.8)

29 How might external influences on a country influence the accounting regulatory system? (section 6.8)

30 How might external influences on a country influence the types of accounting measurement rules adopted? (section 6.8)

31 How might external influences on a country influence the type of accounting disclosure rules adopted? (section 6.8)

32 How might external influences on a country influence the type of accounting measurement and disclosure practices voluntarily adopted by companies? (section 6.8)

References and further reading

Annisette, M. (2000) 'Imperialism and the professions: the education and certification of accountants in Trinidad and Tobago', *Accounting, Organizations and Society*, 25: 631–659.

Australian Stock Exchange (June 2003) *International Share Ownership (Comparison of Share Owners)*, ASX.

Baydoun, N. and Willett, R. (2000) 'Islamic corporate reports', *Abacus,* 36(1): 71–90.

Berglof, E. (1997) 'A note on the typology of financial systems', pp. 151–164 in Hopt, K.J. and Wymeersch, E. (eds) *Comparative Corporate Governance: Essays and Materials*. Berlin: Walter de Gruyter.

Chaderton, R. and Taylor, P.J. (1993) 'Accounting systems of the Caribbean: their evolution and role in economic growth and development', *Research in Third World Accounting*, 2: 45–66.

Chua, W.F. and Poullaos, C. (2002) 'The Empire Strikes Back? An exploration of centre–periphery interaction between the ICAEW and accounting associations in the self-governing colonies of Australia, Canada and South Africa, 1880–1907', *Accounting, Organizations and Society*, 27: 409–445.

Chui, A.C.W., Lloyd, A.E. and Kwok, C.C.Y. (2002) 'The determination of capital structure: is national culture the missing piece to the puzzle?', *Journal of International Business Studies*, 33(1): 99–127.

Cooke, T.E. and Curuk, T. (1996) 'Accounting in Turkey with reference to the particular problems of lease transactions', *European Accounting Review*, 5(2): 339–359.

Cooke, T.E. and Wallace, R.S.O. (1990) 'Financial disclosure regulation and its environment: a review and further analysis', *Journal of Accounting and Public Policy*, 9: 79–110.

Daniel, P., Suranova, V.Z. and de Beedle, I. (2001) 'The development of accounting in Slovakia', *European Accounting Review*, 10(2): 343–359.

Doupnik, T.S. (1987) 'The Brazilian system of monetary correction', *Advances in International Accounting*, 1: 111–135.

Doupnik, T.S. and Salter, S.B. (1995) 'External environment, culture, and accounting practice: a preliminary test of a general model of international accounting development', *International Journal of Accounting*, 30(4): 189–207.

Drummond, J. (2001) 'A risk-free return? It's forbidden', *Accountancy*, April: 98–99.

Frost, C.A., Gordon, E.A. and Hayes, A.F. (2006) 'Stock exchange disclosure and market development: an analysis of 50 international exchanges', *Journal of Accounting Research*, 44(3), June: 437–483.

Gambling, T. and Karim, R. (1986) 'Islam and social accounting', *Journal of Business Finance and Accounting*, 13(1): 39–50.

Hail, L. and Leuz, C. (2006) 'International differences in the cost of equity capital: do legal institutions and securities regulation matter?', *Journal of Accounting Research*, 44(3), June: 485–531.

Hope, T. and Gray, R. (1982) 'Power and policy making: the development of an R&D standard', *Journal of Business Finance and Accounting*, 9(4): 531–558.

Karim, R.A.A. (2001) 'International accounting harmonization, banking regulations and Islamic banks', *International Journal of Accounting*, 36: 169–193.

King, N., Beattie, A., Critescu, A.-M. and Weetman, P. (2001) 'Developing accounting and audit in a transition economy', *European Accounting Review*, 10(1): 149–171.

La Porta, R., Lopez-de-Silanes, F., Shleifer, A. and Vishny, R.W. (1997) 'Legal determinants of external finance', *Journal of Finance*, 52(3): 1131–1150.

La Porta, R., Lopez-de-Silanes, F., Shleifer, A. and Vishny, R.W. (1998) 'Law and finance', *Journal of Political Economy*, 106(6): 1113–1155.

La Porta, R., Lopez-de-Silanes, F., Shleifer, A. and Vishny, R.W. (2002) 'Investor protection and corporate valuation', *Journal of Finance*, 57(3): 1147–1170.

Lewis, M. (2001) 'Islam and accounting', *Accounting Forum*, 25(2): 103–127.

Maali, B., Casson, P. and Napier, C. (2006) 'Social reporting by Islamic banks', *Abacus*, 42(2): 266–289.

Neu, D. and Ocampo, E. (2007) 'Doing missionary work: the World Bank and the diffusion of financial practices', *Critical Perspectives on Accounting*, 18(3), March: 263–389.

Parker, R.H. (1989) 'Importing and exporting accounting: the British experience', pp. 7–29 in Hopwood, A.G. (ed.) *International Pressures for International Change*. London: Prentice Hall/ ICAEW.

Puxty, A.G., Willmott, H.C., Cooper, D.J. and Lowe, T. (1987) 'Modes of regulation in advanced capitalism: locating accountancy in four countries', *Accounting, Organisations and Society*, 12(3): 273–291.

Sian, S. (2006) 'Inclusion, exclusion and control: the case of Kenyan accounting professionalisation project', *Accounting, Organisations and Society*, 31: 295–322.

Stulz, R.M. and Williamson, R. (2003) 'Culture, openness and finance', *Journal of Financial Economics*, 70: 313–349.

Uche, C. (2007) *The accounting profession in British West Africa*. Edinburgh: ICAS.

United Nations (1991) *Accountancy Developments in Africa: Challenge of the 1990s*. New York: United Nations CTC.

Wagenhofer, A. (2001) 'Austria – Individual accounts', in Ordelheide, D. and KPMG (ed.) *Transnational Accounting*, 2nd edn. London: Macmillan.

Yapa, P.W.S. (2003) 'Accounting education and training in ASEAN: the Western influence and the experience of Singapore, Malaysia, Indonesia and Brunei Darussalam', *Research in Accounting in Emerging Economies*, 5: 267–292.

Zeff, S.A. (1972) *Forging Accounting Principles in Five Countries*. Champaign, IL: Stipes Publishing.

Cultural influences on accounting rules and practices

Learning outcomes

After reading this chapter you should be able to:

● Understand what is meant by the term 'culture', and describe the cultural dimensions identified by a number of different researchers.

● Describe the relationship between culture and organizational structures.

● Describe the accounting values identified by Gray, and explain how they might be related to culture.

● Evaluate research which has used these accounting values and assess their significance for those seeking international harmonization.

7.1 Introduction

In Chapter 6 we looked at a range of institutions that can influence accounting rules and practices, and saw how they help to explain why accounting has differed across countries. However, this is not the whole story. This chapter looks at another influence on accounting, namely culture – both the culture of a country and the culture or subculture of accountants.

The institutions of a country are set up and run by people. Accounting regulations are similarly set up by people and accounting is carried out by people. Different people often think and act in different ways. They have different tastes, different beliefs and different attitudes. However, these are not completely random: people often share many similar tastes, beliefs and attitudes. While we will define 'culture' more fully below, we can think of these common attributes as the 'common culture' of a group. The group which shares such a common culture may be the country or society as a whole, or it may be a smaller group of people such as accountants!

If we return to the influences on an accounting system, a similar model to Exhibit 6.1 is reproduced in Exhibit 7.1. We can see how accounting may be affected or influenced by societal culture and accounting culture. Differences in the culture of a society are reflected in the ways in which society organizes itself. The factors discussed in the previous chapter, namely the ways in which the economic system is organized, the ways in which companies are set up, controlled and financed, the legal system and the organization of professions, are all influenced by the culture of the country. But culture may also have a more direct influence on accounting. It influences account preparers, regulators, auditors and users, and so should influence also the types of rules they set out and the practices they follow.

This chapter goes on to explain more fully what is meant by 'culture'. It then looks at some of the evidence on cultural differences across societies, exploring ways in which culture can affect business – in particular how it affects the ways in which businesses are organized, who makes decisions in organizations and what motivates employees. Finally, the cultural values of accountants are discussed and the possible links between accounting and culture are explored.

7.2 Defining culture

7.2.1 The culture of a country

'Culture' in the sense that it is used here refers to the set of common ideas, beliefs and values that are shared by the members of a group of individuals. There are very many alternative definitions of culture and much work has been done in describing and measuring various aspects of culture. However, in the business and accounting literature, the most important work is undoubtedly that carried out by Hofstede, an organizational psychologist. He defined culture as 'the collective programming of the mind which distinguishes the members of one human group from another'.[1]

---

[1] Hofstede (1984).

Exhibit 7.1	The influences on an accounting system

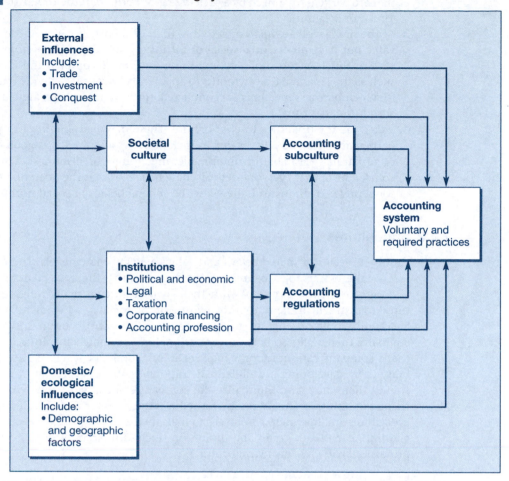

Source: Adapted from Gray (1988). Copyright Accounting Foundation. Reproduced by kind permission of Blackwell Publishers.

This definition highlights three important points about culture:

- Culture is collective, rather than being a characteristic of any one individual.
- It is not directly observable, but it can be inferred from people's behaviour.
- It is of interest only to the extent that it helps to differentiate between groups – due to cultural differences, groups will behave in different and definable ways.

Cultural differences exist at a number of different levels. Hofstede identified four:

1 *Symbols* are the most superficial of the four: they comprise words, gestures, pictures or objects that have particular meanings for a cultural group. An example might be the meaning that different societies tend to attach to Coca-Cola. Coca-Cola can be seen as the most obvious thing to drink on a hot day, or it may be seen as a drink only suitable for the young. It may be seen as being desirable, indicating sophistication and affluence, or it may be seen as an unwelcome example of US international dominance.

2 *Heroes* are individuals (whether real or imaginary) who embody those characteristics that are particularly prized by a society (e.g. Superman in the USA, Asterix in France or Tintin in Belgium).

3 At the next level are *rituals* or activities that, of themselves, have little or no extrinsic value but have an essential social or intrinsic value. They range from simple rituals, such as different forms of greeting, through to more complex and formalized rituals such as the Japanese tea ceremony, to apparently purposive activities such as the ways in which business meetings are conducted. (Indeed, it has been argued[2] that much of accounting is a ritual.)

4 *Values* are the final core level of culture. These may be thought of as preferences for particular states of being. Examples include views about what is good or evil, natural or unnatural, desirable or undesirable and honest or dishonest. This does not, of course, mean that everyone acts on these beliefs or that they describe everyone's personal preferences. Instead, they describe general beliefs or social norms.

7.2.2 Subcultures

Culture in terms of shared beliefs and values exists at many levels. There is societal culture or the culture of a country. Inside any country there are a number of distinct, although overlapping, groups with their own cultures (usually referred to as 'subcultures' to distinguish them from the culture of the society as a whole). Different regional areas and ethnic or religious groups may share distinct subcultures. At the level of the company there will also be an organizational or corporate subculture. Indeed, one way that a company can successfully manage at least moderate levels of uncertainty or instability is by developing a well-defined corporate culture: everyone in the organization should then know and internalize the company's aims, will know what is expected of them and how they should react. This reduces the need for written rules, regulations and procedures and may help employees to make better decisions in new circumstances.[3] In addition, each work group and profession, including accountants and the accounting profession, will have its own subculture.

7.2.3 The dimensions of culture

Culture is a complex phenomenon, too complex to be easily described or measured. However, there have been many attempts to unbundle it into a number of underlying dimensions, each of which is less complex. Each dimension covers one aspect of culture which has then been described, measured and quantified. Different cultural or subcultural groups have then been measured on each dimension and compared with each other. There have been a large number of attempts at doing this and while they disagree upon the precise dimensions or factors that are relevant, they all agree that a small number of dimensions or factors are sufficient to compare and describe societies.

One of the earliest of these attempts was by Kluckholn and Strodtbeck (1961) who used six dimensions developed from asking questions about societies, as shown in Exhibit 7.2. Another anthropologist, Edward Hall, also carried out similar work focusing instead upon only four questions, also shown in Exhibit 7.2.

---

[2] Gambling (1987).

[3] See, for example, Balaga and Jaeger (1984); Harrison and Carroll (1991); Sorensen (2002).

| Exhibit 7.2 | Possible cultural dimensions |

Questions asked by Kluckholn and Strodtbeck:

1 What do members of a society assume about the nature of people? (Good, bad, or some combination?)

2 What do members of a society assume about the relationship between people and the environment? (Live in harmony or subjugate environment?)

3 What do members of a society assume about the relationship between people? (Act as individual, member of group or collective?)

4 What is the primary mode of being? (Accept status quo or not?)

5 What is the conception of space? (Amount of personal space? Public expression of emotions?)

6 What is the dominant temporal orientation? (Past, present or future?)

Dimensions used by Hall:

1 Context: The amount of information that must be explicitly stated if a message or communication is to be successful.

2 Space: Ways of communicating through the specific handling of personal space.

3 Time: Monochronic or sequential handling of tasks versus polychronic or the simultaneous handling of tasks.

4 Information flow: Structure and speed of messages between individuals and organizations.

Source: From Gannon *et al.* (1994).

In what is still the largest cross-country study of employees of any one organization (IBM), Hofstede developed four cultural dimensions, as reproduced in Exhibit 7.3. It is noteworthy that in this initial work, the four dimensions generated did not, unlike the other two attempts described, include a temporal or time-based dimension.

Hofstede has, rightly, been criticized for his choice of terminology, and in particular the use of the terms 'masculinity versus femininity'. It has been argued by many writers that this terminology reinforces notions of gender differences that may, at best, be considered suspect. Later writers have instead used various terms such as 'human heartedness' or 'nurturing'. Of the alternatives proposed, 'nurturing' best describes the same set of characteristics without ascribing either gender or sex differences to them. We will also use this term instead of masculinity/femininity.

Hofstede measured his four dimensions for each of a range of 50 countries and three geographical groupings of countries.[4] The results obtained by Hofstede for a number of countries discussed in this book are reproduced in Exhibit 7.4. (Note that Hofstede did not look at China nor indeed at any of the other then communist countries, and he looked at only one African country, South Africa, and one Arab country, Iran.)

The interpretation of these scores and rankings is set out in Exhibit 7.5. Hofstede used cluster analysis to identify groupings of countries and from his clusters proposed dividing lines separating one of the pairs of characteristics from the other. Exhibit 7.5 also sets out

---

[4] Hofstede (1991).

| Exhibit 7.3 | Cultural dimensions identified by Hofstede (1984) |

Individualism versus collectivism

Individualism stands for a preference for a loosely knit social framework in society wherein individuals are supposed to take care of themselves and their immediate families only. Its opposite, collectivism, stands for a preference for a tightly knit social framework in which individuals can expect their relatives, clan, or other in-group to look after them in exchange for unquestioning loyalty. . . . The fundamental issue addressed by this dimension is the degree of interdependence a society maintains among individuals. It relates to people's self-concept: 'I' or 'we'.

Large versus small power distance

Power distance is the extent to which the members of a society accept that power in institutions is distributed unequally. This affects the behaviour of the less powerful as well as of the more powerful members of society. People in large-power-distance societies accept a hierarchical order in which everybody has a place which needs no further justification. People in small-power-distance societies strive for power equalization and demand justification for power inequalities. The fundamental issue addressed by this dimension is how a society handles inequalities among people when they occur.

Strong versus weak uncertainty avoidance

Uncertainty avoidance is the degree to which the members of a society feel uncomfortable with uncertainty and ambiguity. This feeling leads to beliefs promising certainty and to maintaining institutions protecting conformity. Strong uncertainty-avoidance societies maintain rigid codes of belief and behaviour and are intolerant towards deviant persons and ideas. Weak uncertainty-avoidance societies maintain a more relaxed atmosphere in which practice counts more than principles and deviance is easily tolerated. The fundamental issue addressed by this dimension is how a society reacts to the fact that time runs only one way and that the future is unknown: whether it tries to control the future or to let it happen.

Masculinity versus femininity (low versus high nurturing)

Masculinity stands for a preference in society for achievement, heroism, assertiveness and material success. Its opposite, femininity, stands for a preference for relationships, modesty, caring for the weak and the quality of life. The fundamental issue addressed by this dimension is the way in which a society allocates social (as opposed to biological) roles to the sexes.

the dividing points specified by Hofstede. For example, any country scoring more than 50 on the individualism/collectivism dimension could be described as being individualistic. Countries scoring less than 50 would instead be described as being collectivist.

Others have attempted to create measurements of cultural dimensions that may be used in empirical testing. For example, Schwartz (1994), using 41 cultural groups, classified national cultures into six types (Conservatism, Intellectual and Affective Autonomy, Hierarchy, Mastery, Egalitarian Commitment, Harmony) which in turn were summarized into cultural dimensions (Conservatism, Mastery and Hierarchy).

7.2.4 Critique of Hofstede's work

While many researchers in accounting and management have used Hofstede's work, it has not been uncritically received. There has been much debate regarding its usefulness.

Exhibit 7.4 Scores and rankings for individual countries from Hofstede's cultural dimension research

Country	Individualism versus collectivism		Large versus small power distance		Strong versus weak uncertainty avoidance		Low versus high nurture	
	Score	Rank	Score	Rank	Score	Rank	Score	Rank
Australia	90	2	36	41	51	37	61	16
France	71	10/11	68	15/16	86	10/15	43	35/36
Germany	67	15	35	42/44	65	29	66	9/10
Japan	46	22/23	54	33	92	7	95	1
Netherlands	80	4/5	38	40	53	35	14	51
UK	89	3	35	42/44	35	47/48	66	9/10
USA	91	1	40	38	46	43	62	15
Arab countries	38	26/27	80	7	68	27	53	23

Some of the criticisms made arise because researchers and writers have used the cultural dimensions or the scores provided by Hofstede in an inappropriate manner, although other criticisms are much more fundamental, calling into question the usefulness of Hofstede's work for understanding culture.

Hofstede (1991) has warned against the inappropriate use of his work. In particular, it must always be remembered that the dimensions are intended to discriminate between national cultures and not between individuals. The 'average' or 'typical' individual does not exist and cultural stereotypes can often be more misleading than helpful. Hofstede also argues that the dimensions are not intended to discriminate between subcultural groups such as those based upon gender, generation, social class or organization. This might seem to suggest that Hofstede would not support the application of his work to the accounting subgroup as done by Gray. However, this is not what Hofstede is arguing.

Exhibit 7.5 Interpretation of Hofstede's scores

Characteristics	Score		Rank	Country
Greatest individualism		91	1	USA
Dividing point	50			
Greatest collectivism		6	53	Guatemala
Largest power distance		104	1	Malaysia
Dividing point	44			
Smallest power distance		11	53	Austria
Strongest uncertainty avoidance		112	1	Greece
Dividing point	56			
Weakest uncertainty avoidance		8	53	Singapore
Lowest nurturing		95	1	Japan
Dividing point	50			
Highest nurturing		5	53	Sweden

Gray uses the work to discriminate between accountants or accounting in different countries, a valid comparison, and does not use them to discriminate, for example, between accountants and lawyers in the UK, an invalid use of Hofstede's work.

There have been several critiques of the work of Hofstede from a theoretical perspective. For example, McSweeney (2002) criticizes Hofstede's work on a number of grounds including the tendency to equate cultural groups with countries, while Baskerville (2003) also argues that the quantification, measurement and discussion of cultural dimensions is not the best way to think about culture.[5] Trompenaars,[6] instead, argues that the use of linear scales which have two ends, both of which preclude the other value construct, is not the most useful way to think about culture. In contrast, he argues that each end of the dimension is linked to the other and they should be integrated together and thought of in terms of complementarity rather than in terms of opposition.

Despite these criticisms, Hofstede's work has been used in literally hundreds of empirical studies not only in accounting but across the entire range of social science disciplines. An obvious reason for this is the fact that Hofstede reports specific numbers for each country, allowing researchers to use these as inputs into further statistical analysis and testing. However, even if it is accepted that the approach adopted by Hofstede is a valid one, there are several reasons to believe that the numbers he generated should not be uncritically accepted and used in further empirical studies.

The study took place over the period 1968–72, so it is now more than 35 years old. Over this period, the world has witnessed major changes. In many areas, cultures have moved towards each other, with US cultural values gaining in global importance, while other aspects of local or country-specific cultures are gaining more local prominence.[7]

The study was administered among employees in IBM. IBM was quite a unique company, with a very strong corporate culture, and therefore it tended to attract certain types of employees.[8] The subculture of IBM would have been quite strong, so reducing the size of inter-country differences found in the study.

The study was designed by and administered by individuals from a limited number of developed western countries who may not have had the knowledge necessary successfully to investigate very different cultures. To quote Hofstede:

> When the surveys were administered, not only Western but also non-Western respondents were confronted with Western questions. They dutifully answered them, but could the results really be supposed to express their values to the full?

> (1991, p. 160)

Evidence on this is offered by Michael Bond who developed the Chinese Value Survey (CVS)[9] with the help of researchers from Taiwan and Hong Kong and then administered it to students in 23 countries worldwide. The CVS again found four significant factors or dimensions – human heartedness, moral discipline, integration and long-term orientation. The first three of these were significantly correlated to three of Hofstede's dimensions, although it is important to realize that they are not direct or one-to-one alternatives or substitutes for Hofstede's dimensions. The most directly comparable was 'human heartedness', significantly related to only one of Hofstede's dimensions – nurturing. 'Moral discipline'

---

[5] See Hofstede (2003) for a reply to Baskerville.
[6] Trompenaars and Hampden-Turner (1997); Trompenaars (2003).
[7] See, for example, Ellwood (2001) or Steger (2003).
[8] Chposky and Leonis (1988); Slater (2002).
[9] Hofstede and Bond (1988).

Exhibit 7.6	Short- versus long-term orientation

Short-term orientation	Long-term orientation
Respect for traditions	Adaptation of traditions to a modern context
Respect for social and status obligations irrespective of cost	Respect for social and status obligations within limits
Social pressure to keep up with others even if this means overspending	Thrift
Small savings, little money to invest	Large savings, funds available for investment
Quick results expected	Perseverance
Concern with 'face'	Willingness to subordinate oneself for a purpose
Concern with possessing the truth	Concern with respecting the demands of virtue

and 'integration' were both found to be significantly correlated to the same two of Hofstede's dimensions – power distance and individualism. In contrast, none of the CVS dimensions correlated with uncertainty avoidance which appears not to be universal but instead is unique to western societies. Instead the CVS derived a different dimension – 'Confucian dynamism' or long-term orientation (LTO). This is more similar to the temporal dimension developed by Kluckholn and Strodtbeck. Exhibit 7.6 illustrates the main differences between short- and long-term orientations.

This illustrates the fact that if other questions had been asked, different cultural constructs may have been generated. For example, Hofstede ignored religion, which can also affect attitudes towards business and accounting.[10]

Much of the data collected was not actually used in generating the dimensions. While 63 questions were asked, mainly using Likert 5-point scales, only the central tendency or the mean answers were used in the analysis. Important data on the extent of agreement or disagreement inside each country was therefore ignored. If there is little consensus inside a country then culture is unlikely to explain differences even if the mean scores for each country are quite different from each other. This omission of important data was then compounded by combining the answers to specific questions in such a way as to deliberately make the scales used for each of the four constructs approximately equal in size, even if the underlying extent of agreement or disagreement varied across the four constructs. This means that the resulting scores are ranks only and should not be used in any statistical tests requiring interval data.

The final constructs are actually based on the answers to very few of the questions asked. In particular, uncertainly avoidance and power distance are both based upon the answers to only three questions and these questions were chosen mainly on the basis of theoretical or a prior reasoning rather than statistical testing. See Exhibit 7.7 for the actual questions used. Individualism and nurturing instead were each based upon a

---

[10] Hamid *et al.* (1993).

| Exhibit 7.7 | Questions used to generate power distance and uncertainty avoidance scores |

Power distance scores were computed 'on the basis of country mean scores for the three questions:

(a) Nonmanagerial employees' perception that employees are afraid to disagree with their managers.

(b) Subordinates' perception that their boss tends to take decisions in an autocratic or persuasive/paternalistic way.

(c) Subordinates' preference for anything but a consultative style of decision-making in their boss – that is, for an autocratic, a persuasive/paternalistic or a democratic style.'

Uncertainty avoidance index has 'been compiled on the basis of the country mean scores for the three questions:

(a) Rule orientation: agreement with the statement "Company rules should not be broken – even when the employee thinks it is in the company's best interest".

(b) Employment stability: Employees' statement that they intend to continue with the company for (1) one year at the most, or (2) from 2 to 5 years.

(c) Stress, as expressed in the mean answer to the question: "How often do you feel nervous or tense at work?" '

Source: Hofstede (1984), pp. 75 and 121.

factor analysis of 14 work goals questions. This suggests that the four cultural dimensions generated are not the only ones that could have been generated and others might have been generated if the data had been analyzed in a different way.

None of this means that the cultural constructs generated should be dismissed and indeed Hofstede provides a great deal of theoretical support for them. However, it does mean that the actual figures generated should not be used as measures of the culture of an entire country and be used in statistical tests requiring interval or ratio scales.

This suggests that while it may be valid to use large questionnaires to generate cultural values, it is not valid to go further and use these constructs to generate linear scales and then map countries on these scales to form classifications of countries. Indeed, this is the approach taken by Hampden-Turner and Trompenaars (2000) who have sampled some 46,000 managers in 46 countries including a significant number from the ex-communist world and several from Africa and Asia (i.e. the countries used gave far less of a developed western world bias than does Hofstede's work). Using questions on moral dilemmas and views of how organizations work, they generated six dimensions.

These are:

- Universalism (rules, codes, laws and generalizations) and particularism (exceptions, special circumstances, unique relations).
- Individualism (personal freedom, human rights, competitiveness) and communitarianism (social responsibility, harmonious relations, cooperation).
- Specificity (atomistic, reductive analytic, objective) and diffusion (holistic, elaborative synthetic, relational).
- Achieved status (what you have done, your track record) and ascribed status (who you are, your potential and connections).

- Inner direction (conscience and convictions are located inside) and outer direction (examples and influences are located outside).
- Sequential time (time is a race along a set course) and synchronous time (time is a dance of fine coordinations).

7.3 Culture and business

7.3.1 Culture and leadership style

Even if there is disagreement over the validity of specific attempts to quantify the culture of a country, it is generally agreed that culture, however defined, is one of the factors affecting how a society organizes itself. It will affect businesses and accounting in a variety of ways. If we look first at the relationship between business and culture, Hofstede (1991) suggested that culture influences both the preference for particular leadership styles and organizational structures and the motivation of employers and employees. Hofstede went on to describe how the cultural dimensions he had identified were linked to various organizational characteristics. For example, he argued that leadership styles would be particularly affected by individualism and power distance. If a country is highly individualistic, then leadership styles and structures would tend to be based upon the satisfaction of personal needs. Individual self-interest would feature strongly and personal relationships and loyalties would have relatively little relevance. In collectivist societies leadership would be more of a group phenomenon. Leaders would be successful only if they emphasize the group. Employee welfare would be relatively more important. Culture would also affect the degree of participation – whether extensive and real, consultative, symbolic or non-existent.

While these differences have little direct impact upon financial accounting, they have obvious implications for management accounting. Leadership style affects who makes what decisions in the company. This affects the accounting information system, which must be designed to ensure that decision makers receive the relevant information. The performance evaluation system must be designed so that performance measures reflect decision-making authority.

7.3.2 Culture and motivation

Motivation is also affected by culture. Individualism versus collectivism and high versus low nurturing seem to be particularly important. The importance of theories of motivation for financial accounting can be seen, for example, in agency theory. This is one of the most important theories to emerge in accounting in recent years and it has implications for the design of corporate governance systems and the regulation of auditing and financial reporting. The theory seeks to explain the behaviour of corporate managers. Agency theory assumes that managers are motivated by self-interest (high individualism), in particular by their remuneration including perks (low nurturing). Given these assumptions, it follows that managers will maximize their own income even at the expense of the owners of the company. Controls have to be put in place to prevent this happening. These include auditing and financial reporting, both of which monitor the behaviour of managers. However, this monitoring is not sufficient to ensure that managers act in the best interests of owners. Other contracts such as debt covenants are also used to limit managers' freedom of action. Share options and profit-based performance bonuses may, for example, act to bring managers' interests into harmony with those of the external shareholders. Thus, financial reporting and auditing regulations, other contractual arrangements and managers' preferences for particular measurement and reporting practices are all premised upon certain, usually implicit, assumptions about the behaviour of managers.[11]

If the culture of a country is very different from that implicitly assumed by agency theory with, in particular, higher scores on both collectivism and nurturing, agency theory may not provide such a good explanation of managers' behaviour. This means that the optimal amount and type of regulatory structures and rules may also be very different.[12] One example of an obvious and striking cultural difference may be seen in the case of Tanzania. This society is relatively collectivist with the extended family being particularly important. Thus, one of the earliest Tanzanian accounting standards (TSSAP 2 issued in 1983) includes extensive disclosure requirements with respect to related party transactions.[13] What is striking about TSSAP 2 is the way in which 'related parties' are defined primarily in personal terms, being mainly seen as family members. In contrast, the international standard defines related parties primarily in business terms. While 'close members of the families' fall under the international definition of related parties, far more emphasis is placed upon business associates and other parties with direct or indirect control or influence (see Case study 7.1 for extracts from the respective requirements).

7.3.3 Culture and organizational structures

Finally, culture also affects organizational structures. This has obvious implications for both management and financial accounting. One example is Japanese companies, as will be discussed in more detail in Chapter 16. Japanese corporate groups are often based upon a multitude of relationships such as supplier, customer and debt relationships and common directorships. Rather than there being majority share ownership by a clearly defined parent company there are often relatively small share cross-holdings throughout the group. This affects the usefulness of group statements which are based upon the assumption that a group is made up of a parent company, subsidiaries and sub-subsidiaries, all organized in a hierarchical structure.

Hofstede argued that the two cultural constructs that most affect how organizations are structured are power distance (which primarily influences superior–subordinate relationships) and uncertainty avoidance (which primarily influences the amount and type of rules in place). Hofstede also identified the types of business organizations which should be most common in particular countries, as illustrated in Exhibit 7.8.[14] (Note that this brief and simple description offers only an extremely simplified picture. As with any generalization, many organizations will be structured very differently, and what Hofstede describes may be best thought of as a tendency towards preferring particular styles of organization.)

Exhibit 7.8 shows us that, for example, countries characterized by relatively high power distance and strong uncertainty avoidance should tend to favour organizations run on fully bureaucratic lines. Here, explicit formal rules are more likely to prescribe

---

[11] Jensen and Meckling (1976); Fama (1980); Eisenhardt (1989).

[12] Chwastiak (1999); Kaplan and Ruland (1991); Ogden (1993).

[13] National Board of Accountants and Auditors (1983).

[14] Hofstede (1984), p. 216.

Exhibit 7.8	**Organizational types as identified by Hofstede (1984)**

	A	B	C	D
Power distance	Low	High	Low	High
Uncertainty avoidance	Weak	Weak	Strong	Strong
Organization type	Implicitly structured	Personnel bureaucracy	Workflow bureaucracy	Full bureaucracy
Implicit model of the organization	Market	Family	Well-oiled machine	Pyramid
Countries	Anglo/US Scandinavian Netherlands	South East Asian	Germany Finland Israel	Latin Med. Islamic Japan

Source: Hofstede (1984), p. 216.

behaviour. Power and authority tend to depend upon the position held rather than upon personal characteristics. In contrast, in countries such as the UK, the USA or Australia, which can be characterized by relatively small power distance and weak uncertainty avoidance, organizations should tend to be at least implicitly modelled upon the marketplace.

Thus, relatively less emphasis tends to be placed upon formal rules. Personal attributes and performance are both important in determining an individual's power and authority, while performance measures will be based upon the outcomes achieved rather than the actions undertaken.

7.4 Culture and accounting

7.4.1 Accounting subculture

Culture will influence the organizational structures and decision-making processes of companies and so in turn also influence the accounting and disclosure choices of individual companies. But culture will also have a more direct impact upon accounting practices. In the previous chapter we saw how the institutions and environment of a country can influence its accounting system. Culture will influence the institutions of a country while the subculture of accountants will also be influenced by the culture of the wider society. The system is a dynamic one in the sense that culture influences institutions and accounting while the accounting system provides feedback, influencing society's institutions and culture, as shown earlier in Exhibit 7.1.

The unique professional or job-related factors influencing accountants will not normally be strong enough to override completely or obliterate society-wide cultural differences. Thus, for example, the culture of the UK is different from the culture of (say) Japan, Germany or Korea and the subculture of UK accountants should therefore also be different from the subculture of accountants from Japan, Germany or Korea. The fact that all these accountants perform similar, although not identical, jobs should not be enough to obliterate all cultural differences between the three groups, although it may reduce them. Given the importance of society-wide culture and the influence of this on subcultures, we would expect to find that Hofstede's 'cultural dimensions' are systematically linked to a number of similar 'subcultural dimensions' or 'accounting values'.

7.4.2 Accounting values

If we return to Hofstede's cultural dimensions or values, the two that seem to have the most direct relevance to accounting are 'uncertainty avoidance' and 'individualism'. In a high-uncertainty-avoidance country, institutions will tend to be organized in ways that minimize uncertainty. Rules and regulations will tend to be explicit and prescriptive, and they will tend to be detailed, all embracing and rigid. Low-uncertainty-avoidance countries will tend to be less concerned with reducing uncertainty, they will tend to have fewer rules, perhaps relying more on general principles, and the rules that exist will be more likely to contain options. Individualism, on the other hand, affects motivation. It should therefore affect preferences for particular earnings, measurement rules and disclosure practices. It will also influence the extent to which people are happy to accept rules and controls imposed from above or will be willing to use their personal or professional initiative and be prepared to take risks. This should in turn affect their willingness to accept uniform accounting rules in preference to a more permissive system involving the use of professional discretion.

The work of Hofstede was extended by Gray (1988) who identified four 'accounting values' or 'subcultural dimensions'. '*Professionalism* versus *statutory control*' and '*uniformity* versus *flexibility*' both describe attitudes towards regulation, in particular attitudes towards the type of control system and the level or extent of control that is preferred. '*Conservatism* versus *optimism*' is concerned with attitudes towards measurement. Attitudes towards uncertainty are particularly important here. The final value, '*secrecy* versus *transparency*', is concerned with attitudes towards disclosure. Exhibit 7.9 reproduces Gray's definition of each of these four accounting values.

Exhibit 7.9 Accounting values identified by Gray (1988)

Professionalism versus statutory control
A preference for the exercise of individual professional judgement and the maintenance of professional self-regulation, as opposed to compliance with prescriptive legal requirements and statutory control.

Uniformity versus flexibility
A preference for the enforcement of uniform accounting practices between companies and the consistent use of such practices over time, as opposed to flexibility in accordance with the perceived circumstances of individual companies.

Conservatism versus optimism
A preference for a cautious approach to measurement so as to cope with the uncertainty of future events, as opposed to a more optimistic, laissez-faire, risk-taking approach.

Secrecy versus transparency
A preference for confidentiality and the restriction of disclosure of information about the business only to those who are closely involved with its management and financing, as opposed to a more transparent, open and publicly accountable approach.

Exhibit 7.10 The relationship between cultural dimensions and accounting values

Cultural dimension	Relationship to accounting values			
	Professionalism	Uniformity	Conservatism	Secrecy
Individualism	+	–	–	–
Uncertainty avoidance	–	+	+	+
Power distance	–	+	NR	+
Nurturing	NR	NR	+	+

Key: +   Positive relationship. For example, the *higher* individualism is, the *higher* professionalism will be.

 –   Negative relationship. For example, the *lower* uncertainty avoidance is, the *higher* profession-alism will be.

 NR   No relationship.

Gray also argued that Hofstede's societal cultural values will be systematically linked to his accounting values. The hypothesized relationships between the two are illustrated in Exhibit 7.10, which describes which of Hofstede's cultural dimensions are most strongly associated with each of Gray's four accounting values. Gray also hypothesized that the four accounting values influenced different parts of the accounting system. He argued that professionalism and uniformity influenced the regulatory system, in terms of both the institutional arrangements made for regulation and the methods of enforcement used, while conservatism and secrecy instead influenced the practice of accounting in terms of the measurement system adopted and the disclosures made. This can be seen diagrammatically in Exhibit 7.11.

7.4.3 Applying cultural analysis to accounting

Despite the problems discussed in section 7.2.4, there has been a considerable amount of work in most fields of accounting investigating the importance of culture. For example,

Exhibit 7.11 The relationship between accounting values and accounting systems

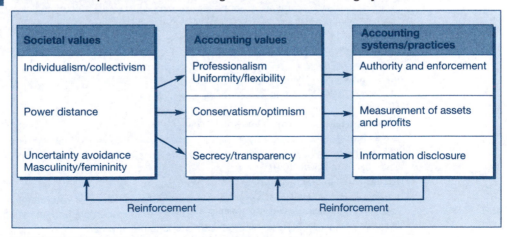

Source: Radebaugh *et al.* (2006), p. 50.

it has been used to explore the behaviour of accountants and accounting firms.[15] It has been used extensively in management accounting to explore issues of management control[16] and the behaviour of individuals in organizations,[17] in international business to explore corporate decision making[18] and in social accounting to explain international differences.[19]

In the field of international accounting it has been used to help explain corporate and accounting bodies' lobbying of the IASB,[20] differences in users' views on accounting rules,[21] interpretations of accounting terminology[22] and the application of specific rules[23] and differences in the accounting regulatory systems of various countries including the English-speaking countries of the UK, the USA, Australia and Canada in comparison with the Asian countries of Singapore, Hong Kong and Taiwan,[24] and New Zealand and India.[25] In each case the two groups of countries are culturally quite dissimilar and the studies were fairly successful in doing this. In contrast, other studies argued that culture fails to explain many of the accounting differences between France and Germany or Malaysia and Singapore.[26] These pairs of countries are culturally more alike than are the groups of countries in the former studies. Culture has also been used at the level of the individual country to explain accounting regulations and corporate behaviour.[27] Finally, it has been used to try to explain levels of disclosure. Again, it appears that culture is helpful in explaining broad patterns or levels of disclosure, while there is also some limited evidence that religion as well as Hofstede's cultural dimensions may be a factor affecting disclosure.[28]

Several of these studies have explored the importance of Gray's accounting values.[29] However, there are also problems with measuring Gray's accounting values. Auditors or other accountants can be asked their views on various issues, but this is not easy, and when done it tends to be restricted to studies which explore very specific and quite narrow decision-making scenarios.[30] A more common approach is to look instead directly at the accounting system. Thus, for example, rather than looking at attitudes towards conservatism, studies have looked at the importance of conservatism in the measurement rules and practices of countries. They have then tested the hypothesis that, for example, countries that have more uncertainty avoidance and more collectivism will have relatively more conservative measurement rules. This approach therefore tests the relationship between a country's culture and its accounting system rather than testing the

---

[15] See, for example, Soeters and Schreuder (1988) or Cohen *et al.* (1992).

[16] Harrison and McKinnon (1999); Chow *et al.* (1999).

[17] Harrison (1992).

[18] Leung *et al.* (2005).

[19] Perera and Mathews (1990).

[20] MacArthur (1996); MacArthur (1999).

[21] Ngangan *et al.* (2005).

[22] Doupnik and Richter (2003); Doupnik and Richter (2004).

[23] Tsakumis (2007).

[24] Kirsch (1994).

[25] Chanchani and Willett (2004).

[26] Fechner and Kilgore (1994); MacGregor *et al.* (1997).

[27] Chow *et al.* (1995); Haniffa and Cooke (2002).

[28] Zarzeski (1996); Archambault and Archambault (2003).

[29] For a review of several of these see Doupnik and Tsakumis (2004).

[30] See, for example, Patel *et al.* (2002).

relationship between a country's culture and the subculture of its accountants or the relationship between accounting values and accounting systems. However, as we have seen, accounting systems are influenced by many factors. There may be a relationship between Hofstede's values and accounting systems without the necessity for or any help from any intervening accounting values.

7.4.4 Examples of studies using accounting values

To give some idea of how culture has been used in international accounting, two studies will be described in more depth. The first one examines whether Gray's accounting values are related to Hofstede's cultural scores and the second one looks at the relationship between Hofstede's measures and disclosure.

Gray's accounting values are concerned with values and beliefs of accountants. It is an immense task to measure these directly, especially in the international area. Salter and Niswander (1995) instead therefore looked at the accounting systems themselves and tested the relationship between certain features of accounting systems and Hofstede's cultural values. Gray's value of professionalism relates to the exercise of professional judgement and professional self-regulation. This was proxied by the use of the true and fair override and the system for regulating the profession. Uniformity refers to consistency and flexibility of rules and was therefore proxied by the legal system and variety of practices used in each country. Differences in attitudes towards conservatism were measured by two variables based upon the use of specific rules that either aggressively reduce reported earnings whenever possible or that prohibit practices that might unduly increase assets or profits. Finally, secrecy was proxied by two variables measuring the extent of disclosure.

The ways in which they measured the four accounting values are described in Exhibit 7.12. This study provides some support for Gray's arguments. As discussed above, Gray argued that the two cultural dimensions most important for accounting are individualism and uncertainty avoidance. Using the scores provided by Hofstede and applying the analysis to 29 countries in 1989 and 1990, Salter and Niswander found that uncertainty avoidance was related to all four of Gray's accounting values. In contrast, individualism helped to explain only one of the four accounting values, namely secrecy: the more individualistic countries tend to disclose the most. There was also little support for any relationship between accounting values and either power distance or nurturing.

Hope (2003) instead explored the issue of the extent to which corporate disclosures are significantly related to cultural values. Prior research has suggested that corporate disclosures are related to the legal system of a country;[31] however, it is unclear how this relates to culture. Therefore, Hope set out to examine the question of what was the relationship between culture and legal systems and disclosure: are both culture and legal systems important or is only one of these two sufficient to explain differences in disclosure levels?

Hope ran a series of multiple regressions with the dependent variable being the level of disclosure of companies in 39 to 42 countries. The independent variables included the scores for the four cultural values of Hofstede and two other cultural variables plus the legal system (code or common law) and a number of control variables that help explain the disclosure practices of the individual company, namely firm size, leverage and stock market listing behaviour, plus the number of analysts following the company which

---

[31] See in particular Jaggi and Low (2000).

| Exhibit 7.12 | The measurement of accounting values |

Accounting value	Measurement used		
Professionalism	Score for audit perspective + professional structure, where:		
	Audit perspective	1	Conforms with legal requirements
		2	Fairly, consistently present, in conformity with
		3	True and fair, in conformity with
		4	True and fair
	Professional structure	0	Law/legislated
		1	Practitioner body
Uniformity	*De jure*	0	Common law system
		1	Code law system
	De facto	Number of practices with high level of uniformity (less than 25% or greater than 75% compliance rate)	
Conservatism	Conservatism 1	Use of various practices that reduce assets or income	
	Conservatism 2	Use of various practices that increase assets or income	
Secrecy	Disclosure index	Two used, each designed to measure the level of disclosure	

Source: Salter and Niswander (1995), p. 385. Used with the permission of the *Journal of International Business Studies*.

should proxy for the richness of the information environment of the company, with companies with a richer disclosure environment also having more analysts following. Overall, he was unable to rule out the conclusion that culture was important. The regression results were very similar whether the legal system or the cultural system was included in the regression, while culture was incrementally significant or was important even when the legal system was already included in the model. However, while these results clearly suggest that the cultural system may be important, there was little support for the specific hypothesis of Gray. All four of Hofstede's variables were found to be significant in at least some of the regressions, and there is little to suggest that uncertainty avoidance and individualism were any more significant than the other two cultural constructs. In addition, the direction of the relationships between the individual constructs and disclosure were by no means always in the hypothesized directions. This suggests that while culture may well be important, the specific relationships and how to model them successfully are still far from clear.

7.5 Is culture an important influence on accounting?

There are many supporters of the view that culture has a significant influence on accounting. Indeed, this is fairly incontrovertible: culture, in the sense of how people think and feel and their values, beliefs and attitudes, affects their behaviour. Accounting regulations and practices are an outcome of human behaviour.

The models linking accounting and culture suggest that culture acts as an intervening factor. Culture modifies the influence of environmental and external factors. It also influences the values or subculture of accountants and the institutions of a society. These in turn both influence accounting systems. Given the complexity of these relationships, it would not be too surprising to find that some countries have similar cultures but dissimilar accounting systems, while other countries have similar accounting systems but dissimilar cultures. It is the complex combination or interaction of all these factors that is important.

Even if there is a clear and consistent connection between culture and accounting, researchers may have failed to uncover it. Most studies of accounting rely upon the works of Gray and Hofstede (not least because Hofstede provides quantified measures for a range of countries). Hofstede has reduced a very complex phenomenon down to four dimensions. While these dimensions were statistically significant, they explained just 49 per cent of the differences across the countries in Hofstede's sample. Thus, either there are omitted variables or there is a fairly large amount of unexplainable or random differences across, and presumably also inside, countries. Unfortunately, all we have are the raw or mean scores for each country. We really need more information than this. Anyone using Hofstede's scores really also needs to know how typical or representative the scores are for each cultural dimension. Do most people have very similar beliefs, attitudes and values, or not? If the people of a society are culturally very similar, culture is more likely to help to explain their accounting system. If instead a country is culturally heterogeneous with people holding very different views or values, then it is far less likely that a measure of 'average culture' will help to explain the accounting system.

While there are many supporters of Hofstede who argue that his work helps us to understand differences in accounting internationally, there is far from universal support for this. Similarly, while there are many who find the work of Gray very helpful in explaining accounting differences, there are problems involved in this work. There are practical problems involved in turning the hypothesis into testable assertions and, even if the theory is correct and there is a significant relationship between societal cultures and accounting systems, it may not be easy to prove such a relationship empirically. Not only are there problems in defining and measuring 'culture', but similar problems exist with respect to the definition and measurement of 'accounting values' and 'accounting systems'.

Culture probably provides a far better explanation of accounting in some countries than it does in others and a far better explanation of some aspects of accounting systems than it does of other aspects.

The previous chapter looked at how accounting has been exported and imported between countries. Even many of the developed countries which have developed systems of regulation and rules over centuries to reflect local needs have imported many of their practices from other countries through a variety of means. However, as a generalization it is possible to say that countries such as the UK, Germany or the USA developed their accounting systems over a large number of years as the needs of the country changed. As such, it seems reasonable to hypothesize that there will be a significant relationship between their accounting systems and their country-wide culture. Other countries, most particularly many of the developing countries, have imported much or even most of their accounting systems. As such, it might be expected that there is far less of a relationship, and perhaps even virtually no relationship, between the indigenous culture and the accounting system and certainly in a world of international accounting standards, even if the relationship holds, it will increasingly be less and less important.

Gray's theory is concerned with the values of accountants. It has two parts to it. Firstly, it hypothesizes that accounting values are linked to societal culture and, secondly, that accountants influence accounting systems. Even if the first of these is correct, the second may not always be correct. The accounting system of a country consists of a number of different parts or subsystems. Authority and enforcement are concerned with the institutions of regulation, while measurement and disclosure are concerned with both the specific rules included in the regulations and the voluntary practices of companies. In some countries, accountants will be important in all three of these. In other countries, accountants may have little or no influence in one, two or even all three of these subsystems. In these cases, Gray's hypothesis may only hold for parts of, or indeed none of, the accounting system.

Summary and conclusions

This chapter has looked at the influence of culture on accounting. We followed Hofstede in defining culture as 'the collective programming of the mind that distinguishes the members of one human group from another'. This was then broken down into the four dimensions of:

- individualism versus collectivism
- large versus small power distance
- strong versus weak uncertainty avoidance
- high versus low nurturing.

The chapter then went on to show how culture can affect business, in particular how it can influence leadership styles, the motivation of employers and employees and organizational structures. Culture can also more directly influence accounting by influencing the subculture of accountants. Four 'accounting values' were described:

- professionalism versus statutory control
- uniformity versus flexibility
- conservatism versus optimism
- secrecy versus transparency.

Finally, the chapter concluded by reviewing a number of empirical studies. From these, and other similar studies, it can be concluded that culture appears to provide a useful first step in understanding or explaining differences between the accounting systems of many countries. This is especially so when we are seeking to explain general patterns across a large number of countries. It may also be helpful in explaining some of the ways in which specific rules or methods are actually applied in different countries. However, as might be expected, it is far less helpful in explaining differences in the accounting systems between relatively similar countries or in explaining differences in specific detailed rules.

Key points from the chapter:

- Culture is defined as the collective programming of the mind which distinguishes the members of one human group from another.

- Culture is collective, not individual. It is not directly observable but can be inferred from people's behaviour.
- Culture in business affects leadership style, motivation and organizational structures.
- Gray (1988) derived four pairs of accounting values from combinations of Hofstede's dimensions of culture.
- Empirical research has found some support for the existence of accounting values as predicted by Gray.
- There are views that support, and views that challenge, the idea that culture is an important influence on accounting.
- There are criticisms of Hofstede's study of cultural dimensions.
- Gray's analysis provides a useful framework for categorizing accounting systems.

Case study 7.1 Accounting for related parties in Tanzania and internationally

Tanzania: TSSAP 2
'Related party' transactions

The term 'related party' shall include:

(a) the chief executive of the enterprise, his [*sic*] spouse and children;
(b) every member of the board of directors or their equivalent, however designated, along with each member's spouse and children;
(c) the parents, brothers and sisters of those mentioned in (a) and (b) above, and
(d) any body corporate which has an influence over the composition of the board of directors of the enterprise.

There shall be a full disclosure of loans of every description made during the accounting period or outstanding at any time during the accounting period to or from any person coming within the definition of 'related party' with particulars of:

(a) nature and conditions of such loans;
(b) identity of the party;
(c) maximum amount outstanding at any time during the accounting period;
(d) rate of interest, if any, applicable to the loan;
(e) details of any guarantee or securities available.

There shall be a disclosure of safari [i.e. holiday] and other imprests and all forms of temporary borrowings outstanding on the Balance Sheet date from any person falling within the definition of the 'related party' provided the amount outstanding exceeds five thousand shillings, stating particulars of:

(a) amount outstanding;
(b) purpose of the imprest or other form of temporary accommodation;
(c) how long the amount has been outstanding;
(d) steps taken for the recovery of the amount.

▶

Case study 7.1	(Continued)

There shall be a disclosure also of the interest of 'related parties' in:

(a) shares and debentures of the enterprise;
(b) contracts in force at any given time during the accounting period or any transaction in which any of the 'related parties' has or had an interest which is of significance to the enterprise.

IASB: IAS 24

Scope:

3. This Standard deals only with those related party relationships described in (a) to (e) below:

(a) enterprises that directly, or indirectly, through one or more intermediaries, control, or are controlled by, or are under common control with, the reporting enterprises (This includes holding companies, subsidiaries and fellow subsidiaries);
(b) associates;
(c) individuals owning, directly or indirectly, an interest in the voting power of the reporting enterprise that gives them significant influence over the enterprise, and close members of the family of any such individual.
(d) key management personnel, that is, those persons having authority and responsibility for planning, directing and controlling the activities of the reporting enterprises, including directors and officers of companies and close members of the families of such individuals; and
(e) enterprises in which a substantial interest in voting power is owned, directly or indirectly, by any person described in (c) or (d) or over which such a person is able to exercise significant influence. This includes enterprises owned by directors or major shareholders of the reporting enterprise and enterprises that have a member of key management in common with the reporting enterprise.

Disclosure

20. Related party relationships where control exists should be disclosed irrespective of whether there have been transactions between the related parties.
22. If there have been transactions between related parties, the reporting enterprise should disclose the nature of the related party relationships as well as the types of transactions and the elements of the transactions necessary for an understanding of the financial statements.
24. Items of a similar nature may be disclosed in aggregate except when separate disclosure is necessary for an understanding of the effects of related party transactions on the financial statements of the reporting entity.

Source: TSSAP 2, *Information Required to be Disclosed in Financial Statements* (National Board of Accountants and Auditors, 1983); IAS24, *Related Party Disclosures* (IASB, 1994).

Questions

The following questions test your understanding of the material contained in the chapter and allow you to relate your understanding to the learning outcomes specified at the start of this chapter. The learning outcomes are repeated here. Each question is cross-referenced to the relevant section of the chapter.

Understand what is meant by the term 'culture', and describe the cultural dimensions identified by a number of different researchers

1 What is meant by the terms 'culture' and 'subculture'? Why are the two different? (section 7.2)

2 Why might accountants have a particularly strong subculture? (section 7.2)

3 Describe your country in terms of the cultural dimensions described by Hofstede. (section 7.2)

4 Using the data provided in Exhibits 7.4 and 7.5, describe each of the countries and place them each into relevant groups. (section 7.2)

5 What are the main differences and similarities between the cultural dimensions of Hofstede, and Hampden-Turner and Trompenaars? (section 7.2)

Describe the relationship between culture and organizational structures

6 How might each of Hofstede's cultural dimensions affect corporate leadership styles? (section 7.3.1)

7 How might each of Hofstede's cultural dimensions affect organizational structures? (section 7.3.3)

8 How might each of Hofstede's cultural dimensions affect what factors motivate employees? (section 7.3.2)

Describe the accounting values identified by Gray, and explain how they might be related to culture

9 Describe Gray's four accounting values and describe how they are linked to Hofstede's cultural dimensions. (section 7.4)

10 Describe your country in terms of the four accounting values of Gray. (section 7.4)

11 Does your description of your country's accounting values and cultural dimensions, as defined by Hofstede, support the hypothesized link between the two as described in Exhibit 7.8? (section 7.4)

12 How are Gray's accounting values linked to the system of accounting regulation? (section 7.4.3)

13 How are Gray's accounting values linked to accounting measurement rules and practices? (section 7.4.3)

14 How are Gray's accounting values linked to accounting disclosure rules and practices? (section 7.4.3)

Evaluate research which has used these accounting values and assess their significance for those seeking international harmonization

15 What are the main practical problems involved in measuring accounting values? (section 7.4.4)

16 Why might Gray's work be more appropriate for developed than developing countries? (section 7.5)

17 Why might Gray's work be more appropriate in explaining general patterns or differences rather than differences in specific measurement and disclosure rules? (section 7.5)

References and further reading

Archambault, J.J. and Archambault, M.E. (2003) 'A multinational test of determinants of corporate disclosure', *International Journal of Accounting*, 38: 173–194.

Balaga, B.R. and Jaeger, A.M. (1984) 'Multinational corporations: control systems and delegation issues', *Journal of International Business Studies*, Fall: 25–40.

Baskerville, R.F. (2003) 'Hofstede never studied culture', *Accounting, Organizations and Society*, 28: 1–14.

Buhr, N. and Freedman, M. (2001) 'Culture, institutional factors and differences in environmental disclosure between Canada and the United States', *Critical Perspectives on Accounting*, 12: 293–322.

Chanchani, S. and Willett, R. (2004) 'An empirical assessment of Gray's accounting value constructs', *International Journal of Accounting*, 39: 125–154.

Chow, L.M., Chau, G.K. and Gray, S.J. (1995) 'Accounting reforms in China: cultural constraints on implementation and development', *Accounting and Business Research*, 26(1): 29–49.

Chow, W.C., Shields, M.D. and Wu, A. (1999) 'The importance of national culture in the design of and preferences for management controls for multinational operations', *Accounting, Organizations and Society*, 24: 441–461.

Chposky, J. and Leonis, T. (1988) *Blue Magic: The People, Power and Politics Behind the IBM Personal Computer.* New York: Facts on File.

Chwastiak, M. (1999) 'Deconstructing the principal-agent model: a view from the bottom', *Critical Perspectives in Accounting*, 10(4): 425–441.

Cohen, J.R., Pant, L.W. and Sharp, D.J. (1992) 'Cultural and socioeconomic constraints on international codes of ethics: lessons from accounting', *Journal of Business Ethics*, 11(9): 687–700.

Doupnik, T.S. and Richter, M. (2003) 'Interpretation of uncertainty expressions: a cross-national study', *Accounting, Organizations and Society*, 28(1): 15–35.

Doupnik, T.S. and Richter, M. (2004) 'The impact of culture on the interpretation of "in context" verbal probability expressions', *Journal of International Accounting Research*, 3(1): 1–20.

Doupnik, T.S. and Tsakumis, G.T. (2004) 'A critical review of test's of Gray's theory of cultural relevance and suggestions for further research', *Journal of Accounting Literature*, 23: 1–48.

Eisenhardt, K.M. (1989) 'Agency theory: an assessment and review', *Academy of Management Review*, 14(1): 57–74.

Ellwood, W. (2001) *The No-Nonsense Guide to Globalization.* London: Verso.

Fama, E.F. (1980) 'Agency problems and the theory of the firm', *Journal of Political Economy*, 88(2): 288–307.

Fechner, H.H.E. and Kilgore, A. (1994) 'The influence of cultural factors on accounting practice', *International Journal of Accounting*, 29(4): 265–277.

Gambling, T. (1987) 'Accounting for rituals', *Accounting, Organizations and Society*, 12(4): 319–329.

Gannon, M.J. and Associates (1994) *Understanding Global Culture: Metaphorical Journey, through 17 Countries.* London: Sage.

Gray, S.J. (1988) 'Towards a theory of cultural influence on the development of accounting systems internationally', *Abacus*, 24(1): 1–15.

Hamid, S., Craig, R. and Clark, F. (1993) 'Religion: a confounding cultural element in the international harmonisation of accounting?', *Abacus*, 29(2): 131–148.

Hampden-Turner, C.M. and Trompenaars, F. (2000) *Building Cross-Cultural Competence: How to Create Wealth From Conflicting Values.* Chichester: John Wiley & Sons.

Haniffa, R.M. and Cooke, T.E. (2002) 'Culture, corporate governance and disclosure in Malaysian countries', *Abacus*, 38(3): 317–349.

Harrison, G.L. (1992) 'Cross cultural generalisability of the relation between participation, budget emphasis and job related attitudes', *Accounting, Organizations and Society*, 17: 319–339.

Harrison, G.L. and McKinnon, J.L. (1999) 'Cross-cultural research in management control system design: a review of the current state', *Accounting, Organizations and Society*, 24: 483–506.

Harrison, J.R. and Carroll, G.R. (1991) 'Keeping the faith: a model of cultural transmission in formal organisations', *Administrative Science Quarterly*, 36(4): 552–582.

Hofstede, G. (1984) *Culture's Consequences: International Differences in Work-related Values*. Beverly Hills, CA: Sage.

Hofstede, G. (1991) *Cultures and Organisations: Software of the Mind*. London: McGraw-Hill.

Hofstede, G. (2003) 'What is culture? A reply to Baskerville', *Accounting, Organizations and Society*, 28: 811–813.

Hofstede, G. and Bond, M.H. (1988) 'The Confucius connection: from cultural roots to economic growth', *Organizational Dynamics*, 16(1): 5–21.

Hope, O.K. (2003) 'Firm-level disclosures and the relative roles of culture and legal origin', *Journal of International Financial Management and Accounting*, 14(3): 218–248.

Jaggi, B. and Low, P.Y. (2000) 'Impact of culture, market forces and legal system on financial disclosures', *International Journal of Accounting*, 35(4): 495–519.

Jensen, M.C. and Meckling, W.H. (1976) 'Theory of the firm: managerial behaviour, agency costs and ownership structure', *Journal of Financial Economics*, 3: 305–360.

Kaplan, S.E. and Ruland, R.G. (1991) 'Positive theory, rationality and accounting regulation', *Critical Perspectives on Accounting*, 2: 361–374.

Kirsch, R.J. (1994) 'Towards a global reporting model: culture and disclosure in selected capital markets', *Research in Accounting Regulation*, 8: 71–110.

Kluckholn, F. and Strodtbeck, F. (1961) *Variations in Value Orientations*. Evanston, IL: Row, Paterson.

Leung, K., Bhagat, R.S., Buchan, N.R., Erez, M. and Gibson, C.B. (2005) 'Culture and international business: recent advances and their implications', *Journal of International Business Studies*, 36: 357–378.

MacArthur, J.B. (1996) 'An investigation into the influence of cultural factors in the international lobbying of the International Accounting Standards Committee on E32: Comparability of financial statements', *International Journal of Accounting*, 31: 213–237.

MacArthur, J.B. (1999) 'The impact of cultural factors in the lobbying of the International Accounting Standards Committee on E32: Comparability of financial statements – an extension of MacArthur to accounting member bodies', *Journal of International Accounting, Auditing and Taxation*, 8(2): 315–335.

MacGregor, A., Hossain, M. and Yap, K. (1997) 'Accounting in Malaysia and Singapore: culture's lack of consequences?'. in Baydoun, N., Nishimula, A. and Willett, R.J.W. (eds) *Accounting in the Asia-Pacific Region*. Singapore: John Wiley & Sons.

McSweeney, B. (2002) 'Hofstede's model of national cultural differences and their consequences: a triumph of faith – a failure of analysis', *Human Relations*, 55(1): 89–118.

National Board of Accountants and Auditors (1983) *Tanzanian Statement of Standard Accounting Practice No.2: Information Required to be Disclosed in Financial Statements*. Dar Es Salaam: NBAA, June.

Ngangan, K., Saudagaran, S.M. and Clarke, F.L. (2005) 'Cultural influences on indigenous users' perceptions of the importance of disclosure items: empirical evidence from Papua New Guinea', *Advances in International Accounting*, 18: 25–71.

Ogden, S.G. (1993) 'The limitations of agency theory: the case of accounting-based profit sharing schemes', *Critical Perspectives on Accounting*, 4: 179–206.

Patel, C., Harrison, G.L. and McKinnon, J.L. (2002) 'Cultural influences on judgments of professional accountants in auditor-client conflict resolution', *Journal of International Financial Management and Accounting*, 13(1): 1–31.

Perera, M.B.H. and Mathews, M.A. (1990) 'The cultural relativity of accounting and international patterns of social accounting', *Advances in International Accounting*, 3: 215–251.

Radebaugh, L.H., Gray, S.J. and Black, E.L. (2006) *International accounting and multinational enterprises*, 6th edn. New York: John Wiley & Sons.

Salter, S.B. and Niswander, F. (1995) 'Cultural influence on the development of accounting systems internationally: a test of Gray's [1988] theory', *Journal of International Business Studies*, 26(2): 379–398.

Schwartz, S.H. (1994) 'Beyond individualism/collectivism: new cultural dimensions of values', pp. 85–99 in Kim, U., Triandis, H.C., Kagitcibasi, C., Choi, S.-C. and Yoon, G. (eds) *Individualism and Collectivism: Theory, Method and Applications*. Thousand Oaks, CA: Sage.

Slater, R. (2002) *Saving Big Blue: Leadership Lessons and Turnaround Tactics of IBM's Lou Gerstner.* New York: McGraw-Hill.

Soeters, J. and Schreuder, H. (1988) 'The interaction between national and organisational cultures in accounting firms', *Accounting, Organizations and Society*, 13(1): 75–85.

Sorensen, J.B. (2002) 'The strength of culture and the reliability of firm performance', *Administrative Science Quarterly*, 47(1): 70–91.

Steger, M.B. (2003) *Globalization: A Very Short Introduction*. Oxford: Oxford University Press.

Trompenaars, F. (2003) *Did the Pedestrian Die?* Oxford: Capstone.

Trompenaars, F. and Hampden-Turner, C. (1997) *Riding the Waves of Culture: Understanding Cultural Diversity in Business*, 2nd edn. London: Nicholas Brealey.

Tsakumis, G.T. (2007) 'The influence of culture on accountants' application of financial reporting rules', *Abacus*, 43(1): 27–48.

Zarzeski, M.T. (1996) 'Spontaneous harmonization effects of culture and market forces on accounting disclosure practices', *Accounting Horizons*, 10(1): 18–37.

The classification of accounting systems

Learning outcomes

After reading this chapter you should be able to:

● Explain why it is important to classify accounting systems.

● Distinguish deductive from inductive approaches to classification.

● Distinguish simple from complex classification systems.

● Explain the advantages and limitations of the different types of classification systems.

● Evaluate published research which develops or uses classification systems.

8.1 Introduction

In Chapters 6 and 7 we looked at a range of factors which may influence accounting. This discussion leads to two questions. Firstly, if accounting systems are or were influenced in systematic ways by environmental factors, then is it possible to find patterns or systematic, explicable differences and commonalities in the accounting systems of different countries? Secondly, which, if any, of the many factors discussed in the last two chapters are most important in explaining accounting patterns? This chapter seeks to provide some answers to these questions by classifying or placing accounting systems into groups of similar systems. The chapter will describe the main types of accounting classification systems that exist, and evaluate their usefulness.

We have been asked, 'Why retain this chapter when harmonization with international accounting standards is already widespread and is increasing?' Our answer is that accounting systems consist of more than the financial statements and notes that come within the scope of IFRS. Accounting systems provide information beyond the measurement and disclosure rules of accounting standards. The methods of classification described in this chapter can be extended to companies that do not have to follow IFRS or to voluntary accounting practices.

All systems of classification depend upon being able to differentiate between important and unimportant differences. Only some accounting differences will be important. Others may have a large impact on reported figures but still not be very important because either the effect on profit or equity is easily seen, or they are transitory differences and can be changed relatively easily without affecting any other aspects of the accounting system. The use of straight-line or accelerated depreciation, for example, may have a large impact on reported profits but the difference is not significant from a theoretical viewpoint. Both are methods of allocating the cost of an asset to the periods that benefit from its use and, as such, are in harmony with each other. Other differences may have relatively little impact upon the reported figures but be important and difficult to standardize. Whether or not a company capitalizes leased assets, for example, may have little effect on its reported profits, but it is very important from a theoretical perspective. The alternative treatments of leased assets reflect very different definitions of an asset. Non-capitalization is based upon a legal definition of assets while capitalization takes an economic perspective instead. These views are not compatible or in harmony with each other.

If we want to gain a complete picture of differences across accounting systems, we must differentiate between significant or fundamental differences and non-significant or non-fundamental differences. Looking only at the impact of differences upon reported figures or only at the number of techniques that are different is not enough.

Classifying accounting systems contributes to this aim. Classifications attempt to place cases (here, the accounting systems of countries) into systematic categories or groups. A good classification system is one where each country's accounting system can be placed in one, and only one, group. The accounting systems of countries in any one group should share the same important or underlying features while also being quite distinct from the accounting systems in the other groups. Differences in unimportant features or transitory differences should not affect the classification system – indeed, the number of differences between countries placed in the same category might be quite large and may even be larger than the number of differences between countries placed in different categories.

8.2 Reasons for classifying accounting systems

There are several reasons for classifying accounting systems. A good classification system should provide a simple way of describing and analyzing complex phenomena. In the absence of a classification system, anyone who wants to know about accounting for individual companies in Greece, for example, must list and describe all the main accounting rules and practices in Greece, such as the methods used to value fixed assets, inventory, intangibles and leases and the rules for consolidation, deferred taxation, foreign currency translation, etc. If the same person then wants to know about accounting for similar entities in Spain, a similarly long list will be required. A simpler approach would be to turn to classification studies which might show that Greece and Spain are in the same group as France, having government-imposed systems based upon Romanic law with tax rules also influencing the reported figures. While this does not tell us the specific accounting rules of Greece or Spain, we would now have a set of expectations regarding the specific rules and practices of each country. Time and effort can then be concentrated on learning about those rules or practices that are different from what is expected – hopefully a very much smaller list of items.

Classification therefore offers a way to simplify a complex world. Classifications may also help domestic and international standard setters. At the level of the individual country, standard setters may be able to look at other countries in the same group for guidance on how they have solved similar problems. This should help them to see which solutions are most likely to be successful, having worked in other countries in the same group, and which will probably be unsuccessful, having failed in other group members. In an international setting, regional or international standard setters may see which countries should be relatively easy to harmonize (those countries in the same group) and which will probably be the hardest (countries in the most widely separated groups). They can also see which issues should be easy to harmonize (issues that are not fundamental) and which issues will probably be far more difficult (fundamental issues).

8.3 Types of classification schemes

There have been many attempts at classifying accounting systems and many different types of classification schemes have been used. They differ in terms of the type of reasoning used, whether inductive or deductive. They also differ in degree of complexity. Both inductive and deductive classifications vary from the very simple to the complex. The simplest schemes are those which use discrete yes/no or 0/1 categories. More complex schemes may use several different classificatory features or variables, while the most complex involve several layers (or hierarchies).

This chapter will continue by describing the main features of each of these different types of classifications. Once the main types of classification systems have been introduced, some of the more important classification studies will be looked at.

8.3.1 Inductive classifications

Inductive classifications do not rely upon a theory of accounting to develop categories, instead they are data driven. They start with data in the form of the specific accounting rules or practices of a number of countries. Typically, they use a large number of countries and an even larger number of accounting rules and/or practices. Groups or categories of countries are then generated by a variety of statistical techniques. Some studies have also gone a stage further and tried to explain the resultant categories by reference to the business, economic or cultural features of each country. Typically, data on a range of features, such as those discussed in Chapters 6 and 7, that might help explain accounting rules or practices would also be collected for each country. Various statistical tests would then be run to see which of these features could be used to generate the same country groupings – or, in other words, which features appeared to 'explain' the groups initially found.

8.3.2 Deductive classifications

Deductive classification schemes (sometimes called intuitive or a priori classifications) decide upon the relevant categories on the basis of the knowledge or beliefs of the classifier. They start with statements such as 'I believe that . . .' or 'I think that the most important features or factors are . . .'. One example of this would be to classify accounting systems on the basis of the valuation system used. For example, all strict historical cost systems would be placed into one category, systems using a modified historical cost system would be placed into a second category, and fully fledged inflation accounting systems would be allocated to the third group. Other examples are that, in some accounting systems, the financial statements must comply with all laws; in other systems, information is presented fairly and in conformity with laws and regulations, so that they have to disclose extra information if this is required for 'fair' presentation. A third category is those where the statements must give a true and fair view even if this means that not all rules or regulations are always fully followed.

These are examples of possible classifications that use certain features of the accounting system itself to group countries. However, it is more common to find deductive classifications that instead classify countries on the basis of various of the business or cultural features discussed earlier. Examples include classifications based upon the type of legal system, financial system or cultural values. These classifications are based upon the argument that the accounting system of a country is the outcome of specific business or cultural features. If we choose the correct or relevant features or descriptors, the resulting groups of countries should have accounting rules or practices that are substantially similar inside each group and substantially different across the groups.

Many of the proposed deductive classification schemes have not been tested to check whether or not the accounting systems inside each group are indeed similar to each other while also being dissimilar to those in the other group(s). However, the validity of these classifications can be tested. To do this, countries would be assigned to the hypothesized categories using deductive reasoning. Various statistical tests would then be applied to the accounting rules or practices of the countries in each category to see whether or not the hypothesized or suggested classifications are indeed valid.

8.3.3 Complexity of classification schemes

Within either of the inductive or deductive systems of classification there may be a range of complexity of the classification schemes used. This section describes the increasingly complex approaches that have been taken.

8.3.3.1 Discrete classifications

The simplest inductive and deductive classifications would categorize or place accounting systems into discrete or mutually exclusive groups. For example, some countries use common law while others use code law, so accounting systems could be classified into two systems on the basis of whether the country uses one or other type of legal system. While this is a very simple classification it is intuitively appealing and several deductive classifications have used the legal system as the classification factor, as discussed below. Empirical studies also support the usefulness of this classificatory variable.[1]

The type of legal system is a binary variable – code versus common law – and so it provides a basis for two groups of countries. The advantage of such binary classifications is that they are very simple and easy to use: it is generally clear to which category each accounting system belongs. Other classificatory variables may be used which lead to three or more groups. At least in theory, a classification exercise could result in an infinite number of groups. However, the most useful classifications contain a limited number of groups, since as the classification scheme becomes more complex and the number of groups increases, the problem of deciding which countries fit into which groups also increases.

8.3.3.2 Classifications using continuous variables

An alternative approach to using discrete or categorical variables is to classify countries using continuous classificatory variables. For example, we might use the influence of tax rules as a classificatory variable. Countries could then be placed along a continuum ranging from the complete independence of tax rules and financial reporting rules to complete dependence, where external financial statements are identical to those used for taxation. Even where a continuous grouping or classification factor is used, countries can still be classified into two or more discrete groups. But now a second decision must also be made – namely, where along the continuum do we place the break point(s), or what are the critical value(s) of the grouping variable that differentiates between the groups? If we have chosen a sensible grouping factor, this should be fairly obvious. For example, if countries tend to cluster at the two extremes of 'little or no influence of tax rules' and 'heavy dependence on tax rules', then there are two groups of countries, and it will be fairly obvious which countries fit into which group.

8.3.3.3 Multidimensional mapping

A slightly more complex way of classifying accounting systems is to use 'multidimensional mapping'. Rather than classifying on the basis of one grouping factor only, this method groups accounting systems on the basis of a number of factors or features, n, where n can range from 2 to infinity. In effect, an n-dimensional picture or map is produced and countries are located on each dimension depending upon the specific values of each grouping factor. The simplest of these are two-dimensional maps, as illustrated by Exhibit 8.1. Two-dimensional classifications are fairly easy to understand and easy to represent graphically; however, there is no reason why more complex classifications cannot be developed using more dimensions or factors.

---

[1] Salter and Doupnik (1992).

| Exhibit 8.1 | A possible two-dimensional classification |

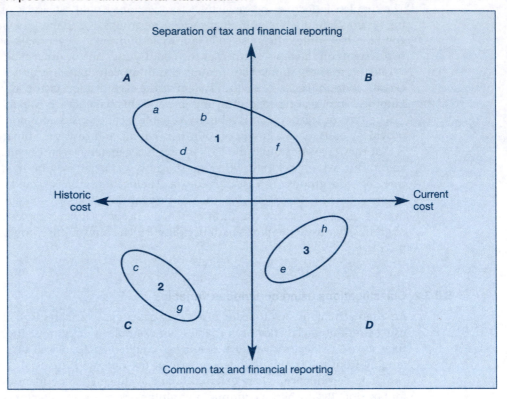

The advantage of multidimensional mapping is that it can be used to classify more complex phenomena. For example, a two-dimensional classification might be based upon:

● the independence or interdependence of tax and financial reporting rules; and
● the use of historical or current costs.

While we are using two continuous classification variables we can still place accounting systems into discrete groups. As can be seen in Exhibit 8.1, each accounting system or country is initially placed onto what may be thought of as a map of accounting systems. Countries where tax and financial accounting are kept separate, with the latter based upon historical costs, would be placed in sector *A*. Those where tax and financial accounting are kept separate, but the latter uses current costs, would be placed in sector *B* etc. The exact location of each country in each quadrant would depend upon the strictness of historical cost rules and the extent to which tax rules impact upon financial reporting. Let us assume that the eight countries, *a–h*, have been correctly placed onto the map. As a second stage we can group these countries into discrete categories. From their positions on the map, as shown in Exhibit 8.1, we appear to have three groups or categories. Category or group 1 contains the four countries *a*, *b*, *d* and *f*, group 2 contains the two countries *c* and *g*, while group 3 contains the remaining two countries, *e* and *h*.

8.3.3.4 Hierarchical classifications

All of the possible classification schemes looked at so far place countries' accounting systems into discrete categories or groups. For example, in Exhibit 8.1 we have three groups

Exhibit 8.2 A possible hierarchical classification

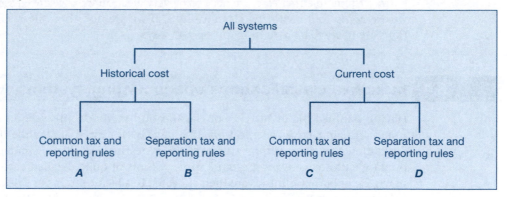

of countries. Anyone interested in comparing the countries classified might want to know whether an accounting system placed in group 1 was more similar to those in group 2 or those in group 3. They might hypothesize, for example, that groups 2 and 3 are the two groups that are most alike. However, the classification scheme does not tell us this, we have to hypothesize it for ourselves.

Hierarchical classifications attempt to answer this type of question. The use of hierarchical classification systems in accounting was first proposed by Nobes (1984), although similar classifications have a long history in the natural sciences. A hierarchical classification using the same two factors as before is presented in Exhibit 8.2. While countries are placed in one of four groups, *A–D*, we can now see the relationship between the groups and understand the linkages between the countries. In particular, this classification tells us that the more important or fundamental classificatory factor is the type of cost system. Countries that are placed in either of groups *A* or *B*, both historical cost, should have more similar accounting systems than would countries that are placed, for example, in groups *A* and *C*, both common tax and reporting rules.

8.3.4 Problems of classification in accounting

Despite the large number of attempts at classification in the accounting literature, classification in accounting is contentious. There are obvious technical problems involved in carrying out any classification study. Which is the best statistical method to use? Is the data used of sufficient quantity and quality? But there are also more fundamental problems. In particular, as will be discussed below, while most of the earlier attempts at classification were attempts to classify 'accounting systems', they failed to explain adequately what this means. It could mean a variety of different things – the regulatory system and the rules that apply to all companies, or those that apply to listed companies only or to group accounts only. Alternatively, it could instead encompass the actual practices of companies, either their measurement or disclosure practices – or both. Again, this could be for all companies or just some types of companies. This lack of careful consideration and description of what is meant by an accounting system has been criticized by a number of writers and, in particular, by Roberts (1995).

Roberts argues that if we cannot agree on exactly what an accounting system is, then we have to accept that all we can do is either to classify certain coherent parts of the system, in other words entire subsystems – for example, measurement rules only – or to classify a number of rules or practices which are an incomplete representation of the entire system. In either case, we need to be very clear on why we are classifying and what we are going to do with the classifications. If we are not, then the resultant classifications are likely to be used in inappropriate ways.

8.4 Inductive classifications of accounting systems

Having outlined the main types of classification methods, this section briefly looks at some of the inductive classifications that have been carried out. While there are important differences across various studies of this type, they all follow a similar approach. The primary data source is most often a survey of lots of quite detailed accounting rules or practices, or both. Countries are then allocated to specific groups or categories using various statistical techniques.

8.4.1 Nair and Frank's study

Nair and Frank (1980) present one of the earliest inductive classifications. Despite the fact that the study uses data that is now more than 30 years old, it remains an important inductive classification that provides interesting perspectives on the historical development of accounting. Importantly, they argue that we should not use all accounting issues to categorize countries. In particular they argue that a classification based upon disclosure issues might be quite different from a classification based upon measurement issues.

They therefore split the 1973 and 1975 Price Waterhouse (PW)[2] data into measurement issues and disclosure issues and developed two classifications – one based upon measurement issues and the other based upon disclosure issues. The data was fed into a factor analysis program. This is a method of reducing a large number of variables into a smaller number of factors by grouping similar variables together into one factor. Countries are then described in terms of this reduced set of factors rather than the underlying data and groups of countries are then formed by allocating countries to categories based upon their factor loadings.

To see how this is done, assume that we are classifying three countries 1–3 and, having used factor analysis, we find that the underlying data can be described by just three factors, A–C. The factor weightings for the countries are as follows:

Factor	A	B	C
1	0.9	0.05	0.05
2	0.4	0.3	0.3
3	0.3	0.4	0.3

If we classify on the basis of the highest factor weightings, as done by Nair and Frank, we would allocate countries 1 and 2 to one group as they each have the highest weighting on factor A, and country 3 to the other group. However, if we instead use a rather more sophisticated method, namely discriminant analysis, we would allocate on the

---

[2] PW undertook three surveys in 1973, 1975 and 1979 covering from 30 countries in 1973 to 64 in 1979. In each study, PW partners from each country were asked about a variety of accounting practices. The issues covered included both measurement and disclosure issues, varying from a total of 233 items in 1973 to 267 in 1979.

| Exhibit 8.3 | Nair and Frank's groups based upon measurement issues (1973 data) |

1	2	3	4
Australia	Argentina	Belgium	Canada
Bahamas	Bolivia	France	Japan
Fiji	Brazil	Germany	Mexico
Ireland	Chile	Italy	Panama
Jamaica	Colombia	Spain	Philippines
Kenya	Ethiopia	Sweden	USA
Netherlands	India	Switzerland	
New Zealand	Paraguay	Venezuela	
Pakistan	Peru		
Singapore	Uruguay		
South Africa			
Trinidad and Tobago			
UK			
Zimbabwe			

Source: Nair and Frank (1980). Reproduced with kind permission of the American Accounting Association.

basis of their factor loadings on all three factors. Now, country 1 would be allocated to one group and countries 2 and 3 would be allocated to the other group – a result that is more appropriate.

Looking first at Nair and Frank's results for measurement issues, the groups generated from 1973 data are as reported in Exhibit 8.3.

Five factors were extracted from the 1973 measurement data. No country had its highest loading on the fifth factor, so four groups were formed. These groups generally appear to make sense. They may be thought of as being:

Group 1: Commonwealth group
Group 2: Latin American group
Group 3: Continental European group
Group 4: US-led group.

The analysis was just as successful when the 1975 data was used, although now six factors were extracted. Five groups were formed, four being quite similar to those found using the 1973 data plus group 5, which contained only one country, Chile. The disclosure-based groups are generally less easy to characterize (although from a purely statistical point of view the classifications are just as successful). As shown in Exhibit 8.4 seven groups were derived from the 1973 disclose data.

Group 1 is again a Commonwealth group which, with the exception of the omission of The Netherlands, is identical to the 1973 measurement group. Group 4, the US-led group, is again very similar to that found using 1973 measurement data, with the only differences being the addition of The Netherlands and the omission of Japan, which is instead placed in group 2. The other four groups are difficult to explain; in particular there is no clear rationale or explanation for group 2 which contains Japan, two Commonwealth Asian countries (Pakistan and India), two South American countries (Bolivia and Peru) and Germany, a result that has no intuitive appeal. The disclosure groups are generally not very stable, with many countries changing groups between 1973 and 1975, suggesting that the classification is not too successful.

| Exhibit 8.4 | Nair and Frank's groups based upon disclosure issues (1973 data) |

1	2	3	4	5	6	7
Australia	Bolivia	Belgium	Canada	Argentina	Sweden	Switzerland
Bahamas	Germany	Brazil	Mexico	Chile		
Fiji	India	Colombia	Netherlands	Ethiopia		
Ireland	Japan	France	Panama	Uruguay		
Jamaica	Pakistan	Italy	Philippines			
Kenya	Peru	Paraguay	USA			
New Zealand		Spain				
Singapore		Venezuela				
South Africa						
Trinidad and						
Tobago						
UK						
Zimbabwe						

Source: Nair and Frank (1980). Reproduced with kind permission of the American Accounting Association.

Nair and Frank also attempted to seek explanations for the groups obtained by using 14 cultural and economic variables to discriminate among the 1975 groups of countries. The variables chosen included language variables, which they argued acted as proxies for cultural and historical links, various GNP-based variables reflecting the stage of economic development and a series of trading bloc variables. The analysis met with some success with two trading bloc variables, the use of French and per capita income being important in explaining the measurement groups, and the use of German and English, the importance of the agricultural sector and three trading bloc variables helping to explain the disclosure results. However, these explanations of group membership are far from conclusive. Indeed, they had little success when using these variables to predict rather than to explain group membership.

There are several ways in which we can assess the success of inductive classifications. Statistical analysis is obviously important, and this suggests that Nair and Frank have been at least moderately successful. But, more important, we need to ask ourselves, 'Do the groups appear to make sense?' Again, it would appear that the classifications are reasonably successful, but not a total success. Some of the groups found by Nair and Frank make intuitive sense, but others do not. Likewise, some of the groups are fairly stable, but others are not.

There are a number of possible explanations for why the analysis was not more successful. The analysis was based upon the PW data which has been strongly criticized, especially by Nobes (1982). He highlights four problems with these surveys. That they contain a number of mistakes; other answers, while correct, give a misleading picture; the questions chosen tend to exaggerate UK/US differences; and, most importantly, the data was not developed for this purpose. As Nobes (1982, p. 63) argues:

> When classifying plants or animals, biologists largely ignore the most obvious characteristics. That is, they do not carry out factor analysis on animals by weight, colour, number of legs, nature of body covering, length of life, etc. This would merely lead to a classification of that data. It would group man with ostriches, dolphins with sharks, bats with owls, and so on.

A number of later studies have instead used other data sources, including specially developed surveys of accountants[3] and surveys of actual financial statements.[4]

8.4.2 D'Arcy's study

One particularly interesting recent study is by d'Arcy (2001). This study is unusual in that it concentrates solely upon accounting rules for listed companies rather than practices. The data used applies to 14 countries plus the IASC and is based upon the information contained in Ordelheide and KPMG (1995). It therefore has a clear focus – *de jure* harmonization – so meeting many of the concerns of Roberts (1995) regarding the applicability of the databases used and the purpose of the classification.

One problem of course concerns the choice of variables. In this case, that was dictated primarily by data availability. Only those items that could be analyzed into required/forbidden/permitted were included, resulting in 129 variables or 88 topics.[5] This of course raises again the issue of whether or not these are the 'correct' items to be used. Indeed, Nobes (2004) argues that this study also swamped important questions with trivial questions. He gives the examples of six questions on negative goodwill but only two on positive goodwill, or five questions on hyperinflation and none on leasing. While it is undoubtedly true that the database, like any, is not as exhaustive as it might be, d'Arcy (2004) counters that the rules used are important, so that it is not trivia swamping important items, but rather that not all important items are included.

The statistical methods used were a marked improvement on prior studies. Two methods were used, simple matching similarity coefficients, or SM, and cluster analysis. SM counts the number of items for which a pair of countries have the same rules. Not surprisingly, the SM was highest for Austria and Germany (91.5 per cent). The lowest was France and the USA (29 per cent), while most pairs ranged between 50 per cent and 70 per cent agreement. Australia was unusual in that all pairs except that with the IASC were less than 60 per cent, so prompting d'Arcy to describe it as having an 'outsider position'.

The cluster analysis was carried out using a variety of different methods and some different non-equal weighting schemes. While there were some differences in terms of exactly when a particular country joined a cluster, each method resulted in the same four quite distinct clusters. Thus, the first pair of countries to 'join' a cluster, being statistically the most similar, were Germany and Austria followed by France and Belgium which then joined the other two to form a four-country European grouping. This group was later joined by Switzerland, Denmark, The Netherlands and the UK to form cluster one, a European cluster. This was later joined by a rather more heterogeneous group, or cluster two, of Sweden, Spain and Japan. The third cluster, also more heterogeneous than the European group or cluster one, was the three-country group of the USA, Canada and the IASC. Australia remained a separate one-country cluster for the longest time, finally joining the USA group only under a final two-cluster solution. This can be seen in Exhibit 8.5 which reproduces the cluster result graphically.

While the methodology applied is clearly a significant improvement on earlier studies, some results might be thought of as unexpected. Firstly, there is no UK–US

---

[3] See, for example, Doupnik and Salter (1993).

[4] See, for example, Choi and Bavishi (1980).

[5] These answers were converted into dichotomous or binary data, with 1/0 being required yes and forbidden no, 0/1 being required no and forbidden yes, and 0/0 required no and forbidden no, that is the item is permitted.

Exhibit 8.5	Clusters found by d'Arcy (2001)

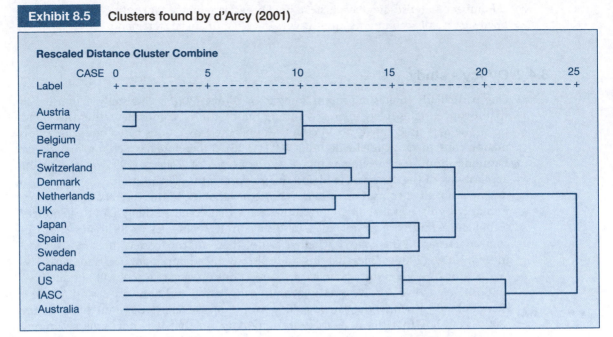

Source: D'Arcy (2001), Fig. 1. Dendogram average linkage between groups.

group. However, there has been considerable debate recently on whether or not such a group exists, as discussed in section 8.5.5 below, and it can easily be argued that actually this is not a surprising result. Much more surprising is Australia which appears to be quite different from any other country.

Nobes (2004) gives a detailed critique of the work in which he criticized the database used for a number of reasons. In particular that it contains a number of misunderstandings and mistakes. He analyzes in detail the mistakes he thinks were made with respect to Australia, the USA and the UK and then compares these countries with Germany. Now, instead of finding that of these four countries, the UK and Germany are the most similar, Australia and the UK, Australia and the USA, and the UK and the USA are all more similar than Germany and the UK. Some of these differences undoubtedly are caused by mistakes, as detailed by Nobes, but some of them also appear to be due to differences in interpretation. D'Arcy (2004) details several of the areas where the differences appear due to interpretation rather than downright mistakes as well as arguing that indeed Australia has had several rules that are quite distinct from those found elsewhere.

More evidence on this issue is given by Lewis and Salter (2006) who instead looked only at one single item, the size of the difference in earnings based upon US GAAP and domestic GAAP in 1999, 2001 and 2003 as reported in the 20-F statements of foreign companies that list in the USA. Their results provide at least some support for d'Arcy in that they found that the USA, Canada, Australia and the IAS group together with, in two of the three years, Sweden also. In contrast, the UK grouped with The Netherlands and, in two of the three years, Span and France also, thus suggesting that EU harmonization efforts may have succeeded in bringing together the practices of EU countries.

Exhibit 8.6	Some questions asked in the Price Waterhouse (1979) survey

Question 2
Financial statements are drawn up on the premise that the business will continue in operation indefinitely.

Question 10
Departures from the going concern concept are disclosed.

Question 29
Fixed assets are stated at cost of acquisition or construction, *less* accumulated depreciation.

Question 47
In historical cost statements, revaluation reserves that arise when fixed assets are stated at an amount in excess of cost are available for charges arising on subsequent downward revaluation of fixed assets.

Question 27
The basis on which fixed assets are stated is disclosed.

Question 185
The amount written-off deferred development costs is disclosed.

8.4.3 Some problems of using survey data

There are several problems with using a data set of questions about accounting practices or rules. The questions asked related to several different types of accounting issues. Exhibit 8.6 lists a few of the questions contained in the 1979 PW survey.[6]

From this, it can be seen that the PW surveys included questions on broad concepts and underlying principles as well as questions on specific issues inside each of the financial statements – both measurement and disclosure issues. The questions inputted into the statistical analysis are then accorded equal importance. However, some of the questions asked are very important, others are trivial, while others cover issues that are of importance to only a few companies. If the survey includes all of these types of questions the statistical analysis cannot differentiate between important and unimportant ones and will treat all questions in the same way. Therefore, unimportant issues may swamp important issues so that the resultant classifications may be either very unstable or incorrect.

If we were to design a database of accounting issues to be used as the basis for developing an inductive classification scheme we would have to decide which issues are important and which are unimportant. To do this, we would have to decide whether to include both regulations and practices or whether instead to limit the database to just regulations or just practices. A classification based upon regulations or *de jure* issues might be quite different from one that was based upon practices or *de facto* issues. As we have seen earlier, in some countries the accounting regulations are set with the needs of the tax authorities or creditors in mind. Discretionary accounting practices and disclosures may instead be designed to meet the needs of stock market participants.

---

[6] Fitzgerald *et al.* (1979).

We would also have to consider the question of which types of organization should be covered by our database. In the UK, this is not really a problem. All but the very smallest UK limited liability companies have to follow the same Companies Acts and accounting standards[7] while the stock market requires very few additional disclosures. In other countries, such as the USA, there are very different requirements for listed companies (regulated by the Securities and Exchange Commission or SEC) and non-listed companies (regulated at the state rather than the federal or country-wide level). In much of Europe the important distinction is instead between the individual company and the group. As discussed in Chapter 14, while listed companies follow IFRS, unlisted companies in many EU countries such as France follow quite different domestic rules which have been mainly regulated by the government. The rules are mainly designed to meet the needs of the government, the tax authorities and creditors. They tend not only to result in relatively conservative profit measures but to be also highly uniform, giving companies little discretion or choice in what methods to use. Therefore, if our database of accounting issues was restricted to issues that applied to group financial statements we might find that France, the UK and the USA were all placed in the same group. If instead our database were limited to issues applying to individual company financial statements we would probably find that the UK and France were placed in different groups. (The USA might even be totally excluded from our database as listed companies have to report only group financial statements.)

8.5 Deductive classifications of accounting systems

Having looked at some of the inductive classification schemes that exist, we now discuss in this section some of the more important deductive classifications that have been proposed in the past.

As discussed in section 8.3, deductive classifications are usually indirect classifications. They use as classificatory factor(s) those characteristics that influence or help explain the accounting systems of countries. Many of the more important influences on accounting were discussed in Chapters 6 and 7. We saw that there were very many influences on accounting and many factors that helped to explain regulations or practices. We therefore need to select the most important factors. Fortunately, this is not quite as difficult as it might at first seem.

Many of the factors that influence accounting are closely related to each other. For example, the legal and tax systems tend to be highly related. Code law countries tend to have less of a separation between tax and accounting regulations than do common law countries. The same countries will therefore tend to be classified in the same ways whichever of these two factors is used. Therefore, when classifying countries we could choose to use either the legal system or the tax system as a basis for classification, but we would not need to use both. We can also make our task easier by ignoring some countries. Obviously, we would like a classification system that correctly groups all countries and if we cannot correctly classify all countries we should try to refine and improve our analysis. But we can omit some groups of countries and still develop useful classification schemes. Most of the classifications in the literature, for example, have ignored or excluded the ex-communist countries and most less developed countries.

---

[7] While listed companies have to follow IFRS, and unlisted ones have to follow FRS, there are relatively few differences between the two sets of standards.

Three types of factors have been used as classificatory variables in the past, namely:

- the objectives of accounting
- the political, economic or cultural environments of countries
- external influences on countries.

Examples of classifications using each of these types of factors will now be explored. However, before doing this, a word of caution is in order. Accounting in many countries has undergone some major changes in recent years. Increasing internationalization of companies and the work of the IASB have led to some major changes in both rules and practices of many countries. It must therefore be remembered that each of these classifications may only apply to one point in time and their results or conclusions are unlikely to be equally valid or indeed at all valid now.

8.5.1 Mueller's classifications

Accounting classifications can be traced back to the early work of Hatfield (1966), first published in 1911, who noted similarities between the USA and the UK and between France and Germany. The modern work really began with Mueller (1967) who, using casual observation, divided accounting systems into four types – largely, but not exclusively, based upon the objectives of accounting:

1 **Macroeconomic systems**, such as Sweden at that time, where the most important function of accounting was to provide data to facilitate governmental direction of the economy.
2 **Microeconomic systems**, such as The Netherlands, where accounting is seen as a branch of business economics, and is aimed primarily at aiding the objectives of the individual business.
3 **Independent discipline systems**, such as the USA and the UK, where accounting is seen as a service function derived from business practices and is characterized by the use of professional judgement.
4 **Uniform systems**, such as France or Germany, where accounting is seen as a means of government administration and control.

The grouping variable is fairly complex, involving as it does the ways in which accounting has developed and the ways in which it is viewed in a country. Although Mueller offered typical examples of countries in each category, it was often not clear where other countries fit – or, indeed, if they fit at all – into any of the four groups.

While Mueller treated the four groups as distinct categories, placing each country into only one of the four groups, later writers have used his ideas but modified the analysis. Rather than using these concepts to classify countries into four separate groups, they have been used to develop a 2 × 2 classification which combines the characteristics into pairs. One axis is then the micro/macro orientation of the accounting system – whether the primary objective of accounting statements is seen as the provision of information useful for the economy as a whole or information useful to the individual company or corporate stakeholder. The other axis measures the way in which regulations are set – whether a uniform system or a system of independent and flexible rules. For example, Oldham (1987) proposed such a classification, as illustrated in Exhibit 8.7. Illustrating some of the changes then occurring in accounting, Oldham produced two different classifications, the one reproduced in Exhibit 8.7, which illustrates the position in the mid-1980s, and a second classification, reproduced in Exhibit 8.8, which refers to the position a decade earlier, in the mid-1970s.

Exhibit 8.7 Oldham's proposed classification using Mueller's accounting variables: the mid-1980s

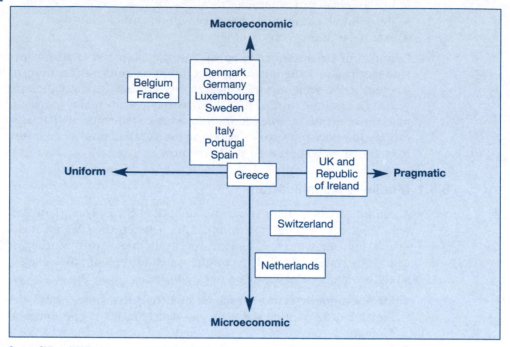

Source: Oldham (1987).

Exhibit 8.8 Oldham's proposed classification using Mueller's accounting variables: the mid-1970s

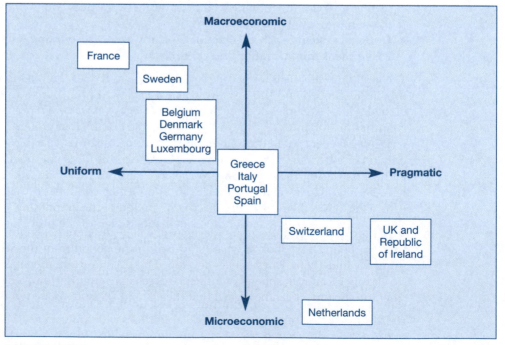

Source: Oldham (1987).

8.5.2 Spheres of influence

Mueller's classification was based upon features of the domestic institutional or cultural environment of countries. However, as discussed earlier, the accounting rules and practices of countries are typically influenced also by external factors. In some countries most of the rules and practices have been imported from elsewhere, with little or no local adaptation. Therefore they bear little or no relation to specific features of that country, such as the stage of business development or business complexity. Such a mismatch between the internal business or cultural environment and accounting is likely to be particularly common in developing countries. Cooke and Wallace (1990), for example, provided evidence suggesting that developed and developing countries should be categorized separately. They looked at the financial disclosure regulations of a number of countries and tried to match these with a variety of economic and cultural features. They found that the relationship between disclosure regulations and features internal to the country was stronger for developed countries than it was for developing countries. Interestingly, and somewhat surprisingly, they also found that the stage of economic development does not help to explain the extent of regulation. This provides clear evidence that, at least for developing countries, we cannot successfully classify if we use only factors that are internal to the country. As discussed in Chapter 6, the accounting regulation of developing countries will often be highly influenced by trade partners or past colonial or other links to particular developed countries.

This idea of exporting or importing accounting rules and practices leads to an alternative type of classification system, which is best illustrated by the work of Seidler (1967). He discussed what he termed 'spheres of influence' and identified three systems:

- **British**: The UK and countries influenced by the UK, including the Commonwealth.
- **American**: The USA and areas influenced by the USA, such as Israel, Mexico and parts of South America.
- **Continental**: Led by France, and including those parts of Southern Europe and South America which base their legal systems on the Code Napoléon.

This is a very simple classification system that, in terms of how it is derived, is almost the complete opposite of Mueller's classification schemes in that it ignores all internal factors. Instead, it looks only at external influences and identifies three countries that Seidler argues have had the greatest success in exporting their accounting systems.

While it might appear to be relatively easy to group countries on the basis of external influences, even here a more complex classification is required. Seidler's three categories are clearly not exhaustive and so the proposed classification does not meet one of the requirements of a good classification system. For example, it excludes Scandinavia; also excluded are parts of Africa, which includes former Portuguese colonies which appear to have a quite distinct accounting system following their former colonial ruler.[8] However, more important than these omissions is the fact that the end product of this type of classification, in terms of the groups developed, will be different depending upon the initial starting point. If we look at what happened in the period from the Second World War until the mid-1960s, when Seidler developed his classification, then it is probably correct to classify US and UK spheres of influence as separate groups. However, if we go back further into history, it can be argued that the UK and US systems are not distinct. The USA

---

[8] United Nations (1991).

was originally very influenced by the UK, with many of the leaders of the US profession in its early days being UK trained.

If we look at what happened to accounting in the 1970s and 1980s, then a far more complex classification scheme would have to be developed. Now EU Directives and European countries would be shown as influencing the UK, while the UK has in turn influenced the EU. Therefore the UK has also influenced accounting in other European countries. A classification developed instead in the 1990s and 2000s would have to show the increasing international influence of US accounting, both through direct pressures or influences and through its indirect influence via the IASB and international stock markets. An up-to-date version of the spheres of influence model would have to be far more complex than the model suggested by Seidler. Indeed, it is not at all clear that Seidler's classification helps at all to explain *current* changes in accounting systems.

8.5.3 Gray's classification

Slightly more complex than any of the categorial classifications looked at so far are classifications using multidimensional mapping. As discussed earlier, any number of dimensions is possible although the simplest forms are those that use only two dimensions or classificatory factors. One example of a two-dimensional classification was developed by Gray (1988). As discussed in Chapter 7, Gray described four accounting values which he hypothesized were linked to the culture of the country. Using these four accounting values, he went on to suggest two two-dimensional maps of accounting systems. One of the most interesting and important things about this work is how Gray defined two types of 'accounting system'. Firstly, he classified countries on the basis of their system of regulation. Two dimensions were considered – who regulates accounting (statutory control versus the profession) and how flexible are the rules that they set (uniform versus flexible). He also produced a second classification based upon the measurement and disclosure rules themselves. The two dimensions used here were the importance of conservatism or prudence and the openness or transparency of the disclosure rules. Countries were then placed on the maps on the basis of judgement, as shown in Exhibit 8.9.

Gray did not use the maps to develop discrete categories or a classification of countries, being content to place countries into the relevant quadrants. However, the work could be extended fairly easily and countries could be classified or placed into discrete groups on the basis of their location on the maps. If we look at the map of measurement and disclosure systems, for example, we could argue that there are two groups of countries. Those countries placed in the quadrant of relatively high secrecy and conservatism fall into one group, while those countries placed in the quadrant of relatively high optimism and transparency form a second.

8.5.4 Hierarchical classifications

8.5.4.1 Nobes's (1984) classification

All the classification schemes looked at so far are categorial classifications. They all place countries into discrete, non-overlapping and hopefully exhaustive categories. As such, they assume that all the countries in any one category share similar characteristics while also being significantly different from the countries in the other categories. In practice, of course, it is not as simple as this. Instead, differences between countries are a matter of degree and some countries placed in the same group will be more alike than are other

Exhibit 8.9 Two-dimensional classifications proposed by Gray

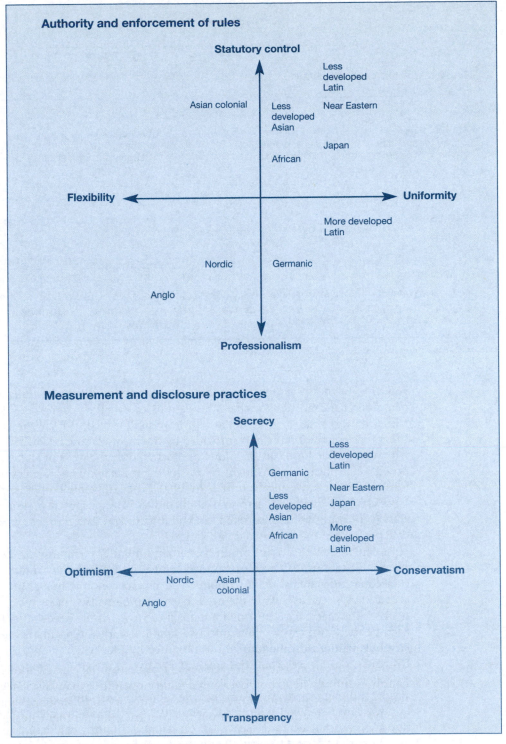

Source: Gray (1988), pp. 12–13. Reproduced by kind permission of Blackwell Publishers.

Exhibit 8.10 Nobes's proposed hierarchical classification of accounting systems (1984)

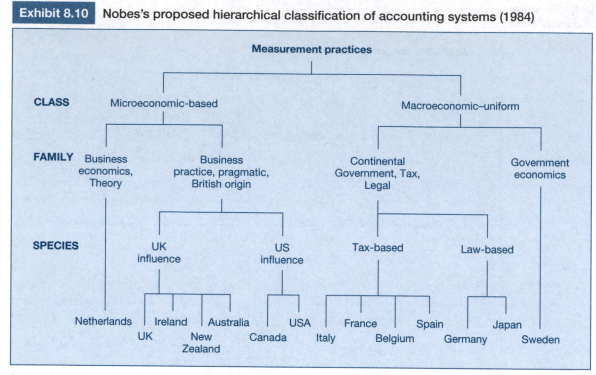

Source: Nobes (1984), p. 94. Reproduced with kind permission of Croom Helm.

countries in the same group. In addition, countries in different groups will share some common characteristics. We therefore want to know which countries or groups of countries are most similar or dissimilar and how similar or dissimilar they are. Answers to these types of questions can be provided by the most complex deductive classifications, which are hierarchical classifications, as illustrated by the work of Nobes (1984). He proposed a classification that sought to classify the measurement practices of listed companies in developed western countries in 1980 – that is, before corporate practices might have changed due to EU harmonization moves. The proposed hierarchy was used to classify 14 countries, as illustrated in Exhibit 8.10, and data on these countries was also collected to test the proposed classification.

As can be seen, this classification has certain similarities with some of the earlier deductive classifications. At the most fundamental level Nobes again argues for two classes of accounting systems, microeconomic and macroeconomic based. In the micro class, accounting is seen as serving the needs of the company itself or its specific stakeholders, while in the macro class the orientation is more towards the needs of society as a whole. Each of these two classes splits into two families, with the resultant four families very largely equating with the four groups proposed by Mueller. Similarly, the two species of UK- and US-influenced countries are similar to two of the groups proposed by Seidler.

This classification was tested by Nobes and the results strongly supported the two classes, although there was relatively little support for the finer categories. The classification was also tested by Doupnik and Salter (1993). They produced an inductive classification applying statistical analysis to data on actual accounting practices. They then assessed whether or not their classification and the categories of countries developed were similar or dissimilar to those suggested by Nobes. While Nobes's original classification scheme was designed to explain measurement practices, Doupnik and Salter tested it using data on both measurement and disclosure practices. In addition, they used data for 1990 rather than 1980 (when the classification was first proposed) and more countries. This is an example of a study that uses cluster analysis as a means of grouping countries.

Despite using very different data from that originally employed by Nobes, Doupnik and Salter's results provide some quite strong support for Nobes's classification. They found two solutions, one with two groups and one with nine groups. At the two-group level, the results clearly support the micro/macro split with the classification being identical to that proposed by Nobes. The nine-group solution also tends to support Nobes's classification.

8.5.4.2 Nobes's (1998) study

In a later study, Nobes (1998) sought instead to explain differences in financial reporting practices and then to use this to develop a hypothetical classification of financial reporting systems. He argued that, of the various factors discussed in the first two chapters of this section, the single most important factor in explaining reporting differences is the financing system. Financing systems can vary across countries in terms of two features: the main source of finance, and the relationship between the company and its finance providers. Finance can be mainly in the form of credit (i.e. debt) or in the form of equity (i.e. shares). The providers of both may maintain an arm's length relationship with the company, where they depend upon the financial statements for information and have no means to influence the company directly, or they may be insiders with a privileged or private relationship to the company through, for example, board membership or other long-term close ties. While not inevitable, outsiders tend to be dominant in strong-equity countries and strong-credit countries tend to be countries where insiders are dominant. This results in two types of financial reporting systems:

- **Type A** – strong equity and outsiders dominant: where the financial reporting system is relatively open, being designed to report to those with no access to other information and the rules for reported earnings are relatively non-conservative.
- **Type B** – strong credit and insiders dominant: where the financial reporting system is relatively non-informative and reported earnings are based upon conservative rules.

Nobes argues that other factors are less important, are closely related to the financing system or are not the factors that actually determine the reporting system. For example, while the level of agreement between taxation and reporting rules may differ across countries in a systematic way, it is not the cause of accounting differences. Rather, the need for accounting for other users such as equity providers meant that tax and reporting rules began to diverge, while the lack of competing users of financial reports meant that the two systems could remain in agreement. Similarly, he argues that culture may help to explain the financing system of countries rather than being a direct determinant of the reporting system. However, culture is rather more complex than this, in that two types of countries may be distinguished. In a manner similar to Seidler's spheres of influence, Nobes argues that there are two types of countries, those that are culturally self-sufficient (CSS) and those that are culturally dominated (CD). Culturally dominated countries will have a mismatch between their accounting systems and their financing systems if only one of them has been imported from a culturally self-sufficient country.

These arguments lead to five propositions, three relating to the type of financial reporting system in existence and two being concerned with the process of change in accounting practices:

P1   If a country is culturally self-sufficient with strong equity outsiders dominant then it will have a Type A system.

P2   If a country is culturally self-sufficient with strong credit insiders dominant then it will have a Type B system.

P3   If a country is culturally dominated it will have the accounting system of the dominant country.

P4   As a country develops a strong-equity outsiders market, it will move towards a Type A system.

P5   Strong-equity outsiders companies in countries where strong-credit insiders are dominant will move to a Type A system.

Nobes provides a number of examples to support these propositions. It is simplest just to quote him on this:

1 New Zealand is a CD country with wholesale importation of British culture and institutions, including a strong-equity outsider system and Class A accounting. Whether the Class A accounting results from the equity market or from direct cultural pressure is not important to the model, it probably arises from both.

2 China is a country without a strong equity-outsider tradition but which seems to be moving towards such a system. Class A accounting is followed.

3 Malawi is a CD country with very weak equity markets but where the accountancy profession has adopted Class A accounting, consistent with its colonial inheritance from the UK.

4 The Deutsche Bank, Bayer and Nestlé are companies from countries with traditionally weak equity markets. These companies are now interested in world equity-outsider markets, so they are adopting Class A accounting for their group accounts.

(Nobes, 1998, p. 180)

In the light of this analysis, Nobes then went on to update his earlier hypothesized classification, as reproduced in Exhibit 8.11. A number of important changes have been made. In particular, he has responded to a number of the criticisms made by Roberts (1995) and the classification system no longer seeks to classify countries. Instead it classifies the accounts of groups of companies. Therefore, the accounting system is the system of financial reporting rules as they apply to particular groups of companies. For example, one system is US GAAP rather than the US as US GAAP does not apply to companies that are not registered with the SEC. Likewise another group is 'standard French' rather than France, as companies can use IASB rules for group accounts if they wish.

In this classification, Nobes equates equity or creditor financing with outsider or insider financing. However, La Porta *et al.* (2000) argue that it is extremely difficult to categorize most countries as either investor or creditor orientated, with many countries such as Italy or France having relatively underdeveloped banking and equity systems. They also document in an earlier (1998) study how equity and debt are not substitutes, but that very often countries with high levels of equity finance also have high levels of debt financing. They argue instead that external finance, whether debt or equity, will only be common if there is strong legal protection for the external parties and that countries with high levels of shareholder protection also tend to have high levels of creditor protection. Thus, it would appear that the more important of Nobes's two variables is the

Exhibit 8.11   Nobes's proposed hierarchical classification of accounting systems (1998)

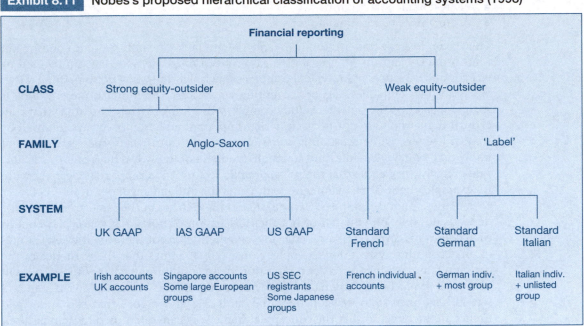

Source: Nobes (1998), p. 181.

extent of internal or external financing rather than whether that finance takes the form of equity or debt. If these arguments are accepted then it would appear that Nobes's hypothesis would be better reframed in terms of the strength of the corporate governance rules, whether these are the procedures adopted by the individual firm or the rules mandated by the country.

8.5.5 Is there an 'Anglo-Saxon' group of countries?

The classifications described so far in this chapter have not all agreed on the question of whether or not there exists an 'Anglo-Saxon' or Anglo-American group of countries. This is a particularly interesting question in the context of the IASB as it has often been accused of being influenced by such a group and of setting standards that are Anglo-American. This debate also illustrates the difficulty of deciding exactly what the key attributes of an accounting system are and therefore what types of accounting systems actually exist.

For example, Alexander and Archer (2000) argue that an Anglo-American group or system of accounting used to exist in that the countries all had micro-orientated professionally set rules but that this reflects the historical position in the 1960s and 1970s, since when the UK and the USA are no longer in the same group. They argue that there are four reasons why people often argue that an Anglo-American group, including both the USA and the UK, exists. Namely:

● Present fairly and true and fair are very similar concepts or they are essentially interchangeable terms.

- The countries in this group all have a propensity to develop conceptual frameworks.
- All are common law countries.
- All are private sector standard setters.

They go on to argue that 'true and fair' and 'present fairly' are not the same concept, but that in the UK and the EU true and fair is an overriding criterion that can be used by either standard setters or individual companies such that they may do something different from the Companies Acts or accounting regulations.[9] In contrast, present fairly is used to mean that the statements fully comply with US GAAP. They also argue that conceptual frameworks are not necessarily that important and are not always followed by standard setters, while illustrating some of the many cases where code law does not imply rigid or inflexible rules and common law does not imply less rules or more flexible rules. Finally, they argue that the private/public sector divide is not that clear cut with, for example, the SEC, a government body, being the ultimate regulator in the USA.

Whether or not this implies that the UK and the USA are in the same group crucially depends not only on whether or not their discussion of how each factor plays out in each country is correct, but also, crucially, on whether or not these are the key features of an accounting system. For example, Nobes (2003) argues that the existence of the true and fair override is not a defining feature of an accounting system. Indeed, it is seldom used in practice by companies, being used only in a few cases where the standard setters have used it to develop their standards. He also argues that Alexander and Archer are incorrect in that the conceptual frameworks are often used by standard setters and that, in particular, discussions of the definitions of assets and liabilities feature frequently in standard setting. Finally, Nobes argues that the type of legal system and who sets the standards are not crucial features of an accounting system. Instead, Nobes argues that an Anglo-American group exists characterized by 'decision making by investors; it plays down the measurement of taxable income and distributable income; it is less worried about prudence; it is more willing to go beyond superficial legal form' (p. 99).

8.6 What conclusions can be drawn?

As we have seen in this chapter, classifications have been developed using a variety of different approaches and there often appears to be little in common between many of the studies. The deductive studies classify on the basis of a wide range of different economic and cultural factors. However, many of these factors are highly correlated so that the resultant groups of countries identified by the various studies are often very similar. These studies suggest, in particular, that there are leading countries in each group. Other countries, often less developed and with historical political and economic links to the leading countries, are influenced by and follow them. When it comes to explaining these groups, the most obvious result is that there are at least two types of accounting systems: a law-based, standardized, macro-based system and a more pragmatic, professionally orientated, micro-based system.

---

[9] True and fair is a concept whose meaning is hotly debated; see *European Accounting Review*, 2(1) (1993) and Evans (2003) for more on this.

Perhaps the main contribution of the deductive studies is not so much to offer classifications of particular countries, but rather to offer descriptions of the key features of national accounting systems and to suggest which factors are influential in their development.

The inductive studies offer a quite different way of developing a classification. Rather than relying upon deductive or a priori arguments they use statistical tests to analyze a large amount of detailed information on accounting rules and/or practices. These studies have a number of weaknesses, particularly the misuse of statistical tests and unthinking use of large data sets. They have also used different types of data and included different countries and different time periods. It is not too surprising, therefore, that the results of the many different classification studies are not always consistent. What is perhaps more surprising is the extent of agreement that there is across the various studies.

Some groups and subgroups clearly emerge from many of the classification studies. In particular, there appear to be:

1 A large Commonwealth group, which may be split into two subgroups of:
   (a) developed Commonwealth; and
   (b) developing Commonwealth.
2 A US-influenced group.
3 A South American group.
4 A European group, which may be split into two subgroups of:
   (a) Central and north Europe; and
   (b) south Europe.

There is also evidence to support the view that no single classification can successfully include all accounting systems, especially when an 'accounting system' is defined to include all aspects of accounting. Disclosure and measurement systems are often sufficiently different to mean that countries need to be classified on the basis of either their disclosure system or their measurement system. While more work needs to be done in this area, different groups will probably also emerge if we consider the practices of different types of companies. For example, countries might be classified quite differently if we looked only at the accounting practices of large listed groups rather than, for example, the practices of individual companies or smaller non-listed groups. In particular, the larger and more international a company is, the more likely it is to follow internationally accepted practices and the fewer differences there should be across companies from different countries.

There are several possible ways forward. We could use increasingly sophisticated statistical methods alongside databases that have been specifically developed for the purpose of classification. This would undoubtedly lead to better classifications as many of the problems of the existing classifications could be avoided. However, the new classifications will probably not be significantly better or very different from those discussed above. Before we can develop new and significantly improved or more useful data sets of accounting rules and practices we need to decide which rules and practices are important and vary in a consistent and predictable manner across countries, and which occur randomly or are temporary or trivial. The most useful way forward is therefore not to carry on replicating past studies using improved data sets or statistical tests, but instead to concentrate upon detailed individual country case studies. Another useful way forward is to look beyond the financial statements to the aspects of financial reporting and disclosure that will continue to be influenced by national institutional and cultural factors, as discussed in Chapter 4.

Summary and conclusions

This chapter has looked at attempts to classify the accounting systems of various countries. All of these classifications attempt to place accounting systems into distinct or non-overlapping groups or categories. The accounting systems inside any one group should share similar characteristics while also being different from the systems placed in the other groups.

The chapter provided an overview of the different types of classifications which are all based upon one or other of two types of reasoning. We saw how deductive or a priori classifications start with a theory of accounting or accounting differences which is used to develop the categories. Key features of the accounting system or the economic, institutional or cultural environment of countries are identified on the basis of prior knowledge and theoretical arguments and these are used to guide the classification of accounting systems. Inductive classifications, in contrast, start with the accounting rules or practices themselves and use various statistical techniques to uncover the underlying groups.

Having discussed the different ways in which classifications can be developed, the chapter went on to describe examples of each of the main types of classification. Several of the more important and more influential empirical studies were discussed. These empirical studies cover a range of different countries, use data from very different time periods and even define an 'accounting system' in quite different ways. As such, they have also come to some quite different conclusions regarding the resultant groups of countries. However, they do share a number of common results and this chapter finished by drawing out conclusions regarding the different types of accounting systems that appear to exist internationally.

Key points from the chapter:

- Classification helps simplify a complex world and helps organize ideas.
- Classification systems may be inductive or deductive.
- The complexity of classification systems increases across discrete, continuous multidimensional and hierarchical approaches.
- Inductive methods generate classification systems from large data sets.
- Deductive methods generate classifications from first principles and then apply them to data.

Questions

The following questions test your understanding of the material contained in the chapter and allow you to relate your understanding to the learning outcomes specified at the start of this chapter. The learning outcomes are repeated here. Each question is cross-referenced to the relevant section of the chapter.

Explain why it is important to classify accounting systems

1 Why might users of accounts be interested in classifications of accounting systems? (section 8.2)

2 Why might accounting regulators, both nationally and internationally, be interested in classifications of accounting systems? (section 8.2)

Distinguish deductive from inductive approaches to classification and simple from complex classification systems

3 What are the main types of classification schemes that have been used to classify accounting systems? Give an example of each type. (section 8.3)

4 Which do you think are the most useful? Why? (section 8.3)

5 What types of factors have been used as classificatory variables in deductive classifications? Give an example of the use of each type of factor. (section 8.3.1)

Explain the advantages and limitations of the different types of classification systems

6 What are the strengths and weaknesses of the inductive approach to classification? (section 8.3.1)

7 What are the strengths and weaknesses of the deductive approach to classification? (section 8.3.2)

Evaluate published research which develops or uses classification systems

8 Of the inductive classification studies described in this chapter, which do you think is the best? Why? (section 8.4)

9 If you were to develop an inductive classification, how would you go about doing it? What are the main problems that you think you would encounter? (section 8.4)

10 Of the deductive classification studies described in this chapter, which do you think is the best? Why? (section 8.5)

11 If you were to develop a deductive classification, how would you go about doing it? What are the main problems that you think you would encounter? (section 8.5)

12 The term 'accounting system' can be taken to mean *de jure* or *de facto* measurement or reporting practices of all companies or certain types of companies. To what extent have the classification studies described in this chapter differentiated between different concepts of an accounting system? (sections 8.4 and 8.5)

13 What evidence is there that the results of classifying countries will be different if different concepts of an accounting system are considered? (For example, to what extent might the groups be different if all companies are considered or if only listed group companies are considered?) (sections 8.4 and 8.5)

14 Which concepts or definitions of an accounting system are likely to be the easiest to classify empirically? Why? (section 8.3.4)

15 Which concepts or definitions of an accounting system are likely to be the hardest to classify empirically? Why? (section 8.3.4)

References and further reading

Alexander, D. and Archer, S. (2000) 'On the myth of Anglo-Saxon financial accounting', *International Journal of Accounting*, 33(4): 539–557.

Choi, F.D.S. and Bavishi, V.B. (1980) 'International accounting standards: issues needing attention', *Journal of Accounting*, March: 62–68.

Cooke, T.E. and Wallace, R.S.O. (1990) 'Financial disclosure regulation and its environment: a review and further analysis', *Journal of Accounting and Public Policy*, 9: 79–110.

D'Arcy, A. (2001) 'Accounting classification and the international harmonization debate – an empirical investigation', *Accounting, Organizations and Society*, 26: 327–349.

D'Arcy, A. (2004) 'Accounting classification and the international harmonization debate: a reply to a comment', *Accounting, Organizations and Society*, 29: 201–206.

Doupnik, T.S. and Salter, S.B. (1993) 'An empirical test of a judgmental international classification of financial reporting practices', *Journal of International Business Studies*, 24(1): 41–60.

Evans, L. (2003) 'The true and fair view and the "fair presentation" override of IAS1', *Accounting Business Research,* 33(4): 311–325.

Fitzgerald, R.D., Stickler, A.D. and Watts, T.R. (1979) *International Survey of Accounting Principles and Reporting Practices*. London: Price Waterhouse International/Butterworths.

Gray, S.J. (1988) 'Towards a theory of cultural influence on the development of accounting systems internationally', *Abacus*, 24(1): 1–15.

Hatfield, H.R. (1966) 'Some variations in practices in England, France, Germany and the US', *Journal of Accounting Research*, Fall: 169–182.

La Porta, R., Lopez-de-Silanes, F., Shleifer, A. and Vishny, R. (1998) 'Law and finance', *Journal of Political Economy,* 106(6): 1113–1155.

La Porta, R., Lopez-de-Silanes, F., Shleifer, A. and Vishny, R. (2000) 'Investor protection and corporate governance', *Journal of Financial Economics,* 58: 3–27.

Lewis, P.A. and Salter, S.B. (2006) 'Europe and America – together or apart: an empirical test of difference in actual reported results', *Advances in International Accounting,* 19: 221–242.

Mueller, G.G. (1967) *International Accounting*. London: Macmillan.

Nair, R.D. and Frank, W.G. (1980) 'The impact of disclosure and measurement practices on international accounting classifications', *Accounting Review*, July: 426–450.

Nobes, C.W. (1982) 'A typology of international accounting principles and policies: a comment', *AUTU Review*, Spring: 62–65.

Nobes, C.W. (1984) *International Classification of Financial Reporting*. London: Croom Helm.

Nobes, C.W. (1998) 'Towards a general model of the reasons for international differences in financial reporting', *Abacus*, 34(2), September: 162–187.

Nobes, C.W. (2003) 'On the myth of "Anglo-Saxon" financial accounting: a comment', *International Journal of Accounting*, 38(1): 95–104.

Nobes, C.W. (2004) 'On accounting classification and the international harmonization debate', *Accounting, Organizations and Society*, 29: 189–200.

Oldham, K.M. (1987) *Accounting Systems and Practice in Europe*, 3rd edn. London: Gower.

Ordelheide, D. and KPMG (eds) (1995) *Transnational Accounting*. London: Macmillan.

Roberts, A. (1995) 'The very idea of classification in international accounting', *Accounting, Organizations and Society*, 20(7/8): 639–664.

Salter, S.B. and Doupnik, T.S. (1992) 'The relationship between legal systems and accounting practices: a classification exercise', *Advances in International Accounting*, 5: 3–22.

Seidler, L.J. (1967) 'International accounting – the ultimate theory course', *Accounting Review*, October: 775–781.

United Nations (1991) *Accounting Developments in Africa*: *Challenge of the 1990s*. New York: United Nations CTC.

9

Measuring harmonization and diversity

Learning outcomes

After reading this chapter you should be able to:

● Understand how comparability indices are used to measure similarities and differences in reported figures.

- Understand how concentration indices are used to measure similarities and differences in accounting methods.
- Measure the comparability of profits and the level of harmonization, using simple examples.
- Understand the approach taken in market-based research investigating earnings 'conservatism'.
- Understand the problems of measuring differences and similarities in narrative and voluntary disclosures.
- Evaluate published research which has used these techniques.

9.1 Introduction

Chapters 6 and 7 looked at reasons why countries have adopted different accounting systems and Chapter 8 looked at the ways in which countries can be placed into groups based upon accounting similarities and differences. This chapter looks instead at the ways in which these accounting similarities and differences can be measured. It also looks at some of the empirical studies that have used these techniques and conclusions are drawn regarding both their strengths and weaknesses and the importance of the results achieved.

As discussed in Chapter 1, differences in the accounting practices of countries are of two types. Similar events can be reported in different ways in different countries. For example, different valuation rules may be used for various assets and liabilities. Secondly, different events may be reported in different countries (e.g. different off-balance-sheet rules may exclude or include specific transactions). Differences in accounting rules or practices can impose significant direct and indirect costs on providers and users of financial statements. Direct costs include extra preparation or analysis costs, indirect costs arise because different decisions may be taken if different information is available.

This chapter begins by looking at the techniques that can be used to quantify or measure the differences and similarities between two or more sets of accounts. It then looks at techniques that seek instead to measure the similarities or differences in the techniques used to produce the figures and differences in the behaviour of earnings across different countries. Finally, it explores methods of measuring differences in the amount and quality of narrative disclosures. In each case it also looks at some of the empirical studies that have used these techniques.

9.2 Similarities and differences in reported figures

One way of comparing financial statements is to measure the extent of the similarities or differences between them. If we can measure and quantify the extent of these, we can see which statements are most alike and which are most different. We can measure changes over time to see if moves towards harmonization are working and we can assess whether or not the differences result in significantly different reported figures.

There are a number of ways to measure the extent of differences or the extent of similarities across financial statements. One approach is to measure the difference in reported earnings and shareholders' funds reported under different GAAP. Here, we could produce one set of financial statements under local rules and another set for the same company using a different set of rules and look at the size of the resultant differences. An alternative approach is to look instead at the methods or rules used by two companies. Here we would count the number of rules that are the same and the number that are different. Each of these two alternatives will give us some idea of how similar or dissimilar the financial statements are. However, they can often give very different results.

There may be a lot of accounting rules that are different between two companies or two countries, but the overall impact of these differences on reported profits and shareholders' funds may be very small. Some of the accounting differences may result in higher profits or shareholders' funds in one country while other differences result in lower figures. The effects may thus cancel each other out. Alternatively, none of the differences in methods or rules may be very important, in that none cause material differences in the figures reported. In other cases there may be very few rules that are different, but each of these different rules may have a significant and consistent impact on profits and shareholders' funds.

When looking at ways of measuring differences in accounting systems we must therefore look at both the differences in the figures reported and the differences in the methods used. The rest of section 9.2 looks at how to measure the extent of similarity or difference in reported figures, then section 9.3 moves on to look at how to measure similarities or differences in the accounting methods used, while section 9.5 looks instead at differences in how quickly good news and bad news are disclosed, or the extent of earnings conservatism.

9.2.1 Foreign GAAP financial statements

To measure the impact on reported figures of accounting differences you need two sets of figures – one set produced using domestic GAAP and the other set reporting the same events but using an alternative set of principles based upon the GAAP of a second country.

As was discussed in Chapter 2, the main reason for providing foreign GAAP statements is the existence of foreign shareholders and foreign stock market listings. Other important explanations of why they are disclosed appear to be the size of the company and the relative importance of foreign operations and the country that the company is headquartered in.[1] However, in practice most often companies do not produce two sets of accounts. Instead they adopt foreign or international standards instead of domestic GAAP, as was illustrated in the examples in section 6.8.4. However, a number of companies do produce a complete set of financial statements under domestic GAAP and a reconciliation statement using foreign GAAP. In particular, many foreign companies listing on US stock exchanges have to provide a reconciliation statement in their annual Form 20-F, filed with the Securities and Exchange Commission, and it is also often reproduced in their domestic country annual report. The net income and shareholders equity reconciliation statements provided by British Telecom (BT) are reproduced in Exhibit 9.1. As can be seen, these statements start with IFRS-based profit and total equity. They then list the significant differences in accounting rules between IFRS and US GAAP. For each of these issues BT discloses the size of the adjustment or the difference between the figures that would be reported under international and US rules. The statements then end by

---

[1] See Tarca (2004).

Exhibit 9.1   Reconciliation statement: British Telecom

35. UNITED STATES GENERALLY ACCEPTED ACCOUNTING PRINCIPLES continued
(II) NET INCOME AND SHAREHOLDERS' EQUITY RECONCILIATION STATEMENTS

The following statements summarise the material estimated adjustments, gross of their tax effect, which reconcile net income and total equity from that reported under IFRS to that which would have been reported had US GAAP been applied.

NET INCOME

Years ended 31 March	Note	2007 £m	2006 £m	2005 £m
Profit for the year in accordance with IFRS		2,852	1,548	1,829
Profit (loss) attributable to minority interests		2	1	(1)
Profit attributable to equity shareholders in accordance with IFRS		2,850	1,547	1,830
Adjustment for:				
Sale and leaseback of properties	a	(29)	(18)	21
Pension costs	b	(195)	(220)	(333)
Capitalisation of interest	c	(5)	(16)	(13)
Financial instruments	d	175	(436)	(415)
Foreign exchange	e	–	39	–
Deferred taxation	f	–	3	3
Impairment of property, plant and equipment	g	(16)	(38)	(24)
Revenue	h	(82)	–	–
Share based payments	i	2	(1)	13
Property rationalisation provision	k	–	–	(5)
Termination benefits	m	–	–	(20)
		2,700	860	1,057
Tax effect of US GAAP adjustments		92	203	240
Net income as adjusted for US GAAP		2,792	1,063	1,297
Basic earnings per American Depositary Share as adjusted for US GAAP[a]		£3.37	£1.26	£1.52
Diluted earnings per American Depositary Share as adjusted for US GAAP[a]		£3.29	£1.25	£1.51

[a]Each American Depositary Share is equivalent to ten ordinary shares.

SHAREHOLDERS' EQUITY

At 31 March	Note	2007 £m	2006 restated[a] £m
Total equity under IFRS		4,272	1,607
Attributable to minority interest		(34)	(52)
Total parent shareholders' equity under IFRS		4,238	1,555
Adjustment for:			
Sale and leaseback of properties	a	(1,095)	(1,067)
Pension costs	b	–	(1,228)
Capitalisation of interest	c	151	164
Financial instruments	d	(7)	3
Deferred taxation	f	(74)	–
Impairment of property, plant and equipment	g	22	40
Revenue	h	(82)	–
Goodwill	j	123	114
		3,276	(419)
Tax effect of US GAAP adjustments		310	581
Shareholders' equity as adjusted for US GAAP		3,586	162

[a]Restatement of deferred tax valuation allowance as set out in note f on page 135.

Source: BT Annual Report and Accounts, 2007, p. 137.

disclosing net income or profits and shareholders' equity under US GAAP. BT also provides a statement describing the main differences between the two GAAP (not reproduced here).

If we look at the reconciliation statement of BT we can see that, for 2007, the total difference in net income between IFRS and US GAAP was not very large, being only £58m. However, much larger differences emerge in 2006 (£484m) and 2005 (£533m) and in the individual components, with pension costs decreasing US income by £195m and financial instruments instead increasing US income by £175m. In the equity statement the largest item, in 2007, is the sale and leaseback of properties as explained in the notes to the reconciliation statement:

(a) Sale and leaseback of properties
Under IFRS, the sale of BT's property portfolio in 2001 is treated as a disposal and the vast majority of the subsequent leaseback is an operating lease. Under US GAAP as BT has a continuing interest in the properties, these properties are recorded on the balance sheet at their net book value, a leasing obligation is recognised and the gain on disposal is deferred until the properties are sold and vacated by BT and the corresponding lease obligation is terminated. Rental payments made by BT are reversed and replaced by a finance lease interest and a depreciation charge.

(BT 2007 Annual report, p. 138)

9.2.2 The comparability index

In the BT example in Exhibit 9.1 we saw that earnings were £58m lower under US GAAP than IFRS GAAP while reserves were £962m lower (before the impact of the differences on tax). However, these figures by themselves tell us relatively little. We need a measure of the differences in the reported figures that takes into account their significance – for a company this size, were these differences significant or not? Also, are they more or less important than differences for other companies or countries? Finally, it would be helpful if our measure of difference yielded figures that made some intuitive sense, so we could understand what the measure meant without having to go back to the original financial statements.

One measure which meets these criteria was suggested by Gray (1980), who developed what he called a **conservatism index**. If we use US GAAP earnings (or shareholders' equity) as a benchmark and look at the impact of moving from US GAAP-based figures to those produced under IFRS GAAP, the index takes the form:

$$1 - \frac{(\text{Earnings}_{USA} - \text{Earnings}_{IFRS})}{|\text{Earnings}_{USA}|}$$

We do not want an index that is negative simply because the company is making a loss. Therefore, absolute earnings are used as the denominator as it ignores the sign of the earnings figures so the index is always positive. The index will take the value of 1.0 if the two earnings figures are the same, it will be greater than 1.0 if IFRS GAAP-based earnings are larger than are US GAAP-based earnings, while an index of between 0 and 1.0 means that IFRS GAAP-based earnings are smaller than are US GAAP-based earnings.

While this index was originally called the 'conservatism index', this term is misleading as accounting methods that result in a lower earnings figure are not always more conservative. For example, the revaluation of fixed assets is not generally thought of as a conservative valuation rule. However, any revaluation will result in higher depreciation charges, and therefore lower earnings. Many other accounting rules are concerned with the question of when costs or revenues are recognized in the income statement rather than being concerned with the amount recognized. Development costs, for example, can be charged to income in the period incurred or capitalized and charged over a number of future periods. These rules therefore result in differences in the pattern of earnings recognition over time but do not affect the total earnings of the entity over its life. This will result in lower earnings in some period(s) but in other period(s) it will result in higher earnings figures. The index is therefore better thought of as an index of how similar or dissimilar the figures are, or how comparable they are. We will therefore instead refer to this index as the **comparability index**.

Just as, in Exhibit 9.1, the difference between US and IFRS GAAP-based earnings and equity was broken down into its constituent parts, the comparability index can also be broken down into partial indices, each one measuring the impact of one accounting issue. For example, if we want to calculate the partial index due to differences in deferred tax we would calculate the index as follows:

$$1 - \frac{\text{Difference due to deferred tax}}{|\text{Earnings}_{USA}|}$$

An example of the calculation of the index for earnings and shareholders' equity is given in Exhibit 9.2.

Exhibit 9.2 **An illustration of the calculation of comparability indices**

	£m
Profit attributable to shareholders – IFRS GAAP	110
Adjustments due to differences in the treatment of:	
Pension costs	10
Deferred tax	(20)
Net income in accordance with US GAAP	100
Shareholders' equity – IFRS GAAP	800
Adjustments due to differences in the treatment of:	
Goodwill	300
Deferred tax	(100)
Shareholders' equity in accordance with US GAAP	1,000

Comparability index calculations

Earnings:		
Total:	$1 - (\text{Profit}_{USA} - \text{Profit}_{IFRS})/|\text{Profit}_{USA}|$	
	$1 - (100 - 110)/100 = 1 - (-0.10)$	= 1.10
Partial:		
Pension costs	$1 - (10/100) = 1 - 0.10$	= 0.90
Deferred tax	$1 - (-20/100) = 1 - (-0.20)$	= 1.20
Shareholders' equity:		
Total:	$1 - (1,000 - 800)/1,000 = 1 - 0.20$	= 0.80
Partial:		
Goodwill	$1 - (300/1,000)$	= 0.70
Deferred tax	$1 - (-100/1,000)$	= 1.10

Exhibit 9.3   Comparison of UK and US GAAP earnings of UK companies

		Number of companies	
	Index value	1988	1994
UK profit less than 90% of US	<0.90	5	4
UK profit between 90 and 95% of US	0.90–0.95	1	1
UK profit between 95 and 105% of US	0.95–1.05	3	2
UK profit between 105 and 110% of US	1.05–1.10	3	1
UK profit more than 110% of US	>1.10	13	17
Total number of companies		25	25
Mean comparability index		1.17	1.25
Range (excluding two outliers): Lowest value		0.65	0.75
Highest value		1.79	2.76

This method has been used in a number of studies that have compared accounting practices across different countries. One of these is Weetman *et al.* (1998) who applied this technique to 25 UK companies which provided reconciliations of reported earnings to US GAAP-based earnings in both 1988 and 1994. The distribution of values of the total indices is reproduced in Exhibit 9.3.

The indices show that earnings were, on average, less under US GAAP in both years, and that the average difference had actually increased over the period. Some of these differences are not material, but fully 18 of the 25 companies had a difference of more than 10 per cent in 1988 and similar differences were found in 21 of the 25 companies in 1994. Especially important were the differences in treatment of goodwill, financial instruments and leasing. While this study is now somewhat old, it provides a very good illustration of why the work of the IASB is so important. Continuing differences of this type of magnitude are obviously likely to have a significant impact upon both the users and preparers of any accounts that are used in any international setting.

9.2.3 The use of reconciliation statements

The comparability index has also been used in a number of other studies that have looked at the differences in reported figures under various GAAP.[2] However, the index is not without its problems. If the reported earnings figure is very small, the index will often be extremely large, which may be misleading. (This is because the change in earnings is being compared with a very small denominator – the benchmark GAAP-based earnings.) More important than this, though, are the problems of data availability. Reconciliation statements are produced by relatively few companies. These companies are generally among the largest and most international of companies. They may not be typical or representative of other smaller or less international companies. Where alternative methods can be used, these companies may not make the same choices as are made by other companies. No company will want to produce two sets of accounts with very different earnings or equity figures unless they have to. This is because many users of the accounts know very little about accounting and may view the figures – and therefore

---

[2] See, for example, Adhikari and Emenyonu (1997); Cañibano and Mora (2000); Emenyonu and Gray (1992); Weetman and Gray (1991).

also the company – with suspicion if it apparently cannot decide how much money it really made. Companies which have to produce reconciliation statements may therefore, where possible, select accounting methods that are acceptable under both domestic and foreign GAAP, so reducing the number of items that are included in the reconciliation statement and the size of the difference between the two sets of figures. For example, Lang *et al.* (2003) found that firms cross-listed on US exchanges adopted less aggressive earnings management and reported more conservative earnings than did similar firms that were not also listed in the USA.[3]

Even if there are no systematic differences between cross-listed and domestic listed firms, it is always dangerous to make generalizations based upon a few cases. The first German company to list on the New York Stock Exchange (NYSE) in 1993 was Daimler-Benz, and this example is often quoted to illustrate how large the differences in earnings can be under different GAAP. On listing for the first time, Daimler-Benz's reported earnings fell from a profit of DM615m under German GAAP to a loss of DM1,839m under US GAAP (giving a comparability index of 2.33). However, to quote only this one year and this company is misleading as much of the difference was due to a one-off adjustment. In other years the differences in reported figures under the two GAAP were very much less. In 1995, for example, the difference was only DM5m on a German GAAP-based loss of DM5,734m. (Recognizing the importance of producing financial statements under an internationally understood and acceptable set of GAAP if they are to be readily used by international investors, Daimler-Benz changed its accounting policies in 1996. It then started producing its full consolidated financial statements under US GAAP.)

Finally, nearly all of the reconciliation statements provided reconcile domestic GAAP figures to US GAAP figures. Thus, it might be relatively easy, for example, to compare IFRS and US practices or Japanese and US practices, but it is much more difficult to compare for example the practices of UK and German unlisted companies.

9.2.4 Simulation studies

Given the problems involved in using reconciliation statements, it would be useful if we could find an alternative way to measure GAAP differences. One possibility is to use simulations. Real companies can be used, or a company can be created using artificial data. The figures can then be recalculated under a number of different accounting methods. If real companies are used, then the samples used can be large enough to be statistically representative of the entire population of companies. If an artificial company is created, we can use average figures derived from all companies or from particular sectors, so creating a typical or average company. Alternatively, we could create an atypical company that illustrates particularly interesting or problematic issues.

A number of simulation studies have been carried out and one of these will be looked at to get an idea of how they work. Walton (1992) compared accounting in the UK and France (more information on this study, including the figures generated, can be found in Case study 9.1, at the end of this chapter). Walton created an artificial construction company that, among other things, had some foreign operations, extraordinary items and leased assets. The case was presented to a number of accountants in the two countries, who produced balance sheets and income statements for the foreign subsidiary and the parent company. While there were some very significant differences between the average

---

[3] See also Joos (2003) for a discussion of this work.

figures generated by the UK and French respondents, for anyone interested in international harmonization, the most important and interesting result (p. 198) was that:

> Variations in treatment within each jurisdiction are quite clear from the results, and it is by no means obvious that a user would obtain a greater consensus by comparing two reports from the same country with each other than by comparing one report from each country.

9.3 Similarities and differences in the accounting methods used

9.3.1 The H-index

So far we have looked at differences in the reported figures of companies that are caused by using different accounting methods. We could instead ignore the actual figures produced and look at the accounting methods used. We would then look at the number of accounting methods that are the same and the number that are different across companies and use this to calculate a measure of how comparable the financial statements are. This method is usually applied to *de facto* practices because the accounting rules in most countries contain options. However, it has also been adapted to measure *de jure* methods.

The comparability or similarity in the accounting methods used by a group of companies increases as fewer alternative methods are used or as the methods used become more concentrated around one alternative. We can use this idea of 'concentration' to measure comparability. In economics, an industry is said to be more concentrated if a small number of companies account for most of the sales of that industry. That is, most customers purchase from the same suppliers. In the same way, financial statements may be said to be more comparable if a small number of alternative accounting methods are used and most companies use the same alternative. That is, most companies choose the same methods. There are many different ways in which industrial concentration can be measured, but one common method is the Herfindahl or H-index. The H-index can also be used to measure the comparability of accounting methods.

The H-index takes the form:

$$\sum_{i=1}^{n} p_i^2$$

where: p_i is the proportion of companies using accounting method i
n is the maximum number of possible methods that can be used.

Exhibit 9.4, panel A, gives numerical illustrations of how to calculate the H-index. This is a simple example of accounting issues 1–3. For each issue two alternative treatments, A and B, are allowed. Assume for the illustration that issue 1 is inventory valuation where the alternatives are (A) FIFO and (B) LIFO. Issue 2 is depreciation where the alternatives are (A) straight line and (B) reducing balance. Issue 3 is development expenditure where the alternatives are (A) capitalize and (B) report as an expense. For issue 1, half of the companies choose method A and the other half use method B, giving an index of 0.50. In contrast, for issue 2 method A is far more popular, being used by 90 per cent of the companies. There is therefore much more consensus and the H-index increases to 0.82. For issue 3 method B is now the more popular, being used by 90 per cent of the companies, so the H-index is again 0.82.

Panel B of Exhibit 9.4 gives information on accounting issues 1–4. For each of these issues four possible alternatives, A–D, exist, although not all are always used in practice.

Exhibit 9.4	Calculation of the Herfindahl index

Panel A

Proportion of companies using method:	A	B	Calculation	H-index
Accounting issue				
1 Inventory valuation	0.50	0.50	$0.5^2 + 0.5^2$	0.5
2 Depreciation	0.90	0.10	$0.9^2 + 0.1^2$	0.82
3 Development expenditure	0.10	0.90	$0.1^2 + 0.9^2$	0.82

Panel B

Proportion of companies using method:	A	B	C	D	H-index
Accounting issue					
1 Inventory valuation	0.25	0.25	0.25	0.25	0.25
2 Goodwill	0.05	0.25	0.25	0.45	0.33
3 Valuation of land	0	0.33	0.33	0.33	0.33
4 Deferred taxation	0	0	0	1.00	1.00

For example, issue 1 is inventory valuation where the alternatives are (A) FIFO, (B) LIFO, (C) average cost and (D) standard cost. Issue 2 is goodwill where the alternatives are (A) write off to revenue reserves, (B) write off to capital reserves, (C) impairment test and (D) amortize over useful life. Issue 3 is valuation of land where the alternatives are (A) value in use, (B) replacement cost, (C) cost adjusted for general prices and (D) historical cost. Issue 4 is deferred taxation on asset revaluation where the alternatives are (A) no recognition until sale, (B) partial recognition of short-term deferrals, (C) deduct from asset value and (D) full provision. Now, the lowest value H-index is 0.25. This is for issue 1, where there is no consensus regarding the best treatment and all four alternatives are equally popular. The highest H-index is 1.0 for issue 4. Here all the companies use method D.

We can see from this that the H-index varies from a low of $1/n$ (where n is the maximum number of treatments permitted, in this case 4), to a high of 1.00, when all companies use the same method.

9.3.2 The C-index

The H-index offers a fairly simple way of measuring comparability. However, it is not a perfect measure. There is no one-to-one relationship between the relative popularity of alternative methods and the resultant values of the H-index so that the index value cannot be interpreted in an unambiguous way. For example, in Exhibit 9.4, Panel B, accounting issue 2 gives an index of 0.33. The H-index is also 0.33 for issue 3 although the distribution of companies across the alternatives is very different. In addition, the H-index cannot cope with multiple reporting. As discussed above, companies may provide a reconciliation statement or other information which allows the user to see the effects of more than one accounting method. In these cases the H-index would be based upon the method used in the main financial statements and would ignore the supplementary disclosures. This will have the effect of underestimating the comparability of the financial statements. The existence of such multiple reporting led van der Tas (1988; 1992) to develop what he calls the compatible or C-index. This is a similar type of index but it can cope with multiple reporting.

Exhibit 9.5	Calculation of the C-index

Number of companies using method:

	A	B	C	Calculation	C-index
Accounting issue					
1 (e.g. depreciation)	15	1	4	$[(15 \times 14) + (1 \times 0) + (4 \times 3)]/[(20 \times 19)]$	0.584
2 (e.g. stock valuation)	7	5	8	$[(7 \times 6) + (5 \times 4) + (8 \times 7)]/[(20 \times 19)]$	0.311

Rather than looking at the proportion of companies that use each accounting method, the C-index instead looks at the number of financial statements that are compatible with each other. It measures the number of pairs of statements that either apply the same accounting method or provide enough additional information to allow users to make comparisons themselves (i.e. the number of compatible reports). The pairs of compatible reports are then compared with the maximum number of possible pairs of reports.

Using a slightly different version of the C-index, one that is slightly easier to use and (it has been argued) also a better index when many countries are being considered,[4] as developed by Archer *et al.* (1995), the C-index takes the form:

$$\frac{\sum (n_i \times (n_i - 1))}{(N \times (N - 1))}$$

where: n_i is the number of companies using method i
N is the total number of companies.

An example of how to calculate the C-index is given in Exhibit 9.5. The methods A, B and C could represent, for example, straight-line, reducing balance and production unit methods of depreciation, or else FIFO, LIFO and average-cost method of valuing stocks of goods.

In this example there are two accounting issues being considered and there are three alternative ways of accounting for each issue. Data is provided on the practices used by 20 companies. There is more consensus over the acceptable treatment for issue 1, where 15 of the 20 companies used method A. For issue 2 no single treatment is particularly popular. The C-index reflects this, being 0.584 for issue 1, but falling to only 0.311 for issue 2. As with the H-index, the C-index will vary from a minimum of 0.0 (where each company uses a different method) to a maximum of 1.0 (where all companies use the same method). The actual values taken by the H- and C-indices will be different (except at these two extremes of 0.0 and 1.0), although they converge towards each other as the number of companies considered increases.

A more detailed explanation and example of the C-index is given in Appendix 9.1 at the end of this chapter.

9.3.3 Measurement of international harmony

The H-index and the C-index both measure harmony or compatibility inside a single country. However, we also need a measure of international harmony. There are several ways to think about international harmony and each can be used to develop a compatibility measure.

---

[4] Morris and Parker (1998).

One approach is to take the world as a whole and have no concern for national boundaries. This might be the perspective taken by an international investor who wants to choose potential investments from a group of companies across a range of countries. To this investor, the home country of each company may not be particularly important. All she wants is to invest in those companies which will provide the best return, irrespective of their country of domicile. To do this, she wants to know the extent to which the financial statements of the group of companies as a whole are compatible. She asks, 'What is the chance that if I pick two companies at random, their accounting practices will be compatible?'

This approach is effectively saying that measuring international harmonization is the same as measuring harmonization in a single country and that the number of countries included is irrelevant. The total C-index would then be applied.

In a study of two or more countries, the total C-index measures *international* harmony defined as the increase in comparability within an international *pool* of accounts brought about when more companies within the pool adopt the same accounting method for an item (Archer *et al.*, 1995). This definition ignores the country of origin of accounts.

A quite different approach is to take account of national boundaries and to ask, 'What is the state of harmonization in each country?', and 'To what extent are companies compatible from one country to the next?' This might be the perspective of a global standard setter who wants to compare the pattern of practices found in different countries.

The question 'What is the state of harmonization in each country?' relates to what Archer *et al.* (1995) call 'within-country' harmonization. The question 'To what extent are companies compatible from one country to the next?' relates to what Archer *et al.* call 'between-country' harmonization.

For a complete picture of international harmonization, each perspective is valuable. It is therefore helpful to have separate indices measuring each type of harmonization. Archer *et al.* suggest that the C-index can be broken down into these two harmonization measures. To see how this works, suppose the world contains two countries. There are 100 companies in total or 50 from each country. A survey shows that 50 companies use the LIFO method of stock valuation while the remaining 50 companies use the FIFO method.

If we ignore the country of origin, the C-index for the 100 companies is 0.49 calculated as:

$$C = \frac{[(50 \times 49) + (50 \times 49)]}{(100 \times 99)} = 0.49$$

Now we decide instead to take note of the national boundaries and we observe the situation as set out in scenario 1 where the two accounting methods are spread equally across each country.

Scenario 1

	Method A (LIFO)	Method B (FIFO)	Total
Country 1	25	25	50
Country 2	25	25	50
	50	50	100

$$\text{Total} \quad C = \frac{[(50 \times 49) + (50 \times 49)]}{(100 \times 99)} = 0.49$$

The within-country C-index is calculated by estimating:

$$\frac{\text{Number of matching pairs in country 1 + Number of matching pairs in country 2}}{\text{Maximum matching pairs in country 1 + Maximum matching pairs in country 2}}$$

$$= [(25 \times 24) + (25 \times 24) + (25 \times 24) + (25 \times 24)]/[(50 \times 49) + (50 \times 49)] = 0.49$$

This result should not surprise us because the pattern of choice within each country is the same as the pattern of choice for the world as a whole.

The between-country C-index is calculated by matching pairs across each country. That is:

$$\frac{\text{Number of matching pairs using method A + Number of matching pairs using method B}}{\text{Maximum possible number of matching pairs}}$$

$$= [(25 \times 25) + (25 \times 25)]/(50 \times 50) = 0.5$$

This result also should not surprise us because the choices are spread evenly across the two countries.

Thus in scenario 1 the total C-index of 0.49 indicates the extent of worldwide compatibility of accounting practice, while the within-country and between-country indices show that there is similar compatibility within each country and across the countries. An international standard-setting body would have to focus attention on two factors: understanding the reasons for companies in each country making different choices; and understanding the relative strength of the standard-setting body in each country. Both aspects would need to be understood in order to assess the likelihood of reaching a compromise on achieving one universal choice.

Now consider scenario 2 where there is total agreement on accounting method in each country but no matching at all across the two countries.

Scenario 2

	Method A (LIFO)	Method B (FIFO)	Total
Country 1	50	0	50
Country 2	0	50	50
	50	50	100

$$\text{Total C} = \frac{[(50 \times 49) + (50 \times 49)]}{(100 \times 99)} = 0.49$$

The within-country index is calculated for each country in turn:

$$\frac{\text{Number of matching pairs in country 1 + Number of matching pairs in country 2}}{\text{Maximum matching pairs in country 1 + Maximum matching pairs in country 2}}$$

$$= [(50 \times 49) + (0) + (0) + (50 \times 49)]/[(50 \times 49) + (50 \times 49)] = 1.0$$

This is the answer we would expect as there is perfect harmonization within each country.

The between-country index is calculated by matching pairs across each country:

$$= [(50 \times 0) + (0 \times 50)]/(50 \times 50) = 0$$

This is again the answer we would expect as there is no harmonization between the two countries.

Scenario 3 shows a calculation where there are three methods of accounting (such as LIFO, FIFO and average-cost methods of stock valuation) to be compared across two countries. The overall index is based on the total number of companies using each method. The within-country index is calculated by reading across the line for each country in turn. The between-country index is calculated by reading down each column of figures.

Scenario 3

Country	Method			Number of companies
	1	2	3	
1	2	5	3	10
2	2	3	10	15
Total	4	8	13	25

	Number of comparable pairs	Total number of possible pairs	Index
Overall index	[(4 × 3) + (8 × 7) + (13 × 12)] = 224	(25 × 24) = 600	0.373
Within-country index	[(2 × 1) + (5 × 4) + (3 × 2) + (2 × 1) + (3 × 2) + (10 × 9)] = 126	[(10 × 9) + (15 × 14)] = 300	0.420
Between-country index	(2 × 2) + (5 × 3) + (3 × 10) = 49	(10 × 15) = 150	0.327

9.3.4 Measurement of harmonization

While there have been a number of studies that have measured the compatibility of financial statements, they have tended to use different indices, different countries, different accounting issues at different levels of fineness and different types of companies.[5] Even without these problems of lack of comparability, there are also some more general problems involved in the interpretation of the C-index.[6] However, while these problems mean that it is difficult to draw anything but very general conclusions from the studies, it is still worth looking at some of the findings.

9.3.4.1 EU harmonization

On of the earliest of these studies, the study by Archer *et al.* (1995), will be described both to give an idea of how C-indices can be used to measure compatibility and to give some ideas on the state of EU comparability prior to the work of the IASB.

---

[5] See, for example, Hellman (1993); Herrman and Thomas (1995); Morris and Parker (1998); Rahman *et al.* (1996); Tay and Parker (1990).

[6] See Aisbett (2001); Krisement (1997).

The C-index and its two components were used to measure changes in harmony across Europe between 1986–87 and 1990–91. This is a period during which the EU attempted to increase accounting harmonization. If this was successful, the level of harmony achieved, as measured by the C-indices, should have increased. A sample of 89 internationally traded companies from eight countries was used, and data was collected from annual reports. This has the advantage that it means that actual practices were considered; however, financial statements often do not provide much detailed information on exactly which accounting methods have been used. This means that the only issues that can be studied are those where companies usually disclose their exact accounting methods; many potentially important issues cannot be examined.

The two areas chosen by this study were deferred tax and goodwill, and five alternative treatments were identified for each (see Exhibit 9.6). The study found that the overall level of compatibility was low, especially for deferred taxation, where the C-index was only 0.149 in 1986–87 and 0.216 in 1990–91. However, the between-country compatibility had increased quite substantially over the period, from 0.108 to 0.186. This was mainly due to a number of Swedish companies changing their practices, coupled with

| Exhibit 9.6 | Compatibility of European financial reporting practices |

Deferred taxation

Possible treatments
A   Nil provision or taxes payable approach
B   Full provision
C   Partial provision
D   Deferred tax recognized, method unspecified or recognized for some companies only
E   No recognition and not known if deferred tax applicable or not

C-indices

	1986–87	1990–91
Within-country	0.371	0.379
Between-country	0.108	0.186
Total index	0.149	0.216

Goodwill

Possible treatments
A   Written-off against profit and loss in year of acquisition
B   Written-off against reserves in year of acquisition
C   Shown as asset and not amortized
D   Shown as asset and amortized over period exceeding one year
E   Other or unspecified treatment

C-indices

	1986–87	1990–91
Within-country	0.583	0.539
Between-country	0.347	0.377
Total index	0.383	0.403

increasing disclosures by the German and Swiss samples. Particularly striking differences emerged between the practices of companies from France, The Netherlands and Sweden, which tended to use the full provision method, and companies from the UK and Ireland, which instead used the partial provision method. For goodwill, the level of compatibility was considerably higher, at 0.383 in 1986–87 and 0.403 in 1990–91, although major differences still existed. Within-country compatibility actually decreased over the period while between-country compatibility increased, due mainly to a number of German companies changing their methods. The main reason that between-country compatibility was not higher was that capitalization and amortization was the almost universal treatment in Belgium and France while immediate write-off to reserves was instead more common in The Netherlands and the UK. Little consensus existed within the samples from Germany, Sweden and Switzerland.

This general move towards increased harmonization in Europe appears to have continued beyond the period examined by Archer *et al*. Again using the C-index, this time on 85 international companies from 13 European countries (EU and non-EU), Cañibano and Mora (2000) instead looked at harmonization between 1991–92 and 1996–97 for the four areas of deferred tax, financial leases, goodwill and foreign currency. They found that in all four areas, harmonization increased. The move was greatest for foreign currency (index moved from 0.34 to 0.53) and the least for goodwill (0.31 to 0.38). One of the two areas covered in Archer *et al*. and in this study was deferred taxation. Similar to Archer *et al*., they found that harmonization increased, again with more Swedish companies changing their practices. These, plus a number of German and Norwegian companies, moved from nil provision to full provision. However, the differences between the practices of companies from France, The Netherlands, Sweden and now also Germany, which tended to use the full provision method, and companies from the UK, which instead used the partial provision method, remained. The second area that both studies considered was goodwill. Here the level of compatibility was higher than that for deferred tax in 1991–92 (0.30), but lower in 1996–97 (0.38). While overall compatibility only increased moderately, there were a significant number of companies which changed their practices. Again, a number of German companies changed from immediate write-off against reserves to amortization. Charging to income in year of purchase did not occur at all in the later period, while several companies from a number of other countries moved from a variety of methods to amortizing over a period in excess of five years.

These results are interesting in the context of institutional moves towards increased harmonization. They are not due to changes in EU rules or domestic standards. Instead, they provide some support for the importance of voluntary harmonization by companies. Of course, while this suggests that at least some companies are recognizing the benefits of increased harmonization, it does not mean that legislative moves towards increased harmonization are not also required.

9.3.4.2 Australia versus the UK and the USA

Another example of a similar type of study, by Parker and Morris (2001), throws some further light on the differences between Australian, US and UK GAAP (as discussed earlier in section 8.5.4). Using 1993 accounts and samples matched by industry and size for 40 companies and 11 practices in each of the UK and Australia, they measured harmonization using the between-country C-index.

Overall, there was very little international harmony, but there were some areas of considerable harmony inside each country (7 of 11 issues for the UK and 5 of 11 for Australia). Perhaps of more interest was their belief that they would find that Australia was more like the USA than the UK as the USA had more influence in Australia than it had in the UK. The results supported this, with Australian GAAP being more like US GAAP than UK GAAP for all issues except the valuation of tangible fixed assets and research and expenditure, where the Australian and US standards were different, and interest on construction of assets and identifiable intangibles where there were no Australian standards. Overall, they concluded that the USA appears to be the cause of partial international harmonization or harmonization across a limited number of countries only, but this partial geographic harmonization actually hinders international harmonization by the IASB for all issues where the international standards conflict with US GAAP.

9.4 Measurement of the impact of the IASB

As might be expected, recent studies looking at both differences in reported figures and differences in the methods used have tended to look at the question of the success of the IASB in achieving harmonization. For example, Murphy (2000) compared a small sample of Swiss companies that did (16) and did not switch (18) from domestic to international GAAP over the period 1988 to 1995 with US, UK and Japanese companies (20 each) which did not use international standards. Any increase in harmonization within the Swiss IAS companies or any increases in harmonization occurring only between the Swiss companies using international standards and the non-Swiss companies could reasonably be thought of as measures of the success of the IASB Comparability Project. However, when using van der Tas's I-index[7] and considering fours items – depreciation, inventory cost method, financial statement cost basis and consolidation – very little evidence of the success of the comparability project was found. Indeed, only in the case of depreciation was the Swiss IAS companies' increase in harmonization significantly greater than that of the non-IAS Swiss companies, while inventory actually became less harmonized in the Swiss IAS companies. When comparing the Swiss and non-Swiss companies it appears that generally practices were becoming more harmonized over the period, but that this applied to both samples of Swiss companies and did not appear therefore to be due solely to the influence of the IASB.

Two aspects of harmonization were included in the measures used in this study, namely the methods used and the disclosures made. For example, the increasing harmonization of cost basis was due to more Swiss companies disclosing what they actually did. While disclosure is obviously desirable, and indeed essential if users are to be able to compare companies in an international setting, increased and therefore more comparable or harmonized disclosure is not the same as more harmonized accounting methods. The IASB will only be successful if it can persuade companies to change their accounting methods as well as improve their disclosures. This suggests that we need to look at both rules and practices.

Other studies have instead looked at how the IASC/IASB rules have changed[8] over the three periods of high flexibility (1973–88), comparability (1989–95) and agreement (1995 onwards) and, not surprisingly, found that they became more harmonized over these periods.

---

[7] The I-index is a modification of the C-index that is more suitable when the number of companies in each country is different. See van der Tas (1988).

[8] Garrido *et al.* (2002).

Haverty (2006) looked instead at the extent of convergence between US GAAP and IFRS as reflected in the reconciliation statements of Chinese firms cross-listed in the USA for the period 1996 to 2002. While this is a sample of only 11 companies, it offers some interesting insights into the impact of the work of the IASB. He examined four accounting figures – net income, net assets, return on net assets and earnings per share – and using Gray's comparability index found that only one of the firms produced comparable figures, in that the differences were less than 5 per cent. Rather surprisingly, he found that for only one firm did all four measures show increased convergence over the period examined, while, in contrast, six firms showed convergence in only one of the four measures. However, the main reason for the differences in reported figures was the fact that the Chinese firms revalued their net assets under IFRS and not under US GAAP. It is likely that the use of revaluation and its practical importance will vary across countries and so these results may not hold for other countries that also use IFRS.

These studies looked at the actual practices of firms. If you are interested in the extent to which countries have implemented IFRS rules then the rules implemented can instead be examined. Now, there are two aspects of harmony – firstly, whether or not the rules cover the same issues and, secondly, if they do, whether they are the same or not. This was the approach adopted by Ding *et al.* (2007) when examining the differences between domestic and international accounting standards across 30 countries in 2001. They firstly calculated a measure of 'absence' for each country, calculated as the number of items for which there was no specific recognition, measurement or disclosure rule. They also calculated a measure of 'divergence' or a measure of the number of items for which national and international rules differed.

Comparing these two measures with five institutional measures, they found that the absence of rules was negatively related to the importance of the stock market and positively related to ownership concentration. The divergence of rules was also negatively related to the importance of the stock market while being positively related to the importance of the accounting profession and the level of economic development. In other words, countries that are economically more successful and have a strong profession are more likely to set their own rules, while countries with rules most similar to the IASB tend to be countries with a shareholder orientation where stock markets are relatively important.

While this study is interesting, it has used a very simple measure of convergence and in practice rules may take a number of different forms. Thus, a particular rule may be required, recommended, allowed or forbidden, or the area may not be regulated. Fontes *et al.* (2005) treated these as five different categories and showed how the differences between two countries can then be measured using a non-parametric or Spearman rank correlation coefficient which provides a simple measure of the extent to which the two systems are similar or dissimilar. Applying this to Portugal, they showed how over time Portugal and the IAS have moved from systems that were negatively correlated to each other to systems of increasing positive correlation.

9.5 Good news, bad news and earnings 'conservatism'

From the perspective of a user of accounting information, what is most important is probably not whether or not the same accounting techniques are being used by two companies or two countries, but rather how different are the figures that are produced by the two systems? Not simply how large are the differences, but are there any consistent differences between the two sets of figures? And, if so, how do the two sets of figures differ? Here, what is important is the pattern of earnings or equity. This is the question that is explored by researchers looking at the question of how conservative earnings are in different countries.

The term 'conservatism' is well known in accounting. It is most commonly used to describe accounting practices that recognize all losses as soon as they are known, but are more cautious about recognizing all gains as soon as they are known. For example, provisions are made against expected losses on long contracts, but profit is only partly recognized on completion of each certified stage of the contract. The words 'asymmetry' ('lack of symmetry') and 'asymmetric' ('not symmetric') are used to describe this unmatched pattern of behaviour. One of the well-known problems of conservatism is that it has different effects on the balance sheet and the statement of profit or loss. Conservatism in the balance sheet can cause over-optimism in the profit or loss (e.g. understating the value of a fixed asset leads to a lower depreciation charge and so a higher profit). Some writers have given a different description of conservatism as a preference for always choosing the option that leads to lower reported values for shareholders' equity, but this view has been discouraged by standard setters.

9.5.1 Basu's model of conservatism

Basu (1997) gave a new interpretation of 'conservatism'. He said it captures the accountant's tendency to require a higher degree of verification for recognizing good news than bad news in financial statements (p. 4). This led Basu to develop what has become known as the Differential Timeliness (DT) model. This is based upon the expectation that earnings reflect bad news more quickly than good news. Basu gave the example that unrealized losses are recognized earlier than unrealized gains. This asymmetry in recognition leads to systematic differences between good news and bad news periods in the 'timeliness' and 'persistence' of earnings. 'Timeliness' measures how quickly an event is reflected in reported earnings. 'Persistence' measures the period of time for which the event continues to have an effect on reported earnings. He used the example of an asset being depreciated over ten years. It is now in its fourth year of operation. Suppose that the enterprise is given the good news that the asset life is now 13 years and so the asset will earn profit for longer. That good news is not reported directly but it results in a lower depreciation charge and so higher earnings. The higher earnings persist for the remainder of the asset life. Suppose instead that the enterprise is given the bad news that the expected asset life is reduced to seven years. The enterprise will apply an impairment test in year 4, causing a sharp reduction in profits in year 4 followed by an even spread of the new depreciation charge on the residual amount. The bad news has a strong immediate effect but less of a persistent effect into future years.

Basu used negative and positive unexpected annual stock returns to represent bad news and good news. Stock returns are measured by the change in share price over a defined period of time. Unexpected returns are the difference between the actual return and the expected return based on a market portfolio and the risk of the specific share. Stock prices reflect market perceptions of a company's performance. Basu relied on a body of previous research which indicated that stock prices anticipate accounting earnings by up to four years. This means that stock prices are the 'leading' variable and earnings are the 'lagging' variable. Basu predicted that if a graph is plotted with annual earnings on the vertical axis and unexpected stock returns on the horizontal axis (Exhibit 9.7), there will be a correlation between the two but the slope of the graph will be steeper for negative

| Exhibit 9.7 | Basu's model of good news, bad news and earnings |

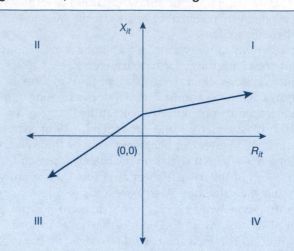

X_{it} and R_{it} are earnings and stock returns, respectively, for firm i in year t. Quadrant I contains observations with positive returns and positive earnings. Quadrant II contains observations with negative returns and positive earnings. Quadrant III contains observations with negative returns and negative earnings. Quadrant IV contains observations with positive returns and negative earnings.

Source: Basu (1997), p. 12.

abnormal returns. The 'bad news' on the left-hand side of the graph will cause earnings to fall faster than the 'good news' will cause earnings to rise on the right-hand side. He also predicted that the intercept on the vertical axis (at the point of zero good and bad news) will be positive because, even though there is neither good news nor bad news, the persistent effect of any previous good news will remain.

Basu tested his hypothesis using US data from 1963 to 1990. The adjusted R^2 (explanatory power) was higher at 6.6 per cent for negative returns than 2.1 per cent for positive returns, which gave Basu support for his claim that bad news has more impact than good news (although both figures for explanatory power are very low). He also found that there were different slopes for the two parts of the graph, as predicted.

Despite the low explanatory power of his results, Basu's paper was significant for comparative research because it led to a series of papers making international comparisons of 'conservatism'. All of these studies are based upon the argument that if there are consistent differences in the accounting systems of different countries we expect this to be reflected in differences in the extent of conservatism, or as argued in one study of international differences:

The underlying premise of our analysis is that a country's legal/judicial system, securities laws, political economy, and tax regime create incentives that influence the behavior of corporate executives, investors, regulators, and other market participants. Such incentives shape the properties of reported accounting numbers through a complex interplay of accounting standards, legal, market, regulatory and political pressures, and reporting discretion exercised by management.

(Bushman and Piotroski, 2006, p. 108)

9.5.2 US/UK comparison

Pope and Walker (1999) applied a similar model in comparing the accounting treatment of extraordinary items in US and UK accounting regimes. Their data covered the period 1976 to 1992 when extraordinary items were a stronger feature in both countries (changes in rules in both countries have subsequently largely eliminated extraordinary items). Their results showed that the degree of 'conservatism' displayed by earnings before extraordinary items under US GAAP was higher than under UK GAAP. However, examination of earnings after extraordinary items showed that the sensitivity of earnings to bad news was higher under UK GAAP than under US GAAP. The explanatory power of their results was 10.5 per cent for earnings after extraordinary items and 13.3 per cent for earnings before extraordinary items. Their results also indicated that an important distinguishing feature of US GAAP conservatism was the relatively slow recognition of good news in earnings.

9.5.3 USA, UK, Australia, Canada, France, Germany and Japan

Ball *et al.* (2000) proposed that earnings would react to good news and bad news at different rates depending on whether the country had a code law or a common law regime. They used the code law/common law distinction as a very crude measure of the extent to which accounting is determined by market supply and demand relative to political forces. They analyzed data for companies in Australia, Canada, the USA, the UK (as examples of common law systems) and France, Germany and Japan (as examples of code law systems) over the period 1985–95. They found that the common law accounting earnings showed greater timeliness than those of code law accounting but that this was almost entirely due to greater sensitivity to economic losses (bad news). They linked this to a desire for greater 'transparency' in disclosure and they regard the more timely reporting as 'high-quality' disclosure. The explanatory power was 4.6 per cent for the code law results and 14.6 per cent for the common law results. When they split the data into two periods, 1985–90 and 1991–95, they found that all countries except Japan showed increased reaction to bad news and concluded that corporate governance measures around the world were causing pressure for more timely reaction. They seemed somewhat unsure about the explanation for Japan.

Their paper contains a full discussion of the limitations of their analysis (pp. 47–49) and it is important to read this discussion before citing the paper simplistically as a conclusion about code law and common law systems. They acknowledge that the most obvious concern is the validity of using stock returns to represent ('proxy' for) economic income. Equating poor public disclosure with uninformed stock prices involves projecting common law precepts onto code law institutions. Code law systems were not designed for public disclosure. Ball *et al.* suggest that this is not a problem as the code law countries will use inside information to inform the market. They assert, without stating the authority (2000, p. 48), that insider-trading laws are fundamentally incompatible with code law governance. A second concern about their model is that the code law/common law categorization is used to represent an economic construct (a variable measure) representing the extent to which accounting is determined by market supply and demand relative to political forces. Their response is that the evidence is consistent with the idea. Another limitation is that their results apply only to listed companies and so are less representative of code law countries in general, where proportionately more companies are unlisted.

9.5.4 Hong Kong, Malaysia, Singapore and Thailand

Ball *et al.* (2003) study the timely recognition of economic losses (measured by negative change in market returns) in Hong Kong, Malaysia, Singapore and Thailand in the period 1984–96 (i.e. before the economic crisis of 1997 in those countries). They make the assumption that these could be described as common law regimes influenced substantially by the UK, US and IAS accounting standards and standard-setting institutions. The results are compared with the 'common law' and 'code law' findings of Ball *et al.* (2000). Hong Kong shows the highest timeliness and Thailand the lowest. The authors compare this with the more market-oriented reputation of Hong Kong compared with Thailand. All are less timely than the common law group studied in Ball *et al.* (2000). This is attributed to the incentives facing managers and auditors in companies dominated by family control and personal networking. These companies are characterized by the authors as having strong incentives to hide large profits and large losses by income smoothing. The explanatory power of the results resembles that of Basu (1997) with an R^2 of 4.5 per cent. They conclude that high-quality standards do not guarantee high-quality financial reporting (1997, p. 260) and that the SEC is 'well advised' (1997, p. 259) in concluding that a condition for acceptance of IAS for financial reporting purposes in the USA is that 'the standards must be rigorously interpreted and applied'. This paper lacks the thorough discussion of limitations found in Ball *et al.* (2000) but all those limitations should be considered in evaluating the US-oriented policy conclusions about the quality of financial reporting.

9.5.5 The EU

There have been a number of studies of various countries in the EU. One of the earliest was by Giner and Rees (2001) who compared France, Germany and the UK, as having two different types of code law and a common law system, respectively. They studied the period 1990 to 1998. The explanatory power of their results for the 'bad news' sample was 8.5 per cent for Germany, 9.9 per cent for France and 11.4 per cent for the UK. The explanatory powers of the 'good news' sample were 0.6 per cent, 1.7 per cent and 0.9 per cent respectively (2001, p. 1311). They agreed with Ball *et al.* (2000) in concluding that bad news is more rapidly incorporated into earnings than is good news. However Giner and Rees observed higher explanatory power for bad news effects in Germany and France compared with Ball *et al.* They found no significant difference between the three countries, which differs from the main result of Ball *et al.* but is consistent with their findings for the shorter time period of 1991–95. Giner and Rees concluded that the differences were disappearing in more recent years despite the different legal traditions. In further analysis they showed that the results for the German sample also showed characteristics of conservatism in which management always make the choice which leads to lower book value of equity.

This work was later extended by Lara and Mora (2004) and by Roanic *et al.* (2004). Lara and Mora used the DT measure as a measure of earnings conservatism as well as an alternative measure of conservatism, namely balance sheet conservatism as developed by Feltham and Ohlson (1995). This defines conservatism in terms of the difference between the book value of the firm and the market valuation of the firm. They found when examining eight European countries that all showed both types of conservatism and that the code law countries were more conservative in terms of balance sheet conservatism than was the UK (the only common law country in the sample). However, contrary to their expectations the UK was not significantly more conservative with respect to earnings (except when compared with Germany). They expected the UK to be more conservative because managers and auditors face higher litigation risk if they fail to disclose bad news, code law countries typically smooth income more to reduce income volatility and higher balance sheet conservatism in code law countries will reduce earnings conservatism. They argue that the result found is probably because differences in corporate ownership patterns have generally declined over time and the differences, at least with respect to large stock-market-listed companies, are now less than is commonly assumed.

Raonic *et al.* (2004) instead extended the analysis to look at European firms that were cross-listed in Europe as these firms are exposed to a number of different regulatory and accounting requirements regimes. Similar to the hypothesis of Giner and Rees, and Lora and Mora, they argued that shareholders in countries where outside shareholders are more important and where regulations are more strictly enforced would be more likely to be able to demand the timely release of bad news. They also used the work of La Porta *et al.* (1997; 1998) as discussed in Chapter 4, to argue that conservatism should depend upon the extent of financial disclosure by the individual company and the importance of the stock market and the degree of regulatory enforcement in that country. For multi-listed firms the scores for each country that they list in were averaged to give a company score. While as in prior works using DT measures the R^2 were for most markets in the region of 10 per cent or less, they found evidence of earnings conservatism in all markets except Zurich. The evidence also suggested that conservatism was influenced by both stock market influences and country-wide regulatory influences, but not by the disclosure practices of the individual company. In particular they found that the exposure to different equity markets tended to result in more timely earnings recognition, while the extent of regulatory enforcement encouraged more conservatism in earnings.

9.5.6 Comment on 'conservatism' research

This type of research focuses only upon certain aspects of conservatism. The term 'conservatism' has no agreed definition and it clearly is not a simple concept. Ball and Shivakumar (2005) split it into two concepts – unconditional and conditional conservatism. Conditional or income statement conservatism is then defined as the tendency to understate net assets by the asymmetric recognition of losses and gains, for example as seen in the old adage 'recognize a loss as soon as it is probable and recognize a gain only if it is certain'. This is the primary focus of DT measures. In addition to this there is unconditional or balance sheet conservatism, the tendency to understate book values leading to book values being lower than the market values of firms.

Givoly *et al.* (2007) describe a number of methodological problems with the DT measure that are likely to be particularly important for research in international accounting.[9] While these do not negate the importance of DT research, collectively they clearly suggest that there are problems with using this measure and that it does tend to underestimate conservatism. Firstly, DT is based on the argument that bad news is reflected in earnings more quickly, but that over time good news will also be reflected in earnings. Thus, at any one point in time earnings reflect relatively up-to-date bad news plus older

---

[9] See Ryan (2006) also for a discussion of other problems and suggested methodological improvements.

good news. This means that earnings reflect the impact of an aggregation of events that occurred over time, sometimes good news will be relatively important and sometime bad news will be relatively important, so that the relationship between earnings and share prices will vary over time as the nature of past events has also varied. Secondly, there will be external events that affect share prices immediately, but affect future earnings and not current earnings at all, for example changes in interest rates or new long-term contracts for the firm. Again this makes the relationship between earnings and share prices unstable over time and reduces the ability of the DT measure to capture conservatism correctly. Finally, if management have discretion over disclosures the timing of disclosures will affect the relationship between earnings and returns and the ability of DT to measure conservatism. This will be a particular problem in the international context where disclosure discretion differs across countries.

These arguments led Givoly *et al.* (2007) to argue that:

> studies that compare the degree of conservatism between countries are more susceptible to the concerns raised here. Countries differ widely in the degree of development of their capital markets, and, hence, in the nature of the information flow. Less developed markets are likely to be characterized by less uniform, more discrete news arrivals. Further, the different legal and regulatory environments of different countries are bound to affect management disclosure policies, and therefore, the DT measure without implying anything about the conservative stance of the reporting firms.

(p. 99)

While this criticism must be borne in mind before uncritically accepting the conclusions of this type of research it is also worth noting the next point they raise:

> . . . not invalidate the notion that an important manifestation of reporting conservatism is the differential timeliness of the earnings response to good versus bad news. To the contrary, this notion is very reasonable and runs to the heart of the conservatism debate. What the evidence does indicate, however, is that the differential timeliness measure likely suffers from considerable measurement error that exceeds those found in other measures of conservatism.

(p. 99)

9.6 Similarities and differences in information disclosure

So far in this chapter we have looked at various ways to compare differences and similarities in the measurement and recognition system and the resultant earnings and equity figures. However, to gain a complete picture of an accounting system we must also look at disclosure practices, including voluntary disclosure practices. There have been a great number of studies that have looked at disclosure practices inside particular countries. Many of these have tried to model the voluntary disclosure decision by measuring the association between the amount of voluntary disclosure and various company-specific factors. Countries looked at include China,[10] Hong Kong,[11] Italy,[12] Japan,[13]

---

[10] Xiao (1999).

[11] Gul and Leung (2004).

[12] Patelli and Prencipe (2007).

[13] Cooke (1991).

Malaysia[14], Mexico,[15] New Zealand,[16] Nigeria,[17] Spain,[18] Sweden,[19] Switzerland,[20] Tanzania,[21] and the UK.[22] There is general support for the proposition that disclosure levels increase as companies get larger. Very often, the listing status of the company and the industry it operates in are also important as are various corporate governance variables. Profitability and leverage, in contrast, generally appear not to be important.

Far less interest has been shown in the question of whether or not disclosure practices differ across countries. Given our discussion in Chapters 6 and 7, we would expect this to be the case. We saw in Chapter 7 that one of Gray's (1988) four accounting values was secrecy versus transparency. We also saw that this accounting value was related to Hofstede's (1984) four cultural dimensions. Gray hypothesized that high transparency or high disclosure levels should be positively related to weak uncertainty avoidance, small power distance, high individualism and low nurturing. Disclosure practices will also be influenced by the institutions of a country. Particularly important for voluntary disclosures might be the corporate financing system. It would be expected that the more dependent companies are upon equity rather than debt financing, and the more dispersed is that share ownership, then the more the company is likely to disclose in its annual report to shareholders.

Voluntary disclosure practices may also be a function of the level of mandatory rules. If mandatory disclosure levels are set very high there is obviously less scope for voluntary disclosure. However, if mandatory levels are high because of cultural or institutional factors in a country, companies may be willing, as discussed above, to disclose more voluntarily. Thus it is not really clear if high mandatory disclosure levels imply high or low voluntary disclosure levels. However, it is not only the absolute amount of voluntary disclosures that will tend to vary across countries. There will often also be significant differences in the types of disclosure made especially with respect to social and environmental information which is likely to depend upon the political, economic and social features of the country, as discussed in Chapter 6.

There are a number of ways to measure the amount of voluntary disclosure made. One of the simplest approaches is to use a scorecard of likely disclosures. If a company discloses the information then it is scored '1', if it has not disclosed the information, but it could have been provided, it is scored '0', while if the item is not relevant for that company then it should not be included in the list of disclosure items for that company but should instead be ignored. Companies can then be compared on the basis of the proportion or percentage of relevant items they each disclose:

$$\frac{\text{Number of items disclosed}}{\text{Maximum number of items that could have been disclosed}}$$

The scores for each company examined from any one country can then be averaged to obtain the country's disclosure score.

---

[14] Haniffa and Cooke (2002).

[15] Chow and Wong-Boren (1987).

[16] Hossain *et al.* (1995).

[17] Wallace (1988).

[18] Wallace *et al.* (1994); Inchausti (1997).

[19] Cooke (1989).

[20] Raffournier (1995).

[21] Abayo *et al.* (1993).

[22] Firth (1979); Linsley and Shrives (2006).

One of the biggest problems with this approach is deciding what items to include: items that are voluntary in one country or one time period may be mandatory in another, and, thus, the items used in surveys in one country and one time period may not be applicable in others. This is a particular problem for cross-national studies of voluntary disclosures. The items included must be voluntary in all countries; however, if the levels of mandatory disclosure are very different, companies in some countries may be disclosing much information voluntarily. But this would not be picked up by the research instrument if it includes only items that are voluntary in all the countries being examined. This is less of a problem in some areas than in others. It is not a major problem, for example when looking at social or environmental disclosures, as most countries have few disclosure requirements in this area.

There has been much debate about whether or not it is sufficient to score each item equally and simply sum the number of disclosures made or whether some items are more important or more significant and should be weighted more highly or whether an item that is disclosed in more detail should be weighted more highly. For example, it might be argued that disclosure of a forecast of income is more important than disclosure of last year's employee turnover rate and so should be scored or weighted twice as highly. Or alternatively, qualitative examples of activities for parts of the company might be scored '1'. A company that discloses information about the same activities but provides quantitative data for all of the company might be scored '3', while financial data covering several years might be scored '5'. Again, the score received by a company would be compared with the maximum possible score it could have got, to produce a measure of the relative level of disclosure.

This type of scoring system is often accused of being too subjective. Certainly, it is not always easy to design a good weighting system and different people may have different views on how items should be weighted. However, the problem of how to measure disclosure quality does not go away if it is ignored, and the decision to score all disclosures equally is a subjective decision, as of course is the decision to use a weighted disclosures score. A more valid reason not to try to weight items according to their importance is the argument that often the extra sophistication is simply not necessary. If we are looking at a fairly large number of items of information, a company that scores relatively high on an equally weighted scoring system will also usually score relatively high on any other type of weighted scoring system. While these are still issues of debate, what is clear is that the disclosure index must, as with the databases used for classifications discussed in Chapter 6, be designed specifically for the purpose it is being used for. If the index is designed for one purpose, but then used without change in a different environment or for a different purpose, it is unlikely to capture what it seeks.[23]

9.6.1 The measurement of environmental and social disclosure

There have been a large number of studies looking at the social or environmental disclosures in a single country, whether for example UK,[24] USA,[25] India,[26] Singapore[27] or Australia.[28] Far less common are studies comparing the practices in different countries,

---

[23] Coy and Dixon (2004).

[24] Gray *et al.* (1995a); Gray *et al.* (2001); Campbell (2004).

[25] Patten (2002); Esrock and Leichty (1998).

[26] Singh and Ahuja (1983).

[27] Tsang (1998).

[28] Deegan and Gordon (1996).

although there have been some.[29] One of the earliest of these was by Roberts (1991), who looked at the disclosures made by large companies, in five European countries (France, Germany, The Netherlands, Sweden and Switzerland). Roberts used a simple checklist of 54 items covering nine areas concerned with either the environment or employee-related matters (see Exhibit 9.8). This study therefore scored companies on the basis of the proportion of these 54 items that were disclosed. While this method is used frequently in studies of voluntary disclosure, it is not used very often in studies that look specifically at only social and/or environmental disclosures. Much more common in these types of studies is content analysis.

Content analysis does not start with a list of possible items of disclosure. Instead it is a method that attempts to measure all the information disclosed that falls into specific categories or types of information. For example, rather than simply asking 'Does this company disclose any of the following 12 items about employees?', it asks 'What is disclosed about employees?' Typically content analysis will start with a number of possible categories of information such as employees or energy consumption or fair trade activities. The volume of disclosure that falls into each category is then counted. To do this, the number of words, sentences or pages of narratives on each category is measured either in absolute terms or as a percentage of the total disclosures. The analysis can also be extended to include other sources of information and not just the annual report and accounts.[30] These studies are interested in the volume of disclosure as they argue either explicitly or implicitly that volume of disclosure is a good measure of the importance of the disclosure.

Analyzing the volume of disclosure is more informative than simply counting the number of items disclosed in those cases where disclosure about an item may be very brief or very extensive. For example, the disclosure checklist in Exhibit 9.8 contains the item 'description of specific examples' of the environmental impacts of products – this could be one sentence giving an example of one product, for example 'Product X has been redesigned and now can be produced using less raw materials' or it may be one or two pages giving detailed quantitative information on a wide range of products and the inputs used to produce them, the resources they consume when in use and their ease of recycling.

However, simply calculating the amount of space devoted to particular types of information is probably not sufficient. The disclosures made could contain good news or bad news, which could be general statements or quantitative or financial information, it could be just a few examples of what are probably the best parts of the company, or it could be an attempt to provide an objective overview of all the activities conducted by the company internationally. It cannot necessarily be assumed that a company that devotes more relative or absolute space to any one type of information is also providing better quality or more informative disclosures. This suggests that we need a way of also capturing the quality of information disclosed. Beattie *et al.* (2004) describe a computerized content analysis method that can be used for analyzing narrative disclosures. This analyzes narrative sentences or parts of sentences on the basis of four characteristics: the time period covered (whether historical, forward looking or non-specific); whether financial or non-financial; whether qualitative or quantitative; and also the topic area covered. They also argue that the overall quality of the narrative disclosures in an annual

---

[29] See, for example, Adams *et al.* (1995); Gamble *et al.* (1996); Laan Smith *et al.* (2005); Roberts (1990).

[30] See Unerman (2000) for more on this.

Exhibit 9.8   Environment- and employee-related disclosure checklist used by Roberts (1991)

Environment protection statement

1	Policies	4	Costs incurred
2	General descriptive statements	5	Outputs/achievements
3	Types of controls employed		

Process-related information

1	Policies	4	Outputs/achievements – qualitative statements
2	Description of specific examples	5	Outputs/achievements – quantitative measures
3	Costs incurred		

Product-related information

1	Policies	3	Outputs/achievements – qualitative statements
2	Description of specific examples	4	Outputs/achievements – quantitative measures

Environment-related investments

1	Policies	4	Outputs/achievements – qualitative statements
2	Description of specific examples	5	Outputs/achievements – quantitative measures
3	Costs incurred		

Research and development activities

1	Policies	3	Overview of all environment related activities
2	Description of specific examples	4	Costs incurred

Energy usage information

1	Policies	5	Improvements achieved – qualitative statements
2	Energy sources used – qualitative statements	6	Improvements achieved – quantitative statements
3	Energy sources used – quantitative statements	7	Improvements achieved – costs
4	Energy sources used – costs		

Political statements

1	Views on legislation	3	Actions undertaken (lobbying, etc.) – specific examples
2	Views on environmental demands	4	Actions undertaken – policies

Employment information

1	Disabled employees – numbers/costs/policies	7	Maternity/paternity leave
2	Trainee policies	8	Share/profit schemes
3	Trainee costs	9	Hours worked
4	Trainee numbers	10	Absenteeism
5	Trainee hours	11	Labour turnover
6	Pay awards	12	Pensioners – numbers/benefits

Health and safety

1	Policies	5	Training activities – quantitative
2	Description actions undertaken – qualitative	6	Accidents – qualitative information
3	Description actions undertaken – financial	7	Accidents – quantitative
4	Training activities – qualitative	8	Illness – time lost

Source: Roberts (1991).

Exhibit 9.9	Explanation of content analysis checklist form

Type	Qualitative
	Quantitative or
	Financial information
Time	Time period covered by disclosures
Area	Information given for:
	All of company
	Specific geographical area(s) or
	Specific line(s) of business only
Extent	Describe all relevant activities of the area or give examples of activities carried out only
Non-narrative	Disclose pictures/diagrams/graphs

report or any other document depends not only on the level of detail of the information provided but also on the spread of disclosure – so that a report that discloses information on only one or two topics will be less informative than one which discloses information on a wide range of topics, even if the level of detail is greater. This is another instance where the H-index can be used, as described in Chapter 8.

A similar type of content analysis form used to measure environmental disclosures is reproduced in Exhibit 9.9, as used by Roberts (1991). This analysis form asks five questions about each relevant type of disclosure. It is similar to the analysis of Beattie *et al.* in that it asks what type of information is disclosed – qualitative or quantitative – and what is the time period covered – past, future or not specified? However, it also considers the extent of the coverage. Very often companies describe their activities for each major division or part of the company, so is this information that is consistently disclosed by all parts of the company, or is it something that just one part of the company thinks is worth disclosing? Finally, is it a statement designed to provide an overview of all relevant activities, or is it just an illustration of an activity? For example, a statement that the company has trained 100 people in new health and safety processes would be a statement about the activities of the entire company; a statement that the subsidiary in Canada trained 20 employees would be an example of an activity only.

One international study using this type of research instrument replicated and extended Roberts's work.[31] Using annual reports from four years later (i.e. 1992 or 1993) and looking at the same five countries plus the UK, this study came to a somewhat different conclusion. It looked at environmental, employee and ethical information and measured the amount of space devoted to a number of issues in each of these three areas. It also measured the number of items that were disclosed in total and the number of items that were disclosed in quantified or financial terms.

The results of this study were interesting in that it found not only that the six countries disclosed significantly different amounts of information, but that the two countries disclosing the most were, firstly, Germany and, secondly, the UK. These two countries are very

---

[31] Adams *et al.* (1998).

different. Germany has a long history of worker participation in corporate management, with works councils being common. It also has a very active and vociferous Green Party. The UK, in contrast, has a relatively small Green movement, the Green Party has not been very important in domestic politics and the UK has no history of works councils, while the trade union movement has substantially decreased in power and influence over the last decade or so. The authors of this work thus conclude that what motivates the voluntary disclosure of social and environmental information in the two countries is probably very different. In Germany, information may well be disclosed as a reaction to external pressures. In the UK, it is more probable that it is disclosed proactively in an attempt to pre-empt such external pressures – if companies can demonstrate that they are acting in socially acceptable ways then perhaps there will be less demand for more regulations and government control of their activities.

More ideas about the reasons for voluntary social and environmental disclosures are provided by Williams (1999) who explored disclosures in seven countries from the Asia–Pacific region. He argued that two of Hofstede's variables are particularly important. While as we saw in Chapter 6 Gray argued that all four of Hofstede's values were linked to secrecy, specifically that 'the higher a country ranks in terms of uncertainty avoidance and power distance and the lower it ranks in terms of individualism and masculinity then the more likely it is to rank highly in terms of secrecy' (Gray, 1988, p. 11), Williams only included uncertainty avoidance and masculinity or nurturing. From the variables discussed in Chapter 5, he also tested the importance of the political system, this time in terms of the level of political and civil repression,[32] legal system, economic development and importance of equity financing. However, of these he found only support for the importance of the cultural variables (both of them) and the political system.

9.6.2 The measurement of other types of disclosure

There have also been a number of studies which have been wider in scope, looking at all or most types of voluntary disclosure. It is difficult to compare these studies or to describe their findings in general terms. They have looked at different countries, different time periods and different types of companies, and have used different disclosure checklists. This section will therefore not attempt to draw generalizations but will instead look at just two of these studies, Meek *et al.* (1995) and Gray *et al.* (1995b), which were interesting studies in that they looked at a wide range of information of three types – strategic, non-financial and financial – all items being voluntary in both the UK and the USA at that time (see Exhibit 9.10). This breakdown of disclosures into three types was necessary as different factors may influence the voluntary disclosure of the different types of information. For example, the disclosure of financial information is likely to be most influenced by corporate financing needs and forms of financing employed. In contrast, disclosure of non-financial information or employee and social information is most likely to be influenced by political and societal pressures for additional disclosures. Thus, companies in one country may tend to disclose relatively large amounts of financial information while companies from another country may instead disclose relatively large amounts of non-financial information.

---

[32] See Belkaoui (1985) and Goodrich (1986) for more on this possible relationship.

Exhibit 9.10 Voluntary disclosure checklist as used by Meek *et al*. (1995)

Strategic information

1 *General corporate information*
1 Brief history of company
2 Organizational structure

2 *Corporate strategy*
3 Statement of strategy and objectives – general
4 Statement of strategy and objectives – financial
5 Statement of strategy and objectives – marketing
6 Statement of strategy and objectives – social
7 Impact of strategy on current results
8 Impact of strategy on future results

3 *Acquisitions and disposals*
9 Reasons for the acquisitions
10 Reasons for the disposals

4 *Research and development*
11 Corporate policy on R&D
12 Location of R&D activities
13 Number employed in R&D

5 *Future prospects*
14 Qualitative forecast of sales
15 Quantitative forecast of sales
16 Qualitative forecast of profits
17 Quantitative forecast of profits
18 Qualitative forecast of cash flows
19 Quantitative forecast of cash flows
20 Assumptions underlying the forecasts
21 Current period trading results – qualitative
22 Current period trading results – quantitative
23 Order book or back-log information

Non-financial information

6 *Information about directors*
24 Age of directors
25 Commercial experience of executive directors
26 Other directorships held by executive directors
27 Employee information

7 *Educational qualifications*
28 Geographical distribution of employees
29 Line-of-business distribution of employees
30 Categories of employees, by gender
31 Identification of senior management and their functions
32 Number of employees for two or more years
33 Reasons for changes in employee numbers or categories
34 Amount spent on training
35 Nature of training
36 Categories of employees trained
37 Number of employees trained
38 Data on accidents
39 Cost of safety measures
40 Redundancy information (general)
41 Equal opportunity policy statement
42 Recruitment problems and related policy

8 *Social policy and value added information*
43 Safety of products (general)
44 Environmental protection programmes – quantitative
45 Amount of charitable donations
46 Community programmes – general
47 Value added statement
48 Value added data
49 Value added ratios
50 Qualitative value added information

Financial information

9 *Segmental information*
51 Geographical capital expenditure – quantitative
52 Geographical production – quantitative
53 Line-of-business production – quantitative
54 Competitor analysis – qualitative
55 Competitor analysis – quantitative
56 Market share analysis – qualitative
57 Market share analysis – quantitative

10 *Financial review*
58 Profitability ratios
59 Cash flow ratios
60 Liquidity ratios
61 Gearing ratios
62 Intangible valuations – except goodwill and brands
63 Dividend pay-out policy
64 Financial summary – for at least six years
65 Restatement of financial information to non-UK/US GAAP
66 Off-balance sheet financing information
67 Advertising information – qualitative
68 Advertising information – quantitative
69 Effects of inflation on future operations – qualitative
70 Effects of inflation on results – qualitative
71 Effects of inflation on results – quantitative
72 Effects of inflation on assets – qualitative
73 Effects of inflation on assets – quantitative
74 Effects of interest rates on results
75 Effects of interest rates on future operations

11 *Foreign currency information*
76 Effects of foreign currency fluctuations on future operations – qualitative
77 Effects of foreign currency fluctuations on current results – qualitative
78 Major exchange rates used in the accounts
79 Long-term debt, by currency
80 Short-term debt, by currency
81 Description of foreign currency exposure management

12 *Share price information*
82 Market capitalization at year end
83 Market capitalization trend
84 Size of shareholders
85 Types of shareholders

Source: Meek *et al*. (1995), pp. 569–570. Used with the permission of the *Journal of International Business Studies*.

Gray *et al.* (1995b) looked at large UK and US multinational companies and compared those that were listed only on their domestic stock exchange with those that were internationally listed (i.e. listed on both the London and New York Stock Exchanges). They were interested in the questions of whether internationally listed companies disclosed more information and disclosed more harmonized information than did domestically listed companies.

For the US sample, they found that internationally listed companies disclosed significantly more information than did domestically listed companies, including significantly more strategic and non-financial information. (This was true after controlling for the possible effect of sample differences with respect to size and multinationality, as measured by the proportion of foreign sales.) For the UK sample, the results were somewhat different, with internationally listed companies disclosing significantly more financial information. They then compared the UK and US samples. For the domestically listed companies, the UK companies disclosed significantly more non-financial information while the US companies disclosed significantly more financial information. For the international group, significant differences also existed, but there was less of a difference between the two countries. Now, the only significant difference was with respect to non-financial information. These results clearly suggest that international listing does not eliminate all country-specific differences in voluntary disclosures. However, it appears to moderate or reduce national differences by, in particular, reducing the difference between the amount of financial information disclosed.

The second study, by Meek *et al.* (1995), looked at the same companies plus a sample of internationally listed European companies from France, Germany and The Netherlands ('internationally listed European companies' were defined as those that listed on either the London or New York Stock Exchange). Using the same disclosure checklist they modelled the voluntary disclosure decision through four regression equations (the four dependent variables being all disclosures; strategic; non-financial; financial information). Exhibit 9.11 reports their findings regarding the amount of disclosure made by the sample companies.

Exhibit 9.11 **The disclosure of voluntary information as found by Meek *et al.* (1995)**

Info.:	Strategic		Non-financial		Financial		Total	
	Mean %	Std dev.	Mean %	Std dev.	Mean %	Std dev.	Mean %	Std dev.
All cos	21.03	13.8	18.06	11.0	16.62	8.9	18.23	7.5
All USA	17.22	10.5	11.89	7.1	16.54	6.8	15.20	5.4
Int. USA	20.03	11.0	14.50	7.4	17.27	7.1	17.09	5.5
Dom. USA	14.43	9.3	9.27	5.7	15.81	6.5	13.32	4.6
All UK	16.83	8.5	25.70	9.1	14.58	9.3	18.73	6.8
Int. UK	17.41	9.7	25.71	10.3	16.92	10.4	19.87	8.0
Dom. UK	16.24	7.3	25.69	8.0	12.24	7.4	17.60	5.2
All Eur.	36.52	16.6	23.01	12.4	19.67	11.8	25.16	8.3
Int. Eur.	36.51	17.5	21.87	13.3	23.19	9.3	26.23	8.4
Dom. Eur.	36.53	15.1	24.16	11.6	16.15	13.2	20.09	8.3

The regression analysis failed to support the hypothesis that disclosure decisions were a function of either profitability or multinationality. All the other independent variables (size, country, industry, leverage and listing status) were significant in at least one of the four regressions. However, none was significant across all four equations (e.g. size was not a significant explanation of the amount of strategic information disclosed). The listing status was significant in explaining the overall level of disclosure and the amount of strategic and financial information. It was not important in explaining the level of disclosure of non-financial information. This, again, supports the assertion that stock market pressures and financing needs are most likely to influence the decision to disclose financial information and other information about the financial and future prospects of the company. In contrast, stock market and financing needs are far less likely to influence decisions regarding the voluntary disclosure of employee and social information.

Summary and conclusions

This chapter has explained the techniques that can be used to measure differences in accounting systems. It has shown how the comparability index can be used to measure the impact of GAAP differences on the reported figures. However, it is not only the difference in reported figures that is important. Standard setters and others interested in international harmonization may also want to measure the degree of difference or similarity in the accounting methods used, as measured by concentration indices. The chapter also explained comparative studies of 'conservatism' as a link between market returns and the reported earnings of a company. Finally, the various ways of measuring voluntary disclosure have been explained and a number of studies reviewed.

Key points from the chapter:

- The comparability index can be used to measure differences in both reported earnings and shareholders' equity and it can also be broken down into partial indices used to measure the impact of differences in the treatment of specific issues.

- The H-index and the C-index both measure differences in the accounting methods used by companies.

- The C-index may be broken down into within-country and between-country harmonization.

- Basu's view of conservatism is based on the expectation that company earnings reflect bad news more quickly than good news.

- Research studies show that the rate of reaction of earnings to good news or bad news is different for common law countries compared with code law countries.

- The level of voluntary disclosure varies across countries.

- Different considerations appear important in determining the level of disclosure of different types of information, and companies in some countries tend to disclose relatively more financial information while companies in other countries tend instead to disclose relatively high levels of social information, including employee and environmental information.

Case study 9.1   A simulation study of UK and French accounting

Walton (1992) explored the impact on the reported figures of differences in the accounting methods used in the UK and France. To do this, he chose a number of accounting issues – some where there are differences in terms of the prescribed rules in the two countries and others where companies have a choice of which methods to use.

The company modelled was a construction company. Specifically, there was a domestic parent company whose premises were compulsorily purchased at a loss and whose new premises were partially financed by a government grant and partially financed by a US-denominated long-term loan. In addition, the parent sold and leased back some plant giving the possibility of showing a profit on the disposal. Finally, an overseas subsidiary was set up to carry out a long-term construction contract. Thus, the case included extraordinary items, long-term foreign currency transactions, the capitalization of interest charges, government grants, leased assets and long-term contracts.

The case study was then presented to a number of auditors and account preparers in both the UK and France. This is not a real company so the results may not apply in practice, but they do provide valuable insights into the types of differences that can exist. The differences in the figures generated by the participants were often very large, especially for the accounts of the subsidiary, as shown in the table. However, the most noticeable, and surprising, conclusion is that for the subsidiary the average responses of the UK participants were more conservative than were the French responses. As shown in the average figures for turnover, profit both before and after interest, net assets and net equity were all less for the UK respondents and often very much less. For example, the average profit before interest calculated by the French sample was 12,793 while for the UK sample it was instead a loss of 12,014.

In contrast, for the parent company, there was little difference in the average figures generated by the UK and French samples – but, this time, the French responses tended to be slightly more conservative and they showed considerably more variability than did the UK responses.

	UK sample		French sample		Conservatism
	Mean	Std dev.	Mean	Std dev.	Index
Overseas subsidiary					
Turnover	136,644	83,407	185,930	36,432	0.735
Profit before interest	(12,014)	50,759	12,793	23,357	−0.939
Interest	(4,675)	5,619	(4,031)	1,654	0.841
Profit after interest	(16,689)	51,344	8,763	22,812	−1.904
Total net assets	168,711	51,670	208,938	23,091	0.807
Net equity	2,911	51,256	28,763	22,812	0.101
Parent company					
Turnover	1,331,733	44,577	1,345,000	76,572	0.990
Profit before interest	340,340	28,012	352,598	78,076	0.965
Interest	19,478	10,374	33,692	19,950	0.578
Profit after interest	320,862	30,012	318,906	86,169	1.006
Extraordinary items	33,770	24,538	58,182	14,444	0.580
Profit after extraordinary	287,092	19,003	260,724	77,221	1.101
Total net assets	865,802	28,802	860,227	86,214	1.006
Net equity	551,862	18,339	538,895	102,203	1.024

Questions

The following questions test your understanding of the material contained in the chapter and allow you to relate your understanding to the learning outcomes specified at the start of this chapter. The learning outcomes are repeated here. Each question is cross-referenced to the relevant section of the chapter.

Understand how comparability indices are used to measure similarities and differences in reported figures

1 What are comparability and partial comparability indices? (section 9.2.2)

2 How are the comparability and partial comparability indices calculated? (section 9.2.2)

Understand how concentration indices are used to measure similarities and differences in accounting methods

3 What is the H- or Herfindahl index and how is it calculated? (section 9.3.1)

4 What is the C-index and how is it calculated? (section 9.3.2)

5 What is the difference between the H-index and the C-index? Which do you think is more useful? Why? (section 9.3)

6 How can the C-index be disaggregated into two indices when it is used on companies from different countries? (section 9.3.2)

7 Which of the two C-index sub-indices identified above is likely to be of more interest to international investors? Why? (section 9.3.3)

8 Which of the two C-index sub-indices is likely to be of more interest to international standard setters? Why? (section 9.3.3)

Measure the comparability of profits and the level of harmonization, using simple examples

9 If you had to quantify the extent of differences between two countries, how might you go about collecting the required information on each of the three types of differences? (sections 9.2–9.5)

10 What problems might you encounter when collecting this information? (sections 9.2–9.5)

11 If you were asked to measure the comparability of UK and US financial statements using the C-index, how would you set about doing it? What problems do you think you would encounter? (section 9.3)

12 If you were asked to do a study to measure the comparability of French and US companies, how would you set about doing it? What problems do you think you would encounter? (section 9.2)

Understand the approach taken in market-based research investigating earnings 'conservatism'

13 How does Basu's model of conservatism relate to what is traditionally understood by the word 'conservatism' in accounting? (section 9.5.1)

Understand the problems of measuring differences and similarities in narrative and voluntary disclosures

14 What were the main findings of Meek, Roberts and Gray when they compared voluntary disclosures of UK and US companies? (section 9.6.2)

15 Given the discussion in Chapters 6 and 7 on why accounting differs across countries, are the results of Meek, Roberts and Gray what you would have expected or not? Why? (section 9.6.2)

16 Do you think the results found will apply to most UK and US companies in the mid-2000s? Why, or why not? (section 9.6.2)

Evaluate published research which has used these techniques

17 What were the main findings of Weetman *et al.* (1998) when they compared the UK and US GAAP-based earnings of UK companies? (section 9.2.2)

18 Given the discussion in Chapters 4 and 5 on why accounting differs across countries, are the results of Weetman *et al.* what you would have expected, or not? Why? (section 9.2.2)

19 Do you think the results found will apply to most UK and US companies in the mid-2000s? Why, or why not? (section 9.2.2)

20 What were the main findings of Walton when he compared UK and French company earnings? (section 9.2.4)

21 Given the discussion in Chapters 6 and 7 on why accounting differs across countries, are the results of Walton what you would have expected, or not? Why? (section 9.2.4)

22 Do you think the results found will apply to most UK and French companies in the mid-2000s? Why, or why not? (section 9.2.4)

23 How did Ball *et al.* (2000) relate earnings conservatism to code law and common law characteristics? (section 9.5.3)

24 How do the findings of Giner and Rees (2001) differ from those of Ball *et al.* (2000)? (section 9.5.6)

25 How do Ball *et al.* (2003) form their conclusions about accounting in Hong Kong, Malaysia, Singapore and Thailand before the Asian economic crisis? (section 9.5.4)

Appendix 9.1 A further explanation of how to calculate the C-index

The C-index takes the form:

$$\frac{\Sigma(n_i \times (n_i - 1))}{(N \times (N - 1))}$$

where: n_i is the number of companies using method i

N is the total number of companies.

This formula is based on mathematical combinations.

Take an example of ten companies where six use method 1 (say FIFO stock valuation) and four use method 2 (say LIFO stock valuation):

Company	A	B	C	D	E	F	G	H	J	K
Method	1	1	1	1	1	1	2	2	2	2

The combinations-based approach asks, 'If you picked up two of these company accounts at random, what is the chance they would use the same accounting method?'

The chance is found by dividing the number of matching pairs by the maximum number of pairs that can be formed.

How many companies match on method 1?

AB	AC	AD	AE	AF
	BC	BD	BE	BF
		CD	CE	CF
			DE	DF
				EF

The answer is 15. If you have learned the formulae for combinations you will know that this can be calculated by the formula:

$$\frac{n(n - 1)}{2}$$

where n is the number of companies using the same method (here it is six companies).

Calculation:

$$\frac{6 \times 5}{2} = 15$$

How many companies match on method 2?

GH	GJ	GK
	HJ	HK
		JK

The answer is 6. This can also be calculated by the formula:

$$\frac{N(N-1)}{2}$$

Calculation:

$$\frac{4 \times 3}{2} = 6$$

The total number of matching pairs is 15 + 6 = 21.

Now ask the question 'What is the maximum number of pairs that could be formed for all companies, disregarding the method used?'

									Count
AB	AC	AD	AE	AF	AG	AH	AJ	AK	9
	BC	BD	BE	BF	BG	BH	BJ	BK	8
		CD	CE	CF	CG	CH	CJ	CK	7
			DE	DF	DG	DH	DJ	DK	6
				EF	EG	EH	EJ	EK	5
					FG	FH	FJ	FK	4
						GH	GJ	GK	3
							HJ	HK	2
								JK	1
								Total	45

Calculation:

$$\frac{N(N-1)}{2} = \frac{10 \times 9}{2} = 45$$

The formula for calculating the C-index is written in full as:

$$\frac{\Sigma(n_i \times (n_i - 1))/2}{(N \times (N - 1))/2}$$

Because both lines have a 'divide by 2' in the formula, this is not shown in the version in section 7.5.2. However, it is important to be consistent. When calculating, either divide by 2 for each line in turn, or calculate both lines of the formula without dividing by 2.

References and further reading

Abayo, A.G., Adams, C.A. and Roberts, C.B. (1993) 'Measuring the quality of corporate disclosure in less developed countries: the case of Tanzania', *Journal of International Accounting Auditing and Taxation*, 2(2): 145–158.

Adams, C.A., Hill, W.Y. and Roberts, C.B. (1995) 'Environmental, employee and ethical reporting in Europe', *Research Report*, 41. London: Chartered Association of Certified Accountants.

Adams, C.A., Hill, W.Y. and Roberts, C.B. (1998) 'Corporate social reporting practices in Western Europe: legitimating corporate activities?', *British Accounting Review*, 30(1): 1–22.

Adhikari, A. and Emenyonu, E.N. (1997) 'Accounting for business combinations and foreign currency translations: an empirical comparison of listed companies from developed countries', *Advances in International Accounting*, 10: 45–62.

Aisbett, S. (2001) 'Measurement of harmony of financial reporting within and between countries: the case of the Nordic countries', *European Accounting Review*, 10(1): 51–72.

Archer, S., Delvaille, P. and McLeay, S. (1995) 'The measurement of harmonisation and the comparability of financial statement items: within-country and between-country effects', *Accounting and Business Research*, 25(98): 67–80.

Ball, R. and Shivakumar, L. (2005) 'Earnings quality in UK private firms', *Journal of Accounting and Economics*, 39(1): 83–128.

Ball, R., Kothari, S.P. and Robin, A. (2000) 'The effect of international institutional factors on properties of accounting earnings', *Journal of Accounting and Economics*, 29: 1–52.

Ball, R., Robin, A. and Wu, J. (2003) 'Incentives versus standards: properties of accounting income in four east Asian countries', *Journal of Accounting and Economics*, 36: 235–270.

Basu, S. (1997) 'The conservatism principle and the asymmetric timeliness of earnings', *Journal of Accounting and Economics*, 24: 3–37.

Beattie, V., McInnes, B. and Fearnley, S. (2004) 'A methodology for analyzing and evaluating narratives in annual reports: a comprehensive descriptive profile and metrics for disclosure quality attributes', *Accounting Forum*, 28: 205–236.

Belkaoui, A. (1985) *International Accounting: Issues and Solutions*. Westport, CT: Quorum.

Bushman, R.M. and Piotroski, J.D. (2006) 'Financial reporting incentives for conservative accounting: the influence of legal and political institutions', *Journal of Accounting and Economics*, 42: 107–148.

Campbell, D. (2004) 'A longitudinal and cross-sectional analysis of environmental disclosure in UK companies – a research note', *British Accounting Review*, 36(1): 107–118.

Cañibano, L. and Mora, A. (2000) 'Evaluating the statistical significance of *de facto* accounting harmonization: a study of European global players', *European Accounting Review*, 9(3): 349–370.

Chow, C.W. and Wong-Boren, A. (1987) 'Voluntary financial disclosure by Mexican corporations', *Accounting Review*, 62(3): 533–541.

Cooke, T.E. (1989) 'Voluntary corporate disclosure by Swedish companies', *Journal of International Financial Management and Accounting*, 1(2): 1–25.

Cooke, T.E. (1991) 'An assessment of voluntary disclosure in the annual reports of Japanese corporations', *International Journal of Accounting*, 26(3): 174–189.

Coy, D. and Dixon, K. (2004) 'The public accountability index: crafting a parametric disclosure index for annual reports', *British Accounting Review*, 36(1): 79–106.

Deegan, C. and Gordon, B. (1996) 'A study of the environmental disclosure practices of Australian companies', *Accounting and Business Research*, 26(3): 187–199.

Deloitte and Touche, VNO-NCW (2002) *Accounting Standards compared: differences between IAS, NL GAAP and US-GAAP*. Deloitte & Touche: available at www.iasplus.com/dttpubs/iasnlus.pdf.

Ding, Y., Hope, O.-K., Jeanjean, T. and Stolowy, H. (2007) 'Differences between domestic accounting standards and IAS: measurement, determinants and implications', *Journal of Accounting and Public Policy*, 26: 1–38.

Emenyonu, E.N. and Gray, S.J. (1992) 'EC accounting harmonisation: an empirical study of measurement practices in France, Germany and the UK', *Accounting and Business Research*, Winter: 49–58.

Esrock, S.L. and Leichty, G.B. (1998) 'Social responsibility and corporate web pages: self-presentation or agenda-setting?', *Public Relations Review*, 24(3): 305–319.

Feltham, G. and Ohlson, J.A. (1995) 'Valuation and clean surplus accounting for operating and financial activities', *Contemporary Accounting Research*, 11: 689–731.

Firth, M.A. (1979) 'The impact of size, stock market listing and auditors on voluntary disclosure in corporate annual reports', *Accounting and Business Research*, 9(36): 272–280.

Fontes, A., Rodrigues, L.L and Craig, R. (2005) 'Measuring convergence of national accounting standards with international financial reporting standards', *Accounting Forum*, 29: 415–436.

Gamble, G.O., Hsu, K. and Tollerson, C.D. (1996) 'Environmental disclosures in annual reports: an international perspective', *International Journal of Accounting*, 31(3): 293–331.

Garrido, P., Leon, A. and Zorio, A. (2002) 'Measurement of formal harmonization progress: the IASC experience', *International Journal of Accounting*, 37: 1–26.

Giner, B. and Rees, W. (2001) 'On the asymmetric recognition of good and bad news in France, Germany and the United Kingdom', *Journal of Business Finance and Accounting*, 28 (9–10): 1285–1332.

Givoly, D., Hayn, C.K. and Natarajan, A. (2007) 'Measuring reporting conservatism', *Accounting Review*, 82(1): 65–106.

Goodrich, P.S. (1986) 'Cross-national financial accounting linkages: an empirical political analysis', *British Accounting Review*, 18(1): 42–60.

Gray, R., Kouhy, R. and Lavers, S. (1995a) 'Corporate social and environmental reporting: a review of the literature and a longitudinal study of UK disclosure', *Accounting, Auditing and Accountability Journal*, 8(2): 47–77.

Gray, R., Javad, M., Power, D.M. and Sinclair, C.D. (2001) 'Social and environmental disclosures and corporate characteristics: a research note and extension', *Journal of Business Finance and Accounting*, 28(3/4): 327–356.

Gray, S.J. (1980) 'The impact of international accounting differences from a security-analysis perspective: some European evidence', *Journal of Accounting Research*, 18(1): 64–76.

Gray, S.J. (1988) 'Towards a theory of cultural influence on the development of accounting systems internationally', *Abacus*, 24(1): 1–15.

Gray, S.J., Meek, G.K. and Roberts, C.B. (1995b) 'International capital market pressures and voluntary annual report disclosures by US and UK multinationals', *Journal of International Financial Management and Accounting*, 6(1): 43–68.

Gul, F.A. and Leung, S. (2004) 'Board leadership, outside directors' expertise and voluntary corporate disclosure', *Journal of Accounting and Public Policy*, 23: 251–279.

Haniffa, R.M. and Cooke, T.E. (2002) 'Culture, corporate governance and disclosure in Malaysian companies', *Abacus*, 38(3), October: 317–349.

Haverty, J.J. (2006) 'Are IFRS and US GAAP converging? Some evidence from People's Republic of China companies listed on the New York stock exchange', *Journal of International Accounting, Auditing and Taxation*, 15(1): 48–71.

Hellman, N. (1993) 'A comparative analysis of the impact of accounting differences on profits and return on equity: differences between Swedish practice and US GAAP', *European Accounting Review*, 2(3): 495–530.

Herrman, D. and Thomas, W. (1995) 'Harmonisation of accounting measurement practices in the European Community', *Accounting and Business Research*, 25(100): 253–265.

Hofstede, G. (1984) *Culture's Consequences: International Differences in Work-Related Values*. Beverly Hills, CA: Sage.

Hossain, M., Perera, M.H.B. and Rahman, A.R. (1995) 'Voluntary disclosure in the annual reports of New Zealand companies', *Journal of International Financial Management and Accounting*, 6(1): 69–85.

Inchausti, B.G. (1997) 'The influence of company characteristics and accounting regulation on information disclosure by Spanish firms', *European Accounting Review*, 6(1): 45–68.

Joos, P. (2003) 'Discussion of how representative are firms that cross-listed in the United States? An analysis of accounting quality', *Journal of Accounting Review*, 41(2), March: 387–396.

Krisement, V.M. (1997) 'An approach for measuring the degree of comparability of financial accounting information', *European Accounting Review*, 6(3): 465–485.

La Porta, R., Lopez-de-Salanes, F., Shleifer, A. and Vishny, R.W. (1997) 'Legal determinants of external finance', *Journal of Finance*, 52(3): 1131–1150.

La Porta, R., Lopez-de-Salanes, F., Shleifer, A. and Vishny, R.W. (1998) 'Law and finance', *Journal of Political Economy*, 106(6): 1113–1155.

Laan Smith, J. van der, Adhikhari, A. and Tondkar, R.H. (2005) 'Exploring differences in social disclosures internationally: a stakeholder perspective', *Journal of Accounting and Public Policy*, 24: 123–151.

Lang, M., Raedy, J.S. and Yetman, M.H. (2003) 'How representative are firms that cross-listed in the United States? An analysis of accounting quality', *Journal of Accounting Review*, 41(2), March: 362–386.

Lara, J.M.G. and Mora, A. (2004) 'Balance sheet versus earnings conservatism in Europe', *European Accounting Review*, 13(2): 261–292.

Linsley, P.M. and Shrives, P.J. (2006) 'Risk reporting: a study of risk disclosures in the annual reports of UK companies', *British Accounting Review*, 38(4), December: 387–404.

Meek, G.K., Roberts, C.B. and Gray, S.J. (1995) 'Factors influencing voluntary annual report disclosures by US, UK and continental European multinational corporations', *Journal of International Business Studies*, third quarter: 555–572.

Morris, R.D. and Parker, R.H. (1998) 'International harmony measures of accounting policy: comparative statistical properties', *Accounting and Business Research*, 29(1): 73–86.

Murphy, A.B. (2000) 'The impact of adopting International Accounting Standards on the harmonization of accounting practices', *International Journal of Accounting*, 35(4): 471–493.

Parker, R.H. and Morris, R.D. (2001) 'The influence of US GAAP on the harmony of accounting measurement policies of large companies in the UK and Australia', *Abacus*, 37(3): 297–328.

Patelli, L. and Prencipe, A. (2007) 'The relationship between voluntary disclosure and independent directors in the presence of a dominant shareholder', *European Accounting Research*, 16(1): 5–34.

Patten, D.M. (2002) 'Media exposure, public policy pressure, and environmental disclosure: an examination of the impact of tri data availability', *Accounting Forum*, 26(2): 152–171.

Pope, P. and Walker, M. (1999) 'International differences in timeliness, conservatism and classification of earnings', *Journal of Accounting Research*, 37(Supplement): 53–87.

Radebaugh, L.H., Gebhardt, G. and Gray, S.J. (1995) 'Foreign stock exchange listings: a case study of Daimler–Benz', *Journal of International Financial Management and Accounting*, 6(2): 158–192.

Raffournier, B. (1995) 'The determinants of voluntary financial disclosure by Swiss listed companies', *European Accounting Review*, 4: 261–280.

Rahman, A., Perera, H. and Ganeshanandam, S. (1996) 'Measurement of formal harmonization in accounting: an exploratory study', *Accounting and Business Research*, Autumn.

Roanic, I., McLeay, S. and Asimakopoulos, I. (2004) 'The timeliness of income recognition by European companies: an analysis of institutional and market complexity,' *Journal of Business Finance and Accounting*, 31(1/2): 115–148.

Roberts, C.B. (1990) 'International trends in social and employee reporting', *Occasional Research Paper*, 6. London: Chartered Association of Certified Accountants.

Roberts, C.B. (1991) 'Environmental disclosures: a note on reporting practices in mainland Europe', *Accounting, Auditing and Accountability Journal*, 4(3): 62–71.

Ryan, S.G. (2006) 'Identifying conditional conservatism', *European Accounting Review*, 15(4): 511–525.

Singh, D.R. and Ahuja, J.M. (1983) 'Corporate social reporting in India', *International Journal of Accounting*, 18(2): 151–169.

Street, D.L., Nichols, N.B. and Gray, S.J. (2000) 'Assessing the acceptability of International Accounting Standards in the US: an empirical study of the materiality of US GAAP reconciliations by non-US companies complying with IASC standards', *International Journal of Accounting*, 35(1): 27–63.

Tarca, A. (2004) 'International convergence of accounting practices: choosing between IAS and US GAAP', *Journal of International Financial Management and Accounting*, 15(1): 60–91.

Tas, L.G. van der (1988) 'Measuring harmonization of financial reporting practices', *Accounting and Business Research*, 18(70): 157–169.

Tas, L.G. van der (1992) 'Evidence of EC financial reporting harmonization: the case of deferred tax', *European Accounting Review*, 1(1): 69–104.

Tay, J.S.W. and Parker, R.H. (1990) 'Measuring harmonization and standardization', *Abacus*, 26(1): 71–88.

Tsang, E.W.K. (1998) 'A longitudinal study of corporate social reporting in Singapore: the case of the banking, food and beverages and hotel industries', *Accounting, Auditing and Accountability Journal*, 11(5): 624–635.

Unerman, J. (2000) 'Methodological issues: reflections on quantification in corporate social reporting content analysis', *Accounting, Auditing and Accountability Journal*, 13(5): 667–680.

Wallace, R.S.O. (1988) 'Corporate financial reporting in Nigeria', *Accounting and Business Research*, 18(72): 352–362.

Wallace, R.S.O., Naser, K. and Mora, A. (1994) 'The relationship between the comprehensiveness of corporate annual reporting and firms in Spain', *Accounting and Business Research*, 25(97): 41–53.

Walton, P. (1992) 'Harmonization of accounting in France and Britain: some evidence', *Abacus*, 28(2): 186–199.

Weetman, P. and Gray, S.J. (1991) 'A comparative international analysis of the impact of accounting principles on profits: the USA versus the UK, Sweden and the Netherlands', *Accounting and Business Research*, 21(84): 363–379.

Weetman, P., Jones, E.A.E., Adams, C.A. and Gray, S.J. (1998) 'Profit measurement and UK accounting standards: a case of increasing disharmony in relation to US GAAP and IASs', *Accounting and Business Research*, 28(3): 189–203.

Williams, S.M. (1999) 'Voluntary environmental and social accounting disclosure practices in the Asia-Pacific region: an international empirical test of political economy theory', *International Journal of Accounting*, 34(2): 209–238.

Xiao, Z. (1999) 'Corporate disclosures made by Chinese listed companies', *International Journal of Accounting*, 34(3): 349–373.

PART 3

Significant influences on international accounting practices

Introduction to Part 3

In Part 1 we provided a general overview of issues relating to global accounting standards, setting the scene for a deeper subsequent study of specific regulatory regimes in Part 3 and specific countries in Part 4. In Part 2 we explained and illustrated methods of analysis and research that are used in comparative studies of financial reporting.

We now move to explain and discuss in more detail the most ambitious and far-reaching influence for harmonization, represented by the work of the International Accounting Standards Board. The US system of Generally Accepted Accounting Principles (US GAAP) is a potential rival to the IASB standards as a global accounting system. It has also provided a strong influence on the development of IASB standards. The European Union (EU) represents a group of member states which all have an interest in applying IASB standards. They also feel that if they are applying the standards they ought to be able to participate in the process in some way. The EU has a total economy of comparable size with that of the USA but has decided to work towards harmonization with IFRS rather than produce 'EU GAAP'. The European Commission also has a history of encouraging harmonization through Directives.

Purpose of Part 3

The chapters of Part 3 have three major aims. The first (in Chapter 10) is to explain the processes by which international financial reporting standards have emerged from a period of more than 30 years in development. The second (in Chapters 11 and 12) is to explain how the national characteristics of the USA and the legal framework of the EU are likely to affect global accounting principles and practice. The third (in Chapter 13) is to indicate the circumstances in which accounting standard setting becomes a political process as much as, or more than, it is a technical process.

Learning outcomes

Specific learning outcomes are set out at the start of each chapter but overall, on completion of Part 3, the student should be able to:

- explain the process by which the IASB has emerged as a global standard-setting body;
- describe and evaluate the development of accounting practice in the USA;
- describe and evaluate the development of accounting harmonization in the EU;
- discuss the political pressures faced by the IASB when its standards are adopted or endorsed by national regulators, considering in particular the EU endorsement process.

10

Developing the IASB's accounting standards

Learning outcomes

After reading this chapter you should be able to:

- Explain the nature and operations of the IASB.
- Understand the challenges facing the IASB in its work.
- Understand the key stages of historical development of international accounting standards.
- Describe the continuing development of the IASB's *Framework*.
- Explain how multinational companies demonstrate their use of global accounting standards.

10.1 Introduction

The main purpose of this chapter is to establish a comprehensive knowledge and understanding of the nature and operation of the International Accounting Standards Board (IASB) and the development of International Financial Reporting Standards (IFRS) that are capable of achieving wide international acceptance. We describe the development of the conceptual framework underpinning IFRS and conclude with a description of the variety of ways in which multinational companies show their use of global standards.

10.2 The IASCF and the IASB

The International Accounting Standards Committee Foundation (IASCF) is an independent body, not controlled by any particular government or professional organization. Its main purpose is to oversee the IASB in setting the accounting principles which are used by businesses and other organizations around the world concerned with financial reporting.

The objectives of the IASCF (and hence of the IASB) as stated in its Constitution[1] are:

(a) to develop in the public interest, a single set of high quality, understandable and enforceable global accounting standards that require high quality, transparent and comparable information in financial statements and other financial reporting to help participants in the world's capital markets and other users make economic decisions;

(b) to promote the use and rigorous application of those standards; and

(c) to bring about convergence of national accounting standards and International Accounting Standards and International Financial Reporting Standards to high quality solutions.

---

[1] Issued 2000, revised 2002 and 2005.

These objectives were seen as giving a more precise focus to the objectives originally written in 1973 (see section 10.2.1).

The updated wording reflects the growing emphasis on the world's capital markets and the move towards rigour in application. The term 'high quality' is also emphasized; this reflects a strong US influence on the constitutional changes that formed the IASB (see Chapters 10 and 11).

10.2.1 From IASC to IASB

The International Accounting Standards Committee (IASC) was formed in 1973 through an agreement made by professional accountancy bodies from Australia, Canada, France, Germany, Ireland, Japan, Mexico, The Netherlands, UK and USA. Its objectives at that time were:

- to formulate and publish in the public interest accounting standards to be observed in the presentation of financial statements and to promote their worldwide acceptance and observance; and
- to work generally for the improvement and harmonization of regulations, accounting standards and procedures relating to the presentation of financial statements.

From 1983 the membership of IASC included all the professional accountancy bodies that were members of IFAC.[2] A joint meeting of all members took place every two and a half years. Although IASC is older than IFAC by four years, the creation of IFAC brought into being a global structure from which IASC could obtain wider authority.[3]

In May 2000 the IASC agreed a change in its Constitution to reflect the changing nature of the work of setting international accounting standards. IASC retained its independence by having its own Constitution that, from 2000, could be altered only by a meeting of the Trustees of the IASCF. Under the 2000 Constitution the members ceased to have a formal role in the decisions of the IASCF. The IASB was established in 2001 as the standard-setting body of the IASCF.

10.2.2 The Trustees

The governance of the IASCF rests with the Trustees. There are 22 Trustees, initially appointed by a Nominating Committee but thereafter taking responsibility themselves for filling vacancies as these arise. Trustees are required to show a firm commitment to the IASB as a high-quality global standard setter, to be financially knowledgeable, and to have the ability to meet the time commitment expected. Each Trustee must have an understanding of, and be sensitive to, international issues relevant to the success of an international organization responsible for the development of high-quality global accounting standards for use in the world's capital markets and by other users. To ensure an adequate geographic representation it is required that six Trustees be appointed from North America, six from Europe, six from the Asia/Oceania region and four from any area, subject to overall geographic balance. Other conditions are attached to the appointment of Trustees in order to ensure a broad spread of interests. The appointment is for a term of three years, renewable once.

---

[2] For membership of IFAC, see www.ifac.org.

[3] A useful historical discussion of the operation of the IASC is provided by Cairns (2002), Ch. 1.

The Trustees meet twice in each year and are responsible for fundraising. They appoint the members of the IASB, the members of the International Financial Reporting Interpretations Committee and the members of the Standards Advisory Council.

10.2.3 The IASB

The IASB, formed in 2001, comprises 14 members, appointed by the IASCF Trustees. Twelve of the Board members commit all their time in paid employment to IASB (described as 'full-time') and two are in part-time employment with IASB. The foremost qualifications for membership of the Board are professional competence and practical experience. Members are appointed for a five-year term, renewable once. The people chosen represent the best available combination of technical skills and background experience of relevant international business and market conditions. The selection is not based on geographical representation. The trustees seek to balance practical experience among auditors, preparers, users and academics. The operation of the IASB is explained in section 10.3.

10.2.4 The International Financial Reporting Interpretations Committee (IFRIC)

The IFRIC emerged in 2002 as a revised version of the Standing Interpretations Committee (SIC). There are 12 voting members of IFRIC, appointed by the IASCF Trustees for renewable terms of three years. The Trustees also appoint a non-voting Chair from the IASB membership or the IASB staff.

The role of IFRIC is:

(a) to interpret the application of IAS and IFRS and to provide guidance on financial reporting issues not specifically included in IAS and IFRS, in the context of the IASB's Framework;

(b) to have regard to the IASB's objective of working actively with national standard setters to bring about convergence of national accounting standards and IAS and IFRS to high-quality solutions;

(c) to publish draft Interpretations for public comment (after clearance by the IASB) and consider comments received; and

(d) to report to the IASB and obtain approval for a final Interpretation.

The procedures followed by IFRIC are set out in its *Due Process Handbook*.[4]

10.2.5 The Standards Advisory Council (SAC)

The SAC provides a forum for participation by organizations and individuals from a wide range of interests and geographic representation. The SAC advises the IASB on agenda decisions and the priorities of the IASB's work, informs the IASB of the views of organizations and individuals on the Council and gives other advice to the IASB or the Trustees. There are around 30 members of the SAC. It normally meets at least three times in a year. Meetings are open to the public.

---

[4] IASCF, *Due Process Handbook for the IFRIC*, January 2007.

Exhibit 10.1	IASCF, sources of operating revenues, 2006

Revenues	2006 (£000)	2005 (£000)
Contributions	10,382	9,374
Revenues from publications and related activities	5,058	4,514
Interest income	568	534
Other income	25	27
	16,033	14,449
Less direct cost of sales from publications etc	(2,922)	(2,753)
Total revenues	13,111	11,696

Source: International Accounting Standards Committee Foundation Annual Report (2006), Statement of Activities, p. 30.

10.2.6 Financing the IASB

From its inception in 1973 the IASC described itself as a 'low-budget organization', relying a great deal on help from persons around the world who were willing to give time to support its activities. Professional accountancy bodies made contributions. International organizations gave grants for specific projects. Sales of publications also made a contribution.

From 2000 the responsibility for fundraising has fallen on the IASCF Trustees. They have continued to raise funds from existing sources but have also explored others such as contributions from multinational companies and stock markets whose needs are served by the IASB. There is a challenge in being seen to raise funds in a balanced way from contributors in many countries so that different countries can be seen to be making fair contributions, especially where those countries find they are not represented on the IASB. There is also a challenge in balancing transparency of information on sources of finance against the desire of some donors to maintain confidentiality. It is important to know that the independent standard setter is not influenced by significant contributors. Hence there is a list of IASCF 'underwriters and supporters' at the end of the annual report. Categories of funders cover Accounting firms, Corporate and other private sector supporters, Central Banks, Government Entities and Other Official Organizations, and Associations.[5] In the 2006 annual report the Trustees discuss the need to put the funding of the IASB onto a more secure basis, such as annual levies, rather than relying so much on voluntary contributions. Exhibit 10.1 sets out the operating revenues for 2006.

10.3 Operation of the IASB

The IASB issues the IFRS. The generic term 'IFRS' is defined as including the new IFRS issued by the IASB, the existing IAS issued by the predecessor IASC, and the Interpretations issued by IFRIC (or its predecessor SIC).[6] This section explains the procedures by which a proposal eventually becomes a standard. It then continues by explaining the

---

[5] IASCF *Annual Report 2006*, p. 39.

[6] IAS 1 (2007) *Presentation of Financial Statements*, para. 11.

IASB's lack of direct powers of enforcement. Finally it discusses the consultation process that establishes acceptance of the IFRS.

10.3.1 Procedure for issuing a standard

In March 2006, following consultation with interested parties, the Trustees approved a *Due Process Handbook* for the IASB.[7] It is based on the following requirements:[8]

- transparency and accessibility
- extensive consultation and responsiveness
- accountability.

Standard setting has six stages:

1 Setting the agenda
2 Project planning
3 Development and publication of a discussion paper
4 Development and publication of an exposure draft
5 Development and publication of an IFRS
6 Regular review and educational activities after an IFRS is issued.

First of all, there has to be an idea. Ideas may come from IASB members, the SAC, other organizations and individuals and the IASB staff. Whatever the source, the priority given to the idea depends on the relevance to users of the information involved and the reliability of information that could be provided; the existing guidance available; the quality of the standard that could be developed; and resource constraints.

Project planning is carried out by a project team from the staff employed by the IASB. The IASB's discussions take place during public meetings, usually held monthly. Any member of the public may attend as an observer. Meeting agendas and observer notes are published on the website in advance of the meeting. Meetings are broadcast on the Internet and archived on the website. Balloting (voting by members) takes place outside meetings, based on a full set of documentation, to ensure that all members vote on all issues.

Liaison activities take place throughout the cycle. There are formal relationships with a range of national standard setters and with the European Financial Reporting Advisory Group (EFRAG) and the Standards Advisory Council (SAC). Liaison also takes place with other interested parties, through giving and receiving invitations to attend discussions and conferences. Working groups, comment letters on documents published for discussion, field visits, field tests and public hearings (including round table discussions) all contribute to the consultation process. Cost/benefit analysis is applied in forming conclusions on proposed standards. Considerable information about the process is published on the IASB's website, some of it in the public domain section and the rest in a 'subscription-only' section.

When documents are issued for consultation a period of 120 days is normally allowed for comment but this may be varied depending on the significance of the project concerned. To provide assurance that consultation has taken place, the IASB follows a 'comply or explain' approach, giving its reasons for omitting any aspect of the consultation

---

[7] IASCF, *Due Process Handbook for the IASB*, March 2006.
[8] IASCF (2006), para. 9.

Exhibit 10.2	Voting procedures of the IASB

Approval by 9 out of 14 members is required for publication of:

An Exposure Draft
An IAS or IFRS
A final IFRIC Interpretation.

A simple majority of those attending a meeting (subject to at least 60% attendance) is sufficient for other decisions, such as publication of a discussion paper.

Source: Based on *Due Process Handbook for the IASB*, March 2006.

process when it publishes a decision summary or a 'basis for conclusions' statement. Voting procedures of the IASB are summarized in Exhibit 10.2.

10.3.2 Power of enforcement

When the IASC was founded its members agreed to use their best endeavours and persuasive influence to ensure compliance with the standards. It was intended that each professional accounting association within the IASC would ensure that the external auditors would satisfy themselves as to observance of the standards and would disclose cases of non-compliance; appropriate action was to be taken against any auditor who did not follow these recommendations. Later, revised wording of the agreement among members acknowledged that IASC pronouncements would not override the standards followed by individual countries. By 1982, the agreement no longer contained the requirement that the auditors should disclose the extent of non-compliance.

The route to enforcement has now moved in the direction of enforcement by national governments requiring the application of IFRS or by applying the powers of national stock exchanges which subscribe to the IOSCO agreement on the acceptance of IFRS. In either case the auditors become involved in the process of approval and enforcement but the audit process is regulated at national level. The development of ISAs by the International Auditing and Assurance Standards Board (IAASB) of the International Federation of Accountants (IFAC) has increased the comparability of auditing work internationally.

10.3.3 Convergence of IFRS and FASB standards

The general approach to liaison has been described in section 10.3.2. An important liaison activity took place at a joint meeting in Norwalk, Connecticut, USA, in September 2002, when the IASB and the FASB pledged to use their best efforts to make their existing financial reporting standards fully compatible as soon as was practical, and to coordinate their future work programmes to ensure that, once achieved, compatibility was maintained. To achieve this, they agreed a programme of short-term and longer term actions to remove a variety of differences.[9] The intensification of this programme during 2004 was explained by the IASB Chair in terms of the window of opportunity given by support from senior business leaders and policy makers in the USA. He also pointed out that no effort to develop truly global standards would be successful without the participation

---

[9] IASCF *Annual Report 2002*, p. 5.

of the USA.[10] Further meetings led to the publication of a *Roadmap for Convergence* with 2008 as the target for completing specific short-term goals and for achieving significant progress in 11 areas of focus.[11] These areas were identified after consultation with the European Commission and the SEC. (More detail is provided in Chapter 11.)

10.4 Changing styles of setting international standards

Various phases have been identified in the standard-setting process operated by the IASC as predecessor of the current IASB (see Exhibit 10.3). It issued IAS. This section discusses those phases and the factors which have influenced a change of direction.

10.4.1 The early standards

The first standards from the IASC in the 1970s were basic, straightforward and largely non-controversial. They had a high level of generality and concentrated primarily on matters of presentation and disclosure rather than more controversial issues of measurement (Nair and Frank, 1981).

10.4.2 Increasing use of permitted alternatives

Standards issued during the 1980s dealt with more complex issues reflecting problematic subjects under active consideration in the leading accounting countries. This led to increasingly frequent use of options within which the prevailing accounting practices of most of the major accounting nations could be accommodated. In this way the IAS did not pose a threat to national differences. It had been noted that most IAS had two acceptable alternative treatments because of the necessity of ensuring that the required 75 per cent of the 14 voting members of the Board voted in favour (see comments of Arthur R. Wyatt, IASC, in Fleming, 1991).

Empirical research studies have from time to time been made on the effectiveness of the IASC. A study of the application of accounting methods by major companies in a range of major accounting nations over the 1970s found that IAS had little impact on

Exhibit 10.3 Phases in the development of the work of the IASC

Stage	
1 Issue of general standards	1973–79
2 Development of more detailed standards	1980–89
3 Reduction of flexibility – Comparability Project	1989–95
4 IOSCO core standards programme	1995–99
5 Convergence and improvements to complete IOSCO conditions	2000–03
6 Stable platform of IFRS	2004–05
7 Roadmap to convergence	2006–08

---

[10] IASB *Insight*, April/May 2004, p. 8.

[11] *A Roadmap for Convergence between IFRSs and US GAAP – 2006–2008*. Memorandum of Understanding between the FASB and the IASB, www.iasb.org.

the accounting practices of the companies surveyed. Except for a few instances, companies which followed a particular accounting method prior to the promulgation of the standard continued to follow the same practice after the standard was issued (Evans and Taylor, 1982). Of the initial 16 standards issued, 8 permitted alternative accounting treatments, and hence allowed flexibility (Choi and Bavishi, 1982). That flexibility was attributed to attempts to accommodate the variety of treatments that existed in reporting standards already adopted by developed countries.

By the mid-1980s other researchers were also observing that the IAS had not succeeded in changing existing national standards, or in establishing new standards. For example, studies showed that in 8 of the 24 international standards issued up to 1984, alternative solutions were permitted (Most, 1984). This was perceived as being due to lack of enforceability. The programme of IAS was seen as having value insofar as it succeeded in codifying generally accepted practice (McKinnon and Janell, 1984). However, by the end of the 1980s there was a high degree of flexibility within the standards.

Purvis *et al.* (1991), analyzing compliance with IAS as indicated in an IASC survey of 1988, found a high level of national conformity with those standards issued early in the life of the IASC but much lower levels of conformity for those issued closer to 1988. The authors observed that the results were not surprising since the nature of the earlier standards, addressing fundamental issues at a general level, meant that countries could comply with minimum need for change, especially in view of the permitted alternative treatments. Furthermore the passage of time permitted countries which initially had non-conforming standards to adopt new ones in line with IAS.

A reaction to the extent of choice in IAS began in 1989 with a project to reduce flexibility. A second phase began in 1995, intended to meet the demands of IOSCO for an acceptable set of core standards.

10.4.3 The Comparability Project

In 1989 the IASC launched a major initiative to bring greater comparability to financial statements.

10.4.3.1 Exposure draft E 32

The initiative was represented by an exposure draft, E 32, which contained proposals to reduce the number of alternative treatments allowed in the IAS issued to date. The exposure draft contained recommendations on matters of free choice that might have had a material effect on the definition, recognition, measurement and display of net income and assets and liabilities in the financial statements of an enterprise. E 32 was seen as the first stage in a continuing process of improvement; it acknowledged that free choice had been necessary in the past to gain acceptance of certain standards.

The IASC also decided to reformat all IAS in such a way as to highlight the significant points of principle in bold italic type. The document would also present, in normal type, explanations of each significant point of principle in the standard.

10.4.3.2 Need for change

The main impetus for these changes was the increase in cross-border financing. Wyatt (in Fleming, 1991) claimed that the American Institute of Certified Public Accountants (AICPA) along with other accounting bodies had agreed in writing to attempt to ensure that the standard-setting bodies in their countries moved towards international standards.

IOSCO encouraged the IASC in its project and, according to Wyatt, intended to encourage securities regulators in member countries to require use of IAS, providing that the IASC could produce results of adequate quality.

10.4.3.3 Statement of intent

The initial proposals contained in E 32 were modified and explained further in a Statement of Intent issued in 1990. The Statement of Intent explained that, where it was not possible to gain agreement on a single recommended approach, there would be a 'benchmark treatment' and an 'allowed alternative treatment'. The word 'benchmark' had gained greater acceptance than the word 'preferred' used in exposure draft E 32. The benchmark treatment was to be regarded as a point of reference for the Board when making its choice between alternatives.

Following on from the Comparability Project, the trend was to make IAS more prescriptive. Some national accounting traditions appear to be at variance with the resulting standards and removal of previously permitted options to focus on one method only has inevitably been a process of robust negotiation. In that process, some observers have identified increasing dominance of accounting principles originating in the USA and the UK.

10.4.3.4 Potential for success

The potential for the Comparability Project to succeed depended on the level of conformity existing at the time of the Project and the subsequent intentions of national standard setters with regard to the subsequent revision of IAS. Research has been undertaken assessing the extent to which the financial reporting practices of countries agreed with the accounting practices contained in the standards issued by the IASC following the Comparability Project. The results showed that there was substantial agreement (Salter *et al.*, 1996; Roberts *et al.*, 1996). Partners in major firms of accountants were asked to indicate the percentage of significant organizations in their country which already followed the recommended accounting treatments (benchmark or allowed alternative) contained in the IAS that were to take effect from January 1995. The average level of national agreement with the IAS was 68.4 per cent. The results for the USA (75.96 per cent) and the UK (74.78 per cent), seen as countries with a strong influence on the development of IAS, were higher than the average but Australia, classed within the 'Anglo-Saxon' sphere of influence, was lower (64.75 per cent). Malaysia (70.80 per cent) has a tradition derived from UK influence. Japan (63.86 per cent) and Germany (57.70 per cent) were lower but the flexibility of group accounting in France contributed to a higher score (71.69 per cent).

In no single country did corporate accounting practice exactly match the revised rules resulting from the Comparability Project. The countries with the least change required in bringing existing practice into line with the revised IAS tended to belong to the UK/US tradition. Countries with the greatest change required were typically those classified as 'code law' countries (see section 4.4.2) which are regarded as adopting a conservative approach to measurement of accounting income and assets.

10.4.3.5 Evaluation of the Comparability Project

The Comparability Project was a bold initiative to reduce options but there are views that it did not entirely succeed because of strong interest groups. It has been suggested that the standard setters of the member states of the EU did not give sufficient signs of unity on issues where the US influence was dominant (a detailed discussion has been provided by Gernon *et al.*, 1990). The Comparability Project did achieve some reduction of options compared with accounting practice in the UK and USA but left a number of allowed alternatives in areas where UK and US practice differed, including amortization of goodwill, deferred taxation, valuation of property, plant and equipment, inventory valuation and accounting for fundamental errors (Weetman *et al.*, 1993).

10.4.4 The Core Standards programme

10.4.4.1 Relations with IOSCO

In its present form IOSCO dates from the mid-1980s. Its objectives include:

- the establishment of standards and effective surveillance of international securities transactions;
- the provision of mutual assistance to ensure the integrity of the markets by a rigorous application of standards and by effective enforcement against offenders.

A working party was established to cooperate with the IASC with a view to identifying accounting standards which security regulators might be ready to accept in the case of multinational offerings. At its annual conference in 1987 a resolution was passed to promote the use of common standards in accounting and auditing practice. In that same year IOSCO became a member of the IASC Consultative Group. IOSCO gave active support to the E 32 Comparability Project, and in 1996 IOSCO accepted observer status on the IASC Board.

10.4.4.2 Identifying the Core Standards

In 1995 the IASC made a significant agreement with IOSCO. The agreement stated that the goal of both IASC and IOSCO was that financial statements prepared in accordance with IAS can be used in cross-border offerings and listings as an alternative to national accounting standards. The achievement of this goal was made conditional on completion of the IASC Work Programme, scheduled for 1999. The Work Programme concentrated on a core set of standards and has come to be referred to more commonly as 'the Core Standards programme'. By March 1996 the Board had revised the target date to March 1998, in response to requests from international companies and from members of IOSCO. The revised target saved 15 months on the original plan.

The Core Standards programme was a very significant step towards helping companies which had a listing on stock exchanges outside their own country and were sometimes required to prepare their financial statements using the generally accepted accounting principles of that country. That condition was applied in particular by the US SEC, and the detail of the additional disclosures was perceived as deterring many companies from seeking a listing in US stock markets.

In effect, IAS were already acceptable for cross-border listings on most major stock exchanges before the Core Standards programme was put in place. The notable exceptions were the USA, Canada and Japan. Japan and Canada indicated by various actions that they were favourably disposed to IAS and so the key factor for acceptability was the US SEC.

10.4.5 IOSCO acceptance and a 'stable platform'

On completion of the Core Standards programme at the end of 1998, the IASC had to turn its attention to making the standards effective, in competition with the influence of US GAAP. Companies in other countries, such as Germany, were looking for global listings, including US listings, and were exploring the relative attractions of US GAAP and IASC standards as the basis for consolidated financial statements.

The reaction to the IASC's initial exploration of the issues indicated that there would be no easy answer. For acceptance of IASC standards in the USA, the SEC indicated that it would expect to see a standard-setting board which had all the features of the FASB, particularly a relatively small number of full-time members and the choice of the best experts available, regardless of geographical origin. The European Commission wanted to see a broader based board with guaranteed geographical spread of representation. During the comment period it became apparent that, to have a credible future in the US capital market, the IASC would need to act in a way consistent with the expectations of the SEC.

Early in 2000 the IASC Board indicated that it approved of a structure based on a board of experts and that it would not pursue the alternative of geographical representation on the board. The geographical spread would come in an SAC which would not have direct standard-setting responsibilities. The SEC then indicated its approval of this direction by issuing a Concept Release as the first stage of the SEC's own consultative process. The Concept Release (February 2000) identified what the SEC regarded as the necessary components of a high-quality financial reporting framework and asked questions about the elements of such a framework. The questions asked were set under various headings:

- Are the core standards sufficiently comprehensive? (Q1–Q3)
- Are the IASC standards of sufficiently high quality? (Q4–Q7)
- Can the IASC standards be rigorously interpreted and applied? (Q8–Q26)

These questions were originally signalled in a press release published by the SEC in April 1996.[12]

The questions on 'high quality' are directed towards how closely the IASC standards resemble US GAAP. Overall the questions focus mainly on interpretation and enforcement, with relatively little enquiry into the intrinsic merits. High-quality standards are said to consist of a comprehensive set of neutral principles that require consistent, comparable, relevant and reliable information that is useful to those who make capital allocation decisions. There were 26 questions, supported by detail described as 'supplementary information' indicating areas where the SEC might have concerns. The problems were seen to lie as much in enforcement as in the standards themselves.

The phrase 'high-quality standards' has appeared in abundance in comments from the SEC, so that the appearance of this phrase in the revised Objectives of the Constitution was not a great surprise. The SEC received a somewhat disappointing number of comments on the Concept Release and did not take it further forward explicitly, although aspects may be seen in subsequent SEC rules.

A further Concept Statement was issued by the SEC in 2007 asking whether US issuers should be allowed to choose between US GAAP and IFRS for their US reporting.

10.4.5.1 IOSCO acceptance

In May 2000 IOSCO announced completion of its assessment of the accounting standards issued by the IASC. The Presidents Committee of IOSCO referred to the 30 standards and related interpretations evaluated by them (described as 'the IASC 2000 standards'). It recommended that IOSCO members permit incoming multinational issuers to use the IASC 2000 standards to prepare their financial statements for cross-border offerings and

---

[12] The press release is not available electronically but is summarized in the *Report on Promoting Global Pre-eminence of American Securities Markets*, SEC, October 1997, ww.sec.gov/news/studies/acctgsp.htm.

listings, as supplemented where necessary by one or more of three supplemental treatments of reconciliation, disclosure and interpretation.

● *Reconciliation* means requiring reconciliation of certain items to show the effect of applying a different accounting method, in contrast with the method applied under IASC standards.
● *Disclosure* means requiring additional disclosures, either in the presentation of the financial statements or in the footnotes.
● *Interpretation* means specifying the use of a particular alternative provided in an IASC standard, or a particular interpretation in cases where the IASC standard is unclear or silent.

This resolution confirmed the good working relationship between IASC and IOSCO but left considerable discretion with the separate market regulators who were the members of IOSCO. It was for each securities commission or regulator to decide whether to accept the IOSCO recommendation and whether to apply supplemental treatments. In particular, if the SEC in the USA were to continue requiring reconciliations to US GAAP there would be a risk that foreign registrants on US stock exchanges would regard this as too costly and troublesome and would apply US GAAP in preference to IASB standards. Chapters 11 and 12 explain in more detail how the regulators in the USA and the EU proceeded from this point.

10.4.5.2 A stable platform for 2005

When the IASB started to plan its Work Programme in 2001, an important focus was the intention of the European Commission to adopt IFRS for all listed companies in member states from 1 January 2005. It was clear that these countries would require time to prepare for the change to IFRS. The IASB decided that only those standards issued by March 2004 would apply from 1 January 2005. Any standards issued after March 2004 would apply from 2006 or later. This would give a 'stable platform' in March 2004 followed by 21 months without further changes.

To achieve the stable platform the IASB put in place an Improvements project to raise the quality and consistency of financial reporting generally. The general phase of improvements removed options in IAS that had caused uncertainty and reduced comparability. This general phase produced a set of revised standards issued in December 2003. Specific improvements were made to IAS 32 and IAS 39. New standards given priority for 2005 were developed in IFRS 2 (share-based payments), IFRS 3 (business combinations), IFRS 4 (insurance contracts) and IFRS 5 (non-current assets and discontinued operations).

10.4.6 Beyond the stable platform

The IASB has continued to develop projects, some on its own initiative and some working with national standard setters. However, by June 2006 the IASB had become aware of some criticisms that it was making too many changes too fast and accordingly the work plan was accompanied by the announcement 'No new major standards to be effective before 2009'. This would give a longer lead time for countries using IFRS to prepare translations and implement new standards in practice. There would be increased opportunity for input on conceptual issues, making more use of discussion papers prior to issuing exposure drafts. Round table discussions would be used to explore specific issues. The IASB claimed its policy would give four years of stability from 2005 to 2009 for those companies adopting IFRS in 2005. New standards continue to appear during this period but companies will not be forced into implementation until 2009. Earlier application will be voluntary.

The Work Plan at December 2007, summarized in Exhibit 10.4, shows the continuing intensity of the ASB's work and the relative influence of the Memorandum of Understanding (MoU) with the FASB.

| Exhibit 10.4 | Summary of Work Plan of IASB at December 2007 |

ACTIVE AGENDA

Projects in MoU with FASB

Short-term convergence projects

- Government grants
- Joint ventures
- Impairment
- Income tax
- Investment properties
- Research and development
- Subsequent events

Other convergence projects

- Consolidation
- Fair value measurement guidance
- Financial statement presentation
- Revenue recognition
- Post-employment benefits
- Leases
- Conceptual framework

Other projects

- Small and medium-sized entities
- Insurance contracts
- Liabilities
- Emission trading schemes
- Common control transactions
- Management commentary

RESEARCH AGENDA

Projects not yet active but included in the MoU with the FASB

- Derecognition
- Financial instruments
- Intangible assets
- Liabilities and equity
- Extractive activities

Source: www.iasb.org/current+projects/IASB+projects.

10.4.7 Small and medium-sized entities

The work of the IASB has been focused on meeting the financial reporting needs of the world's capital markets (see section 10.2) but those capital markets contain only a small proportion of all the business entities of any country. Since its formation in 2001 the IASB has been carrying out a project to develop accounting standards suitable for small and medium-sized entities (SMEs) (see also section 1.4.3). The attraction of such an approach is that one shorter document can contain all the accounting requirements for an SME, which makes accounting far less complicated than having to work through the entire set of full IFRS. Following some preliminary work the IASB published a Discussion Paper in 2004. The responses were encouraging in showing a clear demand for IFRS for SMEs. Many countries would prefer adopting IFRS for SMEs rather than develop a national standard for SMEs. An Exposure Draft was published in 2007.

The Exposure Draft was developed by:[13]

(a) extracting the fundamental concepts from the *Framework* and the principles and mandatory guidance from IFRS; and

(b) considering the modifications that are appropriate with regard to users' needs and cost benefit analysis.

The controversy over having IFRS for SMEs is indicated in the Alternative View reported at the end of the Exposure Draft. One board member felt it was undesirable to develop a separate document because it will lead to non-comparable information (between SMEs and publicly accountable entities and from one SME to another). The board member's main concern was with modification to recognition and measurement – this person felt that the attention should be on modifying disclosure. The board member also pointed to the Constitution of the IASCF which promises a single set of accounting standards.

The evidence of the acceptability of IFRS for SMEs will come with time as they become applied in countries that have already implemented full IFRS for companies that have public accountability.

10.5 The IASB standards

The IASB issues new IFRS, has taken over and is gradually updating the inherited IAS, issues Interpretations as developed by IFRIC and has taken over the inherited SICs. In preparation for the changeover to IFRS in Europe and elsewhere in 2005, the IASB created a 'stable platform' of standards that would remain the same during 2005 and 2006 while the changeover was under way. This 'stable platform' was completed in March 2004.[14] Standards issued after that date took effect from 2007 onwards, although in some cases early adoption was encouraged.

The standards in issue at January 2007 are shown in Exhibit 10.5. In each case the title of the standard is followed by the date of the most recent version and the history of previous major revisions. The IASB makes regular minor revisions to existing standards to reflect the impact of new standards as these are introduced. In the annual handbook of IFRS there is a page at the start of each standard explaining detailed updating

---

[13] Exposure Draft (2007) para. BC66.

[14] IASB *Insight*, April/May 2004, p. 1.

Exhibit 10.5 IASB standards in issue, January 2007

		Comment
IFRS 1	First-time Adoption of International Financial Reporting Standards	Effective date for periods beginning on or after 1 January 2004
IFRS 2	Share-based Payment	Effective date for periods beginning on or after 1 January 2005
IFRS 3	Business Combinations	Effective for business combinations whose agreement date is on or after 31 March 2004
IFRS 4	Insurance Contracts	Effective date for periods beginning on or after 1 January 2005
IFRS 5	Non-current Assets Held for Sale and Discontinued Operations	Effective date for periods beginning on or after 1 January 2005
IFRS 6	Exploration for and Evaluation of Mineral Resources	Effective date for periods beginning on or after 1 January 2006
IFRS 7	Financial Instruments: Disclosure	Effective date for periods beginning on or after 1 January 2007
IFRS 8	Operating Segments (replaces IAS 14)	Effective date for periods beginning on or after 1 January 2009
IAS 1	Presentation of Financial Statements	Revised 2003, superseding 1997 version, which replaced former IAS 1, 5 and 13
IAS 2	Inventories	Revised 2003, superseding 1993 version, superseding 1975 version
IAS 3	Consolidated Financial Statements (withdrawn)	Superseded by IAS 27 and IAS 28
IAS 4	Depreciation Accounting (withdrawn)	Now in IAS 16, 22 and 38
IAS 5	Information to be Disclosed in Financial Statements (withdrawn)	Superseded by IAS 1 (1997)
IAS 6	Accounting Responses to Changing Prices (withdrawn)	Superseded by IAS 15
IAS 7	Cash Flow Statements	Issued 1992, superseding 1977 version
IAS 8	Accounting Policies, Changes in Accounting Estimates and Errors	Revised 2003, superseding 1993 version, superseding 1978 version
IAS 9	Research and Development Costs (withdrawn)	Superseded by IAS 38
IAS 10	Events after the Balance Sheet Date	Revised 2003, superseding 1999 version, superseding 1978 version, reformatted 1995
IAS 11	Construction Contracts	Issued 1993, superseding 1979 version
IAS 12	Income Taxes	Issued 1996, superseding 1979 version, reformatted 1995
IAS 13	Presentation of Current Assets and Current Liabilities (withdrawn)	Superseded by IAS 1 (1997)
IAS 14	Segment Reporting (superseded by IFRS 8)	Issued 1997, superseding 1983 version, reformatted 1995, replaced 2006
IAS 15	Information Reflecting the Effects of Changing Prices (withdrawn)	Withdrawn 2003

▶

IAS 16	Property, Plant and Equipment	Revised 2003, superseding 1998 version; issued 1993, superseding 1982 version
IAS 17	Leases	Revised 2003, superseding 1997 version, superseding 1982, reformatted 1995
IAS 18	Revenue	Issued 1993, superseding 1982 version
IAS 19	Employee Benefits	Amended 2000, issued 1998, superseding 1993 and 1982 versions
IAS 20	Accounting for Government Grants and Disclosure of Government Assistance	Issued 1983, reformatted 1995
IAS 21	The Effects of Changes in Foreign Exchange Rates	Revised 2003, superseding 1993 version, superseding 1983 version
IAS 22	Business Combinations (withdrawn)	Withdrawn March 2004, see IFRS 3
IAS 23	Borrowing Costs	Issued 1993, superseding 1984 version
IAS 24	Related Party Disclosures	Revised 2003, superseding 1984 version, reformatted 1995
IAS 25	Accounting for Investments (withdrawn)	Now in IAS 32, 39 and 40
IAS 26	Accounting and Reporting by Retirement Benefit Plans	Issued 1987, reformatted 1995
IAS 27	Consolidated and Separate Financial Statements	Revised 2003, superseding 2000 version, superseding 1989 version, reformatted 1995
IAS 28	Investments in Associates	Revised 2003, superseding 2000 and 1998 revisions, superseding 1989 version, reformatted 1995
IAS 29	Financial Reporting in Hyperinflationary Economies	Issued 1989, reformatted 1995
IAS 30	Disclosure in the Financial Statements of Banks and Similar Financial Institutions	Issued 1990, reformatted 1995
IAS 31	Interests in Joint Ventures	Revised 2003, superseding 2000 version, amended 1998, issued 1990, reformatted 1995
IAS 32	Financial Instruments: Presentation (formerly Disclosure and Presentation; Disclosure now in IFRS 7)	Changed 2005, revised 2003, superseding 2000 version and 1998 version, issued 1995
IAS 33	Earnings per Share	Revised 2003, issued 1997
IAS 34	Interim Financial Reporting	Issued 1998
IAS 35	Discontinuing Operations (withdrawn)	Withdrawn 2004, see IFRS 5
IAS 36	Impairment of Assets	Revised 2004, superseding 1998 version
IAS 37	Provisions, Contingent Liabilities and Contingent Assets	Issued 1998, supersedes parts of IAS 10
IAS 38	Intangible Assets	Revised 2004, replaces 1998 version
IAS 39	Financial Instruments: Recognition and Measurement	Revised 2003, superseding 2000 version, issued 1998
IAS 40	Investment Property	Revised 2003, issued 2000
IAS 41	Agriculture	Issued 2001

Source: Based on combined volume of International Financial Reporting Standards at 1 January 2007, IASB.

that has taken place. The IASB's website contains summaries of the key aspects of each standard.

Although it is useful to have the standards listed in numerical sequence, for purposes of considering the impact and relevance of the standards it is more convenient to rearrange them according to the accounting issues they address. This rearrangement is presented in Exhibit 10.6.

The IFRIC and SIC standards are listed in Exhibit 10.7. There are relatively few of the latter because many have been withdrawn as they have been taken into revisions of IAS or new IFRS.

Exhibit 10.6 **Classification of IASB standards, by accounting issue**

Disclosure and presentation

General aspects

IFRS 1	First-time Adoption of International Financial Reporting Standards
IAS 1	Presentation of Financial Statements

Specific aspects

IAS 7	Cash Flow Statements
IAS 8	Accounting Policies, Changes in Accounting Estimates and Errors
IFRS 5	Non-current Assets Held for Sale and Discontinued Operations
IFRS 8	Segment Reporting (previously IAS 14)
IAS 24	Related Party Disclosures
IAS 33	Earnings per Share
IAS 34	Interim Financial Reporting

Asset recognition and measurement

IAS 2	Inventories
IAS 16	Property, Plant and Equipment
IAS 36	Impairment of Assets
IAS 23	Borrowing Costs
IAS 25	Accounting for Investments
IAS 38	Intangible Assets
IAS 40	Investment Property

Liability recognition and measurement

IAS 10	Events after the Balance Sheet Date
IAS 37	Provisions, Contingent Liabilities and Contingent Assets
IAS 12	Income Taxes
IAS 17	Leases
IAS 19	Employee Benefits

Financial instruments: assets and liabilities

IAS 32	Financial Instruments: Presentation
IFRS 7	Financial Instruments: Disclosure
IAS 39	Financial Instruments: Recognition and Measurement

Recognition of economic activity

IAS 11	Construction Contracts
IAS 18	Revenue
IAS 20	Accounting for Government Grants and Disclosure of Government Assistance
IFRS 2	Share-based Payment

Measurement of inflation
IAS 29   Financial Reporting in Hyperinflationary Economies

Group accounting
IAS 21   The Effects of Changes in Foreign Exchange Rates
IFRS 3   Business Combinations
IAS 27   Consolidated and Separate Financial Statements
IAS 28   Investments in Associates
IAS 31   Interests in Joint Ventures

Specialist industries
IAS 26   Accounting and Reporting by Retirement Benefit Plans
IAS 41   Agriculture
IFRS 4   Insurance Contracts
IFRS 6   Exploration for and Evaluation of Mineral Resources

Exhibit 10.7   **List of IFRIC and SIC standards, January 2007**

IFRIC 1	Changes in Existing Decommissioning, Restoration and Similar Liabilities
IFRIC 2	Members' Shares in Co-operative Entities and Similar Instruments
IFRIC 4	Determining whether an Arrangement Contains a Lease
IFRIC 5	Rights to Interests arising from Decommissioning, Restoration and Environmental Rehabilitation Funds
IFRIC 6	Liabilities Arising from Participation in an Specific Market – Waste Electrical and Electronic Equipment
IFRIC 7	Applying the Restatement Approach under IAS 29 *Financial Reporting in Hyperinflationary Economies*
IFRIC 8	Scope of IFRS 2
IFRIC 9	Reassessment of Embedded Derivatives
IFRIC 10	Interim Financial Reporting and Impairment
IFRIC 11	IFRS 2 Group and Treasury Share Transactions
IFRIC 12	Service Concession Arrangements
SIC-7	Introduction of the Euro (IAS 21)
SIC-10	Government Assistance – No Specific Relation to Operating Activities (IAS 20)
SIC-12	Consolidation – Special Purpose Entities (IAS 27)
SIC-13	Jointly Controlled Entities – Non-Monetary Contributions by Venturers (IAS 31)
SIC-15	Operating Leases – Incentives (IAS 17)
SIC-21	Income Taxes – Recovery of Revalued Non-Depreciable Assets (IAS 12)
SIC-25	Income Taxes – Changes in the Tax Status of an Enterprise or its Shareholders (IAS 12)
SIC-27	Evaluating the Substance of Transactions Involving the Legal Form of a Lease
SIC-29	Disclosure – Service Concession Arrangements
SIC-31	Revenue – Barter Transactions Involving Advertising Services
SIC-32	Intangible Assets – Web Site Costs

Source: Based on combined volume of International Financial Reporting Standards at 1 January 2007, IASB.

10.6 IASB *Framework*

In 1989 the IASC issued a *Framework* which has been adopted by the IASB and may be regarded as a statement of key principles to be applied in accounting practices (IASC, 1989). The *Framework* is not itself an accounting standard. The purpose of the *Framework* document is to assist:

- the Board in development and review of IAS;
- the Board in promotion of harmonization by providing a basis for reducing the number of alternative accounting treatments permitted by IAS;
- national standard-setting bodies in developing national standards;
- preparers of financial statements in applying IAS and dealing with topics on which IAS do not yet exist;
- auditors in forming an opinion as to whether financial statements conform to IAS;
- users in interpreting financial statements prepared in conformity with IAS;
- those interested in the formulation of IAS by providing information about the approach used by the IASC (now IASB).

The *Framework* deals with:

- the objectives of financial statements;
- the qualitative characteristics that determine the usefulness of information in financial statements;
- the definition, recognition and measurement of the elements from which financial statements are constructed;
- concepts of capital and capital maintenance.

The *Framework* document is concerned with general purpose financial statements which normally include a balance sheet, an income statement, a statement of change in financial position, and those notes and other statements and explanatory material that are an integral part of the financial statements. The term 'financial statements' does not include reports by directors, statements by the Chair, or discussion and analysis by management that may be included in an entity's financial or annual report.

The users of financial statements are identified as present and potential investors, employees, lenders, suppliers and other trade creditors, customers, government and its agents and the public. Although all of the information needs of these users cannot be met by financial statements, it is reasonable to think that providing the information needs of investors will ensure that most of the needs of other users can be satisfied.

10.6.1 A converged framework: IASB and FASB

In October 2004 the IASB and FASB announced that they would develop a common conceptual framework as a foundation for developing principles-based standards that are internally consistent and internationally converged. The FASB already had in place a set of Statements of Financial Accounting Concepts (SFACs), mainly developed in the early 1980s, while the IASB had the *Framework* dating from 1989. The convergence project has been defined in eight phases (see Exhibit 10.8), mainly resembling the separate sections of the 1989 *Framework*.

Exhibit 10.8	Phases of the conceptual framework convergence project

Phase	Topic	Discussion paper	Exposure draft
A	Objectives and qualitative characteristics	July 2006	Qtr 1 2008
B	Elements and recognition	2009	
C	Measurement	Qtr 4 2008	
D	Reporting entity	Qtr 1 2008	
E	Presentation and disclosure	tbd	
F	Purpose and status	tbd	
G	Application to not-for-profit entities	tbd	
H	Remaining Issues, if any	tbd	

'tbd' = date to be determined.

In sections 10.6.2 and 10.6.3 we describe the views of the IASB and FASB as set out in the discussion paper on objectives and qualitative characteristics. In sections 10.6.4 and 10.6.5 we describe the contents of the 1989 *Framework* which is unlikely to change before 2009. Developments towards that change will be described on the IASB website.

10.6.2 Objective of financial statements

The descriptions of objectives of financial statements are set out in Exhibit 10.9. This compares the wording of the Discussion Paper with the existing wording in the IASB *Framework* and the FASB Statement of Financial Accounting Concepts. You should consider the similarities and differences there.

Comments on the Discussion Paper raised three significant issues of concern.

The first, and probably strongest concern, was that the new wording makes no mention of stewardship. The Discussion Paper had anticipated this concern. The two Boards said that fulfilling the stewardship responsibility is part of the overall objective of providing information that is useful for making resource allocation decisions. It does not need a separate statement. There could even be a danger that making a separate statement about stewardship would encourage separation of the effects of management performance from the effects of transactions beyond management control. Those who disagree with this position say that the accounting information needed to assess the stewardship responsibilities of management will not necessarily be produced in a decision-usefulness focus. They want the specific emphasis on stewardship to remain. The IASB staff summary of the comments observed that most of those supporting stewardship were European, which seems to indicate different views where financial reporting may serve needs beyond those of capital markets.

The second concern was the question of identifying users of financial statements. The *Framework* emphasizes a wide range of users. SFAC 1 focuses more specifically on investors and creditors. The Discussion Paper reflects the narrower perspective of SFAC 1.

The third concern was to ask whether the objective should relate only to financial statements or to financial reporting more generally. The IASB is inclined towards a broader view, taking in financial reporting as a whole, but notes that the main focus of both the IASB and FASB has been primarily on financial statements.

| Exhibit 10.9 | Stating the objectives of financial statements |

Discussion Paper 2006

OB2 The objective of general purpose external financial reporting is to provide information that is useful to present and potential investors and creditors and others in making investment, credit, and similar resource allocation decisions.

Source: Discussion Paper: Preliminary Views on an improved Conceptual Framework for Financial Reporting: The Objective of Financial Reporting and Qualitative Characteristics of Decision-useful Financial Reporting Information, IASB/FASB 2006.

IASB Framework 1989

12. The objective of financial statements is to provide information about the financial position, performance and changes in financial position of an entity that is useful to a wide range of users in making economic decisions.

13. Financial statements prepared for this purpose meet the common needs of most users. However, financial statements do not provide all the information that users may need to make economic decisions since they largely portray the financial effects of past events and do not necessarily provide non-financial information.

14. Financial statements also show the results of the stewardship of management, or the accountability of management for the resources entrusted to it. Those users who wish to assess the stewardship or accountability of management do so in order that they may make economic decisions; these decisions may include, for example, whether to hold or sell their investment in the entity or whether to reappoint or replace the management.

Source: *Framework*, 1989.

SFAC 1 (1978)

34. Financial reporting should provide information that is useful to present and potential investors and creditors and other users in making rational investment, credit, and similar decisions. The information should be comprehensible to those who have a reasonable understanding of business and economic activities and are willing to study the information with reasonable diligence.

SFAC 1 Objectives of Financial Reporting by Business Enterprises, November 1978.

10.6.3 Qualitative characteristics

In order that financial statements should be useful to the users, certain qualitative characteristics should be present. That is an uncontroversial view but what causes more debate is the list of characteristics to be applied. Exhibit 10.10 summarizes the key similarities and differences in the Discussion Paper compared with the IASB's 1989 *Framework* and the FASB's 1980 Statement of Financial Accounting Concepts.

10.6.3.1 Relevance

The IASB *Framework* (para. 26) says that information is relevant 'when it influences the economic decisions of users by helping them evaluate past, present or future events or confirming, or correcting, their past evaluations'. FASB Concepts Statement No. 2, *Qualitative Characteristics of Accounting Information*, para. 47, says that, to be relevant, 'accounting information must be capable of making a difference in a decision by helping users to form predictions about the outcomes of past, present, and future events or to

Exhibit 10.10 **Comparison of qualitative characteristics**

[Full references to each document are given in the reference list at the end of the chapter.]

Quality	IASB (1989)	FASB (1980) SFAC 2	IASB/FASB Discussion Paper (2006)
Relevance	1	1	1
Predictive value and confirmatory value	2	2	2
Timeliness	Constraint	2	2
Materiality	2	Constraint	Constraint
Reliability	1	1	–
Faithful representation	2	2	1
Verifiability	2	2	2
Neutrality	2	2	2
Prudence	Discussed	–	–
Conservatism	–	Discussed	–
Completeness	2	2	2
Substance over form	2	–	–
Comparability and consistency	1	1	1
Understandability	1	1	1
Benefits and costs	Constraint	Constraint	Constraint
Balance between qualitative characteristics	Discussed as constraint	Discussed	Focus on costs and benefits

Key: 1 = primary characteristic; 2 = secondary characteristic within primary category.

Constraint = something which puts limits on financial reporting in relation to all the qualitative characteristics.

confirm or correct expectations'. Thus, the definitions differ in whether information must actually *make a difference* in a decision or *be capable of making a difference* in a decision. The Boards concluded that information must be *capable of making a difference* in a decision, to be relevant.

10.6.3.2 Reliability

The Boards took the view that there was no clearly agreed definition of reliability, either in the two existing sets of concepts or elsewhere, and accordingly decided not to include it in the converged framework. The Boards felt that everything to be said about reliability could be found in 'faithful representation' and so promoted it to become one of the four main characteristics.

10.6.3.3 Prudence and conservatism

The Boards took the view that describing *prudence* or *conservatism* as a desirable quality or response to uncertainty would conflict with the quality of *neutrality*. They therefore omitted both from the list of qualitative characteristics.

10.6.3.4 Substance over form

The Boards took the view that faithful representation requires the representation of the economic substance of a transaction rather than relying only on legal form. On this basis it is unnecessary to specify substance over form as a separate characteristic.

10.6.3.5 Timeliness

The Boards considered the two different views of timeliness, an essential component of relevance or a constraint across all characteristics, and initially decided it was essential to relevance. Having considered the comments on the Discussion Paper, the Boards reported in June 2007 that they had tentatively decided that timeliness should be removed as a component of relevance and instead described as an enhancing qualitative characteristic along with comparability, understandability and verifiability.

10.6.3.6 Transparency

Transparency of financial reporting has been much discussed in many quarters. The IASB and FASB debated whether it should be added as a qualitative characteristic. Having considered the various meanings attributed to transparency in accounting, they decided it could be achieved with the qualitative characteristics already defined and did not need separate inclusion.

10.6.4 Elements and recognition

The broad classes of transactions portrayed in financial statements are called elements of financial statements. The elements relating to the measurement of financial position are assets, liabilities and equity. Those relating to the measurement of performance are income and expenses. For an item to be reported in a balance sheet or income statement it must first of all meet the definition of an element and then satisfy the criteria for recognition. These elements are defined as follows:

- an *asset* is a resource controlled by the enterprise as a result of past events and from which future economic benefits are expected to flow to the enterprise;
- a *liability* is a present obligation of the enterprise arising from past events, the settlement of which is expected to result in an outflow from the enterprise of resources embodying economic benefits;
- *equity* is the residual interest in the assets of the enterprise after deducting all its liabilities;
- *income* is increases in economic benefits during the accounting period in the form of inflows or enhancements of assets or decreases of liabilities that result in increases in equity, other than those relating to contributions from equity participants;
- *expenses* are decreases in economic benefits during the accounting period in the form of outflows or depletions of assets or incurring of liabilities that result in decreases in equity, other than those relating to distributions to equity participants.

An item that meets the definition of an element should be recognized (i.e. incorporated in words and numerical amount in accounting statements) if (and only if):

- it is probable that any future economic benefits associated with the item will flow to or from the enterprise; and
- the item has a cost or value that can be measured with reliability.

Items that meet the definition of an element but fail to meet the criteria for recognition may warrant disclosure in the notes to the financial statements if knowledge of the item is considered to be relevant to the evaluation of the results of the enterprise.

10.6.4.1 Assets

An asset is recognized in the balance sheet when it is probable that the future economic benefit will flow to the enterprise and the asset has a cost or value that can be measured reliably. When expenditure has been incurred that meets the definition of an asset but fails the recognition test because it is considered improbable that economic benefit will flow to the enterprise beyond the current accounting period, the transaction should be recognized as an expense in the income statement.

10.6.4.2 Liabilities

A liability is recognized in the balance sheet when it is probable that an outflow of resources embodying economic benefits will result from the settlement of a present obligation and the amount at which the settlement will take place can be measured reliably.

10.6.4.3 Income

Income is recognized in the income statement when an increase in future economic benefits related to an increase in an asset or decrease of a liability has arisen that can be measured reliably.

10.6.4.4 Expenses

Expenses are recognized in income statements when a decrease in future economic benefits relating to a decrease in an asset or an increase of a liability has arisen that can be measured reliably.

10.6.5 Measurement

The IASB *Framework* (1989) is least specific when discussing the measurement methods that should be used in recognizing the elements of the financial statements. It merely lists the different measurement bases that are currently used, namely historical cost; current cost; realizable value; and present value. The *Framework* declines to express a preference for any of these bases of measurement.

In the context of making no recommendation on measurement it is perhaps surprising that the *Framework* ventures into capital maintenance. It offers the guidance that the selection of the appropriate concept of capital (i.e. invested money, invested purchasing power or physical output capacity) and hence the concept of capital maintenance by an enterprise should be based on the needs of the users of its financial statements.

The concept of capital maintenance provides the link between the concepts of capital and profit and imposes some limitation on the measurement processes adopted.

The *Framework* points out that selection from the available concepts of capital main-tenance and measurement bases provides a wide range of accounting models that can be used in the preparation of financial statements. It is claimed that the *Framework* is applicable to the range of accounting models and that at present there is no intention to prescribe one particular model for general adoption.

However, the focus on fair value (see Chapter 5) from both FASB and IASB indicates that eventually this section of the *Framework* will form the basis for a very contentious and lively debate.

10.7 Multinational companies

It has become common for multinational companies to express their accounting results by reference to an internationally accepted approach. This has been perceived as being more acceptable to the investing public and to stock exchange regulators. At present, many companies have two internationally recognized approaches from which to choose – US GAAP and IFRS.

10.7.1 Multinational companies which apply US GAAP

An example of the use of US GAAP as a global standard is seen in Exhibit 10.11 where a Japanese company uses domestic GAAP for individual companies in the group but then applies US GAAP for the group accounts.

10.7.2 Multinational companies which apply IFRS

The use of IFRS by multinational companies depends on the status of IFRS in the home country of the parent company (see Exhibit 10.12).

A straightforward statement of compliance with IFRS is provided by a Swiss company (Exhibit 10.13). Switzerland is not a member state of the EU and can therefore allow companies to comply in full with IFRS.

Research has shown that, historically, companies claiming to comply with IAS did not necessarily comply in all respects. For example, research into behaviour in 1996 (Street *et al.*, 1999) found limited compliance which continued into 1999 (Cairns, 1999). It is

| Exhibit 10.11 | Use of US GAAP, Japanese company |

(1) Basis of presentation and significant accounting policies

(b) Basis of presentation

The Company and its domestic subsidiaries maintain their books of account in conformity with financial accounting standards of Japan. Foreign subsidiaries maintain their books of account in conformity with financial accounting standards of the countries of their domicile.

Certain adjustments and reclassifications have been incorporated in the accompanying consolidated financial statements to conform with U.S. generally accepted accounting principles. These adjustments were not recorded in the statutory books of account.

Source: Canon Inc., Annual Report (2006), p. 62.

Exhibit 10.12 Variations in status of IFRS

- IFRS used as national standards, with explanatory material added.
- IFRS used as national standards, plus national standards developed for topics not covered by IFRS.
- IFRS used as national standards, with some cases of modification for local conditions or circumstances.
- National accounting standards separately developed but based on and similar to the relevant IFRS; national standards generally provide additional explanatory material only.
- National accounting standards separately developed but based on and similar to the relevant IAS in most cases; however, some standards may provide more or less choice than IFRS; no reference is made to IFRS in national standards.
- As in previous case except that each standard includes a statement that compares the national standard with the relevant IFRS.
- National standards developed separately.
- National standards do not exist at the present time.
- No national standards; IFRS not formally adopted but usually used.

Exhibit 10.13 Accounting policy for consolidated financial statements, Swiss company

1. Summary of significant accounting policies

Basis of preparation of the consolidated financial statements
The consolidated financial statements of the Roche Group have been prepared in accordance with International Financial Reporting Standards (IFRS) and comply with Swiss law. They have been prepared using the historical cost convention except that, as disclosed in the accounting policies below, certain items, including derivatives and available-for-sale investments, are shown at fair value. They were approved for issue by the Board of Directors on 1 February 2007 and are subject to approval by the Annual General Meeting of shareholders on 5 March 2007.

Source: Roche (Switzerland), Annual Report (2006), p. 28, www.roche.com.

important for the credibility of the IASB that the claim for compliance is not misleading. Even where companies made clear the areas in which they did not comply, it could nevertheless cause confusion in the minds of those using the accounts. As a result IAS 1 (as revised in 2003) took a strict view on the use of the words 'complying with IFRS':

> An entity whose financial statements comply with IFRSs shall make an explicit and unreserved statement of such compliance in the notes. Financial statements shall not be described as complying with IFRSs unless they comply with all the requirements of IFRSs.
>
> (IAS 1, para. 14)

This strict approach avoids users of financial statements being misled but it also causes problems in understanding where annual reports are substantially in compliance. The SEC in the USA has expressed some frustration with EU companies which are required by the EU regulations to confirm compliance with IFRS as endorsed in the EU. For many companies this may result in full compliance with IFRS but they cannot make that

| Exhibit 10.14 | Statement of accounting policies, Russian company |

Basis of presentation

The Financial Statements were prepared in accordance with the International Financial Reporting Standards, or IFRS, as issued by the International Accounting Standards Board, or IASB, in effect at the time of preparing the Financial Statements. IFRS that was adopted for use in the European Union through the endorsement procedure established by the European Commission does not include IAS 39 'Financial Instruments: Recognition and Measurement' for certain provisions on portfolio hedging of core deposits. Despite this exception, the accounting policies applied in the preparation of the Financial Statements in accordance with IFRS as issued by the IASB did not differ materially from IFRS as adopted for use in the European Union. IFRS differs in various material respects from generally accepted accounting principles in the United States, or US GAAP.

Source: Severstal, Annual Report, 2006, p. 76, www.severstal.com.

statement. Examples of the wording of audit reports of EU companies are shown for France, Germany, The Netherlands and Poland in Chapter 14 (Exhibits 14.14–14.17 respectively).

An increasing number of companies now present financial statements that substantially conform with IFRS. However, because of the strict wording of IAS 1 (revised), some are silent because they do not comply as completely as the IAS requires.

Exhibit 1.1 in Chapter 1 shows the status of IFRS application across a range of countries. It indicates that Russia is moving towards requiring IFRS to be applied. The confusion of the transition is evident in the statement of accounting policies of a Russian company shown in Exhibit 10.14.

Exhibit 1.1 also indicates that India intends to introduce IFRS from 2011. In the meantime accounting in India is strongly indicative of the UK influence in accounting and company law. An attempt by an Indian company to give assurance about 'substantial compliance' with IFRS is shown in Exhibit 10.15.

10.7.3 Reconciliation of IFRS to US GAAP

Until 2008 companies which applied IFRS but had a listing on a US stock exchange were required to provide documentation to the SEC which included a reconciliation comparing the profit and equity measured under IFRS with the same items measured under US GAAP. An example of a reconciliation is shown in Exhibit 10.16. From 2008 the SEC will accept IFRS as issued by the IASB. This kind of detailed reconciliation will remain if IFRS are not exactly those issued by the IASB.

10.7.4 Multinational companies which apply national standards

Some countries are moving towards IFRS but are achieving this through developing their national standards. This leaves the reader of the annual report totally uninformed about the extent of compliance with IFRS – it is necessary to know the state of progress in the national standard setting. Malaysia sets its own standards (Exhibit 10.17).

Korea (Exhibit 10.18) also sets its own standards.

Taiwan is another country that sets its own standards (Exhibit 10.19).

| Exhibit 10.15 | Unaudited financial statements, Indian company |

Financial statements (unaudited) presented in substantial compliance with GAAP requirements of various countries and International Financial Reporting Standards and reports of substantial compliance with the respective corporate governance standards

Over the past decades, the technology and information revolutions have fundamentally transformed economic and political relationships between nations. Thanks to the opening up of financial markets across the globe, investors today have a wide choice of capital markets to invest in. Consequently, the global investor must have access to information about the performance of any company, in any market that he or she chooses to invest in. However, differences in language, accounting practices, and reporting requirements in various countries render performance reports by many companies rather investor-unfriendly.

Today, the strength of a global company lies in its ability to access high-quality capital at the lowest cost from a global pool of investors. Such companies study the needs of global investors and publish financial information in a language and form understood by their existing as well as prospective investors. In the process, financial statistics may have to be restated and financial terminology may need to be translated. Indeed, a key issue in international financial analysis is the restatement and translation of financial reports that describe operations conducted in one environment, but which are the subject of review and analysis in another.

As an investor-friendly company, committed to the highest standards of disclosure, we have been voluntarily providing unaudited financial statements presented in substantial compliance with the GAAP requirements of Australia, Canada, France, Germany, Japan and the United Kingdom, besides those of the United States and India (which information appears separately elsewhere).

Australia, France, Germany and the United Kingdom have adopted the International Financial Reporting Standards (IFRS). We are presenting the unaudited consolidated financial statements for these countries presented in substantial compliance with IFRS. We are also presenting, in US Dollars, financial statements presented in substantial compliance with IFRS. Since there is an ongoing convergence project between US GAAP and IFRS, the IFRS information presented in this Annual Report has been reconciled to our US GAAP information. Financial information presented in Japanese GAAP in this Annual Report has been translated from our US GAAP financial information. The information will be included in the Securities Report to be filed with the Ministry of Finance, Japan. Canadian GAAP financial statements have been presented on the same basis as earlier years and are reconciled to our Indian GAAP financial information.

Further, keeping in mind their local regulations and practices, these countries have formulated their own corporate governance standards. We have provided statements on substantial compliance with these standards in the respective national languages of these countries.

The unaudited consolidated income statements and balance sheets have been presented by converting the various financial parameters, reported in our income statement, into the respective currencies of the above countries. In addition, appropriate adjustments have been made for differences, if any, in accounting principles, and in formats, between India, United States, these countries and IFRS.

Source: Infosys Technologies Ltd, Annual Report 2006, p. 158.

10.7.5 Consolidated statements and parent statements use different accounting systems

The Japanese company illustrated in Exhibit 10.11 explains that national accounting rules are used for the parent company financial statements while US GAAP are used for the consolidated financial statements. For listed companies in the EU it is compulsory to use endorsed IFRS for the group financial statements but there remains a choice for the

Exhibit 10.16 Reconciliation of IFRS and US GAAP results, Stora Enso

Reconciliation of net profit (loss) and shareholders' equity

The following is a summary of the significant adjustments to net profit (loss) and shareholders' equity required when reconciling such amounts recorded in the Group's consolidated financial statements to the corresponding amounts in accordance with U.S. GAAP.

Reconciliation of net profit (loss)

	For the year ended December 31,		
	2004	2005	2006
	€	€	€
		(in millions)	
Reconciliation of net profit (loss)			
Profit (loss) attributable to equity shareholders in accordance with IFRS			
Previously reported	739.7	(130.0)	
Adoption of amendment to IAS 19 (see note 21)	18.2	18.9	
	757.9	(111.1)	585.0
U.S. GAAP adjustments:			
a) Employee benefit plans	(309.7)	(51.0)	(8.9)
b) Reverse acquisition	(51.4)	(63.1)	(20.6)
c) Acquisition of Consolidated Papers Inc.	(167.8)	5.9	7.3
d) Financial instruments	5.1	(83.3)	35.5
e) Impairment of goodwill	(243.9)	8.0	9.0
f) Impairment of fixed assets	(4.4)	191.2	12.7
g) Stock based compensation	(6.0)	3.8	(13.1)
h) Pension surplus refund	1.5	–	–
i) Amortization of goodwill	90.2	–	–
j) Restructuring costs	(10.3)	77.6	70.2
k) Biological assets	(13.8)	4.9	16.2
l) Share of results in associated companies	(17.2)	(78.5)	(10.1)
m) Sale of forest assets	233.7	–	–
n) Minority interest	–	2.2	1.5
o) Buy-outs of minority interest	–	(4.9)	(5.8)
q) Emission rights	–	–	(5.1)
Deferred tax effect of U.S. GAAP adjustments (restated)	(105.1)	(63.7)	(36.3)
Net income (loss) in accordance with U.S. GAAP	369.0	(162.9)	637.5

Reconciliation of shareholders' equity

	As of December 31,	
	2005	2006
	€	€
	(in millions)	
Reconciliation of shareholders' equity		
Equity attributable to equity shareholders in accordance with IFRS		
Previously reported	7,645.3	
Adoption of amendment to IAS 19 (see note 21)	(452.2)	
	7,220.1	7,799.6
U.S. GAAP adjustments:		
a) Employee benefit plans	152.8	(135.6)
b) Reverse acquisition	484.1	463.5
c) Acquisition of Consolidated Papers Inc.	67.1	67.4
d) Financial instruments	–	(2.3)
e) Impairment of goodwill	(243.0)	(208.1)
f) Impairment of fixed assets	252.5	242.0
g) Stock based compensation	17.2	4.1
h) Pension surplus refund	–	–
i) Amortization of goodwill	348.1	335.5
j) Restructuring costs	88.0	158.2
k) Biological assets	(18.5)	(2.1)
l) Share of results in associated companies	(185.3)	(194.4)
m) Sale of forest assets	(353.7)	(367.3)
n) Minority interest	1.2	3.5
o) Buy-outs of minority interest	38.3	32.4
p) Fair value of unlisted securities	(279.4)	(671.5)
q) Emission rights	–	(5.1)
Deferred tax effect of U.S. GAAP adjustments	(194.6)	(119.4)
Shareholders' equity in accordance with U.S. GAAP	7,394.9	7,400.4

Source: Stora Enso (Finland) Form 20-F (2006), from pp. F-101 and F-1029, www.storaenso.com.

Exhibit 10.17 Statement of accounting policies, Malaysian company

1. BASIS OF PREPARATION OF THE FINANCIAL STATEMENTS

The financial statements of the Group and the Company have been prepared in accordance with Financial Reporting Standards (FRSs), the Malaysian Accounting Standards Board (MASB) approved accounting standards in Malaysia for Entities Other Than Private Entities and the provisions of the Companies Act, 1965. During the year, the Group and the Company had adopted new and revised FRSs which are mandatory for financial year beginning on or after 1 January 2006 as described in (a) below.

The financial statements have been prepared under the historical cost convention except as disclosed in the Significant Accounting Policies below.

The preparation of financial statements in conformity with FRSs, the MASB approved accounting standards in Malaysia for Entities Other Than Private Entities and the provisions of the Companies Act, 1965, requires the use of certain critical accounting estimates and assumptions that affect the reported amounts of assets and liabilities and the disclosure of contingent assets and liabilities at the date of the financial statements, and the reported

Exhibit 10.17 *(Continued)*

amounts of the revenue and expenses during the reported period. It also requires Directors to exercise their judgement in the process of applying the Group's accounting policies. Although these estimates and judgement are based on the Directors' best knowledge of current events and actions, actual results may differ.

The areas involving a higher degree of judgement or complexity, or areas where assumptions and estimates are significant to the Group's and the Company's financial statements, are disclosed in note 2 to the financial statements.

(a) Standards, amendments to published standards and Interpretations Committee (IC) interpretations that are effective

[Detailed list and explanations omitted from extract]

A summary of the impact of the new accounting standards, amendments to the published standards and IC interpretations to existing standards on the financial statements of the Group and the Company is set out in note 49 to the financial statements.

(b) Standards, amendments to published standards and IC interpretations to existing standards that are not yet effective and have not been early adopted

The new standards, amendments to published standards and IC interpretations that are mandatory for the Group's financial year beginning on 1 January 2007, which the Group has not early adopted, are as follows:

[Detailed list and explanations omitted from extract]

(c) Standards that are not yet effective and not relevant or material for the Group's operations

[Detailed list and explanations omitted from extract]

Source: Telekom Malaysia Berhad, Annual Report 2006, pp. 223–225.

Exhibit 10.18 Statement of accounting policies, Korean company

SUMMARY OF SIGNIFICANT ACCOUNTING POLICIES

The accompanying non-consolidated financial statements of the Company have been prepared in accordance with Korean Financial Accounting Standards and Statements of Korean Accounting Standards ('SKAS') No. 1 through No. 20 (except for No. 11 and No. 14). The accompanying non-consolidated financial statements were approved by the Company's board of directors on February 13, 2007. Significant accounting policies followed in preparing the accompanying non-consolidated financial statements are summarized as follows.

a. Basis of presentation

The accompanying non-consolidated statutory financial statements have been prepared in the Korean language (Hangul) in conformity with the accounting principles generally accepted in the Republic of Korea ('Korean GAAP'). Certain accounting principles applied by the Company that conform with financial accounting standards and accounting principles in the Republic of Korea may not conform with accounting principles generally accepted in other countries. Accordingly, these financial statements are intended for use by those who are informed about Korean accounting principles and practices. The accompanying non-consolidated financial statements have been condensed, restructured and translated into English with certain expanded descriptions from the Korean language financial statements.

Certain information included in the Korean language financial statements, but not required for a fair presentation of the Company's financial position, results of operations or cash flows, is not presented in the accompanying non-consolidated financial statements. The official accounting records of the Company are maintained and expressed in Korean won, the currency of the country in which the Company is incorporated and operates. The translations of Korean won amounts into U.S. dollar amounts are included solely for the convenience of readers outside of the Republic of Korea and have been made at the rate of ₩930.0 to US$1, the Noon Buying Rate in the City of New York for cable transfers in Korean won as certified for customs purposes by the Federal Reserve Bank of New York on the last business day of the year ended December 31, 2006. Such translations into U.S. dollars should not be construed as representations that the Korean won amounts could be converted into U.S. dollars at the above or any other rate.

Source: SK Telecom, Annual Report 2006, p. 74, www.sktelecom.com.

| Exhibit 10.19 | Statement of accounting policies, Taiwanese company |

2. SIGNIFICANT ACCOUNTING POLICIES

The consolidated financial statements are presented in conformity with the Guidelines Governing the Preparation of Financial Reports by Securities Issuers, Business Accounting Law, Guideline Governing Business Accounting, and accounting principles generally accepted in the R.O.C.

For the convenience of readers, the accompanying consolidated financial statements have been translated into English from the original Chinese version prepared and used in the R.O.C. If there is any conflict between the English version and the original Chinese version or any difference in the interpretation of the two versions, the Chinese-language consolidated financial statements shall prevail.

Source: Taiwan Semiconductor Manufacturing Company Limited and Subsidiaries, Annual Report 2006, p. 126.

parent company's own financial statements. A Finnish company (Exhibit 10.20) illustrates this flexibility and explains the main differences between the parent company approach and the group approach.

10.7.6 Two sets of financial statements

Finally, an interesting example of meeting a range of user needs is shown by the Russian company Gazprom (Exhibit 10.21) which produces a statutory consolidated financial report, based on Russian GAAP, and an IFRS financial report. These give financial statements of quite different appearance and content. A reconciliation statement is provided, linking reported profit in each system. The reconciliation shows that the IFRS reported profit in 2006 is higher than RAR profit, although lower in 2005. This indicates the difficulty of predicting whether one system is more or less prudent than the other. However,

| Exhibit 10.20 | Accounting principles, Stora Enso |

PRESENTATION OF FINANCIAL ACCOUNTS

Stora Enso prepares consolidated annual and interim financial accounts conforming to international financial reporting standards (IFRS). These reports are published in Finnish, Swedish, English and German. In addition, Stora Enso makes an annual reconciliation with US GAAP (Form 20-F).

CONSOLIDATED FINANCIAL STATEMENTS – ACCOUNTING POLICIES

Basis of preparation

The Consolidated Financial Statements of Stora Enso have been prepared in accordance with International Financial Reporting Standards ('IFRS'), as adopted by the European Union, including International Accounting Standards ('IAS') and Interpretations issued by the International Financial Reporting Interpretations Committee ('IFRIC'). However, the differences between full IFRS and EU-adopted IFRS do not impact these

Exhibit 10.20	*(Continued)*

Financial Statements, being the consolidated Financial Statements of Stora Enso Oyj and its subsidiaries which have been prepared under the historical cost convention except as disclosed in the accounting policies below; for example, available-for-sale investments and derivative financial instruments are shown at fair value.

Source: Stora Enso Financials 2006, p. 40.

EXTRACT OF THE PARENT COMPANY FINANCIAL STATEMENTS

Accounting principles

The Parent Company Financial Statements are prepared according to Generally Accepted Accounting Principals in Finland, 'Finnish GAAP'; see Group Consolidated Financial Statements, Note 1. The main differences between the accounting policies of the Group and the Parent Company are:

● The valuation of financial assets, financial liabilities, derivative financial instruments and securities.

● Accounting of post-employment Defined Benefit plans.

● The presentation and accounting for deferred tax.

Source: Stora Enso Financials 2006, p. 106.

Extract from auditors' report

Consolidated financial statements

In our opinion the consolidated financial statements, prepared in accordance with International Financial Reporting Standards as adopted by the EU, give a true and fair view, as defined in those standards and in the Finnish Accounting Act, of the consolidated results of operations as well as of the financial position.

Parent company's financial statements, report of the Board of Directors and administration

In our opinion the parent company's financial statements have been prepared in accordance with the Finnish Accounting Act and other applicable Finnish rules and regulations. The parent company's financial statements give a true and fair view of the parent company's result of operations and of the financial position.

In our opinion the report of the Board of Directors has been prepared in accordance with the Finnish Accounting Act and other applicable Finnish rules and regulations. The report of the Board of Directors is consistent with the consolidated financial statements and the parent company's financial statements and gives a true and fair view, as defined in the Finnish Accounting Act, of the result of operations and of the financial position.

The consolidated financial statements and the parent company's financial statements can be adopted and the members of the Board of Directors and the Managing Director of the parent company can be discharged from liability for the period audited by us. The proposal by the Board of Directors regarding the disposal of distributable funds is in compliance with the Companies' Act.

Helsinki, 6 March 2007

Source: Extract from Stora Enso Financials 2006, p. 109, www.storaenso.com.

there is one item in 2005 which distorts the picture (treatment of treasury share investments where the group holds shares in group companies). Setting aside this item, both years show a higher US profit. The positive adjustments for depreciation indicate faster depreciation in Russia than in the USA. Goodwill is not depreciated (amortized) under US GAAP, causing another positive adjustment. A third positive adjustment arises because certain types of loan interest must be capitalized under US GAAP.

Exhibit 10.21 Income statements and reconciliation statement, Gazprom

OAO GAZPROM CONSOLIDATED STATEMENT OF INCOME
for the year ended 31 December 2006 (in million Roubles)

Note		For 2006	For 2005
	INCOME FROM AND EXPENSES ON ORDINARY ACTIVITIES		
17	Sales of goods, products, works and services (less value added tax, excise tax and other similar mandatory payments)	2,204,888	1,437,981
18	Cost of goods, products, works and services sold	(1,330,031)	(864,531)
18	Commercial expenses	(318)	(293)
18	Management expenses	(91,446)	(77,516)
	Profit from sales	**783,093**	**495,641**
	OTHER INCOME AND EXPENSES		
	Interest income	7,889	5,202
	Interest expense	(47,514)	(41,556)
	Income from investments in other companies	1,660	2,359
19	Other income	2,270,663	1,667,776
19	Other expenses	(2,235,563)	(1,573,353)
	Capitalized profit of associates	37,115	21,903
	Profit before profit tax	**817,343**	**577,972**
14	Deferred tax assets	4,863	2,077
14	Deferred tax liabilities	(31,740)	(16,255)
14	Current profit tax	(208,925)	(135,026)
14	Other similar payments	(2,853)	(1,720)
	Net profit of the reporting period before minority interest	**578,688**	**427,048**
	Minority interest	(26,309)	(6,466)
	Net profit of the reporting period	**552,379**	**420,582**
	FOR REFERENCE:		
	Non-temporary tax liabilities	37,771	3,970
22	Basic earnings per share (in roubles)	24.07	19.30

A.B. Miller
Chairman of the Management Committe

E.A. Vasilieva
Chief Accountant

8 May 2007

Exhibit 10.21 *(Continued)*

OAO GAZPROM
IFRS CONSOLIDATED STATEMENT OF INCOME
FOR THE YEAR ENDED 31 DECEMBER 2006
(In millions of Russian Roubles)

Notes		Year ended 2006	31 December 2005
24	Sales	2,152,111	1,383,545
25	Operating expenses	(1,363,923)	(929,561)
	Operating profit	**788,188**	**453,984**
26	Finance income	97,923	53,890
26	Finance expense	(65,220)	(69,926)
12	Share of net income of associated undertakings and jointly controlled entities	26,363	11,782
	Gain on disposal of available-for-sale financial assets	8,811	385
	Profit before profit tax	**856,065**	**450,115**
	Current profit tax expense	(213,844)	(118,028)
	Deferred profit tax expense	(5,760)	(16,156)
20	Profit tax expense	(219,604)	(134,184)
	Profit for the period	**636,461**	**315,931**
	Attributable to:		
	Equity holders of OAO Gazprom	613,345	311,125
31	Minority interest	23,116	4,806
		636,461	**315,931**
28	**Basic and diluted earnings per share for profit attributable to the equity holders of OAO Gazprom (in Roubles)**	**26.90**	**14.55**

A.B. Miller
Chairman of the Management Committee
20 June 2007

E.A. Vasilieva
Chief Accountant
20 June 2007

The accompanying notes are an integral part of these consolidated financial statements.

▶

27 RECONCILIATION OF PROFIT, DISCLOSED IN CONSOLIDATED STATEMENT OF INCOME, PREPARED IN ACCORDANCE WITH RUSSIAN ACCOUNTING RULES (RAR) TO PROFIT DISCLOSED IN IFRS STATEMENT OF INCOME

	Year ended 31 December	
	2006	**2005**
RAR net profit for the period per consolidated statutory accounts		
Effects of IFRS adjustments:	578,688	427,048
Effect of sales of treasury shares of OAO Rosneftegaz	–	(144,780)
Reclassification of revaluation of RAO UES of Russia (including deferred tax effect of RR 17,725 and RR 4,789 for the years, ended December 31,2006 and 2005, respectively)	(56,129)	(12,397)
Gain of OAO Novatek shares revaluation	(34,984)	–
Differences in depreciation	72,167	59,964
Reversal of Goodwill depreciation	25,069	7,209
Loan interest capitalized	17,275	15,189
Impairment provisions and other provisions	16,431	(16,456)
Fair value adjustment for currency options	1,459	(1,577)
Write-off of research and development expenses capitalized for RAR purposes	(3,438)	(4,222)
Fair value adjustment on commodity contracts	4,169	886
Other effects	15,754	(14,933)
IFRS profit for the period	636,461	315,931

Source: Gazprom, Statutory consolidated financial report (2006), p. 56, and IFRS consolidated financial statements (2006), pp. 4 and 38, www.gazprom.ru/eng/.

Summary and conclusions

This chapter has shown that the IASB has made significant steps towards global convergence of accounting standards for listed companies. The expertise and accumulated experience of the IASB and its predecessor IASC has increasingly been recognized by other international standard setters. However, there is a question mark remaining over the likelihood of unconditional acceptance by the most significant stock market regulators and national legislators. Complementing the work of the IASB, there are many organizations working towards achievement of harmonization and standardization. Not all seek to be active at a global level, some being satisfied with regional action. Multinational companies have moved towards use of global accounting standards, either IFRS or US GAAP, but some are selective in mixing international and national practices.

Key points from the chapter:

- The arguments in favour of global accounting standards are expressed in terms of benefits for preparers, investors and regulators in terms of transparency, comparability, cost saving and understandability.
- The arguments against global accounting standards are that apparent comparability of rules may hide underlying real differences in the transactions and events that are reported; national control of standard setting is lost; the standards are being used in developing countries without regard for their specific needs; and giving monopoly position to one organization may reduce quality through lack of competition.

- The work of the IASB is complemented by that of other organizations, such as the IFAC, harmonizing related aspects such as auditing, corporate governance, education and training, ethics and stock market regulation.
- The IASB has emerged from a process that began with the IASC forming in 1973; there was constant change in the IASC's methods of working as international standards gained greater acceptance.
- IOSCO's acceptance of international accounting standards in 2000 was the key event leading to acceptance of IFRS as being suitable for developed capital markets.
- The decision of the EU to require IFRS for all listed companies from 2005 was a further key event in encouraging the wider acceptance of IFRS.
- It is important to read the 'accounting policies' notes of any multinational company to know what combination of global standards and national standards has been applied by the company.

Questions

The following questions test your understanding of the material contained in the chapter and allow you to relate your understanding to the learning outcomes specified at the start of this chapter. The learning outcomes are repeated here. Each question is cross-referenced to the relevant section of the chapter.

Explain the nature and operations of the IASB

1 Compare the objectives as stated in the 2000 Constitution with those of the 1973 Constitution. What do you learn about the history of the changing nature of the work of the IASC and the intended future direction of the IASB? (sections 10.2 and 10.2.1)

2 What are the benefits and potential limitations of having an International Financial Reporting Interpretations Committee? (section 10.2.4)

3 What are the benefits and potential limitations of having a Standards Advisory Council? (section 10.2.5)

Understand the challenges facing the IASB in its work

4 What mechanisms exist to ensure the independence of the IASB as a standard-setting body? Is there any potential risk that the financing arrangements for the IASB might jeopardize its independence? What other factors may influence independence? (section 10.2.6)

5 Is the process for issuing a standard sufficient to ensure that all interested parties are consulted? What are the benefits and potential limitations of the process? (section 10.3)

6 Is the IASB able to be effective in enforcing its standards? To what extent do established national practices in developed countries inhibit the work of the IASB? (section 10.3.2)

Understand the key stages of historical development of international accounting standards

7 How and why has the nature of the work of the IASC and IASB changed over time? (section 10.4)

8 Was the 1989 Comparability Project a success? (section 10.4.3)

9 What necessitated the implementation of the Core Standards programme? (section 10.4.4)

10 Why was a stable platform for 2005 needed? (section 10.4.5.2)

11 Is it useful to develop IFRS for SMEs? (section 10.4.5.6)

Describe the continuing development of the IASB's Framework

12 Why did the IASC decide it was necessary to issue a *Framework* in 1989? (section 10.6)

13 What are the problems faced by the IASB and FASB in converging the objectives of financial statements? (section 10.6.2)

14 What are the debates between the IASB and FASB in converging the qualitative characteristics of financial statements? (section 10.6.3)

15 What possible explanations are there for the measurement section being the least well-developed section of the *Framework*? (section 10.6.5)

Explain how multinational companies demonstrate their use of global accounting standards

16 What information should readers look for in understanding the use of global accounting standards by multinational companies? (section 10.7)

References and further reading

Barth, M.E., Clinch, G. and Shibano, T. (1999) 'International accounting harmonization and global equity markets', *Journal of Accounting and Economics*, 26: 201–235.

Cairns, D. (1999) 'Exceptions to the rule', *Accountancy International*, November: 84–85, reporting on the *Financial Times International Accounting Standards Survey 1999*, by David Cairns.

Cairns, D. (2002) *A Guide to Applying International Accounting Standards*, 3rd edn. London: Butterworths.

Choi, F.D.S. and Bavishi, V.B. (1982) 'Financial accounting standards: a multinational synthesis and policy framework', *International Journal of Accounting*, Fall: 159–183.

Evans, T.G. and Taylor, M.E. (1982) 'Bottom line compliance with the IASC: a comparative analysis', *International Journal of Accounting Education and Research*, Fall: 115–128.

FASB (1980) SFAC 2, *Qualitative Characteristics of Accounting Information*, Financial Accounting Standards Board, May 1980.

Fleming, P.D. (1991) 'The growing importance of International Accounting Standards', *Journal of Accountancy*, September: 100–106.

Gernon, H., Purvis, S.E.C. and Diamond, M.A. (1990) 'An analysis of the implications of the IASC's Comparability Project', School of Accounting, University of Southern California.

IASB (1989) *Framework*. Approved by the IASC Board in April 1989 for publication in July 1989, and adopted by the IASB in April 2001.

IASB/FASB (2006) *Discussion Paper: Preliminary Views on an Improved Conceptual Framework for Financial Reporting: The Objective of Financial Reporting and Qualitative Characteristics of Decision-useful Financial Reporting Information*. IASB/FASB joint publication.

IASC (1989) 'Framework for the Preparation and Presentation of Financial Statements', in *International Accounting Standards, 1997*. London: International Accounting Standards Committee.

IASCF (2006) *Due Process Handbook for the International Accounting Standards Board*. London: International Accounting Standards Committee Foundation.

Larson, R.K. and Kenny, S.Y. (1995) 'An empirical analysis of international accounting standards, equity markets, and economic growth in developing countries', *Journal of International Financial Management and Accounting*, 6(2): 130–158.

McKinnon, S.M. and Janell, P. (1984) 'The International Accounting Standards Committee: a performance evaluation', *International Journal of Accounting Education and Research*, Spring: 19–34.

McLeay, S., Neal, D. and Tollington, T. (1999) 'International standardisation and harmonisation: a new measurement technique', *Journal of International Financial Management and Accounting*, 10(1): 42–70.

Miles, S. and Nobes, C. (1998) 'The use of foreign accounting data in UK financial institutions', *Journal of Business Finance and Accounting*, 25(3/4): 309–328.

Most, K.S. (1984) *International Conflict of Accounting Standards, a Research Report*. Vancouver: The Canadian Certified General Accountants' Research Foundation.

Nair, R.D. and Frank, W.G. (1981) 'The harmonization of International Accounting Standards, 1973–1979', *International Journal of Accounting Education and Research*, Fall: 61–77.

Purvis, S.E.C., Gernon, H. and Diamond, M.A. (1991) 'The IASC and its Comparability Project', *Accounting Horizons*, 5(2), 25–44.

Roberts, C.B., Salter, S.B. and Kantor, J. (1996) 'The IASC Comparability Project and current financial reporting reality: an empirical study of reporting in Europe', *British Accounting Review*, 28: 1–22.

Salter, S.B., Roberts, C.B. and Kantor, J. (1996) 'The IASC Comparability Project: a cross-national comparison of financial reporting practices and IASC proposed rules', *Journal of International Accounting and Taxation*, 5(1): 89–111.

Street, D.L., Gray, S.J. and Bryant, S.M. (1999) 'Acceptance and observance of International Accounting Standards: an empirical study of companies claiming to comply with IASs', *International Journal of Accounting*, 43(1): 11–48.

Weetman, P., Adams, C.A. and Gray, S.J. (1993) 'Issues in international accounting harmonisation: the significance of UK/US accounting differences and implications for the IASC's Comparability Project', *Research Report*, 33. London: Chartered Association of Certified Accountants.

This chapter also draws on material contained in IASC and IASB publications, particularly:

IASB/IASC Annual Review (various issues).

IASB/IASC Insight (published several times during a year).

IASB/IASC, International Accounting Standards, published annually, various Exposure Drafts and Statements, as indicated in the chapter and on the IASB website, www.iasb.org.

11

The United States of America

Learning outcomes

After reading this chapter you should be able to:

- Explain the development of accounting regulation.
- Understand the impact of the Sarbanes–Oxley Act 2002.
- Explain the key institutional characteristics of the USA.
- Make comparisons of US GAAP with IFRS.
- Understand and explain features of the accounting system and accounting practices in the USA.
- Discuss the US accounting system using the analytical framework of Gray's accounting values.

11.1 Introduction

The combination of US accounting principles and practices is referred to as 'US GAAP', short for 'US generally accepted accounting principles'. The concept of such a set of written principles originates in the USA, although the abbreviation is used in reference to other countries also. Accounting disclosure is characterized by transparency and accounting measurement by general conservatism and historical cost. Such conservatism originated in the stock market crash of 1929, and was modified by business pragmatism and flexibility in response to events of more recent years.[1]

The purpose of this chapter is to explain how the accounting principles and practices of the United States of America (the USA) compare with IFRS and to describe the continuing progress of the convergence project to bring IFRS and US GAAP closer. The US principles and practices are influential beyond the country's national boundary and have, of themselves, provided a means of harmonization for those other countries and business enterprises choosing to follow the US lead. They act also as a block to harmonization where the US regulators require a statement of reconciliation of the differences because a country has adapted IFRS rather than take the precise wording from IASB. The source of the widespread influence of US accounting lies in the country's worldwide political and economic dominance and in the importance of its capital market. The market is closely regulated by an agency of the federal government, the Securities and Exchange Commission (SEC). Those companies which seek a listing for their shares must comply with SEC regulations.

Within this framework of close regulation, there is considerable scope for application of professional judgement in accounting matters. Accounting standards are greater in volume and more detailed than those of almost any other country of the world, but they are set by an independent standard-setting body rather than by statute law. The standard-setting body has been well supported financially, and has therefore researched issues to an extent not feasible in other countries.

---

[1] Zeff (2007).

11.2 The country

The USA is made up of a land mass stretching from the Atlantic to the Pacific Ocean and includes Alaska and Hawaii as states. There are five major units of physical geography. The coastal plain of the east extends down the entire Atlantic coast. Behind the coastal plain rise the Appalachian Mountains in a succession of plateaux and ridges. Moving west, a fertile interior basin is drained by the Mississippi River. Further west again the Rocky Mountains extend from Canada to Colorado and finally the Pacific mountain system contains the Central Valley of California, a rich agricultural area. Mineral resources include iron ore and coal. Agricultural specialization varies according to location and climate. The population is 298 million and has a relatively low growth rate.

The economy showed growth of 3.4 per cent per annum over the period 1995–2005 and general standards of living are high (see Exhibit 11.1).

GDP is created more than three-quarters by services. Manufacturing industry provides only 18.5 per cent of GDP. In manufacturing industry, the highest single contribution is provided by machinery and transport but half of manufacturing industry is diversified into a range of activities. Manufacturing is largely concentrated in a belt reaching from New England to the Midwest. This area contains much of the steel industry, the automotive industry, specialized and electrical engineering and the textile and clothing trades.

The main export product is capital goods, excluding vehicles. The main export destination is Canada. Mexico is the most significant trading partner after Canada, with Japan third. The European Union (EU) takes 21 per cent of US exports, spread across all member states, with the UK being the highest at 4.3 per cent.

The main import product is industrial supplies. The origins of imports are primarily Canada and China. The EU supplies 18 per cent of imports, with Germany being the highest at 5.1 per cent.

Imports exceed exports, giving a negative balance of trade. Inflows of invisibles exceed outflows, reducing the overall negative balance.

From the *Financial Times* annual FT 500 survey there are 184 US companies in the top 500 world companies, measured by market capitalization. The top ten listed US companies are shown in Exhibit 11.2.

Exhibit 11.1 The USA: country profile

Population	298.2 m
Land mass	9,372,610 km^2
GDP per head	US$41,640
GDP per head in purchasing-power-parity	100
Origins of GDP:	%
Agriculture	1.0
Industry	18.5
Services	80.5
	%
Real GDP average annual growth 1995–2005	3.4
Inflation, average annual rate 2001–2006	2.6

Source: *The Economist Pocket World in Figures*, 2008 Edition, Profile Books Ltd.

Exhibit 11.2 Top ten listed US companies

Name	Market cap. $m	Rank in world	Listed UK	Sector
Exxon Mobil	429,566.7	1	Yes	Oil & Gas Producers
General Electric	363,611.3	2	Yes	General Industrials
Microsoft	272,911.7	3	No	Software & Computer Services
Citigroup	252,857.3	4	No	Banks
AT&T	246,206.3	5	No	Fixed Line Telecommunications
Bank of America	228,177.3	8	Yes	Banks
Procter & Gamble	199,293.8	13	No	Household Goods
Wal-Mart Stores	193,642.8	14	No	General Retailers
Altria	184,277.3	15	Yes	Tobacco
Pfizer	179,015.4	17	Yes	Pharmaceuticals & Biotechnology

Source: 'Survey FT 500', at 30 March 2007, www.tt.com.

11.3 Development of accounting regulation[2]

Accounting practices were to some extent imported from the UK by early pioneers establishing business practices in the USA.

11.3.1 Early regulation of accounting[3]

The American Association of Public Accountants, formed in 1886, and the Institute of Bookkeepers and Accountants encouraged a New York State law establishing the profession of Certified Public Accountant in 1896, and similar laws followed in other states. The Association established the *Journal of Accountancy* as a means of professional communication and published a terminology of accounting in 1915. In the early years, maintaining good standards of accountancy practice was very much in the hands of individual practitioners; companies generally did not disclose their accounting practices.

The stock market crash of 1929 caused fundamental changes in many aspects of US business practice. The initial approach was to continue allowing companies relative freedom of choice but to emphasize disclosure. The Securities and Exchange Commission (SEC) was formed by Congress, establishing its rules in 1934 under which it received for filing a copy of the accounts of each listed company. The SEC took a harder line that where listed companies filed accounts which did not have substantial authoritative support, those accounts would not be accepted – effectively, the SEC was deciding on accounting practice.

The American Institute of Accountants (AIA) Committee on Accounting Procedures issued Accounting Research Bulletins (ARBs) between 1939 and 1959. The AIA was renamed as the American Institute of Certified Public Accountants (AICPA) in 1957. Where the SEC felt there was an insufficiently strict approach in the ARBs, it would indicate

---

[2] Wolk *et al.* (2004), Ch. 3.

[3] Zeff (2003a); Zeff (2003b).

that filing of accounts might be refused even though the ARBs had been applied. This caused the AICPA to form the Accounting Principles Board (APB) in 1959. However, the ARBs survived in the form of ARB 43, which was a restatement and revision of the first 40 ARBs. Many parts of ARB 43 remain influential on accounting regulations today.[4]

The APB produced Accounting Research Studies and a series of APB Opinions. These did not dispel the controversies of the earlier periods and there were situations where the SEC indicated dissatisfaction with particular APB Opinions. More generally, it was felt that drafts of APB Opinions were not sufficiently exposed for comment and that resolution of some problems took too long a time. A major enquiry established by the AICPA (called the Wheat Committee) recommended in 1972 the formation of an independent Financial Accounting Standards Board (FASB). In particular, the Wheat Committee noted that the members of the APB were all CPAs, creating a potential conflict of interest; it recommended independence and the broader base of membership seen in the FASB today. A further enquiry, undertaken for the AICPA, by the Trueblood Study Group (AICPA, 1973), identified major objectives of financial statements which were subsequently taken by the FASB as guidance for its approach to standard setting. The present process is discussed further in section 11.7.1.

The FASB was guided in its work by a series of Statements of Financial Accounting Concepts (SFACs) issued in the late 1970s and early 1980s. These statements emphasize a balance sheet approach of defining and recognizing assets and liabilities. Owners' equity is the residual item in the equation. Changes in assets and liabilities must be reported through the income statement. This tends to lead to fluctuations in reported profit when compared with the alternative approach of matching income and expenses in a way that smoothes reported profit from one period to the next.

11.3.2 The Sarbanes–Oxley Act 2002

You have seen in section 3.2.3 how the Sarbanes–Oxley Act of 2002 has changed the procedures for maintaining confidence and assurance in accounting information. These changes have affected all aspects of the US capital market and have affected regulations and practices in many other countries. The Sarbanes–Oxley Act is seen as the most significant piece of securities legislation since the 1930s. This chapter gives more detail of the effect of Sarbanes–Oxley on accounting in the USA.

The accounting problems of Enron[5] emerged as headline news towards the end of 2001. In particular there were problems relating to 'special purpose entities' (SPEs). These SPEs are created to carry out a specific purpose or activity, such as a development project. The SPEs may carry tax benefits or attract a lower cost of financing. If the arrangement meets defined conditions, the SPE is 'off-balance-sheet'. That means the investment is recorded at cost and there is no consolidation. At the time of the Enron decline, the conditions for remaining off-balance-sheet were that the assets must be sold to the SPE and that an independent third party which holds a substantive capital investment (at least 3 per cent of the SPE's total capitalization) must control the SPE and carry the risks and rewards of the SPE's assets.

---

[4] Williams and Carcello (2007), CR.01–02.

[5] Herdman, R., December 2001, 'Testimony concerning recent events relating to Enron Corporation. Evidence before the Subcommittee on Capital Markets, Insurance and Government Sponsored Enterprises and the Subcommittee on Oversight and Investigation, Committee on Financial Services, US House of Representatives', www.sec.gov.news/testimony/1202tsrkh.htm.

In October 2001 Enron announced that shareholders' equity was reduced by $1.2bn because of accounting errors. When one of the SPEs was created, Enron had issued its own shares to the SPE. The intention was that the rising value of the Enron shares would hedge the risk of another investment held by the SPE. In return for the shares issued, Enron received a note (promise) from the SPE. Was this promise an asset for Enron? Initially it was recorded as an asset but in October 2001 Enron and its auditors decided that the item should be deducted from shareholders' equity. This was described at the time as correcting an 'accounting error'.

Enron made a further announcement, in November 2001, that it intended voluntarily to restate its financial statements for 1997 to 2000 and the first two quarters of 2001. The reason was that the company and its auditors had decided that three previously unconsolidated special purpose entities (SPEs) should have been consolidated under GAAP. Enron concluded that three entities no longer met these conditions and so should be consolidated with the group accounts. Such consolidation makes the extent of borrowings across the group clearer in the group balance sheet but also shows a higher level of gearing. These announcements, and others, caused a loss of market confidence that led rapidly to the company filing for bankruptcy.

The accounting concerns raised by these events caused the Act to require new disclosures in financial reports, relating to off-balance-sheet transactions. Chapter 4 explains in more detail how those disclosures are presented. More generally there were concerns about the emphasis placed on detailed rules. A rules-based approach asks, 'How do we stay inside the 3 per cent rule to avoid consolidation?' A principles-based approach asks, 'What gives a fair presentation of the relationship of this special purpose entity to the rest of the group?' The detailed standards and guidance within US GAAP lead down the rules-based approach. Sarbanes–Oxley asked the SEC to study the adoption by the US financial reporting system of a principles-based accounting system.

11.3.3 Principles versus rules[6]

The Sarbanes–Oxley instructions to the SEC on accounting reflected wider concerns of those who asked whether technical compliance with US accounting standards necessarily results in financial reporting that fairly reflects the underlying economic reality of reporting entities.

Three shortcomings of rules-based standards are:

- They contain numerous tests ('bright lines') that may be misused by financial engineers to comply with the letter but not the spirit of standards.
- They contain numerous exceptions ('scope exceptions') to the principles that purport to underlie the standards, resulting in inconsistencies of accounting treatment of transactions and events that have similar economic substance.
- They create a need for detailed implementation guidance, which in turn creates complexity and can even add to uncertainty about the application of the standard.

The SEC reported to the House of Representatives in 2003,[7] as required by Sarbanes–Oxley. The report concluded that neither US GAAP nor international accounting standards, as they existed at that time, were representative of the optimum type of principles-based

---

[6] Study pursuant to Section 108(d) of the Sarbanes–Oxley Act of 2002 on the adoption by the United States financial reporting system of a principles-based accounting system. Report prepared by the SEC.

[7] Ibid.

standard. The SEC had been pointed towards the IFRS as an example of a principles-based system but on close scrutiny it found some IFRS were rules-based standards, while others were principles only and overly general. The SEC defined an optimal standard as making a concise statement of accounting principle where the accounting objective has been specified as an integral part of the standard. There should be few, if any, exceptions or conceptual inconsistencies in the standard. The standard should provide an appropriate amount of implementation guidance. It should also be consistent with a coherent conceptual framework of financial reporting. The SEC called its vision the 'objectives-oriented approach'. It felt that a principles-only approach would provide insufficient guidance to make the standards operational. Increased reliance on the judgements of preparers and auditors could increase the likelihood of disagreements on accounting treatments. This in turn could lead to an increase in litigation.

In the view of the SEC, objectives-oriented standards charge management with the responsibility to capture the economic substance of transactions and events, but defined specifically within the objectives of the standard. The SEC felt that objectives-oriented standards may require less use of judgement than either rules-based or principles-only standards. This would improve consistency and compliance with the intent of the standards.

The SEC explained that an objectives-oriented system would lower the cost to investors and analysts of understanding the standards. They could focus on the objectives of the standard. Quality, consistency and timeliness of financial reporting could be improved. Convergence between US GAAP and international standards would be made easier because standard setters would agree on a principle more rapidly than they would agree on a highly detailed rule. Finally the SEC demonstrated that the FASB was already beginning the change to objectives-oriented standards.

The FASB responded in July 2004,[8] welcoming the SEC's study and agreeing with the recommendations. The FASB intends to make objectives and principles of standards clearer in writing future standards but also indicated that it intends to continue giving implementation guidance, examples and interpretive guidance. It also acknowledges that the SEC will continue to provide guidance as it deems necessary. The Board felt it would take several years for preparers and auditors to make the behavioural changes necessary to exercise professional judgement rather than request detailed rules. Actions had been taken, in consultation with AICPA and Emerging Issues Task Force (EITF), to make the FASB the only designated standard setter in the USA. This would reduce some of the proliferation of rules that was developing previously. The FASB hopes to create a searchable database of authoritative guidance but this will take some years. In the meantime the FASB has made its standards accessible by giving free-of-charge access on its website and making existing guidance more accessible. In working with the IASB on coordination projects, the FASB will replace rules-based standards with principles-based standards as they come up within the project.

11.3.4 Consolidated financial statements[9]

Consolidated financial statements have been published in the USA since the end of the nineteenth century. They are produced so commonly that single company statements are generally published only by entities having no subsidiaries. There is no law in the

---

[8] FASB (2004a).

[9] Williams and Carcello (2007), Ch. 4.

USA that mandates their publication; the requirement to publish has emerged within US GAAP, the most important requirements being ARB 51, dating from 1959, and the more recent SFAS 94. SFAS 94 is close to requiring that all majority-owned subsidiaries be consolidated. Other standards address particular aspects of consolidation and the totality sets the consolidation policy to be followed under US GAAP.

Business combinations are normally accounted for using the purchase (acquisition) method of accounting. On relatively rare occasions, where there is a uniting of interests by exchange of equity shares, the pooling of interests (merger) method has previously been required by APB Opinion 16. Pooling of interests allowed profits to be combined without calculation and amortization of goodwill.

In 1999 the FASB voted to end the pooling of interests method. This reflected the concern of the SEC that pooling of interests had been misused and should not continue. It also voted to reduce the maximum goodwill amortization period from 40 years to 20 years, aligning with the International Accounting Standards. There were objections from industry, led by financial executives through FEI (see section 1.3.5), with appeals to Congress.[10] The Chair of the Senate Committee investigating the issue proposed a periodic impairment test as a better solution. Further actions in the Senate threatened to delay progress for the FASB. This episode provides an example of the strong political pressure that can be exerted on accounting in the USA. The outcome was that in July 2001 the FASB produced SFAS 141, banning pooling of interests in business combinations initiated after that date, and SFAS 142, setting a goodwill impairment test rather than amortization over a specific asset life.[11] SFAS 141 'Business Combinations' supersedes APB Opinion 16. SFAS 142 'Goodwill and Other Intangible Assets' supersedes APB Opinion 17.

Also in 1999 the FASB consulted on changes to a consolidation policy focused on the idea of control, which would be a significant change from the traditional approach based on majority ownership. At the end of 1999 the FASB reaffirmed a commitment to the idea of control and promised a Statement in due course. However, in January 2001 the FASB announced that there was not sufficient support to proceed with a standard.

Joint venture accounting has not been addressed specifically, although it is included in the FASB's long-term project on consolidation. The present treatment is that joint ventures are accounted for using equity accounting. Proportionate consolidation is generally not used because the SEC objects; however, the SEC has made an exception for extractive industries such as oil and gas.

11.4 Institutions

11.4.1 Political and economic system

The USA is a federal republic of separate states. Each state has its own Constitution, but the separate states unite under a federal government operating under a federal constitution. The federal government has the power to impose taxes, the responsibility for national defence and foreign relations, the power to create a national currency and the authority to set country-wide laws regulating commercial and business practice. States also have power to regulate business practice.

---

[10] Zeff (2002), pp. 51–52.
[11] Williams and Carcello (2007), 23.09–23.10.

The federal constitution divides the federal government into the executive, the legislative and the judicial branches. The President of the USA leads the executive branch, while the legislative branch consists of the Congress, the House of Representatives and the Senate. The judicial branch is led by the Supreme Court and, below it, a system of federal courts. Each of the three branches of the US Constitution is independent but there are checks and balances. The President has a power of veto over legislation, but the veto may be overcome by a two-thirds majority of both the House of Representatives and the Senate. The judiciary may declare acts of the executive unconstitutional.

The President is elected every four years, and only permitted two terms in total. The members of the House of Representatives and Senate are also elected. One-third of Senate members are elected by rotation every two years; House of Representatives members are elected every two years. Depending on swings in political mood, it is possible for the majority in the Senate and the House of Representatives to be of a different political party from the President.

The economic system is that of the open market. Historically, the nature of the economic system has developed and changed as the political climate has changed and as technological change has allowed exploitation of new opportunities. The USA has always attracted high wealth in terms of human capital, more than once because persecution elsewhere drove individuals to seek freedom there. Development of the railways opened up the country to industrial production, which has now declined in relation to service industry, though it remains a strong minority element of the economy.

Since the early 1980s the US economy has shown the highest growth rate of GDP of the G7 countries; it has been much higher than the OECD average. Following the crash of some 'dot.com' companies in 2000 there was very little growth of GDP in 2001, but after that it started to grow again, driven by household and government spending. The spending was encouraged by low interest rates.[12] However, since 2004 the trend in growth rate of GDP has slowed, mainly because of tighter limits on how quickly employment can grow.[13] Although the USA holds the first position for size of the economy, China is moving up the league tables very rapidly.[14]

11.4.2 Legal system

The political doctrine of separation of powers in the federal constitution means that business may be affected by each of the executive, the legislative and the judicial arms. Independent regulatory agencies are also in existence as a fourth arm to the processes of the legal system. However, the Chair and chief accountant of the SEC are appointed by the executive (President). (Regulatory agencies are under the rule of the executive, and so there is not a fourth arm to the Constitution; however, the regulatory agencies are approved by Congress.)

Legislation is introduced through committees of each House of Congress. If compromise is required to meet the requirements of each separate House, it will be negotiated in committee before being submitted to the full House of Representatives and Senate. Implementation of the law through the courts begins in federal districts, each having a federal court called a District Court which applies federal law. Appeal from the District

---

[12] 'Finance and Economics: off the bottom', *The Economist*, London, 3 July 2004, 372(8382), p. 82.

[13] OECD (2007).

[14] Leaders: 'Switching engines; the world economy', *The Economist*, London, 24 February 2007, 382(8517), p. 16.

Court is made to the Courts of Appeal, and the Supreme Court reviews decisions of the lower federal courts.

The federal government has general regulatory powers, but much regulation of business enterprises is by state law. One general theme of the federal legislative approach is 'truth in securities', leading to regulation of those who issue shares to the public. Another is free and open competition, leading to what is called 'antitrust legislation'. This makes illegal any restraint of trade created by unfair business combinations, including those established on the basis of what some might regard as mutual trust but others would see as conspiracy.

The legal system of the USA is that of the common law family but has developed uniquely US characteristics; it is therefore not surprising to find similarly unique aspects to the development of accounting law in the USA.

11.4.2.1 Federal and state law

Federal law deals with matters such as the registration of securities, taxation and antitrust law. Powers not specifically delegated to the USA by the Constitution are reserved to the states. State laws apply to matters such as enforcement of contract, agency, conveyancing, bills of exchange, and debtor–creditor relationships; they also overlap with federal law on issues such as securities, taxation and antitrust law.

There is some element of competition between federal and state law. This leads also to interesting competition between states in attracting businesses. Many leading companies are registered in Delaware. This is because, in 1913, the state legislature of New Jersey introduced a restrictive approach to corporations. The corporations transferred their registration to Delaware, which had a flexible incorporation law. Delaware has subsequently developed expertise in matters of business law. The restriction in New Jersey was short-lived but the corporations stayed in Delaware.

One important feature of US law is its Freedom of Information Acts, which give access to government papers that might in other countries be locked away. The openness of practices of governmental administration leads to openness in non-governmental organizations (NGOs) also. Information lodged with the government later becomes available as a government paper.

11.4.2.2 Types of business organization

Businesses may operate as sole traders, partnerships or corporations. Corporations are established and governed by the law of the state in which they are incorporated. A foreign company may incorporate in any state, regardless of where the production facilities and management are located. Incorporation is achieved by filing articles of incorporation and bylaws with the relevant state official. State laws will cover matters such as the initial capital required; classes and powers of voting stock; corporate powers; the number of directors and their duties; payment of dividends; requirements for accounting records; and the cessation of the company. A corporation may acquire and hold its own shares.

All corporations have a board of directors elected by the shareholders and responsible to them for the running of the company. Directors and officers have duties of loyalty and care to the corporation. Any shareholder has the right to sue on behalf of the corporation where there has been a perceived breach of duty. The corporation is a taxable entity. The USA has many more unlisted than listed companies. The focus of this chapter is on listed companies which are regulated by the SEC. In particular, the SEC prescribes the reporting requirements for published accounting information.

The chief executive officer (CEO) is always a member of the board of a company. The CEO is the focus of attention as the person driving the company; there is relatively little press interest in the directors. Typically a CEO will serve for six to eight years. The directors elect the Chair of the board, although in many cases the CEO is the Chair. Active management is delegated by the directors to paid officials. Directors focus on policy issues.

11.4.2.3 The SEC[15]

The Securities Act 1933 has the intention to create 'truth in securities', aiming to provide information for investors and prohibit misrepresentation. Any company planning to offer its securities for sale must register with the SEC, which imposes regulations based on registration forms requiring extensive disclosure. Domestic US companies must prepare an annual registration form referred to as '10-K'. Foreign companies seeking to offer securities for sale in the USA must present an annual registration form called a '20-F' and in some cases must restate their financial statements using US GAAP or provide a reconciliation statement. The essential power of the SEC lies in its authority to reject the filing of accounts: without that filing a company cannot continue to have a stock exchange listing. This gives the SEC effective control over accounting practice without being directly a standard-setting body.

The SEC is a federal agency, and has a strong tradition of being activist in its work. There are detailed rules on what information should be provided, where it should be lodged and where it should be sent. The SEC largely controls information issued by companies. It interacts with state law on some matters of specific disclosure but is prevented by the Supreme Court from encroaching too much on state law. The most important disclosure regulations are Regulation S-X, covering financial statements, and Regulation S-K, covering non-financial disclosure about the operations of the business. These are voluminous, and can be found on the SEC's website, www.sec.gov (see also Chapter 4).

The SEC monitors all trading on the stock exchanges. It has an electronic filing system called EDGAR (Electronic Data Gathering Analysis and Retrieval) whereby companies may lodge information electronically. Access to the EDGAR filings is available through the World Wide Web.

The SEC was one of the parties that came under criticism in the many comments on Enron. With its 'activist' reputation, how could the scrutiny by SEC staff have failed to notice that all was not well with the financial statements lodged with them? The Sarbanes–Oxley Act 2002 directed the SEC to take specific actions in relation to its oversight procedures (see section 3.2.3) and in relation to its rules on disclosures (see section 15.3).

The SEC also continues to update its rules on its own initiative. In 2002 it issued a rule requiring all but the smallest domestic listed companies to accelerate filing dates and to require disclosures on website access to reports. From 2002 the filing period for the annual report was reduced progressively, over a period of three years, from 90 days to 60 days. The quarterly report deadline was similarly reduced from 45 days to 35 days. Companies subject to these changes were also required to disclose in their annual reports the company's website address, information on whether the company makes available free of charge, on or through its website, filings such as the 10-K (annual), 10-Q (quarterly) and 8-K (current information) reports.

---

[15] www.sec.gov.

One of the problems identified by the SEC in its own internal review is that it had developed a reactive culture that failed to identify danger ahead of time. It was generating one-third of its investigations itself while the remainder were initiated by external sources such as complaints or 'whistleblowers'. The SEC has set a more proactive target of reviewing one-third of reporting companies each year, focusing on the largest. An Office of Risk Assessment was established in 2004 to identify and prioritize current risks.

In 2007 the SEC established the SEC Advisory Committee on Improvements to Financial Reporting to examine the US financial reporting system with the goals of reducing unnecessary complexity and making information more useful and understandable for investors[16] (see also section 11.7.1.6).

11.4.3 Corporate governance

Corporate governance, as a means of promoting trust, loyalty and commitment among the various parties, has grown in the USA over many years but its precise nature has depended on the concerns of the time regarding the behaviour of corporate entities. The most significant *de jure* change to corporate governance regulation in the USA is seen in the Sarbanes–Oxley Act of 2002 (see section 3.2.3). Has it had an impact *de facto*? In a survey of 500 companies for the Financial Executives International, second quarter 2004, 49 per cent of respondents said there was no noticeable change; 29 per cent had reduced non-audit business with the audit firm and were using other firms; and the quality of internal control had increased significantly in 23 per cent of respondents.

In the 1990s the SEC began to question the way in which some companies appeared to 'manage' their profit figures by techniques such as overstating restructuring charges, using provisions in acquisition accounting to overstate future earnings, recognizing sales before completion or when the customer has the right to reverse the transaction, and deferring expenses as assets (see section 3.2 on the numbers game).

11.4.3.1 Audit committees

One result of the SEC's concern about earnings management was the formation of the Blue Ribbon Committee on Improving the Effectiveness of Corporate Audits. The Committee reported in 1999 with recommendations for change which included requiring listed companies to have an audit committee on which at least three directors were independent and financially literate. New rules on audit committees were then produced variously by the SEC, the New York Stock Exchange, the American Stock Exchange, the National Association of Securities Dealers and the FASB. The SEC in particular required a declaration of the independence of the audit committee, the use of an audit committee charter, and the inclusion in the annual proxy statement of a report by the audit committee.

However, the presence of audit committees conforming to these rules did not appear to prevent the major corporate collapses of 2001 and 2002, with the result that Sarbanes–Oxley legislated further on the role and composition of audit committees. Key points were:

● The audit committee has responsibility for the appointment, compensation and oversight of any registered public accounting firm employed to perform audit services.

---

[16] http://www.sec.gov/about/offices/oca/acifr.shtml.

- The audit committee must have a procedure to receive, retain and treat complaints received by the company about accounting, internal controls and auditing.
- The audit committee must have the authority to take independent legal advice or other advice as it deems necessary.
- The company must give appropriate funding to the audit committee.
- The audit committee must approve non-audit services provided by the audit firm.
- The external auditor must report to the audit committee on all critical accounting policies and practices to be used, all the alternative GAAP discussed with management, and the implications of the choices made.
- Audit committee members must be a member of the board of directors, but otherwise be independent.
- Companies must disclose whether at least one member of the audit committee is a 'financial expert'.

The New York Stock Exchange issued new rules in August 2002.[17] These stated that an audit committee must fulfil a list of functions, as follows:

- Have at least three independent directors, all financially literate and of whom at least one has accounting or financial management expertise.
- Have a formal written charter and code of business conduct, approved by the board of directors.
- Assist the board's oversight of integrity and compliance of the financial statements.
- Hire and fire the external auditors.
- Obtain and review a report by the independent auditors, at least annually, describing the company's internal quality control procedures, any material issues raised about quality control in previous reviews, and all relationships between the independent auditor and the company.
- Discuss the annual financial statements, quarterly financial statements and management's discussion and analysis (MD&A) disclosures with management and with the independent auditor.
- Discuss earnings press releases and earnings guidance provided to analysts and rating agencies.
- Meet separately, periodically, with management, with internal auditors and with independent auditors.
- Review, with the independent auditor, any audit problems and the response of management.
- Set clear policies for hiring employees or former employees of the independent auditor's firm.
- Report regularly to the board of directors.
- Carry out annual performance evaluation of the work of the board of directors.

This is clearly a demanding list of activities and makes the work of the independent non-executive director more burdensome.

11.4.3.2 Institutional shareholders

The emphasis on 'stakeholders' as a wider constituency encourages corporations to be accountable and report to a wider group. In practice, the market for stocks and shares

---

[17] Listed company manual section 303A.00 Corporate Governance Standards.

remains the primary mechanism for corporate governance. In particular, it is noticeable that major institutional shareholders will use their voting power at company meetings to express their views on corporate governance and are aware that they are expected to show an element of social responsibility as well as safeguarding their position as investors.

11.4.3.3 Structure of the board of directors

Members of the board of directors have wide-ranging backgrounds, and the company's operations may be widely dispersed. Directors receive information quite frequently because of the obligation on listed companies to report quarterly to shareholders. The board of directors meets relatively infrequently, delegating detailed matters to committees of the board. These might cover remuneration packages, finance, public policy, planning, human resources and similar matters. The most important are the audit committee, the compensation committee, the nominating committee and the executive committee.

It is a condition of stock exchange listing that a corporation has an audit committee to review all aspects of external and internal auditing. The audit committee must comprise independent (non-executive) directors. Compensation committees also comprise the independent directors and decide the remuneration packages of senior executives including the CEO. Nominating committees screen policy proposals put forward by the CEO and offer advice on the composition and membership of the board of directors. Executive committees deal with urgent business between meetings of the main board. For corporations progressing at a steady rate, the committee structure is the effective form of governance and the board of directors takes an oversight role, becoming more active in intervention only where a crisis is looming.

11.4.3.4 Remuneration of CEOs

There are often references to the package of remuneration available to the CEO which, in the USA, is referred to as 'compensation'. It means the basic salary paid in cash plus all the other benefits received such as membership of a health care scheme; use of a company car; contributions to a retirement benefit package; bonus payments related to corporate performance and profits; and options (rights) to purchase ordinary shares at an agreed price over a stated period of time. The long-term performance-related aspects are a much greater proportion of the total package than in other countries. In 2006 CEO remuneration on average consisted of 16 per cent salary, 26 per cent bonus and 58 per cent long-term incentives.[18] There was a strong correlation between cash payment (salary plus bonus) and company financial performance.

This compensation package has the potential to make the CEO self-seeking where the profits of the company are threatened or the CEO's position in the business is at risk. Restricting the compensation package might reduce the CEO's entrepreneurial spirit, and so the present emphasis in corporate governance is on disclosure to shareholders of the full compensation package and the use of a compensation committee comprising the non-executive members of the board of directors. The requirement to produce a

---

[18] The Wall Street Journal/Mercer Human Resource Consulting 2006 *CEO Compensation Survey and Trends*, April 2007, www.mercerHR.com.

Compensation Discussion and Analysis[19] since 2006 has led to more active shareholder interest in questioning compensation packages.

11.4.4 Taxation system

The US Congress passes the laws that govern income taxes. The legislation is contained in the Internal Revenue Code and administered by the Internal Revenue Service (IRS). Generally, taxes are imposed on each company separately, but an affiliated group of domestic corporations may file a consolidated return and be taxed as one corporation. It is relatively unusual to find a country allowing tax to be based on the group as a whole.

11.4.4.1 Corporate income tax

Taxable income is determined as the excess of taxable revenue over deductible expenses. The general rule is that all revenue is taxable and expenses are deductible provided they are ordinary and necessary. The resulting taxable profit may differ from the accounting profit because the tax code is intended to generate revenue for the government in a manner consistent with specific social and economic goals, while financial accounting information is intended to be useful to investors and lenders. US corporations are taxable on their worldwide income.

Accrual accounting is used for tax purposes in the USA. However, some expenses such as losses on sales of assets (e.g. buildings) must be realized in cash before they are allowed to be deductible. The tax rules also cover revenue recognition, tax rates and tax credits. Some revenue and expenses are not taxable – a fine imposed for an illegal activity, for example, would not be allowable as an expense. Timing differences occur where the expense is recognized differently under tax rules compared with accounting practice, due to accelerated depreciation, delayed revenue recognition and delayed recognition of expenses.

Accelerated depreciation is used for tax purposes but not necessarily for accounting profit. Under the Modified Accelerated Cost Recovery System, assets are placed in various groups defined by asset life; a depreciation schedule is available for each class. The effect of the acceleration is to write off substantially more than 50 per cent of the cost in the first half of the asset's life: the percentage written off in the early years is greatest for the shortest life group.

An example of delayed revenue is where the business uses the percentage of completion method to report contract profits for accounting purposes but uses the completed contract method for taxation purposes. An example of delayed expenses is a provision for repairs under warranty where the tax rules require the actual repair cost to be incurred.

Companies pay federal taxes and local state taxes, the local taxes being deductible in determining income for federal tax purposes. The federal government may give tax credits, which are direct reductions of the income tax itself, in contrast to tax deductions which reduce the level of taxable income.

11.4.4.2 Tax on distributions

Dividends paid by domestic corporations to US citizens and residents are taxable to such individuals. Dividend income paid to a non-resident alien is generally subject to a withholding tax.

---

[19] http://www.sec.gov/news/press/2006/2006-123.htm.

11.4.5 Corporate financing system

11.4.5.1 Equity investors

The US stock exchanges[20] provide an important primary market for raising new capital. They attract listings by foreign registrants which seek to raise capital in the US market. The stock exchanges are also a secondary market for the purchase and sale of shares already in issue. At the end of 2006 there were 2,280 companies having their common stock (ordinary shares) listed on the New York Stock Exchange (NYSE), of which 451 were foreign registrants. On NASDAQ there were 3,133 listed, of which 321 were foreign registrants.[21] NYSE acquired Euronext N.V. in 2007.

The NYSE share ownership survey[22] showed that in 1998 households remain a strong influence on the US stock market (see Exhibit 11.3) although the percentage was reducing. (Compare this table with the data for some other countries in Exhibit 6.5.) The survey also shows that there was a relatively low percentage of 'rest of the world' investors. Listed US companies were mainly directing their information at US investors.

Exhibit 6.3 indicates the relative size of the US stock market in relation to those of Europe. New York is now ahead of London in the number of international companies listed. For many years New York had relatively few international listings and this was attributed to the strict reporting requirements in the USA, explained later. It might appear that companies are conquering their fears of the US regulatory system. Exhibit 6.4 shows that the US and Japanese markets together dominate world stock markets by size.

The two major national stock exchanges are the New York Stock Exchange (NYSE) and the American Stock Exchange (AMEX), and there are five regional stock exchanges. There is an over-the-counter (OTC) market for unlisted stocks. Dealers in the OTC market are regulated by the National Association of Securities Dealers which uses an electronic Automatic Quotation system (NASDAQ). A stock may be listed on an exchange

Exhibit 11.3	Percentage of corporate stock in the USA owned by investor sectors, 1990 and 1998

Ownership sector	1990	1998
Direct Household Holdings	51.0%	41.1%
Indirect Household Holdings, through personal trusts and estates, life insurance companies, private pension funds and mutual funds	21.0%	27.5%
Total Household	72.0%	68.3%
Rest of the World	6.9%	7.2%
State and Local Government Retirement Plans	7.6%	11.4%
Defined Benefit Private Pension Plans	8.8%	5.6%
Mutual Funds not owned by Households	1.5%	5.0%
Other Non-Household Investors	3.2%	2.2%

Source: From Table 16, *Shareownership 2000*, NYSE.

---

[20] www.nysedata.com/factbook/main.asp.

[21] www.world-exchanges.org/.

[22] *Shareownership 2000*, NYSE, www.nyse.com. Unfortunately this biennial survey was discontinued after 2000.

and traded in the OTC market. Trading such stocks in the OTC is called the 'third market'. Transactions may occur directly between buyers and sellers in what is called the 'fourth market'.

The stock exchanges are approved and regulated by the SEC in order to ensure the market's fairness, competitiveness and efficiency. There was concern in the past that investors were not necessarily receiving the best price, and trading rules are now in place to ensure fairness.

11.4.5.2 Bank lending

Commercial banks are prevented from owning controlling blocks of shares in non-banking companies. They may not underwrite issues of shares or link with investment banks which do so. The basis of these restrictions is historical: the banks were blamed significantly for the stock market crash of 1929. Banks do act as trustees, holding shares on behalf of clients, but the banks prefer the clients to exercise their voting rights directly. The main financial link between banks and corporations is therefore that of lender and borrower. However, the concept of 'relationship banking', where the bank provides services beyond the loan facility, is relatively unfamiliar; the bank may not always have the closer knowledge of the business which might be found in some continental European companies.

11.4.5.3 Mergers and acquisitions[23]

The ability of corporations to merge is restricted by antitrust legislation which seeks to prevent monopoly positions arising. Where a merger or acquisition is not prevented by antitrust law, the process of acquisition is regulated by state law and federal law. There is no equivalent of the voluntary self-regulation applied by the Takeover Panel in the UK. The SEC requires that acquisitions of 5 per cent or more of voting shares are to be disclosed within ten days; changes of more than 1 per cent thereafter must be notified. Tender offers are regulated by the SEC under the Williams Act 1968. Under a tender offer, the prospective purchaser offers a price for a specified quantity of shares. The company issues the tendered shares at the best price offered.

Contested takeover bids have led to defensive practices which may not be in the best interests of all shareholders – 'Poison pills' allow management, at short notice, to place blocks of shares with friendly persons in order to block a bid; 'Crown jewels' provisions place a desirable asset with a friendly corporation elsewhere; 'Greenmail' means paying a price above the market price for shares held by an investor who is threatening to start a takeover bid; 'Supermajority' means requiring a 75 per cent majority vote to remove directors. All these tactics would be forbidden under the UK Takeover Code. They are contested from time to time under state law, but survive or emerge in a modified form.

11.4.6 The accounting profession

The historical development of the accounting profession has been described in an earlier section. It no longer has a direct role in setting accounting standards, but remains the professional organization to which many of those involved in standard setting belong. The AICPA retains exclusive authority in the private sector for promulgating auditing rules. The Auditing Standards Board (ASB) of the AICPA issues Statements on Auditing

---

[23] Sudarsanam (2003).

| Exhibit 11.4 | Membership of the AICPA, 2006 |

Total membership	330,525
Public accounting	40.4%
Business and industry	43.6%
Local, state and federal government	3.8%
Education	2.3%
Retired and Miscellaneous	9.9%

Source: AICPA website, www.aicpa.org.

Standards, and members of the AICPA must adhere to all applicable Statements on Auditing Standards in conducting audits. Audit is required by the SEC in the case of listed companies. For other companies, it is voluntary or else carried out at the request of a third party such as a bank lender.

The AICPA has sought to curb what is sometimes called 'opinion shopping', which refers to the practice where listed companies offer the audit to the firm which gives the most sympathetic interpretation of GAAP. As well as strengthening professional standards of conduct, the AICPA has sponsored a major enquiry into the needs of users of financial reporting. The result of this enquiry, referred to as the Jenkins Report, was published in 1994 and is explained in section 11.7.1.6.

On a wider spectrum than the AICPA, specialization has developed in aspects of the accountancy profession. Specialist professional examinations in the USA now recognize Certified Public Accountants; Certified Internal Auditors; Certified Management Accountants; and Chartered Financial Analysts. The AICPA itself has membership divisions reflecting various activities, being divided almost equally between public practice (accountancy firms) and industry, as shown in Exhibit 11.4.

In the 1990s there were six leading accounting firms in the USA, often referred to as the 'big 6', which undertook the audits of some 97 per cent of companies listed on the NYSE. These were Andersen Worldwide, Ernst & Young, Deloitte & Touche, KPMG Peat Marwick, Coopers & Lybrand and Price Waterhouse. Merger to form Pricewaterhouse-Coopers (PwC) led to the 'big 5' and the dissolution of Andersen in the aftermath of Enron reduced this to the 'big 4'. These firms still carry out most of the audits of listed companies, so audit activity has become increasingly concentrated.

11.5 External influences

The USA has developed by importing know-how and expertise. That includes accounting, which travelled to the USA with early pioneers from the UK. Accounting practice in the USA has subsequently been imbued with increasingly national characteristics. (Section 6.8.3 provides more details on this process of import and export of accounting ideas.) In more recent years, the USA has exported its brand of accounting to countries under its economic influence, particularly Canada, Central and South America, and countries in South East Asia (see also Case study 6.2). Canada, Chile and Mexico are examples of countries falling under the US sphere of influence.[24]

---

[24] CICA (2002).

US influence on Japanese accounting is discussed in Chapter 16. One particularly significant export has been the idea of setting standards through a professional route rather than by government regulation, culminating in an independent standard-setting body.

As a founder member of IASC, the USA has had a significant influence on global accounting practices. The IASB Framework for the Preparation and Presentation of Financial Statements (1989) owes much of its development and direction to the prior work of the FASB published earlier in the 1980s as a series of Statements of Financial Accounting Concepts (SFACs). Opinions are divided as to whether the US influence has been excessive or not.[25] The transition to the IASB, outlined in Chapter 10, indicates a strong continuing role for US influence.

11.6 Comparison with IFRS

As explained earlier, the regulation of accounting practice lies jointly in the hands of the FASB and the SEC. They have different sets of regulations but the SEC, in accepting filing of financial statements, effectively endorses the authority of the independent FASB. Chapter 10 explains the role of the SEC as a member of the International Organization of Securities Commissions (IOSCO), which has accepted a core set of IASB standards as common usage for international companies seeking international listings.

11.6.1 Moving towards acceptance of IFRS

US interest in international accounting was demonstrated by an Act of Congress, signed by the President in October 1996, confirming the importance of IAS in attracting foreign corporations to gain access to listing in the US markets. To that end, Congress urged the SEC to support vigorously the development of high-quality IAS. In 2005 the SEC agreed to a roadmap which committed the SEC to eliminating the US GAAP reconciliation requirement, with the intention that eligible firms listing on US exchanges could choose whether to report under IFRS or US GAAP.[26] A target date of 2009 was set, although this initially appeared to be a target rather than a commitment from the SEC. However, the political interest became stronger, and in April 2007 the political leaders of the EU and USA (Chancellor Merkel and President Bush) signed a Framework for Advancing Transatlantic Economic Integration between the EU and the USA. This led the SEC to announce that, for the financial year ending after 15 November 2007, reconciliation would not be required for IFRS as issued by the IASB. A condition for acceptance in the USA is for the US regulators to be satisfied that IFRS are applied and interpreted faithfully, consistently and thoroughly across different jurisdictions and across different industrial sectors.[27] In particular the SEC staff review filings. In 2006 they reviewed the annual reports of more than 100 foreign private issuers containing financial statements prepared for the first time using IFRS.[28] The staff wrote to some companies asking for

---

[25] Flower (1997); Cairns (1997).

[26] SEC Chairman Cox, International Financial Reporting Standards Roadmap Roundtable, 6 March 2007.

[27] Remarks before the Federation of European Accountants: International Financial Reporting Standards and the US Capital Market, Ethiopis Tafara, Director, Office of International Affairs, US Securities and Exchange Commission, Brussels, 1 December 2005.

[28] Staff observations in the review of IFRS financial statements, July 2, 2007, www.sec.gov/divisions/corfin/ifrs_staffobservations.htm.

additional information, they asked other companies to revise their financial statement presentation and they asked others to enhance the disclosure. The letters to the companies and their replies are all available on the SEC website. The main areas of comment were as follows.

11.6.1.1 Assertion of compliance with IFRS

The SEC staff looked for an explicit and unreserved statement of compliance with IFRS. Most auditors gave opinions on compliance with the version of IFRS accepted by the jurisdiction of the company's home country. Most companies gave this same assertion but also said they complied with IFRS as issued by the IASB.

11.6.1.2 Manner of presentation

The SEC staff found different income statement formats used by companies in the same jurisdiction and in the same industry. The staff asked for clarification about the description of some income statement subtotals and some additional calculations of earnings per share.

11.6.1.3 Common control entities

The SEC staff observed a variety of treatment of common control entities. This is because IFRS 3 did not at that stage cover common control companies.

11.6.1.4 Transactions for which there is no IFRS coverage

Where there is no relevant IFRS coverage, IAS 8 requires companies to look to the most recent pronouncements of their own standard-setting bodies. Where this was done the SEC staff asked for a specific statement of which standard-setting body pronouncements had been used.

11.6.1.5 Scattering of disclosures

The SEC staff found that some disclosures required by the IFRS were located in different places, including locations outside the audited financial statements. Comments were made on missing or unclear items.

11.6.2 Similarities and differences, IFRS and US GAAP

The IASB and FASB have jointly undertaken a short-term project to eliminate some differences between IFRS and US GAAP. Several differences were eliminated in a revision of IFRS in 2003, taking effect from 2005 as the 'stable platform' for implementation of IFRS in the EU. This 'short-term convergence project' was the result of an agreement between the two Boards in September 2002 called the 'Norwalk agreement' (from the place of their meeting). It is essential to refer to a source of information such as the 'iasplus' website[29] for updated briefings on how this project has progressed. Exhibit 11.5 shows the position at March 2007 indicating some of the main similarities and differences and the operation of the short-term and longer term convergence processes.

---

[29] www.iasplus.com.

Exhibit 11.5 Comparison of accounting practices in the USA with requirements of IFRS: key similarities and differences

DISCLOSURE AND PRESENTATION

General aspects

IFRS 1 First-time adoption of IFRS

IFRS 1: The general principle is that companies must make full retrospective application of all IFRS in place at the time of first adoption, unless IFRS 1 allows specific exemptions	US GAAP: There is no specific standard but the same general principle applies, unless specific exemptions are allowed in an SFAS

IAS 1 Presentation of Financial Statements

IAS 1: Requires specific line items but no overall format specified	US GAAP: Separate standards and SEC rules specify particular line items but no overall format specified
IAS 1: One year comparative financial information required	US GAAP: SEC regulations for public listed companies require two years' comparative financial information

Specific aspects

IAS 7 Cash Flow Statements

IAS 7: Three main sections to cash flow statement, direct and indirect methods allowed	US GAAP: SFAS 95 generally in agreement with IAS 7, some detailed differences on classification of interest received and paid, and overdrafts in cash

IAS 8 Accounting Policies, Changes in Accounting Estimates and Errors

IAS 8: Changes in accounting policy are accounted for as an adjustment to prior periods in the opening balance of retained earnings	US GAAP: SFAS 154, taking effect for accounting periods starting after 15 December 2005, has a similar approach, eliminating a previous US difference

IFRS 5 Non-current Assets Held for Sale and Discontinued Operations

IFRS 5: A discontinued operation is a reportable segment or a major component of one	USA GAAP: SFAS 144 is generally in agreement. USA is less restrictive on definitions of 'discontinued', more disclosures required

*IAS 14/ IFRS 8 Segment Reporting**

IAS 14: Requirement for primary and secondary segments to be identified, with detailed disclosure requirements (see also Chapter 5) IFRS 8 (effective from 2009): Segment information is based on the information to be identified according to information used by management to make decisions (see also Chapter 5)	US GAAP: SFAS 131 is similar to IFRS 8, less rigorous than IAS 14 on secondary disclosure

▶

Exhibit 11.5 *(Continued)*

IAS 24 Related Party Disclosures

IAS 24: Requires disclosure of nature and extent of transactions with related parties, nature of relationship and the amounts involved. Compensation of management personnel is disclosed in total and by categories of compensation	US GAAP: SFAS 57 is generally in agreement with IAS 24. Management compensation is not required by any SFAS but is required of listed companies by SEC regulations

IAS 33 Earnings per Share

IAS 33: Requires basic and diluted income from continuous operations per share; net profit or loss per share	US GAAP: SFAS 128 requires basic and diluted income from continuing operations, discontinued operations, extraordinary items, cumulative effect of change in accounting policy, net profit or loss per share

IAS 34 Interim Financial Reporting

IAS 34: Not mandatory but, if used, interim period is a discrete reporting period	US GAAP: If interim reporting is required by SEC, APB 28 regards interim period as an integral part of the full year

ASSET RECOGNITION AND MEASUREMENT

IAS 2 Inventories
ARB 43 is generally in agreement with IAS 2 but there are some differences, e.g.:

IAS 2: LIFO is prohibited IAS 2: Reversal of inventory write-downs is required if certain criteria are met	US GAAP: LIFO is permitted US GAAP: Prohibits reversal of inventory write-downs US GAAP does not prohibit costs of idle capacity and spoilage in inventory*

IAS 16 Property, Plant and Equipment
ARB 43, APB 6 are generally in agreement

IAS 16: Measurement may be at historical cost or revalued amount IAS 16: Major overhaul or inspection is part of cost of asset IAS 16: Residual value is current net selling price, assuming asset is already of the age and condition expected at end of useful life	US GAAP: Revaluation is not permitted US GAAP: Allows choice: treat as expense, defer and amortize until next overhaul; add to cost of asset US GAAP: Residual value is discounted present value of expect proceeds of future sale

IAS 36 Impairment of Assets*

IAS 21: Impairment is recorded when carrying amount of an asset exceeds the higher of the value-in-use (discounted present value of expected cash flows) and fair value less costs to sell	SFAS 121: Impairment is recorded when carrying amount of an asset exceeds the expected future cash flows on an undiscounted basis

IAS 23 Borrowing Costs*

IAS 23: Permits capitalization in some circumstances but does not require this	SFAS 34: Requires capitalization in some circumstances

▶

IAS 38 Research and Development Costs*

IAS 38: Capitalize development costs if certain conditions are met	SFAS 2: Development expenditure may not be capitalized

IAS 38 Intangible Assets
US GAAP generally in agreement on applying an impairment test.

IAS 38: Revaluation permitted if the intangible asset trades in an active market	SFAS 142: Revaluation not permitted

IAS 40 Investment Property*

IAS 40: Option of historical cost model with depreciation or fair value model with value changes through profit and loss	ARB 43: Fixed assets recognized at cost and must be depreciated

LIABILITY RECOGNITION AND MEASUREMENT

IAS 10 Events after the Balance Sheet Date
US GAAP generally in agreement on distinguishing adjusting and non-adjusting events.

IAS 37 Provisions, Contingent Liabilities and Contingent Assets

IAS 37: Best estimate to settle the obligation. Discounting required	SFAS 5: Most probable outcome to settle the obligation. Tends towards low end of range of possible amounts Discounting only allowed where timing of cash flows is fixed and determinable
IAS 37: Recognize restructuring provisions if a detailed plan is announced	IAS 27: Recognize restructuring provision if a transaction or event leaves little or no discretion to avoid future transfer of assets to settle the liability

IAS 12 Income Taxes
IAS 12 and SFAS 109 are in broad agreement but there are differences in details that are being addressed in the short-term convergence project.

IAS 17 Leases
SFAS 13 is generally in agreement with IAS 17. Both distinguish finance leases from operating leases.

IAS 17: Gain on sale and leaseback of a finance lease is recognized over the lease term	SFAS 13: Gain on sale and leaseback of a finance lease is recognized over the useful life of the asset

IAS 19 Employee Benefits
US GAAP is generally in agreement; SFAS 87, 88, 106, differences in detail.

Financial instruments: assets and liabilities

IAS 32 Financial Instruments: Presentation

IFRS 7 Financial Instruments: Disclosures
Generally in agreement; SFAS 133, different treatment of convertible debt instruments.

IAS 39 Financial Instruments: Recognition and Measurement
SFAS 133 is generally in agreement on fair value measurement in primary statements.

IAS 39: Requires subsequent reversal of an impairment loss under specified circumstances	USA does not allow subsequent reversal of an impairment loss

Exhibit 11.5 *(Continued)*

RECOGNITION OF ECONOMIC ACTIVITY

IAS 11 Construction Contracts
ARB 45 is generally in agreement.

IAS 11: Where percentage of completion cannot be determined* the cost recovery method is used	ARB 45: Where percentage of completion cannot be determined* the completed contract method is used

IAS 18 Revenue[†]
US GAAP generally in agreement in SFAC 5 but more detailed in specific standards. A proposed comprehensive standard is on the agenda of IASB and FASB.

IAS 20 Accounting for Government Grants and Disclosure of Government Assistance*
SFAS 116 generally in agreement.

IAS 20: Grants are recognized in income statement when the conditions of receipt are met and there is reasonable assurance that the grant will be received	SFAS 116: Revenue recognition is delayed where there are conditions attached to the grant, until the conditions are met
Grants that relate to assets are either deducted from cost or deferred to be recognized as income over the period of the asset's life	Contributions for the purchase of long-lived assets are reported in the period received

IFRS 2 Share-based Payment
SFAS 123 is generally in agreement on the fair value model to be applied. Differences exist in detail of application.

MEASUREMENT OF INFLATION

IAS 29 Financial Reporting in Hyperinflationary Economies

IAS 29: Where a subsidiary's functional currency is that of a hyperinflationary economy, financial statements are restated in a measurement unit current at the balance sheet date	US GAAP: Where a subsidiary's functional currency is that of a hyperinflationary economy, use the reporting currency (US$) as functional currency; no adjustment for inflation

GROUP ACCOUNTING

IAS 21 The Effects of Changes in Foreign Exchange Rates
SFAS 52 generally in agreement.

IFRS 3 Business Combinations[†]
SFAS 141, SFAS 142 generally in agreement on purchase method, use of impairment test and no pooling of interests. Nature of impairment test is different.

IFRS 3: Minority interest stated at minority's share of fair value of acquired identifiable assets and liabilities	US GAAP: Minority interest stated at minority's share of pre-acquisition carrying value of net assets
Business combination involving entities under common control not specifically covered in IFRS 3. Entities elect either for purchase or for pooling of interest method	Business combination involving entities under common control generally recorded at predecessor cost

▶

IAS 27 Consolidated and Separate Financial Statements

IAS 27: Subsidiary defined in terms of control by parent, with control defined based on voting power or power to govern. Control also defines special purpose entities (SPEs)	US GAAP: Bipolar model distinguishes a voting interest model and a variable interest model. Control is defined by voting power SPEs identified by variable interest that will absorb the majority of expected losses or receive a majority of expected returns
IAS 27: Parent and subsidiaries must conform their accounting policies	US GAAP: No specific requirement to conform accounting policies

IAS 28 Investments in Associates
APB 18 generally in agreement. USA does not require associate accounting policies to conform to those of investor.

IAS 31 Interests in Joint Ventures*

IAS 31: Permits either the equity method or proportionate consolidation	US GAAP: Generally requires equity method (except for construction and oil and gas industries)

*A topic within the short-term IASB/FASB convergence project 2006–08.

†A topic on the Active Agenda for FASB and IASB consideration.

Note: In this exhibit, 'generally in agreement' indicates broad comparability in principle. US accounting standards are very much more detailed in aspects of practical application.

Key: ARB, Accounting Research Bulletin
        APB, Accounting Principles Board Opinion
        SFAS, Statement of Financial Accounting Standard.

US companies do not specifically acknowledge that their accounting practices are related to the IASB standards; this may be taken to confirm the relatively low profile of IASB standards in the scheme of what comprises 'generally accepted accounting principles' (see section 11.7.2.1).

11.7   The accounting system

11.7.1 Current regulations

Since 1973, standards have been set by the FASB.[30] This is an independent, private sector organization, financed by a spread of contributions from accountancy firms, industry, organizations representing investors and creditors, and other related organizations. The FASB comprises seven members who must maintain total independence of other business activity during their term of office. The seven members of the FASB have diverse business backgrounds, and so could be said to be 'professional' in general terms; they are not all recruited from professional accountancy firms.

There is a substantial secretariat supporting the FASB, and an extensive consultative process, called 'due process', has been put in place. The FASB sponsors systematic and thorough research prior to developing a standard. The principle of openness is an essential element of the work of the FASB, extending to holding public hearings to discuss exposure drafts of standards; their deliberations are open to public attendance.

---

[30] http://www.fasb.org/.

The 'due process' of consultation on developing standards involves:

- appointing a task force of experts to advise on the project;
- sponsoring research studies and reviewing the existing literature on the subject;
- publishing a discussion of issues and potential solutions;
- holding a public hearing;
- issuing an exposure draft for public comment.

The result of the process is a Statement of Financial Accounting Standards (SFAS) and enforcement is effectively through the audit process. Implicitly there is a position of power for the SEC because it may refuse to accept a filing by a corporation where the auditor is not satisfied. The AICPA expects its members to apply FASB pronouncements. The report of the auditors to a public company does not refer directly to SFASs but uses the wording 'fairly present . . . in accordance with generally accepted accounting principles'.

The FASB is complemented by an Emerging Issues Task Force (EITF), which considers new issues requiring rapid guidance. Its views are published and are influential, without carrying the compulsion of an SFAS.

11.7.1.1 SEC Committee on Improvements in Financial Reporting (CIFiR)

The potentially broad range of the CIFiR remit is indicated in Exhibit 11.6.

Shortly after the formation of the CIFiR its chairman described his vision of the role of the Committee.[31] In particular he noted the SEC's proposal to permit non-US companies to use IFRS in SEC filings without quantitative reconciliations to US GAAP and the SEC's call for comment on whether US companies should be permitted to

---

Exhibit 11.6   Extract from charter of CIFiR

Article B:
The Committee should consider the following areas of inquiry:

- the current approach to setting financial accounting and reporting standards, including (a) principles-based vs. rules-based standards, (b) the inclusion within standards of exceptions, bright lines, and safe harbors, and (c) the processes for providing timely guidance on implementation issues and emerging issues;

- the current process of regulating compliance by registrants and financial professionals with accounting and reporting standards;

- the current systems for delivering financial information to investors and accessing that information;

- other environmental factors that may drive unnecessary complexity, including the possibility of being second-guessed, the structuring of transactions to achieve an accounting result, and whether there is a hesitance of professionals to exercise judgment in the absence of detailed rules;

- whether there are current accounting and reporting standards that do not result in useful information to investors, or impose costs that outweigh the resulting benefits (the Committee could use one or two existing accounting standards as a 'test case', both to assist in formulating recommendations and to test the application of proposed recommendations by commenting on the manner in which such standards could be improved); and

- whether the growing use of international accounting standards has an impact on the relevant issues relating to the complexity of U.S. accounting standards and the usefulness of the U.S. financial reporting system.

Source: http://www.sec.gov/rules/other/2007/33-8817charter.pdf.

---

[31] Pozen, R. (2007) 'Time to bridge the information gap for all investors', *Financial Times*, 9 August, p. 23.

choose between IFRS and US GAAP. He indicated that CIFiR would have an advisory role in this discussion.

11.7.1.2 Generally accepted accounting principles

The origins of the phrase 'generally accepted accounting principles' in the USA lie in the APB Opinion No. 4 (issued by the AICPA in 1970), which refers to these principles being rooted in 'experience, reason, custom, usage, and . . . practical necessity'. The principles are said there to 'encompass the conventions, rules and procedures necessary to define accepted accounting practice at a particular time'.

The emphasis on GAAP in the USA necessitates having comprehensive and authoritative statements. This in turn has led the FASB to develop a significant volume of Statements of Financial Accounting Standards (SFASs) and an even greater volume of interpretations. The SFASs and the interpretations are quite lengthy in their detail and make a sharp contrast with the IFRS which are primarily statements of broad standards.

A hierarchy[32] of US GAAP is set out in the US Auditing Standard SAS 69 (1992) as follows:

- FASB Statements and Interpretations, APB Opinions and AICPA Accounting Research Bulletins [this is a set of documents for which the IASB equivalent would be IFRS];
- Rules and interpretative releases of the SEC [the UK equivalent would be the FSA Listing Rules];
- FASB Technical Bulletins, AICPA Industry Audit and Accounting Guides and AICPA Statements of Position;
- AICPA AcSEC Practice Bulletins and consensuses of the FASB Emerging Issues Task Force (EITF);
- AICPA accounting interpretations, implementation guides (Qs&As) published by FASB staff and practices that are widely recognized and prevalent either generally or in the industry.

SAS 69 also indicates that other accounting literature may be considered, extending through various professional guidance to textbooks, handbooks and articles. IAS are contained in this miscellaneous grouping.

Acceptance of this list by the FASB was subsequently indicated by its inclusion in SFAS 111, 'Rescission of FASB Statement No. 32 and Technical Corrections', whereby the wording of SAS 69 was incorporated as a technical correction to APB 20, 'Accounting Changes'. However, in the debate following Enron, and in response to the SEC's recommendations, the FASB decided to define its own GAAP hierarchy rather than relying on an auditing standard. In September 2006 a draft revision of the hierarchy was issued by the FASB containing a list, in descending order, broadly similar to that of SAS 69 but with some updating to reflect more recent sources. If the accounting treatment is not specified in that list of sources then an enterprise may look to 'other accounting literature' of which the FASB Concepts Statements would normally be more influential than others in that category.

11.7.1.3 Fair presentation

The US equivalent of the phrase 'true and fair view' found in European accounting is the somewhat different wording 'fairly presented in conformity with generally accepted accounting principles'. It is different because of the specific emphasis placed on GAAP.

---

[32] 'Hierarchy' here means a list of items in descending order of importance.

The European interpretation of 'true and fair' is not uniform, but the UK view is that 'true and fair' stands above any specific set of rules. Some commentators have drawn the distinction by describing the US approach as highly legalistic when compared with a much more judgemental approach in the UK. This perception is another way of expressing the 'rules versus principles' debate, explained in section 11.3.3.

11.7.1.4 'Safe harbor' protection for forward-looking statements

The AICPA formed a Special Committee on Financial Reporting in 1991, chaired by E.L. Jenkins, as part of the AICPA's broad initiative to improve the value of business information and the confidence of the public in that information. Extensive research was undertaken to ascertain the views of investors and creditors. Key recommendations were that, to meet users' changing needs, business reporting must:

- provide more information with a forward-looking perspective, including management's plans, opportunities, risks and measurement uncertainties;
- focus more on the factors that create long-term value, including non-financial measures indicating how key business processes are performing;
- align information reported externally better with the information reported to senior management to manage the business.

However Jenkins noted that the legal environment in the USA at that time discouraged companies from disclosing forward-looking information and recommended that companies should not expand reporting of forward-looking information until there were more effective deterrents to undesirable legal actions.

The Private Securities Litigation Reform Act of 1995 extends the basic legislation of the Securities Act of 1933 and the Securities Exchange Act of 1934, allowing the SEC to clarify what is called a 'safe harbor' of protection against legal action in respect of forward-looking statements, provided these are made outside the financial statements and notes. To obtain the protection companies must state the factors that could affect the financial performance or cause actual results to differ from any estimates made in forward-looking statements. Companies give the requisite statement in the Form 10-K, with duplication wholly or partly in the published annual report.

11.7.1.5 Frequency of reporting

In addition to the annual report, the SEC requires listed companies to produce quarterly reports. Interim reporting is covered by APB 28. US interim reports usually include both the current interim period and a cumulative year-to-date period, together with comparative figures for the previous year. Each interim period is viewed as an integral part of the annual period. This means that while operating cost and revenues will generally be reported in the interim period to which they relate, discretion exists to allocate other costs across interim periods. When APB 28 was issued there was a dissenting view that it was not sufficiently strict in its guidance on allocation to interim periods. The IASB indicates in IAS 34 a general principle of the 'year-to-date' approach, where the events of the interim period are reported as they occur.

Under APB 28 the cumulative effect of a change in accounting principle is always included in net income of the first interim period of the company's accounting year, regardless of when the accounting change occurred. The IASB indicates in IAS 34 a preference for restatement of the comparative figures for the corresponding previous period so that accounting changes do not appear in any one interim period. The differences between US GAAP and IFRS are not addressed in the short-term convergence project.

11.7.1.6 SEC concerns over flexibility

In 1999 the SEC officials expressed concern over the misuse of accounting policies in order to 'manage' earnings. They indicated that accounting fraud was increasing because of the temptation to sacrifice sound reporting practices in order to meet the expectations of investors. Examples of excessive flexibility were premature recognition of revenue, excessive accruals or manipulation of accruals for loan losses and restructuring charges, improper write-downs of assets that continued to be used in operations, and unreasonable lives for depreciation and amortization. Such matters are not in themselves fraudulent, because the rules allow such flexibility, but if there is an intention to deceive then the acts may become fraudulent. SEC staff reports on investigations are published on the SEC website, www.sec.gov.

11.7.1.7 Special industry standards

The FASB sets special industry standards, based on direct action by the FASB rather than the less direct approach of the UK where the ASB franks (approves) the industry's own proposals. FASB industry standards cover the oil and gas industry where there have on occasions been differences of opinion between the FASB and the SEC. The example of SFAS 69, 'Disclosures about Oil and Gas Producing Activities', is interesting because it requires disclosure of financially relevant information beyond that conventionally expected in published accounts. In particular, it requires disclosure of proven oil and gas reserve quantities, capitalized costs relating to oil and gas producing activities, costs incurred on oil and gas exploration and development activities, results of production activities, and a discounted cash flow measure of future cash flows expected from proven reserves. The requirement to report proven reserves was given high publicity in 2004 when Royal Dutch/Shell had to revise its estimates downwards four times, causing delay to the annual report for 2003.[33]

Other industries covered by FASB standards include banking and thrift institutions; broadcasters; cable television companies; motion picture films; records and music; franchisors; insurance enterprises; the mortgage banking industry; real estate (property) companies; and regulated industries. These industries may also be subject to other regulatory bodies setting accounting requirements (see Exhibit 11.7).

The US approach in developing specific industry standards is quite different from the more general approach of the IASB. The only specialized international standards are IAS 26, 'Accounting and Reporting by Retirement Benefit Plans', IAS 30, 'Disclosures in the Financial Statements of Banks and Similar Financial Institutions', IAS 41 'Agriculture' and IFRS 4 'Insurance Contracts'.

11.7.1.8 Tax law and impact on accounting practice

Tax law and accounting law are separate but there may be situations where accountants find it convenient, or even necessary, to use the tax-based approach in the accounting statements. This reduces the flexibility available in principle. An example lies in inventory valuation and the use of LIFO (see section 11.7.3.8).

---

[33] 'Shell accounts get signed off at last', *Financial Times*, 25 May 2004, p. 21.

NOTES TO FINANCIAL STATEMENTS

NOTE ONE:
SUMMARY OF SIGNIFICANT ACCOUNTING POLICIES

General

Southern Company (the Company) is the parent company of four traditional operating companies, Southern Power Company (Southern Power), Southern Company Services (SCS), Southern Communications Services (SouthernLINC Wireless), Southern Company Holdings (Southern Holdings), Southern Nuclear Operating Company (Southern Nuclear), Southern Telecom, and other direct and indirect subsidiaries. The traditional operating companies, Alabama Power, Georgia Power, Gulf Power, and Mississippi Power, are vertically integrated utilities providing electric service in four Southeastern states. Southern Power constructs, acquires, and manages generation assets and sells electricity at market-based rates in the wholesale market. SCS, the system service company, provides, at cost, specialized services to Southern Company and the subsidiary companies. SouthernLINC Wireless provides digital wireless communications services to the traditional operating companies and also markets these services to the public within the Southeast. Southern Telecom provides fiber cable services within the Southeast. Southern Holdings is an intermediate holding company subsidiary for Southern Company's investments in synthetic fuels and leveraged leases and various other energy-related businesses. Southern Nuclear operates and provides services to Southern Company's nuclear power plants.

On January 4, 2006, Southern Company completed the sale of substantially all of the assets of Southern Company Gas, its competitive retail natural gas marketing subsidiary, including natural gas inventory, accounts receivable, and customer list, to Gas South, LLC, an affiliate of Cobb Electric Membership Corporation. As a result of the sale, Southern Company's financial statements and related information reflect Southern Company Gas as discontinued operations for all periods presented. For additional information, see Note 3 under 'Southern Company Gas Sale.'

The financial statements reflect Southern Company's investments in the subsidiaries on a consolidated basis. The equity method is used for subsidiaries in which the Company has significant influence but does not control and for variable interest entities where the Company is not the primary beneficiary. All material intercompany items have been eliminated in consolidation. Certain prior years' data presented in the financial statements have been reclassified to conform with the current year presentation.

The traditional operating companies, Southern Power, and certain of their subsidiaries are subject to regulation by the Federal Energy Regulatory Commission (FERC) and the traditional operating companies are also subject to regulation by their respective state public service commissions (PSC). The companies follow accounting principles generally accepted in the United States and comply with the accounting policies and practices prescribed by their respective commissions. The preparation of financial statements in conformity with accounting principles generally accepted in the United States requires the use of estimates, and the actual results may differ from those estimates.

Regulatory Assets and Liabilities

The traditional operating companies are subject to the provisions of Financial Accounting Standards Board (FASB) Statement No. 71, 'Accounting for the Effects of Certain Types of Regulation' (SFAS No. 71). Regulatory assets represent probable future revenues associated with certain costs that are expected to be recovered from customers through the ratemaking process. Regulatory liabilities represent probable future reductions in revenues associated with amounts that are expected to be credited to customers through the ratemaking process. Regulatory assets and (liabilities) reflected in the balance sheets at December 31 relate to:

(in millions)	2006	2005	Note
Deferred income tax charges	$ 896	$ 937	(a)
Asset retirement obligations-asset	61	81	(a)
Asset retirement obligations-liab	(155)	(139)	(a)
Other cost of removal obligations	(1,300)	(1,295)	(a)
Deferred income tax credits	(293)	(313)	(a)
Loss on reacquired debt	293	309	(b)
Vacation pay	121	117	(c)
Under recovered regulatory clause revenues	411	351	(d)
Building lease	51	52	(d)
Generating plant outage costs-asset	56	54	(d)
Under recovered storm damage costs	89	366	(d)
Fuel hedging-asset	115	24	(d)
Fuel hedging-liability	(13)	(127)	(d)
Other assets	55	56	(d)
Environmental remediation-asset	57	58	(d)
Environmental remediation-liab	(32)	.(36)	(d)
Deferred purchased power	(38)	(52)	(d)
Other liabilities	(50)	(32)	(d)
Plant Daniel capacity	(6)	(19)	(e)
Overfunded retiree benefit plans	(508)	–	(f)
Underfunded retiree benefit plans	697	–	(f)
Total	$ 507	$ 392	

Note: The recovery and amortization periods for these regulatory assets and (liabilities) are as follows:

(a) Asset retirement and removal liabilities are recorded, deferred income tax assets are recovered, and deferred tax liabilities are amortized over the related property lives, which may range up to 60 years. Asset retirement and removal liabilities will be settled and trued up following completion of the related activities.

(b) Recovered over either the remaining life of the original issue or, if refinanced, over the life of the new issue, which may range up to 50 years.

(c) Recorded as earned by employees and recovered as paid, generally within one year.

(d) Recorded and recovered or amortized as approved by the appropriate state PSCs.

(e) Amortized over a four-year period ending in 2007.

(f) Recovered and amortized over the average remaining service period which may range up to 21 years. See Note 2 under 'Retirement Benefits.'

In the event that a portion of a traditional operating company's operations is no longer subject to the provisions of SFAS No. 71, such company would be required to write off related regulatory assets and liabilities that are not specifically recoverable through regulated rates. In addition, the traditional operating company would be required to determine if any impairment to other assets, including plant, exists and write down the assets, if impaired, to their fair value. All regulatory assets and liabilities are to be reflected in rates. See Note 3 under 'Alabama Power Retail Regulatory Matters,' 'Georgia Power Retail Regulatory Matters,' and 'Storm Damage Cost Recovery' for additional information.

11.7.2 Annual reporting

11.7.2.1 Basic information package

The requirements of the SEC are considerable, and the most convenient starting point is the basic information package. The five classes of information are:

- market price of, and dividends on, common equity, and related security matters;
- selected financial data;
- management's discussion and analysis (MD&A);
- audited financial statements and supplementary data;
- other information.

The information must be presented in its entirety to the SEC, but there are various ways of achieving this. It may all be included in the annual report to the SEC on Form 10-K,[34] which is a document of considerable length (as much as 100–200 pages) and generally uninteresting appearance (one type of font and no illustrations or graphics). Alternatively, companies may choose to present some or most of the basic information package in the annual report to shareholders, with a much reduced Form 10-K in which there is a reference to portions of the annual report and the statement for the annual meeting, which are to be read as part of the 10-K filing. Some information required for the 10-K does not normally appear in the annual report, such as lists of legal proceedings being taken against the company, detailed descriptions of the business and a detailed description of land and buildings held by the company.

Other information may be included in the proxy statement which accompanies the notice to shareholders convening the annual general meeting. In particular, there is more about corporate governance; the directors' compensation package ('compensation' means the rewards of all kinds that they receive as directors); the report of the audit committee; information on related party transactions; and the distribution of major shareholdings. An example is provided by Wal-Mart Stores (Exhibit 11.8).

Exhibit 11.8 Wal-Mart Stores, Inc.: proxy statement (extracts)

AUDIT COMMITTEE REPORT

Wal-Mart's Audit Committee consists of three directors, each of whom has been determined by the Board to be 'independent' as defined by the current listing standards of the NYSE and the applicable rules of the SEC. The members of the Audit Committee are James I. Cash, Jr.; Roland A. Hernandez, the chair of the Audit Committee; and Christopher J. Williams. Dr. Cash was appointed to the Audit Committee upon his election to the Board on June 2, 2006, replacing J. Paul Reason. M. Michele Burns also served on the Audit Committee until February 20, 2006. The Audit Committee is governed by a written charter adopted by the Board. A copy of the current Audit Committee charter is available on Wal-Mart's corporate Web site at www.walmartstores.com in the Corporate Governance section of the Investors Web page. In addition, the Audit Committee charter is available in print at no charge to any shareholder who requests a copy from Wal-Mart's Investor Relations Department by submitting a request through the Investors Web page or by writing to the Investor Relations Department at: Wal-Mart Stores, Inc., Investor Relations Department, 702 Southwest 8th Street, Bentonville, Arkansas 72716-0100.

Wal-Mart's management is responsible for Wal-Mart's internal control over financial reporting, including the preparation of Wal-Mart's consolidated financial statements. Wal-Mart's independent accountants are responsible for

---

[34] http://www.sec.gov/about/forms/form10-k.pdf.

Exhibit 11.8 *(Continued)*

auditing Wal-Mart's annual consolidated financial statements in accordance with the standards of the Public Company Accounting Oversight Board. The independent accountants are also responsible for issuing a report on those financial statements and an attestation report on management's assessment of Wal-Mart's internal control over financial reporting. The Audit Committee monitors and oversees these processes. The Audit Committee is responsible for selecting, engaging, and overseeing Wal-Mart's independent accountants.

As part of the oversight processes, the Audit Committee regularly meets with management of the Company, the Company's independent accountants, and the Company's internal auditors. The Audit Committee often meets with each of these groups separately in closed sessions. Throughout the year, the Audit Committee had full access to management and the independent accountants and internal auditors for the Company. To fulfill its responsibilities, the Audit Committee did, among other things, the following:

- reviewed and discussed with Wal-Mart's management and the independent accountants Wal-Mart's audited consolidated financial statements for fiscal 2007;

- reviewed management's representations that those consolidated financial statements were prepared in accordance with generally accepted accounting principles and fairly present the results of operations and financial position of the Company;

- discussed with the independent accountants the matters required by Statement on Auditing Standards 61, as modified or supplemented, and SEC rules, including matters related to the conduct of the audit of Wal-Mart's consolidated financial statements;

- received written disclosures and the letter from the independent accountants required by Independence Standards Board Standard No. 1 relating to E&Y's independence from Wal-Mart and discussed with E&Y its independence from Wal-Mart;

- based on the discussions with management and the independent accountants the independent accountants' disclosures and letter to the Audit Committee, the representations of management and the report of the independent accountants, recommended to the Board that Wal-Mart's audited annual consolidated financial statements for fiscal 2007 be included in Wal-Mart's Annual Report on Form 10-K for fiscal 2007 for filing with the SEC;

- reviewed all audit and non-audit services performed for Wal-Mart by E&Y and considered whether E&Y's provision of non-audit services was compatible with maintaining its independence from Wal-Mart;

- selected and engaged E&Y as Wal-Mart's independent accountants to audit and report on the annual consolidated financial statements of Wal-Mart to be filed with the SEC prior to Wal-Mart's annual shareholders' meeting to be held in calendar year 2008;

- monitored the progress and results of the testing of internal controls over financial reporting pursuant to Section 404 of SOX, reviewed a report from management and internal audit regarding the design, operation and effectiveness of internal controls over financial reporting, and reviewed an attestation report from E&Y regarding the effectiveness of internal controls over financial reporting; and

- received reports from management regarding the Company's policies, processes, and procedures regarding compliance with applicable laws and regulations and the Statement of Ethics, all in accordance with the Audit Committee's charter.

The Audit Committee submits this report:

James I. Cash, Jr.
Roland A. Hernandez, Chair
Christopher J. Williams

AUDIT COMMITTEE FINANCIAL EXPERT

Wal-Mart's Board has determined that James I. Cash, Jr., Roland A. Hernandez, and Christopher J. Williams are 'Audit Committee Financial Experts' as that term is defined in Item 407(d)(5)(ii) of Regulation S-K, promulgated by the SEC, and are 'independent' under Section 10A(m)(3) of the Exchange Act and the requirements set forth in the NYSE Listed Company Manual.

AUDIT COMMITTEE SERVICE

Roland A. Hernandez, who is the chair of the Audit Committee, currently serves on the audit committees of three other public companies and serves as the Chairman of one such other public company's audit committee. The Board has determined that such service does not impair the ability of Mr. Hernandez to serve effectively on the Audit Committee.

CODE OF ETHICS FOR THE CEO AND SENIOR FINANCIAL OFFICERS

You may review Wal-Mart's Code of Ethics for the CEO and Senior Financial Officers on Wal-Mart's corporate Web site at www.walmartstores.com in the Corporate Governance section of the Investors Web page. Wal-Mart's Code of Ethics for the CEO and Senior Financial Officers supplements the Statement of Ethics, which is applicable to all directors, Executive Officers, and Associates and is available on Wal-Mart's corporate Web site at www. walmartstores.com in the Corporate Governance section of the Investors Web page. A description of any substantive amendment or waiver of Wal-Mart's Code of Ethics for the CEO and Senior Financial Officers or the Statement of Ethics will be disclosed on Wal-Mart's corporate Web site at www.walmartstores.com in the Corporate Governance section of the Investors Web page for a period of 12 months after the amendment or waiver. Copies of Wal-Mart's Code of Ethics for the CEO and Senior Financial Officers and of the Statement of Ethics are also available in print at no charge to any shareholder who requests a copy from the Wal-Mart Investor Relations Department by submitting a request through the Investors Web page or by writing to the Investor Relations Department at: Wal-Mart Stores, Inc., Investor Relations Department, 702 Southwest 8th Street, Bentonville, Arkansas 72716-0100.

SUMMARY COMPENSATION

This table shows the compensation for fiscal 2007 for each of the Company's Named Executive Officers.

Name and Principal Position	Fiscal year ended Jan. 31,	Salary ($) (1)	Bonus ($) (2)	Stock Awards ($) (3)	Option Awards ($) (4)	Non-Equity Incentive Plan Compensation ($) (5)	Change in Pension Value and Nonqualified Deferred Compensation Earnings ($) (6)	All Other Compensation ($) (7)	Total ($) (8)
H. Lee Scott, Jr. President and CEO	2007	1,300,000	0	15,274,351	8,081,272	4,285,840	308,390	422,680	29,672,533
Thomas M. Schoewe Executive Vice President and CFO	2007	700,385	0	3,989,665	1,534,178	1,162,122	85,603	135,101	7,607,054
John B. Menzer Vice Chairman, Chief Administrative Officer	2007	1,000,000	0	6,141,744	2,827,292	2,435,700	186,679	154,321	12,745,736
Michael T. Duke Vice Chairman, Responsible for International	2007	900,000	0	4,648,859	2,358,174	2,462,670	94,793	169,900	10,634,396
Eduardo Castro-Wright Executive Vice President and President and CEO, Wal-Mart Stores Division	2007	721,154	50,000	3,609,065	499,264	1,177,255	52,813	92,162	6,201,713

Exhibit 11.8 *(Continued)*

RELATED-PARTY TRANSACTIONS

This section discusses certain direct and indirect relationships and transactions involving Wal-Mart and any director, Executive Officer, director nominee, beneficial owner of more than five percent of the Shares, and any member of the immediate family of the foregoing. Wal-Mart believes that the terms of all of the following transactions are comparable to terms that would have been reached by unrelated parties in arms-length transactions:

During fiscal 2007, Frank C. Robson, the brother of Helen R. Walton, a beneficial owner of more than five percent of the Shares, personally and through partnerships or trusts, leased two store locations to Wal-Mart. Wal-Mart paid Mr. Robson or his related entities rent and other expenses of $866,513 under the leases during fiscal 2007. The Company anticipates that, in fiscal 2008, it will pay Mr. Robson, personally and through partnerships or trusts, approximately $707,000 in rent and other expenses pursuant to such leases.

During fiscal 2007, a manufacturing company and certain of its subsidiaries, which are owned by Jim C. Walton, a director and beneficial owner of more than five percent of the Shares, recorded consolidated sales of products to Wal-Mart in the amount of $233,550. The Company anticipates that it will purchase additional products in fiscal 2008 pursuant to purchase orders placed from time to time in the ordinary course of business totaling approximately $325,000.

During fiscal 2007, a banking corporation and certain of its bank subsidiaries, which are collectively owned by Jim C. Walton; S. Robson Walton, a director, Executive Officer, and beneficial owner of more than five percent of the Shares; and the Estate of John T. Walton, a beneficial owner of more than five percent of the Shares, made payments to Wal-Mart in the aggregate amount of $556,952 for banking facility rent and related ATM surcharges. The banking corporation and its affiliates made additional payments to Wal-Mart pursuant to similar arrangements that were awarded by Wal-Mart on a competitive-bid basis. The leases of banking facility space in various stores remain in effect, and it is anticipated that such banking corporation and its affiliates will pay Wal-Mart approximately $555,000 in fiscal 2008 pursuant to those leases not awarded on a competitive bid basis.

Stephen P. Weber, a manager in Wal-Mart's Information Systems Division, is the son-in-law of Michael T. Duke, an Executive Officer. For fiscal 2007, Wal-Mart paid Mr. Weber a salary of $94,454, a bonus of $15,960, and other benefits totaling $16,610 (including Company contributions to Mr. Weber's Profit Sharing/401(k) Plan account and health insurance premiums). For Mr. Weber's performance in fiscal 2007, he also received a grant of stock options to purchase 314 Shares at an exercise price of $47.26 and 213 restricted stock rights. Mr. Weber continues to be an Associate, and in fiscal 2008, he may receive compensation and other benefits for his services to Wal-Mart in amounts similar to those received during fiscal 2007.

Mauricio Castro-Wright, a director of operations in Brazil, is the brother of Eduardo Castro-Wright, an Executive Officer. For fiscal 2007, Wal-Mart paid Mauricio Castro-Wright a salary of $191,259, a bonus of $82,398 and other benefits having a value of $80,149 (including Company contributions to Mr. Castro-Wright's Profit Sharing/401(k) Plan account, SERP account, and payments related to his expatriate assignment). For Mauricio Castro-Wright's performance in fiscal 2007, he also received a grant of stock options to purchase 733 Shares at an exercise price of $47.26 per Share and 496 restricted stock rights. Mauricio Castro-Wright continues to serve as a director of operations in Brazil, and in fiscal 2008, he may receive compensation and other benefits for his services to Wal-Mart in amounts similar to those received during fiscal 2007.

During fiscal 2007, Springdale Card & Comic Wholesale, Inc., which is owned by the son of David D. Glass, a director and former Executive Officer, had sales to Wal-Mart in the amount of $2,514,085. Wal-Mart may purchase additional products from Springdale Card & Comic Wholesale, Inc. in fiscal 2008 pursuant to purchase orders that are placed from time to time in the ordinary course of business.

Roland A. Hernandez, a director of Wal-Mart, beneficially owns more than ten percent of Inter-Con Security Systems, Inc. ('Inter-Con'). Wal-Mart and Inter-Con have conducted business since 1995, which was prior to Mr. Hernandez's joining the Board in 1998. During fiscal 2007, Wal-Mart paid Inter-Con, through its subsidiary operating in Mexico, approximately $841,124 for security services. The Company anticipates that it will continue to purchase security services from Inter-Con during fiscal 2008 in amounts similar to or greater than amounts paid in fiscal 2007.

Source: Wal-Mart proxy statement 2006, pp. 15, 16, 19, 35, 51, www.wal-mart.com.

It is essential for the interested reader to request the annual report, the 10-K filing and the proxy statement in order to have the benefit of the full BIP intended by the SEC. The main features of each section of the BIP are as follows:

- *Market price of, and dividends on, common equity, and related security matters.* This provides investors with information including the markets in which the stock is traded, the quarterly share price for the past two years, the approximate number of ordinary shareholders, and the frequency and amount of dividends paid over the past two years.
- *Selected financial data.* This is intended to highlight key items including the net sales or operating revenue, income or loss from continuing operations, income (in total and per share) and total assets.
- *Management's discussion and analysis.* The MD&A is explained in more detail in the next section.
- *Audited financial statements and supplementary data.* The company must present income statements and statements of cash flow in respect of the current period and the previous two years. Balance sheets must be presented at the year-end and for the previous year-end. Notes to the accounts are also required.
- *Other information.* This is quite substantial, and covers a brief description of the business; major operating developments such as acquisitions of assets or bankruptcies of parts of the organization; segment information; description of major properties currently owned; description of major active legal proceedings; information about management such as background, remuneration and major transactions between management and the company; and selected industry-specific disclosures, such as for banking, insurance and other regulated industries.

11.7.2.2 Management discussion and analysis

The management discussion and analysis (MD&A) is a report required by Regulation S-K of the SEC. The full title is the 'Management's discussion and analysis of financial condition and results of operations'. It is one of the most important disclosures made by the company. The full version will in many cases be printed in the annual report. Some companies give an edited summary in the financial report, referring the reader to the 10-K registration for the fuller version.

A flexible format is permitted for the MD&A, but the following five items must be covered:

- specific information about the company's liquidity, capital resources and results of operations;
- the impact of inflation and changing prices on net sales and revenues and on income from continuing operations;
- material changes in line items of the consolidated financial statements compared with the prior-period amount;
- known material events and uncertainties that may make historical financial information not indicative of future operations or future conditions;
- any other information the company believes necessary for an understanding of its financial condition, changes in financial condition and results of operations.

The reference to 'future operations and future conditions' reflects a desire of the SEC to give a forward-looking aspect to the MD&A. The encouragement to give forward-looking information is backed by a 'safe harbor' law which is intended to protect forward-looking statements made in good faith (see section 11.7.1.4 and section 4.3).

11.7.2.3 Financial statement formats

In the annual report of US companies there are four primary financial statements:

- balance sheet
- income statement (statement of earnings, profit and loss account)
- cash flow statement
- statement of changes in shareholders' equity (stockholders' equity), including comprehensive income.

These four financial statements, augmented by footnotes and supplementary data, are interrelated. Collectively, they are intended to provide relevant, reliable and timely information essential to making investment, credit and similar decisions, thus meeting the objectives of financial reporting. Companies are required to report comprehensive income under SFAS 130.

Balance sheet

There is no universal form of balance sheet. The objectives are clarity and adequate disclosure of all pertinent and material facts. Some use the account form (a two-sided balance sheet corresponding to debit and credit), others use a report form (where the debit and credit sections of the account form are placed one above the other) and others again use a financial position form which corresponds to the vertical form used in the UK. Within the account form the assets are shown on the left-hand side, starting with cash and proceeding to the least liquid assets. The liabilities are on the right-hand side, starting with current liabilities and proceeding to long-term liabilities and equity. In all cases, there is classification of the main categories of assets and liabilities.

As an example, Sears, Roebuck and Co. uses the report form (Exhibit 11.9), while Altria Inc. uses the account form (Exhibit 11.10).

Income statement

There are essentially two forms of income statement (profit and loss account). One is the multiple step and the other the single step approach. Both require columns of comparative figures for two previous years. The multiple step approach sets out various intermediate balances, including gross profit, as in Altria (Exhibit 11.11).

The single step approach presents one grouping of all revenue items, another grouping of expenses and a resulting net income figure. Pfizer uses the single step approach (Exhibit 11.12). Those who favour the single step approach argue that it is more neutral in its presentation while the multiple step approach makes assumptions about priority of cost recovery. Combinations of both methods may be used; there is no rigid format or chart of accounts. The title 'statement of income' is most widely used, but not universal. Some use 'statement of earnings' and some use 'operations statement'. Both the single step and the multiple step income statements have separate sections for discontinued items, extraordinary items and the effect of a change in accounting principle.

Exhibit 11.13 shows the flexibility of income statement presentation. In panel (a) Wachovia segments its net interest income from its fee income on the face of the income statement, which also includes line item details. In panel (b) Colgate-Palmolive presents a highly summarized consolidated statement of income, with supplemental details of line items reported in the notes.

A particular feature of the income statement is the separate disclosure of the results of discontinued operations. IFRS 5 is mostly comparable with SFAS 144, 'Accounting for

Exhibit 11.9 Sears, Roebuck and Co.: report form of balance sheet

SEARS, ROEBUCK AND CO.
Consolidated Balance Sheets

millions, except per share data	February 3, 2007	January 28, 2006
ASSETS		
Current assets		
Cash and cash equivalents	$ 3,968	$ 4,440
Accounts receivable...	847	811
Merchandise inventories	9,907	9,068
Prepaid expenses and other current assets	372	372
Deferred income taxes	312	516
Total current assets	15,406	15,207
Property and equipment		
Land	2,105	2,146
Buildings and improvements	5,981	5,920
Furniture, fixtures and equipment	2,408	2,268
Capital leases	352	367
Gross property and equipment	10,846	10,701
Less accumulated depreciation	(1,714)	(878)
Total property and equipment, net	9,132	9,823
Goodwill	1,692	1,684
Tradenames and other intangible assets	3,437	3,448
Other assets	399	411
TOTAL ASSETS	$30,066	$30,573
LIABILITIES		
Current liabilities		
Short-term borrowings.......................................	$ 94	$ 178
Current portion of long-term debt and capitalized lease obligations............	613	570
Merchandise payables	3,312	3,458
Income taxes payable..	359	449
Other current liabilities	3,965	3,917
Unearned revenues...	1,073	1,047
Other taxes...	636	731
Total current liabilities	10,052	10,350
Long-term debt and capitalized lease obligations	2,849	3,268
Pension and postretirement benefits	1,648	2,421
Minority interest and other liabilities	2,803	2,923
Total Liabilities	17,352	18,962
SHAREHOLDERS' EQUITY		
Preferred stock, 20 shares authorized; no shares outstanding	—	—
Common stock $0.01 par value; 500 shares authorized; 154 and 160 shares outstanding, respectively.....................................	2	2
Capital in excess of par value	10,393	10,258
Retained earnings	3,688	2,198
Treasury stock—at cost	(1,437)	(642)
Accumulated other comprehensive income (loss)	68	(205)
Total Shareholders' Equity	12,714	11,611
TOTAL LIABILITIES AND SHAREHOLDERS' EQUITY	$30,066	$30,573

Exhibit 11.10 Altria, Inc.: account form of balance sheet

Consolidated Balance Sheets
(in millions of dollars, except share and per share data)

at December 31,	2006	2005
Assets		
Consumer products		
Cash and cash equivalents	$ 5,020	$ 6,258
Receivables (less allowances of $101 in 2006 and $112 in 2005)	6,070	5,361
Inventories:		
Leaf tobacco	4,383	4,060
Other raw materials	2,498	2,232
Finished product	5,305	4,292
	12,186	10,584
Other current assets	2,876	3,578
Total current assets	26,152	25,781
Property, plant and equipment, at cost:		
Land and land improvements	1,056	989
Buildings and building equipment	7,973	7,428
Machinery and equipment	20,990	20,050
Construction in progress	1,913	1,489
	31,932	29,956
Less accumulated depreciation	14,658	13,278
	17,274	16,678
Goodwill	33,235	31,219
Other intangible assets, net	12,085	12,196
Prepaid pension assets	1,929	5,692
Other assets	6,805	8,975
Total consumer products assets	97,480	100,541
Financial services		
Finance assets, net	6,740	7,189
Other assets	50	219
Total financial services assets	6,790	7,408
Total Assets	**$104,270**	**$107,949**

Source: Altria, Inc., Annual Report (2006), pp. 46–47, www.altria.com.

at December 31,	2006	2005
Liabilities		
Consumer products		
Short-term borrowings	$ 2,135	$ 2,836
Current portion of long-term debt	2,066	3,430
Accounts payable	4,016	3,645
Accrued liabilities:		
Marketing	2,450	2,382
Taxes, except income taxes	3,696	2,871
Employment costs	1,599	1,296
Settlement charges	3,552	3,503
Other	3,169	3,130
Income taxes	933	1,393
Dividends payable	1,811	1,672
Total current liabilities	25,427	26,158
Long-term debt	13,379	15,653
Deferred income taxes	5,321	8,492
Accrued pension costs	1,563	1,667
Accrued postretirement health care costs	5,023	3,412
Minority interest	3,528	4,141
Other liabilities	3,712	4,593
Total consumer products liabilities	57,953	64,116
Financial services		
Long-term debt	1,119	2,014
Non-recourse debt		201
Deferred income taxes	5,530	5,737
Other liabilities	49	174
Total financial services liabilities	6,698	8,126
Total liabilities	64,651	72,242
Contingencies (Note 19)		
Stockholders' Equity		
Common stock, par value $0.33\frac{1}{3}$ per share		
(2,805,961,317 shares issued)	935	935
Additional paid-in capital	6,356	6,061
Earnings reinvested in the business	59,879	54,666
Accumulated other comprehensive losses	(3,808)	(1,853)
Cost of repurchased stock (708,880,389 shares		
in 2006 and 721,696,918 shares in 2005)	(23,743)	(24,102)
Total stockholders' equity	39,619	35,707
Total Liabilities and Stockholders' Equity	$104,270	$107,949

Exhibit 11.11 Altria, Inc.: multiple step approach in income statement

Consolidated Statements of Earnings
(in millions of dollars, except per share data)

for the years ended December 31,	2006	2005	2004
Net revenues	$101,407	$97,854	$89,610
Cost of sales	37,480	36,764	33,959
Excise taxes on products	31,083	28,934	25,647
Gross profit	32,844	32,156	30,004
Marketing, administration and research costs	14,913	14,799	13,665
Domestic tobacco headquarters relocation charges		4	31
Domestic tobacco loss on U.S. tobacco pool		138	
Domestic tobacco quota buy-out		(115)	
International tobacco Italian antitrust charge	61		
International tobacco E.C. agreement			250
Asset impairment and exit costs	1,180	618	718
Gain on redemption of United Biscuits investment	(251)		
(Gains) losses on sales of businesses, net	(605)	(108)	3
Provision for airline industry exposure	103	200	140
Amortization of intangibles	30	28	17
Operating income	17,413	16,592	15,180
Interest and other debt expense, net	877	1,157	1,176
Earnings from continuing operations before income taxes, minority interest, and equity earnings, net	16,536	15,435	14,004
Provision for income taxes	4,351	4,618	4,540
Earnings from continuing operations before minority interest, and equity earnings, net	12,185	10,817	9,464
Minority interest in earnings from continuing operations, and equity earnings, net	163	149	44
Earnings from continuing operations	12,022	10,668	9,420
Loss from discontinued operations, net of income taxes and minority interest		(233)	(4)
Net earnings	$ 12,022	$10,435	$ 9,416
Per share data:			
Basic earnings per share:			
Continuing operations	$ 5.76	$ 5.15	$ 4.60
Discontinued operations		(0.11)	
Net earnings	$ 5.76	$ 5.04	$ 4.60
Diluted earnings per share:			
Continuing operations	$ 5.71	$ 5.10	$ 4.57
Discontinued operations		(0.11)	(0.01)
Net earnings	$ 5.71	$ 4.99	$ 4.56

Source: Altria, Inc. Annual Report (2006), p. 48.

Exhibit 11.12 Pfizer: single step approach in income statement

Consolidated Statement of Income
Pfizer Inc and Subsidiary Companies

(MILLIONS, EXCEPT PER COMMON SHARE DATA)	YEAR ENDED DECEMBER 31,		
	2006	2005	2004
Revenues	**$48,371**	$47,405	$48,988
Costs and expenses:			
Cost of sales[(a)]	**7,640**	7,232	6,391
Selling, informational and administrative expenses[(a)]	**15,589**	15,313	15,304
Research and development expenses[(a)]	**7,599**	7,256	7,513
Amortization of intangible assets	**3,261**	3,399	3,352
Acquisition-related in-process research and development charges	**835**	1,652	1,071
Restructuring charges and acquisition-related costs	**1,323**	1,356	1,151
Other (income)/deductions—net	**(904)**	397	803
Income from continuing operations before provision for taxes on income, minority interests and cumulative effect of a change in accounting principles	**13,028**	10,800	13,403
Provision for taxes on income	**1,992**	3,178	2,460
Minority interests	**12**	12	7
Income from continuing operations before cumulative effect of a change in accounting principles	**11,024**	7,610	10,936
Discontinued operations:			
Income from discontinued operations—net of tax	**433**	451	374
Gains on sales of discontinued operations—net of tax	**7,880**	47	51
Discontinued operations—net of tax	**8,313**	498	425
Income before cumulative effect of a change in accounting principles	**19,337**	8,108	11,361
Cumulative effect of a change in accounting principles—net of tax	**—**	(23)	—
Net income	**$19,337**	$ 8,085	$11,361
Earnings per common share—basic			
Income from continuing operations before cumulative effect of a change in accounting principles	**$ 1.52**	$ 1.03	$ 1.45
Discontinued operations	**1.15**	0.07	0.06
Income before cumulative effect of a change in accounting principles	**2.67**	1.10	1.51
Cumulative effect of a change in accounting principles	**—**	—	—
Net income	**$ 2.67**	$ 1.10	$ 1.51
Earnings per common share—diluted			
Income from continuing operations before cumulative effect of a change in accounting principles	**$ 1.52**	$ 1.02	$ 1.43
Discontinued operations	**1.14**	0.07	0.06
Income before cumulative effect of a change in accounting principles	**2.66**	1.09	1.49
Cumulative effect of a change in accounting principles	**—**	—	—
Net income	**$ 2.66**	$ 1.09	$ 1.49
Weighted-average shares—basic	**7,242**	7,361	7,531
Weighted-average shares—diluted	**7,274**	7,411	7,614

[(a)]Exclusive of amortization of intangible assets, except as disclosed in *Note 1K. Amortization of Intangible Assets, Depreciation and Certain Long-Lived Assets*.
Source: Pfizer, Annual Report (2006), p. 37, www.pfizer.com.

Exhibit 11.13 Flexibility in the income statement

(a) WACHOVIA CORPORATION AND SUBSIDIARIES

CONSOLIDATED STATEMENTS OF INCOME

	Years Ended December 31,		
(In millions, except per share data)	2006	2005	2004
INTEREST INCOME			
Interest and fees on loans	$ 21,976	13,970	9,858
Interest and dividends on securities	6,433	5,783	4,639
Trading account interest	1,575	1,581	1,147
Other interest income	2,281	2,355	1,644
Total interest income	32,265	23,689	17,288
INTEREST EXPENSE			
Interest on deposits	9,119	5,297	2,853
Interest on short-term borrowings	3,114	2,777	1,503
Interest on long-term debt	4,783	1,934	971
Total interest expense	17,016	10,008	5,327
Net interest income	15,249	13,681	11,961
Provision for credit losses	434	249	257
Net interest income after provision for credit losses	14,815	13,432	11,704
FEE AND OTHER INCOME			
Service charges	2,480	2,151	1,978
Other banking fees	1,756	1,491	1,226
Commissions	2,406	2,343	2,554
Fiduciary and asset management fees	3,248	3,011	2,819
Advisory, underwriting and other investment banking fees	1,345	1,109	911
Trading account profits	535	286	151
Principal investing	525	401	261
Securities gains (losses)	118	89	(10)
Other income	2,132	1,338	889
Total fee and other income	14,545	12,219	10,779
NONINTEREST EXPENSE			
Salaries and employee benefits	10,903	9,671	8,703
Occupancy	1,173	1,064	947
Equipment	1,184	1,087	1,052
Advertising	204	193	193
Communications and supplies	653	633	620
Professional and consulting fees	790	662	548
Other intangible amortization	423	416	431
Merger-related and restructuring expenses	179	292	444
Sundry expense	1,967	1,829	1,728
Total noninterest expense	17,476	15,847	14,666
Minority interest in income of consolidated subsidiaries	414	342	184
Income from continuing operations before income taxes	11,470	9,462	7,633
Income taxes	3,725	3,033	2,419
Income from continuing operations	7,745	6,429	5,214
Discontinued operations, net of income taxes	46	214	–
Net income	$ 7,791	6,643	5,214
PER COMMON SHARE DATA			
Basic			
Income from continuing operations	$ 4.70	4.13	3.87
Net income	4.72	4.27	3.87
Diluted			
Income from continuing operations	4.61	4.05	3.81
Net income	4.63	4.19	3.81
Cash dividends	$ 2.14	1.94	1.66
AVERAGE COMMON SHARES			
Basic	1,651	1,556	1,346
Diluted	1,681	1,585	1,370

Source: Wachavia Corporation, Annual Report, 2006, p. 66.

(b) COLGATE-PALMOLIVE

CONSOLIDATED STATEMENTS OF INCOME

For the years ended December 31,	2006	2005	2004
Net sales	$12,237.7	$11,396.9	$10,584.2
Cost of sales	5,536.1	5,191.9	4,747.2
Gross profit	6,701.6	6,205.0	5,837.0
Selling, general and administrative expenses	4,355.2	3,920.8	3,624.6
Other (income) expense, net	185.9	69.2	90.3
Operating profit	2,160.5	2,215.0	2,122.1
Interest expense, net	158.7	136.0	119.7
Income before income taxes	2,001.8	2,079.0	2,002.4
Provision for income taxes	648.4	727.6	675.3
Net income	$ 1,353.4	$ 1,351.4	$ 1,327.1
Earnings per common share, basic	$ 2.57	$ 2.54	$ 2.45
Earnings per common share, diluted	$ 2.46	$ 2.43	$ 2.33

15. Supplemental Income Statement Information

Other (income) expense, net	2006	2005	2004
Minority interest	$ 57.5	$ 55.3	$ 47.9
Amortization of intangible assets	16.3	15.6	14.3
Equity (income)	(3.4)	(2.0)	(8.5)
Gains on sales of non-core product lines, net	(46.5)	(147.9)	(26.7)
2004 Restructuring Program	153.1	80.8	65.3
2003 restructuring activities	—	—	2.8
Pension and other retiree benefit	—	34.0	—
Investment losses (income)	(5.7)	19.7	(8.7)
Other, net	14.6	13.7	3.9
Total Other (income) expense, net	$ 185.9	$ 69.2	$ 90.3

Interest expense, net	2006	2005	2004
Interest incurred	$ 170.0	$ 145.0	$ 126.0
Interest capitalized	(3.4)	(2.5)	(2.3)
Interest income	(7.9)	(6.5)	(4.0)
Total Interest expense, net	$ 158.7	$ 136.0	$ 119.7
Research and development	$ 241.5	$ 238.5	$ 223.4
Advertising	$1,320.3	$1,193.6	$1,063.0

Source: Colgate-Palmolive, Annual Report, 2006, pp. 32, 49.

the Impairment or Disposal of Long-lived Assets'. The US rules are less restrictive on the definition of a discontinued operation and require information on pre-tax and post-tax income.[35] Historically the US practice (under APB Opinion No. 30 in 1973) predated the first international standard on the subject in 1992 and probably influenced it. There may be discussion to accompany the financial statement disclosure, as in Textron (see Exhibit 11.14).

---

[35] IAS Plus, *Key Differences Between IFRS and US GAAP*, 2007.

Exhibit 11.14   Reporting the results of discontinued operations: Textron

Our consolidated financial statements and related footnote disclosures reflect the sold businesses of Fastening Systems, InteSys, OmniQuip and the Small Business Direct financing business as discontinued operations, net of applicable income taxes, for all periods presented in accordance with SFAS No. 144, 'Accounting for the Impairment or Disposal of Long-Lived Assets'.

We generally use a centralized approach to the cash management and financing of our manufacturing operations and, accordingly, do not allocate debt or interest expense to our discontinued businesses. Any debt and related interest expense of a specific entity within a business is recorded by the respective entity. General corporate overhead previously allocated to the businesses for reporting purposes is excluded from amounts reported as discontinued operations.

In August 2006, we completed the sale of our Fastening Systems business to Platinum Equity, a private equity investment firm, for approximately $613 million in cash and the assumption of $16 million of net indebtedness and certain liabilities. There was no gain or loss recorded upon completion of the sale. The purchase price is subject to final adjustment based on the audited net asset value, net debt and cash balances at the closing date. We currently are negotiating with Platinum Equity and expect to finalize the purchase price in early 2007.

Prior to the consummation of the sale of the Fastening Systems business, we recorded impairment and other charges of $120 million in 2006 and $387 million in 2005, which are described below.

In September 2005, our Board of Directors approved management's recommendation to explore strategic alternatives for the Fastening Systems business. Based on the approval of this recommendation and the likelihood of execution, we determined that an impairment indicator existed for both the Fastening Systems' goodwill and its long-lived assets. In our assessment of potential impairment of the goodwill, we estimated the fair value of the business using independent third-party valuations. This fair value amount then was compared with the carrying amount of the business. As the carrying amount exceeded the fair value, we then measured the amount of goodwill impairment loss. The excess of the fair value of the business over the fair value amounts assigned to its assets and liabilities represents the implied fair value of goodwill. The carrying amount of the goodwill exceeded the implied fair value of that goodwill, resulting in an impairment loss of $335 million, which was recorded in the third quarter of 2005.

In December 2005, our Board of Directors authorized the divestiture of the Fastening Systems business, and we recorded an after-tax charge of approximately $52 million, which included $37 million related to previously deferred foreign currency translation losses and $7 million in curtailment losses for employee retirement plans. After these charges, we assessed the estimated fair value of the business and determined that no further adjustment to the carrying value was required at that time. In the second quarter of 2006, we recorded an additional $120 million after-tax impairment charge to record the business at the estimated fair value less cost to sell at that time based on offers received from potential purchasers.

In 2005, we recorded a net $46 million gain on disposal primarily related to a tax benefit recorded upon the sale of InteSys.

Operating results of these discontinued businesses, primarily related to Fastening Systems, are as follows:

(In millions)	2006	2005	2004
Revenue	$ 1,101	$ 1,936	$ 1,994
(Loss) income from discontinued operations before special charges	(94)	(388)	72
Special charges	–	(11)	(91)
Loss from discontinued operations	(94)	(399)	(19)
Income tax (expense) benefit	(11)	40	9
Operating loss from discontinued operations, net of income taxes	(105)	(359)	(10)
Gain on disposal, net of income taxes	–	46	–
Loss from discontinued operations, net of income taxes	$ (105)	$ (313)	$ (10)

At December 30, 2006, assets of discontinued operations included current assets of $69 million related to the sale of the Fastening Systems business, and liabilities of discontinued operations included current liabilities of $57 million, representing liabilities retained upon the sale of the Fastening Systems business.

Source: Textron, Annual Report 2006, p. 46, www.textron.com.

Cash flow statement

The FASB has prescribed the nature of the cash flow statement in SFAS 95. The reconciliation of operating profit and cash flow from operating activities is generally included as part of the statement rather than as a note. The categories within the cash flow statement and the level of disclosure are very similar to those of IAS 7. IAS 7 is flexible on the classification of interest received and paid, while SFAS 95 requires these items to be classified as an operating activity. IAS 7 allows overdrafts to be included in cash if they form an integral part of cash management. SFAS 95 excludes overdrafts from 'cash'.[36]

Statement of changes in shareholders' equity (stockholders' equity)

This statement is required by SFAS 130 but there is considerable variety of presentation. It may include changes in the following components:

- preferred shares
- common shares (at par value or at stated value)
- additional paid-in capital
- retained earnings
- treasury shares (repurchased equity)
- valuation gains and losses unrealized (marketable equity securities)
- cumulative translation gains and losses (foreign operations).

SFAS 130, 'Reporting Comprehensive Income', was issued in 1997. It requires that comprehensive income items which bypass the income statement should be reported in a financial statement, displayed as prominently as any other financial statement. Such items might include foreign currency translation adjustments and gains or losses on certain securities. There is no format specified for this statement of comprehensive income. A similar idea is already established in the UK with a statement of total recognized gains and losses. IAS 1 requires a statement of changes in equity but does not specify a presentation of comprehensive income. An example of a statement on comprehensive income is provided by Dow Chemical Company which emphasizes the changes in share owners' equity (Exhibit 11.15).

11.7.2.4 Notes to the accounts

There are extensive requirements for notes to the accounts. Cross-referencing from the primary financial statements to the notes is not always clear so the reader is obliged on occasions to work backwards from the notes rather than forwards from the financial statements. Notes to the accounts may result from FASB standards, SEC regulations, AICPA guidance and other parts of the collection of 'US GAAP'.

Extensive disclosures are required regarding financial instruments and derivative financial instruments, covering many aspects of treasury management within the company. Notes to the accounts give detailed information on the costs of post-retirement benefits, including pensions. Employee stock option plans are described in the notes. Contingent losses and liabilities are reported in the notes where they are reasonably possible. If they are probable, then they must be included in the primary financial statements. SFAS 5 defines 'probable' and 'possible'. Environmental liabilities are to be disclosed, although substantial management judgement is needed in deciding the precise nature of the disclosure. Another important area of disclosure is that of related party transactions where 'related parties' are subject to a wide definition.

---

[36] IAS Plus, *Key Differences Between IFRS and US GAAP*, 2007.

Consolidated Statements of Stockholders' Equity

(In millions) For the years ended December 31	2006	2005	2004
Common Stock			
Balance at beginning and end of year	$ 2,453	$ 2,453	$ 2,453
Additional Paid-in Capital			
Balance at beginning of year	661	274	8
Stock-based compensation	169	387	266
Balance at end of year	830	661	274
Unearned ESOP Shares			
Balance at beginning of year	(1)	(12)	(30)
Shares allocated to ESOP participants	1	11	18
Balance at end of year	–	(1)	(12)
Retained Earnings			
Balance at beginning of year	14,719	11,527	9,994
Net income	3,724	4,515	2,797
Dividends declared on common stock	(1,438)	(1,292)	(1,264)
Accrued dividends on deferred stock	(18)	(31)	–
Balance at end of year	16,987	14,719	11,527
Accumulated Other Comprehensive Loss			
Unrealized Gains on Investments at beginning of year	11	41	43
Unrealized gains (losses)	31	(30)	(2)
Balance at end of year	42	11	41
Cumulative Translation Adjustments at beginning of year	(663)	301	(199)
Translation adjustments	651	(964)	500
Balance at end of year	(12)	(663)	301
Minimum Pension Liability at beginning of year	(1,312)	(1,357)	(1,315)
Adjustments	1,147	45	(42)
Balance at end of year, 2006 prior to adoption of SFAS No. 158	(165)	(1,312)	(1,357)
Reversal of Minimum Pension Liability under SFAS No. 158	165	–	–
Recognition of prior service cost and net loss under SFAS No. 158	(2,192)	–	–
Pension and Other Postretirement Benefit Plans at end of year	(2,192)	–	–
Accumulated Derivative Gain (Loss) at beginning of year	15	38	(20)
Net hedging results	(127)	227	107
Reclassification to earnings	39	(250)	(49)
Balance at end of year	(73)	15	38
Total accumulated other comprehensive loss	(2,235)	(1,949)	(977)
Treasury Stock			
Balance at beginning of year	(559)	(995)	(1,759)
Purchases	(746)	(68)	(15)
Issuance to employees and employee plans	335	504	779
Balance at end of year	(970)	(559)	(995)
Net Stockholders' Equity	$ 17,065	$ 15,324	$ 12,270

Consolidated Statements of Comprehensive Income

(In millions) For the years ended December 31	2006	2005	2004
Net Income Available for Common Stockholders	$ 3,724	$ 4,515	$ 2,797
Other Comprehensive Income (Loss), Net of Tax (tax amounts shown below for 2006, 2005, 2004)			
Unrealized gains (losses) on investments:			
Unrealized holding gains (losses) during the period (net of tax of $30, $(7), $20)	61	(21)	24
Less: Reclassification adjustments for net amounts included in net income (net of tax of $(16), $(6), $(16))	(30)	(9)	(26)
Cumulative translation adjustments (net of tax of $(39), $(29), $101)	651	(964)	500
Minimum pension liability adjustments (net of tax of $657, $26, $(25))	1,147	45	(42)
Net gains (losses) on cash flow hedging derivative instruments (net of tax of $(39), $8, $9)	(88)	(23)	58
Total other comprehensive income (loss)	1,741	(972)	514
Comprehensive Income	$ 5,465	$ 3,543	$ 3,311

11.7.2.5 Critical accounting estimates

In a release dated December 2003,[37] the SEC reminded companies of the importance of providing disclosures about critical accounting estimates or assumptions in their MD&A. There had been a previous reminder, in 2001,[38] that under the MD&A requirements at that time companies should address material implications of uncertainties associated with the methods, assumptions and estimates underlying the company's critical accounting measurements.

The guidance to companies is that they should consider whether they have made accounting estimates or assumptions which are material in nature and in impact. The additional disclosures should supplement, not duplicate, the description of accounting policies already given in the notes to the financial statements. Exhibit 11.16 shows how Colgate-Palmolive Company explains its critical accounting estimates which are in the specific areas of uncertainty relating to insurance risks.

11.7.2.6 Voluntary disclosure

The FASB published, in 2001, a research report *Improving Business Reporting: Insights into Enhancing Voluntary Disclosure* to help preparers improve their business reporting by voluntary disclosure.

11.7.2.7 Interactive data

The SEC announced in 2007 a project to make its filings of annual and interim reports more accessible to investors by providing interactive data. This development was confirmed following a trial run during 2007 involving 36 companies supplying their filing returns using the XBRL computer language which allows a 'tag' to be attached to each item of information in the report. The SEC explained on its website:

> Interactive data pinpoints all of the facts and figures trapped in these dense documents, allowing investors to immediately pull out exactly the information they want, and instantly compare it to the results of other companies, performance in past years, industry averages—however the investor wishes to slice and dice the data. Sophisticated tools to analyze financial data could be developed and become available to the average investor. Meanwhile, for the financial pros and financial publishers, analyzing companies could become cheaper and easier, as inputting and re-keying costs are lower and resources are freed to focus on creating better analytical tools. [39]

The use of XBRL will make it easier for users to make comparisons across data filings. For XBRL to be effective there has to be a standard dictionary ('taxonomy') of terminology, which is likely to reduce diversity in financial reporting. There is a danger that companies increase their use of 'boilerplate' wording (standard paragraphs or phrases, all used identically).

11.7.3 Assets and liabilities

11.7.3.1 Capitalization of borrowing costs

SFAS 34 requires that borrowing costs are normally reported through the income statement. However, in specific circumstances the interest cost may be added to the asset cost (referred to as capitalization of borrowing costs) in order to obtain a measure of acquisition

---

[37] SEC (2003).

[38] SEC (2001).

[39] http://www.sec.gov/spotlight/xbrl/interactivedata.htm#idata_what.

| Exhibit 11.16 | Disclosure of critical accounting estimates, Colgate-Palmolive Company |

Critical Accounting Policies and Use of Estimates

The preparation of financial statements requires management to use judgment and make estimates. The level of uncertainty in estimates and assumptions increases with the length of time until the underlying transactions are completed. Actual results could ultimately differ from those estimates. The accounting policies that are most critical in the preparation of the Company's Consolidated Financial Statements are those that are both important to the presentation of the Company's financial condition and results of operations and require significant or complex judgments and estimates on the part of management. The Company's critical accounting policies are reviewed periodically with the Audit Committee of the Board of Directors.

In certain instances, accounting principles generally accepted in the United States of America allow for the selection of alternative accounting methods. The Company's significant policies that involve the selection of alternative methods are accounting for shipping and handling costs and inventories.

- Shipping and handling costs may be reported as either a component of cost of sales or selling, general and administrative expenses. The Company reports such costs, primarily related to warehousing and outbound freight, in the Consolidated Statements of Income as a component of Selling, general and administrative expenses. Accordingly, the Company's gross profit margin is not comparable with the gross profit margin of those companies that include shipping and handling charges in cost of sales. If such costs had been included in cost of sales, gross profit margin as a percent of sales would have decreased by 770 bps from 54.8% to 47.1% in 2006 and decreased by 750 bps and 720 bps in 2005 and 2004, respectively, with no impact on reported earnings.

- The Company accounts for inventories using both the first-in, first-out (FIFO) method (approximately 80% of inventories) and the last-in, first-out (LIFO) method (approximately 20% of inventories). There would have been no impact on reported earnings for 2006, 2005 and 2004 had all inventories been accounted for under the FIFO method.

The areas of accounting that involve significant or complex judgments and estimates are pensions and other postretirement benefits, stock options, asset impairment, tax valuation allowances, and legal and other contingencies.

- In pension accounting, the most significant actuarial assumptions are the discount rate and the long-term rate of return on plan assets. The discount rate for U.S. plans was 5.80%, 5.50% and 5.75% as of December 31, 2006, 2005 and 2004, respectively. Discount rates used for the U.S. defined benefit and other postretirement plans are based on a yield curve constructed from a portfolio of high-quality bonds for which the timing and amount of cash outflows approximate the estimated payouts of the U.S. plans. For the Company's international plans, the discount rates are set by benchmarking against investment-grade corporate bonds rated AA or better. The assumed long-term rate of return on plan assets for U.S. plans was 8.0% as of December 31, 2006, 2005 and 2004. In determining the long-term rate of return, the Company considers the nature of the plans' investments, an expectation for the plans' investment strategies and the historical rate of return. The historical rate of return for the U.S. plans for the most recent 15-year period was 9%. In addition, the current rate of return assumption for the U.S. plans is based upon a targeted asset allocation of approximately 33% in fixed income securities (which are expected to earn approximately 6% in the long-term), 63% in equity securities (which are expected to earn approximately 9.25% in the long-term) and 4% in real estate and other (which are expected to earn approximately 6% in the long-term). A 1% change in either the discount rate or the assumed rate of return on plan assets of the U.S. pension plans would cumulatively impact future Net income by approximately $10. A third assumption is the long-term rate of compensation, a change in which would partially offset the impact of a change in either the discount rate or the long-term rate of return. This rate was 4.0% as of December 31, 2006, 2005 and 2004. (Refer to Note 10 to the Consolidated Financial Statements for further discussion of the Company's pension and other postretirement plans.)

- The most judgmental assumption in accounting for other postretirement benefits is the medical cost trend rate. The Company reviews external data and its own historical trends for health care costs to determine the medical cost trend rate. The assumed rate of increase is 10% for 2007, declining 1% per year until reaching the ultimate assumed rate of increase of 5% per year. The effect of a 1% increase in the assumed long-term medical cost trend rate would reduce Net income by approximately $4.

● Effective January 1, 2006, the Company adopted SFAS 123R, 'Share-Based Payment,' (SFAS 123R) using the modified prospective method. SFAS 123R requires companies to recognize the cost of employee services received in exchange for awards of equity instruments, such as stock options and restricted stock, based on the fair value of those awards at the date of grant. The Company uses the Black-Scholes-Merton (Black-Scholes) option pricing model to determine the fair value of stock-option awards under SFAS 123R. The weighted average estimated fair value of each stock option granted for the year ended December 31, 2006 was $10.30. The Black-Scholes model uses various assumptions to determine the fair value of options. These assumptions include expected term of options, expected volatility, risk-free interest rate and expected dividend yield. While these assumptions do not require significant judgment, as the significant inputs are determined from independent third-party sources, changes in these inputs, however, could result in significant changes in fair value. A one year change in term would result in a 15% change in fair value. A one percent change in volatility would change fair value by 4%.

● Asset impairment analysis performed for goodwill and intangible assets requires several estimates including future cash flows, growth rates and the selection of a discount rate. Since the estimated fair value of the Company's intangible assets substantially exceeds the recorded book value, significant changes in these estimates would have to occur to result in an impairment charge related to these assets. Asset impairment analysis related to certain fixed assets in connection with the 2004 Restructuring Program requires management's best estimate of net realizable value.

● Tax valuation allowances are established to reduce tax assets such as tax loss carryforwards, to net realizable value. Factors considered in estimating net realizable value include historical results by tax jurisdiction, carryforward periods, income tax strategies and forecasted taxable income.

● Legal and other contingency reserves are based on management's assessment of the risk of potential loss, which includes consultation with outside legal counsel and advisors. Such assessments are reviewed each period and revised, based on current facts and circumstances, if necessary. While it is possible that the Company's cash flows and results of operations in a particular quarter or year could be materially affected by the one-time impacts of the resolution of such contingencies, it is the opinion of management that the ultimate disposition of these matters will not have a material impact on the Company's financial position, or ongoing results of operations and cash flows. (Refer to Note 13 to the Consolidated Financial Statements for further discussion of the Company's contingencies.)

The Company generates revenue through the sale of well-known consumer products to trade customers under established trading terms. While the recognition of revenue and receivables requires the use of estimates, there is a short time frame (typically less than 60 days) between the shipment of product and cash receipt, thereby reducing the level of uncertainty in these estimates. (Refer to Note 2 to the Consolidated Financial Statements for further description of the Company's significant accounting policies.)

Source: Colgate-Palmolive Company, Annual Report (2006), pp. 27–29.

cost that more closely reflects the enterprise's total investment in the asset. Capitalization is also used so as to charge a cost that relates to the acquisition of a resource that will benefit future periods against the revenues of the periods benefited. In the circumstances set out in SFAS 34 the capitalization is mandatory (compulsory). The types of asset to which borrowing costs may be attached are assets under construction or completed investments intended for sale or lease. In contrast, IAS 23 makes capitalization available as a policy choice, without compulsion. This difference is not included in the short-term convergence project.

| Exhibit 11.17 | Altria: capitalization of software costs |

> **Costs of computer software**
>
> Software costs: Altria Group, Inc. capitalizes certain computer software and software development costs incurred in connection with developing or obtaining computer software for internal use. Capitalized software costs are included in property, plant and equipment on the consolidated balance sheets and are amortized on a straight-line basis over the estimated useful lives of the software, which do not exceed five years.

Source: Altria Group, Annual Report (2006), p. 64, www.altria.com.

11.7.3.2 Capitalization of software development costs

SFAS 86 requires that, after technological feasibility has been established, there must be capitalization of all costs incurred for a computer software product that is sold, leased or otherwise marketed. The standard also sets methods for amortization. The Accounting Standards Executive Committee has issued Statement of Position 98-1 *Accounting for the Costs of Computer Software Developed For or Obtained For Internal Use*. The SoP changes previous practice which was to treat such items as an expense of the period. IASB standards do not include this type of industry-specific standard. Exhibit 11.17 (Altria) shows how the company reported the new accounting policy on the first occasion that it was applied.

11.7.3.3 Depreciation

The definition of depreciation has a long history from ARB 43, emphasizing the allocation of cost. ARB 43 specifically stated that it was a process of allocation, not valuation. For income tax purposes, many companies use accelerated depreciation (as allowed by SFAS 109) but this is used relatively rarely in the published accounts of listed companies. One case, showing use of accelerated depreciation as a means of dealing crudely with the additional cost of asset replacement, is General Electric, giving the explanation set out in Exhibit 11.18.

11.7.3.4 Valuation of tangible fixed assets

The prohibition on revaluation of fixed assets dates from ARB 43 and APB 6. It is consistent with the cost model permitted by IAS 16. The prohibition on revaluation extends to investment properties. Some real estate companies (property companies) present historical cost accounts but provide supplementary notes on current value information.

| Exhibit 11.18 | General Electric: accounting policies (extract) |

> **Depreciation and amortization**
>
> The cost of GE manufacturing plant and equipment is depreciated over its estimated economic life. U.S. assets are depreciated using an accelerated method based on a sum-of-the-years digits formula; non-U.S. assets are depreciated on a straight-line basis.

Source: General Electric, Annual Report (2006), p. 75, www.ge.com.

11.7.3.5 Impairment of assets

There is more interest in reduction in the value of fixed assets, referred to as impairment. The current regulation is found in SFAS 144 'Accounting for the Impairment or Disposal of Long-lived Assets'. Previous rules in APB 4 and then SFAS 121 were not clear on when and by how much an impairment should be recognized. The test for impairment in SFAS 144 requires that an impairment loss should be recognized if, and only if, the sum of the future *undiscounted* cash flows is less than the carrying amount of the asset. This caused difficulty for the IASC Core Standards project because the IASC Board believed this test carried too high a risk that the recognition of impairment would be delayed. The Board's rule in IAS 36 is to compare the *discounted* cash flows with the carrying amount, causing earlier recognition.

Where impairment is to be recognized, SFAS 144 states that the recoverable amount is fair value defined as the price for sale or purchase of the asset between willing parties. IAS 36 requires that recoverable amount should be based on the higher of net selling price and value in use. In many cases both approaches will lead to the same answer but IAS 36 may sometimes result in a higher recoverable amount based on value in use.

Finally, SFAS 144 prohibits reversal of an impairment loss where the asset value recovers. IAS 36 specifies circumstances where reversal is required. The differences between SFAS 144 and IAS 36 are not being addressed in the short-term convergence project.[40]

11.7.3.6 Intangible assets

'Intangible assets' are stated at historical cost *less* accumulated amortization. For many years APB 17 prescribed straight-line depreciation over a maximum of 40 years. Even in the case of brand names, where it might be argued that the asset life is longer, the view of the standard was that 40 years was the maximum period. All intangible assets were treated in a similar manner. In 1999 the FASB appeared to be considering reducing the maximum period of amortization from 40 years to 20 years to align with the international standards. Then, in a complete turnaround, FASB took a major change of direction resulting in a new standard SFAS 142 'Goodwill and Other Intangibles', issued in 2001, replacing amortization by requiring an annual goodwill impairment test. The change to SFAS 142 received high-profile political attention, as explained in section 11.3.4. It appeared that a more flexible approach to amortization had been offered as a 'sweetener' to the abolition of pooling of interest accounting under SFAS 141.

Under a separate standard, SFAS 2, research and development (R&D) expenditure is one instance of intangible assets where there is a strong element of conservatism that all expenditure should be reported through the income statement as incurred. It has also been suggested that concern about measurement reliability led in this case to rigid uniformity. This is in contrast to IAS 38, which modifies this approach with a requirement that development costs meeting specific criteria should be capitalized. However, as noted in Chapter 2, there has been continued pressure to base the international practice on expense treatment only. Dow Chemical Company (Exhibit 11.19) explains how environmental costs may be closed as assets where there is an expected future benefit (see section 10.6.4 for the definition of an asset).

---

[40] IAS Plus, *Key Differences Between IFRS and US GAAP*, 2007.

Exhibit 11.19 Environmental costs as assets, Dow Chemical Company

Extract from Significant Accounting Policies

Environmental costs are capitalized if the costs extend the life of the property, increase its capacity, and/or mitigate or prevent contamination from future operations. Environmental costs are also capitalized in recognition of legal asset retirement obligations resulting from the acquisition, construction and/or normal operation of a long-lived asset. Costs related to environmental contamination treatment and cleanup are charged to expense. Estimated future incremental operations, maintenance and management costs directly related to remediation are accrued when such costs are probable and reasonably estimable.

Source: Dow Chemical Company, Form 10-k, p. 62.

11.7.3.7 Marketable securities

Marketable securities must be carried in the balance sheet at the lower of cost or market value on a portfolio basis. This is conservative in the overall approach, but less conservative in permitting the loss on one investment to be set against a gain on another. Current and non-current investments must be separated. Reductions in value of the current investment portfolio must be taken through the income statement, but those in relation to non-current investments are taken to a separate component of shareholders' equity. SFAS 133 requires disclosure of the fair value of financial instruments where practicable. SFAS 133 is considerably more detailed and rules based than IAS 39 but both apply the same principles of fair valuation.

11.7.3.8 Inventory and long-term contracts

Valuation of inventory is covered in ARB 43 (1953), requiring the lower of cost or market value. Cost may be determined using a range of techniques which include FIFO, LIFO and average cost. 'Market value' is defined as current replacement cost subject to an upper limit of net realizable value and a lower limit of net realizable value less a normal profit margin. IAS 2 differs in requiring the lower of cost and net realizable value. In a revision that indicated some independence of the IASB from US influence, IAS 2 (2003) prohibits the use of LIFO. Around two-thirds of US companies use LIFO in whole or in part (see, for example, the tobacco products company Altria, Exhibit 11.20). A strong factor is that the Internal Revenue Service (IRS) requires that if LIFO is used for tax purposes it must be used for financial reporting purposes.

Accounting for long-term contracts is dealt with in ARB 45 (1955). Both percentage of completion and completed contract methods are permitted, although there is a preference expressed for the former. IAS 11 requires percentage of completion. IAS 2 differs from US GAAP in prohibiting the use of LIFO and in permitting a reversal of inventory write-down. These differences are not considered in the short-term convergence project.

11.7.3.9 Financial instruments

SFAS 133, issued in 1996, specifies disclosure rules for derivative financial instruments and hedging activities. SFAS 137 deferred the date of implementation of SFAS 133 to fiscal years beginning after June 2000, to allow companies time to modify their information systems and to issue SFAS 138, effective with SFAS 133. There are hundreds of pages of guidance on SFAS 133 and its related documents. The fundamental principles are (i) derivative instruments should be reported in financial statements because they meet the definitions of

Exhibit 11.20 | **LIFO inventory valuation, Altria**

ACCOUNTING POLICIES [extract]

Inventories: Inventories are stated at the lower of cost or market. The last-in, first-out ('LIFO') method is used to cost substantially all domestic inventories. The cost of other inventories is principally determined by the average cost method. It is a generally recognized industry practice to classify leaf tobacco inventory as a current asset although part of such inventory, because of the duration of the aging process, ordinarily would not be utilized within one year. Altria Group, Inc. adopted the provisions of SFAS No. 151, 'Inventory Costs' prospectively as of January 1, 2006. SFAS No. 151 requires that abnormal idle facility expense, spoilage, freight and handling costs be recognized as current-period charges. In addition, SFAS No. 151 requires that allocation of fixed production overhead costs to inventories be based on the normal capacity of the production facility. The effect of adoption did not have a material impact on Altria Group, Inc.'s consolidated results of operations, financial position or cash flows.

Note 6.

Inventories:

The cost of approximately 28% and 34% of inventories in 2006 and 2005, respectively, was determined using the LIFO method. The stated LIFO amounts of inventories were approximately $0.6 billion lower than the current cost of inventories at December 31, 2006 and 2005.

Source: Altria Inc., Annual Report 2006, pp. 54 and 58, www.altria.com.

assets and liabilities, (ii) fair value is the only relevant measure, (iii) changes in the fair value of derivative instruments are included in net income, and (iv) special accounting for 'hedged' items should be restricted to qualifying items. Changes in the value of 'fair value' hedges are included in net income. 'Other comprehensive income' is used to report changes in the value of 'cash flow' hedges and foreign currency hedges of net investments in a foreign operation. These rules on reporting hedges are similar to IAS 39 but may cause significant adjustments in reconciliations from GAAP in other countries.

11.7.3.10 Off-balance-sheet transactions

Section 11.3.2 explains the concerns raised about special purpose entities (SPEs) following the collapse of Enron. The SPEs were off-balance-sheet (not consolidated as subsidiaries) because an independent third party (defined as a holding of 3 per cent or more of the equity of the SPE) controlled the entity and carried the risks and rewards. Even before Enron there were warnings that 3 per cent seemed a very low level of outside interest. In 2003 an FASB Interpretation (FIN 46) was introduced to clarify the treatment of 'variable interest entities' (as a new description of SPEs). The variable interest could relate to variability of net income or loss, or to variability of fair values of assets. FIN 46 requires the 'primary beneficiary' of the variable interest to consolidate the results of the variable interest entity. It also specifies disclosures.

However, the SPE is only one example of off-balance-sheet finance. There is no single standard in the USA which deals with off-balance-sheet transactions in general terms. Similarly, the IASB has no specific standard on the subject. Various separate FASB standards address specific issues such as sale and repurchase of products and sale of real estate with conditions attached. Disclosures are required about some long-term obligations which establish commitments to future cash outflows. These and other specific standards restrict the scope for off-balance-sheet transactions in particular situations.

FASB standards continue to take a more flexible approach to consolidation of subsidiary companies which does leave scope for assets and liabilities remaining off-balance-sheet. The usual condition for establishing that control exists is ownership of a majority shareholding. There is no concept of 'dominant interest' or of entities which closely resemble subsidiaries (quasi-subsidiaries), although the FASB has a long-term project in progress. Also, as mentioned earlier, joint ventures are generally reported using equity accounting where the investment appears as a single line item. Proportional consolidation is rare.

11.7.3.11 Deferred taxation

Consistent with the balance sheet approach of the FASB's conceptual framework, SFAS 109 requires the deferred taxation liability to be accounted for on the basis of the full liability which the enterprise will eventually have to meet. A change in the expected liability will result in an expense in the income statement. The move from the earlier APB 11, based on the matching of income and expenses in any accounting period and having little regard to the resulting balance sheet figure, reflects the FASB's intention to move to a balance sheet approach.

11.7.4 Income statement and economic activity

11.7.4.1 Share-based payments

Share-based payments are called 'stock compensation' in the USA. The accounting treatment of share-based payments in IFRS 2 is controversial. The subject has raised similar controversy in the USA. Emerging high-tech companies took advantage of the rapidly rising stock market to pay staff in options rather than expend large amounts of cash. These companies were strongly opposed to reporting an expense that would lower profit, or lead to reported losses and so increase the cost of capital.[41] Under APB 25 the employer can choose to measure the cost as the intrinsic value at the date the option is granted. That is generally zero because the market price is below the amount that the employee must pay to acquire shares under the option agreement. SFAS 123 establishes a method of accounting for stock-based compensation that is based on fair value. Because of the strong opposition SFAS 123 encouraged, but did not require, the use of fair value. SFAS 148 provides transition alternatives for voluntarily measuring compensation using a fair value method. As part of the convergence process between FASB and IFRS, FASB has indicated that it will move towards the fair value approach only, as in IFRS 2.[42]

11.7.4.2 Extraordinary items

There is a debate in measuring profit about the relative merits of the **all-inclusive concept** and the **current operating performance concept**. The all-inclusive concept takes the view that all items affecting owners' equity, except for dividends and capital transactions, should be included in net income. The current operating performance concept takes the view that net income should report normal, recurring items of profit and loss

---

[41] Wolk *et al.* (2004), p. 395.

[42] IAS Plus, *Key Differences Between IFRS and US GAAP*, 2007.

relating only to the current period. In moving towards comprehensive income the FASB appeared to favour the all-inclusive concept. However, it also continues to permit separate disclosure of extraordinary items, which reflects the current operating performance concept. US rules permit the separate reporting of extraordinary items, with strict rules for defining these. Extraordinary items are transactions and other events that are (a) material in nature, (b) unusual in nature, and (c) infrequent in occurrence.[43] Extraordinary items are disclosed separately in the income statement, net of tax. Professional judgement is required to identify extraordinary items. Some areas of GAAP require specific items to be treated as extraordinary. The most common items are expropriations of property, gains or losses due to a major casualty, and losses resulting from prohibition under a new law or regulation.

IAS 1 prohibits extraordinary items. The reasons given[44] indicate that the IASB prefers the all-inclusive concept of profit.

11.7.4.3 Earnings per share

The FASB issued SFAS 128, 'Earnings per Share', in March 1997. It was the result of an intention to simplify existing standards in the USA and make these compatible with international standards. SFAS 128 requires that entities with simple capital structures present a single figure of 'earnings per common share' on the face of the income statement, whereas those with complex capital structures should present both primary and fully diluted earnings per share.

There had been criticism that the former standard, APB Opinion No. 15, was arbitrary and unnecessarily complex. Although it required companies to report the primary earnings per share and the fully diluted earnings per share, in practice the disclosure note on earnings per share was often of considerable length because the earnings per share figure was reported separately for each class of share and, in each case, before and after discontinued operations. Earnings per share figures were also reported separately for income before extraordinary items, for extraordinary items alone and for cumulative effects of accounting changes. This variety and detail may have provided an example of professionalism meeting a variety of user needs but in practice it appears to have created potential overload of information. An example of the former complexity of the earnings per share disclosure is provided in the extract from General Motors contrasting the report for 1996 with that of 2006 (see Exhibit 11.21).

There was at one stage a difference of opinion between the FASB and the IASC on the approach to be taken in calculating the fully diluted earnings per share (EPS). The FASB took the view that diluted earnings per share was information on past performance which had predictive value as indirect input to a predictive process. The IASC initially took the view that fully diluted earnings per share provided a forward-looking warning signal. It tried to accommodate both approaches in E 52, but after receiving comment moved towards the US position in issuing IAS 33 in 1997. That in turn allowed the FASB to harmonize by issuing SFAS 128. Differences remained between IASB and FASB in some matters of detailed calculation; these have been taken into consideration by FASB in subsequent exposure drafts amending SFAS 128. The direction of convergence appears to be that the US position is moving towards that of the IASB.[45]

---

[43] APB 30 para. 2.

[44] IAS 1 (2003) paras BC14 to BC18.

[45] Williams and Carcello (2007), p. 14.24; PwC (2006), p. 75.

Exhibit 11.21 General Motors: earnings per share disclosure

(a) As presented in 1996

Earnings attributable to common stocks (Note 20)	1996	1995	1994
$1-2/3 par value from continuing operations before cumulative effect of accounting changes	$ 4,589	$ 5,404	$ 4,296
Income (loss) from discontinued operations (Note 2)	(5)	105	349
Cumulative effect of accounting changes (Note 1)	–	(52)	(751)
Net earnings attributable to $1-2/3 par value	$ 4,584	$ 5,457	$ 3,894
Income from discontinued operations attributable to Class E (Note 2)	$15	$ 795	$ 444
Class H before cumulative effect of accounting change	$ 283	$ 265	$ 249
Cumulative effect of accounting change (Note 1)	–	–	(7)
Net earnings attributable to Class H	$ 283	$ 265	$ 242
Average number of shares of common stocks outstanding (in millions)			
$1-2/3 par value	756	750	741
Class E (Notes 2 and 20)	470	405	260
Class H	98	96	92
Earnings per share attributable to common stocks (Note 20)			
$1-2/3 par value from continuing operations before cumulative effect of accounting changes	$ 6.07	$ 7.14	$ 5.74
Income (loss) from discontinued operations (Note 2)	(0.01)	0.14	0.46
Cumulative effect of accounting changes (Note 1)	–	(0.07)	(1.05)
Net earnings attributable to $1-2/3 par value	$ 6.06	$ 7.21	$ 5.15
Income from discontinued operations attributable to Class E (Note 2)	$ 0.04	$ 1.96	$ 1.71
Class H before cumulative effect of accounting change	$ 2.88	$ 2.77	$ 2.70
Cumulative effect of accounting change (Note 1)	–	–	(0.08)
Net earnings attributable to Class H	$ 2.88	$ 2.77	$ 2.62

Reference should be made to the notes to consolidated financial statements.

Source: General Motors, annual report (1996), p. 59.

(b) As presented in 2006, extract from income statement

	2006	2005	2004
Basic earnings (loss) per share			
Earnings (loss) before cumulative effect of a change in accounting principle	$ (3.50)	$ (18.23)	$ 4.78
Cumulative effect of a change in accounting principle	–	$ (0.19)	–
Earnings (loss) per share, basic	$ (3.50)	$ (18.42)	$ 4.78
Diluted earnings (loss) per share			
Earnings (loss) before cumulative effect of a change in accounting principle	$ (3.50)	$ (18.23)	$ 4.76
Cumulative effect of a change in accounting principle	–	$ (0.19)	–
Earnings (loss) per share, basic	$ (3.50)	$ (18.42)	$ 4.76

Source: General Motors Annual Report (2006), p. 99, www.gm.com (Note 22 gives more detailed explanations).

11.7.5 Group accounting

11.7.5.1 Business combinations and consolidated financial statements

The development of group accounting has been described in section 11.3.4. Convergence discussions between IFRS and US GAAP have been divided into phases reflecting the challenge of reaching agreement on a range of issues.

Under IAS 27 the basis of consolidation policy is control, looking to governance, risks and benefits. Under US GAAP the traditional focus[46] has been on majority voting rights. Companies must also consolidate a 'variable interest equity' where the investor is the primary beneficiary based on assessment of risks and rewards.[47] A variable interest occurs where a contractual, ownership or other pecuniary interest in an entity changes with changes in the value of the entity's net assets (excluding variable interests).[48]

For SPEs the IFRS applies the same principles as it does to all other commercial entities in determining whether control exists. In the USA consolidation depends on the qualifying criteria. The criteria look to whether the SPE has sufficient equity 'at risk'.

Convergence of SFAS and IFRS in the areas of business combinations and consolidated financial statements has been a major challenge for developing beyond the stable platform period.

One major change in the USA is the replacement of ARB 51 (Consolidated Financial Statements) with a new standard taking forward many of the principles of ARB 51 but changing the approach to minority interest, renamed as 'non-controlling interest'. FASB accepts the idea of reporting the non-controlling interest as a separate component of shareholders' equity, moving its perception from that of 'parent company theory' to 'entity theory'.[49]

11.7.5.2 Procedures for acquisition accounting[50]

US GAAP allows only the acquisition method in accounting for a business combination. IFRS 3 also deals with the acquisition method. There are some differences in detail that are being considered by FASB and IASB together. The date on which the consideration is measured may be different. IFRS 3 uses the acquisition date (the date on which control passes) while the US GAAP takes the closing date of the deal, which could be later. The measurement of minority interest is different. IFRS 3 takes the minority's percentage of fair values. US GAAP takes the minority's percentage of the book value (carrying amount) in the accounting records of the acquired company. Negative goodwill is recognized immediately as a gain under IFRS 3. The US procedure allocates the negative goodwill by sharing it across certain non-financial assets acquired. Any excess is recognized as an extraordinary gain.

For entities under common control, US GAAP requires the pooling of interests method to be used. IASB did not reach agreement on this issue by the date of the 'stable platform' in March 2004 and has included it in Phase II of the IASB's business combination project. In the meantime merger accounting continues to be used in such circumstances. The intended convergence with IASB standards took a further step in July 2004

---

[46] See ARB 51.

[47] FIN 46(R).

[48] Williams and Carcello (2007), pp. 8.17–8.18.

[49] Williams and Carcello (2007), p. 8.30.

[50] IAS 1 (2003) paras BC 14 to BC 18.

with an FASB publication on 'tentative decisions' as an indication of the direction of FASB thinking.[51] This was not an exposure draft and comments were not invited.

11.7.5.3 Segment reporting

In June 1997 the FASB issued SFAS 131 'Disclosures about Segments of an Enterprise and Related Information'. It superseded SFAS 14, which had for some years required segmental disclosure of turnover, profits and assets analyzed by industry and geographical segments. SFAS 14, in turn, had been prompted by earlier requirements of the SEC in relation to reports filed on Form 10-K. The move to SFAS 131 was prompted by an emerging debate on the definition of segments. The view in the USA and Canada has been that the enterprise should be allowed to base segments on the organizational structure of the enterprise, even where such segments cover more than one industry or geographical area. The IASC had, at one stage in its discussion, preferred to concentrate on diversity of industry and geography which requires segmental analysis on this basis. The resulting revision of IAS 14 was a compromise which accommodated the position in SFAS 131, but left some flexibility for other countries which prefer the approach based on geographical and industry-based risk and reward. US GAAP is more flexible than IAS 14 on the accounting basis for reporting. IFRS require the amounts to be based on IFRS GAAP but US companies base the amounts on whatever basis is used for internal purposes. The reason given by FASB for requiring companies to disclose segment data based on how management make their decisions was that this was a response to requests from analysts for better information about segments.

11.8 Gray's accounting values

11.8.1 Professionalism versus statutory control

Gray's (1988) analysis, based on Hofstede's (1984) framework, indicates an expectation of strong professionalism. This means a preference for the exercise of individual professional judgement and professional self-regulation. The practical reality is complex, because the standard-setting process is self-regulatory and makes considerable use of professional expertise. However, standard setting is subject to indirect statutory control through the SEC which may, if it chooses, exercise a strong influence on particular accounting practices. The accountancy profession is independent and self-regulating so that the institutional arrangements do support the classification of strong professionalism. Professional judgement is exercised in the format of presentation and the use of notes to the accounts; on the other hand, professionalism is limited by industry standards and by some of the factors listed in later sections as indicative of other aspects of Gray's classification.

A litigious society ready to take action against professional accountants and auditors causes them to seek refuge in the protection of statute and regulation. It was hoped that the Private Securities Litigation Reform Act (1995) would put a stop to disgruntled investors bringing frivolous lawsuits against companies and their professional advisors.

---

[51] FASB (2004b).

11.8.2 Uniformity versus flexibility

Gray's classification, based on Hofstede, indicates high flexibility. By way of contrast it has been suggested[52] that US accounting shows a mixture of both finite uniformity and rigid uniformity. Finite uniformity is seen as the attempt to equate prescribed accounting methods with the relevant circumstances in generally similar situations. The example given is the rule in SFAS 13 on long-term leases where percentages are used to draw the line for capitalization. The percentage is to some extent arbitrary but ensures comparable practice. Another example is the rule on capitalization of borrowing costs in specific circumstances. Rigid uniformity means prescribing one method for generally similar transactions. An example is SFAS 2, requiring all research and development expenditure to be reported in the income statement as incurred. IAS 38 requires capitalization of development costs that meet specific criteria. This difference may be addressed by FASB in its short-term convergence project.

However, flexibility is evident in matters such as depreciation accounting and inventory valuation and in the separation of tax law from accounting practice.

11.8.3 Conservatism versus optimism

Gray's (1988) classification was one of optimism which is defined in his paper as a laissez-faire, risk-taking approach contrasting with conservatism as a cautious approach to measurement. This seems at variance with the US insistence on historical cost accounting and the refusal to allow revaluation. Gray classifies the USA as optimistic in relation to countries such as Germany and France. The sources cited date from the 1970s and early 1980s so it may be that his view of relative optimism was based on the absence in the USA of the excessive provisions found in some continental European practices prior to the implementation of the Fourth Directive. There is also mention of the practice of secret reserves, existing in continental Europe, not being found in the USA or the UK.

The US picture in practice is not totally clear because the caution in banning revaluation, having a long history linked to the 1929 stock market crash, is in contrast to the reluctance to take the harder line on impairment, compared with the preference of the IASB and previously of the IASC. Permitting LIFO stock valuation is probably explained more by the influence of tax law than by the influence of conservatism. Providing in full for deferred taxation could be seen as conservative, but it could also be seen as a professional approach to applying a balance sheet approach consistently. However, the view of a distinguished US academic, commenting on a draft of this section, was 'please do not even try to characterize US accounting as other than conservative. It simply is conservative to the point of being inconsistent in theory.'

Nevertheless, both FASB and the SEC have taken a turn towards fair value since the 1990s. Zeff (1999) traces the progress of both bodies in 'lurching' towards current value accounting based on ideas of 'fair value'.

11.8.4 Secrecy versus transparency

Gray's (1988) classification of US accounting as highly transparent is supported by the extensive disclosure requirements imposed by the SEC, as well as those of the FASB standards. However, it must be remembered that the SEC regulates only listed companies

---

[52] Wolk *et al.* (2004), Ch. 9.

and there are many more unlisted companies in the USA about which much less is known. Research evidence suggests that there is voluntary disclosure by US multinational companies, although less extensive than the voluntary disclosures provided by UK multinational companies.[53] US multinational companies might reply that they already disclose more under compulsion. Specific elements of secrecy remain in off-balance-sheet transactions which are not regulated by any particular standard. On the other hand, the move towards openness and informativeness is reinforced by the AICPA in the work of the Jenkins Committee.

Summary and conclusions

Using the scores developed by Hofstede (1984), Gray's method of analysis predicts that the accounting system in the USA will be characterized by strong professionalism, strong flexibility, strong conservatism and strong transparency. That strong professionalism has been embedded in the historical development of the accountancy profession and the responsibility taken by the profession for setting accounting standards. The FASB continued this professional approach as an independent standard setter. Statutory control by the SEC was a reserve power, rarely implemented in practice. The collapse of Enron changed the global perception of the professionalism of US accounting and the governance system within which it operated. The Sarbanes–Oxley Act generated an unprecedented amount of new rules and legislation but at the same time questioned the extent to which US accounting had come to rely on detailed rules rather than applying principles to accounting decisions. The FASB survived the investigations and questioning of the system of corporate reporting, but had to promise to reconsider the balance of principles and rules.

'High quality' and 'transparency' are key words used frequently in commentaries and exhortations from the SEC. Transparency is seen in the very extensive disclosures required by law and practice, particularly in the basic information package required by the SEC of all listed US companies. Quality is addressed in the SEC's concerns over, and investigations into, earnings management. Flexibility is seen in the lack of prescribed formats of presentation and the separate existence of tax law and accounting law. The traditional insistence on historical cost would place the USA in a highly conservative category, but other aspects of detail in practice, such as capitalization of some expenditure, give glimpses of practices which are not always directed towards conservatism. The developing use of fair values is a further change to the perception of conservatism.

Key points from the chapter:

- The USA has given a lead over many years in matters of regulating corporate reporting and setting standards. The SEC has been imitated in many countries, the FASB gives a model for an independent standard-setting body, and the Sarbanes–Oxley Act has set new standards for regulation of corporate governance and regulation, notwithstanding the crisis of confidence that made it necessary.

- US GAAP remain as a potential global accounting system to rival IFRS but the FASB and SEC are working with the IASB towards 'converging' the two systems. Section 11.6 shows the main areas of difference that will remain after the short-term convergence projects are completed.

---

[53] Meek *et al.* (1995).

- The 'principles versus rules' debate will continue but it seems unlikely that the US regulators will sacrifice the control they hold through writing detailed rules. These may become 'guidance' or 'interpretations' but there will remain limits on the extent to which professional judgement is exercised.

- When analyzing the annual corporate reports of US companies it is essential to cover the full package of annual report, Form 10-K and proxy statement.

Questions

The following questions test your understanding of the material contained in the chapter and allow you to relate your understanding to the learning outcomes specified at the start of this chapter. The learning outcomes are repeated here. Each question is cross-referenced to the relevant section of the chapter.

Explain the development of accounting regulation

1 To what extent do early developments in accounting practice indicate the likely directions of professionalism/statutory control, uniformity/flexibility, conservatism/optimism and secrecy/transparency in current practice? (section 11.3.1)

Understand the impact of the Sarbanes–Oxley Act 2002

2 What were the problems that Sarbanes–Oxley was intended to remedy? (section 11.3.2)

3 How has Sarbanes–Oxley affected corporate governance? (section 11.3.2)

4 What is meant by the 'principles versus rules' debate'? (section 11.3.3)

Explain the key institutional characteristics of the USA

5 How does the political and economic system of the USA fit into the classifications described in Chapter 4? (section 11.4.1)

6 How does the legal system of the USA fit into the classifications described in Chapter 4? (section 11.4.2)

7 How does the corporate governance system of the USA compare with the descriptions given in Chapter 3? (section 11.4.3)

8 How does the taxation system of the USA compare with the descriptions given in Chapter 4? (section 11.4.4)

9 How does the corporate financing system of the USA compare with the descriptions given in Chapter 4? (section 11.4.5)

10 How does the accounting profession in the USA compare with the descriptions given in Chapter 4? (section 11.4.6)

11 How do the external influences on and by accounting practice in the USA compare with those described in Chapter 4? (section 11.5)

12 Which institutional factors are most likely to influence US accounting practice? (section 11.4 generally)

Make comparisons of US GAAP with IFRS

13 In which areas does accounting practice in the USA depart from that set out in IASB standards? (section 11.6)

429

14 For each of the areas of departure which you have identified, describe the treatment required or applied in the USA and identify the likely impact on net income and shareholders' equity of moving from US accounting practice to the relevant IASB standards. (section 11.6)

15 What explanations may be offered for these departures from IASB standards, in terms of the institutional factors described in the chapter? (link sections 11.4 and 11.6)

Understand and explain features of the accounting system and accounting practices in the USA

16 What are the most difficult problems facing accounting in the USA in the process of converging FASB accounting standards with IFRS? (link sections 11.6 and 11.7)

Discuss the US accounting system using the analytical framework of Gray's accounting values

17 Identify the key features supporting a conclusion that professionalism is a characteristic of US accounting. (link section 11.8.1 to section 11.7)

18 Explain which institutional influences cause professionalism, rather than statutory control, to be a characteristic of US accounting. (link section 11.8.1 to section 11.4)

19 Discuss whether a classification of professionalism is appropriate for present-day accounting practice. (section 11.8.1)

20 Identify the key features supporting a conclusion that flexibility, rather than uniformity, is a dominant characteristic of US accounting. (link section 11.8.2 to section 11.7)

21 Explain which institutional influences cause flexibility, rather than uniformity, to be a dominant characteristic of US accounting. (link section 11.8.2 to section 11.4)

22 Discuss whether a classification of strong flexibility is appropriate for present-day accounting practice. (section 11.8.2)

23 Identify the key features supporting a conclusion that optimism, rather than conservatism, is a dominant characteristic of US accounting. (link section 11.8.3 to section 11.7)

24 Explain which institutional influences cause optimism, rather than conservatism, to be a dominant characteristic of US accounting. (link section 11.8.3 to section 11.4)

25 Discuss whether a classification of optimism is appropriate for present-day accounting practice. (section 11.8.3)

26 Identify the key features supporting a conclusion that transparency, rather than secrecy, is a characteristic of US accounting. (link section 11.8.4 to section 11.7)

27 Explain which institutional influences cause transparency to be a characteristic of US accounting. (link section 11.8.4 to section 11.4)

28 Discuss whether a classification of transparency is appropriate for present-day accounting practice. (section 11.8.4)

References and further reading

Adams, C., Weetman, P., Jones, E.A.E. and Gray, S.J. (1999) 'Reducing the burden of US GAAP reconciliations by foreign companies listed in the United States: the key question of materiality', *European Accounting Review*, 8(1): 1–22.

AICPA (1973) *Objectives of Financial Statements: Reports of the Study Group on the Objectives of Financial Statements*. New York: American Institute of Certified Public Accountants.

AICPA (1994) *Improving Business Reporting – A Customer Focus*: *Meeting Information Needs of Investors and Creditors, Comprehensive Report of the Special Committee on Financial Reporting.* New York: American Institute of Certified Public Accountants (The Special Committee was chaired by Edmund L. Jenkins, partner in Arthur Andersen).

Cairns, D. (1997) 'The future shape of harmonisation: a reply', *European Accounting Review*, 6(2): 305–348.

CICA (2002) *Significant differences in GAAP in Canada, Chile, Mexico, and the United States*, Canadian Institute of Chartered Accountants, regular updating of a Joint study (1995) *Financial Reporting in North America*, undertaken by the Canadian Institute of Chartered Accountants, the Instituto Mexicano de Contadores Públicos, AC, and the Financial Accounting Standards Board of the United States, assisted by KPMG Peat Marwick LLP and published jointly.

Collins, W., Davie, E.S. and Weetman, P. (1993) 'Management discussion and analysis: an evaluation of practice in UK and US companies', *Accounting and Business Research*, 23(90): 123–137.

FASB (2001) *Improving Business Reporting*: *Insights into Enhancing Voluntary Disclosures*. Business Reporting Research Project, Steering Committee Report. Financial Accounting Standards Board. Available at www.fasb.org.

FASB (2004a) *Response to SEC study on the adoption of a principles-based accounting system*, July 2004. Available at www.fasb.org.

FASB (2004b) *Summary of FASB tentative decisions on business combinations*, July 2004. Available at www.fasb.org.

Flower, J. (1997) 'The future shape of harmonisation: the EU versus the IASC versus the SEC', *European Accounting Review*, 6(2): 281–303.

Gray, S.J. (1988) 'Towards a theory of cultural influence on the development of accounting systems internationally', *Abacus*, 24(1): 1–15.

Hofstede, G. (1984) *Culture Consequences*: *International Differences in Work-Related Values.* Beverly Hills, CA: Sage.

Meek, G.K., Roberts, C.B. and Gray, S.J. (1995) 'Factors influencing voluntary annual report disclosures by US, UK and continental European multinational corporations', *Journal of International Business Studies*, Third Quarter: 555–572.

OECD (2007) *Economic Surveys*: *United States*, May 2007. Paris: Organization for Economic Cooperation and Development.

PwC (2006) *Similarities and differences – A comparison of IFRS and US GAAP.* Pricewaterhouse-Coopers, October.

SEC (2001) Cautionary advice regarding disclosures about critical accounting policies, Release No. 33–8040, December.

SEC (2003) Interpretation: Commission guidance regarding management's discussion and analysis of financial condition and results of operations, Release No. 33–8350, December.

Street, D.L., Nichols, N.B. and Gray, S.J. (2000) 'Assessing the acceptability of international accounting standards in the US: an empirical study of the materiality of US GAAP reconciliations by non-US companies complying with IASC standards', *International Journal of Accounting*, 35(1): 27–63.

Sudarsanam, P.S. (2003) *Creating Value from Mergers and Acquisitions*: *The Challenges, an Integrated and International Perspective.* Harlow: FT Prentice Hall.

Weetman, P. and Gray, S.J. (1990) 'International financial analysis and comparative corporate performance: the impact of UK versus US accounting principles on earnings', *Journal of International Financial Management and Accounting*, 2(2/3): 111–129.

Weetman, P. and Gray, S.J. (1991) 'A comparative international analysis of the impact of accounting principles on profits: the US versus the UK, Sweden and The Netherlands', *Accounting and Business Research*, 21(84): 363–379.

Weetman, P., Jones, E.A.E., Adams, C. and Gray, S.J. (1998) 'Profit measurement and UK accounting standards: a case of increasing disharmony in relation to US GAAP and IASs', *Accounting and Business Research*, 28(3): 189–208.

Williams, J.R. and Carcello, J.V. (2007) *GAAP Guide Level A 2007*. Kingston upon Thames: CCH Wolters Kluwer.

Wolk, H.I., Dodd, J.L. and Tearney, M.G. (2004) *Accounting Theory: Conceptual Issues in a Political and Economic Environment*, 6th edn. Mason, OH: Thomson South-Western.

Zeff, S.A. (1999) 'Sitting on the fence', *Accountancy International*, July: 68–69.

Zeff, S.A. (2002) '"Political" lobbying on proposed standards: a challenge to the IASB', *Accounting Horizons*, 16(1): 43–54.

Zeff, S.A. (2003a) 'How the US accounting profession got where it is today: Part 1', *Accounting Horizons*, 17(3): 189–205.

Zeff, S.A. (2003b) 'How the US accounting profession got where it is today: Part 2', *Accounting Horizons*, 17(4): 267–286.

Zeff, S.A. (2007). 'The SEC rules historical cost accounting: 1934 to the 1970s', *Accounting and Business Review, IAPF Special issue*: 49–62.

Journals/professional magazines

Financial Times (UK)

Journal of Accountancy (USA)

Economic Surveys. Paris: Organization for Economic Cooperation and Development.

Harmonization across the European Union

Learning outcomes

After reading this chapter you should be able to:

● Explain the origins and nature of the European Union.

● Explain how laws are made in the European Union.

● Explain the effect of the IAS Regulation.

● Understand the role and nature of EU Directives in accounting and auditing.

● Explain how the EU is modernizing its approach to accounting legislation and guidance.

12.1 Introduction

The purpose of this chapter is to show an approach to accounting regulation where separate countries surrender some of their power in matters of company law to a supra-national body. The reporting practices of member states, and the regulatory framework of financial reporting, have all been influenced by membership of the European Union (EU). Chapter 10 deals with particularly interesting characteristics of a selection of member states. This chapter sets the scene more generally by explaining the origins of the EU, the formation of community law and the common features which bind all member states in matters of accounting.

12.2 Origins and nature of the EU

The present-day EU emerged from the European Communities created in the 1950s by a series of treaties:

● the European Coal and Steel Community (ECSC), 1950 (Treaty of Paris)
● the European Economic Community (EEC), 1957 (Treaty of Rome)
● the European Atomic Energy Community, 1957 (Euratom Treaty).

At that stage the emphasis was on industrial and trading partnerships between member states. The three communities became called collectively the 'European Communities' in

1965. Over the years the emphasis on political linkage, as well as trading cooperation, has become more apparent. The Single European Act of 1986 set the aim of removing all barriers, whether physical, technical or fiscal. The title 'European Union' was adopted in the Treaty on European Union signed at Maastricht in 1991. By the end of 1992, the structure for a Single Market was largely complete.

12.2.1 Purpose of the union[1]

The founders of the European Communities wanted to achieve a closer union among the peoples of Europe. This was stated in terms of achieving freedom of movement of persons, services and capital. The political ambitions varied, with some participants desiring to move eventually to a federation of European states and others more cautiously seeking only commercial benefits. Over the years there have been proposals for European integration and union on an increasingly ambitious scale, within the original aims of freedom of movement of persons, services and capital.

For those concerned with the practice of financial accounting and reporting, the most important of these aims is the freedom of movement of capital. Much of the work of the Council and Commission in the 1970s and 1980s related to bringing company law of member states into closer agreement. In the 1990s, more publicity was given to the harmonization of laws relating to the movement of persons and services, but the work on company law continued to develop. Haller (2002) explains how market forces were driving the harmonization of accounting in advance of the formal decision to require all listed companies to apply IFRS. He discusses the challenges facing the EU regulators in exercising influence on the development of IFRS, the technical challenges facing preparers and users of accounts, and the debate over the best interests of small and medium-sized unlisted companies.

12.2.2 Main institutions[2]

Of the three treaties creating the European Communities, the most significant was the Treaty of Rome which led to the establishment of the European Parliament and the Court of Justice. In 1965 the Merger Treaty established a single Council of Ministers and a single Commission covering all three Communities.

The Council of Ministers is the legislative body, which means that it issues the laws. On receiving a proposal from the Commission (see below), the Council of Ministers will usually consult with the European Parliament before issuing legislation. The Council must act within the scope of the treaties and must base its actions on the proposals of the Commission.

The Commission is the civil service of the EU, and Commissioners have considerable power. The Commission watches over the implementation of the treaties in each member state. It initiates policy and sets in place the procedures to implement policy, it helps Council meetings arrive at an agreed basis for action and it has power to administer some of the rules.

The European Parliament is a body which is consulted on matters for legislation but it does not set legislation. Parliament may question the Commission and may, in theory, dismiss its members. There is also some scope for the exercise of a power of veto, preventing legislation from being issued.

---

[1] Fairhurst (2007), pp. 3–5.
[2] Fairhurst (2007), Ch. 3.

The Court of Justice is the highest court for matters relating to community law. It examines the legality of Acts of the Council and of the Commission. It can also provide guidance to national courts in the interpretation of community law.

12.2.3 Member countries

The member states of the EU are listed in Exhibit 12.1.

The six countries which signed the Treaty of Rome were Belgium, West Germany, France, Italy, Luxembourg and The Netherlands. In 1972 Denmark, the Republic of Ireland and the United Kingdom joined the European Communities. The 1980s saw a Mediterranean enlargement, bringing into membership Greece (1981), Spain (1986) and Portugal (1986).

Reunification of Germany brought the former German Democratic Republic ('East Germany') into membership in 1990. Closer links with countries in the European Free Trade Association (EFTA) brought Sweden, Austria and Finland into membership in 1995. At that point the total membership was 15 countries.

Many East European states signed 'Europe Agreements' following the Copenhagen Summit of 1993. These agreements encouraged a relationship that would lead to convergence and regional cooperation and would eventually provide a route to full membership. It is a condition for new entrants to the EU that they take steps to incorporate the company law directives within their national laws. In March 1998 accession negotiations began with Hungary, Poland, Estonia, the Czech Republic, Slovenia and Cyprus. In October 1999 the Commission recommended member states to open negotiations with Romania, Slovakia, Latvia, Lithuania, Bulgaria and Malta. In May 2004 the Enlargement of the EU admitted ten new member states that had met the conditions for membership. These were the Czech Republic, Cyprus, Estonia, Latvia, Lithuania, Hungary, Malta, Poland, Slovenia and Slovakia. In January 2007 Bulgaria and Romania became members. The countries of Turkey, Croatia and the former Yugoslav Republic of Macedonia continue to work towards meeting the conditions for membership.

12.2.4 The European Economic Area (EEA)[3]

The Agreement creating the European Economic Area was negotiated between the Community and seven member countries of the European Free Trade Area (EFTA) and signed

---

Exhibit 12.1 **Member states of the EU from January 2007**

The Republic of Austria	The Hellenic Republic (Greece)	The Republic of Poland
The Kingdom of Belgium	The Republic of Hungary	The Portuguese Republic (Portugal)
The Republic of Bulgaria	The Republic of Ireland	The Republic of Romania
The Republic of Cyprus	The Italian Republic	The Slovak Republic (Slovakia)
The Czech Republic	The Republic of Latvia	The Republic of Slovenia
The Kingdom of Denmark	The Republic of Lithuania	The Kingdom of Spain
The Republic of Estonia	The Grand Duchy of Luxembourg	The Kingdom of Sweden
The Republic of Finland	The Republic of Malta	The United Kingdom of Great
The French Republic (France)	The Kingdom of The Netherlands	Britain and Northern Ireland (UK)
The Federal Republic of Germany		

---

[3] http://europa.eu.int/comm/external_relations/eea/.

in May 1992. Subsequently one of these (Switzerland) decided after a referendum not to participate, and three others (Austria, Finland and Sweden) joined the Union. The EEA was maintained[4] because of the wish of the three remaining countries – Norway, Iceland and Liechtenstein – to participate in the Single Market, while not assuming the full responsibilities of membership of the EU. The Agreement gives them the right to be consulted by the Commission during the formulation of Community legislation, but not the right to a say in the decision making, which is kept exclusively for member states. All new Community legislation in areas covered by the EEA (which includes the Fourth and Seventh Directives) is integrated into the Agreement through a Joint Committee Decision and subsequently made part of the national legislation of the EEA EFTA States. This means that Norway, Iceland and Liechtenstein are closely related to EU member states in matters of accounting rules.[5]

12.3 How laws are made[6]

There are two aspects to community law. Basic legislation, contained in treaties and protocols, sets out fundamental obligations of member states. When member states agree to accept the basic legislation, they give up some of their sovereign power over national affairs. This basic legislation passes directly into the law of the nation and there is no need for a member state to initiate its own laws. Secondary legislation creates obligations on the governments of member states which citizens of those states may refer to in courts of law. Consequently the member states are expected to incorporate secondary legislation in their national laws.

The levels of legislation encountered in matters of financial reporting are:

1 **Regulation**. A regulation has general application and is directly binding on all member states.
2 **Directive**. A directive explains a set of desirable outcomes, which must be achieved by member states – it indicates to member states a variety of options which they can use to achieve the required outcomes; member states select the option or options which best suit national circumstances.
3 **Decision**. A decision may be issued for a particular purpose such as an antitrust or a competition case – it is binding on the persons to whom it is addressed.
4 **Recommendations and opinions**. Recommendations and opinions are also issued, but do not have binding force.

12.4 Impact of IASB standards on accounting in the EU

In November 1995, the European Commission announced that it would look to the IASC to carry forward the work of harmonization. This reversed earlier indications by the Commission that it would wish to develop a programme of European standards. The change of approach probably reflected acknowledgement of the continued diversity of measurement

---

[4] EEA Agreement, updated May 2004, full text on http://secretariat.efta.int/Web/EuropeanEconomicArea/ EEAAgreement/EEAAgreement.

[5] Ibid., Annex XXII.

[6] Fairhurst (2007).

practices across EU countries, despite achievements of harmonization in disclosure and presentation. By 1995 it was becoming apparent that only the IASC would be in a position to meet the needs for harmonization within a relatively short timescale.

As part of the new accounting strategy adopted by the Commission at the end of 1995, the Contact Committee on the Accounting Directives carried out work to analyze the degree of conformity between rules contained in the IAS and the content of the European Accounting Directives. This was intended to provide information to help each member state decide on whether, and to what extent, national companies could apply the IAS. The major review was carried out in 1995 but was then extended for subsequent issues of IAS. Reports are published on the website of the European Commission.

This strategy was not without its critics in the late 1990s, because the Directives were becoming increasingly out of date. It was suggested that inconsistency with the Directives may not necessarily have reflected badly on an IAS that represented more current thinking on an accounting issue.

The IOSCO endorsement of the IAS in May 2000 and the IASC's agreement on restructuring along lines favoured by the US SEC (see section 1.7.5) were met with newspaper comments suggesting that the regulators would carry on wrangling, and that Brussels had lost its 'voice' in matters of international accounting standards.[7] The first comment reflected a concern that the European Commission would set up committees to carry out a process of reviewing the IASs with a view to taking the 'reconciliation' route as a way of preserving the independence of the Commission in matters of accounting regulation. The second comment led to a suggestion that the future debate on IAS would be one-sided without a strong input from the European Commission.

In June 2000 the Commission published its outline financial reporting strategy to require listed companies to use IAS by 2005. This was part of a wider target to implement the Commission's Financial Services Action Plan by the same date. However, the Commission also indicated that it would apply a two-level endorsement mechanism through political and technical review.[8] One view expressed at the time was that the endorsement mechanism could indicate a desire by the Commission for a Europeanized version of the IAS, which would in turn encourage the USA to continue requiring reconciliations to US GAAP. The contrast was made, in comment, between global consensus and regional variation.

The response of the Commission was that endorsement was necessary because it would be unwise to delegate accounting standard setting unconditionally to a private organization over which the EU had no influence. This response reflected the Commission's continuing concerns about the new IASB, established in 2000, not being representative. The endorsement mechanism was seen as keeping open a dialogue with the IASB. Legislative details published in February 2001 indicated that the Commission would keep a firm control of the political aspects of the process.

For many years the accounting regulation in company law of member states had been affected mainly by two Directives – the Fourth and Seventh Directives. Member states incorporated these two Directives in their national company law. They took options, where available, to reflect national needs. When the EU took the decision to require all listed companies to use international accounting standards in preparing group accounts, the decision was implemented by a Regulation. We explained in section 12.3 that this was more powerful than any Directive and it also took precedence over Directives. So

---

[7] Robert Bruce, *The Times*, 25 May 2000; Michael Peel, *Financial Times*, 25 May 2000.

[8] http://europa.eu.int/comm/internal_market/en/company/accounts/news.

member states were obliged to apply and enforce the Directive as part of their law. The Directives remained effective for companies not required to follow the Regulation. This meant that national company law continued to apply for such companies.

Armstrong *et al.* (2007) examined the European stock market reaction to 16 events associated with the adoption of IFRS in Europe. They found that investors reacted positively to events that increased the likelihood of IFRS adoption and negatively to events that decreased it. The results indicated that European equity investors expected net benefits from IFRS adoption associated with convergence and increased information quality.

In the following sections we first describe the new Regulation which brings IFRS to European listed companies. We then describe in detail the Fourth and Seventh Directives, which continue to dictate the shape of national legislation for companies not affected by the Regulation.

12.5 The IAS Regulation

In 2002 the European Commission confirmed its target of IAS adoption by 2005. The Regulation (EC) No. 1606/2002 of the European Parliament and the Council (19 July 2002) on the application of international accounting standards is called 'the IAS Regulation'. Its purpose is to harmonize the financial information presented by public listed companies in order to ensure a high degree of transparency and comparability of financial statements. The Regulation is relatively short. For details of its application we have to look to the Comments issued by the Commission in November 2003.[9]

12.5.1 Scope of the Regulation[10]

The Regulation applies to the consolidated financial statements of listed companies[11] for their financial years commencing on or after 1 January 2005. Member states have the option of permitting or requiring the use of IAS for the individual accounts of companies with a listed group and for the accounts of any unlisted groups or individual companies.[12] International accounting standards are defined in the Regulation as IAS, IFRS, SIC-IFRICs and any other standards issued by the IASB.[13]

As explained earlier, a Regulation is directly applicable in member states. This is different from a Directive, which is an instruction to member states on the content of their national laws. Because the Regulation is directly applicable, member states must ensure that they do not seek to apply to a company any additional elements of national law that are contrary to, or conflict with or restrict, a company's compliance with IAS.[14]

12.5.2 Languages

Adopted IFRS and interpretations are available in all Community languages. They are published in the *Official Journal* of the EU and are also available on the website.[15] Some

---

[9] EC (2003b).

[10] EC (2002).

[11] EC (2002) Article 4.

[12] EC (2002) Article 5.

[13] EC (2002) Article 2. Unfortunately the Regulation predates the IASB's decision to use 'IFRS' as the general description – see Chapter 1.

[14] EC (2003b) section 3.1.

[15] http://europa.eu.int/comm/internal_marke/accounting/index_en.htm.

caution is needed on the part of those using such translations where there is a time lag between the issue of new IFRS and their adoption by the European Commission. The 'EU-endorsed' version of a standard may not necessarily be the most recent update from the IASB.

12.5.3 Adopting IFRS in Europe: 'endorsed' IFRS

The Commission decides on the applicability of international accounting standards within the Community.[16] It is assisted by an Accounting Regulatory Committee[17] and is advised by a Standards Advice Review Group[18] and an independent technical group EFRAG.[19] The tests for adoption[20] are that the standards:

- do not contradict specific principles of the Fourth and Seventh Directives;
- are conducive to the European public good; and
- meet the criteria of understandability, relevance, reliability and comparability, required of financial information needed for making economic decisions and assessing the stewardship of management.

A standard that is adopted is said to be 'endorsed'. If a standard is awaiting endorsement, or is rejected, it may be used as guidance if it is not inconsistent with endorsed standards. If a rejected standard is in conflict with adopted standards, it may not be used. When the Commission first announced the endorsement process, there were fears expressed that this would be used to create 'European IFRS' by selecting some IFRS and rejecting others. The Commission's reply was that the EU cannot give its powers to a body (the IASB) that is not subject to EU jurisdiction, and it is necessary for the EU to endorse standards as part of its duty in setting laws for member states.

12.5.3.1 The Accounting Regulatory Committee

The Accounting Regulatory Committee (ARC) consists of representatives from member states. It is chaired by the Commission. The Committee was set up by the Commission in accordance with the requirements of Article 65 of the IAS Regulation. The ARC has its own procedures, published on the internal market website. Its function is to provide an opinion on Commission proposals to adopt (endorse) an international accounting standard. The IAS Regulation gives a great deal of power to the Commission to control the ARC's agenda because the ARC only gives an opinion, not a decision, and because the ARC has to wait for the Commission to make a proposal. The opinion of ARC may be decided on a majority vote.

The greatest test faced by the ARC in 2004 was the question of endorsing IAS 39. At its meeting in July 2004,[21] the ARC was advised that full endorsement of IAS 39 would be divisive. Some member states supported endorsement, others were opposed. The Commission was exploring an intermediate solution that would endorse IAS 39 with the exception of the fair value option (see section 2.5.2.2) and a limited number of provisions

---

[16] EC (2002) Article 1.

[17] EC (2002) Article 6.

[18] Commission Decision 2006/505/EC, 14 July 2006.

[19] www.efrag.org/.

[20] Regulation Article 3.2.

[21] Meeting report 9 July 2004, ARC/2004-07-09, website of internal market.

dealing with hedge accounting of core deposits. The chairman of the ARC underlined the exceptional nature of the situation facing the ARC, where he saw the EU having to remedy the inability of the IASB and the European banking industry to come to a mutually satisfactory solution on particular matters of concern to bankers. Member states supporting full endorsement asked whether they could adopt it voluntarily, to avoid problems of incomplete application of IFRS.

12.5.3.2 The Standards Advice Review Group

In July 2006 the Commission decided to appoint an independent advisory group on accounting. There are seven members of the Standards Advice Review Group (SARG) whose task is to advise the Commission on the endorsement process of IFRS and IFRICs. SARG will assess whether EFRAG (see below) gives well-balanced and objective opinions. There are seven members of SARG, appointed for their experience and competence at the EU level. It might be asked why the Commission felt it necessary to establish SARG in 2006 when EFRAG had existed since 2001. The press release announcing the first appointments said, 'Since EFRAG is a private body, it is important to establish appropriate institutional infrastructure ensuring that its endorsement advice is objective and well-balanced.'

12.5.3.3 EFRAG

EFRAG is the European Financial Reporting Advisory Group. It is a private institution that was set up in 2001 by organizations active in the area of financial reporting. Its activities are:

- providing proactive advice to the IASB;
- advising the Commission on the acceptability of IFRS for endorsement in Europe;
- advising the Commission on any resulting changes to be made to the accounting directives and related topics.

EFRAG differs from the ARC and SARG. EFRAG is not defined in the IAS Regulation (although there is indirect reference to it) and therefore the Commission has no regulatory obligation to listen to EFRAG. In March 2006, EFRAG's role was formalized in a Working Arrangement with the European Commission, which states that EFRAG will provide advice to the Commission on all issues relating to the application of IFRS in the EU. Within EFRAG there is a Technical Expert Group (TEG) which carries out proactive work and provides endorsement advice. EFRAG is an observer of some IASB projects and is proactive in working with national standard setters. It would like to strengthen and extend its position but that raises issues for the continuing role of national standard setters.

12.5.4 Formats

The IAS Regulation applies directly to consolidated accounts of listed companies. Member states cannot impose their own formats.[22] The Comment on the IAS Regulation suggests that the application of IAS 1 will lead to balance sheets and profit and loss accounts that follow the same principles as those used in the Directives. The profit and loss account may use disclosure by function or by nature (see Exhibit 12.4 later). The balance sheet will present assets either in order of liquidity or using a current/non-current

---

[22] EC (2003b) section 4.2.

distinction. The Regulation is less prescriptive than the Directives and so it may be that in future some companies will begin to experiment with new forms of presentation.

12.5.5 Choices for member states

The Comments emphasize the importance of comparability under the IAS Regulation. This will be achieved where member states do not seek additional qualitative or quantitative disclosures. However, additional disclosure may be required by national regulators where such information lies outside the consolidated accounts or falls outside the scope of IAS.[23] Member states must not restrict explicit choices contained in the IAS.[24]

12.5.6 Application of national law

Where a company is not subject to the IAS Regulation, it continues to prepare accounts under national laws that are based on the Fourth and Seventh Directives.[25] A member state might require particular IAS to be applied by such companies. In such instances the national law still applies.[26]

12.5.7 Articles of Directives still applying under the IAS Regulation

Some Articles of the Fourth and Seventh Directives deal with publication, audit and other matters that are beyond the scope of IASs. These Articles continue to apply, through national law, alongside the IAS Regulation. (There is a detailed list in the Comments document.)

12.6 Company law directives[27]

Company law directives are published under the authority of the Treaty of Rome (Article 54(3)(g)). The Council and the Commission are required to coordinate 'safeguards' to protect the interests of member states and others, in such a way that these safeguards are equivalent across the EU. The safeguards must be consistent with freedom of movement of goods, persons, services and capital. The laws of member states must be brought sufficiently close to allow proper functioning of the common market.

The Directives are the practical means of achieving these safeguards. The Directives which have been issued in relation to company law are shown in Exhibit 12.2. The date given is that of adoption by the Council of Ministers. Incorporation in national law may take several years from the date of adoption. Where a Directive is particularly controversial, such as the Fifth Directive, its adoption may be delayed for a long time. The draft directive on takeovers was first proposed in 1989 but took on greater importance at the 2000 Lisbon European Summit which set a target for implementation of the Financial Services Action Plan.

---

[23] EC (2003b) section 4.1.
[24] EC (2003b) section 3.1.
[25] EC (2003b) section 3.4.
[26] Ibid.
[27] Fairhurst (2007), p. 58.

Exhibit 12.2	EU company law directives

Directive	Date of adoption	Main purpose
First	1968	Powers of directors and powers of companies
Second	1976 Simplified 2005	Requirements for capital when forming a company; maintaining capital; distinction between private and public companies
Third	1978	Reconstructions within public companies
Fourth	1978	Disclosure of financial information and contents of annual accounts of individual companies
Fifth	–	[proposal] Company structure and employee participation
Sixth	1982	Merger and de-merger of public companies
Seventh	1983	Group accounts
Eighth	1984 Revised 2006	Qualifications and independence of auditors
Ninth	–	[proposal] Relationships within a group structure
Tenth	2005	Cross-border mergers
Eleventh	1989	Disclosure in respect of branches of foreign companies located in the member state
Twelfth	1989	Single member companies – memorandum and articles of association
Thirteenth	2004	Takeover bids
Fourteenth	2007?	[proposed] Mobility of companies

Information about company law directives, including full texts, is available on the website of the Internal Market Directorate General.[28] In the fields of accounting and statutory audit, the work of the Internal Market Directorate General is directed towards:

- improving the quality, comparability and transparency of the financial information provided by companies, ensuring compatibility between the Accounting Directives and IASB standards; and
- improving the quality of statutory audit throughout the EU.

It also cooperates closely with international bodies including the IASB and the International Federation of Accountants.

12.6.1 The meaning of equivalence[29]

The purpose of harmonizing company law across member states is to provide equivalent safeguards throughout the EU. The safeguards do not have to be identical. Equivalence allows a variety of options to be inserted in the Directives. Directives consist of a series of Articles, each containing a separate issue for attention. There are three types of Articles found in Directives, namely:

- uniform rules to be implemented identically in all member states;
- minimum rules which may be strengthened by the national government;
- alternative rules giving member states options (choices).

---

[28] Website of Internal Market DG in English is at the address: http://europa.eu/pol/singl/index_en.htm.
[29] FEE (1993), pp. 15–22.

12.6.2 Use of options in national law

Options are negotiated during the drafting of the Directives as a result of lobbying or persuasion by the representatives of the various member states in the Council and the Commission. The options reflect areas where it was most difficult to obtain agreement at the negotiation stage.

In some cases the national government decides which options to adopt. As an example of options taken by governments, the Seventh Directive provided various options on the definition of 'control' for purposes of defining a subsidiary company. The UK government chose one set of options, while the German government chose another. In both cases, companies had to apply the law of their own country.

In other cases the national government preserves the options in its national law and allows the standard setters or the individual companies to decide which option to apply. It should be noted that the Directives provide minimum standards for national law. It is open to national governments to be more exacting in the national legislation. As an example of options within the national law, the Fourth Directive allowed more than one approach to valuation of assets in a balance sheet. The UK government allowed individual companies to choose either historical cost or an alternative valuation method (current cost). The French government did not allow individual companies the choice of departing from historical cost accounting.

12.6.3 The Fourth and Seventh Directives

Accounting rules are contained in the Fourth and Seventh Directives. The Fourth Directive (1978) set the ground rules for the accounts of individual companies, giving standard formats for the balance sheet and profit and loss account.[30] The Seventh Directive (1983) established a common basis of presentation of accounts for groups of companies. Implementation in national law was faster in some countries than in others (Exhibit 12.3) but

Exhibit 12.3 Implementation of Fourth and Seventh Directives in national law

Country	Fourth	Seventh
Denmark	1981	1990
UK	1981	1989
France	1983	1985
Netherlands	1983	1988
Luxembourg	1984	1988
Belgium	1985	1990
Germany	1985	1985
Ireland	1986	1992
Greece	1986	1987
Spain	1989	1989
Portugal	1989	1991
Italy	1991	1991
Sweden	1995	1995
Austria	1995	1995
Finland	1995	1995

[30] Watts (1979).

all member states now have both Directives implemented. Member states joining in 2004 were required to incorporate the Directives in national law before becoming members. Together the Fourth and Seventh Directives have made a considerable impact on the presentation of companies' financial statements.

12.6.4 Modernization of company law[31]

In September 2001, the Commission set up a Group of High Level Company Law Experts to start a discussion on modernization of company law in Europe. The group reported in 2002 on the takeover bids directive and on recommendations for a modern regulatory European company law framework. From the recommendations the Commission produced an Action Plan in May 2003.[32] Its aims were:

- to strengthen shareholders' rights and protection for employees, creditors and the other parties with which companies deal, while adapting company law and corporate governance rules appropriately for different categories of company;
- to foster the efficiency and competitiveness of business, with special attention to some specific cross-border issues.

The Commission did not seek a European Corporate Governance Code because various studies had indicated an EU-level code was not needed, but said it would encourage member states towards a common approach on specific aspects such as:

- include a Corporate Governance Statement in the annual report of a company;
- develop legislation to help shareholders to exercise their rights to receive and vote on relevant information;
- promote the role of (independent) non-executive or supervisory directors;
- develop a regulatory regime giving shareholders more transparency and influence over directors' remuneration, which includes receiving detailed disclosure of individual remuneration;
- create a European Corporate Governance Forum.

The following sections explain how the Action Plan has been implemented.

12.6.4.1 Directors' remuneration

A Commission Recommendation[33] was issued in December 2004, with the title *Fostering an appropriate regime for the remuneration of directors of listed companies*, applicable to listed companies. The main recommendations were: disclosure of the policy on directors' remuneration; allowing shareholders to vote on the policy; disclosure of the remuneration of individual directors; and shareholders' approval of schemes of share options or other rights to acquire shares. In 2007 the Commission staff reported on the application of the Recommendation in member states.[34] The report concluded that the recommended transparency requirements on the remuneration policy and individual directors' pay appeared to be applied in a majority of member states. However, there had been less progress in respect of the recommendations aimed at giving shareholders more influence over pay policy.

---

[31] http://europa.eu.int/comm/internal_market/en/company/company/modern/index.htm.
[32] COM (2003) 284 final.
[33] 2004/913/EC.
[34] Commission Staff Working Document SEC(2007) 1022.

12.6.4.2 Non-executive directors and supervisory board

A Commission Recommendation[35] was issued in February 2005, with the title *The role of non-executive or supervisory directors of listed companies and on the committees of the (supervisory) board*. The recommendations cover the presence and role of non-executive or supervisory directors and their profile (appointment, qualifications, commitment and independence). In 2007 the Commission staff reported on the application of the Recommendation.[36] They found that member states were largely implementing the Recommendation in their national corporate governance codes, based on the 'comply or explain' principle. The majority of countries had mandatory codes for listed companies, with review of compliance largely relying on stock exchange regulators. Separation of the CEO and Chair of the board varied across member states. The report concluded that improvements in governance need an excellent corporate governance code but also an effective 'comply or explain' regime that works in practice.

12.6.4.3 The European Corporate Governance Forum

The Forum, established by the Commission in 2004,[37] examines best practice in member states with a view to enhancing the convergence of national corporate governance codes and advising the Commission. There are 15 members, all with relevant expertise at a European level. The Forum sets benchmarks by adopting statements indicating basic principles of corporate governance. In its annual report for 2006 the Forum asserts its support for the 'comply or explain' principle. It is observing the developments of risk management and internal controls across member states, but does not feel there is a need to introduce a legal obligation for boards of directors to certify the effectiveness of internal controls at an EU level.

12.6.4.4 Voting rights of shareholders

In January 2006 the Commission published a proposed Directive on voting rights for shareholders in EU companies whose shares are traded on a regulated market. The main proposals are: equal treatment of all shareholders in a similar position, to enable participation and voting at meetings; adequate notice of a general meeting, with facilities for attendance and participation; ability to add items to the agenda; the right to ask questions; the right to appoint a proxy voter; and the ability to vote by post instead of attending the meeting. This proposed Directive, following consultation, is taken into national law of each member state.

12.6.4.5 Board responsibilities and improvement of financial information

The Action Plan of 2003 called for improved disclosures about corporate governance practice. Directive 2006/46/EC, issued in June 2006, amended the Fourth and Seventh Accounting Directives. The new Directive has the objective of facilitating cross-border investments and improving EU-wide comparability and confidence in financial statements. It specifies the collective responsibility of management for drawing up and publishing annual accounts and annual reports. It specifies disclosure requirements relating to related parties, off-balance-sheet arrangements, and requires an annual corporate governance statement.

---

[35] 2005/162/EC.

[36] Commission Staff Working Document SEC(2007) 1021.

[37] http://ec.europa.eu/internal_market/company/ecgforum/index_en.htm.

12.6.4.6 Future priorities

Having achieved all the targets of the 2003 Action Plan by 2006, the Commission consulted on the continuing relevance of the Action Plan and its future content. The majority of respondents felt that the Action Plan was an appropriate reply to the needs of enhancing corporate governance in the EU.[38] The main features of the responses were:

● Self-regulation and exchange of best practice are important.
● The Commission should focus on SMEs.
● Some respondents questioned the distinction between listed and non-listed companies.
● Some mentioned obstacles relating to taxation, accounting, social security and employment rights, absence of a European company register, and the continuity of business licences.

The Internal Market Commissioner, speaking at the end of 2006,[39] confirmed a commitment to Better Regulation principles, with an aim of simplifying the environment in which companies operate.

12.6.5 The Statutory Audit Directive

The need for assurance around the world following the collapse of Enron has led to requirements not only for audit and assurance but also for public oversight of the audit process. The Sarbanes–Oxley Act provided for that oversight in relation to the audit of US listed companies and their subsidiaries. The Statutory Audit Directive of 2006[40] allows for the application of a wide variety of different quality assurance systems in the EU. It requires mutual recognition of the different systems used across member states. In December 2006 FEE published the results of a survey of quality assurance arrangements across Europe, showing that all countries except one have a system of external quality audit in place covering all audit firms or statutory auditors.[41]

12.6.6 Financial Services Action Plan

The Financial Services Action Plan of the European Commission is designed to create a Single European Market. The implementation of the IAS Regulation was one strand of this Plan. Directives have been used to introduce other community measures which have had an impact on accounting practices. These Directives have covered:

● admission to listing on a stock exchange;
● mutual recognition of listing particulars (where a company resident in one country is allowed to have its shares listed on the stock exchange of another, without rewriting its financial statements);
● disclosure of major shareholdings;
● insider dealing;
● information contained in a prospectus.

---

[38] http://ec.europa.eu/internal_market/company/consultation/index_en.htm.
[39] Commissioner McCreevy made a statement on 21 November 2006 to the European Parliament.
[40] Directive 2006/43/EC, Statutory audits of annual accounts and consolidated accounts, 7 May 2006.
[41] FEE Annual report (2006), p. 11.

The Prospectus Directive 2003/71/EC sets out the initial disclosure obligations for issuers of securities that are offered to the public or admitted to listing on a regulated market in the EU. It enables issuers to raise capital across the EU on the basis of a single perspective.

The Market Abuse Directive 2003/6/EC sets a common framework for managing insider dealing and market manipulation. Inside information is information that is precise, non-public and likely to have a significant impact on the price of a financial instrument.

The Transparency Directive 2004/109/EC requires companies to disclose information at regular intervals through specific channels and in particular ways. Greater transparency is expected to increase confidence and make comparative analysis easier for investors. The Directive requires annual and half-yearly financial reports and also two interim management statements half-way through each six-month period. The detailed requirements include more forward-looking statements. The annual report must be published within four months of the year-end.

12.6.7 Mutual recognition[42]

Stock exchanges each have their own rules to ensure that companies obtaining a listing provide sufficient information to allow a fair market to operate. Prior to 2005 the rules were drawn up in terms of national accounting practices and consequently companies which had a listing on more than one international stock exchange could find themselves preparing more than one set of accounts. To avoid this problem, the stock exchanges in member states agreed that they would recognize accounts prepared under the rules of any other member state. The agreement was 'mutual' because each stock exchange felt it had given something to the financial community by relaxing the rules, and had also gained something from the financial community, by encouraging international listing of shares.

Mutual recognition was based on the reassurance that member states have minimum standards in common because they all apply the Fourth and Seventh Directives. Mutual recognition is less rigorous than the concept of equivalence (explained earlier). Mutual recognition is likely to continue in the areas of financial reporting (such as management discussions) that are not covered by the IAS Regulation.

12.7 The Fourth Directive[43]

Drafting of the Fourth Directive began in 1965[44] when there were only six members of the European Communities but it was completed in 1978 when there were nine members. For Denmark, the UK and Ireland, which all joined the Community in 1978, some relatively late lobbying was required to reflect national concerns. In particular the UK argued forcefully for inclusion of the concept of 'a true and fair view'. The inclusion of the words 'true and fair' caused particular difficulty for translation into the languages of other member states. Not only were the words unfamiliar, but the ideas behind the words were unfamiliar in continental Europe; particular national approaches are dealt with in section 10.7.1. (The influence of the German Chair in the early stages of drafting the

---

[42] FEE (1993), pp. 15–22.

[43] Directive 78/660/EEC of 25 July 1978.

[44] Watts (1979).

Directive is seen in the detailed specification of the format of financial statements; such prescriptive formats were not known in the UK or Ireland prior to the Fourth Directive.)

12.7.1 Objective[45]

The Directive applies to the accounts of an individual company and covers all aspects of the annual accounts. It aims to harmonize accounting principles, presentation, publication and audit by laying down minimum standards to be applied by member states. The intention in preparing the Directive was that investors, lenders and suppliers should find it easier to obtain, understand and rely on the accounts of companies in other member states. The Directive was also aimed at promoting fair competition among member state companies: managers of a business anywhere in the EU should be able to find out as much about a competitor company as the competitor can find out about their business. Furthermore, multinational corporations should not base decisions about location on differences in national accounting requirements.

12.7.2 'True and fair view'[46]

The Fourth Directive imposes an overriding requirement that the annual accounts (comprising the balance sheet, profit and loss account and notes to the accounts) present a true and fair view. In most cases it would be expected that complying with the requirement of the law would be sufficient. However, it may be necessary for companies to disclose more than the minimum specification in order to present a true and fair view. On relatively rare occasions, companies may have to depart from the requirements of the law in order to give a true and fair view. That is permissible but must be explained in the annual report.

The concept of a 'true and fair view' is essentially Anglo-Saxon in origin[47] and was not readily accommodated within some national practices of continental Europe, particularly where tax legislation had traditionally dominated accounting reporting. The first draft of the Directive, issued in 1971, used words such as 'accuracy' and 'principles of regular and proper accounting'. Negotiations following the accession of the UK, the Republic of Ireland and Denmark resulted in the phrase 'true and fair' appearing. The company laws of each member state now include words approximating in translation to 'true and fair view', but the meaning of the words and application of the concept should be considered in the context of juridical tradition and cultural aspects.

It has been suggested that there is a range of positions on the meaning of 'true and fair view'.[48] In the UK and Ireland, it may be used by standard setters to justify general rules and may be used by companies to justify overriding the specific requirements of law. In Germany, it is clear that the idea of a 'true and fair view' cannot be used to override the requirements of law. Between these two extremes lies a range of interpretations in various member states.

In The Netherlands 'true and fair' may be used by directors and auditors as a basic principle for interpretation of the law and guidelines. It is used in setting guidelines but is not used to override the requirements of the law. In France and Spain 'true and fair' has been used by law makers to allow some move towards substance rather than form. It may be

---

[45] Coleman (1984).
[46] Parker and Nobes (1994).
[47] Alexander and Archer (2000); Alexander and Archer (2003); Nobes (2003).
[48] Parker and Nobes (1994), p. 80.

used by companies as a justification for overriding the law, but only very exceptionally. It is used by directors and auditors as a basic principle for interpretation of the law. In Italy 'true and fair' may be used by directors and auditors as a basic principle for interpretation of the law but it is unlikely that it would be used to justify a departure from the law.

12.7.3 Framework of principles

There is no separate European framework of principles. However, the Fourth Directive includes Article 31 setting out accounting principles for valuation:

- the company must be presumed to be a going concern unless evidence exists to the contrary;
- methods of valuation must be applied consistently from one period to the next;
- valuation must be made on a prudent basis and in particular:
  - only profits made may be included in the financial statements;
  - all foreseeable liabilities and potential losses arising in the year should be taken into account, even where they become apparent between the balance sheet date and the date on which it is drawn up;
  - account must be taken of depreciation, irrespective of whether there is a profit or a loss;
- all income and charges must be brought into account (i.e. the accruals concept is applied);
- components of asset and liability items must be valued separately;
- the opening balance sheet of a year must correspond to the closing balance sheet of the previous year.

12.7.4 Disclosure and presentation

The Fourth Directive includes Articles 9, 10 and 23–26, which list items for disclosure in the balance sheet and profit and loss account. The order of presentation may not be varied but there is some latitude allowed, such as the insertion of subtotals. National standard-setting bodies may add further requirements. Companies have the discretion to provide more information than is prescribed by the Directives.

The layout of the annual accounts is prescribed in **formats**. There are descriptions of formats in the Articles of the Fourth Directive setting out the order of line items for one type of balance sheet and two types of profit and loss account, with a choice of horizontal and vertical presentation for both. Examples of some of the prescribed formats are set out in the Appendix to this chapter.

The first example in the Appendix is a full horizontal balance sheet as set out in Article 9. It shows, by using a variety of symbols, information required from all companies, information not required from small companies, and information not required from small companies or in published accounts of medium-sized companies. In that example, each line item carries a label. The major headings are labelled with capital letters A, B, C, and so on. The next level of headings is labelled with Roman numerals I, II, III, and so on. The third level of headings is labelled with Arabic numerals 1, 2, 3, and so on. Line items labelled with capital letters and Roman numerals must appear on the face of the balance sheet. Those labelled with Arabic numerals may appear in notes to the accounts. The example in the Appendix shows the fullest possible balance sheet where a company places all information on the face of the primary financial statement. Making use of notes to the accounts and the alternative classifications shown for some line items, plus concessions for company size, may reduce the density of information in particular cases.

A full vertical balance sheet is set out in Article 10. The second example in the Appendix shows the application of Article 10 where a company desires to produce a minimum balance sheet taking advantage of the concessions for small companies and making use of the facility for notes to the accounts.

There are four Articles dealing with formats of the profit and loss account because two quite different approaches are allowed, each in horizontal and vertical form. One approach permits the costs to be analyzed by **type of expenditure** (e.g. purchase of goods, payment of wages and salaries) while the other gives categories based on the **function of the expenditure** (e.g. the function of selling goods is identified as cost of goods sold, while paying wages and salaries is reported as either administrative or distribution functions). This is also called the **operational basis**. These two approaches reflect different national practices in existence when the Directive was written. The resulting differences in presentation occur at the start of each type of profit and loss account, and are set out for comparison in Exhibit 12.4. The type of expenditure basis is more detailed on the face of the profit and loss account, but has the disadvantage of not showing the gross profit or loss. Under the functional basis more detailed notes to the accounts are required, so the overall provision of information is the same under each.

Exhibit 12.4 Comparison of alternative forms of vertical profit and loss account (based on Articles 23 and 25) (see also Appendix 12.1)

Type of expenditure	Functional basis (operational basis)
1 Net turnover	1 Net turnover
2 Variations in stocks of finished goods and in progress	
3 Work performed by the undertaking for its own purposes and capitalized	2 Cost of sales (including value adjustments)
4 Other operating income	
5 (a) Raw materials and consumables (b) Other external charges	3 Gross profit or loss
6 Staff costs	
(a) Wages and salaries (b) Security costs, with a separate indication of those relating to pensions	4 Distribution costs (including value adjustments)
7 (a) Value adjustments in respect of formation expenses and of tangible and intangible fixed assets (b) Value adjustments in respect of current assets, to the extent that they exceed amounts that are normal in the undertaking concerned	5 Administrative expenses (including value adjustments)
8 Other operating charges 9–21 Same as 7–19 for *functional basis*	6 Other operating income 7–19 Same as 9–21 for *type of expenditure*

12.7.5 Recognition and measurement

There are no criteria stated for recognition, but there is the general requirement that profits may only be reported when they are 'made'. The word 'made' is not defined, but has generally been equated with 'realized' (also not defined). The restriction to realization of profit has an inevitable consequence on asset recognition in many instances. Since the Directive does not define 'made', a great deal of discretion is therefore left to national law and national standard setters. This area includes potentially controversial issues such as profits on long-term contracts, franchise income, fees received in advance of services rendered, and recognition of income for those who provide finance through leasing arrangements.

The general rule of measurement is that historical cost accounting must be applied, although there is an option in the Fourth Directive (Article 33) by which member states may permit or require companies or any classes of companies to:

● value tangible fixed assets with limited useful economic lives, and stocks, by the replacement value method;
● value by other methods designed to take account of inflation the items shown in the annual accounts, including capital and reserves;
● revalue tangible fixed assets and financial fixed assets.

Where national law provides for use of any these valuation methods, it must define their content and limits and the rules for their application (Article 33).

The Fourth Directive contains specific valuation rules for certain assets:

● Fixed assets with a limited useful economic life must be depreciated so as to write off their value systematically over the useful life (Article 35).
● Goodwill, research and development costs and formation expenses must in general be written off over five years. In exceptional circumstances, member states may permit a longer period (Article 37.1) (see section 12.8.3 for the treatment of goodwill arising on consolidation).
● Current assets must be valued at purchase price or production cost. Value adjustments must be made where the market value is lower than purchase price or production cost (Article 39).
● Member states have options on the valuation of stocks of goods. They may permit the purchase price or production cost of stocks of goods of the same category, either on the basis of weighted average prices, or on the basis of first-in–first-out (FIFO) or last-in–first-out (LIFO) (Article 40).
● Member states have the option to permit use of the equity method of valuing holdings in affiliated companies (the Fourth Directive left open the precise definition of 'affiliated' but the Seventh Directive gave guidance as a holding of 20 per cent or more) (Article 59).

The recognition of liabilities is largely governed by the requirement for prudence, as explained earlier. There are fewer valuation rules than for assets, but particular items are:

● under the heading 'accruals and deferred income', account must be taken of the income and charges of the year, irrespective of the date of receipt or payment (Article 31);
● where the amount repayable under any debt is greater than the amount received (e.g. a discount on issue of a debenture loan) the difference may be shown as an asset and amortized, to be written off no later than the time of repayment of the debt (Article 41);

- deferred taxation liabilities may be recognized, but there is no rule specified for valuation (Article 9/10, Article 43);
- provisions for contingencies and charges must not be in excess of the amount necessary (Article 42).

12.7.6 Measurement approaches

As already explained, the Fourth Directive carries an initial presumption of historical cost accounting. Inflation accounting is considered in the Directive, where member states may permit or require companies or any classes of companies to:

- value tangible fixed assets with limited useful economic lives and stocks by the replacement value method;
- value by other methods designed to take account of inflation the items shown in the annual accounts, including capital and reserves;
- revalue tangible fixed assets and financial fixed assets.

Where national law provides for use of any these valuation methods, it must define their content and limits and the rules for their application (Article 33).

The Fourth and Seventh Directives were written before financial markets developed complex derivative financial instruments. To keep up with such major changes, in May 2001 the Commission published a Directive amending the Fourth and Seventh Directives to align them with IAS 32 and IAS 39. For the first time 'fair value' accounting was permitted under the Directives. It obliged member states to amend national law so as to permit or require companies to adopt fair value accounting methods. It gave member states options to limit the scope of the legislation, such as restricting it to listed companies, or to apply it only to consolidated accounts. The use of fair value accounting does not extend beyond financial instruments on the assets side of the balance sheet, and it does not apply to the 'traditional' types of liability.

12.8 The Seventh Directive[49]

The Fourth Directive deals only with individual companies standing alone. The essential purpose of writing the Seventh Directive was to define a group. This was an extremely controversial matter because of the range of practices in existence across countries and because of the importance of the definition in relation to tax law in some countries.[50] Many of the issues contained in the Fourth Directive, such as presentation, valuation rules and accounting principles, apply equally well to groups of companies. These matters are incorporated in the Seventh Directive by specific reference to the Fourth Directive.

12.8.1 Origins[51]

For some member states, consolidation is a development of recent years. An act of 1965 in Germany required a form of consolidation to be applied by public companies. Listed companies in France were required to apply consolidation from the early 1970s. The

---

[49] Directive 83/349/EEC of 13 June 1983.
[50] FEE (1993).
[51] Niessen (1993).

Seventh Directive was first published as a draft in 1976 and drew on the long-running experience which could be found in the UK, Ireland and The Netherlands. Consequently the Seventh Directive brought group accounting to some continental European countries which had not previously produced consolidated accounts as a widespread practice.

The Seventh Directive shows the influence of Anglo-Saxon practice, in contrast to the Fourth Directive which may be seen as having a clear base in continental European law. There are, however, some important indications of continental European influence in the definition of 'control'. Some countries regarded the group as being essentially an economic unit, defined by its economic activity, while others preferred to have strict definitions set out in law, defined by legal contracts. The considerable debate on the content of the Seventh Directive is reflected in the number of options it contains.

12.8.2 Extensive use of options

Options relate to aspects of consolidated accounting which were found to be too controversial to allow any agreement in a Directive. There are more than 50 options which represent political compromises rather than strong points of principle. The extent of the options available to member states means that variety of national practice is wide. The Directive has increased the number of companies that are required to produce consolidated accounts, but has not greatly increased harmonization in the practices of consolidated accounting.

12.8.3 Approach to consolidation

Undertakings are required to draw up consolidated accounts which include subsidiaries irrespective of their location. 'Subsidiaries' are defined in terms of control by voting rights or dominant influence established by contract. Member states have the further option to require consolidation of companies managed on a unified basis and companies over which a dominant influence is exercised in the absence of a specific contract (Articles 1–4). Articles 5–15 begin the process of developing the options which are a particular feature of the Seventh Directive (Exhibit 12.5).

Merger accounting is permitted where any cash payment represents less than 10 per cent of the nominal value of shares issued (Article 20). Minority interests must be shown separately and all income of consolidated companies must be included (Articles 21–23). This means that proportional consolidation of income is not permissible for full subsidiaries.

Exhibit 12.5 Options for consolidation

Member states may exempt financial holding companies that neither manage their subsidiaries nor take part in appointments to the board of directors (Article 5). They may also exempt small and medium-sized groups provided no listed company is involved (Article 6). A company is exempted from the requirement to consolidate its own subsidiaries if it is itself a subsidiary, but member states may insist on consolidation by listed companies, whether or not they are themselves subsidiaries. Other exemptions are available to member states under Articles 7–11. Member states may require horizontal consolidation where companies are managed by the same person (Article 12). Subsidiaries may be excluded from consolidation if they are immaterial, or if there would be disproportionate expense or delay (Articles 13–15).

Various practical rules for consolidation are set out in Articles 24–28. These are very detailed and reflect the lack of widespread experience of the process when the Directive was given approval.

Positive goodwill arising on consolidation must be amortized through the profit and loss account or else written off immediately against reserves. Negative goodwill should be taken to profit only if it is realized or is due to the expectation of future costs or losses (Articles 30 and 31).

12.8.4 Similarities to the Fourth Directive

The requirement for a true and fair view is contained in Article 16. Formats of the Fourth Directive are updated and expanded to take account of the additional line items of consolidation (Articles 16 and 17). Goodwill based on fair values should be calculated at the date of first consolidation or at the date of purchase (Article 18).

12.8.5 Valuation rules

The valuation rules of the Fourth Directive must be applied (Article 29). The Article specifies initially that the undertaking which draws up consolidated accounts must apply the same methods of valuation as are used in its individual accounts. However, the Article then provides the option that member states may require or permit the use of other valuation methods in the consolidated accounts, provided such methods are permitted by the Fourth Directive. Most member states give permission for use of other valuation rules, but none requires such an approach. The 'fair value' directive of 2001, explained in section 12.7.6 in relation to the Fourth Directive, applies also to the Seventh Directive.

12.8.6 Associates and joint ventures

Member states may require or permit proportional consolidation for joint ventures (Article 32). Associated companies must be recorded as a single line item, using the equity method of valuation (Article 33). The remainder of the Directive deals extensively with disclosure requirements and transitional provisions.

12.9 Modernization of the Directives

12.9.1 Fair review in the annual report

The European Parliament issued a further Directive in June 2003,[52] to set a level playing field between companies in the EU that apply IFRS and those that do not. This Directive stated the desirability of reflecting the IFRS developments in the Fourth and Seventh Directives, particularly in presenting financial statements and applying fair values in accordance with international developments. The Directive set out various instructions and options for member states, requiring them to bring these into force in national legislation by 1 January 2005.

---

[52] EC (2003a).

Exhibit 12.6	Requirement for a fair review in the annual report

> The consolidated annual report shall include at least a fair review of the development and performance of the business and of the position of the undertakings included in the consolidation taken as a whole, together with a description of the principal risks and uncertainties that they face.
>
> The review shall be a balanced and comprehensive analysis of the development and performance of the business and of the position of the undertakings included in the consolidation taken as a whole, consistent with the size and complexity of the business. To the extent necessary for an understanding of such development, performance or position, the analysis shall include both financial and, where appropriate, non-financial key performance indicators relevant to the particular business, including information relating to environmental and employee matters.
>
> In providing its analysis, the consolidated annual report shall, where appropriate, provide references to and additional explanations of amounts reported in the consolidated accounts.
>
> Where a consolidated annual report is required in addition to an annual report, the two reports may be presented as a single report. In preparing such a single report, it may be appropriate to give greater emphasis to those matters which are significant to the undertakings included in the consolidation taken as a whole.

Source: 2003/51/EC Article 2, para.10.

The Directive also introduces a requirement for a 'fair review' in the annual report. This requirement applies to single companies (as an amendment to the Fourth Directive) and to groups (as an amendment to the Seventh Directive). Exhibit 12.6 sets out the requirement in relation to a consolidated annual report.

12.9.2 Enhancing confidence

On 27 October 2004 the Commission published a proposal for a Directive of the European Parliament and of the Council to amend[53] the Fourth and Seventh Directives. The proposals were agreed and Directive 2006/46/EC was published in the *Official Journal* on 16 August with an implementation date of 5 September 2008.

The stated objective behind the new Directive is further to enhance confidence in the financial statements and annual reports published by European companies. The Directive contains measures covering:

- An option to raise the thresholds used to define small and medium companies.
- An option to use fair value estimates.
- Extended disclosure requirements in respect of related party and off-balance-sheet transactions.
- A requirement to confirm the collective responsibility of directors.
- A requirement for companies trading on a regulated market to produce a Corporate Governance Statement.

---

[53] Council Directives 78/660/EEC and 83/349/EEC.

12.10 Recommendation on environmental issues[54]

We explained in section 12.3 the levels of legislation to be encountered in the area of financial reporting. A Recommendation does not have binding force but is an indication of good practice. In May 2001 the Commission issued a Recommendation on the recognition, measurement and disclosure of environmental issues in the annual accounts and annual reports of companies.

The Commission took the view that there was a need to increase and to harmonize the environmental information flowing through corporate annual reports. The Recommendation covers:

- **Recognition of environmental liabilities**. There may be a legal obligation to prevent, reduce or repair environmental damage. There may be a constructive obligation because of past practice or policy of the enterprise. Where reliable estimates of costs can be made, the liability should be recognized. If the costs cannot be estimated reliably, or the obligation has yet to be confirmed, there will be a contingent liability.
- **Recognition of environmental expenditures**. Environmental expenditures should be recognized as an expense of the period in which they are incurred unless they meet the criteria to be recognized as an asset. They may be treated as an asset if they have been incurred to prevent or reduce future damage or conserve resources, and bring future economic benefits.
- **Measurement of environmental liabilities**. The liability is measured as an estimate of the full amount of the liability, based on the expenditure required to settle the present obligation. The estimate should take into account future technical and legal developments, so far as these will probably occur.
- **Disclosures**. There is a detailed list of recommendations on disclosures, covering matters such as policy and programmes for environmental protection, improvements in this area, environmental performance in the business, and descriptions of all environmental liabilities.

Summary and conclusions

This chapter has explained the origins of the EU and the way in which it has expanded and continues to expand as more countries seek membership. It has explained the process by which laws are made, so that the development of national company law may be understood in its impact on national accounting practices. The IAS Regulation imposes IFRS across all EU listed companies from 2005. For entities that do not fall within the IAS Regulation, the most important aspects of EU accounting law are the Fourth and Seventh Directives. The chapter has explained these in some detail so that the practices of individual countries may be understood against this general background. It has also explained how modernization of the Directives is bringing them closer to the IFRS so that eventually it is likely that all companies will apply similar accounting practices, whether listed or not.

---

[54] EC (2001).

Key points from the chapter:

- The IAS Regulation takes precedence over national laws and standards in requiring listed companies in the EU to apply IFRS.

- Member states of the EU have harmonized their national company laws with the Fourth and Seventh Directives. These harmonized national laws continue to apply to companies not covered by the IAS Regulation.

- The EU Commission retains its rights over the process of EU legislation by 'endorsing' IFRS after they are issued by the IASB. The endorsement is carried out by the Commission on the advice of the Accounting Regulatory Committee, which has political representation from all member states. Advice is also taken from technical experts at EFRAG.

- The Fourth and Seventh Directives contain options that give member states flexibility in harmonizing national laws.

- Modernization of the Directives reflects the need to bring them up to date on matters such as the use of fair values in reporting financial instruments.

- The Commission is using its influence to encourage harmonization of environmental reporting.

Questions

The following questions test your understanding of the material contained in the chapter and allow you to relate your understanding to the learning outcomes specified at the start of this chapter. The learning outcomes are repeated here. Each question is cross-referenced to the relevant section of the chapter.

Explain the origins and nature of the European Union

1 To what extent is accounting practice in member states likely to be affected by the stated purpose of the EU? (section 12.2)

2 In which ways are each of the main institutions likely to have influence or impact on accounting practice in member states? (section 12.2)

Explain how laws are made in the European Union

3 What are the different levels of legislation that may be applied to accounting? (section 12.3)

Explain the effect of the IAS Regulation

4 Why did the EU abandon the idea of developing 'EU accounting standards'? (section 12.4)

5 What is the status of the IAS Regulation? (sections 12.3 and 12.5)

Understand the role and nature of EU Directives in accounting and auditing

6 If a new company law directive were proposed today, what processes would be required? How long might it take for the directive to enter national law of each member state? (section 12.6)

7 Is 'equivalence' the same as 'equality'? (section 12.6)

8 Why is it necessary to have options in Directives? What factors might cause options to be allowed in a new Directive? (section 12.6)

9 What are the most significant features of the Fourth Directive? (section 12.7)

10 Why may the words 'true and fair' have a different effect in different countries? (section 12.7.2)

11 What are the similarities and differences between the 'type of expenditure' format and the 'functional basis' format of the profit and loss account? (section 12.7.5)

12 To what extent do recognition and measurement feature in the Fourth and Seventh Directives? (section 12.7.5)

13 What are the most significant features of the Seventh Directive? (section 12.8)

14 What are the problems in defining a group? (section 12.8.3)

Explain how the EU is modernizing its approach to accounting legislation and guidance

15 Why was there a need to modernize the Fourth and Seventh Directives? (section 12.9)

16 Why did the EU use a Recommendation rather than a Directive to give its views on environmental accounting? (section 12.10)

Appendix 12.1 Formats in the Fourth Directive

Horizontal balance sheet (Article 9)

Assets

A   Subscribed capital unpaid   θ
B   Formation expenses   θ
C   Fixed assets   θ

   I   Intangible assets   ⊗
     1   Costs of research and development   φ
     2   Concessions, patents, licences, trade marks and similar rights
        and assets   φ
     3   Goodwill   •
     4   Payments on account   φ

   II   Tangible assets   ⊗
     1   Land and buildings   •
     2   Plant and machinery   •
     3   Other fixtures and fittings, tools and equipment   •
     4   Payments on account and tangible assets in course of construction   •

   III   Financial assets   ⊗
     1   Shares in affiliated undertakings   •
     2   Loans to affiliated undertakings   •
     3   Participating interests   •
     4   Loans to undertakings with which the company is linked by virtue
        of participating interests   •
     5   Investments held as fixed assets   φ
     6   Other loans   φ
     7   Own shares   •

D   Current assets   θ

   I   Stocks   ⊗
     1   Raw materials and consumables   φ
     2   Work in progress   φ
     3   Finished goods and goods for resale   φ
     4   Payments on account   φ

   II   Debtors   ⊗

(Amounts becoming due and payable after more than one year
must be shown separately for each item)

     1   Trade debtors   φ
     2   Amounts owed by affiliated undertakings   •
     3   Amounts owed by undertakings with which the company is
        linked by virtue of participating interests   •
     4   Other debtors   φ
     5   Subscribed capital called but not paid (unless under A-Assets)   φ
     6   Prepayments and accrued income (unless under E-Assets)   •

   III   Investments   ⊗
     1   Shares in affiliated undertakings   •
     2   Own shares   •
     3   Other investments   φ

   IV   Cash at bank and in hand   ⊗

E   Prepayments and accrued income (unless under D.II.6-Assets)   θ
                                    θ

Liabilities

A   Capital and reserves   θ

    I   Subscribed capital (unless called-up capital shown under this item)   ⊗
    II   Share premium account   ⊗
    III   Revaluation reserve   ⊗
    IV   Reserves   ⊗

        1   Legal reserve, in so far as required   φ
        2   Reserve for own shares, in so far as required   φ
        3   Reserves provided for by the articles of association   φ
        4   Other reserves   φ

    V   Profit or loss brought forward   ⊗
    VI   Profit or loss for the financial year (unless under F-Assets or E-Liabilities)   ⊗

B   Provisions for liabilities and charges   θ

        1   Provisions for pensions and similar obligations   φ
        2   Provisions for taxation   φ
        3   Other provisions   φ

C   Creditors   θ

(Amounts becoming due and payable within one year and after more than
one year must be shown separately for each item and in total)

        1   Debenture loans, showing convertible loans separately   •
        2   Amounts owed to credit institutions   •
        3   Payments received on account of orders in so far as they are
            not shown separately as deductions from stocks   φ
        4   Trade creditors   φ
        5   Bills of exchange payable   φ
        6   Amounts owed to affiliated undertakings   •
        7   Amounts owed to undertakings with which the company is linked
            by virtue of participating interests   •
        8   Other creditors including tax and social security   φ
        9   Accruals and deferred income (unless shown under D-Liabilities)   •

D   Accruals and deferred income (unless shown under C.9-Liabilities)   θ
                                                                                                       θ

Key to symbols
θ   Required from all companies.
⊗   Required from all companies.
•   Not required for small companies.
φ   Not required for small companies or published accounts of medium-sized companies.

▶

Minimum vertical balance sheet (Article 10)

C	FIXED ASSETS		θ
	I Intangible assets	⊗	
	II Tangible assets	⊗	
	III Financial assets	⊗	
D	CURRENT ASSETS (showing separately for debtors amounts due in more than one year)		θ
	I Stocks	⊗	
	II Debtors	⊗	
	III Investments	⊗	
	IV Cash	⊗	
F	CREDITORS (due within one year)		(θ)
G	CURRENT ASSETS		θ
H	ASSETS LESS CURRENT LIABILITIES		θ
I	CREDITORS (due in more than one year)		(θ)
J	PROVISIONS FOR LIABILITIES AND CHARGES		(θ)
L	CAPITAL AND RESERVES	⊗	
	I Called-up capital	⊗	
	II Share premium account	⊗	
	III Revaluation reserve	⊗	
	IV Reserves	⊗	
	V Profit or loss brought forward	⊗	
	VI Profit or loss for year	⊗	

Notes:
1   Items A, B, E and K are omitted here because national law can permit inclusion within other headings as shown in previous exhibit.
2   For larger companies the above layout assumes that national law requires or allows all items preceded by Arabic numerals to be shown in the notes on the accounts.
3   The above layout also shows the form of balance sheet that would be published by small companies if all possible concessions relating to the balance sheet were granted to them (and making assumptions 1 and 2 above).
4   Net current assets will include amounts due from debtors after more than one year.

Key to symbols
⊗   Required from all companies.
θ   Required from all companies.

Profit and loss account
Type of expenditure basis – vertical (Article 23)

1	Net turnover	φ
2	Variations in stocks of finished goods and work in progress	φ
3	Work performed by the undertaking for its own purposes and capitalized	φ
4	Other operating income	φ
5	(a) Raw materials and consumables	φ
	(b) Other external charges	φ
6	Staff costs	
	(a) Wages and salaries	(•)
	(b) Social security costs, with a separate indication of those relating to pensions	(•)
7	(a) Value adjustments in respect of formation expenses and of tangible and intangible fixed assets	•
	(b) Value adjustments in respect of current assets, to the extent that they exceed the amount of value adjustments which are normal in the undertaking concerned	•
8	Other operating charges	(•)
9	Income from participating interests, with a separate indication of that derived from affiliated undertakings	•
10	Income from other investments and loans forming part of the fixed assets, with a separate indication of that derived from affiliated undertakings	•
11	Other interest receivable and similar income, with a separate indication of that derived from affiliated undertakings	•
12	Value adjustments in respect of financial assets and of investments held as current assets	(•)
13	Interest payable and similar charges, with a separate indication of those concerning affiliated undertakings	(•)
14	Tax on profit on ordinary activities	(•)
15	Profit or loss on ordinary activities after taxation	•
16	Extraordinary income	•
17	Extraordinary charges	(•)
18	Extraordinary profit or loss	•
19	Tax on extraordinary profit or loss	(•)
20	Other taxes not shown under the above items	•
21	Profit or loss for the financial year	•

Key to symbols

φ   Small and medium-sized companies may be allowed to combine these items under one item called 'Gross profit or loss'. Small companies may be exempted from publishing, but not from preparing, a profit and loss account.

•   Not required for small companies.

Profit and loss account
Functional (operational) basis – vertical (Article 25)

1   Net turnover   ф

2   Cost of sales (including value adjustments)   ф

3   Gross profit or loss   •

4   Distribution costs (including value adjustments)   (•)

5   Administrative expenses (including value adjustments)   (•)

6   Other operating income   •

7   Income from participating interests, with a separate indication of that derived
    from affiliated undertakings   •

8   Income from other investments and loans forming part of the fixed assets,
    with a separate indication of that derived from affiliated undertakings   •

9   Other interest receivable and similar income, with a separate indication
    of that derived from affiliated undertakings   •

10 Value adjustments in respect of financial assets and of investments held as
    current assets   (•)

11 Interest payable and similar charges, with a separate indication of those
    concerning affiliated undertakings   (•)

12 Tax on profit or loss on ordinary activities   (•)

13 Profit or loss on ordinary activities after taxation   •

14 Extraordinary income   •

15 Extraordinary charges   (•)

16 Extraordinary profit or loss   •

17 Tax on extraordinary profit or loss   (•)

18 Other taxes not shown under the above items   (•)

19 Profit or loss for the financial year   •

Key to symbols

ф   Small and medium-sized companies may be allowed to combine these items with item 3 under one
    item called 'Gross profit or loss'. Small companies may be exempted from publishing, but not from
    preparing, a profit and loss account.

•   Not required for small companies.

References and further reading

Alexander, D. and Archer, S. (2000) 'On the myth of "Anglo-Saxon" financial accounting', *International Journal of Accounting*, 35(4): 539–557.

Alexander, D. and Archer, S. (eds) (2001) *European Accounting Guide*, 4th edn. New York: Aspen Law & Business.

Alexander, D. and Archer, S. (2003) 'On the myth of "Anglo-Saxon" financial accounting: a response to Nobes', *International Journal of Accounting*, 38(4): 503–504.

Armstrong, C., Barth, M., Jagolinzo, A. and Riedl, E.J. (2007) 'Market reaction to the adoption of IFRS in Europe'. Available at www.ssrn.com.

Coleman, R. (1984) 'The aims of EEC company law harmonization: corporate accounting and disclosure issues', in Gray, S.J. and Coenenberg, A.G., *EEC and Accounting Harmonization: Implementation and Impact of the Fourth Directive*. Amsterdam: North-Holland.

COM (2003) Modernising Company Law and Enhancing Corporate Governance in the European Union – A Plan to Move Forward. Communication from the Commission to the Council and the European Parliament. May. COM (2003) 284 final.

Fairhurst, J. (2007) Law of the European Union, 6th edn. London: Pearson Education.

FEE (1993) *Seventh Directive Options and their Implementation*. London: Fédération des Experts Comptables Européens/Routledge.

Haller, A. (2002) 'Financial accounting developments in the European Union: past events and future prospects', *European Accounting Review*, 11(1): 153–190.

Niessen, H. (1993) 'The Seventh Directive on consolidated accounts and company law harmonization in the European Community', in Gray, S.J., Coenenberg, A.G. and Gordon, P.D. (eds) *International Group Accounting – Issues in European Harmonization*. London: Routledge.

Nobes, C. (2003) 'On the myth of "Anglo-Saxon" financial accounting: a comment', *International Journal of Accounting*, 38(1): 95–104.

Ordelheide, D. (ed.) (2001) *Transnational Accounting TRANSACC*, 2nd edn. Basingstoke: Palgrave.

Parker, R.H. and Nobes, C.W. (1994) *An International View of True and Fair Accounting*. London: Routledge.

Watts, T.R. (ed.) (1979) *Handbook on the EEC Fourth Directive*: *The Impact on Company Accounts in the Nine Member States*. London: The Institute of Chartered Accountants in England and Wales.

Company law and accounting information

Updating news on matters of company law and accounting is available through: http://europa.eu.int/comm/internal_market/accounting/index_en.htm.

EC (2001) Commission Recommendation of 30 May 2001 on the recognition, measurement and disclosure of environmental issues in the annual accounts and annual reports of companies. 2001/453/EC.

EC (2002) Regulation (EC) No. 1606/2002 of the European Parliament and of the Council of 19 July 2002 on the application of international accounting standards ('The IAS Regulation').

EC (2003a) Directive 2003/51/EC of the European Parliament and of the Council of 18 June 2003.

EC (2003b) Comments concerning certain Articles of the Regulation (EC) No. 1606/2002 of the European Parliament and of the Council of 19 July 2002 on the application of international accounting standards and the Fourth Council Directive 78/660/EEC of 25 July 1978 and the Seventh Council Directive 83/349/EEC of 13 June 1983 on accounting, Commission of the European Communities, November.

European Union home page

The starting point for information about the EU is: http://europa.eu.int/.

13 Some debates on global standard setting

Learning outcomes

After reading this chapter you should be able to:

- Describe the main international organizations that are encouraging international cooperation.
- Explain the conflicting arguments over the nature of the IASB Constitution.
- Explain the controversies arising in the EU during the endorsement process.

- Discuss the likelihood that a monopoly in standard setting will emerge from the IASB/FASB convergence process.
- Suggest future directions for comparative research in global corporate reporting.

13.1 Introduction

The OECD[1] has defined globalization as 'the process whereby domestic product, capital and labour markets become more integrated across borders'. The EU is the largest economic entity working for such integration. The USA is an economy of comparable size which has influence beyond its borders. Other countries around the world are seeking to attract capital investment and are finding themselves aligning their accounting systems either with IFRS or with US GAAP.

The main purpose of this chapter is to reflect on the debates that have emerged as the IASB has developed its role (see Chapter 10), US GAAP remain a competing force (see Chapter 11) and the EU has taken steps to adopt IFRS and has persuaded the US regulators to remove the requirement for reconciliation between IFRS and US GAAP.

We describe a wide range of organizations working to support international cooperation. We then explain some of the controversies raised by the IASB Constitution and by the endorsement of IFRS in Europe. We ask whether a monopolistic position in standard setting is sustainable in the longer term and we conclude by pointing to continuing opportunities for comparative studies in corporate reporting.

13.2 Organizations supporting international cooperation

Before we move into the detailed study of the various discussions and disagreements, we provide a flavour of the organizations around the world that are seeking to harmonize aspects of international accounting practice or at least to foster understanding. Some are private sector federations of interested bodies, some are governmental or intergovernmental organizations, and some others rely on committed individuals for their continuity.

The following sections explain a variety of leading international accountancy organizations. Some operate at a regional level defined by geographic linking of more than one country or state. Others have a worldwide level of operation, although membership and geographical coverage may vary from one to the next.

13.2.1 Regional accountancy bodies

Regional accountancy bodies are in the main non-governmental organizations (NGOs). Although at the outset a number of these bodies had ambitions to develop accounting standards, little real success has been achieved. Most of these regional professional organizations have concentrated their energies on educational matters, organization of conferences and the general dissemination of information to their members and the wider business community. Some have acted as effective pressure groups at a global level, ensuring that their distinctive regional voice is heard in the international accounting standard-setting process. The leading regional accountancy bodies are listed in Exhibit 13.1.

---

[1] OECD (2007), p. 187.

Exhibit 13.1 The leading regional accountancy bodies

ABWA **Association of Accountancy Bodies in West Africa**
Members are Nigeria, Ghana, Liberia, Sierra Leone and Senegal. www.ifac.org/About/RegionalAccountancyOrgs.php

AFA **Association of South East Asian Nations (ASEAN) Federation of Accountants**
A registered non-governmental organization (NGO) for accounting in ASEAN. The economic linkages fostered by ASEAN led naturally to the linking of professional accountants. Accountancy bodies in Brunei, Indonesia, Kampuchea, Laos, Malaysia, Myanmar, the Philippines, Singapore, Thailand and Vietnam are full members. www.afa-central.org

ASCA **Arab Society of Certified Accountants**
ASCA was established in London in 1984 as an Arab professional institution with an international character. Members are citizens of an Arab country who have passed the examinations of a recognized professional association. It has members in Bahrain, Egypt, Emirates, Jordan, Kuwait, Libya, Oman, Palestine, Saudi Arabia, Syria, Tunisia, Yemen. www.ascasociety.org

CAPA **Confederation of Asian and Pacific Accountants**
Established by professional accountancy bodies as a forum for discussion of accounting problems met by accountants in Asia and Pacific countries. Covers 33 organizations in 23 jurisdictions. www.capa.com.my

ECCAA **Eurasia Council of Certified Accountants and Auditors**
A federation of regional professional accountancy bodies whose working language is Russian. www.globalcipa.net

ECSAFA **Eastern, Central and Southern African Federation of Accountants**
This is a body which aims to build and promote the accountancy profession in the region. www.accaglobal.com/ecsafa

FEE **Fédération des Experts Comptables Européens (Federation of European Accountants)**
Brings together professional bodies from European countries, including but not restricted to the EU, to work towards enhancing European harmonization. www.fee.be

IAA **Interamerican Accounting Association**
Membership covers accountancy bodies in countries of Central and South America. Activities include translation of International Accounting Standards. Works closely with IFAC. www.contadoresaic.org

ICAC **Institute of Chartered Accountants of the Caribbean**
Members are the chartered accountancy bodies of The Bahamas, Barbados, Belize, Guyana, Jamaica, St Kitts and Nevis, St Lucia, Trinidad and Tobago, Antigua and Barbuda. www.icac.org.jm

NRF **Nordic Federation of Public Accountants**
The NRF includes Denmark, Finland, Iceland, Norway and Sweden. www.nrfaccount.se

SAFA **South Asian Federation of Accountants**
Member bodies are located in Bangladesh, India, Nepal, Pakistan and Sri Lanka. www.esafa.org

The lack of any significant progress in standard setting by regional bodies is partly due to the problem of enforcement. Non-governmental bodies generally lack the power to insist on compliance with their rules. For a regional accounting standard-setting body to be effective one of the following methods of enforcement would be required:

● the professional accountancy bodies or auditing authorities of each member state of the region agree to apply or approve the regional standards rather than national variations;

- those who govern companies (management or regulators) in each member state agree to apply or approve the regional standards rather than national variations;
- national legislators or standard setters agree on the use of common regional standards;
- national stock exchanges agree to accept the standards defined on a regional basis.

The first two of these conditions have not generally been achieved, probably because business which crosses national boundaries is international in nature rather than being contained to a specific region linking a group of companies or states. Standardization has required the intervention of wider groupings of accountancy bodies and interested persons, intergovernmental organizations and action by securities markets at an international level.

13.2.2 Wider groupings of accountancy bodies and interested persons

There are organizations which have formed to link accountancy bodies and interested persons across national boundaries (see Exhibit 13.2). These have all formed as a result of various voluntary initiatives. They are not driven by national governments.

| Exhibit 13.2 | Organizations of accountancy bodies and interested persons linking across national boundaries |

IFAC **International Federation of Accountants**
Supports IASB as source of international accounting standards. Important work in the area of auditing is done by IAASB (see below). IFAC also has committees dealing with education, ethics, financial and management accounting, and the public sector. Organizes World Congress of Accountants every five years. www.ifac.org

IAASB **International Auditing and Assurance Standards Board**
A committee of IFAC (see above). Issues International Standards on Auditing. Aims to establish high-quality auditing, assurance, quality control and related services standards and to improve the uniformity of practice by professional accountants throughout the world. www.ifac.org/IAASB

IASB **International Accounting Standards Board**
Founded by private sector professional accountancy bodies with the purpose of issuing International Financial Reporting Standards (section 1.4). www.iasb.org

IFIAR **International Forum of Independent Audit Regulators**
Established in 2006 by a large number of national audit regulators from major jurisdictions around the world. http://www.ifiar.org/

G4 **Group of Four (G4)**
Accountancy bodies in the USA, Canada, the UK, Australia and New Zealand worked together in the late 1990s to provide joint input to the development of the work of IASC and to influence international developments. (G4+1 was the name given to this group plus the IASC.) Dissolved at start of 2001 because of potential duplication with new IASB work.

EAA **European Accounting Association**
International organization bringing together institutional and individual membership from around the world. Organizes annual conference and publishes an academic journal. www.eaa-online.org/home/index.cfm

IAAER **International Association for Accounting Education and Research**
Academic community members concerned with promoting excellence in education and research. www.iaaer.org

Central to international cooperation in accounting is the International Federation of Accountants (IFAC). Formed in 1977, its members are professional accountancy bodies in many countries. The mission of IFAC is to serve the public interest, strengthen the accountancy profession worldwide and contribute to the development of strong international economies by establishing and promoting adherence to high-quality professional standards, furthering the international convergence of such standards, and speaking out on public interest issues where the profession's expertise is most relevant. In relation to its members IFAC acts as leader, facilitator, collaborator and observer.[2]

The IFAC Council contains one representative from each member body. It meets once each year to elect the IFAC Board and to discuss changes to the Constitution. The IFAC Board contains 21 members from 17 countries. These members are elected for three-year terms and are responsible for setting policy and overseeing IFAC operations, the implementation of programmes and the work of IFAC technical committees and task forces. The Board meets three times a year. Detailed work is carried out by the technical committees and task forces, supported by a full-time Secretariat headquartered in New York.

Each committee is given responsibility in particular technical areas of IFAC work covering auditing, education, ethics and the public sector. From the perspective of published financial information perhaps the most important work is that of the IAASB (see Chapter 3). International Standards on Auditing (ISAs) are intended for international acceptance.

IFAC encourages international accountancy cooperation on a sub-global basis. To this end it recognizes specific regional accountancy bodies (see Exhibit 13.3) whose views are actively sought by IFAC committees as representing the distinctive views and interests of their members.

Neither IFAC nor its recognized regional bodies have attempted directly to develop accounting standards at an international level. Instead IFAC accepts that the IASB is the major source of authoritative guidance on standardization of international accounting practices.

Exhibit 13.3 Regional accountancy bodies recognized or acknowledged by IFAC

Recognized by IFAC as regional organizations

CAPA	Confederation of Asian and Pacific Accountants
ECSAFA	Eastern, Central and Southern African Federation of Accountants
FEE	Fédération des Experts Comptables Européens (Federation of European Accountants)
IAA	Interamerican Accounting Association

Acknowledged by IFAC as regional groupings

ABWA	Association of Accountancy Bodies in West Africa
ECCAA	Eurasia Council of Certified Accountants and Auditors
ICAC	Institute of Chartered Accountants of the Caribbean
SAFA	South Asian Federation of Accontants

[2] IFAC Constitution, revised (2003).

Exhibit 13.4	Intergovernmental organizations

EU European Union
The European Commission issues Directives which form a basis for national law within each member country. Accounting Directives (Fourth and Seventh) are largely concerned with harmonization of presentation in financial statements. The Internal Market Directorate General has the main responsibility. http://europa.eu.int/comm/dgs/internal_market/index_en.htm

OECD Organization for Economic Cooperation and Development
Established by 24 of the world's 'developed' countries to promote world trade and global economic growth, OECD is concerned with financial reporting by multinational companies. OECD has a Working Group on Accounting Standards, issues guidelines for multinational companies, carries out surveys and publishes reports. Work extends to Central and Eastern Europe, for example the Coordinating Council on Accounting Methodology in the CIS (former Soviet Union). www.oecd.org/home

ISAR Intergovernmental Working Group of Experts on International Standards of Accounting and Reporting
ISAR operates within the United Nations, with a particular interest in accounting and reporting issues of the developing countries. It carries out surveys and publishes reports, and makes recommendations with regard to transnational companies. www.unctad.org

13.2.3 Intergovernmental organizations

The IASB works closely with a number of intergovernmental bodies. These are shown in Exhibit 13.4. These bodies cooperate with the each other and with the IASB.

Chapter 12 has explained the work of the European Commission in more detail.

13.2.4 Organizations of securities markets and analysts

Exhibit 13.5 lists some of the coordinating organizations for securities markets, analysts and fund managers.

Securities markets regulators are particularly interested in the presentation of accounting information as a means of ensuring an efficient market. They have the power to accept or refuse a company's access to the market. The regulators seek to apply strict accounting requirements but also want to avoid undue restrictions which will inhibit growth of the market. They are able to enforce regulations on those companies which seek to raise finance through the stock market.

Analysts who are writing reports on companies need some reassurance about comparability and need to be aware of the usefulness of a standard approach to accounting practice when making international comparisons.

13.2.5 Preparers' organizations

Financial Executives International (FEI)[3] is a US-based association for corporate finance executives. It was founded in 1931 as the Controllers Institute of America and became the Financial Executives Institute in 1962. In November 2000 it opened membership to financial executives around the world and took the 'International' description into its

---

[3] www.fei.org.

| Exhibit 13.5 | Organizations of securities markets and analysts |

IOSCO	International Organization of Securities Commissions Securities regulators around the world come together to promote high standards in the operation of securities markets. www.iosco.org		Research). A US body which educates and examines investment analysts, and carries out research. www.cfainstitute.org
CESR	The Committee of European Securities Regulators Established by a European Commission Decision of June 2001 to improve coordination among securities regulators, CESR acts as an advisory group to the European Commission. Works to ensure consistent and timely implementation of legislation in member states. www.cesr-eu.org	EFFAS	European Federation of Financial Analysts' Societies EFFAS has developed the European method of financial analysis. This involves a standardized approach to the classification and presentation of financial statements. www.effas.com
CFA Institute	Chartered Financial Analysts Institute (Formerly AIMR: Association for Investment Management and	FEAS	Federation of Euro-Asian Stock Exchanges FEAS has 41 members, all emerging stock exchanges in Eastern Europe, Central and South Asia and the Middle East. www.feas.org

title. One aspect of FEI's activity is lobbying standard setters as a representative of chief finance officers. Zeff (2002) suggests that the challenges given by FEI to the FASB on controversial issues give an indication of the type of political pressure that the IASB may face in future.

The European Association of Listed Companies (EALIC), formed in 2002, represents European listed companies in making representations to the European Commission and other European authorities on matters relating to the legal and regulatory framework for listed companies.

13.3 Developing the IASCF Constitution

13.3.1 From IASC to IASB

A very thorough account of the transition from IASC to IASB is provided by Camfferman and Zeff (2007) in a chapter entitled 'Towards a world standard setter'. The following paragraphs owe a great deal to that chapter, which well merits reading in full.

In the second half of the 1990s the IASC was beginning to sense potential rivals for an international standard-setting role. The FASB and the G4+1 were two such rivals. IOSCO's endorsement of the core standards revision was seen as a critical factor for the IASC's continuing pre-eminence. A working party was formed to make recommendations on the IASC's Constitution. There were two competing models for taking forward the work of the IASC. One was to focus on efficiency and independence of the standard-setting process, the other was to focus on the geographical spread of representation.

A discussion paper *Shaping IASC for the future* was published at the end of 1998. There were three levels of action envisaged – the Standards Development Committee, the Board and the Trustees. Reasonable geographical spread featured in the proposed composition of all three bodies. The SDC would draw its membership from national standard setters.

Camfferman and Zeff describe the varied responses to this discussion paper. Many respondents focused on the detail of the proposal – what powers should be available for each level of action, how many participants there should be in each and how they should be nominated. The SEC, FASB and European Commission raised more fundamental questions. The SEC and FASB wanted to see the new organization formed as an international standard setter in its own right, taking it closer to the structure of the FASB. The European Commission thought the proposals were already too close to replicating the FASB.

The proposal changed to focusing on a single board, appointed by trustees, when the IASC met in Warsaw in mid-1999. The idea was proposed by the chairman and the secretary-general who wanted to move the debate along. They proposed a standard-setting board with some full-time and some part-time members, large enough to give a spread of geographical representation. The issue of geographical representation versus expert membership continued to be debated. An interesting comment in Camfferman and Zeff (p. 470) is that both the SEC and the European Commission argued for the centrality of legitimacy. For the SEC this required technical expertise, due process and independence. For the European Commission it required responsiveness to the needs of the national governments and intergovernmental bodies that formed the IASC.

Camfferman and Zeff then document a series of letters in which influential persons set out the conditions under which they could support a new standard-setting body, and the various responses in the continuing discussions of the IASC working party and the IASB Board. The outcome is described by Camfferman and Zeff (p. 492) as a victory for the SEC and those who preferred the independent-expert model, and a defeat for the European Commission and those who preferred a constituency-based model. Chapter 10 describes the constitutional model for the IASB which emerged in 2001.

13.3.2 Review 2005

The IASC Foundation (IASCF) published its Review of the Constitution and Proposals for Change in November 2004. The main revisions involved: a broader geographical representation across the Trustees; an independent IASB benefiting from diverse experience; assurance of adequate consultation; and improved Trustee oversight of due process and consultative issues.

In March 2005 Alexander Schaub, Chairman of the Accounting Regulatory Committee, wrote to the IASCF with five concerns:

1 There should be a formal appointments process for the Trustees of the IASCF. The Trustees should not select their own successors.
2 The composition of the IASB, IFRIC and the Trustees should correspond more closely to the jurisdictions that apply the standards or have undertaken to make them mandatory. It was pointed out that only seven members of the IASB came from countries where IAS were required for listed companies.
3 The Board of Trustees should take a closer involvement in the activities and work programme of the IASB.
4 The funding process should be more coherent. Relying on voluntary contributions leads to potential conflict of interest. The ARC welcomed the Trustees' intention to move to a different funding basis.

5 The ARC supported the proposal to increase the majority voting in the IASB from eight to nine. The ARC would prefer it to be ten.

The IASCF resisted the pressure for using geographical representation as a basis for appointing IASB members. The Trustees continue to appoint new Trustees but commit themselves to consultation with national and international organizations of auditors, preparers, users and academics. It seems significant that regulators are not mentioned specifically.

13.4 EU endorsement of IFRS

We explained in Chapter 12 (section 12.4) that the European Commission's ambitions to develop European accounting standards independently came to an end in 1995 when the Commission announced that it would look to the IASC (now the IASB) to carry forward the work of harmonization of standards. Section 13.4.1 indicates the initial satisfaction with endorsing IFRS as the way forward. Section 13.4.2 describes the first major difference of opinion between the Commission and the IASB over the endorsement of IAS 39. Section 13.4.3 indicates the intervention of the European Parliament in the endorsement of IFRS 8.

13.4.1 Acceptance of IFRS as the way forward

The formal declaration of acceptance of IFRS was made in the IAS Regulation issued in 2002.[4] The 'context' available on the Internal Markets website (see Exhibit 13.6) indicates there was agreement, based on consultation, on taking this way forward.

Exhibit 13.6	Context to the IAS Regulation 2002

> On 13 June 2000 the Commission adopted a Communication entitled 'The EU's Financial Reporting Strategy: The way forward', in which it suggested that all listed companies should be required to prepare consolidated accounts in accordance with international accounting standards from 2005. On 17 July 2000 the Ecofin Council welcomed the Communication; it emphasised that the comparability, accuracy and transparency of European companies were an essential aspect of the integration of European financial markets and of their international competitiveness. Furthermore, the harmonisation of these statements is considered essential for the *Financial Services Action Plan*. In addition, the companies concerned support the adoption of a set of unique internationally recognised rules since this would facilitate the marketability of securities, cross-border mergers and acquisitions, and the raising of finance. The EU legislation on company accounting was adopted in the 1970s and needs to be updated if it is to meet the needs of today's investors. The securities of any one company are, in fact, often held by an internationally diverse group of investors.

Source: http://europa.eu/scadplus/leg/en/lvb/l26040.htm.

---

[4] Regulation (EC) No. 1606/2002 of the European Parliament and of the Council of 19 July 2002 on the application of international accounting standards.

13.4.2 Dissatisfaction over IAS 39

IAS 39 was approved in December 1998 in order to meet IOSCO's target for the Core Standards project (see section 10.4.4). It was issued in March 1999, with contents very similar to the US GAAP existing at the time. There had not been sufficient time or resources to develop an ideal standard; this was a practical solution seen as an 'interim' measure. It did contain the essence of fair value measurement for derivatives and stricter rules on what could be regarded as hedges in matching the gains and losses on two separate transactions. IAS 39 took effect from 2001 and was therefore high on the list of priorities for the newly formed IASB. An exposure draft of improvements to IAS 32 and IAS 39 was published in June 2002 with 2 of the 14 IASB members dissenting.

One concern with IAS 39 is that its strict approach to defining hedges would not reflect the commercial reality of hedging transactions. Retail banks explained that they do not hedge one transaction against another specific transaction; they balance all the risk exposures they face in different markets and different countries.

By 2002 the intention of the EU to adopt IFRS was known. This allowed the EU to become a strong voice in the debate on IFRS. Financial institutions expressed particular concern. Such was the high profile of concern in France that the French President, Jacques Chirac, wrote in July 2003 to the EC President, Romano Prodi, saying that increasing use of fair values would lead to excessive volatility in the economy and that IAS 39 could lead to financial instability in the EU.

The IASB had to demonstrate more clearly that it was carrying out sufficient consultation and entered into active discussions with some of the strongest opponents, particularly European bankers and insurers. Round table discussions were also held.

During 2004 dissatisfaction continued. IAS 39 as revised at the end of 2003 contained an unrestricted fair value option[5] and a relatively tight definition of what could be matched in hedging. Comments on the revision indicated that the restrictive definition on hedging did not reflect business practice, particularly in banking.

A dinner held in January 2004, hosted by Commissioner Bolkestein,[6] brought together representatives from the IASB, the banking industry, the Basle Committee, CESR, CEIOPS and the ECB with a view to facilitate the emergence of a solution on IAS 32 and 39. The five key issues identified included the two continuing points of contention, namely macro-hedging and the fair value option. Participants at the dinner had agreed to the creation of a High Level Consultative Group to work on achievable solutions.

In February 2004 the IASC Foundation invited regulators and participants in the European financial services sector to form a High Level Working Group to advise the IASB.[7] The group was announced in September 2004.[8]

In April 2004 the IASB published an Exposure Draft allowing 'macro-hedging' which gave a larger, less restrictive, view of what constituted a hedge. However, it did not deal sufficiently with the major concerns of some bankers and insurers.[9]

At a meeting of the ARC on 14 June 2004, four member states opposed adoption of the version of IAS 39 current at the time, fifteen member states were in favour of proceeding

---

[5] The 'fair value option' means that entities have a choice to designate any financial asset or any financial liability to be measured at fair value, with gains and losses reported through profit and loss.

[6] Summary of ARC meeting, 3 February 2004.

[7] IASCF Press Release, 10 February 2004.

[8] IASCF Press Release, 21 September 2004.

[9] Ernst & Young (2006), p. 1048.

immediately with the endorsement of IAS 39 as it stood, on the basis of the balance sheet presentational solution for cash flow hedges proposed by the IASB and its commitment to examine seriously the proposal of the European Banking Federation on interest rate margin hedges. Six were not in a position to give their views.

The IASB discussed the responses to its April 2004 Exposure Draft in September 2004 and noted that there was disagreement from a large majority of all categories except regulators.[10] However, the IASB also recognized that reverting to unrestricted fair value would not satisfy the regulators. The IASB expressed a desire to understand better the concerns of some bank regulators.

By September 2004 the EU position was hardening. Two issues were identified as needing attention. One was the use of the full fair value option and the other was the hedge accounting condition.[11] Some regulators felt the full fair value option gave too much scope for discretion. Some banks said the hedge accounting provisions made it impossible for them to hedge their core deposits on a portfolio basis.

This position was not supported in all member states. The chairman of the Financial Reporting Council wrote to the EU Commissioner in June 2004 supporting full endorsement of IAS 39.[12] The UK Accounting Standards Board supported the full hedging provisions and the unamended fair value option[13] but above all emphasized the need for clarification as companies started to prepare their financial statements for conversion to IFRS in 2005.

Following a 'qualified majority' vote of the ARC on 1 October 2004, the European Commission adopted a Regulation on 19 November 2004, endorsing IAS 39 *Financial Instruments: Recognition and Measurement*, with the exception of two 'carve-outs'. The first carve-out related to certain provisions on the use of the full fair value option, the second to certain provisions on hedge accounting. The Commission stressed that these carve-outs were exceptional and intended to be temporary, pending publication by the IASB of the necessary improvements to the original IAS 39 standard.

After extensive consultation with third parties, the IASB in June 2005 published an amended version of IAS 39, *Recognition and Measurement – the Fair Value Option (FVO)*, which restricted the use of the option to designate any financial asset or any financial liability to be measured at fair value through profit and loss. The amended standard received support, both from the financial services industry as well as from the European Central Bank and the Basle Committee of banking supervisors.

The ARC approved the necessary Regulation to adopt the amended standard by the end of September 2005. Adoption was made retroactive to 1 January 2005, so that companies could apply the amended standard for their 2005 final statements.[14] The controversial stages in the development of IAS 39 from the end of 2003 to 2005 are summarized in Exhibit 13.7.

The overall effect of the continuing debate and disagreement throughout 2004 and 2005 was to cause significant uncertainty for companies preparing their first IFRS financial statements for the year ended 31 December 2005. Consider the problem where comparative

---

[10] IASB Update, December 2004, p. 2.

[11] Explanatory memorandum of the Commission Services on the proposal for a Regulation adopting IAS 39, 24 September 2004.

[12] Letter from Sir Bryan Nicholson to Commissioner Bolkestein, 16 June 2004.

[13] ASB Inside Track 41, October 2004, pp. 1–2.

[14] Press release of European Commission, IP/05/884, 8 July 2005.

Exhibit 13.7	Controversial stages in the development of IAS 39	
Date	**Action by IASB**	**Action by EU Commission and ARC**
August 2003	Exposure draft of improvement to IAS 39 (macro-hedging)	
December 2003	Revised version of IAS 39 issued by the IASB	
March 2004	IAS 39 revised to reflect macro-hedging	
June 2004		Meeting of ARC indicates concern over IAS 39
September 2004	Financial Instruments Working Group established by IASCF	
November 2004		Qualified acceptance of IAS 39 with 'carve-out'
December 2004	Amendment issued to IAS 39 for transition and initial recognition of profit or loss	
January 2005	Effective date of IAS 39 (Revised 2004)	
April 2005	Amendment issued to IAS 39 for cash flow hedges of forecast intragroup transactions	
June 2005	Amendment to IAS 39 for fair value option	
August 2005	Amendment to IAS 39 for financial guarantee contracts	
September 2005		ARC approved June 2005 version

Source: Derived from www.iasplus.com and EU Internal Market website.

figures for 2004 are required in the 2005 annual report and therefore companies needed to have their accounting information in an IFRS form, at least internally to the organization, from the start of 2004. They were also required to publish a reconciliation statement showing how the UK GAAP financial statements for the year ended 31 December 2004 would appear when converted to IFRS. This statement had to appear before the interim results for 2005 were published, soon after June 2005. It is not difficult to imagine the frustration of many listed companies across the EU when they had to wait until September 2005 to find out what they should have known early in 2004.

The IASB learned from this experience that the process of consultation on IFRS would in future need to take a different direction, with active consultation and formal dialogue involving key parties. The political art of finding compromise solutions became a new aspect of standard setting.

13.4.3 IFRS 8 segmental reporting

We have explained in Chapter 5 the main technical aspects of the IASB's change from IAS 14 to IFRS 8 with the aim of converging IFRS and US GAAP. We also explained that the change was controversial because some thought that the US standard SFAS 131, on which IFRS 8 is based, was less rigorous than IAS 14 had been. In the press release of November 2006 the IASB Chairman, Sir David Tweedie, said:

> IFRS 8 continues our work to eliminate major differences between IFRSs and US GAAP and to improve financial reporting. The IFRS adopts the management approach to segment reporting set out in SFAS 131. It therefore gives users of financial statements the opportunity to query how the entity is controlled by its senior decision maker. It does this by enabling entities to provide timely segment information at little extra cost.
>
> The Board will continue to examine the merits for a requirement of country-by-country disclosure as suggested by supporters of the Publish What You Pay campaign. A group of Board members will discuss this issue with other interested organisations.

We have explained in Chapter 1 the concerns of the Publish What You Pay campaign.[15]

When the European Commission considered the question of endorsing IFRS 8 for application in the EU, it received unanimous support from the European Financial Reporting Advisory Group (EFRAG), in February 2007. In the light of that technical advice the ARC supported unanimously the Commission proposal to adopt IFRS 8 in the EU. However, when the Draft Regulation appeared before the European Parliament, the Committee on Economic and Monetary Affairs (ECON) of the European Parliament passed a motion[16] in April 2007 criticizing the endorsement of IFRS 8. It said that endorsing IFRS 8 would effectively incorporate the US standard SFAS 131 into EU law. The Committee asked the Commission to carry out an impact assessment and said that if the Commission did not do this then the Parliament would carry out its own impact assessment. The Parliament had not previously chosen to express strong views on the Accounting Regulation but now recognized its powers by saying:

> Accounting standards are incorporated in the law through comitology under regulatory procedure with scrutiny.

'Comitology'[17] is a word used in the European Constitution to describe the way in which the Commission implements legislation by working with committees on which member states are represented. The Parliament is able to monitor the introduction of legislation and can object to measures proposed by the Commission. These are the powers that the Parliament used against the endorsement of IFRS 8. It seems that the Parliament has become more aware of its powers in relation to the Regulation than it had been previously.

Two examples of the public opposition to IFRS 8 are:

1 Letter to the EC Commission (9 May 2007) from the Chair of the Accounting and Auditing Practices Committee of the International Corporate Governance Network. This letter pointed to the potential risks arising from allowing greater management discretion.
2 Comment by UK Members of Parliament on 8 May 2007 criticizing the lack of geographical segment reporting.

The Parliament's intervention caused the Commission to agree that IFRS 8 would not be endorsed before 30 September 2007 and further to agree to consult interested parties and carry out an analysis of potential impacts of adopting IFRS 8. A questionnaire was issued as part of the analysis. The Commission also requested information generated by field

---

[15] www.publishwhatyoupay.org/English and also www.soros.org.
[16] Motion B6-0157/2007 on Draft Regulation 1725/2003 as regards IFRS 8.
[17] http://europa.eu/scadplus/glossary/comitology_en.htm.

studies, research work and internal analysis.[18] The consultation was announced at the end of May 2007 for response by the end of June.

There was some unease that Europe was again being put in a position where endorsed IFRS were not the same as IASB-issued IFRS. However, at the start of September 2007 the Commission published the outcome of its impact assessment. This left the way open to full endorsement of IFRS 8 which was confirmed in November 2007.[19]

In the impact assessment the Commission formed five conclusions:

- The use of the management approach has an overall positive effect on the quality of the segment information, whose usefulness and relevance would increase.
- The increased usefulness and relevance of the segment information based on the management approach outweigh concerns expressed about the comparability of financial reports.
- IFRS 8 appropriately addresses the global needs of financial statements' users for geographical disclosures and would not reduce this information in practice compared with IAS 14.
- IFRS 8 would not create problems relating to corporate governance in the EU.
- IFRS 8 provides appropriate segment reporting rules for smaller listed companies.

The final paragraph of the report gives a perspective on the factors driving the convergence process from an EU viewpoint:

> The Commission Services believe that it is crucial to consider any question regarding the endorsement of accounting standards under the IAS Regulation in the context of the overall development of one global set of standards. One of the overarching objectives of global standard setting is that IFRS is recognised in all jurisdictions, including the USA, without requirement for reconciliation. One of the main prerequisites for achieving this is convergence between IFRS and other GAAPs.

13.4.4 IFRS 12 Service Concession Arrangements

IFRIC 12 is a statement of guidance issued in November 2006 in response to questions about transactions that were not covered by existing standards. It gives guidance on the accounting by operators for public-to-private service concession arrangements. Examples of such arrangements are found where a government makes a contract with a private company to build and operate a school or a hospital. The government pays an annual fee to the private company and in the contract has some control over how the service is provided in the public interest. Some government bodies allow a private company to build a road or a bridge and then charge tolls to users. The accounting challenge of such arrangements is that they take the asset (the school or the hospital, the road or the bridge) off the balance sheet of the government and also off the balance sheet of the private contractor. The asset for the private contractor is the right to receive income.

IFRIC 12 covers public-to-private service concessions where (a) the grantor (the public sector body awarding the contract) controls or regulates what services the operator must provide with the infrastructure, to whom it must provide them, and at what price; and (b) the grantor controls – through ownership, beneficial entitlement or

---

[18] *Accountancy*, July (2007), p. 84.

[19] 'Endorsement of IFRS 8 *Operating Segments* Analysis of Potential Effects – Report', MARKT F3D (2007), http://ec.europa.eu/internal-market/accounting/docs/ifres8-operatingsegment-report.pdf.

| Exhibit 13.8 | Impact of IFRIC 12 |

GAZ DE FRANCE PRESS RELEASE FEBRUARY 2007 [EXTRACT]

Annual sales by division/segment

In millions of euros	2005	2006	Change (%)
Energy Supply & Services			
Exploration – Production	1,139	1,659	46%
Purchase – Sale of Energy	17,265	20,481	19%
Services	1,924	2,181	13%
Infrastructures			
Transmission & Storage – France	2,124	2,227	5%
Distribution – France	3,426	3,289	−4%
Transmission & Distribution – International	2,275	3,570	57%
Adjustments & other	−5,281	−5,765	
GROUP TOTAL (1)	22,872	27,642	21%
GROUP TOTAL excluding the impact of IFRIC 12 accounting interpretations	22,385	27,245	22%
GROUP TOTAL excluding the impact of IFRIC 12 accounting interpretations and with average weather conditions	22,233	27,484	24%

Impact of IFRIC 12 on reported 2005/2006 sales

IFRIC 12	1st quarter	2nd quarter	3rd quarter	4th quarter	Total
2005	93	125	115	154	487
2006	92	98	88	119	397

Source: Press Release, Gaz de France, 14 February 2007.

otherwise – any significant residual interest in the infrastructure at the end of the term of the arrangement.[20]

EFRAG recommended support for IFRIC 12 but noted that three members dissented. The aspects causing dissent were as follows:

(a) The operator will not recognise any of the infrastructure that falls within the scope of IFRIC 12. One EFRAG member disagrees with this principle.

(b) To the extent that the contract involves construction, upgrade and operations phases, the construction and upgrade phases should be accounted for together but separately from the operations phase. One EFRAG member disagrees with this principle.

(c) If the operator provides construction or upgrade services, it will recognise either (and in some cases both) a financial asset (ie a receivable) or an intangible asset (ie a right to charge for usage). Two EFRAG members disagree with this principle.

---

[20] Letter from EFRAG to the Director General for Internal Markets, 23 March 2007.

(d) Whether the operator has a financial asset or an intangible asset will depend on whether the operator's income from providing services under the contract is exposed to demand risk. Two EFRAG members disagree with this principle

EFRAG does not name the dissenting members but it is clear from other contexts that the main objector is Spain. When the IASC Foundation Trustees met in Madrid in July 2007 they issued a statement which said, 'In accordance with their usual practice of meeting stakeholder representative groups from the local jurisdiction, the Trustees met senior representatives from the Bank of Spain, the Madrid Stock Exchange and the Spanish Securities Commission.'

At the ARC meeting of 16 March 2007 the report included the following item:

One Member State argued (as during the last meeting) clearly against endorsement of IFRIC 12. The main reasons for this are that IFRIC 12 did not reflect a true and fair view and therefore did not reflect the economic activities. A specific standard, which could address the specific characteristics of the industry, would be much more preferable. The IASB should be working towards such a standard. In the meantime this Member State proposed, as a 'transitional solution', amending IFRIC 12 to allow, under the intangible asset model, the use of the percentage of completion method as established in IAS 18.

The ARC chairman explained that the procedures for making changes to IFRS are very limited.

IFRIC 12 does not address accounting for the government side of service concession arrangements. The International Public Sector Accounting Standards Board (IPSASB, a board operating under the International Federation of Accountants) has started its own project on service concession arrangements from the perspective of the public sector partner.[21] It seems likely that the debate on accounting for public/private partnerships will continue for some time.

An example of the impact of IFRIC 12 is shown in Exhibit 13.8 opposite.

13.5 Is monopoly of standard setting sustainable?

The widening acceptance of IFRS, either by direct adoption or by incorporation in national standards, appears to be creating a monopoly position for the IASB as a privately constituted body. The only significant challenge to the IASB is from the FASB standards. The convergence project described in Chapter 10 appears to be leading towards one system of accounting standards for all once the IASB and FASB standards become indistinguishable. The question of choosing between IASB and FASB standards has been debated for some time.[22]

13.5.1 Competition between IASB and FASB?

It is now hard to believe that in the late 1990s the FASB regularly published documents of considerable length and detail setting out the differences between IFRS and SFAS. Dye and Sunder (2001) asked why FASB and IASB standards should not be allowed to compete in the USA.

---

[21] IASB Press Release, 30 November 2006.

[22] Hoarau (1995); Kirby (2001); Holthausen (2003); Tarca (2004).

They presented several arguments supporting the monopoly position of the FASB in the USA:

1 The FASB has an unrivalled experience and world leadership in making accounting rules.
2 There is an increased risk of a 'race to the bottom' under regulatory competition. This means a lowering of the quality of standards due to competition – given a choice it is possible that managers of companies will favour the standards that are less rigorous.
3 Most users of financial statements are unable to understand the complexities of accounting standards.
4 IASB's standards might be diluted to gain international acceptance.
5 IASB might be captured by interests that are hostile to business interests.
6 There are costs associated with experimentation in standard setting.
7 There are economies from the benefits of having many customers all using the same standard.

They then presented arguments in favour of competition:

1 Competition will help to meet the needs of globalized business.
2 Competition increases the likelihood that accounting standards will be efficient.
3 Competition will help protect standard setters from undue pressure from interest groups.
4 Competition allows different standards to develop for different corporate clienteles.
5 Competition allows corporations to send signals by their choice of accounting standards.
6 Competition protects corporations against 'regulatory capture' by narrow interests.
7 The marginal benefits of having many customers will diminish as the number increases.

Sunder (2002) presents a more general discussion of regulatory competition as a model for writing and implementing corporate financial standards. He envisages the SEC's oversight role extending to include organizations overseas whose standards are made available to US registrants. We have subsequently seen this in action with the SEC staff taking a detailed interest in the financial statements of foreign registrants prepared under IFRS. His suggestion for implementing a wider competitive regime is for the members of IOSCO to share responsibility for direct oversight over standard-setting bodies.

Schmidt (2002) applied the ideas of Dye and Sunder to the German capital market. In 2002 the European Commission announced its intention to apply international accounting standards across all listed European companies. In Germany (as explained in Chapter 12), prior to the implementation of the IAS Regulation, the *KapAEG* had allowed corporations to opt for international accounting rules without leaving the local capital market or providing a second consolidated statement for that market. Thus, the costs of applying alternative rules for group accounts could be kept low. Schmidt cited research by Leuz and Verrecchia (2000) showing that the stocks of firms opting for what appeared to be stricter accounting information rules experienced significantly lower bid-ask spreads and higher trading volumes within their respective capital markets. Schmidt suggests that since those variables are proxies for a reduction in the information asymmetry component of a firm's costs of capital, it seems plausible that managers have a substantial interest in attracting investors by showing a commitment to rules that investors perceive as leading to high-quality disclosure.

13.5.2 Coexistence of IASB and FASB?

In an interview with the *Journal of Accountancy* in July 2007 the Chairman of the IASB, Sir David Tweedie, gave a typically frank response to a question following up his explanation of the cooperation between IASB and FASB:

> *JofA*: How is the rest of the world reacting to what you just said?
>
> *Tweedie*: They're jealous, frankly, because they see two gorillas out there and they're in danger of getting squashed between them.
>
> You know we have people saying, 'Well, we're as important, so we'd like to make it a triumvirate.'
>
> And the answer is, 'Sorry. Not many people are following your standards. A lot of people are following US GAAP and a lot of people are following IFRS. But join in and help us both to write the "gold" standard for the world.'
>
> This is one of the reasons I see the IASB's members increasingly coming from many countries not previously represented on the IASB—there are big economies around the world that are not represented on the board, or not well represented. You can see them saying, 'We want to come in, and we also want to have a big say in the future.' And that is understandable.
>
> I suspect that the Trustees who oversee the IASB are going to look at that. If countries put forward the right people of independent mind who are genuinely seeking to improve financial reporting, there's a fair chance those people will be selected for the board. But I'm sure that there will always be a solid core of Americans on the board because you've got a huge economy, and that makes sense.

13.5.3 IASB and FASB merge?

De Lange and Howieson (2006) explored the likelihood that the USA will adopt IASB standards in place of its own as the end to the convergence project. Their paper highlighted the role of nationalistic and political influences on international standard setting. They suggested that the result may be either the continued existence of significant differences between US and IASB accounting standards or, perhaps more likely, a 'domination' of IASB accounting standards by the FASB. They derived this belief from the relatively short-term nature of the political incentives driving convergence efforts between the USA and the IASB. They saw a lack of clear incentives for US firms to adopt international standards, regulatory capture as a result of the relative power of the USA in international affairs vis-à-vis other nations, power struggles between the various regulatory bodies in the USA, and a well-documented history of 'American exceptionalism' as a means of defending US sovereignty in matters of US foreign policy.

13.6 Research issues for comparative studies

Chapter 9 has described some methods for carrying out comparative quantitative studies of accounting issues that differ across countries or jurisdictions. It is also possible to identify, through published research, issues of a qualitative type which allow reflection on differences and their possible causes. Weetman (2006) reflects on the ways in which contemporary research contributes to the academic community's understanding of the rich potential of evidence available on cultural and institutional influences leading to international convergence and diversity. The review uses research papers published in

2005 in leading journals to demonstrate the sources of research findings that help understand the impact of national characteristics on accounting. Some research papers make specific use of the country context to analyze their findings; others take the country as given. Collecting papers of a particular theme can bring out country similarities and differences across subject areas as diverse as management planning and control; the nature of the public interest; audit and accountability; capital market sentiment; social and environmental accounting; accounting history; public sector accounting; and accounting education.

Published research studies comparing IFRS and US GAAP are largely dependent on evidence that predates the general European conversion in 2005. Multinational companies in Austria, Germany and Switzerland had for some years been able to choose between IFRS and US GAAP. This allowed Van der Meulen *et al.* (2007) to compare a sample of earnings of German companies over the period 2000–02. They concluded that the stock market made no distinction in its valuation of the relevance of the earnings figures reported. Taking quality scores available for companies in all three countries allowed Daske and Gebhardt (2006) to identify a significant increase in the quality of financial reporting following the adoption of IFRS.

Baker and Barbu (2007) survey research in harmonization of international accounting over the years 1965 to 2004 to identify thematic and methodological changes. Themes that have been sustained across that period are comparative studies and measures of accounting uniformity. Themes that emerged in the middle of the period relate to conceptual frameworks, environmental factors, studies of accounting directives and studies of the growing influence of the IASC/IASB and the implementation of IAS/IFRS in various countries. Studies of the value relevance (impact on market prices) of IAS/IFRS compared with US GAAP have emerged more recently.

Summary and conclusions

The headlines of global accounting standard setting have focused strongly on the competing claims of IASB standards and US FASB standards. The current focus on convergence of IFRS and US GAAP takes attention away from the many organizations and activities seeking to improve accounting and assurance within and across national borders. Section 13.2 has provided a flavour of the range of organizations supporting international cooperation in accounting, auditing and corporate governance through regional associations, securities markets regulators, governmental bodies, organizations of users of financial statements and organizations of preparers of financial statements.

The process of convergence between IFRS and US GAAP is complex because countries that have already adopted IFRS feel that they do not have a direct involvement in a process which will possibly affect them more than the US companies that do not yet use IFRS. This tension has become evident in the European Union in the debate on specific issues such as the development of the IASB Constitution, the endorsement of IAS 39, the acceptance of IFRS 8 and the application of IFRIC 12. Debates of this kind lead to 'endorsed IFRS' being, from time to time, different from the IFRS in force as specified by the IASB.

Questions have been asked about how the IASB can be sustained in the longer term as a private sector body having no jurisdictional location and reliant on donations and subscriptions. We discuss possible outcomes of the IFRS/US GAAP convergence process, as competition, cooperation or merger. Finally we point to directions for continuing research interest in making comparative international studies of accounting and assurance, with a prediction that this is likely to provide a fruitful area of enquiry for some time to come.

Key points from the chapter:

- International cooperation in accounting and auditing is achieved by a wide range of regional organizations. IFAC brings together accountancy bodies in more than 100 countries to create global initiatives in auditing standards, public sector accounting, ethics and education.

- There is a continuing debate over the composition of the IASB, with the US regulators favouring the existing position based on a small group of experts and the European Commission arguing for a broader geographical representation.

- The 'carve-out' of part of IAS 39, resulting in only partial endorsement, showed the power of lobby groups in Europe to influence the European Commission and caused the IASB and the IASCF Trustees to broaden the consultation process leading to the development of IFRS.

- The concerns expressed in Europe over the proposed endorsement of IFRS 8 showed that the European Parliament is prepared to use its powers to disapprove of a new regulation, when pressure groups make their views known.

- The debate over IFRIC 12 showed that economic considerations in one member state can lead to controversy in the endorsement process even where other countries appear to be largely supportive.

- The convergence process between IFRS and US GAAP is still under way but the end point is not yet clear. It could lead to competition, cooperation or a merger in global standard setting. Views have been expressed on all these possibilities.

Questions

The following questions test your understanding of the material contained in the chapter and allow you to relate your understanding to the learning outcomes specified at the start of this chapter. The learning outcomes are repeated here. Each question is cross-referenced to the relevant section of the chapter.

Describe the main international organizations that are encouraging international cooperation

1 To what extent does the work of other international organizations complement the work of the IASB? (section 13.2)

2 What are the relative benefits and limitations of regional groupings of accountancy bodies, wider international groupings of accountancy bodies, intergovernmental organizations and representative groupings of interests such as securities markets regulators or financial executives? (section 13.2)

Explain the conflicting arguments over the nature of the IASB Constitution

3 What are the arguments in favour of creating a standard-setting board with wide geographical representation? (section 13.3)

4 What are the arguments against creating a standard-setting board with wide geographical representation? (section 13.3)

5 What are the arguments in favour of creating a standard-setting board based on a small number of persons having highly relevant expertise? (section 13.3)

6 What are the arguments against creating a standard-setting board based on a small number of persons having highly relevant expertise? (section 13.3)

Explain the controversies arising in the EU during the endorsement process

7 Explain the reason for dissatisfaction in some EU member states over the endorsement of IAS 39. (section 13.4.2)

8 Explain the controversies in the EU over the endorsement of IFRS 8. (section 13.4.3)

9 Explain the problems for the EU in endorsing IFRIC 12. (section 13.4.4)

Discuss the likelihood that a monopoly in standard setting will emerge from the IASB/FASB convergence process

10 What are the arguments for encouraging competition between the IASB and the FASB? (section 13.5.1)

11 What are the arguments for encouraging coexistence between the IASB and FASB?

12 What are the arguments for merging IASB and FASB?

Suggest future directions for comparative research in global corporate reporting

13 Imagine that you have access to a database of annual reports of listed companies in 20 countries. Suggest three research questions you could ask in evaluating the impact of institutional and cultural factors on corporate reporting practices.

References and further reading

Baker, C.R and Barbu, E.M. (2007) 'Trends in research on international accounting harmonization', *International Journal of Accounting*, 42: 272–304.

Camfferman, K. and Zeff, S.A. (2007) *Financial Reporting and Global Markets: A History of the International Accounting Standards Committee, 1973–2000*. Oxford: Oxford University Press.

Daske, H. and Gebhardt, G. (2006) 'International Financial Reporting Standards and experts' perceptions of disclosure quality', *Abacus*, 42(3/4): 461–498.

De Lange, P. and Howieson, B. (2006) 'International accounting standards setting and US exceptionalism', *Critical Perspectives on Accounting*, 17: 1007–1032.

Dye, R.A. and Sunder, S. (2001) 'Why not allow FASB and IASB standards to compete in the US?', *Accounting Horizons*, 15(3): 257–271.

Hirshleifer, D. and Teoh, S.H. (2003) 'Limited attention, information disclosure, and financial reporting', *Journal of Accounting and Economics*, 36: 337–386.

Hoarau, C. (1995) 'International accounting harmonization: American hegemony or mutual recognition with benchmarks?', *European Accounting Review*, 4(2): 217–233.

Holthausen, R.W. (2003) 'Testing the relative power of accounting standards versus incentives and other institutional features to influence the outcome of financial reporting in an international setting', *Journal of Accounting and Economics*, 36: 271–283.

IASC (1989) 'Framework for the preparation and presentation of financial statements', in *International Accounting Standards, 1997*. London: International Accounting Standards Committee.

Kirby, A.J. (2001) 'International competitive effects of harmonization', *International Journal of Accounting*, 36(1): 1–32.

Leuz, C. and Verrecchia, R.E. (2000) 'The economic consequences of increased disclosure', *Journal of Accounting Research*, 38, Supplement: 91–124.

OECD (2007) *OECD Economic Outlook*, Vol. 2007/1, June.

Schmidt, M. (2002) 'On the legitimacy of accounting standard setting by privately organised institutions in Germany and Europe', *Schmalenbach Business Review*, 54(April): 171–193.

Sunder, S. (2002) 'Regulatory competition among accounting standards within and across international boundaries', *Journal of Accounting and Public Policy*, 21(3): 219–234.

Tarca, A. (2004) 'International convergence of accounting practices: choosing between IAS and US GAAP', *Journal of International Financial Management and Accounting*, 15(1): 60–91.

Van der Meulen, S., Gaermynck, A. and Willekens, M. (2007) 'Attribute differences between US GAAP and IFRS earnings: an exploratory study', *International Journal of Accounting*, 42: 123–142.

Weetman, P. (2006) 'Discovering the international in accounting and finance', *British Accounting Review*, 38(4): 351–370.

Zeff, S.A. (2002) '"Political" lobbying on proposed standards: a challenge to the IASB', *Accounting Horizons*, 16(1): 43–54.

PART 4

From national to international standards

Introduction to Part 4

Part 4 brings together the influence of the IASB, the factors causing similarities and differences, and the relative influences of the USA and EU, to describe the state of financial reporting in a selection of countries. We cover four European countries (France, Germany, The Netherlands and Poland) in a comparative study of the institutional influences and the aspects of corporate reporting which have remained distinctive after harmonization of financial statements through IFRS in 2005. The UK has a separate chapter in its role as part of what is sometimes called the 'Anglo-American' influence on accounting.

Japan was a founder member of the IASC (predecessor of the IASB) but has some problems with implementing IFRS because of a perception in Japan that the underlying business structures are so very different from the western corporations for which IFRS appear to have been developed.

China is included in our chapter coverage because it is an emerging market, committed to applying IFRS in its largest companies, but with many problems of learning how to move from a uniform accounting system to one based on professional judgement.

Purpose of Part 4

The chapters of Part 4 have two major aims. The first is to explain how the national characteristics of a range of countries are likely to affect accounting principles and practice, using an institutional and cultural framework derived from the studies explained in Part 2. The second is to indicate the extent to which national practice is already close to or in harmony with IASB standards and to indicate those areas of national practice which are particularly influenced by national characteristics, and therefore possibly more resistant to broader desires for harmonization.

Structure of country chapters

Each chapter explains national institutions and characteristics under headings based on Chapter 6:

- the country
- overview of accounting regulations
- institutions, broken down into:
  - political and economic system
  - legal system
  - taxation system
  - corporate financing system
  - the accounting profession
- external influences.

The influence of institutional factors has been explained in Chapter 6. The effect of cultural influences has been described in Chapter 7. Classifications from the time of separate national standards were summarized in Chapter 8 and measurement of the differences arising from these influences in Chapter 9. Each of the country chapters will refer you back to the relevant sections of those chapters. It is important to read those chapters again as each country is studied, so that you gain an increased understanding of the relative position of the country and avoid learning about one country in isolation.

The country chapters summarize the overall picture of accounting practice at the present time and then identify key features of interest in national principles and practice. There are discussions of the country's characteristics as represented by Gray's system of classification (described in Chapter 7) because these forces may cause underlying differences in reality even after adoption of IFRS or US GAAP gives an appearance of harmonization.

Choice of countries

Choosing which countries to include in detail was one of the most difficult aspects of writing this book. The total global diversity of accounting practice creates a classification range which makes international accounting a fascinating subject for study. Describing anything less than the total must necessarily give an incomplete picture. However, constraints of time and space necessitate a choice which gives the widest possible taste of the diversity and complexity, leaving an appetite to find out more by using the reference material cited in the chapters.

The choice was influenced by:

- relative size and importance of international capital markets;
- residence of major multinational companies;
- role in the development of IFRS;
- origins of the accountancy profession;
- distinctive national accounting principles and practice;
- accounting classification systems which indicate an expectation of distinctive characteristics.

The choice of France, Germany, The Netherlands and Poland, within the EU member states, was decided on the basis that their accounting practices have been identified as very different in many comparative studies.

There are emerging markets in the Far East which have derived their accounting practices from very different backgrounds. Japanese accounting practice has established an international reputation based on an international capital market. China is developing internationally orientated accounting practices which will be consistent with its development of international business activity.

Learning outcomes

Specific learning outcomes are set out at the start of each chapter but overall, on completion of Part 4, for each country the student should be able to:

- know, in outline, the key characteristics of each country as summarized in published economic indicators;
- know the origins of accounting regulations and the historical development leading to the present state of practice;

- relate institutional factors for each country to the framework set out in Chapter 1 with particular reference to:
  - the political and economic system
  - the legal system
  - the taxation system
  - the corporate financing system
  - the accounting profession
  - external factors;
- relate specific practices to national characteristics and summarize the relative position of the country in the international spectrum of accounting practices.

14 Accounting in EU member states

Learning outcomes

After reading this chapter you should be able to:

- Explain how member states of the EU will continue to have a national role, beyond the IAS Regulation, in setting accounting standards.

- Relate the institutional factors and external influences for a selection of member states to the framework set out in Chapter 6.

- Explain and evaluate the state of oversight and assurance in a selection of member states.

- Explain a selection of corporate reporting issues where national differences in regulation and in practice are likely to persist.

- Describe how comparative research studies have helped advance understanding of similarities and differences in accounting across Europe.

14.1 Introduction

With the enlargement of the EU to 27 members, and the linking of Norway through the EEA Agreement, Switzerland is the only western European country that does not implement the Directives and is not obliged to implement the IAS Regulation (see section 12.5). Nevertheless many large Swiss companies apply IFRS by choice. This harmonization based on IFRS does not, however, mean that all annual reports of companies in the EU will look alike. This chapter gives an overview of the national characteristics that have caused accounting diversity in the past and may continue to cause some diversity for listed companies in those areas of financial reporting not subject to the IAS Regulation and those areas not covered by the Directives. As far as possible we draw comparisons across all EU member states; for more detailed discussion we have chosen France, Germany, The Netherlands and Poland. We begin in section 14.2 with economic diversity, since accounting purports to represent the economic substance of transactions and events. In section 14.3 we compare approaches to implementing the IAS Regulation and contrast different approaches to setting national standards. In section 14.4 we expand some of the institutional factors outlined in Chapter 6 by comparing legal systems, the nature of corporate governance, relative strength of equity markets, the nature of professionalism as supported by professional bodies, the influence of taxation, and historical influences. External influences are outlined in section 14.5. Mechanisms of oversight and assurance are discussed in section 14.6.

In section 14.7 we explain and comment on some areas of accounting practice where diversity persists despite the standardization achieved by IFRS. We pay particular attention to Gray's accounting values of transparency or secrecy. Constraints of space make us selective in the issues we consider; our choice reflects matters that show similarities and diversity in annual reports. (For those who wish to know more of the history of accounting development in France, Germany, The Netherlands and Hungary, there are chapter supplements on the website for this text.)

14.2 The countries

Politically all the member states of the EU have systems of government that meet the conditions for acceptance as members, although the precise nature of the democratic process varies. Nobes (1998) suggested that political differences were unlikely to be key explanations of differences in accounting systems across Europe. Economic diversity is greater, especially with the accession of ten new member states in 2004 and a further two in 2007. This leads to the question of whether harmonization of accounting practices creates fictitious comparability because it masks fundamental differences in the underlying economic substance of the business. At present we cannot answer that question from the evidence available but it will undoubtedly provide a subject for future research.

14.2.1 Economic indicators

Exhibit 14.1 shows key economic indicators, separated into the 15 member states prior to 2004 and the 12 new members who joined in or after 2004. The dominant populations are Germany, France, the UK and Italy, with Poland by far the largest of the new members. The GDP per head is adjusted to purchasing power parity with the USA, applying an adjustment factor to take account of the differences in the price of a standard basket of goods and services. The growth rate of real GDP is shown in the next column, with closer matching among 14 of the 15 older members, but much higher growth in Ireland. The relatively low growth rate in Germany has persisted since reunification. Among the new members, Poland has the highest growth rate. The Human Development Index (HDI) combines GDP with adult literacy and life expectancy as an index of human development. A score above 80 is considered 'high' in world comparisons but it can be seen in the table that the new member states have relatively lower levels than the pre-2004 members. The final two columns show the export market and the import market having the highest percentage of total exports and imports of the country. The importance of Germany as a trade partner is clear.

14.2.2 State ownership and privatization

Political conditions may dictate the extent to which the state takes full or partial ownership in business enterprises. A change in political conditions may lead to privatization where the government of the day seeks to reduce or eliminate state ownership. Governments may start a programme of privatization to reduce public debt or to raise cash for other economic programmes, or they may privatize to move towards a political ideal of free market enterprise. Because the industries under state control are often critical to the economy and security of the country, governments which have privatized enterprises will continue to impose regulations on such enterprises, which may affect their accounting and financial reporting. This section discusses the particular situations of France, as a

Exhibit 14.1	Comparison of economic indicators

	Population	GDP per head $PPP	Annual growth of GDP 1995–2005	HDI	Largest single export market	Largest single source of imports
Austria	8.2m	37,330	2.1%	94.4	Germany	Germany
Belgium	10.4m	35,660	2.1%	94.5	France	Netherlands
Bulgaria	7.7	3,460	2.0%	81.6	Italy	Italy
Cyprus	N/A	N/A	N/A	N/A	N/A	N/A
Czech Republic	10.2m	12,190	2.5%	88.5	Germany	Germany
Denmark	5.4m	47,910	2.1%	94.3	Germany	Germany
Estonia	1.3m	10,080	6.6%	85.8	Finland	Finland
Finland	5.2m	37,150	3.5%	94.7	Russia	Germany
France	60.5m	35,150	2.2%	94.2	Germany	Germany
Germany	82.7m	33,800	1.4%	93.2	France	France
Greece	11.1m	20,290	3.8%	92.1	Germany	Germany
Hungary	10.1m	10,820	4.1%	86.9	Germany	Germany
Ireland	4.1m	49,220	7.4%	95.6	USA	UK
Italy	58.1m	30,340	1.3%	94.0	Germany	Germany
Latvia	2.3m	6,880	6.9%	84.5	Estonia & Lithuania	Germany
Lithuania	3.4m	7,540	5.9%	85.7	Russia	Russia
Luxembourg	N/A	N/A	N/A	N/A	N/A	N/A
Malta	N/A	N/A	N/A	N/A	N/A	N/A
The Netherlands	16.3m	38,290	2.2%	94.7	Germany	Germany
Poland	38.5m	7,880	4.2%	86.2	Germany	Germany
Portugal	10.5m	17,460	2.1%	90.4	France	Spain
Romania	21.7m	4,540	2.1%	80.5	Italy	Germany
Slovakia	5.4m	8,590	4.3%	85.6	Germany	Germany
Slovenia	2.0m	17,180	3.9%	91.0	Germany	Germany
Spain	43.1m	26,090	3.5%	93.8	France	Germany
Sweden	9.0m	39,740	2.7%	95.1	USA	Germany
UK	59.7m	36,830	2.7%	94.0	USA	Germany

Source: *The Economist Pocket World in Figures*, 2008 Edition, Profile Books Ltd.

country with a history of waves of state ownership followed by privatization, Germany, where public ownership remains substantial in particular sectors, and Poland, as a country currently in the transition of privatization of state-owned enterprises.

Some of the largest French companies are partly under state ownership. From 1945 onwards there was a move to reconstruct the economy by creating joint enterprise bodies owned by government and private enterprise. That began a tradition of state intervention mixed with private enterprise partnership. France has been subjected to waves of nationalization and privatization of industry, depending on the government in power. A wave of nationalization in the early 1980s was followed by a programme of privatization starting in 1993, but in 1997 a further change of government influenced the process of privatization. Since 1997 the government has raised private sector capital by selling significant state shareholdings in airline companies, banks, defence, insurance and telecom companies. However, by 2000 the state still owned some 1,500 enterprises, employing over 1 million people. Retaining some major shareholdings in state control was seen as a political compromise of a socialist government facing the pressures of capitalism.[1] By 2003 six companies (Air France, France Télécom, La Poste, EDF/GDF, RATP and SNCF) represented the bulk of the economic weight represented by state-owned firms. Plans to reduce state ownership of these companies further were in place[2] although public support appeared relatively low.[3] In particular, the French government announced in September 2004 that it would reduce its holding in France Télécom below 50 per cent, which would allow the company to offer its shares in making future acquisitions, rather than having to offer cash.[4] Previous legislation, which required the state to retain a majority stake, had inhibited the company in raising equity finance and had led to high borrowing. From a governance perspective there is also a potential question about the capacity of the state to provide effective governance over state-owned enterprises. In moving away from this position, without losing the political principle, a State Ownership Agency was announced (Agence des participations de l'état) to watch over state holdings and exercise its rights as a shareholder in state-owned companies.[5]

The OECD[6] provides an example of the extent of public ownership in Germany. The federal government owns the bank Kreditanstalt für Wiederaufbau which in turn owns over 40 per cent of the postal service provider Deutsche Post. Deutsche Post owns a majority stake in Postbank and almost 40 per cent of Deutsche Telekom. The federal government also owns the railways operator Deutsche Bahn. As the postal and railway activities expand internationally the federal government takes an increasing indirect stake in commercial activities abroad. In the energy sector there is municipal ownership of much of the electricity and gas distribution network. The OECD also points to relatively high levels of state aid, particularly in helping regional development in the east of Germany.

In Poland, at the date of accession to membership of the EU, there was a continued state presence in companies being sold as joint-stock companies. An OECD survey[7] published at that time recommended that the privatization process should be accelerated to reduce public debt, boost productivity and enhance investor confidence. The survey suggested that where the state has retained an interest, and even a majority holding, in joint-stock companies whose shares are sold on the stock market, this denies the companies the chance of raising equity capital, limits the scope to hire the best staff, and has probably contributed to low offer prices and lack of interest in companies already on sale. Selling off only a minority shareholding in state-controlled enterprises would perpetuate a system of state ownership and politically appointed managers. The survey recommended seeking strategic external investors to encourage risk taking and to improve corporate governance. A further survey in 2006[8] found that although privatization had continued, rapid reduction in public ownership had not been given a high priority and there seemed to be a reluctance to relinquish direct state control.

---

[1] *Financial Times* Survey, 'France', 14 June 2000, p. vi.

[2] OECD (2003a), pp. 86–89.

[3] *Financial Times*, 5 June 2005, www.ft.com.

[4] *Financial Times*, 2 September 2004, p. 21.

[5] OECD (2003a), pp. 86–89.

[6] OECD (2006a), pp. 126–127.

[7] OECD (2004), p. 18.

[8] OECD (2006b), p. 35.

14.3 International standards; national choices

This section explains how each national regulator intends to implement the IAS Regulation, indicating that there appears to be a continuing role for national standard setters beyond the consolidated accounts that are covered by the Regulation. We then describe in more detail the national standard-setting systems for France, Germany, The Netherlands and Poland.

14.3.1 Implementing the IAS Regulation

The IAS Regulation (see section 12.5) is compulsory for the consolidated accounts of companies admitted to trading on a regulated market of a member state. However, it is not compulsory for the accounts of the individual companies within the group. The Regulation gives member states options to permit or to require individual companies to apply IFRS in their financial statements. Exhibit 14.2 shows the intentions of member states as indicated to the Internal Markets Directorate of the EU at May 2006. Member states appear to have been particularly cautious where the tax system is linked to the accounting system because a change to IFRS could have significant implications for the amount of tax revenue and the distribution of the tax burden. Member states also appear cautious where company law sets rules on distributable profits. The responses of member states on the intended treatment of non-listed groups and individual companies (not shown in the table)[9] are even more cautious.

The spread of answers in Exhibit 14.2 means that national standard-setting bodies continue to have a role. In some cases that role covers individual companies within groups; in other cases it covers consolidated accounts of unlisted companies or individual companies within unlisted groups. In December 2000 the Fédération des Experts Comptables Européens (FEE) published a detailed report on the range of approaches to setting national accounting standards at that time. Exhibit 14.3 summarizes the split between public sector and private sector standard-setting bodies. Sections 14.3.2 to 14.3.5 describe four different types of national standard setter.

14.3.2 France

Under a law passed in 1998, a Comité de la Réglementation Comptable (CRC) was set up with 12 members. The CRC is devoted to making mandatory, for all or some enterprises, the accounting standards which are prepared by the Conseil National de la Comptabilité (CNC)[10] or other institutions. For the first time in France, there was a body with the power to impose accounting standards. Previously the CNC had an advisory role under the Ministry of Finance. The CRC approves all new accounting rules, subject to ratification by the appropriate government ministers. The CRC must act within the framework of the accounting law, but is empowered to prepare the necessary rules for applying the law. Prior to 1998, companies could present consolidated accounts according to internationally recognized standards but with considerable flexibility as to what was meant by 'internationally recognized standards'.[11] This resulted in French companies 'shopping

---

[9] http://ec.europa.eu/internal_market/accounting/docs/ias/ias-use-of-options_en.pdf.

[10] www.minefi.gouv.fr/directions_services/CNCompta/.

[11] *FT World Accounting Report*, January 1997, pp. 9–10; May 1997, p. 6.

Exhibit 14.2	Member states' intentions with regard to individual companies

Answer	Questions to member state	
	*Will you use the option to **permit** IFRS in the annual accounts for individual listed companies?*	*Will you use the option to **require** IFRS in the annual accounts for individual listed companies?*
Yes	Denmark – financial entities yes, others yes until 2009 Finland Germany – for information only Iceland, yes for 2005, 2006 Ireland Liechtenstein Luxembourg Netherlands Norway Poland Slovenia UK	Cyprus Czech Republic Denmark – financial entities yes, others yes until 2009 Estonia Greece Iceland, yes from 2007 Italy, except for insurance Lithuania Malta Portugal
No	Austria Cyprus Czech Republic Denmark, other than financial entities after 2009 Estonia France Greece Hungary Italy Latvia Lithuania Malta Norway Portugal yes, except for banks and financial institutions Slovakia Spain Sweden	Austria Finland France Germany Hungary Ireland Latvia Liechtenstein Luxembourg Netherlands Norway Poland Slovakia Slovenia Spain Sweden UK
Undecided	Belgium – to consider tax and legal issues	Belgium – to consider tax and legal issues

Source: Extract from *Planned Implementation of IAS Regulation*, May, 2006, EU internal market website.

around' for the basis of presentation of their group accounts (Ding *et al*., 2003). The flexibility of French GAAP for consolidated accounts before the introduction of IFRS for listed companies is illustrated in Exhibit 14.4.

The CRC is chaired by the Minister for the Economy, Finance and Industry. Other members are the Minister of Justice, the Secretary of State for the Budget, the Presidents of the Bourse, the CNC, the CNCC and the OEC, three representatives of enterprise and employer interests and representatives of the civil and criminal courts. During 1999 the

| Exhibit 14.3 | Setting accounting standards in Europe: private or public sector body |

Private sector	Public sector
Austria	Belgium
Denmark	Czech Republic
Germany	Finland
Italy	France
Netherlands	Hungary
Slovenia	Luxembourg
Sweden*	Portugal
Switzerland	Romania
UK and Ireland	Spain
	Sweden*

*Sweden has two standard-setting bodies.

Source: *Accounting standard-setting in Europe*, FEE, December 2000, www.fee.be.

CRC adopted a ruling on a new draft of the Plan Comptable Général (PCG)[12] and approved a new methodology for consolidated accounts.[13] The PCG was further updated in 2005. Ministerial approval remains a final condition for any CRC recommendation. The CNC continues issuing opinions in its advisory role and so it is essential that the CRC and CNC work harmoniously. In May 2007 the Ministry for the Economy, Finance and Industry announced the first stages of reform of the CNC. This reflected the need to make the CNC more flexible in adapting to the world of IFRS and influencing the IASB

| Exhibit 14.4 | French GAAP in consolidated accounts, Total |

Accounting policies

The Consolidated financial statements of TOTAL and its subsidiaries (together, the Company or Group) have been prepared in accordance with generally accepted accounting principles in France (French 'GAAP') and comply with the principles and methodology relative to Consolidated financial statements, Regulation No. 99–02 approved by the decree dated June 22, 1999 of the French Accounting Regulations Committee.

Furthermore, the Company applies the standards issued by the Financial Accounting Standards Board (FASB) which are compatible with the French Regulations and, which contribute, in their current wording, to better reflect the assets and liabilities of the Company and the best comparability with the other oil majors, namely those from North America. The exceptions to the use of FASB standards are presented in the Annual Report as well as in the annual report of the Company under US Generally Accepted Accounting Principles (Form 20-F).

Source: Total Annual Report (2003), p. 145, www.total.com.

---

[12] http://www10.finances.gouv.fr/fonds_documentaire/reglementation/avis/avisCNCompta/pcganglais/pcganglais1.htm. Text of 1999 version of PCG in English but without more recent updates.

[13] *Accountancy International*, July 1999, p. 57.

standard-setting process. The intention was to give the new CNC three commissions – one for IFRS, one for standards relating to private companies and one for public sector accounting.[14]

14.3.3 Germany

The German Accounting Standards Committee (Deutsches Rechnungslegungs Standards Committee, DRSC)[15] was formed in 1998 using the model of the FASB in the USA. It takes a legal mandate from the German Commercial Code (HGB) (para. 342) and comprises seven independent experts. Its standards are approved by the Ministry of Justice.

In respect of individual companies, Exhibit 14.2 indicates that the Federal Ministry of Justice does not intend to *require* individual companies to use IFRS in their financial statements for regulatory purposes and that it will *permit* the use of IFRS only for purposes of providing information, so the DRSC will continue to have a role in developing national standards for individual companies within listed groups and for unlisted companies.

The DRSC website explains that enterprises preparing consolidated financial statements in accordance with the HGB should apply German Accounting Standards (GAS). Enterprises whose securities are publicly traded and which prepare exempting consolidated financial statements in compliance with internationally recognized accounting principles do not have to apply GAS. From 2005 all enterprises which list securities have been exempted from applying GAS. However, enterprises applying international accounting principles continue to apply GAS to the extent that international accounting principles do not include any requirements.

14.3.4 The Netherlands

There are three stages to accounting regulation in The Netherlands. The first is the Civil Code, the second is the Enterprise Chamber (see section 14.6.4) and the third is The Council for Annual Reporting (Raad voor de Jaarverslaggeving, or RJ). The RJ is not part of the formal legal system but is an essential element in the implementation of the law. It was established in 1982, replacing an earlier body set up in 1971 at the request of the government, and it operates under the oversight of the Social Economic Council. The RJ acts on behalf of the Foundation for Annual Reporting and comprises representatives of three interest groups – users, preparers and auditors. The users are represented by the two main trade unions and a representative from the Dutch Financial Analysts' Society, the preparers are represented by the principal industrial confederation, and the auditors are represented by their professional body, NIVRA. It is interesting to note the emphasis placed on employees as users.

The RJ reviews the accounting principles which are applied in practice and gives its opinion on the acceptability of those principles within the framework of the law. Opinions are published as Guidelines for Annual Reporting. Part of the work of the RJ is to give opinions on IASB standards.

The composition of the RJ[16] reflects the fundamental legal requirement of financial accounts that the bases underlying the valuation of assets and liabilities and the determination of the financial results comply with standards acceptable in the business environment.

---

[14] *World Accounting Report*, June 2007.

[15] http://www.standardsetter.de/drsc/news/news.php (select English-language option).

[16] Hoogendoorn (2001), p. 700.

The Council does not in itself have statutory powers or duties and there is no government representative on the RJ. Its opinions have no statutory backing, although they do provide an important frame of reference for the auditor and for the courts in arriving at views on the application of accounting policies. The RJ contains a range of interest groups working together to achieve a consensus. It cannot strictly be proposed as an example of professionalism because the influence of NIVRA is only one of the voices on it, but it indicates the potential for interesting social interaction where statutory control is not imposed.

Section 14.6.1.1 explains the oversight work of the Autoriteit Fianciele Markten or AFM under the Act on the Supervision of Financial Reporting.

Revaluation to a replacement cost (current cost) basis is allowed in Dutch accounting standards as an alternative to historical cost, indicating the flexibility of Dutch accounting *de jure*. However, examples of replacement cost accounting are relatively rare. Prior to 2005, one case was Heineken (Exhibit 14.5, Panel A). It would have been permissible for

---

Exhibit 14.5 Heineken, change from replacement cost to historical cost

Panel A: Notes describing replacement cost accounting, Heineken

Tangible fixed assets
Except for land, which is not depreciated, tangible fixed assets are stated at replacement cost less accumulated depreciation. The following average useful lives are used for depreciation purposes:

Buildings	30–40 years
Plant and equipment	10–30 years
Other fixed assets	5–10 years

The replacement cost is based on appraisals by internal and external experts, taking into account technical and economic developments. Other factors taken into account include the experience gained in the construction of breweries throughout the world. Grants received in respect of investments in intangible fixed assets are deducted from the amount of the investment. Projects under construction are included at cost.

. . .

Current assets
Stocks purchased from third parties are stated at replacement cost based on prices from current purchase contracts and latest prices as at balance sheet date. Finished products and work in progress are stated at manufactured cost based on replacement cost and taking into account the production stage reached.

Stocks of spare parts are depreciated on a straight-line basis taking account of obsolescence. If the recoverable amount or net realizable value of stocks is less than their replacement cost, provisions are formed in respect of the difference. Advance payments on stocks are included at face value.

Receivables are carried at face value less a provision for credit risks and less the amount of deposits on returnable packaging.

Securities are carried at the lower of historical cost and quoted price, or estimated market value in the case of unlisted securities.

Cash is included at face value.

Revaluations
Differences in carrying amounts due to revaluations are credited or debited to group equity, less an amount in respect of deferred tax liabilities where applicable.

Source: Heineken Annual Report (2004), pp. 84–85, www.heinekeninternational.com.

Panel B: Historical cost measurement in 2005

Notes to the reconciliation balance sheet as at 1 January 2004

1 Property, plant & equipment are €363 million lower due to the change from statement at estimated replacement cost to historical cost.

. . .

5 The impact on Inventories is zero because the change from estimated replacement cost to historical cost is compensated by the reclassification of certain returnable packaging materials from property, plant & equipment assets to inventories.

Notes to the reconciliation balance sheet as at 31 December 2004

1 Property, plant & equipment are €354 million lower due to the change from statement at estimated replacement cost to historical cost.

. . .

5 Inventories are slightly higher due to the combination of the change from estimated replacement cost to historical cost and the reclassification of some returnable packaging materials from property, plant & equipment to inventories.

Source: Heineken Annual Report (2005), pp. 107–108.

Heineken to continue this practice from 2005 under IAS 16 but the company chose to revert to historical cost measures (Exhibit 14.5, Panel B). No reason is given in the 2005 annual report.

14.3.5 Poland[17]

Polish accounting is regulated by the Accounting Act of 1994 with subsequent amendments, particularly those of 2002 and 2004. Together these harmonize with the Fourth and Seventh Directives and bring Polish accounting closer to IFRS. During 2003 the Polish Accounting Committee[18] was established to prepare and issue standards to implement the Act. The first standard was issued by the Committee in September 2003. Polish Accounting Regulations take into account the specific economic circumstances of Poland as well as the requirements of the EU. In areas unregulated by the Act, reference may be made to IFRS.

From 2005 Polish listed companies followed IFRS completely, but as there are relatively few of these the Polish Accounting Regulations remain important for many companies. The reconciliation of Polish accounting standards to IFRS published by Orlen indicates the gap between the two systems (Exhibit 14.6).

---

[17] Ernst & Young (2004), p. 27.

[18] www.mf.gov.pol.

Exhibit 14.6 Reconciliation of Polish accounting standards to IFRS, Orlen

34. Transformation for IFRS purposes

The Group companies maintain their accounts in accordance with the accounting principles and practices employed by enterprises in Poland as is required by the Accounting Act and related regulations. The financial statements set out above reflect certain adjustments not reflected in the companies statutory books to present these financial statements in accordance with IFRS effective for 2003, except for non-compliance with IAS 29 and IAS 16 as specified in Note 3.

The adjustments to the consolidated financial statements prepared under Polish Accounting Standards ('PAS') are set out below:

	Net profit for the year ended 31.12.2003 in PLN million	Net profit for the year ended 31.12.2002 in PLN million
PAS basis consolidated	1,014	479
Distributions from profit for social activity	(4)	–
Borrowing costs capitalisation, less depreciation	(68)	(25)
Amortisation of CPN goodwill	(10)	(11)
IFRS treatment of negative goodwill	17	8
Deferred tax on the above	53	(17)
Other	(15)	(13)
IFRS Consolidated	**987**	**421**

	Net assets 31.12.2003 in PLN million	Net assets 31.12.2002 in PLN million
PAS basis consolidated	9,130	7,927
Distribution from profit for social activity	–	–
Borrowing costs capitalisation less depreciation	458	526
Goodwill on CPN, net	62	72
IFRS treatment of negative goodwill	(54)	(71)
Deferred tax on the above	(87)	(140)
Other	1	15
IFRS Consolidated	**9,510**	**8,329**

a. Distribution from profit for social activity

According to Polish business practice shareholders of the Company have the right to distribute the profit for the employees benefits, i.e. for bonus payment or for the Company's social fund. Such distributions are presented in statutory financial statements, similarly to dividend payments, through the change in capital. In the financial statements prepared in accordance with IFRS such payments are charged to operating costs of the year, that the distribution concerns.

b. Capitalisation of borrowing costs

In accordance with PAS, borrowing costs are written off to the income statement as incurred net of the amount capitalised related to borrowings for specific capital projects. Borrowing costs incurred on general borrowings are always expensed as incurred. Borrowing costs are capitalised as a part of the costs of the relevant fixed assets up to the date of commissioning and written off to the income statement over the period in which assets is depreciated.

In these financial statements borrowing costs are subject to capitalisation in accordance with allowed alternative treatment of IAS 23 'Borrowing costs' presented in Note 4(i).

c. Goodwill on shares purchased from former CPN employees
The acquisition of CPN's employee shares was recorded for IFRS purposes under the acquisition method of accounting. As a result the Company recognised goodwill of PLN 107m on the acquisition of the 19.43 per cent CPN shares held by the employees.

For PAS, the acquisition of CPN, including the acquisition of the minority shares was pushed back to the earliest financial statements presented under pooling of interests' method.

d. IFRS treatment of negative goodwill
According to PAS, before the amended Accounting Act came into force, the Company released negative goodwill to income during two to five years period subsequent to acquisition. In the IFRS financial statements negative goodwill is recognised in a manner presented in Note 4(c).

e. Deferred tax effects
Adjustments related to above mentioned differences between PAS and IFRS are basis for deferred tax calculation.

f. IFRS treatment of revenues
In accordance with PAS, the Company and certain of its subsidiaries included excise tax charged on the oil product manufactured in their revenues and selling expenses.

For the purpose of these consolidated financial statements prepared under IFRS revenues and selling expenses had been presented net of excise tax of PLN 9,309m and PLN 9,426m for the years ended 31 December 2003 and 31 December 2002, respectively.

Source: Orlen Annual Report (2003), pp. 151–153, www.orlen.pl.

14.4 Institutional influences

14.4.1 Legal systems

14.4.1.1 Range of legal systems

The characterization of continental European countries as 'code law' systems appears too general when the details are considered. The French legal system is of the Romano-Germanic family but has taken on a European characteristic which is identifiably different from the German legal system. Other countries having a legal system similar to that of France include Belgium, Denmark, Italy, The Netherlands, Portugal and Spain.

The German legal system is of the Romano-Germanic family, with the German approach as a unique branch of the European grouping. Consequently German accounting practice, which is strongly contained in law, might be expected to show unique characteristics.

The Dutch legal system is based on laws, jurisprudence (verdicts), treaties and custom. The laws are passed by Parliament. The courts will recognize international treaties and will use long-established customs as an aid to the interpretation of statutes. The system of law in The Netherlands is within the Romano-Germanic family and of the European tradition, alongside France but distinguished from Germany.

Exhibit 14.7 Descriptions of public and private limited companies

	Public limited company	Private limited company
France	SA (Société anonyme)	SARL (Société à responsabilité limité)
Germany	AG (Aktiengesellschaft) (joint-stock company)	GmbH (Gesellschaft mit beschränkter Haftung) (limited liability company)
The Netherlands	NV (Naamloze vennootschap)	BV (Besloten vennootschap)
	Structure-NV is a larger company having at least 100 employees and a works council	Structure-BV is a larger company having at least 100 employees and a works council
Poland	SA (spólka akcyjna) Joint-stock company	Sp.z.o.o. (spólka z organiczoną odpowiedzialnością) Limited liability company

Poland has a code law system. The Polish Commercial Code of 1934 was dormant from 1948 but was gradually reactivated from the 1980s as a market economy began to emerge. It was only in 2000 and 2004 that the Code was modernized in readiness for joining the EU.

14.4.1.2 Types of business organization

Most countries have some form of limited liability company where owners are able to invest in a business and limit their personal loss to the amount of the equity interest in the company. Most countries also distinguish public limited companies from private limited companies (see Exhibit 14.7).

As the descriptions suggest, the public limited company has obligations to a wider public as shareholders, lenders, employees, customers, suppliers and government agencies, while the private limited company has obligations to a narrower range of stakeholders closely connected to the company. Corporate governance obligations, including the requirements of accounting rules, are generally more onerous for public companies, particularly those having a stock market listing.

14.4.2 Corporate governance

The website of the internal market contains a very thorough and detailed comparative study of corporate governance codes across the 15 member states in 2001.[19] This provides an excellent starting point for any comparative study. It can be augmented by

---

[19] *Comparative Study of Corporate Governance Codes Relevant to the European Union and its Member States*, on behalf of the European Commission Internal Market Directorate, January 2002.

reference to the website of the European Corporate Governance Institute (ECGI) where there are links to the codes of separate countries.[20] The rest of this section describes some of the key features of corporate governance in France, Germany, The Netherlands and Poland.

14.4.2.1 France

In France, there is a choice of two distinct systems for Sociétés anonymes, one having a unitary board and the other having separate executive and supervisory boards. The traditional approach is the unitary board, appointed by the shareholders, having a Chair (*president du conseil d'administration*) and a chief executive (*directeur general*). Formerly a *président directeur générale* (PDG) was the Chair and chief executive, elected by the board. As a matter of French law until 2001, the PDG had executive authority and the sole right to represent the company. The Loi relative aux Nouvelles Régulations Economiques 2001 (NRE Act) now allows the supervisory and management roles to be separated.

The PDG has traditionally held a strong position of control over the company and the system of corporate governance has been largely dependent on the PDG's personality. Furthermore, the PDG gains support from loyal shareholders and particularly the shareholder representatives who take places on the board of directors. Undertakings not to sell shares may also be given by major shareholders.[21] A typical PDG may be a professional manager who has developed a career with the business, possibly as a founding owner. The PDG may also be a person brought in from outside because of their connections, particularly where relations with government are important.

The size of a unitary board varies with company size but at least two-thirds of its members must be non-executive. Traditionally the board did not intervene in the day-to-day running of the business. Its role was to hire and fire the PDG, to authorize the raising of new finance and to authorize mergers or other links; meetings were relatively infrequent. The NRE Act emphasizes the responsibility of the board for supervising the operations of the company.

There is legislation dating from 1966 which allows the alternative of a supervisory board (*conseil de surveillance*) resembling that found in Germany. Management is in the hands of a *directoire* (two to seven members) appointed by the supervisory board to run the company. This alternative system of corporate governance is relatively little used.

Companies over a specified size are required to have a *comité d'entreprise* on which the workforce is represented. This reflects the socialist politics of France in the early 1980s. The committee is not as strongly based as the German works council and the control of the company is very much in the hands of the PDG. One or two members of the *comité d'entreprise* attend meetings of the board of directors, but have no voting rights. The board does not deal with day-to-day activities and so it is possible for the PDG to take executive action without extensive consultation with the representatives of the *comité d'entreprise*.

The corporate governance debate in France was encouraged by the publication in 1995 of the report *The Boards of Directors of Public Companies*, from a working group chaired by Marc Viénot. It contained a series of recommendations intended to address the concerns of international investors. In 1999 a review, also chaired by Marc Viénot,

---

[20] www.ecgi.org/codes/all_codes.htm.

[21] Charkham (1994), p. 152.

made recommendations on the role of the Chair and chief executive officer, re-election of directors, executive pay, financial information and audit. It recommended that final consolidated accounts should be available within two months of the period-end and that auditors should advise the board on the choice of accounting framework for the consolidated accounts (IAS or US GAAP where consistent with French GAAP). The recommendations were not mandatory but encouraged voluntary reform and influenced the NRE Act.

Companies in France are allowed by law to distribute voting rights unevenly and may issue new shares during takeover battles without consulting existing shareholders. Such practices are gradually diminishing under pressure from institutional investors. Annual reports contain information on managers' remuneration, including share options.

The Autorité des marchés financiers publishes an annual report on corporate governance and internal control. From the analysis of annual reports in 2005 the AMF concluded there were further improvements in corporate governance reporting and also more evaluation of the work of the boards of directors. It felt the information on internal control remained 'patchy' and supported a reference framework drawn up in 2006 by a Market Advisory Group.[22]

14.4.2.2 Germany

The German system of corporate governance for companies of a substantial size (all AGs and GmbHs of more than 500 employees) is based on a 'two-tier' principle. This means there are two layers of management control: the shareholders and the employees are stakeholders and share in the appointment of the supervisory board; the supervisory board appoints an executive board. In the case of an AG, this is called a *Vorstand*; in the case of a GmbH, it is called a *Geschäftsführung*.

There are strict rules on the composition of the supervisory board. For the largest companies, the membership of the supervisory board is split equally between persons appointed by the shareholders and persons appointed by the employees. Where there are fewer than 2,000 employees, two-thirds of the members are appointed by the shareholders. The Chair of the board is always drawn from the shareholder representatives and has the casting vote in a situation of deadlock.

The area of activity of the supervisory board is prescribed by law and covers:

- the company's accounts for a specified period;
- major capital expenditure and strategic acquisitions or closures;
- appointments to the executive board;
- approval of the dividend.

The main function is to ensure the competence of general management, but a second role is the approval of the annual profit and loss account and balance sheet. Both are audited (where the corporation is at least of medium size) and the supervisory board may question the external auditors. The employees' representatives also function effectively because they draw on material provided by the works councils which allows them to play an effective part in the work of the supervisory board.

Banks often take a seat on the supervisory board of a company. They do this as part of the shareholder representation. The banks have traditionally been pre-eminent as suppliers of capital and they also provide a range of other services. There are therefore strong

---

[22] AMF 2006, *Report on Corporate Governance and Internal Control*, January 2007.

personal links with the company beyond the formal links of the supervisory board. The banks themselves have advisory boards of which industrialists are members, and there are therefore some intricately interwoven links between banks and companies. It has been suggested that the combination of direct ownership, deposited share voting rights, length of lending period and breadth of services provides the following benefits:

- deep relationships between companies and banks whereby the bank becomes a counsel and guide to the company on a long-term basis;
- a considerable flow of information into the banks;
- deep knowledge by the banks about sectors of industry which can be used to the advantage of customers;
- development of well-trained staff in the banks;
- banks having the knowledge, motivation and authority to exert influence on company management.[23]

A 1997 law on aspects of corporate governance, the Law on Control and Transparency in the Corporate Sector (Gesetz zur Kontrolle und Transparenz im Unternehmensbereich (KonTraG)), aimed to match the corporate governance standards of other countries and was influenced significantly by the report of the Cadbury Committee in the UK.[24] The legislation was a response to problem cases arising in prominent companies in the mid-1990s.

The executive board of directors is a decision-making body which acts collectively and therefore the idea of a powerful chief executive has historically been unusual in Germany. The Chair of the board has been held by members of the board in rotation.

Members of the executive board are appointed by the supervisory board, and a two-thirds majority is usually required for this decision. Where such a majority cannot be achieved then a simple majority will suffice, with the Chair having the casting vote. In practice, therefore, shareholders have more potential than employees to influence the composition of the board of directors.

German industrial relations have developed under the principle of co-determination, meaning the right of employees' representatives to participate in decisions that affect them. Central to this is the provision of detailed information, including internal accounting information, at the level of plant, company and group. Co-determination is practised through works councils, which are legally defined trade union bargaining rights and employee board representation. Traditionally, German trade unions have been organized on an industry-by-industry rather than on a craft basis, which tends to encourage industrial harmony. Works councils have existed in Germany since the early 1970s.

In 2001 Professor T. Baums delivered the report of the Baums Commission on corporate governance and the modernization of stock company law. This led to a German code of best practice in 2002 (the Cromme Code), revised 2003 and again in 2007 (see Case study 3.1). The proposals of the Baums Commission aimed to strengthen accountability and transparency.[25] The 2003 revision of the Cromme Code recommended disclosure of the remuneration of individual directors (as is the practice in the USA or UK) but *Company Reporting*[26] found that German companies were resisting this recommendation. These

---

[23] Charkham (1994), Ch. 2, p. 43.

[24] *The Corporate Accountant*, April 1997, p. 1.

[25] Available at www.ecgi.org/codes/all_codes.htm.

[26] *Company Reporting*, August 2004, IAS Monitor, pp. 15–18.

companies disclosed aggregate remuneration of the board of management and the supervisory board, and the number of directors on each. One company stated that, as the important information had been disclosed, a public discussion of the salaries of individual members would not be expedient. Another said it was contrary to the justified right of privacy of board members. The 2007 Code takes a firmer stance,[27] requiring disclosure of the compensation of each member of the management board.

14.4.2.3 The Netherlands[28]

A Dutch corporation is managed by a board of management comprising one or more members. They are all called 'managing directors'. In the UK they would be 'executive directors' and in the USA 'executive officers'. These directors are appointed and dismissed by the general meeting. The managing board as a whole is responsible for the proper management of the corporation. For a structure corporation, the supervisory board appoints and dismisses the managing directors.

For structure corporations (large companies) a supervisory board is a requirement. Other companies may have a supervisory board if they wish to do so. The functions and responsibilities of the supervisory board are laid down in the Civil Code and include the following powers:

- to appoint and dismiss members of the managing board;
- to determine the financial statements;
- to approve certain decisions of the managing board.

In particular, the supervisory board adopts the annual accounts. It has unrestricted access to the corporate premises and the right to inspect the books and records. Each member of the supervisory board must sign the annual accounts, and members of the supervisory board may be personally liable for the consequences of issuing misleading accounts. Since 2004 members of the supervisory board of a structure corporation are appointed by the shareholders' meeting. The supervisory board makes nominations and must, in principle, nominate persons recommended by the works council for up to one-third of the supervisory board members. A simple majority of the meeting of shareholders may dismiss the supervisory board for reasons of lack of confidence.[29]

The works council is compulsory for larger companies. Its purpose is to allow the workforce to debate with the executive board twice a year on important issues. The works council must receive the annual accounts and a report on the company's social policy. It must be allowed to give advice when significant plans are being made and it must be consulted on matters regarding conditions of employment.

Audit committees are found in some companies in The Netherlands, as a relatively recent introduction. An important function of the audit committee is to formalize contact between the supervisory board and the internal and external auditors. It appears that the idea originated around 1978 in the supervisory board of Royal Dutch/Shell, drawing on the company's experience in Canada and the USA. Its use appears limited to larger listed companies, particularly those in the financial sector. The audit committee will typically comprise a mixture of members of the supervisory board, representatives of the financial management and representatives of the internal audit department. Effectively,

---

[27] 2007 Code, section 4.2.4.

[28] Hoogendoorn (2001); Klaassen (2001).

[29] *Doing Business in the Netherlands*, Baker Tilly International (2006).

the audit committee is a subcommittee of the supervisory board. The audit committee will typically meet prior to the annual audit to discuss the audit plan and shortly after completion of the audit to discuss the results of the audit and the annual financial statements.

Internal audit is a strong aspect of the corporate governance of Dutch companies and the management board places heavy reliance on internal audit. The extension of internal audit work to cover operational control matters and risk assessment indicates the evolution of internal audit towards the status of advisor to senior management on a wide range of aspects of the business.[30]

The external auditor is appointed by the general meeting, the supervisory board or the management board (in that order) and may be dismissed by the appointing group or by the general meeting.

In 1997 a committee of the Amsterdam Stock Exchange reviewed (the Peters Report) corporate governance. It made recommendations for companies and their supervisory boards, in a spirit of self-regulation. Many of the recommendations have been adopted voluntarily by listed companies. The Dutch Corporate Governance Code was issued in 2003 by a Corporate Governance Committee (see Exhibit 3.10).

14.4.2.4 Poland

The formal bodies of the joint-stock company are the shareholders' meeting, the management board and the supervisory board. The shareholders' meeting elects the supervisory board, which must have at least three members. The supervisory board elects the management board. The term of office of members of the management board may not exceed five years. Joint-stock companies may issue registered shares or bearer shares. Limited liability companies are not required to have an audit or to have a reserve fund. The minimum share capital is lower than that of a joint-stock company. The company is run by a management board elected by the shareholders' meeting.[31] Joint-stock companies must have an annual audit and must create a reserve fund for potential losses by transferring 8 per cent of the annual profits until the reserve amounts to one-third of the share capital. There is a minimum level of share capital required.

The Polish Corporate Governance Forum[32] proposed a Corporate Governance Code for Polish listed companies in 2002 and subsequently contributed to the 2005 revision of the Code (see Case study 3.6). The third annual rating of corporate governance mechanisms in Polish companies[33] stated that corporate governance risk was lower for companies using legal solutions stipulated in relevant corporate documents which properly safeguarded outside investors' interests, for example through the introduction of supervisory board independent members. The Forum emphasized that the rating did not pass judgements on the independence and qualifications of supervisory board members or on management quality.

14.4.3 Equity capital markets

Exhibit 14.8 shows the top 30 European companies, ranked by market capitalization. The columns indicating listing in London and New York show the potential for a strong 'Anglo-Saxon' influence. These largest companies are all in West European countries, apart

---

[30] Fraser *et al.* (2000).

[31] Ernst & Young (2004), Ch. 3.

[32] http://www.pfcg.org.pl/en/pfcg/index.htm.

[33] Evolution not revolution! Corporate Governance Ratings, 2005 (see website above).

| Exhibit 14.8 | Top 30 European companies, June 2007, with highest Polish company for comparison |

Rank in Europe	Name	Country	Market cap. $000m	London listing	NYSE listing	Sector
1	Gazprom	Russia	245.9	yes	no	Oil and gas
2	Royal Dutch/Shell	UK	214.0	yes	yes	Oil and gas
3	BP	UK	208.8	yes	yes	Oil and gas
4	HSBC	UK	202.1	yes	yes	Banks
5	Total	France	167.1	yes	yes	Oil and gas
6	GlaxoSmithKline	UK	157.0	yes	yes	Pharmaceuticals and biotechnology
7	Nestlé	Switzerland	155.3	yes	no	Food producer and processor
8	Roche	Switzerland	154.6	no	no	Pharmaceuticals and biotechnology
9	EDF	France	152.2			Electricity
10	Novartis	Switzerland	149.7	no	yes	Pharmaceuticals and biotechnology
11	Vodafone	UK	140.4	yes	yes	Telecoms services
12	ENI	Italy	129.9	no	yes	Oil and gas
13	UBS	Switzerland	124.5	no	yes	Banks
14	Royal Bank of Scotland	UK	122.5	yes	yes	Banks
15	Sanofi Aventis	France	117.8	no	yes	Pharmaceuticals and biotechnology
16	Santander Central Hispano	Spain	111.2	no	yes	Banks
17	Telefonica	Spain	108.1	yes	yes	Telecoms services
18	Unilever NV/plc	NL/UK	99.5	yes	yes	Food producer and processor
19	Unicredito Italiano	Italy	99.0			Banks
20	BNP Paribas	France	97.1	no	no	Banks
21	Intesa SanPaolo	Italy	96.6			Banks
22	Siemens	Germany	95.0	yes	yes	Electronic and electrical equipment
23	Arcelor Mittal	France	94.1			Industrial metals
24	Nokia	Finland	93.9	no	yes	IT hardware
25	ING	Netherlands	93.4			Life insurance
26	E.ON	Germany	93.2			Gas, water and multiutilities
27	Barclays	UK	92.5	yes	yes	Banks
28	Allianz	Germany	89.0			Nonlife insurance
29	Rosneft	Russia	88.5			Oil and gas
30	AXA	France	88.4			Nonlife insurance
192	PKO Bank	Poland	16.6			Banks

Source: *Financial Times* FT 500, 2007.

| Exhibit 14.9 | Europe 500, analyzed by country | | |

Country	Number of companies	Country	Number of companies
UK	109	Greece	9
France	73	Norway	9
Germany	49	Portugal	8
Italy	37	Denmark	8
Spain	36	Ireland	7
Switzerland	31	Poland	7
Sweden	22	Czech Republic	3
Russia	21	Netherlands/UK	2
Netherlands	18	Romania	2
Belgium	12	Cyprus	2
Finland	11	Hungary	2
Austria	10	Belgium/Netherlands	1
Turkey	10	Luxembourg	1

from Gazprom and Rosneft of Russia which both have a London listing. The largest Polish company, a telecommunications company, was 192nd in Europe in 2007. Exhibit 14.9 shows the geographical spread of the top 500 European companies.

14.4.3.1 France

Equity investors

We explain in section 6.6.1 that the French stock exchange is now part of Euronext.[34] Euronext is the world's first cross-border exchange business. For regulatory purposes it operates through subsidiaries in the separate countries. Of the 100 companies in the Euronext 100 index, 60 are French and they carry 60 per cent of the weighting of the index.

Historically, French companies have not generally used the stock market as a source of finance but in more recent years there has been an increase in new equity financing. Use of share options to reward management caused greater interest in the stock market from the 1990s onwards.[35] However, there is a view that shareholders have a conservative view of expectations from dividends. Growth of the company, with corresponding increase in value of the shares, is the preference of many shareholders.[36]

There is a tradition of family business in France and some of these family businesses prefer borrowing rather than issuing further shares to raise finance. This, combined with state ownership of some large companies, means that for many years companies preferred to issue bonds to raise new capital, rather than equity. Relatively few listed companies in France have widely dispersed shareholdings.[37] Most companies have major shareholders because of a history of flotation as a subsidiary, because of shareholdings by other

---

[34] www.euronext.com.
[35] Ibid.
[36] Charkham (1994), p. 142.
[37] Charkham (1994), pp. 126–127.

companies or because founders have retained their investment. Such shareholdings have in part been designed to discourage takeovers by creation of cross-shareholdings.

Almost all shares in quoted companies are held in bearer form. That means the person in possession of the share certificate (the bearer) has ownership. Because this makes share certificates vulnerable to theft and fraud, they are generally held by custodian banks as intermediaries; there is no paper certificate. In 2001 Euroclear[38] took over the national central registry, SICOVAM. Companies do not know who many of their shareholders are, and there is no mailing of information to shareholders, although the annual general meeting is advertised and shareholders have the choice of attending. Dividends are not sent to shareholders. They are paid by Euroclear to intermediaries for onward distribution. Since 1987 there has been a new type of share, the identifiable bearer security (*Titre au porteur identifiable*, TPI). The issuing company may request disclosure of the holder's identity. That request is fulfilled by Euroclear France, which sends it to the account keeper, which may be the company itself or a financial institution.

There has been some concern that small shareholders may not be paid sufficient attention, and many companies now make efforts to contact their shareholders. Because companies do not know who owns them, communication relies on press announcements and on information given in briefings to analysts' meetings, which some companies record for the website.[39]

In France, there is no equivalent to the pension funds of the UK or the USA as equity investors. The major insurance companies are significant investors, tending to concentrate their investments, and often having a representative on the company's board of directors.[40]

Regulation of the stock market

The Autorité des marchés financiers (AMF)[41] was established by the Financial Security Act 2003. It is a member of IOSCO, CESR and FSF (see sections 1.3.4 and 3.2.1). It was formed from the merger of the Commission des opérations de bourse (COB), the Conseil des marchés financiers (CMF) and the Conseil de discipline de la gestion financière (CDGF). These bodies were merged to improve the efficiency of France's financial regulatory system and to give it greater visibility. The AMF is an independent public body. Its remit is to safeguard investments in financial instruments and in all other savings and investment vehicles, ensure that investors receive material information, and maintain orderly financial markets. It regulates the activities of Euronext Paris. In particular it monitors companies to ensure that they provide complete, relevant information on a timely basis and in an equitable manner to all market participants (investors, analysts, fund managers, the press and the general public).

14.4.3.2 Germany[42]

Shares in AG companies have traditionally been in the form of bearer shares, which means that possession is evidence of ownership. Consequently they need to be taken

---

[38] www.euroclear.com/wps/portal.

[39] www.renault.com/gb/finance/index_finance.htm.

[40] Charkham (1994), p. 147.

[41] www.amf-france.org (English-language option is available).

[42] Charkham (1994), p. 27; *Accountancy International,* January 2000, p. 67.

care of, and the usual place for safe custody is a bank. Because they are bearer shares, not carrying the owner's name, it is difficult to gain information on the pattern of share ownership. Towards the end of the 1990s the use of registered shares was becoming increasingly popular, replacing the almost exclusive previous use of bearer shares.

Equity investors

The German stock market is third in order of size in the EU, following London and Euronext (Exhibit 6.4), and has grown significantly over the past 15 years (Exhibit 6.5). The domestic companies listed have a market capitalization which is a relatively low percentage of GDP, indicating that equity funding is not as significant to the national economy as are the markets in the UK or the USA. From Exhibit 6.5 it is clear that individual investors are not a major factor in the market. The most significant shareholder group is non-financial corporations, a situation where companies hold shares in each other. Such systems of cross-holdings make companies very secure against takeover bids, but also foster secrecy.

Institutional investors are not in general a strong force in the financing and governance of companies. Because shares are in bearer form and held by banks, there is strong power in the hands of the banks when voting at general meetings is required. The banks hold proxy votes authorized by the owners of the shares; banks are obliged to consult the owners of the shares and have dealt with this obligation by asking for a 15-month proxy covering all the shareholdings of the investor. It would not be unusual for the banks collectively to control more than half of the votes cast at an annual general meeting of a major German company. Deutsche Post, with Ruhr-Universität Bochum, in 2003 surveyed its 820,000 domestic private investors, holding a total of 10 per cent of the share capital, to find how they collect information on stocks. They relied mainly on media reports, with the annual report being relatively low on their list, but 58 per cent read the income statement.

Regulation of the market

Companies seeking a listing must present a prospectus. Listed companies are also required to disclose an interim report. The content of this report is regulated by the Stock Exchange Act (Börsengesetz) and the Ordinance regulating Stock Exchange Listing (Börsenzulassungsverordnung).[43] The Deutsche Börse claims to have high transparency in the operation of the market. It has two segments – the General Standard and the Prime Standard. The General Standard companies must meet the requirements of German securities laws, such as annual and interim reports and ad hoc disclosures in German. The Prime Standard companies must, in addition, give quarterly reports, use IFRS or US GAAP, publish a financial calendar, hold at least one analyst conference each year and make ad hoc disclosures in English as well as in German. Research into the previous Neuer Market (New Market) showed that companies using IAS or US GAAP showed 81 per cent average compliance with IAS and 86 per cent average compliance with US GAAP.[44] General concerns about the regulation of the Neuer Market caused the Deutsche Börse to rearrange its business under the new Prime Standard and General Standard.

---

[43] Ballwieser (2001), pp. 1332–1333.
[44] Glaum and Street (2003).

14.4.3.3 The Netherlands

Equity investors

There is an established stock market in Amsterdam and other related markets including the European Options Exchange, the Amsterdam Futures Market, the Rotterdam Energy Futures Exchange, the over-the-counter (OTC) market and a market for private arrangements.

The Amsterdam Stock Exchange operates within Euronext and is relatively significant in relation to the GDP of the country. However, its high turnover is mainly attributable to a relatively small number of companies and the Amsterdam exchange is not a significant source of new capital. The companies listed are relatively large in market capitalization.

Prior to 2005, the Amsterdam Stock Exchange allowed foreign companies to follow either IASB standards or US GAAP without reconciliation to Netherlands GAAP. Domestic companies could follow Netherlands GAAP or could apply IASB standards, US GAAP or UK GAAP with a reconciliation to Netherlands GAAP.[45] This indicates the relative flexibility of the stock exchange and perhaps reflects the dominance of multinational Anglo/Dutch and Belgian/Dutch companies.

14.4.3.4 Poland[46]

The Warsaw Stock Exchange is the principal market. In its present form it dates from 1991, with structure and regulation guided by the French system. It is a self-regulatory organization whose rules are approved by the Polish Securities and Exchange Commission.[47] It has three divisions – the main floor, the parallel market and the free floor. The main floor is the primary market and requires an issuer to publish audited financial statements for the previous three years. The National Depository of Securities registers and keeps in deposit securities introduced to public trading. Any public offering must be approved by the Securities and Exchange Commission.

A survey by the Warsaw Stock Exchange in 2006 found that 35 per cent of shares were traded by domestic individual investors, 34 per cent by domestic institutional investors and 31 per cent by foreign investors. The greatest change on previous years was the increase in investment by domestic individuals.

14.4.4 Bank lending

14.4.4.1 France

Historically, deposit-taking banks did not participate in the financing of their industrial and commercial customers;[48] merchant banks were the source of lending to business. The two types of banks are, since 1984, similar in status under banking law, all being called *établissements de crédit*. The provision of bank lending is concentrated in a small number of large banks. This factor, in combination with the relative lack of spread of equity shareholding mentioned earlier, means that a few banks are relatively influential in matters of raising corporate finance. Banks also take equity shareholdings in companies. This may be encouraged by the company which sees a source of

---

[45] Klaassen (2001), p. 1922.

[46] Ernst & Young (2004), pp. 8, 60.

[47] Warsaw Stock Exchange, http://www.gpw.pl/index.asp; Polish SEC, www.kpwig.gov.pl/index-ang.htm; both have English-language versions.

[48] Charkham (1994), pp. 144–145.

cheaper capital and a protection against takeover. For the banks, the strategy of increasing their involvement in corporate finance has resulted from comparative evaluation of the systems in Germany and in the UK, with the conclusion favouring the German approach. This gives a long-term orientation to bank financing by loans and by equity investment.[49]

14.4.4.2 Germany

Banks approach lending as a long-term arrangement. This creates what is called 'relationship' banking rather than 'transaction' banking. Bankers have to understand their customers and the industries in which they are located. The major banks have developed a range of services so that a company may receive all types of banking service, including lending, from one source – referred to as *Universalbanken*. Banks take an active part in the corporate governance of companies that they finance. This reduces the information gap between customers and banks and so helps minimize the agency costs of bank lending.

Banks are also shareholders in companies, to a significant extent. This has to some extent happened by accident, because banks will accept equity as repayment of debt when a company falls into difficulties. Because of various regulatory changes in the late 1990s and capital gains tax changes in 2002 there were expectations that financial institutions would reduce their holdings in non-financial companies but the subdued stock markets discouraged large-scale selling.

Bank financing is relatively more important as a source of finance to the corporate sector than in the USA or UK (40 per cent of GDP in Germany in 1999, compared with 12.6 per cent of GDP in the USA).[50] It is commonly asserted in textbooks that the debt:equity ratios of German companies are higher than those of the USA or the UK but this is not borne out by national income statistics[51] (corporate debt in Germany in 2001 was 7.9 per cent compared with 17.1 per cent in the UK and 19.0 per cent in the USA) and is challenged by research (Rajan and Zingales, 1995).

14.4.4.3 The Netherlands

There is an active banking sector. Credit banks grant loans to businesses, and specialist financial institutions offer finance for special purposes such as business start-ups and export finance. Corporate debt was 28.3 per cent of stock market capitalization in 2001.[52] Research into the period 1984–97[53] showed that Dutch companies preferred internal finance over external finance. Among the external finance types they preferred bank loans over shares and preferred shares over bonds.

14.4.4.4 Poland

Traditionally the relationship of Polish banks to Polish companies resembled that of German banks to German companies. However, in recent years banks have become risk averse and have found that they can satisfy their lending plans by lending to the

---

[49] Charkham (1994), p. 146.
[50] OECD (2003b), p. 201.
[51] OECD (2003b), p. 203.
[52] Ibid.
[53] Haan and Hinloopen (2002).

government as a low-risk debtor. So the larger Polish companies have turned to external financing and investment. The very large Polish companies are able to borrow in the USA.

14.4.5 Taxation system

A survey of conditions in the early 1990s showed that corporate income tax revenues in most EU countries were low by international standards, as a percentage of GDP. The relatively low yield, and large variations across EU countries with similar statutory tax rates, were attributed to several factors. The differences in accountancy rules were one explanation, but another was extensive political use of tax relief. The tax reliefs substantially reduced the effective tax rates. A code of conduct on business taxation was agreed in December 1997 to prevent tax reliefs of one country leading to harmful competition among member states.

The relationship between accounting and taxation systems across Europe was the subject of a special issue of *The European Accounting Review* in 1996 (Vol. 5 supplement). Hoogendoorn (1996) summarized the general relationship between accounting and taxation as shown in Exhibit 14.10.

In the group classed as 'independence' there is a range of relationships between the accounting and taxation systems. Where the tax authorities say that they will accept the profit reported under general commercial accounting principles, the preparers of accounts may have taxation consequences in mind when they make their policy selection within general accounting principles. In the group classed as 'dependence' the tax rules may be applied in the commercial accounts and may result in the accounts not conforming to the idea of a 'true and fair view'. Concerns about the relationship between accounting and taxation have continued after 2005 because many countries do not intend to permit or require IFRS for individual companies (see section 14.3.1).

14.4.5.1 France

Companies pay corporation tax based on their accounting profits. The definition of 'profit' for corporate tax purposes is that used for commercial and industrial purposes. Corporate income taxes are paid by individual companies rather than by groups of

---

Exhibit 14.10 The general relationship between accounting and taxation

Independence	Dependence
Czech Republic	Belgium
Denmark	Finland
Ireland	Germany
Netherlands	Italy
Norway	Sweden
Poland	France
UK	

Source: Hoogendoorn (1996), Table 1, p. 786.

companies. However, there are some specific rules for groups of companies. For businesses the taxable income is calculated by starting with the accounting profit as determined by the Plan Comptable Général. Some further adjustments are made for the purposes of tax law. These adjustments involve the exclusion of expenses which relate to personal items associated with the owner of the business. Gifts to customers, expenses of entertaining and travel, and commissions paid to third parties are examples of transactions which are acceptable. The emphasis is on 'normal business practice', but it is essential that the expense item be included in the financial accounts.

The basis of the depreciation calculation is allocation of cost over the useful life of the asset but accelerated depreciation is allowed for specific assets provided it is used in the financial statements. The civil court (Conseil d'État) decided in 1999 that the amortization of goodwill was an allowable deduction when calculating taxable profit, providing the goodwill was a separable asset with a definite end-date to the benefits attached. This clarified previous uncertainty but only where strict conditions are met.[54]

Provisions are widely used in French accounting practice. To be allowable for tax purposes the provision must meet specific criteria which ensure that the provision is probable, that it is specific and that it arises from an event which happened during the year (rather than an event after the balance sheet date).

Capital gains are taxable. Previously a company paid a lower rate of tax on long-term capital gains until distributed, but this now applies only to specified investments. Until December 2004 dividend distributions were taxed under an imputation system. Where a company made a distribution of dividend there was an extra payment of 50 per cent of the net dividend (*avoir fiscal*) and a tax credit of the same amount was released for the shareholder. The *avoir fiscal* was removed by the 2004 Finance Law. Only individual shareholders can benefit from a new reduction equal to 50 per cent of the net dividend.[55]

14.4.5.2 Germany

In Germany, there is a close link between the annual accounts and the tax accounts. The principles of recognition and valuation applied in the commercial accounts must in general be incorporated into the tax balance sheet. On some occasions, tax law requires specific accounting principles which differ from accounting regulations; this is usually to allow a degree of objectivity. The close relationship between accounting and tax principles is referred to as the authoritativeness principle (the *Mabgeblichkeitsprinzip*). (It is also translated in texts as the principle of 'congruency' or 'bindingness'.) The *Mabgeblichkeitsprinzip* states that the generally accepted accounting principles (GoB) form an authoritative basis for tax accounts unless there are other explicit tax rules.[56] Tax accounts are thus derived from commercial accounts. However, the tax legislation is also very detailed in relation to accounting treatment and tax incentives. The availability of tax incentives usually requires the values of tax accounting to be used also in commercial accounting. This has been called 'the reverse authoritativeness principle'. So, in reality, tax practices influence the starting point for preparation of the commercial accounts. In particular there is pressure on German companies to value assets at the lowest amount possible and liabilities at the highest amount possible.[57]

---

[54] *Accountancy International*, January 2000, p. 66.

[55] *Doing business in France* (2006), UHY International.

[56] Crampton *et al.* (2001).

[57] Ballwieser (2001), pp. 1296–1298.

Small businesses in particular prefer to produce one set of accounts which satisfy the tax law as well as the accounting rules. Where the tax burden may be reduced or postponed, businesses will be influenced by that factor in their accounting practice. Tax on companies is levied on each company separately, rather than on a group of companies. Tax reforms agreed by Parliament in July 2000 reduced the corporate tax burden compared with the 1990s and, from 2003, removed capital gains tax on sales of shares by major shareholders, potentially making the capital market more flexible.

From 2001 the imputation system of taxation on dividends was removed and replaced by the 'half-income system'. Only half of the distributed profits of a corporation are included in the shareholder's personal tax base. However no credit is allowed for the corporation tax paid by the company.[58]

14.4.5.3 The Netherlands

In The Netherlands accounting and taxation are formally independent, for both individual accounts and group accounts. Both sets of regulations leave scope for flexibility. Tax law relating to incorporated businesses is contained in the Law on Corporation Tax. Dividends distributed by a Dutch corporation are subject to a withholding tax.

14.4.5.4 Poland

In Poland, taxable income of companies is arrived at by adjusting accounting profits for tax purposes. Tax depreciation rates are prescribed in tax law. There are corporate income tax incentives such as special economic zones. The standard corporate income tax rate was 19 per cent in 2004, which was regarded as a beneficial tax rate.[59] Uncertainty in the tax system has been a significant problem for Polish companies (see Exhibit 14.11).[60]

Exhibit 14.11	Note on uncertainty regarding taxation, TP Group

[Extract from Income Tax note]

Value added tax, corporate income tax, personal income tax or social security regulations are subject to frequent changes which often leads to the lack of reference to well established regulations or legal precedents. There is also a lack of clarity in current regulations which results in contradictions in legal interpretations both within government bodies and between companies and government bodies. Tax settlements and other (e.g. customs or foreign exchange law) may be subject to review and investigation by a number of authorities, which are entitled to impose severe fines, and additional liabilities resulting from such tax audits must be paid together with interest charges. These facts create tax risks in Poland that are substantially more significant than those typically found in countries with more developed tax systems. Tax authorities may examine the accounting records up to five years after the end of the year in which the final tax payments were to be made. As a result liabilities presented in the consolidated financial statements may change later after the final decisions of tax authorities.

Source: TP Group, Annual Report (2006), Income Tax Note 12, p. 60, www.tp-ir.pl.

---

[58] *Doing business in Germany* (2006), UHY Deutschland AG.

[59] Ernst & Young (2004), p. 9.

[60] OECD (2004), p. 179.

This is because prior to 2005 there was no facility for companies to obtain *ex ante* (in advance) tax rulings and there were different interpretations at different local tax offices. Since January 2005 the tax offices have been permitted to publish binding interpretations of the law but this does not reduce the overall complexity.[61] There remains a lag in time between the passage of a tax law and its enactment, and there have been different interpretations at different local tax offices.

14.4.6 The accounting profession

Baker *et al.* (2001) compared the regulation of the statutory auditor in the UK, France and Germany, and concluded that while there might be a movement towards international harmonization of auditing standards across Europe, it is less likely that harmonization of the regulation of statutory auditors will occur. They distinguish significant reliance on recognized professional bodies in the UK from control by quasi-governmental entities in France and Germany. We will see in Chapter 15 that the UK has moved further down the quasi-governmental route since Baker *et al.* carried out their analysis but their observations on the differences in regulation of statutory audit remain interesting. We compare here the nature of the accounting and auditing professions in France, Germany, The Netherlands and Poland.

14.4.6.1 France

The reform of company law in 1967 established the profession of auditor (*commissaire aux comptes*). Historically, the profession of auditor had been separate, in the eyes of the law, from that of accountant. However, in practice most auditors also belong to the accountancy profession. A range of professional bodies existed in the latter part of the nineteenth and the early twentieth century. These were rationalized by government action in formation of the Ordre des experts comptables et des comptables agréés (OEC) in 1945.[62] This was formed as a two-tier body of the *expert comptable* who was authorized to prepare annual accounts and the *comptable agréé* who operated the bookkeeping system.

Ordre des Experts Comptables (OEC)[63]

Only members of the OEC are permitted to call themselves *expert comptable*. They have a monopoly position, protected by law, in the public supply of certain accounting services. Only partners or employees of an accountancy practice may use the title *expert comptable*; those who move to work in industry lose their membership of the professional body. This means there is no professional accountancy body representing accountants working in industry and commerce.

Those seeking membership of the OEC must undergo a period of training and pass professional examinations, including the writing of a dissertation.

An example of the underlying differences in thinking may be seen in a draft conceptual framework published in 1996 by the OECD, rejecting the Anglo-Saxon/US/IASC 'balance sheet approach' and instead emphasizing the importance of the profit and loss account as the essential statement of wealth creation.[64]

---

[61] OECD (2006b), pp. 85–86; *Doing Business in Poland* (2007) UHY International.

[62] Scheid and Walton (2001), p. 306.

[63] Scheid and Walton (2001), p. 306; Standish (2000), Ch. 5.

[64] *FT World Accounting Report*, July 1996, p. 2.

Compagnie Nationale des Commissaires aux Comptes (CNCC)

The CNCC was formed in 1969 as part of a continuing reform of auditing under government jurisdiction. Although the statutory position of the auditor was established by the law of 1867, there was no professional organization at that time and it was only after a reform of the law in 1935 that the duties of the auditor were extended and professional organizations began to appear.

Formation of the CNCC was related to changes in the law which widened the responsibilities of auditors and fixed their fees in relation to the size of the client. They were required to certify the *regularité* (conforming with legal requirements) and the *sincerité* (application of accepted valuation methods in good faith) of the accounts. Most *commissaires aux comptes* are also *experts comptables*, as members of the OEC.

14.4.6.2 Germany

Audit is required for large corporations and large enterprises. According to the law, only *Wirtschaftsprüfer* and firms of *Wirtschaftsprüfer* may act as auditors. For medium-sized limited liability companies there is a second category, the sworn-in auditors (*vereidigter Buchprüfer*) and their firms. Those seeking to become *Wirtschaftsprüfer* normally require a university degree and to have at least four years of practical auditing experience.[65] There is a demanding final examination. As in most other countries, a high degree of independence is demanded of the *Wirtschaftsprüfer*. Links with the company under audit are forbidden, both for the auditor and for the audit firm. There is a body of tax accountants, the Steuerberater (with more than 55,000 members), which would like to have the right to audit but its claims are repeatedly rejected by the legislators.

Legislation sets out the legal position of the *Wirtschaftsprüfer* and the sworn-in auditor. The legislation allows the profession to be self-governing. All *Wirtschaftsprüfer* and sworn-in auditors are required to be members of the chamber of *Wirtschaftsprüfer* (Wirtschaftsprüferkammer) which is a public law body under the official supervision of the Federal Minister of Economics. With around 12,000 persons entitled to describe themselves as *Wirtschaftsprüfer* (Exhibit 14.12), it may be regarded as an elite body. Germany is one of the EU member states (along with Belgium, France and Greece) that restrict membership of the professional associations to those working in public practice. Membership therefore indicates a function rather than an educational background. There is no equivalent professional body for those working in industry or business.

| Exhibit 14.12 | German accounting profession: members of the Wirtschaftsprüferkammer |

Wirtschaftsprüfer Statutory auditor	12,194
vereidigter Buchprüfer Sworn-in auditors	3,988
Statutory audit firms	2,178
Licensed audit firms	148
Others	829
Total number	19,337

Source: Members at 1 July 2004, http://www.wpk.de/english/about/statistics.asp.

---

[65] *Wirtschaftsprüferordnung*, section 9, para.1.

At a conference in 1995 a senior official at the Federal Ministry of Justice invited German accountants to enter detailed discussions about professional standards. The Institute of German Public Accountants and the Wirtschaftsprüferkammer entered into detailed negotiations with the Ministry. The fruits of the discussions were incorporated in the KonTraG.[66] Among other aspects of corporate governance, the law requires German accountants to comment on the company's year-end business report as well as the accounts. They are also required to scrutinize the company's risk management system and mention any risks which might threaten the company as a going concern. This creates a new volume of work and adds new complexity to the statutory audit. Most significant, however, is the change from regarding auditing as an examination of past business alone. The KonTraG requires auditors to express a view about ongoing business.

The Institut der Wirtschaftsprüfer (IDW) has for some time issued statements in the form of professional expert opinions. As a result of the KonTraG, these are now separated into IDW Auditing Standards (IDWAuS) and IDW Accounting Standards (IDWAcS). Standards are supplemented by non-binding Practice Statements.[67]

As a further result of the KonTraG, the IDW published new auditing standards in 1999, bringing aspects of the International Auditing Standards into German auditing principles, subject to German law. A structure is recommended for the long-form audit report which is required by the HGB. The auditor must evaluate management's assessment of the economic situation and future development of the enterprise.[68]

Some proposals from the Ministry were not incorporated in the new law. A clause requiring rotation of auditors was removed and the Ministry was persuaded against its initial intention of increasing statutory liability. The KonTraG stipulates automatic liability of DM2m for statutory audits (previously established at DM500,000 in 1965) and four times that figure for consultancy. In practice lawsuits are rare.

With effect from January 2005 an Auditor Oversight Commission (AOC) has been established, having responsibility for the registration, disciplinary investigation and quality assurance of those who provide statutory audit services. Only persons outside the profession can be members of the AOC.

14.4.6.3 The Netherlands[69]

The origins of the accounting profession may be traced to the last decades of the nineteenth century when the role of accountants developed from bookkeeping to auditing as limited liability companies grew in importance. The separation of management and ownership of companies created a demand for auditors having independent and professional judgement. Other duties such as internal auditing, governmental auditing and management advisory work also developed.

The Netherlands Institute of Accountants was established in 1895 with the purpose of creating statutory rules for the accounting profession, although the rules did not materialize. No further significant legislative action arose until the Chartered Accountants Act of 1962, which reserved the auditing of financial statements for *registeraccountants* (RA). The same law created the Nederlands Instituut van Registeraccountants, NIVRA,

---

[66] *The Accountant*, May 1997, p. 13.

[67] Crampton *et al.* (2001), p. 15.

[68] *Accountancy International*, November 1998, p. 82; October 1999, pp. 51–52.

[69] Hoogendoorn (2001); Klaassen (2001).

as the Dutch Institute of Chartered Accountants. Another body, the Accountants-Administratieconsulenten (AA) came into existence in 1974, providing accounting services directed more at SMEs. Implementation of the Eighth Directive in Dutch law in 1993 gave the right of auditing to both NIVRA and AA, but in practice large companies choose NIVRA members as their auditors.

The education and examination of RAs is considerably more onerous than that required by the Eighth Directive. It lasts from 8 to 12 years, embracing undergraduate and postgraduate study as well as professional training.

NIVRA issues auditing guidelines but does not issue accounting standards or guidelines. It does, however, participate in accounting guidelines through membership of the Council for Annual Reporting. However, departures from the Guidelines for Annual Reporting are not referred to in the report of the independent auditor.

14.4.6.4 Poland

The Act on Auditors and their Self-Governing Body (1994) provides a legal framework for the creation, governance and operation of the National Chamber of Statutory Auditors (NCSA). The Ministry of Finance supervises the NCSA.[70] Of about 7,700 NCSA members, some 4,250 are active.[71] NCSA is a member of IFAC, along with the National Board of Certified Chartered Accountants Association in Poland, created within the Accountants Association of Poland (AAP).[72] AAP is a voluntary organization of accountants, financial specialists, auditors and information technology accounting specialists, existing since 1907. When the Act on Auditors was introduced, the chartered accountant members of AAP were able to register as statutory auditors and NCSA members. A cooperation agreement between AAP and NCSA was signed in 2004. The AAP is not a self-regulatory body within the Polish legal framework. There is a code of professional ethics. The NCSA sets auditing standards. If particular issues are not covered by existing standards the NCSA permits the use of International Auditing Standards. The NCSA is empowered to take disciplinary action for enforcing the code of professional ethics and auditing standards.

14.5 External influences

14.5.1 France

There is a history of independent development of accounting practice in France. Early tendencies towards charts of accounts may be traced to a commission formed in 1918 which included in its remit the idea of standardization. No specific chart appeared in France at that time but in the 1920s Schmalenbach proposed a model chart of accounts in Germany. The German occupation of France in 1940 brought ideas of German economic organization to industry and administration in France; this drew attention to potential deficiencies in French accounting practice and a code was prepared in 1942 as a detailed manual.

---

[70] Jaruga and Schroeder (2001).

[71] World Bank ROSC Report, 2002.

[72] www.skwp.pl has an English-language website.

As a founder member of the EU, France has influenced the content of the directives affecting company law in the community. It has in turn been influenced by other members joining the EU, particularly the UK request that the Fourth Directive should include the requirement for a 'true and fair view' (see Chapter 11).

Colonization of Africa in the late nineteenth century left a legacy of French accounting tradition in many African countries which are now independent. In particular, that legacy reflects the notion that accounting regulations should apply to all business entities, whether or not incorporated, and that there should be a uniform chart of accounts. It has been suggested that the French approach has made it easier to regulate unincorporated businesses and provide bookkeeping training, provided there is adequate literacy among small traders.[73]

14.5.2 Germany

Historically, accounting practice in Germany has developed independently with distinctive national characteristics.[74] As a founder member of the EU, Germany has had a significant influence on the directives affecting company law. Because of historical political links and continuing commercial links, German accounting has an influence on practices in countries such as Austria and Hungary. During periods of occupation of other countries during wartime, the German influence affected some accounting practices in countries such as France, and there is also evidence of a German influence on Japanese accounting. Germany itself was occupied briefly after the Second World War, and there has been a resulting impact on consolidated accounting in some sectors.

As other countries have joined the EU, Germany has found its own approach modified from time to time. This is particularly significant in the case of the 'true and fair view' being imported under UK influence and being seen as an infringement of the tax-driven approach to accounting.

Multinational companies are a vehicle of change in accounting practice. Daimler-Benz (section 9.2.3), as the first German company to obtain a full listing on a US stock exchange, presented its group accounts in US GAAP but continued to prepare the parent company accounts under the German Commercial Code. Both sets of financial statements were audited by independent auditors. Subsequently other German companies took a listing on the New York Stock Exchange. German regulations for group accounts prior to 2005 were flexible so that some companies chose IFRS and others chose US GAAP. This brought greater awareness of different accounting systems to major German companies.

14.5.3 The Netherlands

The accounting system of The Netherlands is very clearly individualistic and has developed under internal national influences.

As a founder member of the EU, The Netherlands influenced the formation of directives. The Netherlands was also a founder member of the IASC. Former colonies of The Netherlands, mainly Indonesia (the former Dutch East Indies), have accounting practices reflecting the Dutch influence. It has been suggested that the Dutch influence made it relatively easy for Indonesia to create national rules closely aligned with IAS.[75]

---

[73] Walton, P., 'Special rules for a special case', *Financial Times*, 18 September 1997, p. 11.

[74] Ballwieser (2001), pp. 1224–1227.

[75] *FT World Accounting Report*, August/September 1996, pp. iii–v.

The large multinational companies which have their base in The Netherlands have created their own mixture of harmonized accounting practices to meet their specific needs and have in some matters influenced domestic practices of competitors.

It has been suggested that a willingness to consider foreign ideas has been a continuing characteristic of Dutch accounting, but uncritical reception has been rare. Until the 1970s unique features of Dutch accounting were a source of pride. Perceptions of the value of harmonization are seen as a feature of more recent years.[76]

14.5.4 Poland[77]

To understand the complexities of accounting developments in Poland it is necessary to understand the history of Poland. It was a significant political and economic entity from the fifteenth to seventeenth century but was then partitioned progressively in the late 1700s, divided among Russia, Prussia and Austria. The legislation of each of these countries affected the partitioned country. Napoleon Bonaparte created the Grand Duchy of Warsaw in 1807, introducing the Napoleonic Code. His defeat in 1815 left that part of Poland under Russian control. As commercial laws developed, one part of Poland experienced Russian laws while the rest developed under the German Commercial Code. In 1918 at the end of the First World War, the Second Republic was created and had to reintegrate the tripartite business and accounting practices. In 1934 the Polish Commercial Code was introduced. From 1939 to 1944 the German system of uniform accounting was imposed in the parts of Poland under German occupation, while Soviet accounting was used in the regions incorporated into the USSR (Russia). The uniform accounting plan adopted in 1946 followed the German model. From the 1950s there was a centrally planned economy under Soviet economic planning. The failure of central planning led to the creation of a social market economy in the 1980s. From the end of the 1980s Poland had the target of EU membership and its accounting laws were changed to reflect the EU Directives.

14.6 Oversight and assurance

This section indicates some of the main developments in mechanisms of oversight and assurance in Europe generally and in France, Germany, The Netherlands and Poland in particular. Chapter 3 gives a broader view of processes of oversight and assurance.

14.6.1 EU-wide initiatives

Responsibility for ensuring compliance with accounting standards remains a national responsibility. This section compares the national processes for oversight and assurance and describes some of the developments in the establishment and operation of audit committees.

14.6.1.1 Public oversight

We have explained in Chapter 3 how the Sarbanes–Oxley Act established a Public Oversight Board in the USA. For Europe the question is whether such initiatives should be taken at national level or across the EU. FEE published a discussion paper in 2003 on the

---

[76] Klaassen (2001), pp. 1915–1916.
[77] Jaruga and Schroeder (2001), pp. 1596–1599.

Exhibit 14.13 Mechanisms of institutional oversight for consolidated accounts of listed companies, 2001

Institutional oversight mechanisms				No institutional oversight system*
Stock Exchange	Stock Exchange Regulator	Review Panel	Other government	
Sweden	Belgium	UK (FRRP)	Denmark	Austria
Norway	France		UK (DTI)	Finland
Switzerland	Italy		Czech Republic	Germany
	Portugal			Ireland
	Spain			Luxembourg
				Netherlands
				Hungary
				Slovenia

*Note that subsequently oversight systems have been developed in some cases – see following description for Germany and The Netherlands.

Source: FEE Survey of Enforcement Mechanisms in Europe, 2001, p. 1.

European coordination of public oversight. It supported the European Commission's view[78] that the practical implementation of oversight should be at national level.

FEE had previously published an investigation of national oversight systems in 2001. In particular it analyzed the oversight of the consolidated accounts of listed companies where there is a review that extends beyond a formal check of the contents. Exhibit 14.13 shows which body, if any, took responsibility for overseeing publication of consolidated accounts of listed companies.

Subsequently in Germany a privately organized review board was set up under the Financial Statements Review Act. The board conducts field reviews of financial statements at the request of the Federal Financial Supervisory Authority. Publication of findings is the main sanction.[79]

In The Netherlands, under the Act on the Supervision of Financial Reporting, the Authority for Financial Markets (Autoriteit Fianciele Markten or AFM) supervises the financial reporting of Dutch listed companies and reviews the annual reports. If necessary the AFM can apply to the Enterprise Section of the Amsterdam Court of Appeal to require a company to amend its financial statements. The 2007 review of 2006 reporting focused on the application of IAS 12 *Income Taxes* and IAS 7 *Cash flow statements*.[80] The AFM focused on IAS 12 because points raised in the 2004 review had recurred in 2005.

The FEE commentary (2003) emphasizes the importance of coordination and recognition of equivalence in quality between the European and US oversight systems. It suggests that this could be achieved through a European Coordination Audit Oversight Board (ECAOB). It would coordinate, rather than duplicate, work at a national level. That suggestion has not so far been taken forward.

---

[78] *International Accounting Bulletin*, Issue 338, 21 November 2003, pp. 1 and 11–14.

[79] *Doing Business in Germany*, PricewaterhouseCoopers (2007).

[80] www.iasplus.com.

14.6.1.2 Audit committees

A comparative study of European corporate governance codes found that by the end of 2001 an audit committee was recommended in, among other countries, Belgium, France, The Netherlands, Spain, Sweden and the UK.[81] The High Level Group of Company Law Experts[82] presented its final report in November 2002 on a modern regulatory framework for company law in Europe. The report provided guidance on the role and composition of audit committees. However, it saw corporate governance as a matter for national codes on corporate governance. The report can therefore be seen as a guide against which to evaluate national codes. The report recommends that the audit committee should comprise non-executive or supervisory directors, the majority of whom should be independent. The responsibilities of the audit committee should be:

- selecting the external auditor for appointment by shareholders;
- setting the terms and conditions for employment of the external auditor;
- monitoring the relationship between the external auditor and the company and its executive management, with particular emphasis on safeguarding auditor independence;
- monitoring the provision of non-audit services, either by prohibiting them or by monitoring them closely;
- meeting the auditors at least once in each quarter, and meeting them annually without the executive directors being present;
- ensuring that the external auditor has all the information required for the audit role;
- receiving the auditors' management letter with comments on the financial statements and considering whether these comments should be disclosed in the financial statements;
- reviewing accounting policies and changes to these;
- monitoring internal audit procedures and the company's risk management system;
- meeting regularly with those who are responsible for the internal audit procedures and risk management systems;
- considering to what extent the findings of the risk management system should be reported in the company's financial statements.

14.6.2 France

The Loi sur la Sécurité Financière (LSF 2003) affects the structure of French accountancy firms, reinforcing the importance of the separation of audit and non-audit activities.[83] It established the Haut Conseil des Commissaires aux Comptes to monitor the audit profession and oversee ethics and independence. It works with the CNCC (see section 14.4.6.1).

The Bouton Report 'Promoting better corporate governance in listed companies' was issued in September 2002. It made recommendations on the Constitution and work of audit committees, reflecting the detail of the report of the EU High Level Group of Company Law Experts (see section 14.6.1.2). It required the audit committee to exclude any corporate officer, but only specified that two-thirds of the committee should be independent directors.[84]

The audit report of Total (Exhibit 14.14, Panel A) is interesting because of the section 'Justification of our assessments', required by law. This section draws attention to particular

---

[81] Smith (2003), Appendix III.

[82] EC Communication May 2003, Reinforcing Statutory Audit in the EU.

[83] Comparative Study (2002), section V.A.6.

[84] http://europa.eu.int/comm/internal_market/en/company/company/modern/index.htm.

Exhibit 14.14 Reports by statutory auditors in France

Panel A: Audit report, Total

Statutory auditors' report on the consolidated financial statements

This is a free translation into English of the statutory auditors' report issued in French and is provided solely for the convenience of English speaking users. The statutory auditors' report includes information specifically required by French law in such reports, whether modified or not. This information is presented below the opinion on the consolidated financial statements and includes an explanatory paragraph discussing the auditors' assessments of certain significant accounting and auditing matters. These assessments were considered for the purpose of issuing an audit opinion on the consolidated financial statements taken as a whole and not to provide separate assurance on individual account captions or on information taken outside of the consolidated financial statements.

This report should be read in conjunction with, and construed in accordance with, French law and professional auditing standards applicable in France.

For the year ended December 31, 2006

To the shareholders,

In compliance with the assignment entrusted to us by the Annual General Shareholder's Meeting, we have audited the accompanying consolidated financial statements of TOTAL S.A. for the year ended December 31, 2006.

The consolidated financial statements have been approved by the Board of Directors. Our role is to express an opinion on these financial statements based on our audit.

I. Opinion on the consolidated financial statements

We conducted our audit in accordance with professional standards applicable in France. Those standards require that we plan and perform the audit to obtain reasonable assurance about whether the consolidated financial statements are free of material misstatement. An audit includes examining, on a test basis, evidence supporting the amounts and disclosures in the financial statements. An audit also includes assessing the accounting principles used and significant estimates made by the management, as well as evaluating the overall financial statements presentation. We believe that our audit provides a reasonable basis for our opinion. In our opinion, the consolidated financial statements give a true and fair view of the assets, liabilities, financial position and results of the Group as at December 31, 2006 in accordance with IFRSs as adopted by the European Union.

II. Justification of our assessments

In accordance with the requirements of article L.823-9 of the Commercial Code relating to the justification of our assessments, we bring to your attention the following matters:

Some accounting principles applied by TOTAL involve a significant amount of judgments and estimates principally related to the application of the successful efforts method for the oil and gas activities, the depreciation of long-lived assets, the provisions for dismantlement, removal and environmental costs, the evacuation of retirement obligations and the determination of the current and deferred taxation. Detailed information relating to the application of these accounting principles is given in the notes to the consolidated financial statements.

Our procedures relating to the material judgments or estimates made by the management and which can result from the application of these accounting principles enabled us to assess their reasonableness.

The assessments were made in the context of our audit of the consolidated financial statements taken as a whole, and therefore contributed to the formation of the unqualified opinion expressed in the first part of this report.

III. Vérification spécifique

In accordance with professional standards applicable in France, we have also verified the information given in the Group management report. We have no matters to report as to its fair presentation and conformity with the consolidated financial statements.

Paris La Défense, April 3, 2007

The statutory auditors

KPMG Audit	ERNST & YOUNG Audit
Département de KPMG S.A.	
René Amirkhanian	Gabriel Galet Philippe Diu

Exhibit 14.14 *(Continued)*

Panel B: Internal control procedures

Statutory auditor's report (Article L 225–235 of the French Commercial Code)

[Free translation of a French language original]

Statutory auditors' report, prepared in accordance with article L 225-235 of the French Commercial Code, on the report prepared by the Chairman of the Board of Directors of TOTAL S.A., regarding the internal control procedures that relate to the preparation and processing of financial and accounting information.

To the shareholders,

In our capacity as statutory auditors of TOTAL S.A., and in accordance with Article L 225-235 of the French Commercial Code, we report to you on the report prepared by the Chairman of your company in accordance with Article L 225-37 of the French Commercial Code for the year ended December 31, 2006.

It is for the Chairman to give an account, in his report, notably of the conditions in which the duties of the Board of Directors are prepared and organized and the internal control procedures in place within the company.

It is our responsibility to report to you our observations on the information and declarations set out in the Chairman's report on the internal control procedures relating to the preparation and processing of financial and accounting information.

We performed our procedures in accordance with professional guidelines applicable in France. These require us to perform procedures to assess the fairness of the information and declarations set out in the Chairman's report on the internal control procedures relating to the preparation and processing of financial and accounting information. These procedures notably consisted of:

- Obtaining an understanding of the objectives and general organization of general control, as well as the internal control procedures relating to the preparation and processing of financial and accounting information, as set out in the Chairman's report;
- Assessing the evaluation given on the adequacy and effectiveness of these procedures, including considering the appropriateness of the evaluation process and the implementation of the tests conducted; and
- Performing the tests relating to the design and execution of these procedures, in addition to our audit procedures related to the accounts, that we believed necessary to confirm the information and conclusions given on this subject in the President's report.

On the basis of these procedures, we have no matters to report in connection with the information and declarations given on the internal control procedures relating to the preparation and processing of financial and accounting information, contained in the Chairman of the Board's report, prepared in accordance with Article L 225-37 of the French Commercial Code.

Paris La Défense, April 3, 2007

The statutory auditors

KPMG Audit   ERNST & YOUNG Audit
Département de KPMG S.A.

René Amirkhanian   Gabriel Galet   Philippe Diu

Source: Total, Registration Document 2006, p. 112.

accounting matters, but without qualifying the audit opinion. This is a variation on the US requirement for directors to draw attention to critical accounting estimates (see Exhibit 11.16). Panel B of Exhibit 14.14 shows the report of the statutory auditors on the report prepared by the chairman of the board of directors on the internal control procedures relating to the preparation and processing of financial information.

14.6.3 Germany

The German Corporate Governance Code (2007) is summarized as Case study 3.1. It presents essential statutory regulations for the management and supervision of German listed companies. It is built on the legal requirement in Germany for a dual board system of management board and supervisory board (section 14.4.2.2).

The German auditor is required to prepare a detailed report for management and the supervisory boards and must also comment on management's appreciation of the financial position and prospects of the company as shown in the directors' report. There is no prescribed wording for an audit report but the opinion must be clearly understandable and must draw clear attention to major problems.[85]

The auditor's report on Deutsche Telekom, a German company, does not refer specifically to the corporate governance code but it does cover the group management report (Exhibit 14.15).

14.6.4 The Netherlands

The Enterprise Chamber[86] is a special chamber of the Courts of Justice which gives rulings on allegations of failure to comply with the legal requirements of financial accounting. The verdicts are specific to the cases considered, but may also have a wider influence. The Chamber may state that the financial accounts are incorrect and may give an order to the company containing precise requirements as to the preparation of financial statements, now or in the future. It may also give instructions of a more general nature which may cause a particular accounting policy to become unacceptable. The verdict may include comment on the auditor, which may in turn lead to professional disciplinary action being taken by the professional body. The audit report of a typical Dutch company gives a 'true and fair' opinion but does not refer to the corporate governance code (Exhibit 14.16). It specifies consistency of the executive report with the financial statements. There are two separate opinions; one for the consolidated financial statements and one for the parent company financial statements.

In relation to the introduction of IFRS for listed companies the Authority for Financial Markets (Autoriteit Fianciele Markten or AFM) has formed a Financial Reporting Committee of 12 external IFRS experts to advise the AFM on the application of IFRS.

14.6.5 Poland

In 2002 and 2005 the World Bank produced Reports on the Observance of Standards and Codes (ROSC) with specific coverage of accounting and auditing.[87] The conclusions in 2002 were mainly of the form 'needs to strengthen', which was perhaps not surprising in a system that is developing rapidly to meet international standards. The 2005 report acknowledged 'very significant progress'. It recommended that further enhancements to the statutory framework were needed and provided a long list of suggestions. In particular the report recommended establishing a public overview body for the National Chamber

---

[85] *Doing Business in Germany*, PricewaterhouseCoopers (2007).

[86] Klaassen (2001), p. 1917.

[87] World Bank (2002) and (2005), www.worldbank.org/ifa/rosc_aa.html.

Exhibit 14.15 Report by statutory auditor in Germany

Auditors' report

We have audited the financial statements of Deutsche Telekom AG, Bonn, comprising the income statement, balance sheet, cash flow statement, statement of recognized income and expense, and the notes to the consolidated financial statements, together with the Group management report for the financial year from January 1 to December 31, 2006. The preparation of the consolidated financial statements and the Group management report in accordance with the IFRSs, as adopted by the EU, and the additional requirements of German commercial law pursuant to § 315a (1) of the German Commercial Code (Handelsgesetzbuch – HGB) are the responsibility of the Company's Board of Management. Our responsibility is to express an opinion on the consolidated financial statements and on the Group management report based on our audit.

We conducted our audit of the consolidated financial statements in accordance with § 317 HGB and German generally accepted standards for the audit of financial statements promulgated by the Institute of Public Auditors in Germany (Institut der Wirtschaftsprüfer – IDW) and additionally observed the International Standards on Auditing (ISA). Those standards require that we plan and perform the audit such that misstatements materially affecting the presentation of the net assets, financial position and results of operations in the consolidated financial statements in accordance with the applicable financial reporting framework and in the Group management report are detected with reasonable assurance. Knowledge of the business activities and the economic and legal environment of the Group and expectations as to possible misstatements are taken into account in the determination of audit procedures. The effectiveness of the accounting-related internal control system and the evidence supporting the disclosures in the consolidated financial statements and the Group management report are examined primarily on a test basis within the framework of the audit. The audit includes assessing the annual financial statements of those entities included in

consolidation, the determination of the entities to be included in consolidation, the accounting and consolidation principles used and significant estimates made by the Company's Board of Management, as well as evaluating the overall presentation of the consolidated financial statements and the Group management report. We believe that our audit provides a reasonable basis for our opinion.

Our audit has not led to any reservations.

In our opinion, based on our findings of our audit, the consolidated financial statements comply with the IFRSs as adopted by the EU, the additional requirements of German commercial law pursuant to § 315a (1) HGB and give a true and fair view of the net assets, financial position, and results of operations of the Group in accordance with these requirements. The Group management report is consistent with the consolidated financial statements and as a whole provides a suitable view of the Group's position and suitably presents the opportunities and risks of future development.

Stuttgart/Frankfurt (Main), February 13, 2007

Ernst & Young AG
Wirtschaftsprüfungsgesellschaft
Steuerberatungsgesellschaft
Stuttgart

| (Prof. Dr. Pfitzer) | (Hollweg) |
| Wirtschaftsprüfer | Wirtschaftsprüfer |

PricewaterhouseCoopers
Aktiengesellschaft
Wirtschaftsprüfungsgesellschaft
Frankfurt (Main)

| (Frings) | (Menke) |
| Wirtschaftsprüfer | Wirtschaftsprüfer |

Source: Deutsche Telekom, Annual Report (2006), p. 198, www.deutschetelekom.com.

of Statutory Auditors (KIBR). It also recommended that the Polish Securities and Exchange Commission (KPWIG) should develop a process for review of financial information based on IFRS.

An example of an audit report for a Polish company is shown in Exhibit 14.17. The auditors give a 'present truly and fairly' opinion. Corporate governance codes are not mentioned but consistency between the management report and the financial statements is noted.

Exhibit 14.16 Audit report, Heineken

Auditor's report

To: Annual General Meeting of Shareholders of Heineken N.V.

Report on the financial statements

We have audited the 2006 financial statements of Heineken N.V., Amsterdam as set out on pages 67 to 121. The financial statements consist of the consolidated financial statements and the Company financial statements. The consolidated financial statements comprise the consolidated balance sheet as at 31 December 2006, the income statement, statement of recognised income and expense and statement of cash flows for the year then ended, and a summary of significant accounting policies and other explanatory notes. The Company financial statements comprise the Company balance sheet as at 31 December 2006, the Company income statement for the year then ended and the notes.

Management's responsibility

The Executive Board is responsible for the preparation and fair presentation of the financial statements in accordance with International Financial Reporting Standards as adopted by the European Union and with Part 9 of Book 2 of the Netherlands Civil Code, and for the preparation of the report of the Executive Board in accordance with Part 9 of Book 2 of the Netherlands Civil Code. This responsibility includes: designing, implementing and maintaining internal control relevant to the preparation and fair presentation of the financial statements that are free from material misstatement, whether due to fraud or error; selecting and applying appropriate accounting policies; and making accounting estimates that are reasonable in the circumstances.

Auditor's responsibility

Our responsibility is to express an opinion on the financial statements based on our audit. We conducted our audit in accordance with Dutch law. This law requires that we comply with ethical requirements and plan and perform our audit to obtain reasonable assurance whether the financial statements are free from material misstatement. An audit involves performing procedures to obtain audit evidence about the amounts and disclosures in the financial statements. The procedures selected depend on the auditor's judgement, including the assessment of the risks of material misstatement of the financial statements, whether due to fraud or error. In making those risk assessments, the auditor considers internal control relevant to the entity's preparation and fair presentation of the financial statements in order to design audit procedures that are appropriate in the circumstances, but not for the purpose of expressing an opinion on the effectiveness of the entity's internal control. An audit also includes evaluating the appropriateness of accounting policies used and the reasonableness of accounting estimates made by management, as well as evaluating the overall presentation of the financial statements.

We believe that the audit evidence we have obtained is sufficient and appropriate to provide a basis for our audit opinion.

Opinion with respect to the consolidated financial statements

In our opinion, the consolidated financial statements give a true and fair view of the financial position of Heineken N.V. as at 31 December 2006, and of its result and its cash flow for the year then ended in accordance with International Financial Reporting Standards as adopted by the European Union and with Part 9 of Book 2 of the Netherlands Civil Code.

Opinion with respect to the Company financial statements

In our opinion, the Company financial statements give a true and fair view of the financial position of Heineken N.V. as at 31 December 2006, and of its result for the year then ended in accordance with Part 9 of Book 2 of the Netherlands Civil Code.

Report on other legal and regulatory requirements

Pursuant to the legal requirement under 2:393 sub 5 part e of the Netherlands Civil Code, we report, to the extent of our competence, that the report of the Executive Board as set out on pages 8 to 61 is consistent with the financial statements as required by 2:391 sub 4 of the Netherlands Civil Code.

Amsterdam, 20 February 2007

KPMG ACCOUNTANTS N.V.

J.F.C van Everdigen RA

Source: Heineken N.V. Annual Report, 2006, pp. 122–123.

Exhibit 14.17 Audit report, Telekomunikacja Polska

Independent Auditors' report

To the Shareholder of Telekomunikacja Polska SA

1 We have audited the attached consolidated financial statements[1] of the Telekomunikacja Polska Capital Group ('the Group'), for which the holding company is Telekomunikacja Polska S.A. ('the Company') located in Warsaw at 18 Twarda St., for the year ended 31 December 2006, containing:
   – the consolidated balance sheet as at 31 December 2006 with total assets amounting to 32,611 million zlotys,
   – the consolidated profit and loss account for the period from 1 January 2006 to 31 December 2006 with a net profit amounting to 2,096 million zlotys,
   – the consolidated statement of changes in shareholders' equity for the period from 1 January 2006 to 31 December 2006 with a net increase in shareholders' equity amounting to 113 million zlotys,
   – the consolidated cash flow statement for the period from 1 January 2006 to 31 December 2006 with a net cash outflow amounting to 797 million zlotys and
   – the additional notes and explanations
   ('the attached consolidated financial statements').

2 The Company's management is responsible for the preparation and fair presentation of these financial statements in accordance with International Accounting Standards and International Financial Reporting Standards as adopted by the European Union. This responsibility includes: designing, implementing and maintaining internal control relevant to the preparation and fair presentation of financial statements that are free from material mis-statement, whether due to fraud or error; selecting and applying appropriate accounting policies; and making accounting estimates that are reasonable in the circumstances.

3 We conducted our audit of the attached consolidated financial statements in accordance with:
   – chapter 7 of the Accounting Act, dated 29 September 1994 ('the Accounting Act'),
   – the auditing standards issued by the National Chamber of Auditors, and
   – International Standards on Auditing,
   in order to obtain reasonable assurance whether these financial statements are free of material misstatement. In particular, the audit included examining, to a large extent on a test basis, documentation supporting the amounts and disclosures in the attached consolidated financial statements. The audit also included assessing the account-ing principles adopted and used and significant estimates made by the Management Board, as well as evaluating the overall presentation of the attached consolidated financial statements. We believe our audit has provided a reasonable basis to express our opinion on the attached consolidated financial statements treated as a whole.

4 In our opinion, the attached consolidated financial statements, in all material respects:
   – present truly and fairly all information material for the assessment of the results of the Group's operations for the period from 1 January 2006 to 31 December 2006, as well as its financial position as at 31 December 2006;
   – have been prepared, in all material aspects, in accordance with International Accounting Standards and Interna-tional Financial Reporting Standards as adopted by the European Union;
   – are in accordance with the provisions of laws affecting the content of the attached consolidated financial statements.

5 Without qualifying our opinion, we draw attention to the following issue:
   As more fully explained in notes 32 (d) and 32 (e) to the consolidated financial statements the Company is a party to a number of legal and administrative proceedings. To the extent the obligations in respect of these proceed-ings could be reliably measured the Company has made provisions in this respect, which represent the Com-pany's best estimate of the amounts that according to the Company's Management Board are more likely than not to be paid. The amount of the liabilities depends on a number of future events, the outcome of which is uncertain and as a consequence the amount of the provisions may change at a future date.

6 We have read the 'Management Board's Report[2] on the Group's activity for the period from 1 January 2006 to 31 December 2006 and the rules of preparation of the annual consolidated financial statements' ('the Directors' Report') and concluded that the information derived from the attached consolidated financial statements recon-ciles with these financial statements. The information included in the Directors' Report corresponds with the relevant regulations of the Decree on current and periodic information.'

on behalf of Ernst & Young Audit Sp.z o.o.Rondo ONZ 1,00-124 Warszawa Reg.No.130

Wojciech Putkownik
Certified Auditor
No.10477/7677

Jacek Hryniuk
Member of Management Board
Certified Auditor
No.9262/6958

Warsaw, 15 February 2007

[1] As presented on pages 36–81.
[2] As included in the Annual Report filed on the Warsaw Stock Exchange
Source: Telekomunikacja Polska SA, annual report (2006), p. 82.

14.7 **Corporate reporting issues**

The IAS Regulation brought *de jure* harmonization to European listed companies from 2005 but only in those areas where IFRS are applicable. The remainder of the corporate report is open to a mixture of national and international influences. This section considers some of them.

14.7.1 'True and fair view'

The idea of a 'true and fair view' was introduced to the Fourth Directive at a late stage in its development. The translations to the languages of member states reflected different perceptions in each country. Parker and Nobes (1994) explored the meaning of 'true and fair' across a range of European countries. Aisbitt and Nobes (2001) examined the implementation of the true and fair view requirement into the laws of Austria, Finland and Sweden. The translation issue will be no less problematic as IAS 1 is taken into national languages. Evans (2003) examined the nature of the IAS 1 wording on 'present fairly' and discussed the likely interpretation in Germany. This section explains the perceptions of 'true and fair view' in national legislation in the period immediately prior to adoption of IAS 1 in the EU.

14.7.1.1 France

The wording used in French legislation is *'une image fidèle'*, translated as 'a faithful picture'. The use of the word 'faithful' had historical precedents and left sufficient ambiguity to satisfy national legislators. Parker and Nobes (1994, p. 80) classify the French approach as allowing the arrival of the true and fair view to permit some change towards substance rather than form. It became available to directors and auditors to be used as a basis for interpretation or for guidance where no rules existed.

14.7.1.2 Germany

The wording in the law which enacts the Fourth Directive is '(*unter Beachtung der Grundsätze ordnungsmässiger Buchführung) ein den tatsächlichen Verhältnissen entsprechendes Bild*'. It is translated as '(in compliance with accepted accounting principles) a picture in accordance with the facts'. The German legislators found it difficult to bring the concept of 'true and fair' into German law, and their wording differs from that of the official German-language version of the directive. Parker and Nobes (1994) classify the German approach to 'true and fair' as one which cannot be used to justify a departure from the law.

14.7.1.3 The Netherlands[88]

The wording of the Dutch law, incorporating the Fourth Directive, uses the phrase *'een getrouw beeld'*, which may be translated as 'a faithful picture'. Nobes's (1984) classification of The Netherlands in respect to 'true and fair view' is that it is used by directors and auditors as the basic principle in interpreting the law and guidelines. The 1970 law had used wording which could be translated as 'presents faithfully, clearly and consistently over time' and also 'presents an insight such that a well-founded opinion can be

---

[88] Zeff *et al.* (1999).

formed'. Thus in The Netherlands, as in the UK and Ireland, the notion of a true and fair view predated the Fourth Directive.

14.7.1.4 Poland[89]

We explained earlier that the 1994 Act was revised in 2000, with the majority of revisions only coming into force in the financial year beginning 1 January 2002. The true and fair requirement is contained in Article 4(1) of both the old and the revised Act and the Polish words used are unchanged (*rztelnie* and *jasno*). The paragraphs are almost identical, but the revision is substantive and consists of omitting the requirement that accounting principles are applied in a way that is *prawidlowo*, namely in accordance with the rules. The explanation of this change lies in a new Article 4(2) which was not present in the 1994 Act. It reads:

> Events, including economic transactions, are included in the books of account and disclosed in the financial statements in accordance with their economic substance.

Also new from 1 January 2002 is Article 10(3) which reads:

> In matters not regulated by the provisions of the Act, the entity, when choosing an accounting principle or policy, may use national accounting standards issued by the Accounting Standards Board so authorised by the Act. In the event of the absence of an appropriate national standard, international accounting standards may be used.

14.7.2 Formats of financial statements

European companies have for many years been accustomed to following the well-defined formats of the Fourth and Seventh Directives (see Chapter 12). Since 2005, group financial statements have been prepared under IAS 1 which is quite flexible on presentation. Individual companies may continue to be regulated by the Directives.

Until the 1990s it was common for groups to include the parent company financial statements in the group annual report published in English. The parent company financial statements followed national practice in presentation and often looked quite different from the group financial statements which took advantage of the flexible approach to consolidated financial statements then existing for companies with foreign listings. Even before 2005 these separate individual financial statements were disappearing from the consolidated annual report. One of the few remaining examples of inclusion of the parent company financial statements is Alcatel (see Exhibit 14.18).

Exhibit 14.18 shows the assets (*actif*) above and liabilities and equity below (*passif*). Liabilities are categorized by their nature but not by date of maturity. The separation of current and non-current liabilities is given in notes to the accounts. The categories gross cost, accumulated depreciation (or provision for depreciation) and net book value are used for all assets, whether current or fixed. This example shows the persistence of the presentation favoured by the parent company prior to the introduction of IFRS for group financial statements. It may be that the different presentations will become less apparent to an international readership if the group accounts in English omit the parent company financial statements.

---

[89] We are indebted to Dr Marek Schroeder, University of Birmingham, for the information in this section.

Exhibit 14.18 Balance sheet of parent company, Alcatel

PARENT COMPANY BALANCE SHEETS AT DECEMBER 31

ASSETS (in millions of euros)	Notes	2006 Gross value	2006 Depreciation	2006 Net value	2005 Net value	2004 value
Intangible assets	**(7)**	**157.4**	**(27.8)**	**129.6**	**21.4**	**1.9**
Land		–	–	–	–	–
Buildings		0.1	(0.1)	–	–	–
Other property, plant and equipment		0.4	(0.4)	–	–	0.1
Property, plant and equipment		**0.5**	**(0.5)**	**–**	**–**	**0.1**
Investments in subsidiaries and associates	(8)	28,849.1	(11,148.0)	17,701.1	7,417.1	10,378.4
Receivables from subsidiaries and associates	(9)	0.6	(0.6)	–	–	–
Other financial assets	(9)	11,968.2	(224.5)	11,743.7	10,873.2	9,602.7
Investments and other non-current assets		**40,817.9**	**(11,373.1)**	**29,444.8**	**18,290.3**	**19,981.1**
Total non-current assets		**40,975.8**	**(11,401.4)**	**29,574.4**	**18,311.7**	**19,983.1**
Accounts receivable and other current assets	(16)	1,981.7	(0.4)	1,981.3	2,423.1	3,257.2
Marketable securities	(10)	784.7	–	784.7	1,625.2	1,720.2
Cash	(10)	1,172.9	–	1,172.9	1,515.2	1,428.9
Total current assets		**3,939.3**	**(0.4)**	**3,938.9**	**5,563.5**	**6,406.3**
Prepayments and deferred charges		26.2	–	26.2	26.2	115.9
Total assets	**(6)**	**44,941.3**	**(11,401.8)**	**33,539.5**	**23,901.4**	**26,505.3**

LIABILITIES AND STOCKHOLDERS' EQUITY

(in millions of euros)	Notes	2006 Before appropriation	2006 After appropriation*	2005 After appropriation	2004 After appropriation
Capital stock		4,619.4	4,619.4	2,857.1	2,610.9
Additional paid-in capital		15,353.6	15,353.6	8,173.5	7,757.6
Reserves		2,148.9	2,237.9	2,148.9	2,134.4
Retained earnings		2,303.8	3,624.5	2,299.7	2,152.2
Net income for the year		1,779.2	–	–	–
Statutory provisions		–	–	–	–
Shareholders' equity	**(12)**	**26,204.9**	**25,835.4**	**15,479.2**	**14,655.1**
Other equity items	**(13)**	**–**	**–**	**–**	**645.0**
Reserves for liabilities and charges	**(14)/(19)**	**191.6**	**191.6**	**192.5**	**2,826.2**
Bonds convertible in new or existing shares (OCEANE)	(15)/(16)	1,022.4	1,022.4	1,022.4	1,022.4
Other bonds and notes issued	(15)/(16)	1,421.3	1,421.3	1,937.3	2,741.8
Bank borrowings and overdrafts	(16)	74.1	74.1	122.7	160.5
Miscellaneous borrowings	(16)	1,617.2	1,617.2	1,003.2	227.6
Financial debt		**4,135.0**	**4,135.0**	**4,085.6**	**4,152.3**
Taxation and social security	(16)	12.6	12.6	15.9	14.7
Other liabilities	(16)	2,995.2	3,364.7	4,067.7	4,211.7
Liabilities		**3,007.8**	**3,377.3**	**4,083.6**	**4,226.4**
Currency translation adjustment		0.2	0.2	60.5	0.3
Total liabilities and shareholders' equity		**33,539.5**	**33,539.5**	**23,901.4**	**26,505.3**

*Proposed.

Source: Alcatel-Lucent Reference document (2006), p. 198, www.alcatel-lucent.com.

14.7.3 Charts of accounts

14.7.3.1 France[90]

Early attempts had been made at creating a chart of accounts, particularly in 1942 (see also section 14.5). In 1946 the government of France established a commission on accounting standards leading to a code (Plan Comptable Général) in 1947 which contained some of the features of the 1942 code. One of the genuinely French features was to have no fixed relationship between management accounts and financial accounts (splitting the chart into two sets of related accounts). The code gradually became standard practice although it was not mandatory under law. It had a strong influence on the training of professional accountants and remained substantially unaltered until the implementation of the Fourth Directive in the 1982 Plan Comptable Général.

The national accounting code (Plan Comptable Général)[91] is at the heart of financial reporting and accounting. The code is revised at relatively infrequent intervals, with amendments and additions occurring more frequently. The 1999 PCG was issued by the CRC with approval of the CNC and under ministerial order. It has been amended subsequently in matters of detail. There are two central objectives of the PCG:

- standardizing the organization of the accounting system of the enterprise;
- standardizing the presentation of financial results and position.

Taken together, these ensure that the accounting records are maintained in a form which permits production of the required form of financial statements.

The PCG is very detailed, using a decimal numbering system to specify major headings and greater levels of detail. The highest level of heading is shown in Exhibit 14.19.

The detailed accounts under each heading are also specified using further digits. Two-digit examples are given in Exhibit 14.20.

Exhibit 14.19 Main classes of financial accounts

Class 1	Capital accounts
Class 2	Fixed asset accounts
Class 3	Stocks and work in progress accounts
Class 4	Accounts for debts receivable and payable
Class 5	Financial accounts
Class 6	Accounts for charges
Class 7	Income accounts

Exhibit 14.20 Examples of two-digit codes in the Plan Comptable Général

21	Tangible fixed assets
40	Suppliers and related accounts
39	Any two-digit account ending in 9 indicates a provision against an asset

---

[90] Griziaux (1999), pp. 1178–1179; Fortin (1991).

[91] Standish (2000); CNC website (2000), www.finances.gouv.fr/CNCompta/.

Exhibit 14.21	Examples of three-digit and four-digit codes

21 – Tangible fixed assets
    211 – Land
        2111 – Undeveloped land
        2112 – Serviced land
        2113 – Underground and above-ground sites
        2114 – Mining sites
40 – Suppliers and related accounts
    401 – Suppliers
        4011 – Suppliers – Purchases of goods and services
        4017 – Suppliers – Contract performance holdbacks
    403 – Suppliers – Bills payable
    404 – Fixed-asset suppliers
        4041 – Suppliers – Fixed-asset purchases
        4047 – Fixed-asset suppliers – Contract performance holdbacks
29 – Provisions for diminution in value of fixed assets
39 – Provisions for diminution in value of stocks and work in progress

Three-digit and four-digit codes are also used for detailed recording (Exhibit 14.21). They can be aggregated to the two-digit level in order to present information for financial reporting.

The PCG contains the following main sections:

TITLE I	–	OBJECT AND PRINCIPLES OF ACCOUNTING
TITLE II	–	DEFINITION OF ASSETS, LIABILITIES, INCOME AND CHARGES
TITLE III	–	ACCOUNTING RECOGNITION AND VALUATION RULES
TITLE IV	–	KEEPING, STRUCTURE AND FUNCTIONING OF ACCOUNTS (including list of accounts codes)
TITLE V	–	FINANCIAL STATEMENTS (annual account, balance sheet, profit and loss account and notes)

Effectively it is a very detailed manual for the preparation of accounts. It does not have the status of a law, but application of the classification is compulsory. Furthermore there are industry-specific versions. The PCG requires interpretation of some of the rules and it is not a full source of information on all matters. It does, however, contain extensive guidelines for explanation of the principles.

The general principles of the PCG are intended to produce a true and fair view (*image fidèle*) by application of prudence, consistency (*régularité*) and faithful reckoning (*sincérité*). The CNC continues to give advice on the PCG. In April 2000 it issued advice relating to liabilities, covering definitions and valuation.

14.7.3.2 Germany

There are two meanings of the phrase 'chart of accounts' in Germany. One is an accounts framework (*Kontenrahmen*), setting an outline chart for companies in a particular sector. The other is a detailed accounts plan (*Kontenplan*) developed by a business for its own use.

Both use a decimal system of classification. Ten classes of accounts, numbered 0–9, are each divided into ten account groups. Each account group has ten account types and each account type has ten sub-accounts; further subdivision is permitted.[92] The numbers so created form the account number.

Charts of accounts have a long history in Germany, first appearing around 1900. A comprehensive system was developed by Schär in 1911, but the leading authority was the work of Schmalenbach published in 1927, called *Kontenrahmen*. Since 1945 it is not mandatory to use a particular *Kontenrahmen* for a sector. Industry frameworks have continued to be issued by the Association of German Industry and have been adapted to take account of the Fourth Directive.

14.7.3.3 The Netherlands[93]

The Civil Code deals with financial statements and related matters in Title 9 of Book 2, *Annual Accounts and Directors' Report*. The 15 sections are shown in Exhibit 14.22.

As explained earlier, there are three sources for companies which intend to follow generally acceptable accounting principles in The Netherlands. The word 'acceptable' is used here rather than 'accepted' because there is no specific book of accounting standards such as that found in the USA or the UK. The first source is to follow the Civil Code as statute law. The second is to take note of the verdicts of the Enterprise Chamber and the third is to apply the recommendations of the Council for Annual Reporting (RJ). This combination is essential as the key rule for accounting in The Netherlands (comparable with achieving a 'true and fair view' in the UK).

| Exhibit 14.22 | Sections of the Civil Code |

1, 2	General provisions
3	Regulations concerning the balance sheet and the notes
4	Regulations concerning the profit and loss account and the notes
5	Special regulations concerning the notes
6	Regulations concerning valuation principles and the principles underlying the determination of financial results
7	Executive directors' report
8	Other data
9	Audit requirements
10	Publication
11	Exemptions based on the size of the company
12	Specific industries
13	Consolidated financial statements
14	Provisions for banks
15	Provisions for insurance companies

---

[92] www.accaglobal.com/members/services/int_mobility/factsheets/germany/procedures.

[93] Klaassen (2001).

The Enterprise Chamber can only react to complaints – it cannot initiate action. The person making a complaint must prove a direct interest in the financial statements of the company and must state the perceived deficiency. The court hears the complainant, the company's view and the auditor's explanation. Because the Chamber is part of a formal legal process, the number of judgments is relatively small. The formation of the Chamber was seen as being an alternative to creating a supervisory body like the US SEC.

As explained earlier (see section 14.3.4), the recommendations of the Council for Annual Reporting (RJ), published in the form of guidelines, are not a statutory requirement. They are, however, regarded as authoritative pronouncements and an important frame of reference for the auditor in forming an opinion on financial statements. Departures from the guidelines of the RJ are possible and are not referred to in the auditor's report.

14.7.3.4 Poland[94]

Uniform charts of accounts were used from 1940 to 1989. Since then, the Accounting Act requires each entity to prepare its own chart of accounts. Model charts of accounts may be used to unify groups of operations and reduce the work of creating a chart. Model charts may be devised by the SEC for listed companies or by the Ministry of Finance for other companies.

The history of charts of accounts in Poland is described by Jaruga and Szychta (1997), tracing the development and changes from German occupation in the 1940s to the first Polish Uniform Plan of Accounting in 1946–49, a reform in the 1950s to a Soviet plan of accounts and then a return to a more 'continental' approach in the late 1980s. Although the law from 1991 allowed companies to design their own chart, the authors reported a prevailing opinion that a standard chart (such as the Model chart) would facilitate training and application. The counter opinion of the regulatory experts was that greater flexibility would result in a better reflection of economic reality.

14.7.4 Business combinations[95]

A survey by FEE (2002), using a mixture of *de jure* and *de facto* analysis, showed the diversity of national practices across 21 European countries in 1999–2000 in the treatment of business combinations. The survey found that the purchase method was allowed in every country studied, while pooling of interest was allowed in most countries but not in Austria, the Czech Republic and Hungary. Of the 96 business combinations examined, 75 used the purchase method and 21 used pooling of interests. Some of the pooling of interest cases were effectively acquisitions but the alternative treatment was allowed under national law.

Most countries required goodwill to be capitalized and amortized. During the period of the survey, nine countries allowed direct write-off against reserves (Austria, the Czech Republic, Denmark, France, Germany, Italy, Luxembourg, The Netherlands and Switzerland). Only one company in the survey used the impairment approach, which had already been established in the USA at that time. There was a wide range of amortization periods used by companies, with 20 years being a common period but phrases such as

---

[94] Jaruga and Schroeder (2001), p. 1603.
[95] FEE (2002).

'up to 20 years' being seen as unhelpful to readers. Some countries presumed a period of five years for amortization in the absence of further information (Belgium, Denmark, Finland, Italy, Poland, Portugal, Sweden).

Some countries allowed IAS or US GAAP for group accounts, giving further flexibility within any country. At the time of the FEE report this flexibility in consolidated accounts applied in Austria, Germany, Finland, the Czech Republic, Denmark, France, Italy and The Netherlands. The application of IFRS to all European listed companies from 2005 was thus a major change in harmonization of group accounting across Europe, in the area of business combinations. Some companies were already applying IFRS, although not always in full.

14.7.5 Secrecy versus transparency

14.7.5.1 France

Gray (1988) (see Chapter 7) classified French accounting as relatively low on the secrecy scale compared with Germany or the less developed Latin countries. This is consistent with the extensive use of notes to the accounts and various types of additional disclosure such as segmental reporting, the management report and the statutory disclosures on corporate social and environmental reporting, sometimes referred to as 'the social balance sheet'.

Notes on the accounts[96]

The balance sheet, profit and loss account and notes to the accounts must be read as a whole. It is specifically stated in the PCG 1999 that the three documents form *un tout*, and it is also stated in the Commercial Code in the phrase *un tout indissociable*.

The notes are regarded as complementing and commenting on the information in the balance sheet and profit and loss account. They may also supply additional information where the rules are not sufficient to give a true and fair view. Their role also covers describing and justifying changes in accounting policies or presentation of information. It is clear from the Commercial Code that the notes should be used to provide the additional information necessary for a true and fair view. Giving additional information in the balance sheet and profit and loss account is not acceptable.

Two sets of notes are required – one for the parent company and one for the group. It should be noted that in English-language versions of group accounts the parent company accounts and notes are often omitted.

Management report

The 1985 Act incorporates the provision of the Seventh Directive for a review of the development of the business and discussion of important post-balance-sheet events, likely future developments and research and development. This may be seen as comparable with the directors' report in UK companies' annual reports. The stock market regulations require the management report to be published with the half-yearly results as well as with the annual report. Stock market reporting obligations add further recommendations about information such as risk disclosures.[97]

---

[96] Parker (1996).

[97] Standish (2000), sections 2.1, 2.2.

Social and environmental reporting

A law relating to company law reform in non-accounting matters, passed in 1977, required French undertakings having a significant number of employees (more than 300) to present to the staff committee a *bilan social*, or employment report.[98] The *bilan social* is not part of the notes to the accounts but is sometimes published in the annual report. It may be regarded as a type of social balance sheet although it is presented as a narrative report. The information required by the law covered employment, wages and related costs, health and safety conditions, other working conditions, staff training, industrial relations and living conditions where these are the responsibility of the employer.

This long-standing recognition of the importance of social reporting was consolidated in the Law on New Economic Regulations (Nouvelles Régulations Économiques, NRE) passed in 2001 and implemented from 2002. It represented a major update of France's company law framework. All companies listed on the main market must report on a number of social and environmental issues. Information is required about the working conditions of employees, equality policies, health and safety arrangements, community and charity work, use of energy sources, measures to limit the company's impact on the environment, compliance with environmental legislation and reduction of environmental risk.

Public access to information

The Ministry of Justice runs, through the Tribunaux de Commerce, the register of commerce. This is where all corporations of any kind must deposit for public access their articles of association. Limited liability corporations must also deposit their annual financial statements.

The Centrale des bilans, run by the Bank of France, receives data voluntarily from 28,000 large companies. The companies receive in return reports about their own relative performance and balance sheets. A further analysis of the company's performance and financial health is available for a fee. The Bank of France also provides information on a company's indebtedness through the Centrale des risques. Ratings of companies for use by lenders are derived from the Centrale des risques and are available through the Fichier bancaire des entreprises.

14.7.5.2 Germany

Gray (1988) classified German accounting as highly secretive by reputation. However, the extent of information provided is quite extensive and the reputation for secrecy may have been created by concentrating on a few items such as hidden reserves. Since 1998 the change in regulation of group accounting and the pressures of competing in international capital markets have resulted in some German companies providing very informative segmental information and detailed management reports. Leuz and Wüstemann (2003) challenge the perception that German accounting is uninformative. They show the importance of private information channels but acknowledge that arm's length or outside investors relying primarily on public disclosures may be less well informed in the German system than they would be in the Anglo-American economies. They also argue that the voluntary changes to IFRS (prior to 2005) did not fundamentally alter the German accounting system and its reliance on private information channels and insider governance. Accounting standards leave discretion and the exercise of that discretion

---

[98] Parker (1996), p. 335; Scheid and Walton (1992), p. 164.

depends on controlling insiders' incentives. Reform to accounting standards must be accompanied by changes to the institutional framework and strengthening of corporate governance.

Notes on the accounts

Notes on the accounts are a mandatory part of the financial statements. The German view is that the balance sheet, profit and loss account and notes must, taken together, produce a true and fair view. The 'true and fair' test is not applied to each element separately. Particularly important use of notes to the accounts are:

- disclosure of methods of accounting and valuation;
- effects of accounting methods applied solely for tax reasons;
- information on receivables and liabilities;
- information on changes in equity as shown in the statement of appropriation of profit;
- information on employees;
- remuneration and benefits of board members;
- information on shareholdings.

Before 1987, notes had to be prepared and disclosed only by public companies and certain large private companies. The extension of notes to financial statements of all companies is therefore regarded as an important change resulting from the Fourth Directive.

Management report

Companies are required by the law (HGB) to prepare a management report. It must be consistent with the financial statements. Additional requirements may be set by the Deutsche Börse.

14.7.5.3 The Netherlands

Management report[99]

The report by the managing board of directors is prescribed in the Civil Code. The report should contain a general review, information on the dividends and financial results, a balance sheet profile and an indication of prospects. In this way, past, present and future issues are discussed. It reports also on issues of employment and research and development activities. The indication of prospects relates to capital investments, finance, employees' development, circumstances related to net sales development and profitability analysis. The requirement to show a true and fair view applies to this report.

There are therefore similarities with the operating and financial review provided by UK companies, the management report provided by German companies and the management discussion and analysis required in the USA.

Environmental report[100]

The Environmental Management Act (1997) established a requirement for an environmental report to the government. Companies in targeted industries agree ('covenant') with the government to provide an environmental report. It is available to interested

---

[99] Klaassen (2001), pp. 1999–2000.
[100] Hoffmann (2003).

parties on demand. The Environmental Reporting Decree (1999) required that certain categories of company (those which have potentially serious effects on the environment) must produce two environmental reports – one for the government and one for the public.

14.8 Comparative research studies

Comparative research studies may focus on similarities and differences in regulation (*de jure* comparisons) or in practice (*de facto* comparisons). Consolidated financial statements of listed companies are the most readily available source of information for *de facto* comparisons. From 2005 onwards the common application of IFRS will change the approach of researchers to *de facto* comparisons. One approach will be to focus on companies that do not apply IFRS (individual companies within listed groups, or else unlisted groups). This will offer greater challenges in gaining access to the information and to collaboration across researchers with suitable language skills and national knowledge. Another approach will be to use statistical analysis to detect underlying differences among the consolidated accounts of companies that claim to be harmonized with IFRS.

There is a large body of comparative research studies across European countries where the evidence has been taken from information published by companies. Section 14.8.1 explains how harmonization studies have been carried out on the basis of information disclosed by companies.

14.8.1 Harmonization studies

The methods used in harmonization studies are explained in Chapter 7. The technical detail of the results of these studies may no longer reflect accounting practice in the respective countries but the research studies remain useful for two reasons. They show how comparative studies of harmonization may be carried out where accounting practices remain beyond the IFRS harmonization process and they show the extent of diversity that existed prior to the universal application of IFRS in consolidated accounts of listed companies.

In section 7.5.4.1 we discuss in detail the research of Archer *et al.* (1995) based on the C-index and the work of Cañibano and Mora (2000), also based on the C-index. We show in that section how this type of research demonstrated the relative progress of the harmonization process in areas of accounting diversity such deferred taxation, goodwill, finance leases and foreign currency translation.

Hermann and Thomas (1995) used the I-index in their comparative study. They found that, of the countries classed as legalistic (Belgium, France, Germany and Portugal), France had the highest bi-country I-index when compared with the fairness-orientated countries (Denmark, Ireland, UK and The Netherlands). This was explained by Hermann and Thomas as reflecting French use of methods of consolidation influenced by the UK and the USA, and the influence of IAS on French group accounting practices. They found that Germany was the only country where all companies sampled used strict historical cost. Depreciation policy in the German sample, based on declining balance in the early years and then straight line in later life, was significantly different from the straight-line approach used by most other companies. This was attributed by Hermann and Thomas to the influence of tax law on accounting practice in Germany. In respect of accounting for goodwill they detected a change in practice in the accounts examined for

1992–93 year-ends, with 20 out of 30 companies capitalizing and amortizing goodwill. They found that the bi-country I-index was relatively high for pairings within the fairness-orientated grouping (Denmark, Ireland, The Netherlands and UK).

Emenyonu and Gray (1992) applied harmonization indexes and chi-square tests to 1989 data. They confirmed the flexibility of measurement practices in consolidated accounts of large French companies, compared with those of German and UK companies. The accounting policies examined were inventory valuation, depreciation methods, goodwill, research and development expenditure and foreign currency translation. In bi-country I-indices, Germany was second lowest to Portugal in harmonization with other EU countries in this range of accounting matters.

One of the problems faced by Emenyonu and Gray was non-disclosure of information. Some companies fail to explain an accounting policy that has been applied. Pierce and Weetman (2002) demonstrated the adjustments required to the C- and H-indices to take account of non-disclosure and applied these adjustments in a comparative study of deferred taxation in Ireland and Denmark over the period 1986 to 1993. The apparent increase in harmonization over the period was explained in part by the improvement in disclosure over the period as companies in both countries gave progressively clearer explanations of how they were accounting for deferred taxation.

Comparisons of mid- and eastern European countries tend to be qualitative descriptions and evaluations rather than quantitative studies. There have been more single country studies than comparative studies but one example of a large-scale comparative study was the special issue of *The European Accounting Review* (1995), Vol. 4(4), covering Eastern Europe.

14.8.2 Statistical analysis

From 2005 consolidated accounts of listed companies in the EU have applied IFRS. Within some IFRS there is a range of choices about measurement that will not be disclosed in the annual reports.[101] Accordingly statistical analysis of the reported accounting figures will be required to detect any variations in choices.

One type of statistical analysis which has been used to make cross-country comparisons follows the 'conservatism' literature (Basu, 1997) which applies econometric analysis (see section 9.5.1).

Giner and Rees (2001) studied companies in France, Germany and the UK over the period 1990 to 1998. They found that in all three countries there was a stronger relationship between bad news and earnings than between good news and earnings.

Lara and Mora (2004) found evidence of balance sheet conservatism and earnings conservatism across eight European countries in the period 1988–2000. They found that code-law-based countries were more balance sheet conservative. They also found that UK companies were more earnings conservative (recognizing bad news fastest compared with good news). While this kind of research still has some technical question marks, especially when it is effectively comparing stock market sentiment more than it is comparing accounting information, it is nevertheless an indication of the way forward in detecting the persistence of national or cultural choices underlying apparent standardization.

Another type of research question that relates accounting to stock market perceptions is to ask, 'What is the value relevance of accounting information constructed under

---

[101] Nobes (2006).

different accounting systems?' Value relevance is measured as the association between stock prices and accounting numbers (measured as earnings and book value of net assets). Share prices reflect, at least in part, the accounting numbers. Arce and Mora (2002) measured value relevance of earnings and book value in eight countries for the period 1990–98. They found that earnings were more value relevant than book value in market-oriented countries, and found the reverse in creditor-oriented countries. They speculated that IFRS could reduce the differences caused by accounting rules, but not those caused by institutional and cultural factors. Repetition of this type of research, once IFRS accounting is established, could give more scope for quantifying institutional and cultural differences across markets.

Summary and conclusions

The EU has made a major contribution to harmonization of accounting disclosure and measurement. The Fourth and Seventh Directives brought significant harmonization of disclosure and have provided a basis for emerging and transition economies to develop their accounting rules in a very short space of time as part of the process of joining the EU. The Directives did not achieve harmonization in measurement. The decision to work towards acceptance of IAS/IFRS rather than develop separate European standards was a major step towards harmonization in measurement as well as in disclosure. The process of endorsement, developing towards 2005, appeared cumbersome and unduly cautious but was justified as protecting regulatory independence of the EU. The disagreements over aspects of IAS 39 were disappointing, but overall the movement towards harmonization for listed groups of companies by 2005 was a major achievement for a large and diverse economic grouping that rivals the USA in size and potential economic influence. Annual reports published since 2005 continued to reflect diversity in areas not regulated by IFRS.

Key points from the chapter:

- The IAS Regulation takes precedence over national laws and the Fourth and Seventh Directives. It applies to the consolidated financial statements of listed groups.

- National legislation may require or permit other entities to apply the IAS Regulation. In the approach to 2005 there was great caution over such moves because of the potential impact on taxable profits and distributable profits.

- The distinction between common law and code law countries will have less influence on accounting practice that is harmonized under the IAS Regulation but may continue to affect those aspects of corporate reporting and assurance that remain under national direction.

- Corporate governance has developed rapidly in all member states, but it is important for users of financial information to understand the accompanying assurance mechanisms.

- Equity capital markets are taking a role in developing transparency and assurance in financial reporting. Again it is important for users of financial information to understand the processes of specific markets.

- The accounting profession continues to be very different in functions and state of development in different countries. This poses a challenge to the implementation and assurance of harmonized standards.

● There are accounting issues where evidence of diversity will continue, explained by institutional and cultural differences. Examples are the meaning of 'true and fair; the importance of charts of accounts; and the relative transparency of management reports or other narrative disclosures.

Questions

The following questions test your understanding of the material contained in the chapter and allow you to relate your understanding to the learning outcomes specified at the start of this chapter. The learning outcomes are repeated here. Each question is cross-referenced to the relevant section of the chapter.

Explain how member states of the EU will continue to have a national role, beyond the IAS Regulation, in setting accounting standards

1 What is the range of choices made by member states in deciding on whether to require or permit IFRS for individual companies within a listed group? (section 14.3.1)

2 What types of standard-setting body are found in France, Germany, The Netherlands and Poland? (sections 14.3.2 to 14.3.5)

Relate the institutional factors and external influences for a selection of member states to the framework set out in Chapter 6

3 How do the legal systems of France, Germany, The Netherlands and Poland fit into the classifications described in Chapter 6? (section 14.4.1)

4 How do the corporate governance systems of France, Germany, The Netherlands and Poland compare with the descriptions given in Chapter 3? (section 14.4.2)

5 How do the corporate financing systems of France, Germany, The Netherlands and Poland compare with the descriptions given in Chapter 6? (section 14.4.3)

6 How do the taxation systems of France, Germany, The Netherlands and Poland compare with the descriptions given in Chapter 6? (section 14.4.5)

7 How do the accounting professions in France, Germany, The Netherlands and Poland compare with the descriptions given in Chapter 6? (section 14.4.6)

8 How do the external influences on accounting practice in France, Germany, The Netherlands and Poland compare with those described in Chapter 6? (section 14.5)

Explain and evaluate the state of oversight and assurance in a selection of member states

9 What are the enforcement mechanisms used across member states to support the application of IFRS? (section 14.6)

10 How does enforcement differ in France, Germany, The Netherlands and Poland? (sections 14.6.1 to section 14.6.4)

Explain a selection of corporate reporting issues where national differences in regulation and in practice are likely to persist

11 What are the problems of comparing the meaning of 'a true and fair view' across member states? (section 14.7.1)

12 What are the benefits of the standard formats introduced by the Fourth and Seventh Directives? (section 14.7.2)

13 Why do some countries have charts of accounts but other countries implement accounting standards without such detailed guidance? (section 14.7.3)

14 What are the similarities and differences in narrative reporting in France, Germany and The Netherlands? (section 14.7.5)

Describe how comparative research studies have helped advance understanding of similarities and differences in accounting across Europe

15 What did research studies find about harmonization in the 1980s and 1990s? (section 14.8.1)

16 What has been discovered in the 'conservatism' studies based on statistical analysis? (section 14.8.2)

References and further reading

Aisbitt, S. and Nobes, C. (2001) 'The true and fair view requirement in recent national implementations', *Accounting and Business Research*, 31(2): 83–90.

Arce, M. and Mora, A. (2002) 'Empirical evidence of the effect of European accounting differences on the stock market valuation of earnings and book value', *European Accounting Review*, 11(3): 573–599.

Archer, S., Delvaille, P. and McLeay, S. (1995) 'The measurement of harmonization and the comparability of financial statement items: within-country and between-country effects', *Accounting and Business Research*, 25(98): 67–80.

Baker, C.R., Mikol, A. and Quick, R. (2001) 'Regulation of the statutory auditor in the European Union: a comparative survey of the United Kingdom, France and Germany', *European Accounting Review*, 10(4): 763–786.

Ballwieser, W. (2001) 'Germany – individual accounts', in Ordelheide, D. (ed.) *Transnational Accounting TRANSACC*. Basingstoke and New York: Palgrave.

Basu, S. (1997) 'The conservatism principle and the asymmetric timeliness of earnings', *Journal of Accounting and Economics*, 24: 3–37.

Cañibano, L. and Mora, A. (2000) 'Evaluating the statistical significance of *de facto* accounting harmonization: a study of European global players', *European Accounting Review*, 9(3): 349–370.

Charkham, J.P. (1994) *Keeping Good Company: A Study of Corporate Governance in Five Countries*. Oxford: Clarendon Press.

Comparative Study of Corporate Governance Codes Relevant to the European Union and Its Member States. Report by Weil, Gotshal & Manges, LLP in conjunction with EASD (European Association of Securities Dealers) and ECGN (European Corporate Governance Network), January 2002. Published by the European Commission, Internal Market Directorate General, http://europa.eu.int/comm/internal_market/en/company/company/news/corp-gov-codes-rpt_en.htm.

Crampton, A., Dorofeyev, S., Kolb, S. and Meyer-Hollatz, W. (2001) *UK: Germany: The main differences between UK and German Accounting Practice*, Deloitte & Touche, www.iasplus.com.

Ding, Y., Stolowy, H. and Tenehaus, M. (2003) '"Shopping around" for accounting practices: the financial statement presentation of French groups', *Abacus*, 39(1): 42–64.

Emenyonu, E.N. and Gray, S.J. (1992) 'EC accounting harmonization: an empirical study of measurement practices in France, Germany and the UK', *Accounting and Business Research*, Winter: 49–58.

Evans, L. (2003) 'The true and fair view and the "fair presentation" override of IAS 1', *Accounting and Business Research*, 33(4): 311–325.

FEE (2002) *FEE Survey on Business Combinations*, March, Fédération des Experts Comptables Européens.

FEE (2003) Discussion paper, *European Enforcement Coordination*.

Fortin, A. (1991) 'The 1947 French accounting plan: origins and influences on subsequent practice', *Accounting Historians Journal*, 19(2), December: 1–25.

Fraser, I., Henry, W. and Wallage, P. (2000) *The Future of Corporate Governance Insights from The Netherlands*. Edinburgh: The Institute of Chartered Accountants of Scotland.

Giner, B. and Rees, W. (2001) 'On the asymmetric recognition of good and bad news in France, Germany and the United Kingdom', *Journal of Business Finance and Accounting*, 28(9–10): 1285–1332.

Glaum, M. and Street, D.L. (2003) 'Compliance with the disclosure requirements of Germany's New Market: IAS versus US GAAP', *Journal of International Financial Management and Accounting*, 14(1): 64–100.

Gray, S.J. (1988) 'Towards a theory of cultural influence on the development of accounting systems internationally', *Abacus*, 24(1): 1–15.

Griziaux, J.-P. (1999) 'France: individual accounts', in Ordelheide, D. (ed.) *TRANSACC: Transnational Accounting*. London: Macmillan.

Haan, L. de and Hinloopen, J. (2002) *Ordering the preference hierarchies for internal finance, bank loans, bonds and shares*, Tinbergen Institute Discussion Paper TI 2002–072/2, www.tinbergen.nl.

Haller, A. (2002) 'Financial accounting developments in the European Union: past events and future prospects', *European Accounting Review*, 11(1): 153–190.

Hermann, D. and Thomas, W. (1995) 'Harmonization of accounting measurement practices in the European Community', *Accounting and Business Research*, 25(100): 253–265.

Hoffmann, E. (2003) 'Environmental reporting and sustainability reporting in Europe: an overview of mandatory reporting schemes in The Netherlands and France', Institute for Global Environmental Strategies, www.iges.or.jp/en/be/pdf/report7.pdf.

Hoogendoorn, M. (1996) 'Accounting and taxation in Europe – a comparative overview', *European Accounting Review*, 5(Supplement): 783–794.

Hoogendoorn, M.N. (2001) 'The Netherlands', in Alexander, D. and Archer, S. (eds) *European Accounting Guide*, 4th edn. New York: Aspen Law and Business.

Jaruga, A. and Schroeder, M. (2001) 'Poland', in Alexander, D. and Archer, S. (eds) *European Accounting Guide*, 4th edn. New York: Aspen Law and Business.

Jaruga, A. and Szychta, A. (1997) 'The origins and evolution of charts of accounts in Poland', *European Accounting Review*, 6(3): 509–526.

Klaassen, J. (2001) 'Netherlands – individual accounts', in Ordelheide, D. (ed.) *Transnational Accounting TRANSACC*. Basingstoke and New York: Palgrave.

Lara, J.M.G and Mora, A. (2004) 'Balance sheet versus earnings conservatism in Europe', *European Accounting Review*, 13(2): 261–292.

Leuz, C. and Wüstemann, J. (2003) *The Role of Accounting in the German Financial System*, Centre for Financial Studies, Johann Wolfgang Goethe Universität, Frankfurt am Main, No. 2003/16.

Nobes, C.W. (1984) *International Classification of Financial Reporting*. London: Croom Helm.

Nobes, C.W. (1998) 'Towards a general model of the reasons for international differences in financial reporting', *Abacus*, 34(2), September: 162–187.

Nobes, C.W. (2006) 'The survival of international differences under IFRS: towards a research agenda', *Accounting and Business Research*, 36(3): 233–245.

OECD (2003a) *OECD Economic Surveys: France*, Vol. 2003/11. Paris: Organization for Economic Cooperation and Development.

OECD (2003b) *OECD Economic Surveys, Germany*, Vol. 2002, Supplement No. 4, January. Paris: Organization for Economic Cooperation and Development.

OECD (2004) *OECD Economic Surveys: Poland*, Vol. 2004/8, June. Paris: Organization for Economic Cooperation and Development.

OECD (2005) *OECD Economic Surveys: Netherlands*, Vol. 2006/2, December. Paris: Organization for Economic Cooperation and Development.

OECD (2006a) *OECD Economic Surveys: Germany*, Vol. 2006/8, May. Paris: Organization for Economic Cooperation and Development.

OECD (2006b) *OECD Economic Surveys: Poland*, Vol. 2006/11, June. Paris: Organization for Economic Cooperation and Development.

OECD (2007) *OECD Economic Surveys, France*, Vol. 2007/13, June. Paris: Organization for Economic Cooperation and Development.

Parker, R.H. (1996) 'Harmonising the notes in the UK and France: a case study in *de jure* harmonisation', *European Accounting Review*, 5(2): 317–338.

Parker, R.H. and Nobes, C.W. (1994) *An International View of True and Fair Accounting*. London: Routledge.

Pierce, A. and Weetman, P. (2002) 'Measurement of de facto harmonisation: implications of non-disclosure for research planning and interpretation', *Accounting and Business Research*, 32(4): 259–273.

Rajan, R.G. and Zingales, L. (1995) 'What do we know about capital structure?', *Journal of Finance*, 50(5): 1421–1460.

Rathbone, D. (ed.) (1997) *The LGT Guide to World Equity Markets 1997*. London: Euromoney Publications.

Scheid, J.-C. and Walton, P. (1992) *European Financial Reporting – France*. London: Routledge.

Scheid, J.-C. and Walton, P. (2001) 'France', in Alexander, D. and Archer, S. (eds) *European Accounting Guide*, 4th edn. New York: Aspen Law and Business.

Smith, R. (2003) *Audit Committees*: *Combined Code Guidance*. A report and proposed guidance by an FRC-appointed group chaired by Sir Robert Smith. Financial Reporting Council, www.frc.org.uk/publications. Appendix III surveys other countries.

Standish, P. (2000) *Developments in French Accounting and Auditing 2000*, available at www.experts-comptables.fr/html/countries/gb/index.html.

Zeff, S.A., Buijink, W. and Camfferman, K. (1999) '"True and fair" in the Netherlands: *inzicht or getrouw beeld?*', *European Accounting Review*, 8(3), 523–548.

Newspapers, journals and web-based sources

FT World Accounting Report, published monthly by Financial Times Publications.

The Corporate Accountant, insert in *The Accountant*, UK monthly published by Lafferty Publications, London.

Ernst & Young (2004) *Doing Business in Poland*, www.ey.com/global/content.nsf/Poland_E/Doing_Business_in_Poland_2004.

AMF: Report on Internal Control and Corporate Governance, http://www.amf-france.org/Styles/Default/affiche_plan.asp?IdSec=6&IdRub=174&IdPlan=236&Id_Tab=0.

15 The United Kingdom

Learning outcomes

After reading this chapter you should be able to:

- Explain the development of accounting regulation.
- Explain the key institutional characteristics of the UK.
- Discuss the meaning of an 'Anglo-Saxon' system of accounting.
- Explain the structure and processes for oversight and assurance.
- Understand and explain features of the corporate reporting system that illustrate the continuing diversity of UK accounting practices.

15.1 Introduction

Accounting practice in the UK has a strong tradition of professionalism in which statute law and accounting standards set general bounds on requirements but the professional accountant exercises judgement in the application of those requirements. The accounting profession is well established and there is a relatively wide requirement for the audit of company accounts.

Tax law has developed separately from accounting law and there is no requirement that accounting profit must be calculated under fiscal rules to be an acceptable base for taxable profit. Membership of the European Union (EU) from 1972 has brought significant changes in UK company law and business regulation.

Company law concentrates primarily on protection of shareholders and creditors. Other sources of authority indicate a concern with wider stakeholders. From time to time there have been concerns to ensure that the needs of employees are addressed and that the public interest is taken into account. This type of concern depends to some extent on the political views of the government of the day. The Companies Act (2006) reflects the theme of 'a better business framework'[1] in the UK government's stated aim of minimizing regulatory complexity.

15.2 The country

The UK comprises The United Kingdom of England, Wales, Scotland and Northern Ireland. The Channel Islands and the Isle of Man have their own treasuries and separate systems of direct taxation. The term 'Great Britain' denotes the main land mass of the British Isles. Great Britain includes England, Scotland and Wales; it is a geographical description rather than a political unit. The term 'British Isles' is also a geographical description, covering England, Wales, Scotland, all of Ireland and the various islands around the coastlines of these countries.

The population is 59.7 million and has a relatively low rate of growth. Population density is greatest in the south-east of England.

The economy has shown growth of 2.7 per cent per annum over the period 1995–2005 (see Exhibit 15.1). Gross domestic product is created 75 per cent by services, 14 per cent by manufacturing industry and 10 per cent by other industry. Agriculture is a relatively small proportion (1 per cent) of gross domestic product.

---

[1] http://www.berr.gov.uk/bbf/index.html.

Exhibit 15.1 The UK: country profile

Population	59.7 million
Land mass	242,534 km^2
GDP per head	US$36,830
GDP per head in purchasing power parity	79.3 (USA = 100)
Origins of GDP:	%
Agriculture	1.0
Industry	23.6
Services	75.4
	%
Real GDP average annual growth 1995–2005	2.7
Inflation, average annual rate 2001–2006	1.7

Source: *The Economist Pocket World in Figures*, 2008 Edition, Profile Books Ltd.

Standards of living are relatively high in terms of life expectancy and a rate of population growth which is lower than the rate of growth of GDP. The rate of inflation, at 1.7 per cent per annum over the period 2001–06, is relatively low and indicates that accounting has not needed to show particular concern for price-adjusted measurement.

Visible imports have exceeded exports for several years. Exports comprise mainly manufactured and semi-manufactured products. The USA remains an important export destination although the EU as a whole takes a larger portion of UK exports. The largest single export market in the EU is Germany. Imports also came from the EU but a significant amount of trade exists with the USA. Trade with Commonwealth countries has fallen significantly since the UK joined the EU. Completion of the Channel Tunnel was a significant factor in allowing commercial freight traffic more ready access to continental Europe.

From the *Financial Times* annual survey, the top 500 world companies at the start of 2007 included 41 UK companies. The top ten UK listed companies are shown in Exhibit 15.2.

Exhibit 15.2 Top ten UK listed companies

Name	Market cap. ($000m)	Rank in Europe	Listed US	Sector
Royal Dutch Shell	109.2	2	yes	Oil & Gas Producers
BP	106.5	3	yes	Oil & Gas Producers
HSBC	103.0	4	yes	Banks
Glaxosmithkline	80.0	6	yes	Pharmaceuticals & Biotechnology
Vodafone Group	71.6	11	yes	Mobile Telecommunications
Royal Bank of Scotland	62.4	14	yes	Banks
Barclays	47.1	27	yes	Banks
AstraZeneca	41.1	35	yes	Pharmaceuticals & Biotechnology
Anglo American	39.7	37	no	Mining
HBOS	39.3	38	no	Banks

Source: 'Survey FT 500', *Financial Times*, March 2007, www.ft.com, www.nyse.com.

15.3 Development of accounting regulation

15.3.1 Company law[2]

The first Companies Act was passed in 1844, allowing limited liability companies to form by incorporation as joint-stock companies; prior to that time a separate Act of Parliament was required for each company formed. The Companies Act set out basic rules for accounting and auditing, but these were not effective until 1900. The company was seen as a private arrangement involving shareholders and directors, and secrecy in business matters was regarded as a virtue.

From 1907, there was a requirement to produce an audited balance sheet, but no stipulation as to format or content. A major change in public opinion about accounting disclosure resulted from the *Royal Mail Steam Packet* case (1932) (*R v Lord Kylsant* (1932) I KB 442, [1931] 1 All ER Rep 179), where a company produced a false prospectus by drawing on 'secret reserves' to give the appearance of profitability. That change in opinion led to the Companies Act 1948 specifying minimum levels of disclosure in annual accounts; an audited profit and loss account and balance sheet; group accounts; and enhancement of the rights and duties of auditors. The 1948 Act concentrated on disclosure and the protection of shareholders and creditors.

Matters of valuation, formats of financial statements and the method of recording transactions were all left to directors. There persisted a strong philosophy of minimal intervention by government and a defence of the rights of directors and shareholders to take decisions on corporate matters. Some changes extending disclosure were made in 1967, concentrating primarily on the report of the directors and additional notes to the balance sheet, and also including the significant improvement of disclosing turnover (sales). The principles of 1948 remained.

The most significant change in approach was taken in 1981 when the Fourth Directive was implemented in UK company law. This brought formats and valuation rules to company law for the first time. Concepts such as prudence, consistency, accruals and going concern were introduced to law, as was the requirement to report only realized profit in the profit and loss account. The 1981 Act was additional to the 1948 and subsequent Acts. All were consolidated in 1985. Implementation of the Seventh Directive was by way of the 1989 Act amending the principal Act of 1985.

The most recent phase of company law development (1998–2001) took the form of an extensive consultation on Company Law Reform.[3] Its aim was to create a modern framework for company law rather than continue to amend a structure created more than 100 years previously. The Companies Act 2006 is the outcome of that consultation.[4]

15.3.2 Consolidated accounts[5]

Evidence of consolidation by particular companies may be traced to the early years of the twentieth century but it was not until the aftermath of the *Royal Mail Steam Packet* case (1932) that the doubts of accountants were overcome. One aspect of that case had

---

[2] Napier (1995); Gordon and Gray (1994), Ch. 2.

[3] For an archive of the company law review process see http://www.berr.gov.uk/bbf/co-act-2006/clr-review/page22794.html.

[4] For the full text of the CA 2006, see http://www.berr.gov.uk/bbf/co-act-2006/index.html.

[5] Ma *et al.* (1991).

been reporting the results of subsidiaries only on receipt of dividends. Group accounting was made compulsory under the Companies Act 1948, based on definitions of a subsidiary which held until the incorporation of the Seventh Directive in the 1989 Act. The Companies Act 1948 gave no guidance on the method of group accounting; not even consolidation was compulsory. It was left to the professional accountant to determine the method of group accounting, and it would have satisfied the requirements of law to staple together all the accounts of parent and subsidiary. In this context, the influence of leading textbook writers was important.

The initial reaction to the Seventh Directive was that UK accounting already satisfied its requirements and the options on definition allowed the approach of the 1948 Act to continue. However, the experiences of the late 1980s, when companies began to avoid consolidation by working round the 1948 definitions, led to adoption of the more widely embracing options in the Seventh Directive which emphasized effective control rather than relying solely on percentage of ownership. The Companies Act 1989 extended the UK definition of a subsidiary and included recommendations on consolidation not previously found in UK law. The problems identified in the USA by the aftermath of Enron did not cause the same concerns with the UK regulation of consolidated accounts because the UK already had an accounting standard FRS 5[6] *Reporting the Substance of Transactions* which required companies to consider the commercial substance of the risks and rewards of investments, rather than focus only on rules based on percentage holdings.

Since 2005 the group accounts of UK listed companies have been required to comply with IFRS. From 2007 the group accounts of AIM[7] companies must also comply with IFRS. Non-listed companies may continue to apply the consolidation process set out in UK GAAP.[8]

15.3.3 Accounting standards

Prior to 1970 there was no system of written accounting standards in the UK. Professional bodies issued guidance to their members. The Institute of Chartered Accountants in England and Wales (ICAEW) in particular had a detailed handbook of recommendations on accounting and auditing matters, which was advisory in nature. Following some well-publicized company failures in the 1960s the major accountancy bodies established the Accounting Standards Committee (ASC), jointly owned by themselves. They each retained the power of veto over any standard and all proposals for new standards had to be approved by the Council of each member body. From 1970 to 1990 Statements of Standard Accounting Practice (SSAPs) were issued by the ASC.

Accounting standards have from time to time tried to meet economic needs of the day. High inflation in the early 1970s stimulated debate and practice in a variety of approaches to the problem. Initial inclinations towards general price levels in current purchasing power accounting then switched to specific price levels in current cost accounting, as advocated by Edwards and Bell (1961).

A major review of the standard-setting process (the Dearing Review) recommended that accounting standards should remain, as far as possible, the responsibility of preparers, users and auditors, rather than becoming a matter of regulation by law. An independent standard-setting body was seen to be necessary, with adequate financial support to

---

[6] ASB (1994).

[7] The Alternative Investment Market, used for transactions in shares of smaller and relatively new companies.

[8] See, for example, *Deloitte ukGAAP 2007* or *PWC Manual of Accounting: UK GAAP 2007*, both published by CCH, Kingston upon Thames.

carry out its work. Dearing also made recommendations about the organization of the standard-setting process.

Most of Dearing's recommendations were adopted in 1990, when the government announced the establishment of the Financial Reporting Council (FRC) and the Accounting Standards Board (ASB) as one arm of the FRC. Companies legislation has subsequently strengthened the role of the FRC and confirmed the authority of the ASB as the UK standard setter (see section 11.6.2.1)

15.4 Institutions

15.4.1 Political and economic system

The UK is a constitutional monarchy, having a parliamentary system of government. There are two Houses of Parliament at Westminster, in London. The House of Commons has over 600 elected members. Called Members of Parliament (MPs), they are elected by the adult population of the UK on a 'first-past-the-post' system. This system of election normally results in one of two political parties taking a clear majority as the basis of government for a term of office lasting up to five years. The House of Lords until 1999 comprised a mixture of hereditary peers of the realm and also life peers appointed in recognition of public service. In 1999 legislation was passed to prevent hereditary peers from sitting or voting and their numbers have been progressively reduced, leaving an appointed second chamber. There is a continuing debate as to whether the House of Lords should remain an appointed second chamber or should change to elected membership. Legislation originates in the House of Commons and after approval there is passed to the House of Lords. In the House of Lords there may be detailed amendments to the proposed legislation, but only rarely is it defeated completely. The House of Commons has the power to restore legislation opposed by the House of Lords: the House of Lords may consequently modify or delay legislation, but cannot prevent its passage.

The House of Commons is led by the Prime Minister who is usually also the leader of the parliamentary party holding the parliamentary majority. The monarch is head of state, but must act on the advice of the government of the day.

The dominant position of the House of Commons and the lack of conflict between the leader of the government and the majority party in Parliament mean that business legislation desired by the government is likely to become law. From 1979 to 1997 the UK had a Conservative government. A marked change of electoral mood led to the election of a Labour government in 1997.

The economic system is generally based on a free market approach. Government regulation is applied to particular aspects of economic activity, such as the control of competition or the prevention of price-fixing arrangements. In 1996 the Bank of England was given independent power to determine interest rates, taking this power from previous control by the government. The purpose of this change was to allow interest rates to move more closely with market forces in the economy.

The period of Conservative government from 1979 saw a policy of privatization of companies which had been in government control, nationalization having dated from the late 1940s. Privatization was seen as a political ideal but also placed large capital funds at the disposal of the government of the day and reduced the borrowing requirements of the public sector. The privatization policy was largely completed before the Labour government came to power and, despite earlier indications that it would reverse this policy, on achieving power the Labour government showed no apparent desire to carry out such reversal. However, regulation of the privatized companies is extensive, particularly for the utilities, covering pricing of products, and provides another means of government control.

Rates of exchange between the pound sterling and other currencies are determined by market forces. The Bank of England has regard to the rate of exchange when setting interest rates. Although the UK is a member of the EU, there has been reluctance to join the European Monetary System (EMS) and take up the euro as a common currency.

15.4.2 Legal system

Statute law is established by Parliament and sits alongside common law which has been established by tradition through the courts of law. There is a national system of law for the UK as a whole but there is also a separate legal system in Scotland, derived from the historical position of Scotland as an independent country prior to the Act of Union in 1707. Business law is usually applicable on a UK-wide basis. There are some separate laws established by the UK Parliament to be applied in Northern Ireland and Wales, recognizing their separate historical origins.

In the seventeenth and eighteenth centuries, trading and commercial companies could be formed only by royal charter or by private Act of Parliament. Company law, allowing relatively straightforward incorporation of business companies, came into existence in the middle of the nineteenth century. The law at that stage was not excessively intrusive, taking the view that the regulation of a company was essentially a matter for the shareholders and the directors. A series of business scandals in the early years of the twentieth century led to the view that more intervention was required through business legislation. This led, in the Companies Act 1948, to much more detailed prescription on disclosure of information and general conduct of the business. That legislation survived, with some modification in 1967. A major revision of company law took place when the UK joined the EU and was required to adopt the Fourth and Seventh Directives. Periodically there is a consolidation of company law which revises and updates previous legislation. The company law provisions of the Companies Act 2006 restate almost all of the provisions of the Companies Act 1985, together with the company law provisions of the Companies Act 1989 and the Companies (Audit, Investigations and Community Enterprise) Act 2004.

Statute law also covers matters such as insolvency, financial services and insider trading on the stock market. There is a strong tradition of judge-made law, passed down through decisions in courts of law which are taken as binding precedent for future cases of a similar type.

Although parliamentary process is required for primary legislation, such as the approval of the Companies Act 2006, some amendments to legislation may thereafter be implemented without debate in Parliament. Thus the Companies Act is amended from time to time by Statutory Instrument. This method is used to change disclosure exemption limits, or to delete minor unwanted items of disclosure or to add new items of detail within an overall existing heading.

The UK legal system may be classified as from the common law family, and of British type. Within the UK, Scots law is based on Roman law. Laws affecting business are set by the UK Parliament but may have an additional section relating to Scots law.

Unincorporated businesses operate as sole traders or partnerships. Both carry the disadvantage that the owner has unlimited liability for the obligations of the business. The need to grow and seek a larger capital base may eventually force the expanding business to seek incorporation as a limited liability company. There are two types of limited

Exhibit 15.3	Differences between public and private companies

Public limited company (plc)	Private company (Ltd)
Minimum two directors	Minimum one director
Minimum share capital £50,000	No minimum share capital
Shares and debentures may be offered to the public by advertisement	Prohibition on offer to the public
Restrictions on making loans to directors	Fewer restrictions on dealing with directors
General prohibition on assisting others to purchase the company's own shares	Giving assistance to purchase own shares is allowed, subject to safeguards for creditors and minority shareholders
Company may purchase its own shares provided fixed capital is not reduced	Own shares may be purchased out of fixed capital

liability company: the public limited company (plc) and the private limited company (Ltd). Exhibit 15.3 sets out the key differences.

15.4.3 Corporate governance[9]

The day-to-day management of companies is in the hands of the board of directors. The single tier board comprises both executive and non-executive directors. It is desirable in public companies for the Chair and the chief executive to be separate persons. The board is led by a Chair who is usually a non-executive director. The board is expected to act as a single group of persons, all taking collective responsibility for the decisions of the board. In practice, everyday activity is delegated by the board to a senior executive director who leads the other executives in running the company.

Directors are elected, and may be removed, by the shareholders in annual general meetings. Directors are required to act as agents of the shareholders, as a body, and in that context have duties defined by law. The directors must act in good faith in the best interests of the company.

15.4.3.1 The Combined Code of Corporate Governance

There have been several reports into corporate governance in the UK. The first, in 1992, known as the 'Cadbury Report', was chaired by Sir Adrian Cadbury.[10] That report set a Code of Best Practice to be followed by company directors. Its recommendations for disclosure of directors' emoluments were taken forward by Sir Richard Greenbury, resulting in the Greenbury Report (1995).[11] The extensive disclosures on directors' remuneration to be found in the annual reports of UK companies reflect the recommendations of Greenbury. The rules for directors' remuneration are now contained in regulation through a statutory instrument.[12] Subsequently, a review chaired by Sir Ronald Hampel published a report (the Hampel Report) in 1998[13] confirming much of

---

[9] Charkham (1994), Ch. 6; Davies (1999).

[10] Available at www.ecgi.org/codes/country_pages/codes_uk.htm.

[11] Ibid.

[12] The Directors' Remuneration Report Regulations 2002, www.hmso.gpv.uk/si/si2002/20021986.htm.

[13] Available at www.ecgi.org/codes/country-pages/codes_uk.htm.

the work of Cadbury and Greenbury and setting a Combined Code containing Principles of Good Governance and a Code of Practice. Hampel took the view that entrepreneurship should not be stifled by excessive regulation.

The Combined Code is now the responsibility of the Financial Reporting Council[14] and is regularly reviewed and updated.

15.4.3.2 Internal control

Following publication of the Combined Code in 1998, The Institute of Chartered Accountants in England and Wales agreed with the stock exchange that it would provide guidance to assist listed companies in implementing the requirements of the Code in relation to internal control. The Internal Control Working Party, chaired by Nigel Turnbull, produced a statement of guidance in 1999,[15] subsequently revised in 2005.[16] This guidance sets out best practice on internal control for UK listed companies, and assists them in applying section C.2 of the Combined Code. The guidance states that the annual report and accounts must include such meaningful, high-level information as the board considers necessary to assist shareholders' understanding of the main features of the company's risk management processes and system of internal control, and should not give a misleading impression.[17]

15.4.3.3 Legislation for a corporate governance statement

Section 12.9.2 explains the EC Directive which will lead to legislation requiring listed companies to produce a Corporate Governance Statement. The UK consultation on the implementation of the measures in the Directive closed on 1 June 2007. The government stated its intention to introduce legislation implementing the Directive with the secondary legislation implementing the accounting provisions under section 15 of the Companies Act 2006.

15.4.4 Taxation system

Companies pay corporation tax while owners of unincorporated businesses pay income tax. The two types of tax operate under different rules and may have different rates of tax applied. However, for the determination of taxable business profits the rules are similar. The starting point is the reported accounting profit, modified by specific aspects of tax law. One description of policy states: 'There is merit in further alignment of taxable and commercial (i.e. accounting) profits. But if there are good policy reasons for departing from following accounting rules the Government is prepared to do so.'[18]

15.4.4.1 Taxable income

A distinction is drawn between income arising from revenue transactions and that arising from capital receipts. Income is subdivided according to its source and different rules

---

[14] http://www.frc.org.uk/corporate/.

[15] Turnbull (1999).

[16] Turnbull (2005).

[17] Ibid., para. 33.

[18] http://www.hmrc.gov.uk/practitioners/int_accounting.htm.

are applied to each source. The aggregate amount is subject to corporation tax. For companies the main sources are:

- trading profit
- non-trading income
- chargeable gains.

Those companies that choose to use IFRS in their individual accounts are able to use those accounts as the starting point for their tax computations.[19] They are not be required to prepare separate UK GAAP accounts for tax purposes. Companies may also choose to continue using UK GAAP for individual company accounts. Under tax law, trading profit is based on reported accounting profit with adjustments specified in tax law. The most significant adjustment is that tax law does not allow accounting depreciation as an expense but substitutes instead a system of capital allowances at prescribed rates. Trading stock may not be valued on a last-in–first-out (LIFO) basis. Profits and losses on the disposal of fixed assets are not included in taxable profits. Provisions are not allowed unless they can be shown to be specific to a defined item of expected loss. Some expenses, such as business entertaining, are not allowed for tax purposes.

Non-trading income includes investment income, rental income, interest and royalties. These are generally taxed on the basis of cash received rather than on an accruals basis.

Chargeable gains are the profits calculated on disposal of fixed assets. Indexation allowances, calculated to eliminate the inflationary element of the gain, were available until 1998.

There is therefore formal independence of the accounting and tax approaches to measurement of profit, and this permits financial reporting to be flexible without fiscal impact. However, despite formal independence there have developed effective interdependencies, primarily because the judgment of the courts in relation to taxable profit is that it should be based on the profits reported under generally accepted accounting principles. Where flexibility exists under accounting practice, there have been instances of choosing the approach likely to lead to the most favourable taxation outcome, and on occasions this flexibility has been challenged in the courts by the tax authorities. The results of such court decisions have had some influence on subsequent accounting practice.

15.4.4.2 Tax treatment of dividends

Dividends are paid to UK shareholders net of a withholding tax. The individual shareholder may set up the amount of the withholding tax against the personal tax bill but large institutional shareholders such as pension funds, which are exempt from tax, may not reclaim the amount withheld. This selective imputation system reflects a change in political power in 1997, ending almost 25 years of a widely applied imputation system. Companies which receive dividend income from other companies may not claim any deduction for the tax withheld and they must pay corporation tax on the dividend income. Relief is available within groups of companies.

15.4.5 Corporate financing system[20]

15.4.5.1 Equity investors

A survey of share ownership in the UK (2004) showed that individuals hold only 14 per cent by value of the equity of listed companies (see Exhibit 15.4). More than 60 per cent

---

[19] http://www.hmrc.gov.uk/practitioners/int_accounting.htm.
[20] Gordon and Gray (1994), Ch. 3.

| Exhibit 15.4 | Beneficial ownership of UK shares, 2004 |

Ownership	Percentage of total equity owned
Rest of the world	32.6
Insurance companies	17.2
Pension funds	15.7
Individuals	14.1
Unit trusts	1.9
Investment trusts	3.3
Other financial institutions	10.7
Charities, churches, etc.	1.1
Private non-financial companies	0.6
Public sector	0.1
Banks	2.7
	100.0

Source: *Share Ownership: a report on ownership of shares as at 31 December 2004*, Office for National Statistics, www.statistics.gov.uk.

is held by insurance companies, pension funds and a range of financial institutions including unit trusts. This relative strength of investment by financial institutions is an unusual characteristic by comparison with other countries. Individuals invest indirectly through saving for pensions, taking insurance and buying investment products provided by financial institutions. Institutional investors tend not to become involved in the management of the company, but where strong concerns arise the institutional investors will use their powers in general meetings. They are increasingly expected to be active in their scrutiny of their investments, as part of good corporate governance.

15.4.5.2 London Stock Exchange[21]

The London Stock Exchange dates from the seventeenth century. For a period of time there were regional trading floors but these closed in the mid-1960s and business focused on London. A major change in the nature of trading operations in the 1980s meant that a dealing floor was no longer maintained, and trading now takes place by use of telephones and computer screens. The main market is the London Stock Exchange, on which companies have a full listing. For new, smaller companies there is the Alternative Investment Market (AIM). It is regulated by the London Stock Exchange but has rules which are less onerous. The AIM may provide a step towards full membership.

Movement on share prices is measured by a number of indices, the most frequently mentioned being the FTSE 100 index. This index is operated jointly by the *Financial Times* and the London Stock Exchange, based on the 100 largest companies measured by market capitalization.

The Official List of securities on the LSE is regulated by the UK Listing Authority (UKLA)[22] as part of the Financial Services Authority (FSA). The UKLA takes charge of admissions to listing but the LSE continues to regulate admission to trading. Annual reports and prospectuses issued by listed companies must comply with the UKLA's Listing Rules.

---

[21] http://www.londonstockexchange.com/en-gb/home.htm.

[22] http://www.fsa.gov.uk/Pages/Doing/UKLA/index.shtml.

The relative importance of the UK stock exchange in Europe can be seen in Exhibit 4.3, although it remains less significant than US and Japanese markets in terms of the market capitalization of listed companies. Exhibit 15.4 shows that individual shareholders are a relatively small group among those investing in equity shares. The 'rest of the world' proportion doubled between 1994 and 2000 but has remained fairly constant since then. The increase in the late 1990s was explained in part by international mergers where the new company was listed in the UK. Also, some companies moved their domicile to the UK. As a technical change to the figures during this period, shareholdings held in UK offshore islands were reclassified as 'rest of the world'. Nevertheless the increase is an indication of the importance of global markets to the major UK companies.

15.4.5.3 Bank lending

London is one of the major banking centres of the world. The Bank of England is the central bank, exercising regulatory control over lending by commercial and merchant banks. Commercial banks are reluctant to become involved in ownership of companies and therefore concentrate on very short-term lending to companies. The medium-term and longer term lending originates with merchant banks or venture capitalists.

Commercial banks also seek to offer services beyond pure lending, particularly for small and medium-sized enterprises (SMEs). They do not play a significant part in corporate governance but may find themselves linked to a customer on a more long-term basis where short-term loans are repeatedly rolled over.

Merchant banks are interested in the larger companies or those medium-sized companies which intend to grow. The merchant banks offer all types of corporate finance services including dealing in foreign exchange markets; swaps; financial futures; forward rate agreements; interest rate and currency options; money market loans and deposits. Strengths of individual banks depend on their chosen specialisms but most will offer advice on takeovers and mergers; corporate reorganization and reconstruction; management buyouts; stock exchange flotations; and bond issues on foreign currency markets.

15.4.5.4 Mergers and acquisitions[23]

Activity in takeovers and mergers varies with economic cycles. Accounting practice distinguishes a true merger from an acquisition, but in practice nearly all business combinations in the UK involve one party acquiring another. Takeover activity is regulated by the Takeover Panel,[24] a self-regulating mechanism which has existed since 1968. It sets a code of practice for takeovers and can impose penalties ranging from a private reprimand to removal of the shares from stock exchange listing. The underlying themes of the code are openness, timeliness and even-handedness.

Government policy to discourage creation of monopolies is administered by the Competition Commission. The Commission will investigate a proposed acquisition and is required to state whether the proposal is, or is not, against the public interest.

Accounting information often plays an important part in takeovers, especially where these are contested. The LSE sets out rules for disclosure in circulars issued in connection with a takeover proposal. The Takeover Code dictates who shall receive such information; often companies will voluntarily exceed the minimum requirement and more

---

[23] Sudarsanam (2003).
[24] www.thetakeoverpanel.org.uk.

may be learned about the parties involved than would ordinarily appear in the annual report.

15.4.5.5 Private equity funds[25]

There has been a rapid increase in 'private equity' as a form of business finance. This means that groups of individuals or financial institutions raise finance from private sources to acquire businesses. Typically, an individual or group of individuals sets up a limited liability partnership (LLP) and raises capital from a group of investors. The LLP has a limited life, such as ten years. The investors aim to raise finance privately, to acquire businesses which they can improve and then sell again, possibly by a stock market flotation. The finance may be taken up in the form of loans or as additional equity investment. Some of the private equity investors have acquired companies previously listed on a stock exchange. Concerns have been expressed about the accountability of private equity investors because they are not listed companies themselves and so are not as closely scrutinized as a listed company would be.

15.4.6 The accounting profession[26]

The UK has a long history of professional accountancy bodies. Over time specialist groupings have emerged. The major professional bodies are:

- The Institute of Chartered Accountants in England and Wales (ICAEW)
- The Institute of Chartered Accountants of Scotland (ICAS)
- The Institute of Chartered Accountants in Ireland (ICAI)
- The Association of Chartered Certified Accountants (ACCA)
- The Chartered Institute of Management Accountants (CIMA)
- The Chartered Institute of Public Finance and Accountancy (CIPFA).

All set examinations as a precondition of membership. Those persons wishing to become company auditors must obtain the status of Registered Auditor, which normally means membership of the ICAEW, ICAS, ICAI or ACCA, together with relevant practical experience.

Before 1990 these professional bodies worked together, through the Accounting Standards Committee (ASC), in setting accounting standards. The process was found to be too slow and was accused of being controlled too closely by the profession. In 1990 the ASB was established as an independent authority and the professional bodies lost their power of veto over the issue of a standard. They continue to make representations to the ASB and to contribute indirectly through the work of members.

Concern has been expressed in the UK about the concentration of audits of major listed companies in the four international accounting firms ('Big 4'), auditing over 90 per cent of all companies listed on the main market. The Financial Reporting Council and the Department of Trade and Industry commissioned a report on competition and choice in the UK audit market, carried out by the consultancy firm Oxera.[27] This has created a framework of continuing debate on the risks and benefits of concentration of the assurance process.

---

[25] Special Report, Private Equity, *Financial Times*, 24 April 2007.

[26] POB (2006).

[27] FRC (2006a).

15.5 External influences

Historically, UK accounting has developed as an approach which has been exported to other parts of the world, particularly the countries which were once colonies but today form part of the Commonwealth.[28] Those countries, on gaining independence, looked to wider global practices and adapted their UK-based accounting systems to include practices found in major trading partner countries. It has been suggested that accounting in the USA is an adaptation, rather than wholesale adoption, of the UK accounting system, carried to that country by pioneering accountants emigrating to the USA.[29]

15.5.1 'Anglo-Saxon' influence

The description 'Anglo-Saxon' or 'Anglo-American' is frequently encountered in research studies and professional commentaries. The countries that are linked by this description are primarily the UK, Ireland, the USA, Canada, Australia and New Zealand. Alexander and Archer (2000) suggested, and then challenged, four hypotheses that would support the validity of 'Anglo-Saxon accounting' based on claims for shared characteristics (see Exhibit 15.5). Based on their challenge, they questioned the existence of a single identifiable 'Anglo-Saxon' system.

Nobes (2003), in support of the idea of an 'Anglo-Saxon' accounting system, suggested a different hypothesis:

> Anglo-Saxon accounting (compared to other forms of accounting) is oriented towards decision-making by investors; it plays down the measurement of taxable income and distributable income; it is less worried about prudence; it is more willing to go beyond legal form.

Alexander and Archer (2003) replied by saying that they felt Nobes underestimated the power and use of the 'true and fair override' and that the 'rules v principles' debate (see section 8.3.3) was still not resolved.

15.5.2 Influence of EU membership

The most significant inward influence on UK accounting has been membership of the EU.[30] To meet the requirements of membership, the UK was required to make significant changes in company law to adopt the various directives. In particular, the concept of having formats and valuation rules contained in company law was seen as a major change resulting from the Fourth Directive. However, the UK also had an influence on accounting in the EU. At the date of UK membership, the Fourth Directive was still in draft form and did not give any scope for the 'true and fair' approach which was the UK tradition. The 'true and fair' amendment to the Fourth Directive was a very significant concession to UK requests. Subsequently the UK has moved to use of IFRS in line with a scope and a timetable set by EU Regulation.

---

[28] Parker (1995).
[29] Parker (1989).
[30] Nobes and Parker (1984); Nobes (1993).

| Exhibit 15.5 | Debating the 'Anglo-Saxon' influence |

Arguments for and against the existence of an 'Anglo-Saxon' system of accounting

1 True and fair view

For: There is a close relationship between 'true and fair view' (TFV) and 'fair presentation' (FP).

Against: 'True and fair view' in the UK is an overriding requirement. Complying with the law does not guarantee a true and fair view. Professional judgement is needed. Courts of law will regard accounting standards as important evidence of true and fair. However, the views of experts about the opinion of the profession are very important. Professional judgement may choose an answer that does not comply with law or standards.

'Fair presentation' in the USA is expressed as 'fair presentation in accordance with US GAAP'. There is a definition of US GAAP based on written standards and guidance (see Chapter 8). So US accounting does not try to go beyond the law and the standards.

2 Conceptual frameworks

For: There is a common practice of developing 'conceptual frameworks' (CF) for financial accounting and reporting.

Against: Alexander and Archer say that conceptual frameworks are created to give an appearance of self-regulation. They have little practical relevance but they create a set of 'beliefs' that make the standard setters appear independent of the law makers.

3 Common law system

For: They all share a common law legal system, which distinguishes them from countries having a code law system.

Against: There can be flexibility or rigidity in either kind of legal system. It does not help to define 'Anglo-Saxon' accounting. The USA has a very detailed set of financial accounting standards that must be applied, so the legal system is largely irrelevant as a description of accounting practice. The Netherlands is said to have flexible accounting with professional judgement, similar to UK and US accounting, but it has a legal system based on code law. Germany has a code law system but the accounting rules are written with flexibility for interpretation by professional experts.

4 Setting accounting standards

For: Private sector regulation of accounting takes precedence over public sector regulation.

Against: In the USA, Congress sets the laws for the SEC. The SEC accepts accounting standards written by the FASB. SEC can overrule FASB. Congress can overrule SEC and FASB. So the public sector aspect is very strong.

Source: Based on Alexander and Archer (2000).

Multinational companies are an agent for the import and export of international practices. Where these companies have found themselves producing different sets of financial statements for different jurisdictions, they have tended to choose options which were common to more than one country. Such companies have from time to time referred to their own attempts to find common approaches to specific issues, or frustration at the lack of common approaches.

15.6   Oversight and assurance

The corporate failure of Enron and other companies in the USA in early 2002 prompted the UK government to ask, 'Could it happen here?' The answer was 'Yes it could, although perhaps less likely.'[31] The Chancellor of the Exchequer and the Department of Trade and Industry[32] put in place specific initiatives on accounting and auditing in addition to continuing work on implementing the recommendations of the Company Law Review (2001). These initiatives were:

- the Co-ordinating Group on Accounting and Auditing Issues (CGAA), set up February 2002, interim report July 2002, final report January 2003;
- the Higgs investigation of the effectiveness of non-executive directors, set up February 2002, issued consultation paper June 2002, final report January 2003;
- the CGAA, which published an interim report in July 2002, commissioned a separate group, chaired by Sir Robert Smith, to develop code guidance for audit committees, set up September 2002, final report January 2003;
- a review of the regulatory regime of the accountancy profession, announced by Secretary of State for Trade and Industry, July 2002, in response to CGAA interim report, consultation document issued October 2002, final report January 2003;
- a government White Paper 'Modernising Company Law' containing proposals for company law reform, issued July 2002.

15.6.1 Review of the regulatory regime of the accountancy profession[33]

Since 2004 the regulatory regime of the accountancy profession has been located within the framework of the Financial Reporting Council (FRC). The recommendations of a review by the Co-ordinating Group on Accounting and Auditing Issues (CGAA),[34] published in 2003, included the following:

1. The FRC should take over the functions of the Accountancy Foundation (established in 2000 to oversee the regulation of the profession) to create a unified and authoritative structure with three clear areas of responsibility:

   (a) setting accounting standards;
   (b) enforcement or monitoring of accounting standards;
   (c) oversight of the major professional bodies.

2. The independent regulation and review of audit should be strengthened significantly. Responsibility for setting independence standards for auditors and for monitoring the audit of listed companies and other significant entities should be transferred from the accountancy professional bodies to the independent regulator.

Subsequently the FRC was asked to extend its remit to cover aspects of the work of the actuarial profession.

---

[31] Smith (2003), p. 21.
[32] Now called the Department for Business, Enterprise and Regulatory Reform (BERR), www.berr.gov.uk.
[33] Review (2003).
[34] Co-ordinating Group (2003).

15.6.2 The Financial Reporting Council[35]

The FRC is the UK's independent regulator responsible for promoting confidence in corporate reporting and governance. Its functions, since 2004, are:

- promoting high standards of corporate governance;
- setting, monitoring and enforcing accounting and auditing standards;
- setting actuarial standards;
- statutory oversight and regulation of auditors;
- operating an independent investigation and discipline scheme for public interest cases;
- overseeing the regulatory activities of the professional accountancy and actuarial bodies.

Some of the FRC's functions are supported by statutory powers, through company law, while other functions have no statutory backing but derive their authority from widespread support from the FRC's stakeholders.

The FRC draws members from across the financial, business and professional communities at the highest levels. Its original remit of setting and enforcing accounting standards has been enlarged significantly, reflecting confidence in its strategy, operations and proactive role. The FRC has six subsidiary boards, five of which are described in the following sections. The separate boards are independent in exercising their respective functions. The FRC is funded jointly by the accountancy profession (through the Consultative Committee of Accountancy Bodies), business (through a levy collected by the Financial Services Authority) and the government.

15.6.2.1 The Accounting Standards Board[36]

The ASB was established in 1990 as an independent standard-setting body. It is recognized for that purpose under the Companies Act 2006. There had been criticism of its predecessor, the Accounting Standards Committee (ASC), because of the dominance of that committee by professional accountancy bodies and its apparent lack of power to take bold decisions on difficult accounting issues. The ASB spent the first five years of its existence remedying the perceived defects of the UK national standards, but from the mid-1990s it engaged increasingly with other national standard setters and with the IASB to influence the direction taken by international accounting standards. The ASB has expressed a strong commitment to align UK national standards with IFRS so that eventually all companies will produce financial statements on a similar basis, whether acting under the IAS Regulation or under national standards. The ASB has established experience of developing a separate standard for small companies. This is called the FRSSE (Financial Reporting Standard for Small Enterprises). The advantage for small companies is that if they choose to follow the FRSSE they do not have to be concerned about the detail of the larger body of full standards.

15.6.2.2 The Financial Reporting Review Panel[37]

The FRRP seeks to ensure that the annual accounts of public companies and large private companies comply with the requirements of the Companies Act 2006 and applicable

---

[35] www.frc.org.uk/about/.

[36] http://www.frc.org.uk/asb/about/.

[37] http://www.frc.org.uk/frrp/about/.

accounting standards. Where the accounts of a company do not comply with the requirements of the Act, the legislation gives power to the courts to order preparation of a revised set of accounts, at the cost of the directors who approved the defective accounts. This procedure gives statutory support to UK accounting standards, even though the ASB is an independent private body. The FRRP gives relatively few rulings in any one year and the censured companies appear to be average performers suffering temporary performance difficulties, rather than perennial underperformers.[38]

15.6.2.3 The Professional Oversight Board[39]

The POB contributes to the achievement of the FRC's fundamental aim of supporting investor, market and public confidence in the financial and governance stewardship of listed and other entities by providing:

- independent oversight of the regulation of the auditing profession by the recognized supervisory and qualifying bodies;
- monitoring of the quality of the auditing function in relation to economically significant entities;
- independent oversight of the regulation of the accountancy profession by the professional accountancy bodies.

The POB also has oversight of the actuarial profession.

15.6.2.4 The Auditing Practices Board[40]

The APB was established in April 2002, replacing a previous APB that had been in place since 1991. The APB is committed to leading the development of auditing practice in the UK and the Republic of Ireland so as to:

- establish high standards of auditing;
- meet the developing needs of users of financial information;
- ensure public confidence in the auditing process.

Since 2005 the APB has issued UK and Ireland versions of the International Standards on Auditing (ISAs UK and Ireland) (see IAASB in section 3.3.1). The ASB consults in the UK using each new or revised ISA as an exposure draft for comment. When the ISA is issued in the UK it is augmented by reference to specific aspects of UK regulation.

15.6.2.5 The Accountancy Investigation and Discipline Board[41]

The AIDB replaces the work of the Joint Disciplinary Scheme previously operated by ICAEW and ICAS, extending its role to cover the ACCA, CIMA and CIPFA; the ICAI continues to deal separately with Irish accountants to take account of the separate legal and political circumstances. The AIDB focuses on cases of public interest. Other cases continue to be dealt with by the individual accountancy bodies. Accountancy bodies may refer cases to the AIDB but the AIDB may also call in cases that have come to its attention. The scheme operates independently, with a majority of members being non-accountants.

---

[38] Peasnell *et al.* (2001).

[39] http://www.frc.org.uk/pob/about/.

[40] http://www.frc.org.uk/apb/about/.

[41] http://www.frc.org.uk/aidb/about/.

15.6.3 Implementing the Transparency Obligations Directive

The Transparency Obligations Directive of the EU has been implemented in the UK through the Disclosure and Transparency Rules (DTR) of the UK Listing Authority.[42] The DTR require companies listed on a regulated market to publish their annual reports within four calendar months of the financial end (previously the time limit was six months). Half-yearly reports must apply IAS 34, must include an interim management report, and must be published within two calendar months of the end of the six-month period. Preliminary announcements are voluntary but if issued must comply with stated requirements. An Interim Management Statement must be issued partway through each half-yearly period, giving a brief update on events since the most recent annual or half-yearly report. The DTR set out general principles for the content of the interim management statement. Effectively this brings a form of quarterly reporting to the UK market. The year 2007 brought in a theme of more disclosure more often. The firm of Deloitte, in explaining the new rules, asked, 'Will all then be clear? Or, will this reporting in a more regimented fashion simply lead to more bland reporting rather than focused commentary as appropriate?'[43]

15.6.4 Audit committees

We have explained in section 15.4.3.2 that as part of the process of revising the Code, the government asked the CGAA to develop guidance on audit committees. A Group was formed under the chairmanship of Sir Robert Smith. The Group reviewed experience in other countries and noted developments in the USA, the EU and elsewhere. The Smith Report (2003) defined the primary role of audit committees as ensuring the integrity of financial reporting and the audit process by ensuring that the external auditor is independent and objective and does a thorough job, and by fostering a culture and an expectation of effective oversight.[44]

The key functions of audit committees were listed as:

- Monitor the processes which ensure the integrity of the financial statements of the company.
- Review the company's financial control and risk management systems.
- Monitor and review the effectiveness of the company's internal audit function.
- Make recommendations to the board in relation to the appointment of the external auditor and approve the remuneration and terms of engagement of the external auditor following appointment by the shareholders in general meeting.
- Monitor and review the external auditor's performance, independence and objectivity.
- Develop and implement policy on the engagement of the external auditor to supply non-audit services.

The Smith Report recommended that the directors' report in the company's annual report should include a separately identifiable section on the activities of the audit committee. An example of an audit committee's report is given as an appendix to the Smith Report, along with specimen terms of reference for the audit committee.

---

[42] http://www.fsa.gov.uk/pubs/ukla/list_dec06.pdf. The rules apply to accounting periods starting on or after 20 January 2007.

[43] *Clear all year: considering new rules and practice in interim reporting*, Deloitte & Touche LLP (2007).

[44] Smith (2003) para. 7.

One important aspect of the work of the audit committee is defining the meaning of 'independent' non-executive director. For this, Smith refers to Higgs[45] who states that the director must be independent in character and judgement and there must be no relationships or circumstances that could affect, or appear to affect, the director's judgement. Higgs listed the kinds of relationships that would indicate lack of sufficient independence. The conditions for independence were confirmed in the Combined Code on Corporate Governance (2003).[46]

15.6.5 Non-executive directors

Section 15.4.3.2 explains the establishment of the Higgs review of the role and effectiveness of non-executive directors. The evidence used in the review included the 250 responses received to the consultation paper, survey data on the population of non-executive directors in 2,200 UK listed companies, an opinion poll survey of 605 executive directors, non-executive directors and Chairs of UK listed companies, and in-depth interviews of 40 directors of FTSE 350 companies. This evidence was made available on the review's website. The recommendations of the Higgs Report are now seen in the Combined Code (2003). The areas covered are listed in Exhibit 15.6.

One of the most controversial recommendations of Higgs was that at least half the members of the board, excluding the Chair, should be independent non-executive directors. In the Combined Code this condition is modified for smaller companies to require at least two independent non-executive directors. One of the non-executive directors should be identified as the senior non-executive director. This person should be available to shareholders whose concerns have not been met through the normal channels of chief executive and Chair. The Chair should meet the tests of independence at the time of appointment but it is recognized that the independence diminishes as the Chair becomes more involved in working with the company. There must be separate roles defined by the board for the Chair and for the chief executive.

There were fears that the Higgs Report would deter suitably qualified persons from agreeing to become non-executive directors because of the additional burden and the risk of legal actions against directors of the company. Higgs recommended that companies should be able to provide insurance cover for all directors to cover the costs of defending legal actions. The Tyson Report (2003) resulted from a government request for investigation into broadening the base of non-executive directors.[47]

| Exhibit 15.6 | Topics covered in the Higgs Report on non-executive directors |

The board	Tenure and time commitment
The Chair	Remuneration
The non-executive director	Resignation
The senior independent director	Audit and remuneration committees
Independence	Liability of directors
Recruitment and appointment	Relationships with shareholders
Induction and professional development	Smaller listed companies

---

[45] Higgs (2003), Annex A, section A.3.4.
[46] FRC (2006b) para. A.3.1.
[47] Tyson (2003).

15.7 Corporate reporting issues

15.7.1 Professionalism versus statutory control

The history of accounting practice in the UK is strongly dependent on professional expertise developing practices to satisfy the general requirements of the law. This is consistent with the development of other professions such as law and medicine.

When the law was required to adopt a more prescriptive approach in relation to incorporating the Fourth and Seventh Directives in national law, those drafting the law made extensive use of options in order to preserve the capacity for professional judgement. The preservation of the concept of a 'true and fair view' was a particularly important aspect of the strength of professionalism in the UK, because it allowed continuation of the practice of evolving generally accepted accounting principles. The reforms of supervision of the accountancy profession under the POB have introduced more layers of oversight and accountability but there is still a core expectation of professional values in applying legislation and standards for corporate reporting.

15.7.2 True and fair view

There is no definition of the phrase 'a true and fair view' although much has been written about it. The ASB has sought the advice of legal counsel on the matter and that advice is presented as an appendix to the *Foreword to Accounting Standards*. The emphasis is very much on the dynamic nature of the concept. 'What is required to show a true and fair view is subject to continuous rebirth' (Appendix, para. 14). The legal opinion is that the courts will hold that compliance with accounting standards is necessary to meet the true and fair requirement. The courts would probably give special weight to the view of the ASB as a standard-setting body.

It thus seems inescapable that accounting standards are a necessary component of a true and fair view, although they may not in themselves be sufficient in all situations. Professional judgement remains an essential additional element. A particular feature of the application of a 'true and fair view' is FRS 5 *Reporting the Substance of Transactions* which seeks the commercial substance of transactions and events. In the discussion of the transition to IFRS in 2005, concerns were expressed in the UK that there was no IASB standard to parallel FRS 5.

The history of accounting practice in the UK is strongly dependent on professional expertise developing practices to satisfy the general requirements of the law. This is consistent with the development of other professions such as law and medicine.

When the law was required to adopt a more prescriptive approach in relation to incorporating the Fourth and Seventh Directives in national law, those drafting the law made extensive use of options in order to preserve the capacity for professional judgement. The preservation of the concept of a 'true and fair view' was a particularly important aspect of the strength of professionalism in the UK, because it allowed continuation of the practice of evolving generally accepted accounting principles.

The Companies Act 1985 used phrases such as 'in accordance with principles generally accepted, at the time when the accounts are prepared' but did not define 'principles generally accepted'. There were strong indications from case law that the courts of law would have careful regard to accounting standards set by the ASB. Popularization of the abbreviation 'UK GAAP' may be attributed to the book of that title first published by

Exhibit 15.7	True and fair override, Kingfisher

Accounting policies

Accounting conventions

The financial statements of the Company and its subsidiaries are made up to the nearest Saturday to 31 January each year. The financial statements of the Company and its subsidiaries are prepared under the historical cost convention, except for land and buildings that are included in the financial statements at valuation, and are prepared in accordance with applicable accounting standards in the United Kingdom.

However, compliance with SSAP 19 'Accounting for Investment Properties' relating to depreciation on investment properties and FRS 10 'Goodwill and Intangible Assets' relating to the capitalisation and amortisation of goodwill both require a departure from the requirements of the Companies Act 1985 as explained below.

Source: Kingfisher Annual Report (2004), p. 27. www.kingfisher.com.

the accountancy firm of Ernst and Young in the late 1980s and subsequently revised regularly (Davies *et al.*, 1999). The abbreviation may, however, be found earlier than that in the documents lodged with the SEC by companies having a full listing on a major US stock exchange, where the companies were creating terminology which would appear familiar to US readers.

The use of the phrase in the UK must be seen in the context of the statutory requirement for financial statements to present a 'true and fair view' which is widely regarded in UK accounting practice as having a broader range than the US phrase 'fairly present'.

When company law was revised in 1985 the 'true and fair override' was seen as an important principle because there could be occasions when professional judgement would compel the accountant to break compliance with the law in the interests of presenting a true and fair view. A survey by *Company Reporting* in 2004[48] showed that while one-quarter of companies invoked the true and fair override, nine out of ten cases were a consequence of company law not keeping up with accounting standards. In particular a departure arises because under the UK standard on investment properties (SSAP 19), investment properties are revalued but not depreciated. The standard on impairment (FRS 10) allows an impairment test and no amortization. Company law requires depreciation and amortization for all fixed assets of finite life. The survey results suggest that the UK concern for retaining the 'true and fair override' in IAS 1 (see section 2.2.2) may be overstated since from 2005 the IAS Regulation is the law and so conflict between IFRS and the law disappears. An example of the 'true and fair override' in UK accounting standards, prior to the conversion to IFRS, is shown in Exhibit 15.7 where Kingfisher applied the accounting standards SSAP 19 and FRS 10 but in doing so departed from the requirements of the Companies Act.

15.7.3 Formats of financial statements

The formats set out in the Fourth Directive were incorporated in the Companies Act 1985 (consolidating earlier legislation). Accounting details of a similar type were incorporated in the Companies Act 2006 by supplementary regulations. For many years the law has set out two formats of balance sheet and four formats of profit and loss

---

[48] *Company Reporting*, June 2004, pp. 3–8.

account, thus permitting both vertical and horizontal arrangements. In practice, most companies choose the vertical form of balance sheet and the vertical form of profit and loss account in the functional version. This allows the matching of cost of goods sold against turnover to report gross profit. A smaller number of companies use the version of the profit and loss account which shows type of expenditure. The IAS Regulation is less prescriptive than the Directives. Consequently it has been interesting to observe companies' choices of formats and wording since 2005. Although IAS 1 does not prescribe headings, many UK companies have changed to 'income statement' from the traditional 'profit and loss account'.

IAS 1 requires a statement of changes in equity but allows a range of ways of achieving this. The Statement of Recognised Income and Expense reflects a development in the UK from 1993, when the ASB proposed the Statement of Total Recognised Gains and Losses (STRGL) as an additional primary financial statement to report the total of all gains and losses of the reporting entity that are recognized in a period and are attributable to shareholders. The first line of this statement is taken from the profit and loss account which reports the net profit realized for shareholders, but it continues by adding in unrealized items, particularly increases in value of fixed assets and foreign currency translation effects. The information contained in the STRGL could in principle be found in the note of movements on reserves, but these were not easy to find or to understand. The ASB felt that creating a new primary statement, to be presented in close proximity to the profit and loss account, would draw attention to the unrealized gains and losses.

Initial response to the ASB had asked that the STRGL should be extended to provide a complete reconciliation of movements in shareholders' funds. The ASB decided the reconciliation would be useful but preferred a separate note which would not divert attention from the components of performance in the STRGL. Thus the presentation of information for companies applying UK accounting standards remains different from that of companies reporting under IAS 1. An example of a statement of recognized income and expense is shown for Tesco in Exhibit 15.8.

15.7.4 Narrative reporting

Gray (1988) classified UK accounting as strongly transparent. Notes to the accounts and additional voluntary disclosures are evidence of such transparency. The operating and financial review, interim reporting, corporate social responsibility reporting and disclosures regarding directors' remuneration are examples of transparency in UK reporting practice. It has been observed that non-financial disclosures in annual reports of major companies are greater in the UK than in the USA or in continental European countries.[49]

There has been a strong tradition of leading UK companies making voluntary disclosures well ahead of the minimum requirement of the law. This is particularly so where the companies have multinational activities. Such companies are using the annual report to project their image on international stock exchanges. However, as the regulations and guidance on disclosure grow in size and complexity it becomes increasingly difficult to identify the information that is genuinely volunteered. This section indicates the main sources of guidance specific to UK companies.

---

[49] Meek *et al.* (1995).

Exhibit 15.8 | Group statement of recognized income and expense

GROUP STATEMENT OF RECOGNISED INCOME AND EXPENSE Year ended 24 February 2007

	notes	2007 £m	2006* £m
(Loss)/gain on revaluation of available-for-sale investments	14	(1)	2
Foreign currency translation differences		(65)	33
Total gain/(loss) on defined benefit pension schemes	23	114	(443)
(Losses)/gains on cash flow hedges:			
– net fair value (losses)/gains		(26)	44
– reclassified and reported in the Income Statement		(12)	(5)
Tax on items taken directly to equity	6	12	133
Net income/(expense) recognised directly in equity		22	(236)
Profit for the year		1,899	1,576
Total recognised income and expense for the year		1,921	1,340
Attributable to:			
Equity holders of the parent		1,920	1,327
Minority interests		1	13
		1,921	1,340

*Results for the year ended 25 February 2006 include 52 weeks for the UK and the Republic of Ireland and 14 months for the majority of the remaining International businesses.

Source: Tesco Annual Report (2007), p. 45, www.tesco.com.

15.7.4.1 Notes to the financial statements

Notes to the financial statements are required by company law and, for listed companies, by stock exchange regulations. Where the primary financial statements fail to show a true and fair view, this cannot be rectified by providing information in the notes, which provide additional explanation to support what is contained in the financial statements.

15.7.4.2 Operating and financial review[50]

The operating and financial review (OFR) was introduced in 1993 as a form of disclosure recommended by the ASB in a non-mandatory statement of best practice. The ASB saw the OFR as a framework for the directors to discuss and analyze the performance of the business and the factors underlying its results and financial position, in order to assist users to assess for themselves the future potential of the business.

There was no standard format for the OFR because directors were encouraged to design the OFR in a manner best suited to the needs of the business and its users. The ASB was keen to avoid the stereotyped image of some of the management discussion and analysis (MD&A) documents issued in the USA. Essential features of the OFR were a top-down structure; a balanced and objective account; reference to matters discussed previously which have not turned out as expected; analytical discussion; explanations of ratios calculated; and analysis of trends. In discussing trends it should indicate trends and factors which have affected the results but are not expected to continue in the

---

[50] ASB (1993b); ASB (2003); ASB (2005); ASB (2006).

future, and also known events, trends and uncertainties which were expected to have an impact on the business in the future.

The Final Report of the Company Law Review Steering Group (section 15.3.1) recommended a mandatory OFR. The *Financial Times*[51] summarized some of the comments on the government's draft proposals. One strongly supportive view was that the OFR would become the spinal column of narrative reporting, with more detailed reports running off it. One broadly supportive commentator nevertheless feared it might be taken over by corporate social responsibility reporting. Another was concerned that a mechanistic approach with boilerplate text would result. Some thought directors would be inhibited in making forward-looking statements because there was no 'safe harbour' provision (see section 11.7.1.4) but the Department of Trade and Industry rejected that idea as unworkable.

Following the usual consultation process, legislation was introduced by Statutory Instrument with the intention of making the OFR mandatory from 2005 in parallel with a Business Review introduced to satisfy the requirements of the EU Modernization Directive. The ASB introduced a Reporting Standard setting out in more detail how the OFR would be prepared. However, at a late stage in 2005 the Chancellor of the Exchequer announced that the mandatory requirement would be removed. The ASB, which had not been consulted about this change of position, had no choice but to withdraw the Reporting Standard and reinstate the document as a non-mandatory Reporting Statement.[52] The Chancellor's stated reason for the change of direction was that introducing an OFR by legislation would 'gold plate' the implementation of the EU Modernization Directive and would impose an unnecessary burden on business. The less demanding Business Review remained mandatory.

In a survey of annual reports published between August 2005 and 2006, the firm of Deloitte[53] observed that only 20 per cent published a section formally described as an OFR but a further 55 per cent showed clear recognition of the OFR guidance. Another 20 per cent showed some recognition of OFR guidance. The Reporting Statement allows flexibility in presentation of the OFR material and does not insist on a separate section with the specific heading. The average length of an OFR, either formal or showing clear recognition, was 25 pages in the top 350 companies, 13 pages in the mid-tier and 9 pages for the smallest listed companies. The report comments on the practical difficulties of surveying OFR information because of the flexibility of presentation but it is also supportive of the usefulness of an OFR in helping directors to carry out their reporting responsibilities.

15.7.4.3 Business Review

The requirements for the Business Review are set out in the Companies Act 2006, section 417. The directors' report must contain a business review that provides:

- a fair review of the company's business; and
- a description of the principal risks and uncertainties facing the company.

The requirement for a Business Review extends to all companies other than those defined as 'small'. All Business Reviews must provide a balanced and comprehensive

---

[51] *Financial Times*, 2 August 2004, Fund Management Weekly Review, p. 3.

[52] For a detailed explanation see the Introduction to ASB (2006).

[53] *Write to reason: surveying OFRs and narrative reporting in annual reports*, Deloitte & Touche LLP (2006).

analysis of the development and performance of the company's business during the financial year and the position of the business at the end of the year. Quoted companies[54] must provide additional information to include:

- the main trends and factors likely to affect the future development, performance and position of the company's business;
- information about environmental matters, the company's employees and social and community issues;
- information about persons with whom the company has contractual or other arrangements that are essential to the business of the company.

Analysis of the business performance must include discussion of key performance indicators that can be used as a point of reference.

15.7.4.4 Corporate governance reporting

As a result of the work of the corporate governance initiatives described in sections 15.4.3, the annual report of a major UK company will now contain a statement on corporate governance, a statement on internal controls, a report from the Remuneration Committee, and a statement on the going-concern status of the company, as well as a statement of the directors' responsibilities.[55] Exhibit 15.9 shows the introduction to the corporate governance report of GlaxoSmithKline and also the section describing communication with shareholders.

| Exhibit 15.9 | Corporate governance report, GlaxoSmithKline |

Corporate governance

This section discusses GlaxoSmithKline's management structures and governance procedures. It contains the company's reporting disclosures on corporate governance required by the Combined Code on Corporate Governance of the Financial Reporting Council (Combined Code), including the required statement of compliance. Further, the company reports on compliance with the US laws and regulations that apply to it.

The Board	54
Corporate Executive Team	55
Governance and policy	56
Dialogue with shareholders	58
Annual General Meeting	59
Internal control framework	59
Committee reports	60
The Combined Code	62
US law and regulation	63

Dialogue with shareholders

Financial results are announced quarterly.

The company reports formally to shareholders twice a year, when its half-year and full-year results are announced. The full-year results are included in the company's Annual Report and Annual Review, which are published for shareholders. The company's half-year results are

▶

---

[54] A quoted company has its equity share capital included in the official list of the UK stock market or an EEA state, or is admitted to dealing in the New York Stock Exchange or NASDAQ (CA 2006, s. 385).

[55] *Company Reporting*, February 2000, pp. 3–8.

Exhibit 15.9 *(Continued)*

published in a national newspaper shortly after release. The CEO, CFO and President, Pharmaceutical Operations give presentations on the full-year results to institutional investors, analysts and the media.

There are webcast teleconferences after the release of the first, second and third quarter results for institutional investors, analysts and the media. The Annual Report, Annual Review and quarterly results are available on the company's website.

The Annual General Meeting (AGM) takes place in London, and formal notification is sent to shareholders at least one month in advance. At the Meeting, a business presentation is made to shareholders and all Directors able to attend are available, formally during the AGM, and informally afterwards, for questions. Committee Chairmen ordinarily attend the AGM to respond to shareholders' questions. The entire Board was in attendance at the company's AGM in May 2006. All resolutions at the AGM are decided on a poll as required by the company's Articles of Association. The results of the poll are announced to the London Stock Exchange and posted on the company's website. Details of the 2007 AGM are set out in the section 'Annual General Meeting' (see page 59).

To ensure that the Non-Executive Directors are aware of and understand the views of major shareholders about the company, the Board has in place a process focusing on sector-specific issues, as well as general shareholder preferences. At its meeting in September, the Board received an external review of shareholder opinion.

The CEO and CFO maintain a dialogue with institutional shareholders on performance, plans and objectives through a programme of regular meetings.

The Group's Investor Relations department, with offices in London and Philadelphia, acts as a focal point for contact with investors throughout the year.

The Chairman meets regularly with institutional investors to hear their views and discuss issues of mutual importance.

The Chairman of the Remuneration Committee meets annually with major shareholders to discuss executive remuneration policy.

All Non-Executive Directors, including new appointees, are available to meet with major shareholders if requested.

The company's website provides access to current financial and business information about the Group.

Source: Annual Report (2006), GlaxoSmithKline, pp. 53 and 58.

15.7.4.5 Interim reporting

We explained in section 15.6.3 that the Disclosure and Transparency Rules (DTR) of the UK Listing Authority[56] require half-yearly reports that apply IAS 34, include an interim management report, and are published within two calendar months of the end of the six-month period. IAS 34 requires the 'discrete' method of reporting, where the interim period is regarded as a distinct accounting period. Seasonal businesses may consequently report markedly different results in each half or quarter of the year.

---

[56] http://www.fsa.gov.uk/pubs/ukla/list_dec06.pdf. The rules apply to accounting periods starting on or after 20 January 2007.

Prior to 2007 compliance with IAS 34 was voluntary. A survey[57] of the half-yearly interim reports of 100 UK listed companies in 2006 found that meeting the challenge of the DTR and IAS 34 in 2007 would require changes from all companies surveyed, although this would not be onerous for those already complying with best practice.

15.7.4.6 Corporate social responsibility reporting

The Kingsmill Report into Women's Employment and Pay (2001)[58] contained a range of recommendations for the government aimed at improving the management of human capital and so tackling the significant earnings gap between men and women in the UK. In relation to corporate reporting Kingsmill recommended improved reporting of human capital management information by both public and private sector organizations, suggesting the OFR as a possible vehicle for such reporting.

A survey by *Company Reporting* in 2004[59] found that companies reporting employee information did so in a specific CSR report or in the Directors' Report. Relatively few used the OFR or a separate HCR section. Information in the Directors' Report tended to be the minimum required by legislation. Those following the spirit of the Kingsmill recommendations were largely using a CSR report. The types of information disclosed were: general employee policies, union and labour relations, communication with employees, career development, remuneration, redundancies and employee satisfaction surveys. Half the companies surveyed addressed health and safety. A few companies produced diversity statistics on gender, ethnicity and disability.

The UK government has established a website as a gateway to corporate social responsibility.[60] It provides links to websites of organizations encouraging 'best practice' in CSR reporting.

15.7.4.7 Preliminary announcements

Under stock exchange rules a listed company is required to make an announcement of its results for the year in such a way that the information reaches all stock market participants at the same time. This is done through an organized announcements service; however, the amount of information announced varies from one company to the next. Some give little more than the annual profit and a summary balance sheet; others provide detail almost as great as that of the annual report which follows later. The ASB issued a non-mandatory statement on preliminary announcements which will improve the timeliness, quality, relevance and consistency of preliminary announcements. The recommendations have similarities to the statement on interim reports.

15.7.4.8 Directors' remuneration[61]

As explained earlier, concerns about corporate governance in the UK led in particular to recommendations of increased disclosure of directors' emoluments and other benefits. The general recommendations of the Cadbury Committee were made specific by the Greenbury Committee and implemented by the stock exchange as requirements for

---

[57] *Clear all year: considering new rules and practice in interim reporting,* Deloitte & Touche LLP (2007).

[58] www.womenandequalityunit.gov.uk/pay/Kingsmill.htm.

[59] *Company Reporting,* July 2004, pp. 3–8.

[60] csr.gov.uk.

[61] www.hmso.gov.uk/si/si2002/20021986.htm.

listed companies. In 1997, the requirements were extended by a statutory instrument to all limited companies, although with less demanding rules for unlisted companies. The statutory instrument was subsequently updated as *The Directors' Remuneration Report Regulations 2002*. The Companies Act 2006 continued the power to set regulations on the detail of directors' remuneration.

Summary and conclusions

In this chapter we have explained the institutional structure which has led to the development of the UK contribution to what is sometimes described as 'Anglo-Saxon' or 'Anglo-American' accounting. Comparison of this chapter with Chapter 11 shows that accounting in the UK has developed in a way that is distinctive from the process creating US GAAP. The mechanisms for oversight and assurance in the UK are also very different from the mechanisms set in place in the USA. The tradition in the UK has been for voluntary self-regulation but in recent years has moved increasingly within a framework set by statute law and administered by private sector bodies under authority of the law.

Characteristics of accounting principles and practice in the UK are related to the predictions made by Gray and others based upon analysis of accounting values. Gray's (1988) method of analysis may be used to predict that the accounting system in the UK will be characterized by strong professionalism, strong flexibility, strong optimism and strong transparency. The profession has a long history of development in the UK and has traditionally operated in a framework where statutory control is limited to prescribing minimum standards only, leaving the profession to determine best practice. Flexibility has been consistent with this professional approach, uniformity in matters such as presentation of formats being a relatively new feature caused by implementation of directives. Optimism, rather than conservatism, is seen in the use of alternative valuation rules to historical cost accounting. Transparency is seen in the extensive disclosures required of companies by way of notes to the accounts.

UK accounting has developed in its own mould but has also been exported to former UK colonies and trading partners. The UK standard-setting body continues to be an active participant in the work programme of the IASB.

Key points from the chapter:

- A history of strong professionalism in accounting has been moderated over the years by increasing regulation, initially through standards volunteered by the profession but more recently tending towards direct or indirect statutory control.

- Corporate governance initiatives, comprising Cadbury, Greenbury and Hampel, have provided guidance that has influenced other countries in their corporate governance codes. Higgs and Smith have added to this guidance in the specific areas of non-executive directors and audit committees.

- The Financial Services Authority sets the listing rules for the London Stock Exchange, including disclosure requirements.

- The idea of 'Anglo-Saxon' influence is frequently mentioned in research and professional papers; there are arguments for and against this system existing in reality.

- Oversight mechanisms have been enhanced since 2002 as a result of company law review and the wider role given to the Financial Reporting Council with its new subsidiaries.

- Accounting issues that may continue to show a separate UK characteristic of listed companies include the application of a 'true and fair view', the formats of financial statements and the range of narrative reporting.

- Gray's (1988) method of analysis may be used to predict that the wider corporate reporting system in the UK will be characterized by strong professionalism, strong flexibility, strong optimism and strong transparency. Regulation imposed outside the UK, particularly the IAS Regulation, modifies this tradition.

Questions

The following questions test your understanding of the material contained in the chapter and allow you to relate your understanding to the learning outcomes specified at the start of this chapter. The learning outcomes are repeated here. Each question is cross-referenced to the relevant section of the chapter.

Explain the development of accounting regulation

1 To what extent do early developments in accounting practice indicate the likely directions of professionalism/statutory control; uniformity/flexibility; conservatism/optimism; and secrecy/transparency in current practice? (section 15.3)

Explain the key institutional characteristics of the UK

2 How does the political and economic system of the UK fit into the classifications described in Chapter 6? (section 15.4.1)

3 How does the legal system of the UK fit into the classifications described in Chapter 6? (section 15.4.2)

4 How does the corporate governance system of the UK fit into the classifications described in Chapter 6? (section 15.4.3)

5 How does the taxation system of the UK compare to the descriptions given in Chapter 6? (section 15.4.4)

6 How does the corporate financing system of the UK compare to the descriptions given in Chapter 6? (section 15.4.5)

7 How does the accounting profession in the UK compare to the descriptions given in Chapter 6? (section 15.4.6)

8 How has membership of the EU affected UK accounting? (section 15.5.2)

9 Which institutional factors are most likely to influence UK accounting practice? (sections 15.4 and 15.5)

Discuss the meaning of an 'Anglo-Saxon' system of accounting

10 What are the arguments that support the description 'Anglo-Saxon accounting system'? (section 15.5.1)

11 What are the arguments against the description 'Anglo-Saxon accounting system? (section 15.5.1)

Explain the structure and processes for oversight and assurance

12 What was the outcome of the review of the regulatory regime of the accountancy profession in 2002? (section 15.6.1)

13 What is the role of the Financial Reporting Council and its subsidiary boards? (section 15.6.2)

14 How does the role of the Department of Trade and Industry bring statutory control to a professionally oriented system of accounting? (section 15.6.3)

15 What is the role of an audit committee in giving assurance on corporate reporting? (section 15.6.4)

16 What is the role of non-executive directors in giving assurance on corporate reporting? (section 15.6.5)

Understand and explain features of the corporate reporting system that illustrate the continuing diversity of UK accounting practices

17 How is the UK perceived in Gray's range of accounting values of 'professionalism/statutory control'? (section 15.7.1)

18 Why is there a strong view from the UK that the 'true and fair override' must be preserved in international accounting standards? (section 15.7.2)

19 Why might different formats be observed when comparing the financial statements of large UK listed companies with those of smaller unlisted companies? (section 15.7.3)

20 What are the aspects of narrative reporting that are characteristic of the UK accounting system? (section 15.7.4)

References and further reading

Alexander, D. and Archer, S. (2000) 'On the myth of "Anglo-Saxon" financial accounting', *International Journal of Accounting*, 35(4): 539–557.

Alexander, D. and Archer, S. (2003) 'On the myth of "Anglo-Saxon" financial accounting: a response to Nobes', *International Journal of Accounting*, 38(4): 503–504.

ASB (1994) FRS 5 *Reporting the Substance of Transactions,* Accounting Standards Board.

ASB (1997) *Interim Reports*, Statement by the Accounting Standards Board.

ASB (1999a) FRS 15 *Tangible Fixed Assets*, Accounting Standards Board, February.

ASB (1999b) *Statement of Principles*, Accounting Standards Board, December.

ASB (2003) *Operating and Financial Review*, Statement issued by the Accounting Standards Board.

ASB (2004) *UK Accounting Standards: A Strategy for Convergence with IFRS*, Accounting Standards Board, March.

ASB (2005) *Reporting Standard 1: Operating and Financial Review*, Accounting Standards Board. Issued May 2005, withdrawn January 2006.

ASB (2006) *Reporting Statement: Operating and Financial Review*, Accounting Standards Board, January.

Cairns, D. and Nobes, C. (2000) *The Convergence Handbook: A Comparison between International Accounting Standards and UK Financial Reporting Standards*. London: Institute of Chartered Accountants in England and Wales.

Charkham, J.P. (1994) *Keeping Good Company: A Study of Corporate Governance in Five Countries*. Oxford: Clarendon Press.

Co-ordinating Group on Accounting and Auditing Issues, *Final Report* to the Secretary of State for Trade and Industry and the Chancellor of the Exchequer, January 2003, URN 03/567, www.dti.gov.uk/cld/cgaai-final.pdf.

Davies, A. (1999) *A Strategic Approach to Corporate Governance*. Aldershot: Gower.

Davies, M., Paterson, R. and Wilson, A. (1999) *UK GAAP*, 6th edn. London: Macmillan.

Deloitte & Touche (2007) *ukGAAP 2007: Financial Reporting for UK Unlisted Entities*. Kingston upon Thames: CCH, Wolters Kluwer.

DTI (2004) Modernisation of Accounting Directives/IAS Infrastructure: A Consultation Document, March, www.dti.gov.uk/cld/current.htm.

DTI (2005) Company Law Reform White Paper. Archived at http://www.berr.gov.uk/files/file13958.pdf.

Edwards, E. and Bell, P. (1961) *The Theory and Measurement of Business Income*. Berkeley, CA: University of California Press.

FRC (2006a) *Discussion Paper: Choice in the UK audit market*, May, Financial Reporting Council, http://www.frc.org.uk.

FRC (2006b) *The Combined Code on Corporate Governance*, June, Financial Reporting Council, http://www.frc.org.uk/corporate/combinedcode.cfm.

Gordon, P.D. and Gray, S.J. (1994) *European Financial Reporting – United Kingdom*. London: Routledge.

Gray, S. and Roberts, C. (1993) 'Voluntary information disclosure: the attitude of UK multinationals', in Gray, S.J., Coenenberg, A.G. and Gordon, P.D. (eds) *International Group Accounting – Issues in European Harmonization*. London: Routledge.

Gray, S.J. (1988) 'Towards a theory of cultural influence on the development of accounting systems internationally', *Abacus*, 24(1): 1–15.

Higgs, D. (2003) *Review of the role and effectiveness of non-executive directors*, Department of Trade and Industry, www.dti.gov.uk/cld/non_exec_review.

Hofstede, G. (1984) *Culture's Consequences: International Differences in Work-related Values*. Beverly Hills, CA: Sage.

ICAEW (2003) *Prospective Financial Information: Guidance for UK Directors*, The Institute of Chartered Accountants in England and Wales, www.icaew.co.uk/pfi.

Ma, R., Parker, R.H. and Whittred, G. (1991) *Consolidation Accounting*. London: Longman Cheshire.

Meek, G.K., Roberts, C.B. and Gray, S.J. (1995) 'Factors influencing voluntary annual report disclosures by US, UK and continental European multinational corporations', *Journal of International Business Studies*, Third Quarter: 555–572.

Napier, C. (1995) 'The history of financial reporting in the United Kingdom', in Walton, P. (ed.) *European Financial Reporting: A History*. New York: Academic Press.

Nobes, C. (1993) 'Group accounting in the United Kingdom', in Gray, S.J., Coenenberg, A.G. and Gordon, P.D. (eds) *International Group Accounting – Issues in European Harmonization*. London: Routledge.

Nobes, C. (2003) 'On the myth of "Anglo-Saxon" financial accounting: a comment', *International Journal of Accounting*, 38(1): 95–104.

Nobes, C.W. (1984) *International Classification of Financial Reporting*. London: Croom Helm.

Nobes, C.W. and Parker, R.H. (1984) 'The Fourth Directive and the United Kingdom', in Gray, S.J. and Coenenberg, A.G. (eds) *EEC and Accounting Harmonization: Implementation and Impact of the Fourth Directive*. Amsterdam: North-Holland.

Parker, R. (1989) 'Importing and exporting accounting: the British experience', pp. 7–29 in Hopwood, A.G. (ed.) *International Pressures for Accounting Change*. London: Prentice Hall/ICAEW.

Parker, R. (1995) 'Financial reporting in the United Kingdom and Australia', in Nobes, C.W. and Parker, R. (eds) *Comparative International Accounting*, 4th edn. Englewood Cliffs, NJ: Prentice Hall.

Parker, R.H. and Nobes, C.W. (1994) *An International View of True and Fair Accounting*. London: Routledge.

Peasnell, K.V., Pope, P.F. and Young, S. (2001) 'The characteristics of firms subject to adverse rulings by the Financial Reporting Review Panel', *Accounting and Business Research*, 31(4): 291–311.

POB (2006) Key facts and trends in the accountancy profession, November, Professional Oversight Board, http://www.frc.org.uk/pob/.

Review (2003) *Review of the Regulatory Regime of the Accountancy Profession*, Report to the Secretary of State for Trade and Industry, January, URN 03/589.

Smith, R. (2003) *Audit Committees: Combined Code Guidance*, A report and proposed guidance by an FRC-appointed group chaired by Sir Robert Smith, Financial Reporting Council, www.frc.org.uk/publications.

Sudarsanam, P.S. (2003) *Creating value from mergers and acquisitions: the challenges, an integrated and international perspective.* Harlow: FT Prentice Hall.

Turnbull, N. (1999) *Internal Control: Guidance for Directors on the Combined Code.* London: The Institute of Chartered Accountants in England and Wales.

Turnbull, N. (2005) *Internal Control: Revised Guidance for Directors on the Combined Code*, Financial Reporting Council, http://www.frc.org.uk/corporate/internalcontrol.cfm.

Tyson (2003) *The Tyson Report on the Recruitment and Development of Non-executive Directors*, http://www.womenandequalityunit.gov.uk/boardroom_diversity/brighter_boards.htm.

Weetman, P. and Gray, S.J. (1990) 'International financial analysis and comparative corporate performance: the impact of UK versus US accounting principles on earnings', *Journal of International Financial Management and Accounting*, 2(2/3): 111–129.

Weetman, P. and Gray, S.J. (1991) 'A comparative international analysis of the impact of accounting principles on profits: the USA versus the UK, Sweden and The Netherlands', *Accounting and Business Research*, 21(84): 363–379.

Weetman, P., Jones, E.A.E., Adams, C. and Gray, S.J. (1998) 'Profit measurement and UK accounting standards: a case of increasing disharmony in relation to US GAAP and IASs', *Accounting and Business Research*, 28(3): 189–208.

Sources of regularly updated information on accounting standards and related matters

UK Accounting Standards Board: http://www.frc.org.uk/asb/.

The London Stock Exchange: http://www.londonstockexchange.com/.

The London Stock Exchange Fact File (annual publication).

16 Japan

Learning outcomes

After reading this chapter you should be able to:

- Understand the key characteristics of the country as summarized in published economic indicators.
- Relate institutional factors for the country to the framework set out in Chapter 6.
- Explain the origins of accounting regulations and the historical developments leading to the present state of practice.
- Explain the position of national accounting practice in relation to the IFRS.

16.1 Introduction

Despite the international pre-eminence of Japanese corporations, it is often quite difficult for a non-Japanese report reader to discover the measurement or disclosure practices of the typical Japanese company. The most obvious reason for this is the problem of language – while most large Japanese companies, including very many not listed on any overseas stock markets, produce English-language annual accounts and reports, these are different from the Japanese-language reports. Unlike the statutory Japanese reports, the English-language ones are normally glossy documents full of photos and graphics with a PR-style review of activities. More importantly, the financial statements are often not the same as those in the Japanese-language statements. They may contain different information, additional notes or even additional statements may be disclosed while other information given in the Japanese accounts is not provided. Japanese financial statements also look somewhat different from UK or US financial statements, which can confuse the unsophisticated user. Companies therefore typically recast their financial statements to make the English-language versions look more like a typical set of US financial statements. This does not affect the reported earnings or equity figures, but many items in the accounts will be reordered or reclassified or even produced solely for foreign readers. Exhibit 16.1 provides

| Exhibit 16.1 | Basis of presentation of English-language accounts: Sumitomo Mitsui |

NOTES TO CONSOLIDATED FINANCIAL STATEMENTS

1. **Basis of Presentation [extract]**

. . . SMFG has prepared the accompanying consolidated financial statements in accordance with the provisions set forth in the Japanese Securities and Exchange Law and its related accounting regulations, and in conformity with accounting principles generally accepted in Japan ('Japanese GAAP'), which are different in certain respects as to application and disclosure requirements of International Financial Reporting Standards.

The accounts of overseas subsidiaries are based on their accounting records maintained in conformity with generally accepted accounting principles prevailing in the respective countries of domicile. The accompanying consolidated financial statements have been restructured and translated into English (with some expanded descriptions and the inclusion of consolidated statements of stockholders' equity) from the consolidated financial statements of SMFG prepared in accordance with Japanese GAAP.

Some supplementary information included in the statutory Japanese language consolidated financial statements, but not required for fair presentation, is not presented in the accompanying consolidated financial statements.

Amounts less than one million yen have been omitted. As a result, the totals in Japanese yen shown in the financial statements do not necessarily agree with the sum of the individual amounts.

The translation of the Japanese yen amounts into U.S. dollars are included solely for the convenience of readers outside Japan, using the prevailing exchange rate at March 31, 2006, which was ¥117.48 to US$1. The convenience translations should not be construed as representations that the Japanese yen amounts have been, could have been, or could in the future be, converted into U.S. dollars at that rate.

Source: Sumitomo Mitsui Financial Group, Annual Report, 2006, p. 79, www.smfg.co.jp.

one example of this. It shows that Sumitomo Mitsui Financial Group not only reclassifies some of the items, but also provides a convenience translation and 'some expanded descriptions and the inclusion of consolidated statements of stockholders' equity' in its English-language accounts. However, the company omits other supplementary information provided in its Japanese-language financial statements.

The main problem for the non-Japanese reader will be understanding an unfamiliar set of GAAP, as Japan is not fully compliant with IFRS or US GAAP. A number of companies, especially those listed in the USA, therefore adjust the Japanese accounts to reflect US GAAP which are also then used as a basis for the audit of the English-language statements. Many of these companies have been doing this for a large number of years and currently there is no general move towards using IFRS instead of US GAAP. This is a form of restatement and it is not always possible to restate the figures without resorting to various estimates and assumptions. For example, Hitachi (2006) states, in its accounting policies, that:

> The consolidated financial statements presented herein have been prepared in a manner and reflect the adjustments which are necessary to conform them with accounting policies generally accepted in the United States of America. Management of the Company has made a number of estimates and assumptions relating to the reporting of assets and liabilities and the disclosure of contingent assets and liabilities to prepare these financial statements. Actual results could differ from those estimates.

(p. 39)

Whichever of these two approaches is used, the figures and formats will not be identical to the Japanese-language accounts and, where different accounting rules are used, companies do not generally quantify the impact on reported figures.

16.2 The country

Japan is made up of a number of islands off the coast of China. Much of the land is extremely mountainous and the population resides in the densely populated coastal areas. As can be seen from the figures in Exhibit 16.2, Japan is a highly successful country,

Exhibit 16.2 Japan: country profile

Population	128.1 million	
Land mass	377,727km^2	
GDP per head	US$35,390	
GDP per head in purchasing power parity	74.6	(USA = 100)
Origins of GDP:	%	
Agriculture	1.7	
Industry	30.0	
Services	68.3	
	%	
Real GDP average annual growth 1995–2005	1.3	
Inflation, average annual rate 2001–2006	−0.3	

Source: *The Economist Pocket World in Figures*, 2008 Edition, Profile Books Ltd.

with an average per capita GDP of over US$35,000 in 2006.[1] Note, however, that Japan has had a very low growth rate over the last ten years, so that it has dropped from third highest per capita GDP in 1998 to twentieth in 2006.

Japan has achieved remarkable growth since the Second World War. It is a highly industrialized and urbanized country that is dependent for its economic success on large international companies. Much of its success is built on trade, with the country being the home of many of the largest companies in the world. For example, the *Financial Times* annual Global 500 survey (2007) listed 49 Japanese companies in the top 500 companies in June 2007, measured by market capitalization. (This was second highest after the USA with 184 and above the UK with 41.) The top ten of these are shown in Exhibit 16.3.

Japan has in the past relied extensively upon exports, resulting in a large balance of payments surplus. Domestic investment has always been high, being approximately 25 per cent of GDP per annum in the early 2000s in comparison with 15–20 per cent in most other developed countries. This has resulted in a low rate of return and calls for a greater amount of inward investment, which has always been exceptionally low (FDI was just 2 per cent of GDP in 2002 compared with 20 per cent in the USA and 41 per cent in the UK).[2] However, inward direct investment is still difficult due to legislation such as the

Exhibit 16.3 Top ten Japanese companies, June 2007

Company	Rank Global 500	Market value $m	Sector	Listed in US	Listed in UK
Toyota Motor	7	230,832	Automobiles and parts	Yes	Yes
Mitsubishi UFS Financial	38	122,186	Banks	Yes	No
NTT DoCoMo	77	84,707	Mobile telecommunications	Yes	Yes
Nippon Telegraph & Telephone	81	83,054	Fixed line telecommunications	Yes	Yes
Mizuho Financial	92	76,316	Banks	Yes	No
Canon	100	71,486	Technology hardware and equipment	No	Yes
Sumitomo Mitsui Financial	105	70,083	Banks	No	No
Honda Motor	119	63,867	Automobiles and parts	Yes	Yes
Takedo Chemical Industries	130	58,218	Pharmaceuticals and biotechnology	No	No
Sony	154	50,868	Leisure goods	Yes	Yes

Source: www.FT.com, www.NYSE.com, www.Londonstockexchange.com.

---

[1] *The Economist Pocket World in Figures*, 2008 edition.

[2] OECD (2004); Beattie (2004).

mergers and acquisitions rules, corporate and country culture and 'complicated and non-transparent administrative procedures and practices that span several government offices as well as non-transparent administrative guidance and industry practice'.[3]

Despite the limited importation of goods and services, Japan has a long history of importing ideas from other countries. As will be discussed below, this includes accounting principles. Foreign influences can be seen both in the regulatory system and in the rules and practices adopted.

16.3 Institutions

16.3.1 Political and economic system

Japan has a liberal-democratic parliamentary system of government and government–business relations may be characterized in terms of cooperation. The government is actively involved in regulating and guiding businesses. A noticeable feature of this system is the bureaucracy, which is far more important and influential than it is in most western democratic societies. Ministerial officials draft legislative bills, brief parliamentary committees and commissions of inquiry and present bills personally to Parliament (the Diet). Particularly important for business is the powerful Ministry of International Trade and Investment (MITI) which, while less influential than many western authors claim, has played a significant role in managing the corporate sector. Also important is the powerful employers' federation, the Keidanren, which, while not a formal part of the political or government system, plays an important role in influencing government–business relationships and the regulation of business, including the regulation of accounting.

One of the most important features of the economic system that affects accounting is the way in which business is organized. Japanese trade was dominated by powerful trading houses which formed the basis of the *zaibatsu* (large financial combines). These groups were broken up after the Second World War and, in an attempt to stop them reforming, the 1946 Anti-monopoly Law (modelled on US laws) prohibited holding companies. However, it is not so easy to regulate business behaviour and the *zaibatsu* have been largely replaced by *keiretsu*. Lacking a holding company, the *keiretsu* tend instead to be quite loose networks of related companies which are centred around a bank, trading company (*sogo shosha*) or large manufacturing company. Typically, the size of shareholdings held by the lead company is small, with minority cross-holdings between group members being important. The group is also maintained through interlocking directorships and meetings of key staff. Intergroup sales and purchases are often also important and long credit terms, especially in times of financial difficulty, are not uncommon. The relationships may also be cemented by a number of other activities such as joint research and development projects. In practice, there are four different types of *keiretsu*:[4]

- the six largest corporate groups consisting of three ex-*zaibatso* groups, including Mitsui, Mitsubishi and Sumitomo;
- three bank groups – Fuyo, Sanwa and Daiichi-Kangyo;
- *keiretsu* organized along vertical lines of production (e.g. Toyota); and
- *keiretsu* organized along vertical lines of distribution (e.g. Panasonic).

---

[3] Invest Japan Forum (2002) as reported by Beattie (2004).

[4] Kumar and Hyodo (2001).

Exhibit 16.4	Mitsubishi Companies

Q1: Is Mitsubishi a single company?

A1: No. 'Mitsubishi' is a community that consists of a multitude of independent companies. The names of most - but not all - of those companies contain the word 'Mitsubishi.' And many of the companies use the three-diamond Mitsubishi mark. But none calls itself simply 'Mitsubishi.'

Q2: You say Mitsubishi is 'a multitude of independent companies.' How do you define Mitsubishi and how many companies are there?

A2: Here at mitsubishi.com, we speak of 'Mitsubishi' in terms of the member companies subject to the company search on this website, which counts to approximately 200. But that is not the one and only definition of Mitsubishi. Another example of definition is the 30 members of the Kinyokai, the informal group of core Mitsubishi companies.

The independence of the Mitsubishi companies makes the 'Mitsubishi' all but impossible to define and thus a clear number the group consists of cannot be stated. If we simply count the number of companies with 'Mitsubishi' in their names existing world wide, that would be around 400. But there are also hundreds of Mitsubishi companies that do not have 'Mitsubishi' in their names.

Q3: Why do the Mitsubishi companies undertake joint endeavors like the 'mitsubishi.com' website if they are separate and independent companies?

A3: The companies conduct their business activities independently and even compete with each other in many fields. But as they share the same founding management *philosophy*, they cooperate in areas of common interest, such as sporting, cultural events and public-interest activities. The companies established a Mitsubishi portal on the Internet, 'mitsubishi.com', to provide a broad perspective on 'Mitsubishi.'

Q4: Do the Mitsubishi companies have some kind of decision-making body that determines overall policy for the companies?

A4: No. But all the companies honor the *Three Principles* prescribed by *Koyata Iwasaki*, the Fourth and final president of the old Mitsubishi organization: 1. Corporate Social Responsibility, 2. Integrity and Fairness, and 3. International Understanding through Trade.

Q5: How did the Mitsubishi companies begin?

A5: The companies trace their *origin* to a shipping company started in 1870 by a man named *Yataro Iwasaki*. Yataro also established businesses in mining, shipbuilding, banking and insurance. He thus laid the foundation for the subsequent growth and *development of the Mitsubishi companies*.

Source: www.mitsubishi.com/e/group/about.html.

The Mitsubishi Group of companies is a good example of such a loose group of companies. Exhibit 16.4 reproduces part of the explanation of the group relationships found on the Mitsubishi website.

The impact of the *keiretsu* on accounting has been much debated. It has been argued for example that they have led to lower levels of disclosure to outsiders and lower profits as less efficient management are protected from the rigours of the corporate control market. However, there is also evidence that such insider relationships actually increase the effectiveness of the monitoring of management and decrease the ability of management to manage earnings so increasing the quality and predictability of accounting numbers.[5]

The economic system also impacts upon particular measurement rules. For example, the collapse of Asia–Pacific economies in 1997 had repercussions in Japan which meant that some banks were not able to collect investments in and loans to other countries,

---

[5] See, for example, Cheung *et al.* (1999); Jiang and Kim (2000); Douthett and Jung (2001).

while the long period of expansion over 50 years saw a pause. This had consequences for accounting and auditing. For example, the poor performance of investments meant that many companies found themselves with large pension fund obligations which led to a review of the accounting for retirement benefits. This led to the introduction of a new standard which is very similar to IAS 19.

16.3.2 Legal system

The legal system is a code-based legal system. While it has been influenced by other countries, such as France and Germany, it also has some unique features. Like other code law countries, business relationships are regulated by the Commercial Code (CC). The CC, being set by the Ministry of Justice, is concerned with ensuring that all parties to a contract are protected, especially lenders and other creditors. The emphasis was therefore placed upon single entity reporting – as it is the legal entity not the group that enters into the legal contracts – and upon prudence or conservatism in reporting performance. However the 2002 tax reforms introduced the concept of a consolidated taxation system which taxes the parent and all 100 per cent owned domestic subsidiaries as a single entity.

One obvious impact of the CC that would be unusual or unfamiliar to a UK or a US reader is with respect to legal reserves. The requirement for legal or statutory reserves is an important aspect of the emphases placed upon creditor protection in the CC. Companies have to transfer an amount equal to at least 10 per cent of cash dividends to a legal reserve each year until that reserve plus any extra paid-in capital amounts to at least 25 per cent of legal capital. This is not distributable, although any reserves in excess of this 25 per cent are distributable. Companies would often also reduce distributable reserves by making relatively large transfers from distributable to appropriated non-distributable reserves. Particularly important are transfers with respect to retirement payments, warranties and repairs.

16.3.3 Corporate governance system[6]

In Japan, the legal framework prescribes two types of mechanisms for corporate governance that apply to most listed companies: a corporate auditors system consisting of general meetings of shareholders, the board of directors, representative directors, executive directors, corporate auditors and the board of corporate auditors ('company with a corporate auditors system'); and a committees system consisting of general meetings of shareholders, the board of directors and committees composed of members of the board of directors (nomination committee, audit committee and compensation committee), representative executive officers and executive officers ('company with a committees system'). The selection is left to individual companies. The committees system is a system that was introduced in April 2003 when the CC was amended. Before such amendment, only the corporate auditors system existed. Under the committees system three committees must be established: a nomination committee, an audit committee and a compensation committee. Each committee should consist of three or more directors, and at least half of the members of each committee should be outside directors. With respect to companies with a corporate auditors system, outside auditors must be nominated, but the appointment of outside directors is not required.

---

[6] Mechanism for Corporate Governance in Japan, Appendix to *Principles of Corporate Governance for Listed Companies*, 2004.

The committees system is more closely comparable with the system found in listed companies in the UK or USA. The corporate auditors system shows that corporate governance mechanisms can be set up differently while still applying principles that are consistent with the OECD (see Chapter 3).

16.3.4 Taxation system[7]

The Japanese corporate tax system has been described as a mixed system. It retains a German influence, seen in the relative importance of the CC in prescribing methods of tax computation, and it has also been influenced by the US system, seen in its reliance upon GAAP.

The Corporation Tax (CT) law is the most important tax law although it is supplemented by Special Taxation Measures which are designed to meet specific policy objectives such as energy conservation, pollution control, regional development and the promotion of small and medium enterprises. These Special Taxation Measures apply to all entities, particular industries or even specific entities as appropriate. The CT law does not contain sufficiently detailed rules to enable companies to calculate taxable income. Instead, it relies upon other sources of authority. In particular, it requires companies to use the CC as the basis for computing much of their taxable income, hence the continental European-style rules that allowances or expenses are permitted for tax purposes only if they are also included in the published accounts. However, the CC is not exhaustive and does not unambiguously define income. The CT law requires companies to use GAAP if there are no specific regulations and where it does not conflict with the CT law.

There is a clear relationship between reported income and taxable income. If a company changes its methods of calculating reportable income then it will probably also change its taxable income. However, the two income measures are not identical. While the CC and GAAP form the basis of taxable income, the CT law also prescribes a number of adjustments to reported income, expenses and allowances. There are a number of reasons for this. In particular, the CT law is also designed to provide tax incentives to encourage companies to meet the government's economic goals – additional or special depreciation over and above economic or ordinary depreciation, for example, is allowed for under the Special Taxation Measures. Special depreciation is recognized as an expense for tax purposes, while under the CC it is reported as an appropriation of retained earnings. The impact of economic policy considerations can also be seen in a number of other areas of accounting including the further use of reserve accounting. Companies are permitted to set up a number of tax-free reserves. Some of these, such as reserves for bad debts, are permitted under both the CT law and CC. A considerable number of other tax-free reserves are instead treated as an expense under the Special Taxation Measures and so deducted from earnings before taxation, while under the CC they are instead treated as appropriations of retained earnings. While the importance of these measures has declined recently, as Japan has increasingly moved towards an 'equity in taxation' perspective, they still remain important. Just how common these reserves still are is illustrated in Exhibit 16.5, which lists the most important reserves permitted in the Special Taxation Measures for fiscal year 2003.[8]

Although the importance of the Special Tax Measures is falling, they are still significant. For example, it is estimated that they cost an estimated ¥1,792bn in terms of lost tax revenues in the 2003 fiscal year falling to Y1,088bn in the 2005 fiscal year, as shown in Exhibit 16.6.

---

[7] For more detail see www.mof.go.jp/english/tax.

[8] Tokyo Stock Exchange annual report (2004).

Exhibit 16.5	Reserves permitted in the Special Taxation Measures

- Overseas investment loss reserve
- Reserve for prevention of mineral pollution in metal mining
- Reserve for prevention of certain disasters
- Reserve for changing the heat quantity of gas
- Reserve for loss in buying-back computers
- Used nuclear fuel reprocessing reserve
- Nuclear plant dismantling reserve
- Reserve for extraordinary casualties
- Special reserve for repair of ships or furnaces
- Reserve for locating new mineral beds
- Reserve for large-scale repair of Shinkansen railways
- Reserve for Kansai or Central Japan International Airport Adjustment
- Reserve for utilisation and accumulation of farmland

Source: Ministry of Finance, www.mof.go.jp/english/tax/taxes2006e.htm.

Exhibit 16.6	The estimated loss of revenue due to Special Taxation Measures for corporations, fiscal year 2005

	Billion yen
A. Special depreciation	
1. Special depreciation on specified equipment	
Anti-pollution equipment	4.0
Seacraft etc.	1.0
2. Special depreciation on medical equipment etc.	8.0
3. Immediate depreciation on low-value assets	40.0
4. Others	15.0
Sub-total	68.0
B. Reserves	
5. For removal and disposal of nuclear material used in power generation	16.0
6. For unusual danger	19.0
7. Others	20.0
Sub-total	55.0
C. Tax credits and income deduction etc.	
8. Credit for conducting research and development	597.0
9. Tax measures to promote reform of structure of energy supply & demand	28.0
10. To promote investment by SMEs	211.0
11. To improve management fundamentals of SME	3.0
12. To improve management fundamentals on information [sic]	100.0
13. Increase in human investment	14.0
14. Others	12.0
Sub-total	965.0
Total revenue loss	1,088.0

Source: Ministry of Finance, www.mof.go.jp/english/tax/taxes2006e.htm.

Exhibit 16.7	Income taxes reconciliation statement

Company A (effective rate below statutory rate)

The Company and its domestic subsidiaries are subject to a number of income taxes, which, in the aggregate, represent a statutory income tax rate of approximately 40% for the years ended December 31, 2006 and 2005, and 42% for the year ended December 31, 2004.

A reconciliation of the Japanese statutory income tax rate and the effective income tax rate as a percentage of income before income taxes and minority interests is as follows:

Year ended December 31	2006	2005	2004
Japanese statutory income tax rate	40.0%	40.0%	42.0%
Increase (reduction) in income taxes resulting from:			
Expenses not deductible for tax purposes	0.3	0.3	0.4
Tax benefits not recognized on operating losses of subsidiaries	–	–	–
Income of foreign subsidiaries taxed at lower than Japanese statutory tax rate	(2.1)	(1.9)	(2.1)
Tax credit for research and development expenses	(4.1)	(3.9)	(4.0)
Other	0.4	0.3	(1.3)
Effective income tax rate	34.5%	34.8%	35.1%

Company B (effective rate above statutory rate in 2007)

The Tokyo Regional Tax Authority investigated prices of sales and purchases with overseas subsidiaries ('transfer pricing'), by comparison with third party transactions, and assessed additional tax reflected in the income statement for 2007.

Year ended March 31	2007	2006	2005
Japanese statutory income tax rate	40.9%	40.9%	40.9%
Expenses not deductible for tax purposes	0.5	0.6	0.7
Equity in earnings of affiliates	(3.3)	(3.3)	(3.2)
Non-taxable dividend income	(0.1)	(0.1)	(0.0)
Tax credit for research and development costs	(1.2)	(1.6)	(2.6)
Correction for transfer pricing taxation	9.1	–	–
Other	(0.2)	2.4	0.5
Effective income tax rate	45.7%	38.9%	36.3%

Companies disclose varying amounts of information on taxes. Typical reconciliations between the statutory tax rate and the effective tax rate actually paid are shown in Exhibit 16.7.

16.3.5 Corporate financing system

The Tokyo Stock Exchange (TSE) is the largest of the Japanese stock markets with 2,174 domestic and 32 foreign companies listed on it at the end of 2003[9] (see Exhibit 4.3).

---

[9] www.mof.go.jp/English/tax/taxes2003e.htm.

For a period in the late 1980s the TSE was the largest in the world, as measured by market capitalization. However, this was followed by major falls in share prices in the 1990s with the market value in 2006 of ¥549,789,300 million having nearly returned to the 1989 high of ¥611,151,800 million.

The TSE underwent a major structural reform, the so-called 'Japanese Big-Bang', in 1998 to make it more competitive and to make share trading more appealing. This included the introduction of off-exchange trading of listed securities, followed in January 1999 by reductions in the listing requirements for medium-sized companies and, in July 1999, by the introduction of the TDnet (Timely Disclosure network) which, *inter alia*, means all listed products are traded via a computerized trading system and the information filed with the TSE is also made available on its website. However, while Tokyo is one of the largest and most modern stock exchanges in the world, it differs from most other large stock markets in that international companies are not important. Unlike exchanges such as the NYSE or Euronext, the number of foreign companies listed has decreased every year since 1991. In 1991 there were 125 listed overseas companies; by the end of 2006 this had fallen to 25 (see Exhibit 16.8). Trading value has fallen by even more, from ¥3,469,227 million in 1987 to only ¥153,788 million in 2006. However,

Exhibit 16.8	**Foreign companies listed on TSE as at end 2006**

Australia	Westpac Banking Corp.	May 1986
Canada	Toronto-Dominion Bank	May 1986
Cayman	Xinhua Finance	Oct. 2004
France	Alcatel Lucent	Dec. 1988
	BNP Paribus	Mar. 2000
	Société Générale	Feb. 2000
Germany	Bayer	Oct. 1988
	Volkswagen	Dec. 1988
	Deutsche Telekom	Nov. 1996
Hong Kong	Henderson Land Development	Feb. 1997
Korea	POSCO	Nov. 2005
Malaysia	YTL Corporation	Feb. 1996
Netherlands	AEGON	Oct. 1988
Spain	Telefonica	Oct. 1985
Switzerland	UBS	June 1998
UK	Barclays	Aug. 1986
	BP	Aug. 1987
	Japaninvest Group	Dec. 2006
USA	AFLAC Incorp	Dec. 1987
	American International Group	Sept. 1987
	Bank of America	July. 1987
	Boeing Company	Oct. 1990
	Dow Chemical Company	Dec. 1973
	JPMorgan Chase & Co.	June 2001
	Merrill Lynch & Co.	Nov. 1986

Source: *TSE Stock Exchange Fact Book*, 2007.

Exhibit 16.9 Share ownership in Japanese stock markets (%)

	1986	1996	2006
Financial institutions	41.5	41.9	31.1
Business corporations	30.1	25.6	20.7
Foreigners	5.3	11.9	28.0
Individuals	20.1	19.4	18.1
Government and others	3.0	1.2	2.1
Total	100	100	100

Source: TSE (2006) Shareholding Survey.

the importance of foreign investors has increased substantially over a similar period as illustrated in Exhibit 16.9.

The more important source of finance for most companies has traditionally been bank loans. In the past, these have tended to be short-term loans, although this is changing and the financing patterns of Japanese companies are beginning to resemble more closely those of US or UK companies. Most large companies tend to have close relationships with a key bank and short-term bank loans are automatically rolled over. (Note that this has the effect of making typical working capital and long-term debt to equity ratios different from what might be expected with UK or US companies.) One of the advantages of being a member of a *keiretsu* is that the central bank is more likely to increase lending in periods of difficulty to prevent a crisis occurring. In many countries, such as the UK, large companies typically have relationships with numerous banks; these may even compete with each other to be the first to call in their loans at the first sign of difficulty.

16.3.6 The accounting profession

The first institute of professional accountants was created in 1927, although the profession in its current form originates in the period following the Second World War as one of the creations of the US occupation forces. The CPA law (1948) required accountants to be suitably trained (in a manner and at a level similar to US accountants). This led to the creation of the Japanese Institute of Certified Public Accountants (JICPA) in 1949, although it was not until 1966 that all CPAs had to be members of the JICPA (see Exhibit 16.10 below).

All companies regulated by the Securities and Exchange Law, large CC-regulated companies, financial institutions and various other types of organizations have to be audited by a registered CPA. The profession itself is very small with only 17,246 CPAs plus a further 5,782 junior accountants (having passed stage 2 of the professional exams) and 163 audit corporations at the end of 2006.[10] However, this represents a significant growth over the last two or three decades mirroring the increase in audit requirements. For example, there were 1,508 CPAs in 1960 growing to 4,162 CPAs and 24 audit corporations in 1970 and 8,799 CPAs and 110 audit corporations in 1990. While this shows a remarkable growth, the absolute size of figures is misleading as the tax accountants, who are much larger in number, do much of the work required by the CT law and they have

---

[10] www.hp.jicpa.or.jp/english.

their own professional body and examinations. A second difference from the UK or USA is that far fewer people train as accountants and subsequently leave the profession to join commercial or financial institutions. This difference can largely be ascribed to cultural differences. Japan is famous for lifetime employment, although its importance tends to be overstated in that it applies only to larger companies and to the more skilled workforce. (Even here, people tend to take early retirement and then continue to work after this on a consultancy or short-term contract basis.) However, lifetime employment policies and the philosophy of group membership and loyalty to the company are far stronger in Japan than they are in most other countries – commercial and financial institutions prefer to train their own staff and place far less emphasis upon external training or professional qualifications.

Despite this, the competition to enter the profession has historically been extremely intense and the success rate has correspondingly been low. The examinations are conducted by the CPA and Auditing Oversights Board (see section 16.5.2, below); the first exam is an entrance exam open to all non-graduates and which tests general literary and mathematical ability. The second stage allows successful candidates to become junior accountants. The success rate in the second set of examinations has historically been below 10 per cent with only about half of the successful candidates going on to pass the third and final set of examinations in their first sitting at the end of a further minimum of three years of training and practical experience.

The JICPA acts to a large extent as a trade body and it does not issue accounting standards. Instead, its functions are limited to the following:

- conducting research on and investigation into practices and systems of accounting, auditing and other related professional services in Japan and overseas;
- providing guidance on auditing, accounting and other related professional services and submitting comments on various exposure drafts published by other organizations;
- providing pre-qualification training courses and programmes for continuing professional education;
- performing quality control reviews; and
- conducting investigative and disciplinary proceedings.

JICPA was also a founding member of both the IFAC and IASB.

16.4 External influences

The development of accounting regulation in Japan is also very largely a history of how Japan has imported help or ideas from overseas. In particular, the early CCs were heavily influenced by practice in continental Europe while the USA played a major role in introducing legislation after the Second World War which created the Securities and Exchange Law, the JICPA and a standard-setting body, the Business Advisory Deliberation Council.

US influence is seen in the English-language reports of Japanese companies. When companies were first required to prepare consolidated financial statements in conformity with Japanese GAAP in 1975, some companies were allowed by special regulation to submit US GAAP consolidated financial statements to the Ministry of Finance in place of Japanese GAAP statements. These were companies registered with the US SEC at the time. Over the period of 30 years further companies became registered with the US SEC but they were not named in the special regulation and so had to produce consolidated financial statements under both sets of GAAP. The list was only updated in 2002. The special regulation does not allow IFRS to be substituted for Japanese GAAP.

16.5 Accounting regulations

16.5.1 Early influences on accounting regulations

Before the Meiji era (1868–1912), Japan was a closed country made up of some 2,000 feudal entities with political power shared between the *shogun* (military leaders) and the *daimyo* (feudal lords). There were no formal courts or written laws, accounting was not regulated and a variety of different types of traditional bookkeeping methods were used. While some of these were extremely sophisticated, they were diary-style single entry systems. This began to change in the 1860s and 1870s when Japan started to look to the west, to develop international trade and to learn from the experiences of other countries. This included, for example, the introduction of double-entry bookkeeping for the first time in Japan in the Yokosuka Steel Works where it was introduced in collaboration with French naval accountants. Particularly important was the Iwakura Mission in 1871, which included over 1,000 officials who went to Europe and the USA to see how businesses were organized and how business–government relationships were structured. Japan also began to import accounting texts from a number of countries and to employ foreign accountants to train local accountants.[11]

The influence of the UK in this period can be seen in the work of Alexander Shand. His system was incorporated into the 1872 National Bank Act which included requirements to prepare annual accounts which had to be examined or audited by government officials. However, continental European influences were more important. The first draft of the Civil Code of 1878 was rejected by Japanese jurists as being too close to the French Code from which it was largely derived. The final 1889 version clearly contained influences from French, German and British law. Similarly, the original draft Commercial Code of 1881 was drafted by a German, and both the final version of the Old Commercial Code of 1890 and its amended version or the New Commercial Code of 1899 retained a strong German flavour. This legal framework remains in place and Japanese accounting in consequence continues to retain certain continental European characteristics.

16.5.2 Development of the triangular legal system

The Japanese regulatory system is similar to many of the code-based European countries. There are three sources of laws that prescribe financial accounting and reporting. These are: the Ministry of Justice via the CC, the Ministry of Finance via the Securities and Exchange Law (SEL), and the tax authorities which have an important indirect influence, resulting in a system that is often referred to as the 'Triangular Legal System'.[12] While the stock market is important, it does not regulate corporate disclosures itself and the accounting profession has been relatively unimportant except with respect to the auditing rules.

---

[11] Someya (1989).
[12] www.jicpa.or.jp/n_eng/e-account.html.

The earliest regulations took the form of CC regulations administered by the Ministry of Justice. These apply to joint-stock (Kabushiki Kaisha) companies whether publicly listed or not. While there is no code of accounts, the rules are relatively uniform and conservative. The most important objective is to protect creditors. The first Commercial Code of 1899 required all companies to produce five documents:

- an inventory (no longer required)
- a balance sheet
- an income statement
- a business report
- proposals regarding profit distribution and reserve accounts.

These documents had to be audited by a statutory auditor, who does not have to be a CPA. This audit is primarily concerned with ensuring that no fraud has taken place rather than attesting to the 'correctness', 'truthfulness' or 'fairness' of the published accounts. It can be more appropriately thought of as being akin to an audit of corporate governance rather than an independent external audit.

The CC was very largely of Germanic origin, although later amendments have reflected Anglo-American influences. Emphasis was originally placed upon the inventory of assets and liabilities which had to be presented to the annual general meeting. The balance sheet had originally to be created from this inventory, rather than being derived from the original books of account. This reflected the legalistic background of the CC. It does not include many detailed accounting rules, these instead being prescribed in legal Ordinances which contain detailed rules regarding the form and content of the prescribed statements.

Until 2004 the CC only applied to single entity financial statements with companies having to submit an annual report to the AGM containing the balance sheet, income statement, business report, profit appropriation and supporting schedules. For year-ends after April 2004, companies instead had to provide designated consolidated statements including the balance sheet and income statement. In addition, the accounting requirements have now been moved from the CC itself to Ministerial regulations, meaning that they no longer need the approval of the Parliament or national Diet, allowing them to be more easily changed.

The Ministry of Finance plays a vital role in regulating listed companies. All listed companies are required, under the SEL, to file audited registration documents and annual and semi-annual accounting reports with both the stock exchange and the Ministry of Finance. The registration documents and the annual report contain similar information including a balance sheet, income statement, statement of appropriations and various supporting schedules or notes. These documents are in addition to those required under the CC. The prescribed form and content are more detailed and the requirements are designed less for creditor protection; instead the needs of shareholders predominate. This means that the SEL accounts include additional disclosures and items may be classified somewhat differently. However, as far as the parent company accounts are concerned, the CC accounts and the SEL accounts should give the same net income and shareholders' equity figures. These statements have to be audited by a registered independent CPA as well as the statutory auditors.

Much of the Ministry's work in this regard was passed down to the Business Accounting Deliberation Council, now renamed as the Business Accounting Council (BAC). While this may have appeared to be quite similar to the standard-setting bodies of countries like the UK or USA, it had certain important differences. In particular it was less independent of the government. Its members were appointed by the Ministry and bureaucrats played an important role in initiating and guiding new rules through the legislative process.

However, this triangular system is now reduced in importance. The standard-setting process has now moved away from the Ministry of Finance and the BAC to a private sector standard-setting body, the Accounting Standards Board.

The history of important accounting and auditing regulations, as seen by the accounting profession, is shown in Exhibit 16.10.

Exhibit 16.10	History of the accounting and auditing system
1890	Commercial Code enacted
1948	Securities and Exchange Law enacted Certified Public Accountants Law enacted
1949	Financial Accounting Standards for Business Enterprises issued Japanese Institute of Certified Public Accountants established as a self-disciplinary association
1950	Regulations Concerning the Terminology, Forms & Preparation Methods of Financial Statements issued Auditing Standards & related rules issued
1951	Audit by CPAs required under the Securities and Exchange Law Licensed Tax Accountant Law enacted
1963	Financial Statements of companies with shares traded over-the-counter became subject to audit
1966	JICPA recognized as a special legal body according to amended CPA law requiring all CPAs to be members of JICPA
1967	First audit corporation formed in accordance with amended CPA law
1973	IASC established with JICPA as a founding member
1974	Audit by CPAs required under the Commercial Code
1975	Accounting Standards for Consolidated Financial Statements issued Audit of banks and insurance companies by CPAs required
1977	CPA audit of interim and consolidated financial statements begun IFAC established with JICPA as a founding council member
1979	Accounting standards for foreign currency transactions issued
1981	An IASC board meeting held in Tokyo Scope of audit by CPAs expanded and strengthened in revised Commercial Code Auditing manual issued by JICPA auditing committee
1987	13th World Congress of Accountants held in Tokyo
1988	Disclosure requirements for segments drastically revised Disclosure requirements for related party transactions and market value information for marketable securities amended
1991	Auditing standards and related rules drastically revised

1992	The CPA Law relating to examinations and other issues amended
1993	Commercial Code amended to strengthen shareholders' rights and statutory auditors' authority and to improve procedures for issuing debentures
1995	Accounting Standards for Foreign Currency Transactions amended
1998	Fiftieth anniversary of the CPA Practice in Japan
1999	Accounting Standards for Financial Instruments issued Commercial Code amended to set forth new Stock Exchange and Transfer System Accounting Standards for Foreign Currency Transactions revised
2001	Accounting Standards Board of Japan (of the Financial Accounting Standards Foundation) established as an accounting standards setter
2002	Business Accounting Council published Opinions concerning Revisions of Auditing Standards, Revisions of Interim Auditing Standards & Accounting Standard for Impairment of Fixed Assets. Commercial Code amended to include Ministerial Decree on Financial Statements of Joint Stock Companies Auditing Standards drastically revised
2003	Certified Public Accountants Law amended
2004	CPA Investigation and Examination Board reorganised into CPAAOB to enhance auditor oversight

Source: www.jicpa.or.jp (July 2007).

16.5.3 The development of the accounting profession, BADC and BAC

Significant external influences can also be seen in the regulation of listed companies. Following the defeat of Japan in the Second World War, the allied occupation under US General MacArthur set out *inter alia* to reform and restructure Japanese business. An important element of this was the disbanding of the 15 most powerful *zaibatsu* or large financial combines which controlled much of Japanese business and the sale of the shares of the constituent companies to the general public. For this to succeed the stock market, which was not very active, had to be reconstructed to provide external shareholders with sufficient security at an acceptable cost to make share ownership an attractive proposition. The occupation forces naturally turned to the USA to provide a model of how to do this and, in an albeit modified form, they imported and imposed the relevant US laws. One of the things required was a highly skilled and highly regarded profession of independent auditors to attest the accounts of listed companies.

The CPA law was passed in 1948, leading to the creation of the Japanese Institute of Certified Public Accountants (JICPA). The Securities and Exchange Commission, an independent body designed to oversee the securities market, was also established in the same year. However, this was disbanded in 1953 and its role transferred instead to the Ministry of Finance (MoF). Of long-term importance was the Securities and Exchange Law (SEL) of 1949 which still forms the basis of the regulation of listed companies. Also created was the Investigation Committee on Business Accounting Systems (ICBAS), an independent body charged with developing accounting standards. It began work by issuing, in 1949, two statements: the 'Working Rules for Preparing Financial Statements' and the 'Financial Accounting Standards for Business Enterprises' (also known as the 'Business Accounting

Principles'). The latter was very heavily influenced by 'A Statement of Accounting Principles' which had been published by the US AICPA in 1938. In 1952 the ICBAS ceased to be an independent body when it was effectively made a part of the Ministry of Finance. It also changed its name to the Business Accounting Deliberation Council (BADC). While the power to regulate accounting had therefore passed from independent bodies to the government and the bureaucracy, the BADC retained an important role. The profession, in the form of JICPA, was represented on this body, as were academics and representatives from the business community (the Keidanren, or the Japanese Federation of Economic Organizations, banks and commercial corporations), the Tokyo Stock Exchange, the Securities Analysts' Association and various other interested parties. All members were appointed by the Ministry of Finance, which also provided the funding.

The BADC issued a number of standards including:

- 'Financial accounting standards for business enterprises' (first issued in 1949 and amended a number of times since then);
- 'Financial accounting standards on consolidated financial statements' (June 1975 and later amendments, revised June 1997);
- 'Standards for the preparation of interim financial statements';
- 'Accounting standards for foreign currency translation';
- 'Consolidated financial reporting';
- 'Tax effect accounting';
- 'Employee retirement benefits';
- 'Financial instruments'.

It also issued a number of interpretations concerned, *inter alia*, with the problems of reconciling financial accounting standards with CC and tax law requirements.

In July 2000 there was a further reorganization with the establishment under the Ministry of Finance of the Financial Services Agency (FSA) with a remit that includes the SEL, securities markets trading rules, the establishment of business accounting standards, planning and policy on corporate finance and the supervision of CPAs and the CPA law. As part of this, the renamed Business Accounting Council (BAC) was brought under the FSA as an advisory body which 'establishes business accounting standards and audit standards, and at the same time conducts investigations and deliberations concerning the unification of cost accounting and the development and improvement of other aspects of the business accounting system, and reports to the Commissioner of the FSA and others'.[13]

16.5.4 The Accounting Standards Board of Japan and the Financial Accounting Standards Foundation

Ten private sector organizations including the Keidanren, JICPA and TSE came together in February 2001 to initiate a private sector standard-setting organization. This led, in July 2001, to the establishment of the Financial Accounting Standards Foundation (FASF) and, underneath this, the Accounting Standards Board of Japan (ASBJ) which then took over from the BAC as the main standard-setting body, while the BAC retained its position as an advisory council to the FSA. the relationship between the FASF and the ASBJ is shown in Exhibit 16.11.

Two main factors led to the creation of this new organization. Firstly, it was recognized that increasing globalization and sophistication of business and financial transactions

---

[13] www.fsa.go.jp.

Exhibit 16.11 Organization of the Financial Accounting Standards Foundation, 2007

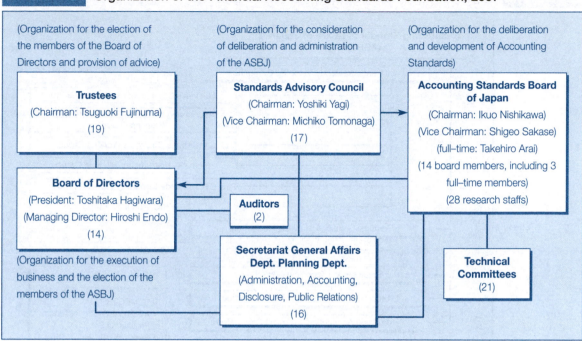

Source: www.asb/or/jp/html_e/fasf/organization.php.

meant that there was an increased need for new standards and, secondly, it was important to establish a system that could collaborate with and respond quickly and efficiently to the IASB and changes to IFRS. Accordingly, the objective of the FASF is to 'contribute to the sound development of financial practices in Japan and sound capital markets by making recommendations and contributions to the international accounting system by studying, researching, and developing generally accepted accounting standards, and by studying and researching disclosure system and various other practices pertinent to business finance systems'.[14] To do this, the FASF carries out five activities:

- study, research and develop generally accepted accounting standards;
- study and research disclosure systems, as well as various other practices pertinent to business finance systems;
- make recommendations based on results of these;
- help develop and improve international accounting standards;
- other business necessary to discharge objectives.

The FASF is managed by a board of directors and by trustees. The former are responsible for fundraising, deciding on members and determining the business plan, while the latter give advice on plans and budgets and select the board members and the auditors. Currently there are 14 directors, only one of which is full-time, with the rest representing industry, audit firms, financial institutions and academia.

The ASBJ is responsible for the development of accounting standards via a number of themed committees as shown in Exhibit 16.12. Exhibit 16.13 provides examples of the

---

[14] www.asb.or.jp.

Exhibit 16.12 Organization of the ASBJ (2007)

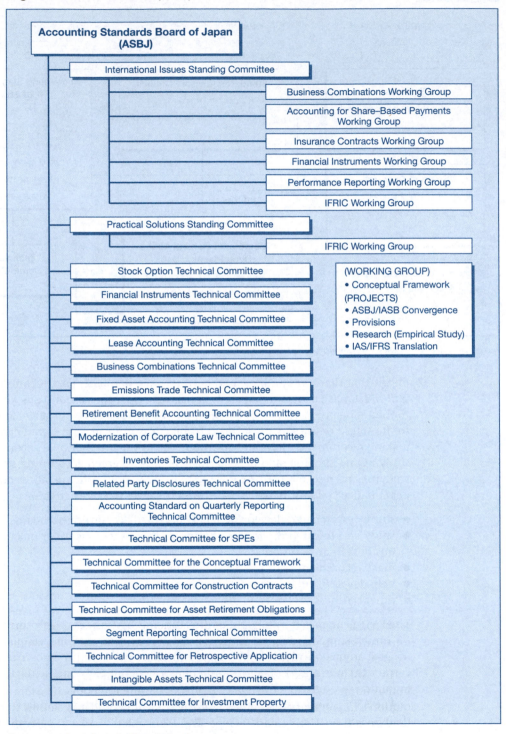

Accounting Standards Board of Japan (ASBJ)

International Issues Standing Committee
- Business Combinations Working Group
- Accounting for Share–Based Payments Working Group
- Insurance Contracts Working Group
- Financial Instruments Working Group
- Performance Reporting Working Group
- IFRIC Working Group

Practical Solutions Standing Committee
- IFRIC Working Group

- Stock Option Technical Committee
- Financial Instruments Technical Committee
- Fixed Asset Accounting Technical Committee
- Lease Accounting Technical Committee
- Business Combinations Technical Committee
- Emissions Trade Technical Committee
- Retirement Benefit Accounting Technical Committee
- Modernization of Corporate Law Technical Committee
- Inventories Technical Committee
- Related Party Disclosures Technical Committee
- Accounting Standard on Quarterly Reporting Technical Committee
- Technical Committee for SPEs
- Technical Committee for the Conceptual Framework
- Technical Committee for Construction Contracts
- Technical Committee for Asset Retirement Obligations
- Segment Reporting Technical Committee
- Technical Committee for Retrospective Application
- Intangible Assets Technical Committee
- Technical Committee for Investment Property

(WORKING GROUP)
- Conceptual Framework
(PROJECTS)
- ASBJ/IASB Convergence
- Provisions
- Research (Empirical Study)
- IAS/IFRS Translation

Source: www.asb.or.jp/html_e/asbj/organization.php.

Exhibit 16.13 Examples of objectives of ASBJ technical committees

Intangible Assets Technical Committee

Objective

The target of this Technical Committee for the time being is to carry out an overall study on major differences in the accounting for intangible assets under Japanese GAAP and other international standards. This study will be carried out from theoretical and practical perspectives and is expected to be issued as a discussion paper.

This discussion paper is intended to be the first step towards the longer-term objective, which is to develop systematic accounting standards related to intangible assets.

The deliberations in this Technical Committee also relates to the ASBJ-IASB convergence project (long-term item).

Segment Reporting Technical Committee

Objective

The proposal on segment reporting has been received from the Theme Advisory Council as the groups (level 2) other than the group important short-term theme (level 1), which says that an effective method to determine business segments should be reconsidered including a study of the 'management approach' used in the US. In addition, because the issue was proposed as a topic for the first phase in the convergence project meeting between the Accounting Standards Board of Japan (ASBJ) and the International Accounting Standards Board (IASB) held in March 2005, the ASBJ set up a working group to study segment reporting for providing information to the IASB which converged with the management approach applied in SFAS 131 investigating the points of revising the current Japanese rule.

Having deepened understanding of the points of revising the current Japanese rule through the study in the working group, this Technical Committee will discuss the basic idea of segments, disclosure items and develop the accounting standard for segment reporting in Japan.

This issue is included in the 'short-term project' in the third meeting of the convergence project between the ASBJ and the IASB held in March 2006.

International Issues Standing Committee

Objective

To contribute to the development of International Financial Reporting Standards (IFRS) by a liaison relationship with the International Accounting Standards Board (IASB).

Source: www.asb.or.jp.

objectives of some of the technical committees which illustrate the sources of the original agenda items. The ASBJ currently has two full-time members plus 11 part-time members. As with the FASF, these include CPAS, academics, business people and representatives from various financial institutions. All members of the founding bodies must comply with the ASBJ standards.

The ASBJ has issued a range of pronouncements including discussion papers on a conceptual framework (in September 2004 and December 2006), exposure drafts, practical solutions, implementation guidance and accounting standards. Recent standards include standards on quarterly financial reporting (March 2007), related party disclosures (October 2006) measurement of inventories (July 2006), share price payments, business divestitures, changes in net assets and presentation of net assets (all December 2006).

16.5.5 The introduction of consolidated accounting

Many specific accounting rules show the influence of foreign practices. Consolidated accounting provides a particularly good illustration of the conscious importing of a foreign practice.

Until the 1960s, consolidated accounts were not produced. However, the 1960s and 1970s were marked by a number of high-profile bankruptcies which were either caused by or made worse by profit manipulation which remained undetected under single entity accounting. In addition, the oil crises of the early 1970s led to a number of mergers and takeovers with companies becoming larger and more complex. A number of Japanese companies also had to produce consolidated accounts to achieve a listing on a foreign stock exchange. For example, Sony was the first Japanese company to list on the NYSE in 1961, closely followed by Honda, Mitsubishi and Matsushita. The NYSE refused to accept single entity accounts. Thus, by 1973, more than 60 Japanese companies had had to produce consolidated accounts. Likewise, a number of US companies wanted to list in Japan and they had to gain permission from the Tokyo Stock Exchange to be allowed to list when producing group or consolidated accounts instead of individual company accounts. By the end of 1973, Citicorp, Dow Chemical and First Chicago Corp. had achieved listings on the TSE on this basis.[15]

It has been argued[16] that these factors all meant that the Japanese perceived their accounts to be of a lower quality or status than those of companies from many other countries. It has also been argued that cultural features were particularly important, especially something that has been called the 'shame culture' of Japan.[17] This is a culture where individuals are motivated by the need to avoid the adverse reactions of others: in other words, values are derived from external stimuli. This prompted them to consider the introduction of consolidated accounts. A second cultural feature was also important in helping to explain the process by which consolidated accounts were introduced, namely the wish to avoid conflict, so that harmony and concessional decision making are both important. This meant that non-governmental groups were consulted over the proposed standards, with the BADC playing an important advisory role. Thus, it took fully 12 years and over 60 meetings of the BADC for the MoF to issue Ordinances on consolidated accounts and another five years before they were tightened and increased in scope. The MoF could have unilaterally imposed them as soon as requested by the Diet in 1965, but did not. It is also interesting to note that the Keidanren (employers' federation) did not oppose the proposals from any theoretical perspective but instead argued that their implementation would be too difficult.

The 1977 rules were heavily influenced by the rules of other countries, in particular the USA, despite controversy over whether or not such rules were appropriate in the Japanese context. (As discussed below, the structure of the typical Japanese group differs quite markedly from the pyramid structure based upon total or majority ownership of subsidiaries and sub-subsidiaries as is typically found in developed western countries.)

Exhibit 16.14 sets out a description of the process that the MoF went through in seeking a consensus over this issue in the period up to the early 1980s.

As consolidation was initially contentious and not supported by the Keidanren, the rules when first introduced were something of a compromise and allowed subsidiaries to

---

[15] McKinnon (1984).

[16] McKinnon (1986).

[17] Cooke (1991).

Exhibit 16.14 History of the regulations for consolidated accounts

1965	Diet requests the Ministry of Finance to improve corporate disclosure under the Securities Exchange Law.
1965	The MoF requests the BADC to prepare an interim report on consolidated financial statements, with the idea of improving corporate disclosure.
1966	The BADC reports to the MoF and the ministry releases an Exposure Draft on Consolidation for public review.
1966	The Keidanren reports that it supports the exposure draft in principle but that it strongly opposes the implementation of consolidation in the near future.
1967	The MoF releases its 'Opinion on Consolidated Statements' which supports the introduction of consolidation.
1971	Diet revises the Securities Exchange Law to require that the financial statement of important subsidiaries be attached to the parent-only statements and calls on the MoF to draft the necessary new provisions and revision clauses for the introduction of consolidation.
1971	The BADC resumes discussion on consolidation.
1975	The BADC releases financial accounting standards for consolidated financial statements.
1976	The MoF issues Ordinances 27 to 30 operational from fiscal periods commencing April 1 1977.
1981	The MoF revises the consolidation Ordinances to make equity accounting mandatory and to tighten the materiality exclusion clause.

Source: McKinnon and Harrison (1985), p. 209.

be excluded if they were not material. In this context, 'material' was defined as being less than 10 per cent of both the combined assets and sales of the parent and the consolidated subsidiaries. Earnings were not included in the definition of materiality, as it would have made the requirements too restrictive. However, this exclusion clause was perhaps too successful in reducing the impact of the consolidation requirements. The MoF estimated that only 27 per cent of all subsidiaries were actually consolidated in 1979–80, most of the rest being excluded because of liberal interpretations of the materiality exclusion clause. The materiality exclusion clause was tightened in 1981, when a 10 per cent income criterion was also added; this meant that many more subsidiaries had to be consolidated. However, Japanese companies still continued to exclude many subsidiaries from consolidation.

A standard issued in June 1997, effective for fiscal periods starting on or after 1 April 1999, changed this position and brought Japanese practice much more into line with IAS 27. The 1997 standard introduced guideline materiality criteria of between 3 and 5 per cent. Perhaps more importantly, it also changed the definition of a subsidiary. Previously, the definition was based exclusively upon ownership. The standard introduced the concept of control into the definition. The standard also had the effect of increasing the amount of information produced in the Japanese-language statements of most companies. It required the consolidated statements, not the parent company statements, to be treated as the more important set of statements and therefore also meant that all companies would produce a consolidated cash flow statement. (Most companies producing English-language statements were already providing a cash flow statement.)

16.5.6 Accounting regulations and the IASB

Japan was one of the founding members of the IASC in 1973 and JICPA members have a long tradition of involvement in the process of setting international accounting standards. However, active involvement in the work of the IASB does not guarantee compliance with IFRS, and Japan has in the past illustrated this point. The standard-setting process as set up after the Second World War was largely independent of the government. Shortly after this, it was successfully captured by the government and the bureaucracy so that the profession played a relatively minor role in setting standards. Japanese rule setters therefore were not greatly influenced by the work of the IASB. However, this position has changed in the last few years, most obviously with the move to a private sector standard-setting system with the FASF and the ASBJ. Japan was increasingly conscious that its standards were often thought of as being inadequate in comparison with most other major countries. It was also conscious of the importance of the IASB and the need to have a voice in international standard setting. These two pressures were largely responsible for the establishment of the new system, as described above in section 16.5.4, and the choice of a structure that is similar to other standard setters such as the USA and UK as well as the IASB.

Initially, Japan expressed support for international convergence but was not prepared fully to endorse the process. The statement by the ASBJ on convergence, reproduced in Exhibit 16.15, explains why Japan has not wholeheartedly endorsed convergence. Indeed, it can be argued that it would be unrealistic given the Japanese culture to expect Japan to endorse fully a system of convergence without firstly knowing exactly what would be involved.

Exhibit 16.15 ASBJ Statement on Convergence, April 2003

- International integration of capital markets and that of market systems including accounting standards are two sides of the same coin. Market infrastructures will be fully integrated when domestic capital markets are internationally integrated. We agree with such result as the ultimate goal, and in our view, convergence represents such ultimate and desirable goal. To promote convergence, sufficient discussion and consensus-building among participants in the domestic market are necessary. Therefore, we cannot make commitment that convergence should always come first even for the matters to which we cannot assent on any terms. However, we think it is also true of the countries that announced the intention of convergence, in particular United States and European Countries.

- ASBJ is positively taking part in international discussions and making every effort to improve our own standards, with our mission in our article of organisation, to contribute to development of international accounting standards. ASBJ will continuously make maximum efforts to contribute to convergence of accounting standards and to enhance harmonisation of our own standards with IFRS.

Source: www.asb.or.jp/e_asbj/ifad_report.html.

However, even prior to the establishment of the ASBJ in July 2001, the BADC had issued a number of important statements that essentially harmonized Japanese practice with IAS. These covered, for March 2000 year-ends, accounting standards on:

- consolidated financial statements policies and procedures
- consolidated statements of cash flows
- interperiod tax allocations
- research and development costs.

For March 2001 year-ends the changes also covered:

- pensions
- financial instruments
- interim consolidated financial statements.

The FSA issued, in April 2004, a list of the differences that it saw between Japanese GAAP and IFRS. This listed only seven areas: financial instruments; business combinations; impairment of assets; retirement benefits; R&D; consolidated financial statements; and investment properties.

In January 2005 the ASBJ announced a joint project with the IASB to achieve convergence. Following a first meeting in March 2005 the two bodies agreed initially to start a phased approach towards convergence in which differences that would be fairly easy to address should be tackled first. This resulted in the ASBJ agreeing to look at five areas: measurement of inventories; segment reporting; related party disclosures; verification of accounting policies applied to foreign subsidiaries; and investment properties. At a later meeting in March 2006 it was agreed to add the three areas of asset retirement obligations, construction contracts and disclosure of financial instruments at fair value. It was also decided to change the approach to a new 'whole picture' approach that classifies differences either as short-term items due for elimination by the end of 2008 or as longer term projects, including performance reporting, revenue recognition, retrospective restatement, scope of consolidation and intangibles.

Exhibit 16.16 summarizes the differences between international and Japanese standards in 2006.

16.6 Auditing

The regulations governing the scope of auditing are set out in Exhibit 16.17.

Auditing standards are developed jointly by the Auditing Standards Subgroup of the BAC and the JICPA Auditing Subcommittee. The JICPA has also issued 36 practical guidelines since 2002 with the 26 still in place in early 2007 being based upon international auditing standards. These bring the Japanese GAAS essentially into line with IAS. In addition, the CPA law was revised as of April 2004 to bring it into line with the US Sarbanes–Oxley Act. It includes prohibitions against various non-audit services and required rotation of audit partners, but not audit firms, at least every seven years. It also established the CPA and Auditing Oversight Board (CPAAOB) within the FSA to enhance auditor oversight. The CPAAOB examines disciplinary actions against CPAs and audit corporations, conducts CPA exams, monitors and reviews internal controls of audit corporations and inspects audit corporations and the JICPA. While similar to international audit rules, the audit report is rather different from a UK-style report. The CC does not contain a complete code of accounts (as, for example, seen in

Exhibit 16.16	Differences between international and Japanese standards, 2006

Uniformity of accounting practices:
Japan: Permit use of different GAAP for foreign and domestic subsidiaries as long as this does not lead to 'unreasonable consequences'. In November 2005 ASBJ issued an exposure draft limiting foreign GAP to US or IFRS. IAS27 and IAS28 require uniform accounting policies.

Scope of consolidation:
Japan: If a Special Purpose Entity is established to transfer financial assets it is excluded from consolidation. IAS27 requires consolidation if substance of relationship indicates control.

Business combinations:
Japan: Requires pooling of interest for certain combinations and in general goodwill is amortized by straight line method over maximum of 20 years. IFRS3 requires purchase method only and IAS36 requires use of annual impairment tests.

Inventories:
Japan: Allow use of cost as well as lower of cost or market, although under review. IAS2 requires use of cost or market.

Impairment of assets:
The two use different rules for measuring any impairment loss.

Capitalization of development costs:
Japan: Costs incurred during development must be expensed. IAS38 requires recognition if certain criteria are met.

Construction contracts:
Japan allows either percentage of completion or completed construction method. IAS11 requires percentage of completion method if it can be estimated reliably.

Employee benefits:
Differences in detail exist including prohibition in Japan of the corridor approach for defined benefit plans as permitted by IAS19.

Leases:
Japan: If finance lease does not transfer ownership, it can be treated as an operating lease. IAS17 does not permit this option.

Source: Corporate Disclosure in Japan, JICPA 2006.

France), and in many areas there are no requirements or, where they exist, they allow companies a wide choice of acceptable methods. However, the accounting system can still best be described as a uniform system of accounting in the sense that the rules have to be applied in the prescribed ways. Thus, the concept of 'true and fair' is not found in Japan. The audit report instead states that the financial statements 'present fairly . . . in conformity with accounting principles generally accepted in Japan'. As we have seen above, these GAAP are codified in many different places – the ASJ, the CC, the SEL and the tax laws. All of these sources of GAAP have to be followed without any possibility of overriding them to produce more useful or relevant information. The audit report itself tends typically to be very similar to US audit reports with users of Japanese reports having to read them quite carefully to see exactly which GAAP have been used, as illustrated in Exhibit 16.18, the audit report of Asahi Glass, a typical Japanese audit report.

Exhibit 16.17 Japanese audit requirements

Certified public accountants have a commitment to the public to provide and enhance the credibility of financial statements by expressing an audit opinion on such financial statements.

GAAS

The CPA audits have been made in accordance with the Auditing Standards codified by the Business Accounting Council (BAC), and audit practice guidelines issued by the JICPA. The Auditing Standards codified by the BAC together with audit guidelines issued by the JICPA are deemed to be the generally accepted auditing standards (GAAS) in Japan.

In Japan, certified public accountants provide audit services in the following areas:

Statutory Audits
The Commercial Code and Related Laws

- Companies (Kabushiki Kaisha) with outstanding common stock of ¥500 million or more or total liabilities of ¥20,000 million or more
- Mutual insurance companies, credit banks (shinyo kinko), credit cooperatives (shinyo kumiai), and labor banks (rodo kinko) specified by relevant laws

The Securities and Exchange Law

- Companies initially listing and already listed on stock exchanges
- Companies initially registering and already registered with the Japan Securities Dealers Association
- Companies initially offering and have offered to the public securities of at least ¥500 million
- Companies with at least 500 shareholders

Other Statutory Audits

- Private schools receiving subsidy from national or local government
- Labor unions
- Political party's subsidy report prepared in accordance with the Political Party Grant Law
- Local Governments
- National universities
- Investment corporations
- Special purpose companies of which the aggregate amount of specific bonds and specific loans is ¥20,000 million or more
- Independent administrative corporations

Non-Statutory Audits

- Religious organizations, non-profit organizations, consumers cooperatives, and healthcare organizations
- Audits in connection with mergers, business transfers, and acquisitions
- Other audits not covered above

Cross-Border Audits

- Japanese companies with cross-border listings
- Operations in Japan of foreign companies

Source: Japanese Institute of Certified Public accountants web page, www.jicpa.or.jp (July 2007).

Exhibit 16.18 Audit report, Asahi Glass, 2006

REPORT OF INDEPENDENT AUDITORS

ChuoAoyama PricewaterhouseCoopers

PRICEWATERHOUSECOOPERS

Kasumigaseki Bldg. 32nd Floor
3-2-5 Kasumigaseki, Chiyoda-ku,
Tokyo 100-6088, Japan

To the Board of Directors of
Asahi Glass Company, Limited

We have audited the accompanying consolidated balance sheets of Asahi Glass Company and its consolidated subsidiaries as of December 31, 2005 and 2004, and the related consolidated statements of income, shareholders' equity, and cash flows for the year then ended, all expressed in Japanese yen. These consolidated financial statements are the responsibility of the Company's management. Our responsibility is to express an opinion on these consolidated financial statements based on our audits.

We conducted our audits in accordance with auditing standards generally accepted in Japan. Those standards require that we plan and perform the audit to obtain reasonable assurance about whether the consolidated financial statements are free of material misstatement. An audit includes examining, on a test basis, evidence supporting the amounts and disclosures in the consolidated financial statements. An audit also includes assessing the accounting principles used and significant estimates made by management, as well as evaluating the overall consolidated financial statement presentation. We believe that our audits provide a reasonable basis for our opinion.

In our opinion, the consolidated financial statements referred to above present fairly, in all material respects, the consolidated financial position of Asahi Glass Company and its consolidated subsidiaries as of December 31, 2005 and 2004, and the consolidated results of their operations and their cash flows for the year then ended in conformity with accounting principles generally accepted in Japan.

As discussed in Note 2 (2) to the consolidated financial statements, the Company changed its policy of accounting for goodwill from the year ended December 31, 2004. Also, as discussed in Note 2 (10), effective as of December 31, 2004, the Companies have adopted the accounting standard for impairment of long-lived assets.

The amounts expressed in U.S. dollars, which are provided solely for the convenience of the reader, have been translated on the basis set forth in Note 3 to the accompanying consolidated financial statements.

March 30, 2006

Source: Asahi Glass Co. Ltd Annual Report (2006), p. 35.

16.7 Information disclosure

As we have seen, Japan has imported many of its regulatory structures and accounting rules. However, many features of Japanese society are quite different from those of other countries. Thus, despite a complex system of accounting regulation, there is with some exceptions relatively little emphasis on – or demand for – information disclosure in general purpose annual reports. Debt financing has traditionally been more important than equity financing and the debt providers (the banks) have not required external financial statements as they are able to demand whatever information they require. Other *keiretsu* members likewise have a variety of formal and informal ways of obtaining the information they want. Thus the need for external monitoring via audited annual accounts has been largely replaced by other corporate governance systems. For example, one study of the role of non-executive directors[18] concluded that bankers and other representatives of groups with intercorporate relationships are often appointed in times of financial difficulty and that these board members are important in monitoring and disciplining corporate behaviour. This behaviour is congruent with the culture of the country. Group consciousness and interdependence leads to relatively high levels of mutual trust, so there is less of a perceived need to monitor corporate behaviour externally. For example, in one study it was estimated that, before the new standards of the last few years, Japanese disclosure requirements were only approximately 40 per cent of those in the USA.[19]

This lack of disclosure has been compounded by the impacts of patterns of financing, group structures and *keiretsu* membership and cultural values, which all mean that the

---

Exhibit 16.19 Forecast information provided by Sojitz Group

Extract from Notice Concerning Revisions to Consolidated and Non-Consolidated Earnings Forecasts for the Fiscal Year Ending March 31, 2005

Following drastic review of its current Business Plan, Sojitz Holdings Corporation (hereinafter referred to as 'Sojitz Holdings' or 'the Company') has formulated a New Business Plan with the aim of enhancing corporate value by quickly restoring market confidence. Guided by its Business Plan, Sojitz Holdings has decided to write-off an amount totaling approximately ¥400 billion (on a consolidated basis) in an effort to instantaneously restore asset quality. The write-off will cover the loss for the complete withdrawal from low-profit businesses including overseas investments and loans and the disposal of real estate holdings.

As a result of its decision to implement these measures, the Company has revised consolidated and non-consolidated earnings forecasts for the fiscal year ending March 31, 2005 as follows.

Consolidated Earnings Forecasts for the Fiscal Year Ending March 31, 2005

As a result of the Company's decision to write-off the amount as identified in its New Business Plan, mentioned above, Sojitz Holdings has revised its earnings forecasts, which were initially announced on May 13, 2004 together with the Company's fiscal 2003 financial results.

Earnings forecasts for the current fiscal year:

[Consolidated]	Billions of Yen		
	Net Sales	Recurring Profit	Net Income (Loss)
Previous Forecast (A)	6,100	85	50
Revised Forecast (B)	5,000	50	−380
Difference (B−A)	−1,100	35	−430
Difference (%)	−18.0%	−41.2%	−
(Reference) Results of Fiscal 2003	5,861.7	48.5	−33.6

[The notice continues with information about non-consolidated financial statements.]

Source: Sojitz Holdings, Notice issued 8 September 2004, revised forecast for year ending 31 March 2005, www.Sojitz_holdings.com/eng/.

---

[18] Kaplan and Minten (1994).

[19] Davis (1989).

Japanese-language annual reports, while providing the information required by law, have tended not to go any further by providing extensive amounts of voluntary information. This is less noticeable in many of the English-language reports, when companies, and in particular those listed in overseas markets, have tended to disclose rather more information. However, even here, the voluntary disclosure levels tend to be less than those found in the reports of similar US or UK companies, though there is some evidence that the level of voluntary disclosure has been increasing, at least over the three years 1989, 1994 and 1998.[20]

However, one area where Japanese companies provide more information than those from other companies is in the area of forecasts, as required by Japanese law. Such forecasts are generally not produced in the English-language reports although one exception to this is the example of Sojitz Group, as shown in Exhibit 16.19. The company issued a forecast in May 2004 at the time of publishing the annual report, but then revised the forecast downwards in September 2004 to reflect an impairment review.

Summary and conclusions

This chapter has shown that, in many respects, Japanese accounting is quite unique. The early continental European (especially German) influences are still important, reflected in the importance of the Commercial Code and its creditor orientation. In contrast, the Securities and Exchange Law bears many traces of its roots in the US system of regulation. However, neither German nor US rules or institutions have been adopted wholesale and the imports have been adapted and changed over time to reflect local influences. Overlaid on this is the recent standard-setting system of the Financial Accounting Standards Foundation and the Accounting Standards Board of Japan. This is an independent system with standards set by members of the profession, business and financial institutions, which reflects a deliberate attempt to introduce a standard-setting system that is similar to that of the IASB, reflecting the desire of Japan to be involved in and influence the moves towards international convergence. The system thus reflects a mixture of quite disparate influences. Indeed, it is has not really been correct to talk of 'Japanese accounting': instead, there is 'Commercial Code accounting', 'SEL accounting' and 'English-language accounting', although it may be argued that the system is increasingly coalescing into a system that is becoming more and more similar to IFRS.

The accounting principles and practices of Japan, at least until the last three or four years when IFRS have been an important influence, are related to the predictions made by Gray (1988), based upon analysis of cultural factors. Using the scores developed by Hofstede (1984) which suggested that the most important cultural dimension for accounting was Japan's strong uncertainty avoidance, Gray's work can be used to predict that the Japanese accounting system should exhibit strong statutory control, be uniform rather than flexible, be relatively conservative and be relatively secretive. Many of these predictions have been supported by the analysis of practices in Japan.

Key points from the chapter:

- Japan has a code law legal system and the Commercial Code is used to regulate all businesses.

---

[20] Singleton and Globerman (2002).

- The Commercial Code contains a number of rules which apply to all companies; the regulations emphasize creditor protection and require relatively few disclosures.

- Many areas of accounting are not covered by the Commercial Code, many of the more important regulations that affect listed companies being the result of the Securities and Exchange Law and, increasingly, accounting standards.

- The taxation system is largely based upon accounting GAAP; however, there are quite a number of areas where the taxation rules have an impact upon accounting and financial reporting practices. In particular, companies typically set up and disclose more special reserves than they would otherwise.

- The accounting profession in Japan is relatively weak in influence.

- Japan has imported many of its institutions from overseas. Many of the early accounting laws were imported from Europe, in particular Germany. Following the Second World War, new regulations and regulatory structures were introduced based upon the US system, although these have been modified to reflect Japanese influences. The Japanese accounting system has therefore been categorized alongside both the USA and Germany.

- Japan has now fully endorsed the IASB convergence project and it has promised to achieve convergence in many, but not all, areas by the end of 2008.

Questions

The following questions test your understanding of the material contained in the chapter and allow you to relate your understanding to the learning outcomes specified at the start of this chapter. The learning outcomes are repeated here. Each question is cross-referenced to the relevant section of the chapter.

Understand the key characteristics of the country as summarized in published economic indicators

1 To what extent does the business environment of Japan provide clues as to possible influences on accounting practices? (sections 16.2 and 16.3)

Relate institutional factors for the country to the framework set out in Chapter 6

2 How does the political and economic system of Japan fit into the classifications described in Chapter 6? (section 16.3.1)

3 How does the legal system of Japan fit into the classifications described in Chapter 6? (section 16.3.2)

4 How does the taxation system of Japan compare with the descriptions given in Chapter 6? (section 16.3.3)

5 How does the corporate financing system of Japan compare with the descriptions given in Chapter 6? (section 16.3.4)

6 How does the accounting profession in Japan compare with the descriptions given in Chapter 6? (section 16.3.5)

7 Which institutional factors are most likely to influence Japanese accounting practice? (section 16.3)

8 How do the external influences on accounting practice in Japan compare with those described in Chapter 6? (section 16.4)

Explain the origins of accounting regulations and the historical developments leading to the present state of practice

9 To what extent do early developments in accounting practice indicate the likely current practice? (section 16.5)

Explain the position of national accounting practice in relation to the IFRS

10 In which areas does accounting practice in Japan depart from that set out in International Financial Reporting Standards? (section 16.5.6)

11 For each of the issues identified above:

● Describe the treatment prescribed in Japanese GAAP.

● Identify the likely impact on income and shareholders' equity of moving from Japanese GAAP to the relevant IFRS. (section 16.5.6)

12 What explanations may be offered for these departures from IFRS, in terms of the institutional factors described in the chapter? (section 16.3)

References and further reading

Beattie, A. (2004) 'Call for foreigners to help break tradition', *Financial Times*, 23 March.

Cheung, J.K., Kim, J.-B. and Lee, J. (1999) 'The impact of institutional characteristics on return-earnings associations in Japan', *International Journal of Accounting*, 34(4): 571–596.

Cooke, T.E. (1991) 'The evolution of financial reporting in Japan: a shame culture perspective', *Accounting, Business and Financial History*, 1(3): 251–277.

Davis, S.M. (1989) *Shareholder Rights Abroad: A Handbook for the Global Investor*. Washington, DC: Investor Responsibility Research Inc.

Douthett, E.B. and Jung, K. (2001) 'Japanese corporate groupings (keiretsu) and the informativeness of earnings', *Journal of International Financial Management and Accounting*, 12(2): 133–159.

Gray, S.J. (1988) 'Towards a theory of cultural influence on the development of accounting systems internationally', *Abacus*, 24(1): 1–15.

Hofstede, G. (1984) *Culture's Consequences: International Differences in Work-related Values*. Beverley Hills, CA: Sage.

Jiang, L. and Kim, J.-B. (2000) 'Cross-corporate ownership, information asymmetry and the usefulness of accounting performance measures in Japan', *International Journal of Accounting*, 35(1): 85–98.

Kaplan, S.N. and Minten, B.A. (1994) 'Appointment of outsiders to Japanese boards: determinants and implications for managers', *Journal of Financial Economics*, 36: 225–258.

Kumar, S. and Hyodo, K. (2001) 'Price–earning ratios in Japan: recent evidence and further results', *Journal of International Financial Management and Accounting*, 12(1): 24–49.

McKinnon, J.L. (1984) 'Application of Anglo-American principles of consolidation to corporate financial disclosure in Japan', *Abacus*, 20(1): 16–33.

McKinnon, J.L. (1986) *The Historical Development and Operational Form of Corporate Reporting Regulations in Japan*. New York: Garland.

McKinnon, J.L. and Harrison, G.L. (1985) 'Cultural influence on corporate and governmental involvement in accounting policy determination in Japan', *Journal of Accounting and Public Policy*, 4: 201–223.

OECD (2004) *Trends and recent developments in foreign direct investment*. Paris: Organization for Economic Cooperation and Development.

Singleton, W.R. and Globerman, S. (2002) 'The changing nature of financial disclosure in Japan', *International Journal of Accounting*, 37: 95–111.

Someya, K. (1989) 'Accounting "revolutions" in Japan', *Accounting Historians' Journal*, 16(1): 75–86.

The Economist Pocket World in Figures, 2007 Edition. London: Profile Books.

Tokyo Stock Exchange (2004) *Principles of Corporate Governance for Listed Companies*.

Learning outcomes

After reading this chapter you should be able to:

- Understand and explain the origins of accounting regulations and the historical development leading to the present state of practice.

- Relate institutional factors for the country to the framework set out in Chapter 6.

- Understand and explain the position of national accounting rules in relation to the IASB standards.

- Understand the characteristics of national accounting practice in terms of Gray's accounting values.

- Explain how research papers contribute to understanding accounting practice and accounting values.

17.1 Introduction

China has become a major economic force in recent years. With nearly one-quarter of the world's population, China has experienced remarkable growth since it began to liberalize its economy in 1979. Since 1994, annual GDP growth has easily exceeded that of any of the successful but far smaller Asian tiger economies (at an annual real growth rate of 9.1 per cent). This has been accompanied by rapid increases in international trade and inward investment through a variety of vehicles including bonds, equity investment and joint ventures. As we will see in this chapter, this has been accompanied by a massive restructuring of China's economic system including its financial institutions and accounting system. New accounting laws, based upon IASB standards, have recently been introduced and the accounting system has undergone substantial changes.

17.2 The country

Exhibit 17.1 provides some details about The People's Republic of China (PRC). What is perhaps most striking is the sheer size of the country and its population. This means that it is a country of contrasts – much of the coastal area is highly industrialized and

Exhibit 17.1 China: country profile

Population	1,315.8 million	
Land mass	9,560,900km^2	
GDP per head	US$1,700	
GDP per head in purchasing power parity	16.1	(USA = 100)
Origins of GDP:	%	
Agriculture	13	
Industry	48	
Services	40	
	%	
GDP average annual growth 1995–2005	9.0	
Inflation, average annual rate 2001–2006	1.5	

Source: *The Economist Pocket World in Figures*, 2008 Edition, Profile Books Ltd.

| Exhibit 17.2 | FT 500 Chinese companies (including Hong Kong China) |

	Name		FT 500 rank	Market capitalization US$bn	Listed UK	Listed USA	Sector
1	Industrial & Commercial Bank of China	China	9	224,787	No	No	Banks
2	China Mobile	HK	16	181,799	No	Yes	Mobile telecom
3	Bank of China	China	23	165,511	No	No	Banks
4	China Construction Bank	China	35	128,529	No	No	Banks
5	China Life Assurance	China	41	116,280	No	Yes	Insurance
6	Sinopec	China	53	104,014	No	Yes	Oil &gas
7	Bank of Communications	China	166	47,069	No	No	Banks
8	Ping An Insurance	China	196	41,673	No	No	Insurance
9	Hutchison Whampoa	HK	202	41,001	No	Yes	General industrial
10	CNOOC	HK	220	37,982	No	Yes	Oil &gas
11	China Merchants Bank	China	265	32,441	No	No	Banks
12	Cheung Kong	HK	302	29,314	No	No	Real estate
13	Sun Hung Kai Properties	HK	310	28,827	No	No	Real estate
14	Hang Seng Bank	HK	327	27,157	No	No	Banks
15	Bank of China	HK	349	25,625	No	No	Banks
16	Foxconn International	HK	424	21,373	No	No	Technology hardware

Source: *Financial Times*, FT 500 (2007), www.londonstockexchange.com, www.nyse.com.

economically successful, with the population having a rapidly rising standard of living. Economic reform began in rural areas with a major government programme to 'Develop the West'. The currency is the renminbi (RMB), also called the yuan.

As can be seen from Exhibit 17.2, China is now home to eight of the FT 500 companies while Hong Kong is home to a further eight. This exhibit reflects the rapid growth of China and its financial sector in particular, with all the Chinese corporations having entered the FT 500 for the first time in 2007.

Recent years have witnessed much debate in both the Chinese and the western press about just how successful China has been in restructuring its economy. With such a large country it is difficult to get accurate data and government statistics were thought to be suspect with growth rates overestimated in the 1990s. However, this seems now not to be the case and it is generally agreed that annual real growth rates of more than 7 per cent have been achieved in every year since 1991. Indeed, even after government attempts to control an overheating economy the first eight months of 2006 recorded a growth rate of 10.7 per cent.[1] However, from Exhibit 17.1, we can see that the per capita GDP of mainland China was only US$1,700 in 2005,[2] implying that China is still a very poor country. However, this figure is somewhat misleading as with a large rural population (approximately 60 per cent of the population live in rural areas) much production is for personal consumption and so is excluded from official statistics. China's largest export market is the USA (21 per cent) followed by Hong Kong (17 per cent) and Japan (12 per cent).

---

[1] www.chinability.com/GDP.htm.

[2] As reported in *The Economist Pocket World in Figures*, 2008.

The size of the country means that it is more difficult to administer and coordinate economic policies. While centralized control of the economy has been of prime importance, in practice the system is often far from uniform. Many of the economic reforms have been applied in a piecemeal fashion. Institutions have been allowed to grow and develop in response to market needs and government control or regulation has often followed, not preceded, market developments. Different parts of the country have been subject to different rules and various government ministries have imposed different sets of rules on the enterprises and institutions under their control. One example of this is Hong Kong. On 1 July 1997, Hong Kong was returned to the control of China. China promised that it would remain as a market-led capitalist system for at least the next 50 years – the 'one country, two systems' policy. That China felt able to do this and that it was prepared to live with such apparently different economic systems coexisting alongside each other is not as remarkable as might at first appear. In an attempt to modernize and increase economic welfare, many of the economic structures of mainland China had already been 'westernized' and China already had experience of running four special economic areas in the coastal region where the economic rules were already far more liberal than those applied elsewhere in the country.

17.3 Institutions

17.3.1 Political and economic system

The Chinese Communist Party dominates the government. The General Secretary of the Party plays an important leadership role. It was the guidance of Deng Xiaoping that took China forward into developing a market-based economic system. Jian Zemin followed as leader, continuing the reform policy, and was succeeded in November 2002 by Hu Jintao.

17.3.1.1 Importing a centralized planning system

When the Communist Party came to power in 1949, the most important task facing it was to achieve rapid socio-economic development without depending in any way on the advanced capitalist nations. The only model then available was the Soviet one, which was imported with almost no major changes. Thus, Soviet-style economic and political institutions were introduced, including centralized planning via a series of five-year plans.

The 1949 Revolution resulted in the public ownership of all enterprises. Public ownership existed in two forms: state enterprises and collectives. Collective enterprises were owned by the people who operated them. State enterprises were held by the state and owned ultimately by the entire population. State ownership was considered to be the ideal; collectives were generally converted into state enterprises once they reached a certain size. The government was the main, probably the sole, user of financial statements. The economy was run by means of a compulsory comprehensive economic plan; perceived demand was converted into specific production targets for each enterprise. Capital, labour, equipment and materials were all allocated to enterprises on the basis of production targets. Similarly, prices and customers were strictly controlled via the plan. The only role of accounting was therefore to provide information to the government for planning purposes, for resource allocation decisions and for monitoring of the plan. Each state enterprise can perhaps be best thought of as being equivalent to a cost centre in a typical western commercial organization. There was no real system of external financial reporting as it is commonly understood. Instead, enterprises had to produce uniform statements describing, among other things, their past production levels and cost data.

The Chinese leadership sought to give the adopted system a Chinese identity. This was seen in the Great Leap Forward of 1958–59 which culminated, most disastrously, in the Cultural Revolution of 1966–76. The Cultural Revolution attempted to ensure that the country retained its socialist nature; in particular, market structures were not to be introduced and no class system was to be allowed to develop. The attempt to prevent a bureaucratic elite developing, by actions such as forcing intellectuals to undertake manual labour and the creation of revolutionary committees of workers to run their factories, resulted in a major collapse of the economy. Following the death of Mao in 1976 the 'Maoist model' was heavily criticized and a new model of socialist development based upon market-orientated principles and institutions began to be created under the leadership of Deng Xiaoping.[3]

Market socialism is a difficult thing to achieve as it involves maintaining the political system and the position of the present political leadership while also undertaking major changes to the economic system. It is difficult to restructure the economy without also calling into doubt the legitimacy and effectiveness of the political system and politicians who ran the previous socialist economic system. This is one of the major reasons why China is adopting a process of piecemeal economic reforms. It also helps to explain why the process is far from smooth and why, at times, political considerations mean that the economic reforms have stalled.

17.3.1.2 The start of economic reform

During the initial period of reform the emphasis was mainly on agricultural reform, with dismantling of the commune system. Some reforms were also made in the commodity markets, with state enterprises being allowed to sell some of their output independently and keep some of their income; some goods were removed from price controls and some private businesses were allowed. Some enterprises were also allowed to raise foreign currency loans and to keep a proportion of any foreign currency that they earned.

From the mid-1980s greater emphasis has been placed on state enterprise reforms. This encompasses a large number of different areas. The finance system has been reformed with commercial banks taking over some of the roles of the central bank. Foreign exchange markets have been established, as have stock markets (see below) and even agricultural products and metals futures markets.

17.3.1.3 Membership of the World Trade Organization

The most important event in China's move towards western markets was its admission to membership of the World Trade Organization (WTO) in December 2001. This committed China to unprecedented liberalization of its markets for goods and services. China agreed to overhaul its legal and business systems and to allow more foreign companies and products to enter its markets.

17.3.2 Legal system

During the period of centralized planning control, the legal system was increasingly seen simply as another tool for the social control of society. Emphasis was placed upon maintaining political control and social order. Other objectives, such as guaranteeing personal

---

[3] White (1993).

liberties or ensuring the smooth functioning of the economy, were given very low priority. Legal reform has also been an important feature of the last two decades. Economic reforms can be successful only if suitable legal controls and protections are developed in parallel with the new market structures. A complete system of contract and commercial law therefore had to be developed almost entirely from the beginning. While there have been a significant number of new codes and statutes introduced, the process is still far from complete.

There are three different levels of legislative power. Accounting has been regulated by institutions at all three levels. Laws are set by the National People's Congress. Below this is the State Council which issues administrative rules and regulations. Finally, national ministries and commissions issue directives and regulations for the particular industries or enterprises under their control. In the past different accounting systems have been employed by different industries and the various ministries have imposed different accounting rules. Recent legal moves have therefore not only involved a move away from the traditional fund-based system towards a westernized system, but also increasingly dismantled industry-specific regulations and moved towards imposing uniform rules on all commercial enterprises, whether foreign owned, joint ventures, equity financed or government owned. However, economic reform and government restructuring probably had a stronger influence than legal factors in the abandonment of industry-specific standards in 2000 when the new accounting system was stipulated.

17.3.3 Taxation system

17.3.3.1 Taxation and economic reform

Until the economic reforms began, enterprises were not taxed on their profits or surpluses – all of these were transferred to the state. Starting in 1979, some enterprises were allowed to keep some of their surpluses which, since 1983, have been taxed. Enterprises with foreign investments were treated rather differently. A series of laws were passed starting in 1980, which established the tax structure for these enterprises. Taxable profits were generally the same as reportable profits although there were some differences. Enterprises were given a number of tax incentives while some items were not deductible for tax purposes. Loss carry-forwards were also allowed.

From 1994, the enterprise taxation system has been considerably simplified. State enterprises are now taxed in the same way as other enterprises and the number of different types of taxes substantially reduced. More important for accounting is the fact that there has been a decoupling of tax and accounting. The financial reporting rules may now differ from the rules used to compute taxable earnings. This means that the influence of the tax rules on financial reporting is likely to decrease over time as new financial accounting rules can be introduced without being constrained by their impact on tax revenues. This period has also witnessed the increasing use of tax incentives to encourage foreign direct investment, especially via the active participation in joint ventures.

17.3.3.2 Business taxes and turnover taxes for foreign investors[4]

Foreign Investment Enterprises, which are PRC legal entities or joint ventures with foreign investment ownership of at least 5 per cent, are subject to Foreign Enterprise Investment Tax on worldwide income. The national rate is 30 per cent, with an additional

---

[4] www.pwccn.com/home.eng (July 2007).

local rate of 3 per cent. Foreign Investment Enterprises in some geographical areas or industries pay a lower national rate.

VAT applies to sales of goods and services. The rate is generally 17 per cent, with a lower rate of 13 per cent applied to some staple goods such as books and publications. Consumption Tax is an additional turnover tax applied to specific 'luxury goods' such as tobacco, alcohol, jewellery and automobiles.

There are many types of Chinese tax applicable to foreign investors, namely Customs Duty, Value Added Tax (VAT), Consumption Tax, Business Tax, Foreign Enterprise Income Tax, Individual Income Tax, Withholding Income Tax, Deed Tax, Land Appreciation Tax, Resources Tax, Stamp Duty, Urban Real Estate Tax, Motor Vehicles Acquisition Tax and Vehicles & Vessels Usage Licence Tax. This variety of taxes, together with the frequent changes of regulation, gives foreign investors the impression that tax is complex. However, the government wishes to encourage foreign investment, so the rules include incentives. These incentives encourage companies to locate in special economic zones, and also encourage export, high-tech and infrastructure projects.

17.3.4 Corporate financing system

17.3.4.1 Listed companies

There are stock markets in the PRC at Shanghai and Shenzhen, and a separate market in Hong Kong.[5] One of the most important differences between the economic reforms of China and those of most of Eastern Europe has been the greater emphasis that China has placed upon establishing a suitable financial infrastructure. Thus, rather than starting by privatizing companies and hoping that stock markets and other necessary financial institutions would then develop naturally as they were needed, China instead began much of its economic reforms at the other end, by setting up the required financial institutions. One of the most important of these institutions is a stock market. If companies are no longer to be financed by the government then there needs to be an active and efficient market in which they can raise public debt and equity.

While there was a stock market in China prior to the communist revolution, it had been closed down in 1949. It was not until the 1980s that moves began to re-establish capital markets. Treasury bonds were first sold to public enterprises in 1981 while, in 1984, state-owned enterprises also started issuing bonds. This was rapidly followed by a number of other developments such as the bond credit-rating service of the People's Bank of China, a nation-wide computerized bond trading network (the Securities Trading Automated Quotations System, STAQS) and foreign-currency-denominated commercial and treasury bonds.

A number of commercial enterprises also started issuing shares in 1984. The Shenzhen Stock Market opened unofficially on 1 December 1990 and the Shanghai Securities Exchange soon after. The number of companies making equity issues initially increased only slowly. For example, by the time Shenzhen Stock Market officially opened in mid-1991, it had only 5 listed companies, increasing to 17 by mid-1992. However, the demand for shares was almost limitless. Individuals had to buy application forms before purchasing shares and such was the demand that over 1 million people gathered in Shenzhen at one point in 1992 to buy these application forms.

There are a large number of different share categories. Government, central and local government agencies have retained ownership in state-owned enterprises (SOEs) that

---

[5] Hong Kong at www.hkex.com.hk; Shanghai at http://sse.com.cn; and Shenzhen at www.szse.cn.

have listed by holding non-tradable state shares. Similar to this are legal person shares which can be held by government agencies, other SOEs or privately owned enterprises and are only traded with permission of the Chinese Securities Regulatory Commission (CSRC). Companies may also issue employee shares which are non-tradable until the firm itself permits, domestic individual or A-shares, that are listed and traded in local currency and were originally available only to Chinese nationals, and foreign or B-shares, originally available only to overseas investors.[6] From December 2002 certain qualified foreign institutional investors (QFII) may purchase A-shares on Chinese stock exchanges as well as listed treasury, convertible and corporate bonds, but they must gain prior approval and must operate within a quota. Since 2001 B-shares have also been available to domestic investors holding foreign currency accounts. In 2003 there were 111 B-share companies but this represented relatively little growth from the 108 listed in 1999. H-shares are denominated in Hong Kong dollars and are also available only to foreign investors. The first companies to list on the Hong Kong and New York markets both gained approval for listing in October 1992, less than two years after the first Chinese stock market opened for business.

Increasing numbers of Chinese companies are now listed, not only in Hong Kong, but also in New York and London, as shown in Exhibit 17.3. As discussed later, China has been actively encouraging foreign investment in its own stock markets.

Companies cannot list on both exchanges and Shanghai is the more important exchange. At the end of 2006 it had 828 listed companies offering A-shares and 54 offering B-shares, while the Shenzhen Stock Exchange had 566 companies offering A-shares and 55 offering B-shares. Additional information on each market is shown in Exhibit 17.4. This illustrates in particular the rapid growth in number of shareholders and the generally high price–earnings ratios achieved.

Any enterprise can issue A-shares if it meets a series of legal requirements, the main ones being:

- It must be aligned with the state's policies of industrial development.
- It must be approved by both the local government and the CSRC.
- The proportion of A-shares to total shares must be at least 25 per cent (or 15 per cent in the case of the largest companies listing in Shanghai) and the proportion of employees to total shares must be less than 10 per cent.
- In the last financial year, the percentage of net assets to total assets must be at least 30 per cent and the ratio of intangible to tangible assets must be less than 20 per cent.
- It must have a good credit record over the last three years.

If a company does not meet these criteria but it is a high-tech, high-growth potential company it may list in the Shenzhen SME board, which was set up in 2004 and three years later had 140 companies listed with an average price–earnings ratio of 57.90.[7] In addition to meeting these criteria, a company can only issue B-shares if it has obtained approval from the State Administration of Foreign Exchange (SAFE) for its use of foreign investment or for its conversion into a foreign-funded enterprise and it must have a stable source of adequate foreign revenue sufficient to pay dividends. The number of companies allowed to issue such shares is limited and generally the proportion of B-shares to A-shares for companies with both is less than 5 per cent.

---

[6] See Zhang and Zhao (2004) for an interesting discussion of resultant price differentials between the two markets.
[7] www.szse.cn.

Exhibit 17.3 Mainland Chinese companies listed in the USA and UK, July 2007

Company	Industry/sector	Listed
New York		
Acorn International	Broadline retailer	May 2007
Aluminium Corporation of China Limited	Aluminium production	December 2001
American Oriental Bioengineering	Food products	December 2006
China Eastern Airlines	Airlines operation	February 1997
China Life Insurance Company	Commercial life insurance	December 2003
China Mobile	Mobile telecommunication	October 1997
China Netcom	Fixed-line telecommunication	November 2004
China Petroleum and Chemical Corp	Oil refining	October 2000
China Southern Airlines	Commercial airline services	July 1997
China Telecom Corporation Limited	Fixed-line telecommunication	November 2002
China Unicom	Telephone communications	June 2000
Guangshen Railway	Rail transportation	May 1996
Huaneng Power International	Holding co./power plants	October 1994
LDK Solar	Electrical components & equipment	June 2007
Mindray Medical internatonal	Medical equipment	September 2006
New Oriental Education & Technology	Specialized consumer services	September 2006
Petro China	Oil and gas exploration	April 2000
Qiao Xing Mobile Communications	Telecommunication equipment	May 2007
Semiconductor Manufacturing International Corporation	Semiconductor manufacturing	March 2004
Simcere Pharmaceuticals	Pharmaceuticals	April 2007
Sinopec Shanghai Petrochemical	Petrochemicals production	July 1993
Suntech Power	Electrical components & equipment	December 2005
Tongjitang Chinese Medicines	Pharmaceuticals	March 2007
Trina Solar	Electrical components & equipment	December 2006
Yanzhou Coal Mining	Coal mining	March 1998
Yingli Green Energy	Electrical components & equipment	June 2007

London		
Air China	Airline	December 2004
China Petroleum and Chemical Corp	Oil refining	October 2000
Datang International Power Generation	Electricity	March 1997
Jiangxi Copper Co	Other mineral extraction & mines	June 1997
Zhejiang Expressway Co	Other construction	May 2000
Zhejiang Southeast Electric Power	Electricity	Sept 1997

Source: Based on www.nyse.com (July 2007); www.londonstockexchange.com (July 2004); www.iaspluscom (July 2007).

Exhibit 17.4 Selected stock market information, 1995–2006

	1995	1996	1997	1998	1999	2000	2001	2002	2003	2004	2005	2006
No. of listed stocks												
SHSE A	184	287	372	425	471	559	630	705	770	827	827	828
SHSE B	36	42	50	52	54	55	54	54	54	54	54	54
SZSE A	127	227	348	400	450	499	494	494	491	522	531	566
SZSE B	34	43	51	54	54	58	56	57	57	56	55	55
P/E SZSE	9.4	36.4	39.9	30.6	36.3	56.0	39.8	37.0	36.2	24.6	16.4	32.7
No. of shareholders												
SZSE A m	5.6	10.9	16.1	19.0	21.5	28.1	31.1	32.6	33.2	34.1	34.7	37.6
SZSE B 000	22	94	103	106	111	127	551	577	597	613	619	635
Market capitalization (bn US$)												
SHSE	31.18	67.63	113.8	131.1	180.0	332.5	340.6	313.1	368.0	321.2	285.1	
SZSE	11.71	53.88	102.6	109.6	146.8	261.2	196.7	160.1	156.2	136.3	115.2	
Trading volume (bn US$)												
SHSE	338.0	1,125.3	1,699.2	1,529.2	2,094.5	3,873.3	2,803.6	2,093.7	2,570.9	3,268.0	2,375.3	
SZSE	11.5	27.4	209.4	137.7	177.2	363.6	192.5	136.2	139.4	195.8	153.4	

Source: Shanghai Stock Exchange (SHSE) *Fact Book 2000–2006*; Shenzhen Stock Exchange (SZSE) *Fact Book 2000–2005*.

17.3.4.2 Privatization

One factor limiting the expansion of stock market activity has been the fact that the state has retained substantial shareholdings in SOEs that have privatized and become listed on the stock market, with the state and legal persons holding 59 per cent of all shares in 2002, only down from 72 per cent in 1993.[8] Even more entities, approximately 84 per cent, were ultimately controlled by the state either directly or indirectly via industry companies, state asset investment bureaux, state asset management bureaux or SOEs.[9] Exhibit 17.5 illustrates the presence of the state as

---

[8] Delios *et al.* (2006).
[9] Liu and Sun (2005).

Exhibit 17.5 Illustration of information provided on ultimate shareholdings, Sinopec 2006

Change in Share Capital and Shareholders

Change in share capital for the year ended 31 December 2006

1. Changes in share capital for the year ended 31 December 2006

	Before change		Change						After change	
	shares	Ratio (%)	Rationed shares	Bonus shares	Shares transferred from reserve funds	Others	Sub-total		Shares	Ratio (%)
I. Shares not in circulation										
1. Promoter's shares comprising,	4,000,000,000	55.56	–	–	–	–	–		4,000,000,000	55.56
State-owned shares	4,000,000,000	55.56	–	–	–	–	–		4,000,000,000	55.56
Domestic legal person shares	–	–	–	–	–	–	–		–	–
Overseas legal person shares	–	–	–	–	–	–	–		–	–
Others	–	–	–	–	–	–	–		–	–
2. Legal person shares	150,000,000	2.08	–	–	–	–	–		150,000,000	2.08
3. Internal staff shares	–	–	–	–	–	–	–		–	–
4. Priority shares or others	–	–	–	–	–	–	–		–	–
Sub-total of Promoter shares	4,150,000,000	57.64	–	–	–	–	–		4,150,000,000	57.64
II. Shares in circulation										
1. RMB ordinary shares	720,000,000	10.00	–	–	–	–	–		720,000,000	10.00
2. Domestic listed foreign shares	–	–	–	–	–	–	–		–	–
3. Overseas listed foreign shares	2,330,000,000	32.36	–	–	–	–	–		2,330,000,000	32.36
4. Others	–	–	–	–	–	–	–		–	–
Sub-total of Shares in circulation	3,050,000,000	42.36	–	–	–	–	–		3,050,000,000	42.36
III. Shares in total	7,200,000,000	100.00	–	–	–	–	–		7,200,000,000	100.00

2. Information on the controlling shareholder and de facto controller of the Company

(1) Controlling shareholder

Name of controlling shareholder:	China Petroleum & Chemical Corporation ('Sinopec Corp.')
Authorised representative:	Chen Tonghai
Registered capital:	RMB86.7 billion
Date of incorporation:	February 2000
Major business:	crude oil and natural gas business includes: exploring for, extraction, production and trading of crude oil and natural gas; processing of petroleum; production of petroleum products, trading, transportation, distribution and sales of petroleum products; production, distribution and trading of petrochemical products.

(2) De facto controller

Name of the de facto controller:	China Petrochemical Corporation ('Sinopec')
Authorised representative:	Chen Tonghai
Registered capital:	RMB104.9 billion
Date of incorporation:	July 1998
Major business:	provide well drilling services, oil well logging services and mine shaft work services; manufacturing of production equipment and maintenance services; project construction services and public works and social services such as water and electricity.

(3) Change of controlling shareholder and de facto controller of the Company
During the Reporting Period, there was no change to the controlling shareholder and the de facto controller of the Company.

(4) Diagram of the ownership and controlling relationship between the Company and the de facto controller

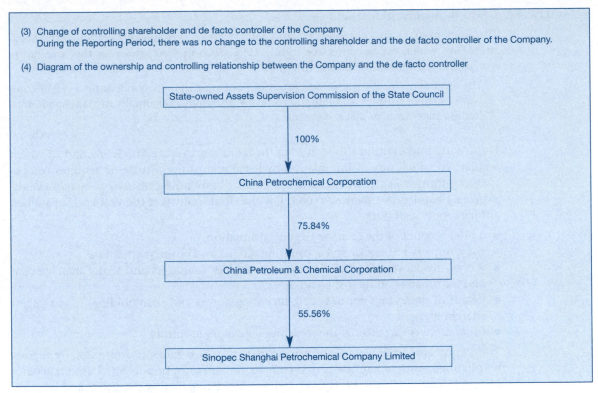

Source: Sinopec Ltd Annual Report (2006), pp. 12 and 14.

controlling shareholder. Not only has continuing state ownership limited the availability of shares for the general public but most of these enterprises have faced a number of corporate governance issues as they have tended to have complex and opaque ownership structures, many continuing management links to the government and disclosure practices more orientated to state ownership that the needs of investors.[10] In 2005 the CSRC therefore announced a new initiative, the 'Administrative Measures on the Split Share Structure Reform of Listed Companies', to convert non-tradable state and legal person shares to tradable shares. By June 2006, 1,006 A-share companies had complied with 343 yet to do so.[11] However, the impact of this will be very slow. To prevent any adverse impact on share prices, the newly converted shares can only be sold over a number of years; currently no more than 5 per cent of state-owned shares can be sold in any three consecutive accounting years. But, eventually, this will substantially increase the number of shares that can be traded. Similarly, all future initial public offerings (IPOs) must also eliminate all non-tradable shares.

---

[10] CFA Institute (2007).

[11] Thompson Financial News, 20 June 2006, quoted in CFA Institute (2007). See Ding and Graham (2007) for a discussion of the role of accounting information in this process and the impact of ideology on the accounting discourse surrounding the event.

17.3.4.3 CSRC regulation of markets

The stock markets are controlled by the CSRC.[12] This has major powers under the Securities Law, which became effective in July 1999. Section 3 sets rules for the continuing disclosure of information, stipulating that:

> The documents for the issuing and listing of shares or corporate bonds announced by companies shall be truthful, accurate and complete; they may not contain any falsehoods, misleading statements or major omissions.

(Article 59)

Particularly important in this section of the Securities Law are Articles 61 and 62 which regulate the disclosure of information by listed companies. Article 62 requires companies to inform the stock market and the public of any price sensitive or 'major' events. Article 61 requires companies to submit, within four months of the year-end, an audited annual report including:

- a brief account of the company's general situation;
- the company's financial and accounting reports and business situation;
- a brief introduction to the directors, supervisors, managers and senior management and information in their shareholdings;
- details of shares and bonds issued, including names and shareholdings of ten largest shareholders;
- other matters specified by the securities regulatory authority.

They must also issue a semi-annual report within two months and quarterly reports within one month of relevant period-end. All of these must be published simultaneously in a corporate disclosure newspaper and website designated by the CSRC and be available at the company's headquarters.

The CSRC issues standards that are applicable to all listed companies that specify what these 'other matters' are. At the end of 2003 there were 19 CSRC standards on content and format of information disclosure. The CSRC revised and reissued *The Standard Form and Content of Information for Disclosure by Companies Making Public Issues No 2: Form and Content of the Annual Report* early in 1999 to increase the amount of disclosure required. A further revision was issued in 2001. It was extended in 2003 to require that managers and financial executives guarantee in writing that the information contained in the financial reports is true and complete. The revised version also standardizes the format of the annual report by including a reporting format in an appendix.[13]

The CSRC has introduced a very large number of other measures to make investment in equities more attractive, with more than 300 guidelines being issued between 1992 and 2003.[14] These include proposals to improve the corporate governance of companies as well as making information more accessible. In particular, it has issued a *Code of Corporate Governance for Listed Companies in China* (issued January 2001)[15] which sets out basic principles for corporate governance and *The Guidelines for Introducing Independent Directors to the Board of Directors of Listed Companies* (2001)[16] which includes basic rules of behaviour for directors and senior managers. This emphasis on corporate governance is reflected in company reporting (see Exhibit 17.6 for an example of some of these disclosures).

---

[12] Website has pages in English: www.csrc.gov.cn.

[13] IAS Plus, *Country Updates*, China, April 2003.

[14] Lin (2004).

[15] An English-language version is on the CSRC website, www.csrc.gov.cn/en/homepage/index_en.jsp.

[16] Ibid.

Exhibit 17.6 Report of the Supervisory Committee, Sinopec, 2006

Report of the Supervisory Committee

In 2006, the Supervisory Committee of the Company conscientiously discharged its supervisory duties in accordance with the 'Company Law' and the relevant legislations, the 'Articles of Association of Sinopec Shanghai Petrochemical Company Limited' and the 'Rules of Procedure for Supervisory Committee Meeting of Sinopec Shanghai Petrochemical Company Limited', thus helping preserve and increase the asset value of the Company, ensuring a standardized operation and safeguarding the shareholders' lawful interests.

Five meetings of the Supervisory Committee were convened during the Reporting Period

(i) The fourth meeting of the fifth session of the Supervisory Committee was convened on 23 March 2006 at the Company's office, and the following was considered and approved:
  (a) the work report of the Supervisory Committee for the year 2005;
  (b) the annual report of the Company for the year 2005;
  (c) the Supervisory Committee's comments and recommendations on the Company's operating results for the year 2005;

(ii) The fifth meeting of the fifth session of the Supervisory Committee was convened on 25 April 2006 at the Company's office, and the following was considered and approved:
  (a) the 2006 first quarterly report of the Company;
  (b) the proposal on the membership changes of the fifth session of the Supervisory Committee.

(iii) The sixth meeting of the fifth session of the Supervisory Committee was convened on 15 June 2006 at Jinshan Hotel, and the following was considered and approved:
  (a) to elect Mr. Gao Jinping as chairman of the Supervisory Committee;

(iv) The seventh meeting of the fifth session of the Supervisory Committee was convened on 28 August 2006 at the Company's office, and the following was considered and approved:
  (a) the 2006 interim report of the Company;
  (b) the Supervisory Committee's analysis and recommendations on the Company's 2006 interim report;

(v) The eighth meeting of the fifth session of the Supervisory Committee was convened on 25 October 2006 at the Company's office, and the following was considered and approved:

  the 2006 third quarterly report of the Company.

Work carried out by the Supervisory Committee during the Reporting Period

During the Reporting Period, members of the Supervisory Committee discharged their duties diligently; conducted meetings on a regular basis; focused on improving the quality of meeting deliberation, attended Board meetings; and promptly furnished comments or suggestions on the operation management of the Company. Major recommendations made to the Company in 2006 were: (i) further strengthen its management to raise the receivable recovery ratio and reduce receivables; (ii) pay more attention to new issues and new problems about product sales as a result of the change in the sales system, so as to enhance and improve the weaknesses in the connection between centralized product sales and specialized companies; (iii) further strengthen the management to lower the Company's on-trip crude oil loss rate in maritime shipment and crude oil loss rate in processing; (iv) further enhance measures to effectively reduce receivables for auxiliary businesses, particularly clearing up receivables of three years or above, while striving for the reduction of receivables for the core businesses; (v) further strengthen the management and application of inventories, reducing inventories' hold on capital; and (vi) further strengthen its management to emphasize economic and technical indicators, in order to control resource and energy consumption, enhance site management quality, and raise the planned target of overall refining yield of petroleum products.

In discharging their routine monitoring duties, regular meetings of the Supervisory Committee Office were convened and the Company's quarterly reports were analyzed quarterly. The main aspects of the Supervisory Committees work

Exhibit 17.6 *(Continued)*

were as follows: First, relevant units (departments/offices) were requested to provide explanations on any specific unusual financial data for clarifying, analyzing and resolving the problem. Secondly, recommendations were made on improving the weaknesses existing in production, operation and management. Thirdly, the Supervisory Committee carried out research into the basic level and enhanced supervision and made recommendations on the enhancement of management and supervision with specific respect to changes in the sales system and the implementation of financial audit at the primary level. The Supervisory Committee, in conjunction with the Company's supervisory departments, monitored performance and inspected specific items. In accordance with the rules of the China Securities Regulatory Commission in respect of annual report disclosures, during 2006 the Supervisory Committee carried out verification of the bad debts written-off, provisions for bad debts and impairment of inventories, disposal of materials which have stayed inactive for three years, guarantee for and trusting of capital and acquisitions and disposals of assets in auxiliary businesses, and so forth.

During 2007, the Supervisory Committee will, in accordance with the newly published Company Law, discharge their supervisory duties diligently and promote a more regulated corporate governance structure. In accordance with the Company's need of implementing the low-cost strategy, the Supervisory Committee will further strengthen inspection and research on problems regarding financial, operation and construction management in line with production operation targets and the full commencement of the structural adjustment program. It will further strengthen the reform and transformation program of the Company's auxiliary businesses, and the supervision and checking of the execution of governance structure and operating system of enterprises remaining after the clean-up and shake-up investment at subsidiary level. The Supervisory Committee will also further strengthen the supervision and checking of the execution of the Company's internal control system. Through supervision and checking, the preservation and value enhancement of the Company's assets can be ensured and the lawful interests of all shareholders of the Company can be safeguarded.

Company's operation in compliance with legislation

During the Reporting Period, a check-and-balance mechanism was set up and enhanced by the Supervisory Committee in accordance with the Company Law, Corporate Governance Standards for Listed Companies and other legislations, and the corporate governance structure was promoted and regulated. The Supervisory Committee discharged their duties and authorities diligently by monitoring the management's enforcement of the Company Law, Corporate Governance Standards for Listed Companies and other legislations as well as the execution of resolutions made at the shareholders' meetings and board meetings. The Supervisory Committee also monitored the board of directors' decision-making procedures and the execution of the internal control system. No acts of the Board, general management team or its senior management staff in discharging their duties were found to have been in breach of the laws and regulations of China or the Company's Articles of Association or in prejudice to the Company's or shareholders' interests. The Supervisory Committee believes that in 2006, in light of the volatile rise of international crude oil prices to high levels and reaching record highs, the Company was able to: follow the working plans of Sinopec and Sinopec Corp.; establish the low-cost strategy; effectively ensure long-cycle, safe and stable operation of production facilities; gradually carry out professional centralized management, reforms of auxiliary businesses and clean-up and shake-up investment at subsidiary level; and effectively strengthen internal management of the enterprise. Production operations remained steady in general, with positive progress reported for work in various aspects.

Source: Sinopec Ltd Annual Report (2006), pp. 76–78.

Under revised CSRC guidelines issued in January 2003, managers and financial executives must guarantee in writing that the reports contain no major errors or misleading information (see Exhibit 17.7). As revised in December 2003 the rules also require additional disclosure in the annual report relating to the use of funds of the listed companies by controlling shareholders and related parties and also provision of financial guarantees to these parties.

Exhibit 17.7	Written confirmation to annual report issued by directors, supervisors and senior management

Written Confirmation to the 2006 Annual Report Issued by Directors, Supervisors and Senior management of Sinopec Shanghai Petrochemical Company Limited

Pursuant to the requirements of No. 68 of the Securities Law and 'No. 2 Content And Format of Annual Report' of 'Standard of Content and Format on Information Disclosure for Publicly Listed Companies' (2005 Revision), we, being directors, supervisors and the senior management of the Company, having carefully studied and reviewed the Company's 2006 annual report, are in the opinion that: the Company was in strict compliance with the financial system operation of listed companies and the 2006 annual report gave a true and fair view of the financial position and operating results of the Company. The unqualified auditors reports of the Company issued by KPMG Huazhen and KPMG, respectively, were true and fair. We warrant that the information contained in the 2006 annual report is true, accurate and complete, and that there are no false or misleading statements contained in or material omissions from this report. We jointly and severally accept full responsibility for the authenticity, accuracy and completeness of the information contained in this report.

Signature:
Directors:

Rong Guangdao	Du Chongjun	Han Zhihao	Shi Wei
Li Honggen	Dai JinBao	Lei Dianwu	Xiang Hanyin
Chen Xinyuan	Sun Chiping	Jiang Zhiquan	Zhou Yunnong

Supervisors:

Gao Jinping	Zhang Chenghua	Wang Yanjun	Lu Xiangyang
Geng Limin	Liu Xiangdong	Yin Yongli	

Senior Management:

Zhang Jianping	Tang Chengjian	Zhang Jingming

Source: Sinopec Ltd Annual Report (2006), p. 210.

17.3.5 Accounting profession

As might be expected, one of the problems that China is facing is the extreme shortage of qualified accountants. Until the reforms began, all that was required at the enterprise level was people who could follow the prescribed systems and record the required transactions. The only professional accountants were the 10,000 or so who had qualified before the communist revolution.[17]

The Accounting Society of China (ASC) was the first accounting body to be set up after the beginnings of the reforms, in January 1980. The ASC is an academic body which seeks to foster education and research. It was the first body to become involved in standard setting when, in 1987, it formed a committee to establish a conceptual framework and promote accounting standards. Its work was superseded by Ministry of Finance initiatives when the ministry formed a similar working group. This was the first stage in setting and enforcing authoritative standards.[18]

---

[17] Blake and Gao (1995).
[18] Hao (1999).

The main accounting professional body, the Chinese Institute of Certified Public Accountants (CICPA), was set up in 1988. Government influence can be seen most obviously in its membership, with the Chair of CICPA being the Ministry of Finance Vice-Minister in charge of accounting affairs. Following merger with the Association of Certified Public Auditors (ACPA) in 1996, the membership rose to approximately 5,600 accounting firm members or 140,000 individual members by mid-2006 with 69,700 practising members and slightly more non-practising members.[19] In 1996 it became a member of the Confederation of Asian and Pacific Accountants (CAPA) and a year later it joined IFAC.

While the CICPA does not set accounting standards, it has issued a number of important guidelines or codes of conduct on professional ethics, education and training and practice review which all of its members are expected to follow. Much of the work of CICPA is carried out in six special and one professional committee: an Auditing Standards Committee to develop independent auditing standards, a Discipline Committee to discipline firms and members, an Appeal Committee to consider appeals of decisions of the Discipline Committee and a Rights-protecting Committee to protect the rights of the profession and its members, an Education and Training Committee, a Finance Committee, an Editorial Committee and a Professional Advisory Committee. Some ideas of the impact of the Discipline Committee can be seen in the fact that 268 cases against members were heard in 2004, rising to 448 in 2005.[20]

The CICPA drafts 'Independent Auditing Standards' which are issued by the Ministry of Finance.[21] During 2005 the Auditing Standards Committee agreed to converge its auditing standards with international auditing standards and issued a series of exposure drafts essentially to achieve this. Exhibit 17.8 reproduces the joint statement of the Auditing Standards Board and the International Accounting Standards Board explaining this policy and the progress made by the end of 2005. Exhibit 17.9 lists the auditing standards issued as at the beginning of 2007.

In February 2006, the Ministry of Finance held a ceremony to release the new Accounting System for Business Enterprises alongside 48 new Auditing Standards for Certified Public Accountants that substantially bring Chinese auditing standards into line with international auditing standards. These auditing standards must be used by all Chinese firms from 1 January 2007. The country is also moving towards implementing the latest IFAC code of ethics, with this being undertaken by the CICPA in 2006–07.

Some idea of the effectiveness of the increased regulation of accounting and accountants can perhaps be seen in the October 2006 CICPA press release reproduced in Exhibit 17.10.

Exhibit 17.11 reproduces the 'Report of the PRC auditors' of the 2006 Chinese accounts of the Sinopec Shanghai Petrochemical Co. Ltd. This report, with its reference to 'China's Auditing Standards for the Certified Public Accountants', the 'Accounting Standards for Business Enterprises and the Accounting Regulations for Business Enterprises issued by the Ministry of Finance' and the opinion that the 'financial statements comply with the requirements . . . and present fairly, in all material respects', can be compared with the 'Repot of the International Auditors' [sic] of the 2006 IFRS-based

---

[19] www.cicpa.org.cn/english.htm.

[20] CICPA reply to IFAC SMO self-assessment questionnaire, August 2006.

[21] Xiao *et al.* (2000).

| Exhibit 17.8 | Joint statement of Chinese Auditing Standards Board and IASB, 2005 |

Joint Statement of the Secretary-General of the China Accounting Standards Committee and the Chairman of the International Accounting Standards Board

08 November 2005

The China Accounting Standards Committee (CASC) and the International Accounting Standards Board (IASB) held a successful convergence meeting on accounting standards on 7 and 8 November 2005 in Beijing. The meeting was co-chaired by China's Vice-Minister of Finance and Secretary-General of the CASC Mr Wang Jun and IASB Chairman Sir David Tweedie. Mr Liu Yuting, member of CASC and Director-General of the Accounting Regulatory Department of the Ministry of Finance, and key members of the accounting standard-setting team of the Accounting Regulatory Department attended the meeting. Three IASB members joined Sir David: Warren McGregor, Patricia O'Malley, and Tatsumi Yamada, as did two IASB directors Wayne Upton and Paul Pacter. This high level meeting followed a series of CASC-IASB staff working meetings that lasted over one week in October.

Both parties agree that establishing and improving a single set of high quality global accounting standards is the logical consequence of the trend of economic globalisation. International convergence takes time to happen. It is a goal to which the IASB as well as national accounting standard-setters of all jurisdictions in the world should continue to make sustained efforts. China stated that convergence is one of the fundamental goals of their standard-setting programme, with the intention that an enterprise applying CASs should produce financial statements that are the same as those of an enterprise that applies IFRSs. How to converge with IFRSs is a matter for China to determine.

The IASB notes that, as their national standards converge with IFRSs, some countries add provisions and implementation guidance not included in IFRSs to reflect the circumstances of those countries. This is a pragmatic and advisable approach with which China agrees.

During the past year, China has issued Exposure Drafts of the Basic Accounting Standard for Business Enterprises and 20 specific standards. China expects to issue two more Exposure Drafts. At the same time, China has also begun a review of its 16 existing CASs. As a result, China's accounting standards system for business enterprises is being developed with a view to achieve convergence of those standards with the equivalent IFRSs. The IASB applauds and expresses admiration for the enormous progress already made towards convergence.

The two parties acknowledged that differences between CASs and IFRSs still exist at the moment on a limited number of matters, including reversal of impairment losses, disclosure of related party relationships and transactions, and accounting for certain government grants. Both parties agreed to work to eliminate those differences as quickly as possible. They noted, however, that these are relatively small matters as compared with the matters on which the CASC's recent work has achieved such significant progress towards convergence.

During the discussions, the IASB identified a number of accounting issues for which China, because of its unique circumstances and environment, could be particularly helpful to the IASB in finding high quality solutions for IFRSs. These include disclosure of related party transactions, fair value measurements and business combinations of entities under common control. The CASC has agreed to assist the IASB in researching and providing recommendations on these issues. Similarly, in reviewing the revisions to the EDs, existing standards, and the implementation guidance, the CASC will get assistance from the IASB as well.

As a result of the success of this joint meeting, the CASC and the IASB have agreed to continue to meet periodically and strengthen the exchange and co-operation between the two parties, to achieve convergence of the Chinese Accounting Standards for Business Enterprises with the International Financial Reporting Standards.

Source: www.iasb.org.

Exhibit 17.9 Auditing standards for use from 1 January 2007

PRC	Name	International
1	General standard for assurance engagements	
1101	Objectives & general principles governing an audit of financial statements	ISA 200
1111	Audit engagement letters	ISA 210
1121	Quality control for audits of historical financial statements	ISA 220R
1311	Audit working papers	ISA 230R
1141	Consideration of fraud in an audit of financial statements	ISA 240
1142	Consideration of laws and regulations in an audit of financial statements	ISA 250
1151	Communications with those charged with governance	ISA 260
1152	Communications between predecessor and successor CPAs	–
1201	Planning an audit	ISA 300
1211	Understanding the entity and its environment and assessing the risks of material misstatement	ISA 315
1212	Consideration relating to entities using service organizations	ISA 402
1221	Materiality	ISA 32I
1231	Procedures in response to assess risks of material misstatement	ISA 330
1301	Audit evidence	ISA 500
1311	Supervisory physical inventory count	ISA 501PtA
1312	Confirmation	ISA 505
1313	Analytical procedures	ISA 520
1314	Audit sampling and other means of testing	ISA 530
1321	Audit of accounting estimates	ISA 540
1322	Auditing fair value measurements and disclosures	ISA 545
1323	Related parties	ISA 550
1324	Going concern	ISA 570
1331	Audit of opening balances on initial engagements	ISA 510
1332	Subsequent events	ISA 560
1341	Management representations	ISA 580
1401	Using the work of other CPAs	ISA 600
1411	Considering the work of internal auditing	ISA 610
1421	Using the work of an expert	ISA 620
1501	Auditors' reports	ISA 700R
1502	Modified auditors' reports	ISA 701
1511	Comparatives	ISA 710
1521	Other information in documents containing audited financial statements	ISA 720

| Exhibit 17.10 | Importance of auditing by CICPA |

CICPA: Over half of listed companies exaggerate profits

More than half of China's listed companies would have exaggerated profits in their 2005 annual reports if certified accountants had not stopped them, the China Institute of Certified Public Accountants (CICPA) said.

In a report released Thursday, the CICPA said 776 Chinese listed firms out of a total of 1,371 were ready to declare 38.8 billion yuan (4.9 billion U.S. dollars) of fictive profits in their 2005 draft annual reports if accountants had not intervened.

Certified public accountants also struck 109.4 billion yuan of asset value from the books of 590 listed firms.

According to CICPA sources, all accounting firms are required to file a copy of their auditing reports with CICPA. The CICPA report was compiled from an analysis of these reports.

CICPA officials said the report shows that China's certified public accountants have become bolder and more professional in fulfilling their duties.

False accounting has been a thorny issue in China. The Ministry of Finance said earlier this week that its probe of 39 property firms shows that these firms failed to report profits totaling 3.3 billion yuan in 2005.

As property prices soar in China, property firms have vehemently denied reports that their profit level is much higher than most industries.

The probe shows that the 39 firms had a profit margin of 26.79 percent rather than the 12.22 percent shown in their accounting books.

Source: http://www1.cei.gov.cn/ce/doc/cen1/200611102475.htm.

accounts of the same company as shown in Exhibit 17.12. This report is designed for use in the Hong Kong Stock Exchange and it refers instead to 'Hong Kong Standards on Auditing issued by the Hong Kong Institute of Certified Public Accountants', IFRS and 'the disclosure requirements of the Hong Kong Companies Ordinance' and the opinion that the statements present a 'true and fair view of the state of affairs'.

The CICPA also assists the Ministry of Finance in organizing the national CPA exams and in approving the registration of CPAs. The 1993 Law of Certified Public Accountants gave the Ministry of Finance power to supervise CPAs, auditing firms and accountancy bodies. It was made responsible for developing the national CPA exams and authorizing the establishment of CPA firms. It has also taken steps to improve professional attitudes. These include reorganizing CPA firms to be independent of government ownership and to assume legal liability for their work.[22] Currently, there is no requirement for members to have any particular accountancy education although they must have passed the National Uniform CPA examination and have some relevant college or similar education. However, this is under review and new regulations requiring an undergraduate degree and more accounting education are to be introduced. In addition, they must have at least two years' practical experience with a CPA firm if they are to become practising members. The CICPA also organized compulsory CPD for its practising members.

---

[22] Yunwei and Pacter (2000).

Exhibit 17.11 Chinese-based audit report, Sinopec Shanghai Petrochemical Company Ltd

Report of the PRC Auditors

KPMG Huazhen

To the shareholders of Sinopec Shanghai Petrochemical Company Limited

We have audited the accompanying financial statements of Sinopec Shanghai Petrochemical Company Limited ('the Company'), which comprise the consolidated balance sheet and balance sheet as at 31 December 2006, and the consolidated income statement and profit appropriation statement, income statement and profit appropriation statement, consolidated cash flow statement and cash flow statement for the year then ended, and notes to the financial statements.

Management's Responsibility for the Financial Statements

The Company's management is responsible for the preparation of these financial statements in accordance with the Accounting Standards for Business Enterprises and the Accounting Regulations for Business Enterprises issued by the Ministry of Finance of the People's Republic of China. This responsibility includes: designing, implementing and maintaining internal control relevant to the preparation of financial statements that are free from material misstatement, whether due to fraud or error; selecting and applying appropriate accounting policies; and making accounting estimates that are reasonable in the circumstances.

Auditors' Responsibility

Our responsibility is to express an opinion on these financial statements based on our audit. We conducted our audit in accordance with China's Auditing Standards for the Certified Public Accountants. Those standards require that we comply with ethical requirements and plan and perform the audit to obtain reasonable assurance whether the financial statements are free from material misstatement.

An audit involves performing procedures to obtain audit evidence about the amounts and disclosures in the financial statements. The procedures selected depend on the auditors' judgment, including the assessment of the risks of material misstatement of the financial statements, whether due to fraud or error. In making those risk assessments, the auditors consider internal control relevant to the entity's preparation of the financial statements in order to design audit procedures that are appropriate in the circumstances, but not for the purpose of expressing an opinion on the effectiveness of the Company's internal control. An audit also includes evaluating the appropriateness of accounting policies used and the reasonableness of accounting estimates made by management, as well as evaluating the overall presentation of the financial statements.

We believe that the audit evidence we have obtained is sufficient and appropriate to provide a basis for our audit opinion.

Opinion

In our opinion, the financial statements comply with the requirements of the Accounting Standards for Business Enterprises and the Accounting Regulations for Business Enterprises issued by the Ministry of Finance of the People's Republic of China and present fairly, in all material respects, the consolidated financial position and financial position of the Company as at 31 December 2006, the consolidated results of operations, results of operations, consolidated cash flows and cash flows of the Company for the year then ended.

KPMG Huazhen	Certified Public Accountants
	Registered in the People's Republic of China
	Hu Qiong
Beijing, the People's Republic of China	**Wang Wenli**
	29 March 2007

Source: Sinopec Ltd Annual Report (2006), p. 145.

Exhibit 17.12   Hong-Kong-based audit report, Sinopec Shanghai Petrochemical Company Ltd

Report of the International Auditors

Independent Auditors' Report
To the shareholders of Sinopec Shanghai Petrochemical Company Limited
(Established in The People's Republic of China with limited liability)

We have audited the consolidated financial statements of Sinopec Shanghai Petrochemical Company Limited ('the Company') set out on pages 89 to 144, which comprise the consolidated and company balance sheets as at 31 December 2006, and the consolidated income statement, the consolidated statement of changes in equity and the consolidated cash flow statement for the year then ended, and a summary of significant accounting policies and other explanatory notes.

Directors' responsibility for the financial statements

The directors of the Company are responsible for the preparation and the true and fair presentation of these financial statements in accordance with International Financial Reporting Standards promulgated by the International Accounting Standards Board and the disclosure requirements of the Hong Kong Companies Ordinance. This responsibility includes designing, implementing and maintaining internal control relevant to the preparation and the true and fair presentation of financial statements that are free from material misstatement, whether due to fraud or error; selecting and applying appropriate accounting policies; and making accounting estimates that are reasonable in the circumstances.

Auditors' responsibility

Our responsibility is to express an opinion on these financial statements based on our audit. This report is made solely to you, as a body, and for no other purpose. We do not assume responsibility towards or accept liability to any other person for the contents of the report.

We conducted our audit in accordance with Hong Kong Standards on Auditing issued by the Hong Kong Institute of Certified Public Accountants. Those standards require that we comply with ethical requirements and plan and perform the audit to obtain reasonable assurance as to whether the financial statements are free from material misstatement.

An audit involves performing procedures to obtain audit evidence about the amounts and disclosures in the financial statements. The procedures selected depend on the auditors' judgement, including the assessment of the risks of material misstatement of the financial statements, whether due to fraud or error. In making those risk assessments, the auditors consider internal control relevant to the entity's preparation and true and fair presentation of the financial statements in order to design audit procedures that are appropriate in the circumstances, but not for the purpose of expressing an opinion on the effectiveness of the entity's internal control. An audit also includes evaluating the appropriateness of accounting policies used and the reasonableness of accounting estimates made by the directors, as well as evaluating the overall presentation of the financial statements.

We believe that the audit evidence we have obtained is sufficient and appropriate to provide a basis for our audit opinion.

Opinion

In our opinion, the financial statements give a true and fair view of the state of affairs of the Company and of the Group as at 31 December 2006 and of the Group's profit and cash flows for the year then ended and have been properly prepared in accordance with International Financial Reporting Standards promulgated by the International Accounting Standards Board and the disclosure requirements of the Hong Kong Companies Ordinance.

KPMG

Certified Public Accountants
8th Floor, Prince's Building
10 Chater Road
Central, Hong Kong

29 March 2007

Source: Sinopec Ltd Annual Report (2006), pp. 87–88.

17.4 External influences

Accounting in China has a very long history. Both accounting and auditing systems were highly developed, at least as regards the recording of economic and financial transactions, more than 2,000 years ago. Indeed, the emergence of the first form of accounting can be traced back to the Shang Dynasty (1500 to 1000 BC). However, accounting failed to develop rapidly after this due at least partially to domestic political upheavals. Thus, until the early part of the last century single entry bookkeeping predominated. Western accounting methods began to be imported into the country in the 1920s although they were still relatively underdeveloped when the PRC was formed in 1949.

With the change to a communist system, China adopted wholesale the Soviet system of accounting. Despite attempts at developing a unique Chinese political and economic system, during the period of both the Great Leap Forward (1958–59) and the Cultural Revolution (1966–76), the accounting system remained largely unchanged until economic liberalization began in the late 1970s.

China is now attempting to find a unique development path combining socialist social structures with capitalist markets. This has involved major changes in the ways in which enterprises are organized with the introduction of profit measures and private ownership. This means that the accounting system has also had to be radically restructured, starting virtually from the beginning. This has encompassed all aspects of accounting, including not only financial accounting and reporting by both domestic enterprises and foreign joint ventures, but also stock market regulations, auditing regulations and accounting education.

As discussed in Chapter 4, it is obviously neither feasible nor sensible to develop a brand new accounting system without reference to the models established elsewhere. This has meant that China began to import western accounting rules as exemplified by, in particular, IFRS. These are being deliberately imported into China by the Chinese authorities rather than being imposed by more powerful players. However, the authorities were probably aware of strong encouragement towards IASB standards from joint venture companies, the World Bank, the International Monetary Fund and foreign accounting firms.[23]

17.5 Accounting regulations

If you are studying China as an external observer, the current accounting system can best be understood if you first understand the key features of the previous accounting system, which was very different from that of any western capitalist country. This section will therefore include an outline of the system of accounting that was in place before the current accounting reforms began. It will then describe the process of continuing development in accounting regulation and practices in China.

17.5.1 Uniform accounting regulation

Prior to reform, the accounting regulations, known as the Uniform Accounting Regulations (UAR), were set either directly by the Department of Administration of Accounting

---

[23] Xiang (1998); Xiao *et al.* (2000).

Affairs (a part of the Ministry of Finance) or, in the case of specific industries, by the ministry responsible for that industry and then approved by the Ministry of Finance. The UAR consisted of a system of many uniform plans, each in turn containing detailed rules or regulations covering both costing and financial reporting matters. Accounting was controlled by the Ministry of Finance, because it was seen as only one of the many tools available to ensure the efficient functioning of businesses.

The system was a uniform one, with enterprises having to follow detailed regulations. This may be seen in the treatment of depreciation, for example, with only straight-line depreciation being permitted for most enterprises. Approved useful lives were set by regulation and enterprises were allowed to use different depreciation rates only if they had prior approval. However, while the accounting rules were detailed and rigidly imposed, different systems were developed for enterprises in different sectors or industries.

A major difference from western commercial accounting concerned the use of fund accounting. This is not a type of funds flow statement but rather a way of categorizing accrual-based assets and liabilities. The balance sheet categorized both assets and liabilities on the basis of their function. This practice originated because of the need to control the activities of enterprises to ensure that they met the national plan. Three categories were used:

- fixed funds
- current funds
- specific funds.

Fixed funds were similar to fixed assets in that they included the physical assets of the enterprise used by labour to generate output. However, intangible assets were not included and land was also generally excluded. Land is seen as belonging to the people and therefore it cannot be owned by an enterprise, although, increasingly, rights to use land were valued and traded. This practice still continues; indeed it is interesting to see that the Chinese regulations for valuation of these are less conservative than the international standards, as illustrated by the Sinopec (2006) accounts:

> Under IFRS land use rights are carried at historical cost less accumulated amortization, under PRC accounting rules and regulations, land use rights are carried at revalued amount less accumulated depreciation.

Income was calculated in a somewhat different way. Reflecting the state control of the economy, it was calculated after a number of appropriations such as a public welfare fund for employees' collective welfare facilities, which would be treated as profit distributions in western companies. This system is now changing. For example, the Sinopec (2006) accounts state that:

> Pursuant to the shareholders meeting of 15 June 2006, the Company's Articles of Association was revised that [sic] the Company is no longer to set aside statutory public welfare fund from the net profit available for appropriation, pursuant to the notice 'Cai Qi [2006] No 67' issued by the Ministry of Finance, the balance of the statutory public fund of . . . was transferred to the statutory surplus reserve.

Administration and workshop expenses were also treated as product costs. This was an important difference because many enterprises were producing to centralized plans that could involve stockpiling unsaleable inventory. Including such expenses as product costs meant that they were not being charged to the income statement but instead appearing as assets in the balance sheet. Not having any overriding principle of conservatism meant that this practice could continue for long periods.

With the economic liberalization of the 1980s which increased enterprises' freedom of action, and with evermore enterprises investing in other enterprises, it became increasingly easy to circumvent the restrictions on the use of the different funds. Also, as enterprises became increasingly free to make their own operating and investment decisions, and as private ownership increased in importance, the state had less need to dictate how enterprises should use any particular source of finance. Therefore, the need to use fund accounting decreased greatly, opening the way for the introduction of western accounting principles. At the same time the tradition of uniform accounting rules remained strong.

17.5.2 Stages of financial accounting reforms

The reform of financial accounting can be divided into four phases.[24] The first phase involved regulations for foreign joint ventures. These regulations started in 1979 with the 'Law on Sino-Foreign Joint Ventures'. This was little more than a statement of principles and it was followed by a series of more detailed laws. These included a joint venture income tax law and laws on contracts and foreign exchange. The first accounting-related laws were passed in March 1985, being the 'Accounting Regulations for Sino-Foreign Joint Ventures' and 'Charts of Account and Accounting Statements for Industrial Sino-Foreign Joint Ventures'. Following further changes in the economic system, including the further development of foreign exchange markets, these regulations were replaced, in 1993, by 'Accounting Regulations for Enterprises with Foreign Investments' and 'Charts of Accounts and Accounting Statements for Industrial Enterprises with Foreign Investments'. The 1985 regulations were particularly important as they were the first move away from fund accounting towards international practices.

Enterprises started to issue equity shares in 1984. Thus, the second stage of reform involved the introduction of regulations for domestic or Chinese-owned public companies. This started in May 1992 when the Ministry of Finance and the National Committee of Economic Structure Reform jointly promulgated 'Accounting Regulations for Share Enterprises'. This was an important development as it was the first set of regulations which adopted international accounting practices for use by purely domestic enterprises.

The third and crucial reform was the 'Accounting System for Business Enterprises (ASBE)' (also called the Enterprise Accounting System, EAS) issued in November 1992 and effective from 1 July 1993. The ASBE was a major attempt both to unify the accounting systems used by different industries and to move financial accounting towards international accounting practices.[25]

The fourth stage of reform is still taking place and involves establishing a complete set of accounting standards issued by the Accounting Standards Committee. The ASC was set up in October 1998 by the Ministry of Finance to oversee the development of a complete set of Chinese GAAP. It is a consultative body comprising experts from relevant departments of the government, local accounting firms and academics. This phase has

---

[24] Roberts *et al.* (1995).

[25] Tang *et al.* (1994).

involved the phasing out of industry-specific regulations and their replacement by a set of standards designed to bring Chinese accounting into line with international standards, although industry-specific guidelines still exist.

17.5.3 Accounting regulation from 1992 to 2000

The 1992 Accounting System for Business Enterprises (ASBE) was the first major piece of accounting legislation that applied to all enterprises irrespective of their form of ownership. It was also the first attempt to introduce regulations that applied equally to all industries rather than relying, as in the past, on industry-specific regulations. However, the move from a series of uniform fund-based accounting systems to one western-style system involves major changes for enterprises, and it would have been unrealistic to expect them to be able to change quickly and easily. Thus, there were several transitional arrangements set up, including various voluntary industry-specific accounting systems, each based upon the ASBE but designed to make the move from the respective UAR as simple as possible.

The ASBE involved a change in the function of financial accounting. It has been suggested that prior to the accounting reforms, financial accounting served four objectives:[26]

- to reflect, analyze and assess the implementation of the state plan;
- to reflect the source of funds obtained by enterprises and the ways funds are applied, and to evaluate fund utilization and turnover in operation;
- to ensure legitimacy of the sources of funds and fund application;
- to provide financial and cost information in order to improve operation and management of enterprises for greater economic benefit.

The ASBE introduced the idea of reporting to all external users. Article 11 set out the objectives of accounting information as:

> Accounting information must be designed to meet the requirements of national economic control, the needs of all concerned external users in order to understand an enterprise's financial position and operating results, and the needs of management to strengthen financial practices and administration.

> (Tang *et al.*, 1994)

It is worth noting that the government was the first-named user group in this objective. It was intended that the ASBE of 1992 would be replaced by a full set of 30 accounting standards within three years. This project was financed by the World Bank with Deloitte Touche Tohmatsu acting as consultants. However, once Deloitte Touche Tohmatsu started work it found that the task was larger than it had originally envisaged and that it would take considerably longer than anticipated to educate many of the SOEs in the new system and to ensure that they were fully willing and able to introduce new western-style accounting standards. Tang (2000) lists a number of reasons for this. He argues that many accountants did not understand either the theoretical reasoning behind the conceptual frameworks found in a number of other countries or why the old system needed to be changed. In addition, the unique circumstances of China meant that several of the underlying principles found in other countries were inappropriate. The government was identified as an important user; indeed it was thought to be as important as other users. In addition, given a number of past problems caused by false accounting information, it was felt that the concept of reliability was more important than relevance. Thus, there was much more of a need to

---

[26] Ibid.

assess the likely impacts of the proposed standards and to develop professional competence and expertise than was originally realized.

Although the ASBE of 1992 introduced western-style financial statements, it was not a very detailed set of regulations. They have been considerably strengthened since they were first issued both in terms of rules regarding the operation of the accounting system and in terms of accounting rules themselves. With respect to the former, the Accounting Law was thoroughly revised, effective from July 2000, such that it included:[27]

- an increase in the basic requirements for accounting and bookkeeping, dealing in particular with accounting records kept on computer;
- a clear definition of the responsibilities of the person in charge of a reporting unit;
- a strengthening of the requirements for internal accounting supervision, including the establishment of an effective internal control system by each unit;
- a requirement that accounting personnel must be appropriately qualified;
- increased protection for individuals who report violations of the accounting law; and
- more severe penalties for breaches of the Accounting Law's requirements.

17.5.4 The system from 2000 to 2006

Generally accepted accounting principles in the PRC are set by the law, the Ministry of Finance and the China Securities Regulatory Commission (CSRC). The Accounting Law of the PRC (revised 1 July 2000) replaced the previous law of 1992. In 2000 the State Council issued Financial Accounting and Reporting Rules for Enterprises (FARR) which apply to all enterprises except for very small ones that do not raise funds externally.

The Accounting Law gave the Ministry of Finance the power to establish regulations and systems for accounting. In January 2001 the Ministry of Finance adopted an updated Accounting System for Business Enterprises (ASBE) and in April 2004 introduced the Accounting System for Small Business Enterprises (ASSBE), effective from 1 January 2005. The size criteria for small companies are based upon number of employees or turnover or total assets, although the criteria include enterprises that would be considered to be large in most countries. For example, industrial companies can follow the ASSBE if they have less than 300 employees, while for construction it is 600 employees and for retail it is 100 employees. In addition, they must not raise funds from the public, be a sole proprietor or partnership or be a financial institution. The ASSBE provides a number of simplifications and exemptions from the ASBE in areas such as impairment of assets, equity method investments, finance leases, capitalization of borrowing costs, post-balance-sheet events and production of financial statements.

The Ministry of Finance also continued to develop accounting standards with the advice of the international accountancy firm Deloitte Touche Tohmatsu. The initial stages of this project resulted in a series of standards, as listed in Exhibit 17.13. Although the scope of each of the PRC standards is different, many of the issues addressed in individual standards were also included in the ASBE, which has wider application. The ASBE was consistent with the standards, although usually the individual standards and supporting guidance were more detailed. The Ministry of Finance also issues accounting guidelines. For example, recent guidelines include 'Accounting Guidelines for Enterprises engaged in Guarantee Activities' and 'Temporary Requirement in respect of Share Reforms of Listed Enterprises', both issued in November 2005, 'Temporary Requirement in respect

---

[27] *Accountancy International* (December 1999), p. 52.

Exhibit 17.13 List of PRC accounting standards issued by the Ministry of Finance

No.	Subject	Effective date of current version	Applies to
1	Disclosure of related party relationships and transactions	1 January 1997	Listed enterprises
2	Cash flow statements	1 January 2001	All enterprises
3	Events occurring after the balance sheet date	1 January 1998, amendments from July 2003	All who follow ASBE (starting 2003)
4	Debt restructuring	1 January 2001	All enterprises
5	Revenue	1 January 1999	Listed enterprises
6	Investments	1 January 2001	Joint-stock limited enterprises (from 2001)
7	Construction contracts	1 January 1999	Listed enterprises
8	Changes in accounting policies and estimates and corrections of accounting errors	1 January 2001	All enterprises from 2001
9	Non-monetary transactions	1 January 2001	All enterprises
10	Contingencies	1 July 2000	All enterprises
11	Intangible assets	1 January 2001	Joint-stock limited enterprises
12	Borrowing costs	1 January 2001	All enterprises
13	Leases	1 January 2001	All enterprises
14	Interim financial reporting	1 January 2002	Listed enterprises
15	Inventories	1 January 2002	All who follow ASBE (starting 2003)
16	Fixed assets	1 January 2002	All who follow ASBE (starting 2003)

Source: IAS Plus, *Country Updates*, China, July 2004, www.iasplus.com/country/China.htm.

of Recognition and Measurement of Financial Instruments' (applicable to commercial banks) issued in September 2005 and 'Accounting Guidelines for Enterprises of the Film Industry' and 'Accounting Guideline for Enterprises of the Shipping and Port Industry', both issued in December 2004. These are examples of industry-specific guidance that extend previous experience in China of providing industry-specific rules.

17.5.5 The system from 2007

The second stage of the work of Deloitte Touche Tohmatsu was to develop a further series of standards designed to reduce further the differences between Chinese and international standards. However, these were not introduced until February 2006 when the Ministry of Finance finally released the Basic Accounting Standards for Business Enterprises consisting of 38 standards (see Exhibit 17.14 for a list of these) and a new basic

Exhibit 17.14 Accounting Standards for Business Enterprises, applicable from 1 January 2007

1	Inventories
2	Long-term equity investments
3	Investment properties
4	Fixed assets
5	Biological assets
6	Intangible assets
7	Exchange of non-monetary assets
8	Impairment of assets
9	Employee compensation
10	Enterprise annuity fund
11	Share-based payment
12	Debt restructurings
13	Contingencies
14	Revenue
15	Construction contracts
16	Government grants
17	Borrowing costs
18	Income taxes
19	Foreign currency translation
20	Business combinations
21	Leases
22	Recognition and measurement of financial instruments
23	Transfer of financial assets
24	Hedging
25	Direct insurance contracts
26	Re-insurance contracts
27	Extraction of petroleum and natural gas
28	Changes in accounting policies and estimates and correction of errors
29	Events occurring after the balance sheet date
30	Presentation of financial statements
31	Cash flow statements
32	Interim financial reporting
33	Consolidated financial statements
34	Earnings per share
35	Segment reporting
36	Related party disclosure
37	Presentation of financial instruments
38	First time adoption of Accounting Standards for Business Enterprises

standard or a conceptual framework. The delay was mainly due to concerns by the government and some practitioners about the standards and in particular the role of conservatism in allowing companies to manipulate income and so reduce fiscal revenues and doubts about the abilities of practitioners to understand or implement the new standards. These standards are designed to bring practice very largely into line with IFRS, although the two are not always identical mainly due to unique features of the Chinese legal system. Also introduced were additional annual and quarterly disclosure requirements designed to address the concerns of critics regarding the quality of disclosure. All listed companies must use these standards as from 1 January 2007, while all SOEs and large to medium companies must apply them by the end of 2009.

Exhibit 17.15 provides an illustration of the differences between IFRS and Chinese accounting rules as of 2006, immediately before the introduction of the new Chinese accounting standards which bring China much more into line with international standards.

While the new system of accounting applies to year-ends starting 1 January 2007, companies are required to produce a reconciliation statement explaining all the significant differences between the old and new systems in their 2006 annual accounts. The example of Sinopec is given in Exhibit 17.16.

While the new accounting standards bring Chinese accounting substantially into line with international standards, there are some differences remaining, mainly due to the unique legal system of China. Exhibit 17.17 describes the more important remaining differences.

The move to these new standards will obviously have a significant impact on financial statements. It has been suggested that these changes in the numbers reported may in turn have a number of potentially significant impacts on the reporting entities themselves, as illustrated in Exhibit 17.18.

By November 2006 the Ministry of Finance had issued additional guidance on the implementation of 32 of the 38 new standards.

17.6 Hong Kong China

As discussed above, Hong Kong reverted from British control to Chinese control in July 1997 when it became a Special Administrative Region (SAR) of China. Hong Kong, or, as it is now officially termed, Hong Kong China, had been acquired by the British in stages from 1842 and since then it has been economically highly successful, as can be seen from the economic data given in Exhibit 17.19.

17.6.1 Political and economic system

China has promised that Hong Kong will remain as a market-led capitalist system for at least the next 50 years, described as the 'one country, two systems' policy. Given the tiny size of Hong Kong compared with China, the absorption of Hong Kong into China might seem at first sight to be of little significance to China. However, as we have seen throughout this chapter, China is undergoing a profound process of change. It has introduced many market-based laws and regulations and is moving more and more towards a

Exhibit 17.15 PRC accounting rules, Sinopec Shanghai Petrochemical Company Ltd

Differences between financial statements prepared under PRC Accounting Rules and Regulations and IFRSs

The Company also prepares a set of financial statements which complies with PRC Accounting Rules and Regulations. A reconciliation of the Group's net profit and shareholders' equity prepared under PRC Accounting Rules and Regulations and IFRSs is presented below.

Other than the differences in classification of certain financial statements assertions and the accounting treatment of the items described below, there are no material differences between the Group's financial statements prepared in accordance with PRC Accounting Rules and Regulations and IFRSs. The major differences are:

Notes:

(i) Capitalisation of general borrowing costs
Under IFRSs, to the extent that funds are borrowed generally and used for the purpose of obtaining a qualifying asset, the borrowing costs should be capitalised as part of the cost of that asset. Under PRC Accounting Rules and Regulations, only borrowing costs on funds that are specially borrowed for construction are eligible for capitalisation as fixed assets.

(ii) Valuation surplus
Under PRC Accounting Rules and Regulations, the excess of fair value over the carrying value of assets given up in part exchange for investments should be credited to capital reserve fund. Under IFRSs, it is inappropriate to recognise such excess as a gain as its realisation is uncertain.

(iii) Government grants
Under PRC Accounting Rules and Regulations, government grants should be credited to capital reserve. Under IFRSs, such grants for the purchase of equipment used for technology improvements are offset against the cost of asset to which the grants related. Upon transfer to property, plant and equipment, the grant is recognised as income over the useful life of the property, plant and equipment by way of a reduced depreciation charge.

(iv) Revaluation of land use rights
Under IFRSs, land use rights are carried at historical cost less accumulated amortisation. Under PRC Accounting Rules and Regulations, land use rights are carried at revalued amount less accumulated amortisation.

(v) Pre-operating expenditure
Under IFRSs, expenditure on start-up activities should be recognised as expenses when it is incurred. Under PRC Accounting Rules and Regulations, all expenses incurred during the start-up period are aggregated in long-term deferred expenses and then fully charged to the income statement in the month of commencement of operations.

(vi) Goodwill and negative goodwill amortisation
Under PRC Accounting Rules and Regulations, negative goodwill, acquired before 17 March 2003, and positive goodwill are amortised on a straight line basis over their useful lives.

Under IFRSs, with reference to IFRS 3, 'Business combinations', the Group no longer amortises goodwill effective 1 January 2005. Such goodwill is tested annually for impairment. Also in accordance with the transitional arrangements under IFRS 3, previously recognised negative goodwill was derecognised at the beginning of that period, with a corresponding adjustment to the opening balance of retained earnings.

(vii) Sale of assets to a jointly controlled entity
Under PRC Accounting Rules and Regulations, a listed company that sells fixed assets to its related party, any excess of the net disposal proceeds over the carrying amount of the fixed assets, net of income tax, is recognised in capital reserve.

Under IFRSs, a venturer that contributes non-monetary assets or sells assets to a joint venture, while the assets are retained in the joint venture, the venturer shall recognise a gain or loss to the extent the assets have been sold to the other venturers.

(viii) Changes in fair value of available-for-sale securities
Under PRC Accounting Rules and Regulations, long-term investments in entities in which the Group does not have control, joint control or does not exercise significant influence in their management are stated at cost.

Under IFRSs, investments in available-for-sale equity securities are carried at fair value with any change in fair value, other than impairment losses, recognised directly in equity. When these investments are derecognized or impaired, the cumulative gain or loss previously recognised directly in equity is recognised in the income statement.

Effects on the Group's net profit and shareholders' equity of significant differences between PRC Accounting Rules and Regulations and IFRSs are summarised below:

	Note	Years ended 31 December	
		2006 RMB'000	2005 RMB'000
Net profit under PRC Accounting Rules and Regulations		736,851	1,704,627
Adjustments:			
Capitalisation of borrowing costs,net of depreciation effect	(i)	28,708	26,924
Reduced depreciation on government grants	(iii)	26,760	26,760
Amortisation of revaluation of land use rights	(iv)	3,498	3,498
Reversal of pre-operating expenditure previously written-off	(v)	–	80,605
Goodwill and negative goodwill amortisation	(vi)	7,267	12,599
Sale of assets to a jointly controlled entity	(vii)		
– reclassification of the gain, net of income tax, from capital reserve to income statement		89,329	–
– reversal of the unrealised gain, net of depreciation effect		(50,795)	–
Deferred tax effect of the above adjustments		2,789	(4,564)
Profit attributable to equity shareholders of the Company under IFRSs		844,407	1,850,449

	Note	As at 31 December	
		2006 RMB'000	2005 RMB'000
Shareholders' equity under PRC Accounting Rules and Regulations		19,273,088	19,166,908
Adjustments:			
Capitalisation of borrowing costs	(i)	138,657	109,949
Valuation surplus	(ii)	(44,887)	(44,887)
Government grants	(iii)	(263,919)	(290,679)
Revaluation of land use rights	(iv)	(125,865)	(129,363)
Goodwill and negative goodwill	(vi)	22,415	15,148
Sale of assets to a jointly controlled entity, net of depreciation effect	(vii)	(50,795)	–
Changes in fair value of available-for-sale securities	(viii)	25,822	–
Deferred tax effect of the above adjustments		1,827	2,911
Total equity attributable to equity shareholders of the Company under IFRSs		18,976,343	18,829,987

Source: Sinopec Ltd Annual Report (2006), pp. 204–206, www.sinopec.com.cn.

Exhibit 17.16 Reconciliation between old and new accounting standards, Sinopec Shanghai Petrochemical Company Ltd

Sinopec Shanghai Petrochemical Company Limited
31 December 2006 and 1 January 2007
Reconciliation statement of differences in the consolidated shareholders' equity between the new and old accounting standards

	Note	Amount RMB'000
Consolidated shareholders equity as at 31 December 2006 (old accounting standards)	3(1)	19,273,088
Adjustment:		
1 Financial assets available for sale measured at fair value	3(2)	25,822
2 Income tax	3(3)	(24,672)
3 Minority interests	3(4)	336,013
4 Interest capitalisation of general borrowings	3(5)	138,657
Consolidated shareholders' equity as at 1 January 2007 (new accounting standards)		19,748,908

Sinopec Shanghai Petrochemical Company Limited
31 December 2006 and 1 January 2007
Notes to the reconciliation statement of differences in consolidated shareholders' equity between the new and old accounting standards

In respect of the areas that are not specified in Art. 5 to Art.19 of ASBE 38 and the Opinion, this reconciliation statement of differences is prepared under the following principles:

(1) Upon the adoption of the New Accounting Standards, the Company has accounted for minority interests in the consolidated shareholders' equity in accordance with the Accounting Standards for Business Enterprises No. 33 Consolidated Financial Statements, and the adjustment is reflected in separately-presented items in the reconciliation statement of differences.

Significant items explanation

(1) The figures of consolidated shareholders' equity as at 31 December 2006 (under the Old Accounting Standards) are extracted from the Company's consolidated financial statements for the year ended 31 December 2006 prepared under the Old Accounting Standards. These financial statements were audited by KPMG Huazhen, which issued an auditors' report with unqualified opinion on 29 March 2007. The basis of presentation and the significant accounting policies of these financial statements are set out in the Company's 2006 consolidated financial statements.

This reconciliation statement of differences and its notes should be read in conjunction with the 2006 financial statements.

(2) Financial assets available for sale measured at fair value
According to the requirements to measure financial assets available for sale at fair value under the 'Accounting Standards for Business Enterprises No.22 Recognition and Measurement of Financial Instruments', the Company determined the fair value of the financial assets available for sale as at 1 January 2007 based on the bidding prices in on open market amounted to RMB81,118,700. The Company made the adjustment to increase the consolidated shareholders' equity amounting to RMB25,822,000 based on the differences between the book value and the fair value.

(3) Income tax

In accordance with 'Accounting Standards for Business Enterprises No.18 Income Tax', the Company increased the deferred tax liabilities amounted to RMB24,672,000 on implementation of the new accounting standards as at 1 January 2007 at the first time, the net decrease of retained earnings amounted to RMB 24,672,000.

(4) Minority interests

The Company adjusted the minority interests amounting to RMB336,013,000 in accordance with the new accounting standards.

(5) Interest capitalisation of general borrowings

In accordance with 'Accounting Standards for Business Enterprises No.17 Borrowing Cost', the interest expenses of general borrowing for the construction or production of the qualifying asset should be capitalized as part of the cost of that asset. The Company increased fixed assets and construction in progress by the capitalisation interest of general borrowings amounting to RMB138,657,000 on implementation of the new accounting standards as at 1 January 2007 at the first time, the net increase of retained earnings amounted to RMB 138,657,000.

Source: Sinopec Ltd Annual Report (2006), pp. 201–203.

Exhibit 17.17 Significant remaining differences between Chinese and international standards

ASBE	IAS/IFRS	Significant differences between PRC and international standards
2 Long-term equity investment	IAS 31 Interest in joint ventures	ASBE 2 does not address accounting treatment of jointly controlled operations or assets
3 Investment property	40 Investment property	IAS 40 must use fair value if entity classifies land use rights held for rental as an investment property, ASBE 3 allows use of cost or fair value model
4 Fixed assets	16 Property, plant & equipment	Under ASBE PPE must be shown at cost and not at revaluation
5 Biological assets	41 Agriculture	ASBE 5 uses cost model unless evidence that the entity can reliably obtain fair values, IAS 41 requires fair values unless estimate is clearly unreliable
6 Intangible assets	38 Intangible assets	ASBE 6 only permits use of cost model, IAS 38 allows use of cost of revaluation models
8 Impairment of assets	36 Impairment of assets	ASBE 8 prohibits reversal of all impairment losses, IAS 36 prohibits reversal for goodwill only
9 Employee benefits	19 Employee benefits	Defined benefit plans not addressed in ASBE as not allowed in PRC
10 Enterprise annuity fund	26 Retirement benefit plans	
11 Share-based payments	IFRS 2 Share-based payments	ASBE 11 is more limited in scope reflecting PRC practices

Exhibit 17.17 *(Continued)*

12 Debt restructuring	39 Financial instruments: Recognition & measurement	ASBE 12 does not cover debt derecognition
15 Construction costs	11 Construction costs	ASBE 15 requires all direct costs of obtaining contract to be expensed, IAS 11 permits capitalization if costs meet criteria
16 Government grants	20 Government grants	ASBE 16 only allows grant to be treated as deferred income, IAS 20 also permits deduction from carrying amount of asset
17 Borrowing costs	23 Borrowing costs	ASBE 17 requires capitalization, IAS 23 also permits immediate expensing
19 Foreign currency translation	21 Effects of changes in foreign currency rates	IAS 21 permits presentation of statements in any currency, PRC laws require use of local currency only
21 Leases	17 Leases	ASBE 21 requires leasehold interest in land to normally be treated as intangible, IAS normally requires treatment as operating lease
25 Direct insurance contracts	IFRS 4 Insurance contracts	ASBE 25 contains specific requirements for income, reserves and costs, IFRS 4 does not. IFRS 4 gives guidance on unbundling, ASBE 25 does not
27 Extraction of petroleum and natural gas	IFRS 6 Exploration for & evaluation of mineral resources	ASBE 27 only covers oil & gas. IFRS 6 permits cost or revaluation, ASBE 27 only allows cost method
30 Presentation of statements	1 Presentation of financial statements	ASBE 30 permits analysis of expenses by function only, IAS 1 permits analysis by function or nature
31 Cash flow statements	7 Cash flow statements	ASBE 31 requires use of direct method, IAS 7 permits direct or indirect method. ASBE specifies treatment of interest and dividends, IAS does not
32 Interim financial reporting	34 Interim financial reporting	ASBE 32 does not require statement of changes in equity, but requires complete B/S, income statement
33 Consolidated statements	27 Consolidated & separate FS	ABSE requires use of same year-end for all entities. ABSE only allows use of equity method for jointly controlled entities, IAS 27 also permits use of proportionate consolidation
35 Segment reporting	14 Segment reporting	ASBE applies to all entities, IAS applied only if debt or securities publicly traded
36 Related party disclosures	24 Related party disclosures	ASBE excludes state-controlled enterprises, IAS 24 does not

Source: Deloitte China 'China's new accounting standards' 2006, www.iasplus.com.

Exhibit 17.18 Possible implications of the new accounting standards

Chinese Accounting – New Era, New Challenge

On 15 February 2006, the Ministry of Finance of the People's Republic of China (the 'MoF') formally announced the issuance of the long awaited Accounting Standards for Business Enterprises ('ASBEs') which consist of a new Basic Standard and 38 Specific ASBEs . . .

The impact of applying the ASBEs should not be underestimated. Some of the wider implications of applying these ASBEs are as follows:

Changes in share prices and credit ratings

Where the impact of transition is not transparent, it could make it difficult to assess the underlying performance of the enterprise, leading to damaging market speculation. Therefore it is essential that the impact is effectively communicated to stakeholders.

Impact on key performance indicators (KPIs)

The market may expect KPIs across sectors to be comparable, even though the new ASBEs may affect individual companies in different ways. It is essential that any such differences, and the reasons for them, are explained to stakeholders.

Impact on gearing and liquidity ratios

Loan covenants based on ratios from financial statements may be broken, or become much tighter, leading to uncertainty about the availability of finance. A timely review of agreements should be performed to identify and rectify potential issues.

Increased volatility in results

The new requirements require greater use of fair values and such measurement will lead to increased volatility in results. Entities will need to explain this to stakeholders.

Systems and controls

Systems will need to capture data which may not have been required under current PRC GAAP. The necessary modifications and other requirements must be identified early to enable implementation and testing before full reporting is required.

Training

Accounting staff, and other members of staff making operational decisions, and those charged with governance will need to have sufficient knowledge and understanding of the new requirements under ASBEs. Sufficient training will be required.

Distributions and dividend policy

The new requirements may affect the ability of an enterprise to make distributions. Entities will need to assess the impact on their dividend policy and communicate this clearly to stakeholders.

Taxation

The new ASBEs may have an impact on tax treatments. An accurate assessment of the full tax implications may be difficult to perform until precise details of the taxation authorities' treatment of these changes are known.

Source: Deloitte China, *China's new accounting standards,* 2006, www.iasplus.com.

Exhibit 17.19 Hong Kong and mainland China: country profile

	China	Hong Kong	
Population	1,285.0 million	7.0 million	
Land mass	9,560,900km^2	1,075km^2	
GDP per head	US$1,700	US$25,390	
GDP per head in purchasing power parity	16.1	83.2	(USA = 100)
Origins of GDP:	%	%	
Agriculture	13	0	
Industry	48	10	
Services	40	90	
	%	%	
GDP average annual growth 1995–2005	9.0	3.9	
Inflation, average annual rate 2001–2007	1.5	−0.6	

Source: *The Economist Pocket World in Figures*, 2008 Edition, Profile Books Ltd.

market-led capitalist system as exemplified by the economy of Hong Kong. Given the economic success of Hong Kong, it might be expected that Hong Kong will therefore be an important influence on the rest of China.

17.6.2 Hong Kong Stock Exchange

The securities and futures market in Hong Kong is regulated by the Securities and Futures Commission, which is an independent non-governmental statutory body operating under the authority of the Securities and Futures Ordinance (operational from 2003). It is funded by levies on market transactions and fees charged to the industry.[28] The stock market consists of two markets, the main market for established companies and the Growth Enterprise Market or GEM. This is described on its own website[29] as a 'buyers beware market for informed investors' being designed for high-growth but higher risk companies that lack the history or earnings required for the main market. There were 983 companies on the main market in early 2007, including 100 H-shares and 87 red-chip companies and 197 on GEM (including 43 H- and 4 red-chip). Red-chip companies are companies incorporated in Hong Kong but with at least 30 per cent of their share-holdings being held directly or indirectly by mainland Chinese entities or with at least 20 per cent mainland holdings and a strong influential presence of mainland China linked to individuals on the board. One example of such a company is CNOOC, as illustrated in Exhibit 17.20.

As shown in Exhibit 6.3, Hong Kong is the sixth largest stock market, as measured by market capitalization, being slightly larger than both the German Bourse and Toronto. However, it is dominated by just three stocks with HSBC, China Mobile and China

---

[28] See www.hksfc.org.hk (English-language option).
[29] www.hkgem.com.

Exhibit 17.20 Information on ultimate holding company, CNOOC Limited

Corporate Information

CNOOC Limited (the 'Company') was incorporated in the Hong Kong Special Administrative Region ('Hong Kong'), the People's Republic of China (the 'PRC') on 20 August 1999 to hold the interests in certain entities thereby creating a group comprising the Company and its subsidiaries. During the year, the Company and its subsidiaries (hereinafter collectively referred to as the 'Group') were principally engaged in the exploration, development, production and sale of crude oil, natural gas and other petroleum.

The registered office address is 65/F Bank of China Tower, 1 Garden Road. Hong Kong. In the opinion of the directors, the parent and the ultimate holding company is China National Offshore Oil Corporation ('CNOOC'), a company established in the PRC.

Source: CNOOC Limited Annual Report (2005), p. 78, Notes to the financial statements.

Construction Bank Corporation accounting for approximately 28 per cent of its capitalization and the top 50 corporations accounting for 67 per cent of capitalization as at the end of the first quarter of 2007. The largest group of shareholders is overseas institutional investors at 39 per cent followed by 27 per cent local retail and 26 per cent local institutional with 3 per cent owned by overseas retail shareholders. Looking at the country of residence of the overseas shareholders, the USA accounts for 26 per cent, UK 24 per cent, the rest of Europe 25 per cent and China 5 per cent.

17.6.3 Accounting institutions

The institutions of Hong Kong have all been heavily influenced by the British. This includes the legal system and corporate legislation and the accounting profession.

17.6.3.1 The Hong Kong Society of Accountants

The Hong Kong Society of Accountants (HKSA)[30] has in the past set its examinations in conjunction with the UK-based Association of Chartered Certified Accountants (ACCA). The HKSA Qualifying Programme has mutual recognition with the ACCA qualification and with the CPA Australia. Membership of the HKSA is also open, subject to an aptitude test, to accountants that are professionally qualified in the USA, Ireland, Australia, Canada, South Africa, New Zealand or Zimbabwe as well as the UK. As in the UK, accounting is mainly regulated via statute or company law and accounting standards. Statute, in the form of the Companies Ordinance 1965, was very largely based upon the UK Companies Act 1948. Thus, it sets out basic requirements to disclose group accounts and directors' reports and details certain disclosures inside both the accounts and the directors' report. As far as accounting is concerned, the Act is very much a disclosure act and it does not include any valuation or measurement rules.

---

[30] www.hksa.org.hk.

The Professional Accountants (Amendment) Bill was passed in July 2004. It represented a step taken voluntarily by the HKSA to respond to heightened public expectations. It allowed a change of name from the HKSA to the Hong Kong Institute of Certified Public Accountants. From the end of 2004, members are designated CPA (Certified Public Accountant) or FCPA (Fellow). As of mid-2007, there were 26,402 members, 84.3 per cent CPAs and 15.7 per cent FCPAs, but only 13.6 per cent held practising certificates.

17.6.3.2 Accounting standards

Accounting standards are set by the Financial Accounting Standards Committee (FASC) of the HKSA. Until 1993 these standards were mainly local adaptations of UK standards. From 1993 the Council of the HKSA required the FASC to develop accounting standards to achieve convergence with IFRS.[31] However, it did not uncritically accept international standards but instead it reviewed all international standards and as appropriate included additional disclosure requirements in a Hong Kong standard, or even required a deviation from IFRS. The Urgent Issues and Interpretations Sub-Committee prepared interpretations and guidelines. Also important are auditing standards, issued by the Accounting Standards Committee (ASC) and the Auditing Standards Committee (AUSC), both being committees of the HKSA. Standards are thus professionally set; however, the ASC is made up not only of the international auditing firms' employees but also of members from small audit firms, industry and the stock exchange.

The system changed in the beginning of 2005. From that date Hong Kong ceased to issue its own standards but instead reissued international standards changing only the naming system from IFRS to HKFRS. Where local legislation means that the international standard cannot be adopted with no changes, these are now published with additional guidance in a footnote or appendix. Similarly, Hong Kong has also accepted the international auditing standards and the IFAC professional code of ethics, again with additional guidance if necessary to reflect local legal requirements. International standards now apply to all listed and unlisted entities except small and medium enterprises which use the SME FRF (Small and Medium Enterprise Financial Reporting Framework) and FRS (Financial Reporting Standard), also effective from 1 January 2005. The SME FRS differs from international standards in that it is based solely upon the historic cost convention. While the move towards uncritical acceptance of IFRS is important, the practical impact on most companies is relatively minor as Hong Kong had already achieved significant progress towards harmonization.

If a company fails to comply with standards, there is no legal sanction that can be taken against the company. However, if the failure to comply is not due to the necessity to report a 'true and fair view' the auditor must qualify the accounts. Failure to issue a qualified report would mean that the auditor can, at least potentially, be held liable to professional misconduct. Exhibit 17.21 gives an example of a PRC-based company, China Telecom, which applies Hong Kong GAAP.

Exhibit 17.22 sets out the Hong Kong Stock Exchange reporting requirements for PRC companies that use PRC accounting standards.

---

[31] Preface to Hong Kong Financial Reporting Standards, October 2003.

Exhibit 17.21 Significant accounting policies, China Telecom

2. SIGNIFICANT ACCOUNTING POLICIES

(a) Basis of preparation
The accompanying financial statements have been prepared in accordance with International Financial Reporting Standards ('IFRS') promulgated by the International Accounting Standards Board ('IASB'). IFRS includes International Accounting Standards ('IAS') and interpretations. These financial statements also comply with the disclosure requirements of the Hong Kong Companies Ordinance and the applicable disclosure provisions of the Rules Governing the Listing of Securities on the Stock Exchange of Hong Kong Limited.

These financial statements are prepared on the historical cost basis as modified by the revaluation of certain property, plant and equipment (Note 2(g)) and available-for-sale equity securities (Note 2(k)). The accounting policies described below have been consistently applied by the Group.

The preparation of the financial statements in conformity with IFRS requires management to make judgements, estimates and assumptions that affect the application of policies and the reported amounts of assets and liabilities and disclosure of contingent assets and liabilities at the date of the financial statements and the reported amounts of revenues and expenses during the reporting period. The estimates and associated assumptions are based on historical experience and various other factors that are believed to be reasonable under the circumstances, the results of which form the basis of making the judgments about carrying values of assets and liabilities that are not readily apparent from other sources. Actual results could differ from those estimates.

Source: China telecom Annual Report (2006), p. 93.

Exhibit 17.22 Hong Kong Stock Exchange reporting requirements for PRC companies

Chapter 4 — Accountants' Reports and Pro Forma Financial Information

19A.08   The reporting accountants for a PRC issuer must be qualified and be independent to the same extent as required under rule 4.03 for the reporting accountants of any other issuer.

19A.09   A report will not normally be regarded as acceptable unless the relevant accounts have been audited to a standard comparable to that required in Hong Kong.

19A.10   Reports for PRC issuers will normally be required to conform with the requirements as to accounting standards set out in rules 4.11 to 4.13, except that PRC issuers, which adopt IFRS, will not be required to comply with the requirements in (b)(i) and (ii) of rule 4.11.

Note: *A report for a PRC issuer may, in addition, present in a separate part of the report financial information conforming with applicable PRC accounting rules and regulations provided that the report contains a statement of the financial effect of the material differences (if any) from either of the accounting standards referred to in rule 4.11, as the case may be.*

19A.11   As indicated in rules 4.14 to 4.16, where the figures in the accountants' report differ from those in the audited annual accounts, a statement of adjustments must be submitted to the Exchange enabling the figures to be reconciled.

Note: Paragraphs 4.11–4.13 require companies to provide financial statements in accordance with Hong Kong standards or to disclose and explain departures from such standards. Paragraphs 4.14 – 4.16 require a statement of adjustments made in the accountants' report.

Source: www.hkex.com.hk (August 2004).

17.7 Gray's accounting values

Chapter 5 explains how Gray (1988) derived accounting values from studies of societal value dimensions by Hofstede (1984). Hofstede (1991) included an additional dimension based on Chinese values relating to a long-term versus a short-term orientation. Gray (1988) concluded that China's accounting development and practice should be in the cluster that supports statutory control, uniform practices, a conservative measurement approach and secrecy in disclosure. Chow *et al.* (1995) analyzed the accounting debate of the 1990s and particularly the adoption of accounting standards from 1993 in moving from a rigid and uniform approach towards a more Anglo-Saxon orientation. They concluded that a continuing mix of uniform system and professional standards would be necessary.

17.7.1 Professionalism versus statutory control

As we have seen, the system of accounting is one which relies exclusively upon statutory control. While accounting standards are issued, they are issued by the Ministry of Finance independently of the profession; the CICPA is limited to setting auditing standards and acting as a trade organization for exams and CPA registration. This position is probably inevitable – the state traditionally closely controlled all enterprises by a system of centralized plans and as one part of this system of control it has imposed a highly regulated set of accounting plans. The state is unlikely to give up this power to a professional body unless there is a very good reason to do so. The profession is also still relatively new, small and powerless. As such, it is unlikely to be in a position to offer a strong case for why standard setting should be devolved from the state. The interesting question is what might happen in the future. It remains to be seen whether or not, once the profession expands in size and once the full set of basic accounting regulations are in place, the system will rely less exclusively upon statutory control.

17.7.2 Uniformity versus flexibility

While the accounting system lies at an extreme position on the professionalism/statutory control continuum, it is more difficult to place it on the uniformity/flexibility continuum. The UAR was a uniform system giving enterprises no discretion on how to account for particular transactions or events. This philosophy continues into the new regulations although there are a number of areas where enterprises are given almost complete discretion over the methods to use. The result is a dual approach in which China has retained a uniform accounting system in the ASBE while also developing accounting standards based on IFRS. Xiao *et al.* (2004) explain the coexistence of the two approaches to accounting regulation in terms of the special circumstances of a transforming government, strong state ownership, a weak accounting profession, a weak and imperfect equity market and the inertial effect of accounting tradition and cultural factors.

17.7.3 Conservatism versus optimism

The introduction of the concept of conservatism or prudence into Chinese accounting reflected the changing political system and in particular the move towards economic liberalism introduced by Deng[32] is a relatively new concept for Chinese enterprises, although it appears to be gaining acceptance as an important concept.[33] The Accounting System states that an enterprise should comply with the requirements of the prudence concept. An enterprise should not overstate assets or revenue, or understate liabilities or expenses. It should not provide for any hidden reserve.[34] Previously, prudence was in the regulations but was not an overriding concept and was not universally applied. The reasons for this are twofold. Firstly, prudence had always been regarded as a feature of capitalist accounting which could be used by management to manipulate profits and to exploit the workers. As such, criticisms of the concept used to be found in nearly all Chinese accounting textbooks until the 1980s. Secondly, prudence tends to result in a reduction in reported surpluses or profits. As these were handed back to the state, the introduction of prudence would have resulted in a fall in state revenues.

17.7.4 Secrecy versus transparency

Chow *et al.* (1995) explain that a society like China with large power distance and strong uncertainty avoidance means that the preference for secrecy is relatively high. On the other hand the collectivist culture requires business enterprises to be accountable to society by way of providing information. The government therefore intervenes to prescribe disclosure requirements. ASBE 2001 brought greater transparency to PRC accounting.[35] There remains a strong element of secrecy in the limited range of narrative disclosure required and the relatively low level of voluntary disclosure.

17.8 Empirical studies

17.8.1 Classification studies

China has not been included in any of the empirical studies concerned with classifying accounting systems. If it had been included it would have formed an extra or new group. Until the reforms began it would have been grouped alongside the USSR and other East European countries. Since the Chinese reforms began, China has moved away from a centralized, socialist and plan-based accounting system. Likewise, the countries of Eastern Europe have also been dismantling their accounting systems and replacing them with systems more akin to those in various western countries. If the Chinese accounting reforms described above are compared with those of, for example, Poland, as discussed in Chapter 12, it is clear that the reforms have taken somewhat different directions. We saw in Chapter 12 how Poland has been heavily influenced by the EU and has implemented accounting rules designed to be in harmony with EU rules. China in contrast is attempting to harmonize with the IASB while adapting the standards to meet the continuing unique features of the country. While China has introduced many of the institutions that exist in free markets, SOEs are still important and the state still maintains its

---

[32] Ezzamel *et al.* (2006).

[33] Lin and Chen (1999).

[34] Article 11(12).

[35] Pactor (2001).

socialist orientation with control of the economy and regulation of business being of prime importance. Thus, if China was now to be classified alongside other countries it would probably no longer form a large group with all the countries of Eastern Europe. Instead, it would probably form its own unique group as a country that has a system which shows the influence of international standards while still retaining some characteristics of the pre-reform system.

17.8.2 Comparability measures

We might expect the figures reported by Chinese companies, at least until the introduction of the 2007 rules, to be quite different from those reported from similar companies from other countries, because of differences in the accounting rules and differences in the environment in which the companies act. As we saw above, the concept of conservatism is a new one in China. While historical costs have been used, assets have not in the past been written down below cost. To the extent that inventories are overvalued and liabilities are not recognized, Chinese profits will be relatively overstated. Similarly, R&D capitalization and the capitalization of self-generated intangibles and pre-operating expenses will also lead to a relative overstatement of earnings. However, there are other accounting methods used in China that will in contrast tend to reduce reported earnings. The use of LIFO, one-off fixed asset revaluations and excess depreciation charges will all reduce reported earnings. Whether the overall effect is one of reducing or increasing earnings in contrast with the equivalent UK or US firm is not obvious.

In the years before the ASBE (2001) there were significant differences between PRC accounting and IAS-based accounting. An idea of the differences between IAS and PRC standards can be gained from the work of Chen *et al.* (1999) who examined the reconciliation statements of between 34 and 50 companies with B-shares listed on the Shanghai Stock Exchange for each of the years 1994–97 (making a total of 165 cases in all). In most cases it was found that IAS-based earnings were the more conservative. Thus, in 133 cases PRC-based earnings were the larger and in only 29 cases were they smaller than IAS-based earnings. In no case did restatement to IAS turn a loss into a profit, although in contrast there were 18 cases when the reconciliation turned a profit into a loss. In each year the PRC-reported earnings were, on average, significantly larger than the IAS-based earnings. The five items that accounted for the largest differences in the two sets of earnings figures were found to be:

- foreign currency translation
- bad debts
- fixed assets valuation, revaluation and depreciation
- accrued expenses
- long-term investments.

Although the average differences were large (mean differences varying across the four years from 17.9 per cent to 30.1 per cent) these differences are likely to become less important over time. Five differences are largely eliminated by the ASBE 2001 (inventory valuation, bad debt allowances, long-term investment valuation, deferred tax and use of equity or cost method). Chen *et al.* (1999) suggested that these five items accounted for approximately 40 per cent of the differences in reported earnings. In addition, the differences in foreign currency treatment were caused by capitalizations created when the monetary reforms were first introduced. These are likely to be fully amortized by now and will no longer affect the earnings figures produced.

17.8.3 Disclosure studies

Ferguson *et al.* (2002) asked, 'What is the level of voluntary disclosure in the annual reports of wholly state-owned PRC enterprises listed on the Hong Kong Stock Exchange?' This was the first empirical examination of former wholly owned SOEs listed internationally. These are the Chinese companies that issue H-shares.

Ferguson *et al.* tested for, and found, greater voluntary disclosure by H-share companies, particularly in financial and strategic disclosures. They suggested several possible reasons:

- Keeping secret might be seen as 'bad news', causing investors to reject the shares ('adverse selection').
- Investors are afraid of things that are kept secret by managers ('information asymmetry').
- H-share companies do not fear competitors because they have government protection and so do not fear losing cash flows through loss of market share.
- H-share companies want to attract investors.
- H-share companies are not afraid of attracting the attention of regulators ('political costs').
- H-share companies want to raise finance at the lowest cost of capital, so focus on financial and strategic disclosures.

Their second test aimed to show that voluntary disclosure by red-chip firms will be lower than that by H-share firms (red-chip are the highest rated Hong Kong companies, so called by comparison with 'blue-chip' which are the highest rated UK companies). Their reasoning was that red-chip firms face higher risks from competition (proprietary costs).

The authors suggested that H-share firms may reflect state-initiated disclosure policies rather than management policy. The government of PRC wants to lower the cost of capital in order to raise more capital and expose Chinese companies to investors.

They next compared nine companies issuing H- and A-shares with 18 companies issuing A-shares only, in the consumer electronics industry. Disclosure by the 'H and A' group was significantly higher than that of the 'A-alone' group. They concluded that disclosure practices of H-share PRC companies listing in Hong Kong are sensitive to the needs of investors and are not driven by state ownership alone. They also appear to be sensitive to management's assessments of costs and benefits. However, there is evidence of state-encouraged disclosure policies. The research is limited by the small size of samples.

Chen and Cheng (2007) instead looked at the effect of some of the initiatives of the CSRC to make the market more efficient. In particular during the period they studied, 1999 to 2003, the CSRC introduced a number of corporate governance improvements as well as measures designed to reduce the difference between CAS and IAS disclosures, especially the requirement that companies should, if possible, use the same rules for both CAS and IAS accounts. They demonstrated that the changes in the extent of harmonization with IFRS were primarily due to the CSRC change in disclosure rules rather than any improvements in corporate governance at the individual firm level.

17.8.4 Value relevance of accounting information

There have been a number of studies looking at the value relevance of accounting information, or the extent to which accounting information is reflected in share prices. China is a particularly interesting country in which to explore this issue given the existence of both A- and B-shares, with A-share companies issuing only PRC-based accounting information and AB-share companies also issuing IFRS-based information.

It might be expected that the information disclosed by AB-share companies would be more value relevant than that issued by A-companies as more information is disclosed by these companies; however, this does not always appear to be the case. For example, Chen *et al.* (2001) documented that in the earlier years of the stock markets (1991–98) the A-market appears to be more value relevant. In a later study Lin and Chen (2005) looked specifically at the question of whether Chinese accounting standards (CAS) were more informative than international ones (IAS) for the period 1995 to 2000. Looking at both stock prices and returns, they found that CAS-based numbers were generally more relevant than IAS reconciliations, although the latter did have some value relevance. They offered a number of suggestions for why these counter-intuitive results might hold. It might be because investors were more familiar with the CAS system of regulation and disclosure coupled with close links between reported CAS profits and taxation and therefore a closer link between pre-tax profits and dividends. In addition, the government had often interfered in the market during this period and so influenced stock price behaviour and increasing market inefficiency. Finally, the B-shares tend to be thinly traded and because, during this period, Chinese investors could only invest in A-shares, there was a large price difference between the two markets.

Zhang and Ding (2006) looked at a later period, 2001 to 2004, and found some systematic differences in share price behaviour between the two types of companies. In particular, they found that AB-share companies had a lower bid-ask spread implying that the market for these companies was more efficient. However, they also had a greater return volatility implying that these companies perhaps attracted more transient investors.

Summary and conclusions

This chapter has described a country of contrasts. China has undergone profound changes in recent years. The economic system is still changing and the country is in the midst of introducing many new accounting standards. China has moved from a system of public ownership of all enterprises to a mixed system with increasing private ownership of both small and large companies. Many companies now freely trade their shares on both domestic and overseas stock markets. However, the economic changes are still not completed and many parts of the economy are still owned and controlled by the state.

The communist system led to a uniform accounting system; the recent economic reforms have resulted in the introduction of new accounting laws and regulations, the most important being the ASBE (2001) and the 38 new 2007 ASBE standards. However, the system can probably still be characterized in terms of low professionalism[36] and high secrecy.[37] It is rather more difficult to characterize the system in terms of conservatism and uniformity. In some areas, the system is still very rigid or uniform. In other areas, the system may be characterized by extreme flexibility. There remains a need for stronger assurance processes, to discourage false accounting or fraudulent reporting. While conservatism or prudence is a new concept, in some areas the system is very conservative,

---

[36] See Xiang (1998).
[37] See Chow *et al.* (1995).

while in other areas it is far from conservative. Finally, there is the impact of the IASB; however, it remains to be seen what the impact will be on either reported figures or stock market behaviour.

Key points from the chapter:

- The accounting system of China has a strong tradition of a uniform accounting system.
- The uniform accounting system developed under a communist political system to serve the needs of the state and state-controlled enterprises.
- Moving to a market-based economy has required major changes in accounting which have developed gradually since the 1980s.
- The Accounting Standards for Business Enterprises (1992) marked a significant stage in the move to a market-based economy.
- China began a process of matching its standards to International Accounting Standards prior to becoming a member of the World Trade Organization.
- The development of PRC standards that are consistent with IFRS is now largely complete.
- The accounting profession is at a relatively early stage in development and needs the detailed rules of the ASBE.
- Hong Kong continues to apply different accounting rules and has its own regulatory system for the stock market. Some PRC companies have their shares traded as 'H'-shares on the Hong Kong exchange.

Questions

The following questions test your understanding of the material contained in the chapter and allow you to relate your understanding to the learning outcomes specified at the start of this chapter. The learning outcomes are repeated here. Each question is cross-referenced to the relevant section of the chapter.

Understand and explain the origins of accounting regulations and the historical development leading to the present state of practice

1 What are the aspects of accounting in China between 1949 and 1980 that may give particular problems in applying western-based international accounting standards? (sections 17.5.1 and 17.5.2)

2 Why has accounting in China become of wider interest to western business since the early 1980s? (sections 17.5.2 and 17.5.3)

3 How did accounting in China develop between 1992 and 2000 to meet the requirements for becoming a member of the World Trade Organization? (section 17.5.3)

Relate institutional factors for the country to the framework set out in Chapter 6

4 How does the political and economic system of China fit into the classifications described in Chapter 6? (section 17.3)

5 To what extent does the business environment of China under the communist regime provide clues as to possible influences on accounting practices? (section 17.3)

6 To what extent does the current reform in the business environment of China provide clues as to possible influences on accounting practices? (section 17.3)

7 How does the taxation system of China compare with the descriptions given in Chapter 6? (section 17.3.3)

8 How does the corporate financing system of China compare with the descriptions given in Chapter 1? (section 17.3.4)

9 How does the accounting profession in China compare with the descriptions given in Chapter 6? (section 17.3.5)

10 Which institutional factors are most likely to influence Chinese accounting practice? (section 17.3)

11 How do the external influences on accounting practice in China compare with those described in Chapter 6? (section 17.4)

Understand and explain the position of national accounting rules in relation to the IASB standards

12 In which areas does accounting practice in China depart from that set out in International Accounting Standards? (section 17.5.5)

13 For each of the areas of departure which you have identified, describe the treatment required or applied in China and identify the likely impact on net income and shareholders' equity of moving from Chinese accounting practice to the relevant IASB standard. (section 17.5.5)

14 What explanations may be offered for these differences from IASB standards, in terms of the institutional factors described in the chapter? (section 17.3)

15 What are the most difficult problems facing accounting in China as it seeks full harmonization with the IASB standards? (section 17.5.5)

Understand the characteristics of national accounting practice in terms of Gray's accounting values

16 Identify the key features supporting a conclusion that strong statutory control is a characteristic of Chinese accounting. (section 17.7.1)

17 Identify the key features supporting a conclusion that uniformity, rather than flexibility, is a dominant characteristic of Chinese accounting. (section 17.7.2)

18 Identify the key features supporting a conclusion that conservatism is not a dominant characteristic of Chinese accounting. (section 17.7.3)

19 Identify the key features supporting a conclusion that secrecy is a characteristic of Chinese accounting. (section 17.7.4)

20 Why is the location of Hong Kong China in accounting classification studies likely to remain different from that of mainland China? (sections 17.6 and 17.7)

Explain how research papers contribute to understanding accounting practice and accounting values

21 How might China be located within the classification studies reported in Chapter 6? Why has it not appeared in such classification studies previously? (section 17.8.1)

22 Is it likely that comparability studies may continue to help foreign users to understand accounting information produced by Chinese companies? (section 17.8.2)

23 What may be learned from disclosure studies of Chinese companies reporting in Hong Kong? (section 17.8.3)

References and further reading

Blake, J. and Gao, S. (eds) (1995) *Perspectives on Accounting and Finance in China*. London: Routledge.

CFA Institute, (2007) *China Corporate Governance Survey.*

Chen, C.J.P., Gul, F.A. and Su, X. (1999) 'A comparison of reported earnings under Chinese GAAP vs IAS: evidence from the Shanghai Stock Exchange', *Accounting Horizons*, 13(2): 91–111.

Chen, C.J.P., Chen, S. and Su, X. (2001) 'Is accounting information value relevant in the emerging Chinese stock markets?', *Journal of International Accounting, Auditing and Taxation,* 10: 1–22.

Chen, J.J. and Cheng, P. (2007) 'Corporate governance and the harmonization of Chinese accounting practices with IFRS practices', *Corporate Governance,* 15(2), March: 284–293.

Chow, L.M., Chau, G.K. and Gray, S.J. (1995) 'Accounting reforms in China: cultural constraints on implementation and development', *Accounting and Business Research*, 26(1): 29–49.

Delios, A., Wu, Z.J. and Zhou, N. (2006) 'A new perspective on ownership identities in China's listed companies', *Management and organization Review,* 2(3): 319–343.

Deloitte Touche Tohmatsu (2006) *China's new accounting standards*, August.

Ding, S. and Graham, C. (2007) 'Accounting and the reduction of state-owned stock in China', *Critical Perspectives in Accounting,* 18: 559–580.

Ezzamel, M., Xiao, J.Z. and Pan, A. (2006) 'Political ideology and accounting regulation in China', doi:10.1016/j.aos.2006.09.008.

Ferguson, M.J., Lam, K.C. and Lee, G.M. (2002) 'Voluntary disclosure by state-owned enterprises listed on the stock exchange of Hong Kong', *Journal of International Financial Management and Accounting*, 13(2): 126–152.

Gray, S.J. (1988) 'Towards a theory of cultural influence on the development of accounting systems internationally', *Abacus*, 24(1): 1–15.

Hao, Z.P. (1999) 'Regulation and organisation of accountants in China', *Accounting, Auditing & Accountability Journal*, 12(3): 286–302.

Hofstede, G. (1984) *Culture's Consequences: International Differences in Work-related Values.* Beverly Hills, CA: Sage.

Hofstede, G. (1991) *Cultures and Organisations: Software of the Mind.* London: McGraw-Hill.

Lin, T.W. (2004) 'Corporate governance in China: recent developments, key problems and solutions', *Journal of Accounting and Corporate Governance*, 1: 1–23.

Lin, Z.J. and Chen, F. (1999) 'Applicability of the conservatism accounting convention in China: empirical evidence', *International Journal of Accounting*, 34: 517–537.

Lin, Z.J. and Chen, F. (2005) 'Value relevance of international accounting standards harmonization: evidence from A- and B-share markets in China', *Journal of International Accounting, Auditing and Taxation*, 14: 79–103.

Liu, G.S. and Sun, S.P. (2005) 'The class of shareholding and its impact on corporate performance – a case of state shareholding composition in Chinese publicly listed companies', *Corporate Governance: An international Review*, 13(1): 46–59.

Pacter, P. (2001) 'Emerging trends', *Accountancy*, May: 100.

Roberts, C.B., Adams, C.A., Woo, R.W.K. and Wu, X. (1995) 'Chinese accounting reform: the internationalisation of financial reporting', *Advances in International Accounting*, 8: 201–220.

Tang, Y. (2000) 'Bumpy road leading to internationalisation: a review of accounting development in China', *Accounting Horizons*, 14(1): 93–102.

Tang, Y.W., Chow, L. and Cooper, B.J. (1994) *Accounting and Finance in China*, 2nd edn. Hong Kong: Longmans.

White, G. (1993) *Riding the Tiger: the Politics of Economic Reform in post-Mao China*. London: Macmillan.

Xiang, B. (1998) 'Institutional factors influencing China's accounting reforms and standards', *Accounting Horizons*, 12(2): 105–119.

Xiao, Z., Zhang, Y. and Xie, Z. (2000) 'The making of independent auditing standards in China', *Accounting Horizons*, 14(1): 69–89.

Xiao, Z., Weetman, P. and Sun, M. (2004) 'Political influence and coexistence of a uniform accounting system and accounting standards: recent developments in China', *Abacus*, 40(2): 193–218.

Yunwei, T. and Pacter, P. (2000) 'Revolution in accounting in China', *Accounting and Business*, January: 18–20.

Zhang, L. and Ding, S. (2006) 'The effect of increased disclosure on cost of capital: evidence from China', *Review of Quantitative and Financial Accounting*, 27: 383–401.

Zhang, Y. and Zhao, R. (2004) 'The valuation differential between class A and B shares: country risk in the Chinese stock market', *Journal of International Financial Management and Accounting*, 15(1): 44–59.

Index